SUICIDE IN CANADA

Edited by Antoon A. Leenaars, Susanne Wenckstern, Isaac Sakinofsky, Ronald J. Dyck, Michael J. Kral, and Roger C. Bland

The Canadian National Task Force on Suicide found that suicide rates in Canada, especially among youth, exceed those in many other countries around the world, including the United States. Health-care professionals and social-service providers identify suicide as one of the most important areas in which they need information. Yet there has been a lack of comprehensive prevention response, little change in public policies, and support for research is lacking.

Compiled by Canada's leading experts on suicide, this collection provides long-awaited information that focuses specifically on Canada. It addresses suicide as a multidimensional problem with biological, psychological, cultural, sociological, personal, and philosophical aspects. The contributions integrate both critical analysis and personal experience. There are accounts from Inuit elders, from women who have survived the loss of a family member, and from workers at a crisis line. Among the topics covered are the development of suicide prevention; theory and research; First Nations and Inuit peoples; family, community, and government approaches; distress centres; survivors; and the debate over the right to die.

Suicide in Canada does more than simply describe recent developments in suicidology in Canada – it is a call for action that will save lives. It will be of immediate use to psychiatrists, psychologists, nurses, social workers, crisis workers, and researchers.

ANTOON A. LEENAARS practises psychology in Windsor, Ontario, and is affiliated with the University of Leiden, The Netherlands.

SUSANNE WENCKSTERN is a psychological associate for the Board of Education, City of Windsor.

ISAAC SAKINOFSKY is a professor of psychiatry at the University of Toronto and head of the Suicide Studies Program at the Clarke Institute for Psychiatry.

RONALD J. DYCK is director of the Prevention and Promotion Branch, Alberta Health.

MICHAEL J. KRAL is associate professor of psychology at the University of Windsor.

ROGER C. BLAND is professor and chair of psychiatry at the University of Alberta.

Suicide in Canada

EDITED BY ANTOON A. LEENAARS,

SUSANNE WENCKSTERN,

ISAAC SAKINOFSKY, RONALD J. DYCK,

MICHAEL J. KRAL, and ROGER C. BLAND

UNIVERSITY OF TORONTO PRESS
Toronto Buffalo London

© University of Toronto Press Incorporated 1998
Toronto Buffalo London
Printed in Canada

ISBN 0-8020-0738-4 (cloth)
ISBN 0-8020-7791-9 (paper)

Printed on acid-free paper

Canadian Cataloguing in Publication Data

Main entry under title:

Suicide in Canada

ISBN 0-8020-0738-4 (bound)   ISBN 0-8020-7791-9 (pbk.)

1. Suicide – Canada.   I. Leenaars, Antoon A., 1951–   .

HV6548.C3S85 1997   362.2809'71   C97-931454-2

University of Toronto Press acknowledges the financial assistance to its publishing program of the Canada Council for the Arts and the Ontario Arts Council.

The publication of this book was assisted by the Ontario Mental Health Foundation.

To the Inuit and First Nations
Peoples of This Land

Contents

Foreword

My name is Lucien Taparti. This is a recording of my words from my own experience. There are a lot of problems that come from the land, and when you get older you tend to get more problems. But when I was younger, there seemed to be hardly any problems, because we were living in a small settlement with only a few iglus [houses]. Now I am sixty-six years old. I was born in 1926 in Wager Bay. Some solutions to the problems can arise easily, but some are hard to understand. So if no one understands me, I can be asked and I'll be available. I don't want anyone to misunderstand me. I want to be understood clearly and I want to say that which will make sense.

In the past we hardly used to hear of suicides in our communities and would hear of them every so often only, because there were less people. Only once in a blue moon you'd hear of suicides in one of the communities. But nowadays, in one year there would be quite a few suicides. It's hard to grasp the problem. I feel we should look for solutions and start giving this matter more consideration/attention.

I noticed in Iqaluit during our meeting [annual conference of the Canadian Association for Suicide Prevention / L'Association canadienne pour la prévention du suicide (CASP/ACPS), Iqaluit, May 1994] that there are many of us in Canada whose children have committed suicide. They are anyone, whether they are Inuit, qablunaat (non-natives), or Dene, and every one of them feels the same way. Not one person feels differently.

When I had eight children I was happy. I grew up with no father and my children had a father so I was happy about this. That's why I was never worried about them, because they had a father. And I felt they were comfortable and I never really showed my love to them, that's how I am. I raised them the same way and gave all of them the same amount of love, even though they might have thought otherwise. Even though I am like that, I have experienced the biggest loss. Since I was born I have experienced losing relatives, losing my older brother, losing my father. The biggest loss was my own child, who shot himself and died. I thought that I felt the biggest hurt. Since the incident, I realized that you can't point fingers at anyone in society, you can't blame anyone. But after experiencing this yourself, you tend to point at yourself. That's exactly how I felt, because I am the father. Why did my child do this? That is what I felt. You don't want this to happen again.

And also, another son of mine froze to death almost a year after the suicide. Since then, you tend to point to yourself, being the father. I can talk about my own feelings about this, but I can't really talk about it any further.

Even with what happened, my children are still around. There are six of them and I have two adopted children and I have grandchildren now. We will all go to the same place some day and our time will come some day. My children and grandchildren will go through the same.

I don't want to blame the young people only, and I don't want to put them down. When their minds have time to be changed there is time for rectifying the problems. Perhaps if they could talk to their friends about any of their problems earlier, then they would be a lot happier, and they wouldn't be as afraid of others. And perhaps they wouldn't feel as alone, because they would know that they live with others. If they could start thinking of these things and remembering them.

The resources, such as the church groups, the police, the social workers, and the justice groups, help in the communities. But when it comes to us, the people in the communities, I wonder if we are going to be silent about this or are we going to try to do something about this before our elders die off.

A person's life is precious and it seems like the elders knew this. Even though the people were capable once, later they forgot these things. For example, they have forgotten the hunting of the animals and the heavy labours of survival on the land. Even though these people know they need help, they don't really ask for help, so it becomes a burden for them in their mind.

So how could we rectify this, working in our communities – not only in the harsh land, but all of us in Canada? We have to start helping, because we all feel the same way and we live the same way. We all have the same lives. So we need to look for resources that would help in our communities.

I want people to consider how we could work together more in their communities. We need to teach our young people of their own culture, whether it be Inuit culture, qablunaat's culture, or Dene culture. Some of us who are using modern ways, and people who knew the old ways then, would be able to say that we are using a new way.

I think we have to start asking ourselves, 'Where can we get help with suicidal people?' It is essential that we each ask ourselves this. The Inuit must ask themselves. We Canadians will have to ask how we could start to initiate things and how we could rectify problems more so and promote the issue more, so that suicide could decline. It's obvious now that we'll have to really work together on this issue.

When I went to Iqaluit in the spring of 1994, it seemed like it was useless, for they [CASP] had already started their meeting. I went there and I felt that I wouldn't be of benefit, that I wouldn't give anything that would be of help. From within myself, they had made me cry a lot, but quite a few people came with tears, whether they were old or not. That's what I saw. Little did I know that I had to voice my concerns too. I also realized that I have to seek some solutions.

Even though there are resources out there for people already, there are many people who commit suicide. Many of us have experienced losing someone. That's why I really want to talk about it. If I were silent, I know it wouldn't be of help. We have to be visible and if we are visible then that's how the problem will become visible.

To the people who I have met on this issue, I would say that whether we could come up with solutions, I would like them to strive harder. I don't want them to dwell on grief too much, or to think that they are not useful. We are all capable of coming up with solutions.

We really have to start thinking of ways to rectify things. I'm sure this can be achieved somehow, but I don't know the answer to it. If solutions came from a larger community it could be a starting point, and even if they think they couldn't come up with solutions, they would be able to do so. Just as long as they have appropriate laws (rules) that they'd use. As long as the rules are capable of being followed. I'll use snow as an example: it is worked on by different people – some are very good with snow and some are able to work with it but not as well. That's why we use different types of snow to work with. Snow was our means of survival, even when we were young and even when we became adults. I wasn't worried at all, knowing that we'll get an iglu, even when there was going to be a blizzard. That was one of the laws and I followed it; so that was our life and the iglus were where our lives were. That's how we used to live in the winter time.

If we started tackling different things that we were capable of doing on our own, we couldn't really think of other things to get into. Soon as we were capable to do things that we had to follow, we didn't have much to be concerned with, not like our young people I see today. That's how it is with our culture from the harsh region; our cultures are all different and we need to keep our culture visible. If we ignore the issue, it is obvious that it won't get rectified.

We all have different lives, different cultures, and we can't say that the qablu-naat have a strong culture. All of us came from our ancestors and if we could grasp that back then there were less suicides, perhaps we could start utilizing our culture for prevention. We'll have to know more about the cultures of our ancestors, and try to follow them and try to help each other more. We can use many peoples' cultures, whether they may be the qablunaats', the Dene's, or even the Inuit's culture. If we can be more aware of people's cultures, I'm sure we would be able to come up with something that would be of benefit.

Our ancestors went through hardships, and everyday too they had work to do – everyday, whether it was summer, fall, winter, or spring. They always had things to do that were useful. During the whole year they'd work on things that had to be done, from the springtime throughout the whole summer, and in winter time things that were readied to be used. When they started trapping foxes in the winter they would try and catch what they could for survival, everyday. The blizzards would be the only days that no one would go to. Those were the only days they didn't go out in the land. They would also keep in mind when the weather would clear up. Because they wanted their lives to be organized and to progress better and they all had the same goal, that's how they lived. They had loved ones, they had children, they had wives, they had relatives, and they wanted to teach someone. Seems like today we should do the same, but the big difference is losing people due to suicide.

We have to think of ways to develop things in the community that will benefit the people. We can learn from past experiences. We often go through hard times, but they pass, and later we could look back and think that at one time we felt it would have never passed. As Inuit we could depend on one another; we have family, our father, grandfather, brother, and other relatives we could lean on. And I myself am a grandfather and even further a great-grandfather. Any mistakes could be corrected, because, as I have learned from my experiences, we learn from our mistakes.

In the past it was not always happy. People were scattered around in the land. We would walk everywhere in the summer and sleep on caribou skin when it was available. We would have a gun and knife and hunt daily. This was our culture. We worked very hard to feed our families. We caught our meat for the winter and we had to feed the dogs. We would use the skin to keep us warm and for us to sleep on. The caribou skin was very important, very useful. We worked hard to survive. When we needed to sleep we would use snow to build our iglus.

Nowadays, when a person is lost on the land we have radios to help us look for them. And we know that he will make it home to his family.

We were very busy growing up, we would have to work until everything was done. We have to work towards having a good future. For example, when I first came to Rankin Inlet there was no littering anywhere, the land was clean. Nowadays, you see caribou carcasses everywhere, and if we want to keep our land and live better we need to stop littering. This does not happen only in Rankin Inlet, but all over the place. Even though we have Renewable Resource officers this does not disappear, and we need funds to clean up the mess. We need to develop ways to deal with this. A lot of times not only young people leave carcasses on the land, even the elders might do it. Because often they will look for caribous with fat and if a caribou does not have fat on its body they will leave it right where they shot it. I think we need to work together because I know everybody equally worries about this. We need to work together and correct these problems. We need to voice our concerns for them to be dealt with. We could give our ideas, and if an idea is not right we could discuss it and work together to better things for our people.

I want to encourage the young people to be strong; even though they might go through hard times, they always pass. Their time will come when they will leave this land. My mother used to say that our elders should be approached so that they could talk to us and counsel us, and we should be thankful to them, this is the way of the people.

When I was able to take care of myself I thought I didn't need anybody anymore, but my mother never stopped teaching me about the facts of life. She taught me about how to plan for the future. She told me that I have a future, problems will come up in the future, and accidents could happen. I myself thought that her words did not make sense. I didn't realize that she too has lived a hard life and she is just teaching me from experience. I would not talk back to my mother because it was not acceptable. I had to realize that our lives have changed and that all my children are individuals and think differently and act differently from each other. We have to think of their future and make them realize that problems do pass. In our communities we have utilized the search and rescue associations more often than we did in the past. One of the reasons is that we do not take enough time to teach our children life skills, and because of that we should not criticize them if they are not able to survive out in the land. I think that we should learn from each other instead of getting upset when someone tries to correct our behaviours. In the past we were taught how to build iglus and this was a way for our fathers to trust us out on the land. Our parents taught us how to survive. They believed in us and I really feel that when a person believes in you, you are able to do better. We were taught about weather predictions and our parents were able to give us things to survive within the harsh land. Nowadays there are snow machines, which often contribute to accidents, and it seems colder now when you go out on the land. We were taught patience and told that we could only be safe by being patient. When it was stormy out we would have to wait for the storm to calm down before we went anywhere. We grew up with only a few assets. We would walk a great distance to get home from hunting. I was able to survive because my parents taught me and I would listen to them.

I have gone through a lot of hardship. I am glad that I am able to say that I am sixty-six years old. I was attacked by a polar bear on April 6, 1988; I was unconscious for about one hour. I can now say that I'm doing better these last five years. I am watching my children grow. I am grateful to the Lord and to the people who were able to get me to where I am. My son, who was nineteen, brought me back to Rankin Inlet, and it was amazing because he did not know much about the land. We talk to our children or sometimes scold them so that they could do better in life. I know that I could have learned from my father if I had listened. This is why I scold my children sometimes, because I love them and want them to do good in life.

Nowadays there are restrictions in life. Policies that are followed. We are told that when our children are sixteen they are able to do as they please because they are adults. I understand this. My son went through hardship when he was trying to take me back home, but we were able to get back safely. My child was the one that saved my life because he was able to take me back home. I am glad that I am able to watch my grandchildren grow.

I am talking today because of those people who take their lives and how we could help those people who think of this way to escape. We need to think of how to help them understand that this is not the way to go. We need to develop solutions for them. We need to help those who have initiated solutions.

As elders we often say that life has changed and the weather has changed, but one of the reasons I think is that we don't go out enough and get fresh air. We are aware that search and rescue committees are essential. We each have a purpose in life and we need to work with our young people to make them realize that they are important. Perhaps we could take them somewhere, where we could talk to them and make them understand that we need them because they are the future. We used to travel in any condition and I have found unusual things in the past. There are a lot of elders who are able to talk to the young people and teach us about the facts of life. We need to better utilize funds to develop programs for our youth. You need to learn from experience. I have just talked about my life experience. We need to initiate programs because I feel I should have done this in the past, but it's unfortunate that we end up just waiting for somebody else to do things. These are the things that I wanted to talk about. I might have forgotten some things but these are things that I understand

and I feel I'm done in talking. I'm really appreciative of the assistance with this book. I wish the book and all people success. Smile every day and you will receive one from myself and others that you smile at.

LUCIEN TAPARTI
Rankin Inlet, Nunavut

Preface

Suicide is a major mental-health problem and public-health problem in Canada. Canada's suicide rate ranks above average in comparison to countries around the world and, for example, is higher than that of the United States (National Task Force on Suicide, 1987, 1994; Leenaars, 1995). The impact of suicide in terms of expected years of life lost is enormous. Suicide is so prevalent in Canada, especially among youth, that UNICEF has recently called it a major tragedy.

Suicide is a traumatic event that eventually touches most of our lives. Yet, few people understand suicide sufficiently. Professionals identify suicide as one of the most important areas for which they require greater information; yet, like most people, they overly espouse myths about this problem. Our National Task Force on Suicide (1987) noted that suicide often receives minimal focus in training centres, hospitals, schools, and universities. There is, thus, a need for more information.

Suicide is a multidimensional malaise. It is an event with biological, psychological, cultural, sociological, personal, and philosophical aspects. Thus, the response must be equally diverse (Caplan, 1964). The intent of this book is to introduce the reader to our malaise and our need to act. The volume is uniquely Canadian, providing a specific focus on Canada's multiculturalism and geographic characteristics. We hope to address our national diversity. At the same time, however, we hope the book will be of interest to international readers who, according to the World Health Organization (Bertolote, 1993), encounter similar obstacles around the world.

This book addresses suicide among Canada's Aboriginal people. The rate of suicide among our First Nations and Inuit peoples is well above the national average (Royal Commission on Aboriginal Peoples, 1995). Thus, we address the need to discuss suicide among Aboriginal people, while simultaneously addressing other important Canadian topics. By 'important' we mean topics that have emerged and have been identified as the principal areas in the field today in Canada.

The process of creating the book itself is reflective of the Canadian scene and is a sort of 'coming of age.' The volume itself did not arise from a government document or an administrative decision; rather, it grew from the grass roots. Researchers, clinicians, crisis workers, survivors, and many people have called for Canadian information on suicide. It was this need that served as the impetus for this volume. The book itself, in fact, presents a multidisciplinary approach, representing how suicide needs to be addressed in Canada. A diversity of people is needed in suicide prevention, from practitioners to community participants to researchers, reflecting differing conceptual, theoretical, and ethical viewpoints. We hope that this book will be a challenge to future Canadian researchers, clinicians, crisis workers, theoreticians, and others to reduce the prevalence of suicidal behaviour in Canada.

Canada has much work to do. The 1987 National Task Force on Suicide, at the release of its document *Suicide in Canada*, noted Canada's lack of productivity in this area, and made many recommendations. Yet, it was predicted (Tanney, Lakaski, Leenaars, and Syer-Solursh, 1987) that few, if any, of the recommendations would be implemented. More recently, the Royal Commission on Aboriginal Peoples (1995) at the release of its document *Choosing Life*, called for similar action among Aboriginal people. Yet, at the recent conference of the Canadian Association for Suicide Prevention (CASP), Brant Castellano, Tizya, and Connors (1995) expressed concern about the lack of action to that report too. The World Health Organization has, in fact, established goals and provided directions worldwide to address suicide (Bertolote, 1993). Despite some important provincial steps, Canada, at a federal level, has not taken up the call. Is this reflective of Canada's melancholia? Will we remain in our sick bed, as Margaret Atwood (1972) predicted, while our people die ... while our young people kill themselves ... while our Inuit continue to suffer from cultural genocide ...?

We would be remiss if we did not make specific note of the inadequate support for research in Canada. It is now well established that people in Canada must do their own research on suicide (Leenaars, 1995). The borrowing of America's research findings alone may well result in less than adequate conclusions within the Canadian context. Yet, there is a lack of support for the necessary research. Indeed, Canada's support is, on a per capita basis, among the lowest in the major countries reporting to the Organization for Economic Cooperation and Development (Lipset, 1990). Support is needed but will likely not be forthcoming. Thus, we ourselves must begin to support the next generations of researchers; otherwise Canada will forever be in the dark ages in understanding its unique malaise.

Our book is a new pathway towards knowledge about suicide in Canada. It is the first of its kind. The strength of the volume is that it gives voice to the people working in suicidology in our country. Each of the authors is one of Canada's leading suicide preventionists, a diverse and talented group. The list of authors was generated over time by the senior editor, beginning in 1988 with the establishment of the Canadian Association for Suicide Prevention. After we formally started the book project in 1994, we reviewed many names and concluded with the current list, recognizing regrettably that some people would be omitted. There were a few authors who were invited but never submitted papers, owing to various factors; a few simply expressed that they were too old now to write. Our overall acceptance rate, however, was above 90 per cent. We are honoured with the final list, a talented group that includes many voices.

The views of the authors in this volume cover a wide range and are grouped under the following perspectives: history; epidemiology and the Canadian scene; theory and research; First nations and Inuit experience; family, community, and government approaches; distress centres; survivorship; and the right-to-die debate. These are the important issues in suicidology today in Canada.

The first part, on history, provides some personal vignettes on the development of suicide prevention in Canada, concerning such topics as the first hospital unit and the establishment of crisis centres and of the Canadian Association for Suicide Prevention. We strongly agree here with George Santayana, when he said, 'Those who cannot remember the past are condemned to fulfill it.'

The section on epidemiology and the Canadian scene presents the current nomothetic knowledge of suicide in Canada, addressing special Quebec realities and our cultural diversity. The section concludes with a chapter on the difference between suicide in Canada and in the United States, reporting that although there are great similarities, there are enough differences to warrant Canada's own study of this issue.

The third part, on theory and research, provides a few reflections on the current directions of scholarly thought on suicide. Next, as noted, a special focus on suicide among the First Nations and Inuit is presented, followed by a section on family, community, and government approaches. This section emphasizes that Canada's vast geographical domain and its different ethnic mix call for an approach that considers the unique roles of the Canadian family, its communities, and government. Part 6 outlines suicide among youth and the response to youth suicide in communities and schools. Next, the role of distress centres in Canada is outlined, highlighting how, since the 1970s, the establishment of prevention centres has marked a major effort at reducing suicide.

Part 8 goes beyond suicide, exploring the impact of suicide on survivors. During the 1980s, survivors of suicide have begun to receive the concern and attention in Canada that their difficult emotional experience warrants. Our final section addresses the issue of the right to die. The debate about the right to die centres on one of the most controversial and elusive issues facing people today in Canada and across the world. We end on this topic, not only because it is a current issue, but also because it raises new issues that suicide preventionists and people in general will be facing in the near future. In this way, we hope to serve as a stimulus for thought, a hope of all sound books.

The book is, thus, intended to be expansive in its breadth. The multiplicity of editors, we hope, has equally allowed us to be multifarious. The diverse voices herein will help us understand our staggering tragedy and, most important, develop appropriate and effective prevention methods.

To conclude, this edited volume concerns the current general state of the art of suicidology across Canada. This book, we hope, will integrate the diversity of insights and directions in the field and add to the literature. At the same time, the volume is intended to be part of the larger health framework, seeking 'to foster and improve the health of Canadians' (Federal/Provincial/Territorial Advisory Committee, 1994). Most of all, we hope it will help to save lives.

As a final note, in order ultimately to prevent suicide, we must respect *all* people. This is an important teaching of one of Canada's greatest teachers, Chief Dan George. We must promote well-being for all. That is why the editors met in Lake Louise in the Canadian Rockies to review the book and to produce this preface. Lake Louise is the spiritual home of suicidology in Canada. We hope that our readers will join us in promoting the well-being of Canadians.

THE EDITORS
Lake Louise, 14 October 1995

REFERENCES

Atwood, M. 1972. *Survival*. Toronto: Anansi.
Bertolote, J. 1993. *Guidelines for the Primary Prevention of Mental, Neurological and Psychosocial Disorders: Suicide*. Geneva: World Health Organization.
Brant Castellano, M., R. Tizya, and E. Connors. 1995. (October). 'Choosing Life: An Open Discussion on Suicide among Aboriginal Peoples.' Keynote panel presented at the Conference of the Canadian Association for Suicide Prevention, Banff, AB.

Caplan, G. 1964. *Principles of Preventive Psychiatry*. New York: Basic Books.

Federal/Provincial/Territorial Advisory Committee. 1994. *Strategies for Population Health*. Ottawa: Supply and Services Canada.

Leenaars, A. 1995. 'Suicide and the Continental Divide.' *Archives of Suicide Research* 1: 39–58.

Lipset, S. 1990. *Continental Divide*. New York: Routledge.

National Task Force on Suicide. 1987. *Suicide in Canada*. Ottawa: Health Canada.

– 1994. *Suicide in Canada: Update*. Ottawa: Health Canada.

Royal Commission on Aboriginal Peoples. 1995. *Choosing Life: Special Report on Suicide among Aboriginal People*. Ottawa: Supply and Services Canada.

Tanney, B., C. Lakaski, A. Leenaars, and D. Syer-Solursh. 1987 (May). 'Canadian Perspectives: Suicide in Canada.' Panel presented at the combined conference of the American Association of Suicidology and International Association for Suicide Prevention, San Francisco, CA.

PART I: HISTORY

History can produce a meaningful perspective on a wide array of topics. This is as true about suicidology as about any other field. Regrettably, little has been written about the early events in this field in Canada.

History is not merely a repository of facts. Histories are constructions. One avenue to our past is the idiographic approach, which calls for the use of personal documents – logs, notes, memoirs. This was our pathway to Canada's early history. We asked people in the suicide-prevention movement to write an anamnesis.

The first section outlines Canadian suicidology's history and development. It provides some comment on issues in the field, and consists of brief vignettes concerning topics ranging from the first hospital unit to the establishment of crisis centres and of the Canadian Association for Suicide Prevention.

1

History: Vignettes of the Development in Suicide Prevention

ANTOON A. LEENAARS, MENNO BOLDT, EDWARD A.
CONNORS, PATRICIA HARNISCH, GERRY G.
HARRINGTON, KAREN G. KIDDEY, MARCIA B. KRAWLL,
KAREN LETOFSKY, BERND OSBORG, RICHARD F.
RAMSAY, ISAAC SAKINOFSKY, and GORDON WINCH

History, if viewed as more than a catalogue of past events, could produce a meaningful perspective on a wide array of fields of study. This is as true about suicidology as about any other field.

Undoubtedly, some readers will question whether historical study can possibly be useful. How could a history of suicidology, especially in one country (e.g., Canada), be a legitimate source of knowledge? Is it not merely anecdotal fact? Are not significant events only occurring today? Is it not the future that will provide the best perspective? However, another perspective (see Kuhn, 1962; Leenaars and Diekstra, 1995) would argue that any human endeavour is ultimately based upon past achievements, achievements that some particular community acknowledges as supplying the foundation for further development.

Suicidology has a long history. Plato and Aristotle, for example, discussed the issue. Yet, it is only at the turn of the twentieth century that Emile Durkheim and Sigmund Freud began legitimate study of suicide and its application to prevention. Contemporary suicidology, in fact, began even later with Edwin Shneidman's discovery (Leenaars, 1993; Shneidman, 1969) of several hundred suicide notes in a coroner's vault in 1949 in Los Angeles. The 'falcrum moment,' as Shneidman himself called it, came a few moments later when he had a glimmering that the vast potential value of the notes could be immeasurably increased if he did not read them, but rather, using John Stuart Mill's method of difference, compared them blindly in a controlled experiment with simulated suicide notes. The seeds for the contemporary study of suicide and its prevention were then sown.

Contemporary suicidology is now almost fifty years old. Yet, despite the fact that the concern about suicide predated the European presence in Canada, contemporary suicidology in Canada is much younger, maybe twenty-five years at best. This fact of history is critical because there are distinct differences between suicide and its prevention in Canada and in the United States (Leenaars, 1995). Canada has its own history in suicidology. Regrettably, little is known about the critical foundations in Canada, even by people in the field. It is the intent of this essay, as of the rest of this volume, to address this lack, although this essay is by no means exhaustive.

Because of this short history, we were able to ask various important players to tell their story themselves. (There are other people who equally should be included in our list; regrettably, many were unable to participate. An obvious lack is the discussion of the history in Quebec – e.g., Quebec Association of Suicidology and Suicide Action, Montreal – despite an invitation.) Of course, the truth is that the authors in this volume have been a part of our history in suicidology. Yet, the people in this essay have laid some of the early Canadian foundations. They are the people, following Shneidman into the vault, who have sown the seeds for further development in suicide prevention in Canada.

To end this brief introduction, we shall quote another key person in the history of Canadian suicidology, whose premature death was a deep loss to our field. Clare Brant wrote: 'One of the favourite phrases is, "We look back to find a new direction." If you get lost, you try to find out where you came from. Look back to find a new direction' (1987: 181).

Thus, we shall let the key people themselves speak to allow for direction, or a foundation, for suicidology in Canada to spring forth.

The History of Suicide amongst Tribal People in Canada (Connors)

The history of suicide amongst the original tribal people of North America shows the drastic shifts in health status that has accompanied the transition from tribal society to civilized society. All of the accumulated evidence appears to point to a drastic decline in most indicators of health since the point of contact with European civilization in 1492. It is becoming a well-known fact that the European newcomers to this land viewed their society as superior and sought to destroy or convert the tribal peoples to their 'civilized' ways. This period of more than five hundred years of genocide has taken a heavy toll on the tribal people of North America, as has been the case globally wherever civilized society has attempted to colonize tribal peoples. It is estimated that from thirty to fifty million tribal people were killed worldwide during the process of colonization, 'including the complete annihilation of every tribal person in Newfoundland, Tasmania and Banda Neira'(Gawitrhá, 1991: 122).

While history paints a tragic picture for North American tribal people, this devastation did not occur without forewarning. Most tribal people of North America have prophecies that foretold the coming of the European to North America and the suffering, ill health, and death that would occur amongst the tribal people as a consequence of this contact. However, almost all of these prophecies also tell of a time of healing that will mark the re-establishment of a state of health amongst tribal people as they rediscover the powerful healing knowledge from their pasts. Many of these prophecies also indicate that a true time of healing will follow for all races on this planet as the tribal people help all other races to reconnect with the wisdom from their tribal roots in order to re-establish balance between all life forms. It is believed that this healing will be necessary if we are to survive on this planet.

Many people have already recognized the signs that indicate we are now in the time of healing, when the tribal people of North America will reconnect with their tribal healing knowledge and begin their ascendancy to a healthier state. A sense of hope and optimism is growing in First Nations communities across Canada as these prophecies continue to unfold.

It is against this historical backdrop and through these prophecies that the history of suicide amongst tribal peoples in Canada can best be understood. Violence directed at oneself or towards others within one's own tribal community was a relatively rare occurrence in the past within tribal society. While there had to be enough of these behaviours demonstrated to warrant the creation of totems and taboos to discourage their expression, the incidence of such behaviours appears to have been extremely limited by the time of contact. In the case of suicide, the only recorded occurrences of this behaviour suggest that these actions, while rare, did occur. However, when such acts occurred they appear to have been consistent with the social structure and beliefs of tribal society. In other words, suicide was not a meaningless act of aggression against oneself or others, but was an act of self-sacrifice that was meant to promote the health and viability of the larger community.

In the case of the warrior who forfeited his life when facing certain death, his suicidal act was inspired by the honour he and his relatives received from his promoting the continuance of the tribe. The native person who took her/ his life after being treated disrespectfully, or not in accordance with tribal custom, invoked the tribe to correct the imbalance within the tribe by dealing harshly with the transgressor. Many of the people who violated tribal custom in such a way as to dishonour a person's spirit, such that the person would choose to leave this life, were banished from the tribe. Therefore, the suicide resulted in a re-establishment of balance within the community and the main-tenance of a healthy lifestyle. The suicidal action was not egocentrically moti-vated but ecocentrically guided (i.e., behaviour directed by a concern for maintaining health and survival of the group by maintaining balance between all of creation). The native person who took his/her life after a precious loved one died tragically and honourably often did so in order to further mark the value of their loved one's action in support of the healthy growth and survival of the community. Often the honourable suicide and related honourable events became part of the community folklore through story and/or song, which continued to promote the value that no greater love hath a man or woman than to give his/her life for the healthy continuation of his/her people. This certainly was the thinking of those native elders who, when they had decided they had become too much of a burden on their people, chose their time to enter into the next life. However, even this time was considered to be determined by the Creator and the suicide was, therefore, a spiritually condoned act.

If one understands the form of tribal thought before its transformation through the process of acculturation, it is possible to recognize that suicide was viewed in a very different light than it is considered today (Rupert Ross [1992] offers valuable insights into tribal thought in his book *Dancing with a Ghost*). In fact, suicide in tribal culture was both rational and adaptive when viewed in the context of survival of the tribe and maintaining equilibrium within all of the creation.

Since contact with civilized society, the prophecies of the declining health of North American tribal people have continued to unfold. As the process of acculturation has continued, suicidal behaviour among tribal people in this country has shifted from a rate that was, in all likelihood, lower than that of the European population to a present-day rate that is on average six to seven times that of the current Canadian population. This steady rise in the suicide rate amongst the tribal people of Canada has occurred throughout the period of acculturation/genocide. As the rate has increased it is apparent that the meaning and purpose of suicide has changed within tribal communities. The behaviour that once was viewed as a functional act has been transformed into a meaningless behaviour within communities that are often devoid of beliefs and values. It appears as though communities that are most disconnected from their tribal identities, and/or that of the dominant Canadian society, suffer the highest rates of suicide (Berry, 1990; Westlake Van Winkle and May, 1986). The evidence is mounting to support the belief that the effort by the dominant Canadian society to force the tribal people of Canada to assimilate is the major reason for the decline in health of this people. Similarly, this assimilative pressure is likely behind the significantly higher rates of suicide witnessed amongst the tribal people of Canada.

There is sufficient reason to believe in a healthier future despite the rather bleak pictures that the current suicide rates of Canadian tribal people seem to paint. The prophecies forecasting a healthier future for tribal peoples have started to unfold. Many communities are beginning to reconnect themselves with the essential values and beliefs that have formerly supported a healthier lifestyle and environment for their members. Within these communities it is evident that the social structures are starting to reform as values and beliefs re-emerge, allowing the people to make meaning of life and to discover their life purpose.

These changes are being witnessed within tribal communities like Alkali Lake, British Columbia, which transformed from reporting 95 per cent alcoholism to 5 per cent alcoholism in a ten-year period. The signs of the healing times were also apparent in Edmonton, Alberta, during July 1992, when approximately 2000 tribal people from around the planet gathered to celebrate the emerging health within their peoples. This gathering, called Healing Our Spirits Worldwide, was truly a powerful sign of the healthier path that the tribal people of Canada are now treading. If these and other signs are true indicators that we are now in the 'healing times,' we can expect to see a decline in the suicide rates amongst the tribal people of Canada during the years to come.

In the meantime, perhaps we should recognize the large numbers of tribal youth who are taking their lives as a reflection of the ill state that our current Canadian society has achieved. Our participation in forming a society that supports oppression and inequities to the degree that a significant portion of our youth choose death over life does not speak well for our 'civilized' society. Hopefully, these tragic losses will awaken us to the awareness that our current social structures are not promoting the health and well-being that we desire for all of our citizens. Perhaps it is time that we all look to our tribal pasts for the knowledge that helped sustain healthier states for all of creation. The social structures developed within tribal society seem to provide healthier environments that promote life.

Our children are crying out to us:
'We want a new world, and we want it now.'
They have a right to it.
All of us have that right.
We are the ones who are going to have to make this new world.
We are going to have to learn again
how to respect each other as men and women.
Understanding of respect is one of the strongest principles
held in the belief system of the Native today.

Arthur Solomon (1994: 58)

Suicide Intervention (Osborg)

It is obviously impossible for one such as myself to give a totally objective view of suicide prevention in Canada, since there was too much personal involvement – intellectual, emotional, and financial. It has been part of my experience from early childhood onwards. It is still a background noise – now in my eighties – in my present-day existence.

The roots of suicide prevention in this country are old. It was in 1961 that I was first alerted to the need for such a service by a brother-priest. I had made a death-bed promise to him to carry on the work in March of 1962. Subsequently, I became a member of the Order of St Luke, the Physician, an Anglican order dedicated to spiritual/liturgical healing as well as such efforts as suicide prevention. The order, which is now ecumenical, started to operate its first suicide-prevention service in Berlin in 1948 during the airlift. I became aware of this work during a visit to Europe in 1967. However, the concept of suicide-prevention was already developing in North America. In 1963 I attended my first suicide prevention conference in Philadelphia, where the idea was tentatively discussed. During my next visit there in 1964 some private conversations alerted me to the need for the introduction of the service in Canada. It was during that same year that the Salvation Army began a 'flying service' in Toronto, providing intervention to suicidal people in their homes.

My own personal involvement stems from the Berlin visit in 1967. The order's records showed that in 1948 about 6000 persons committed suicide in Berlin (with a population of perhaps one million). Nineteen forty-eight was the year of the airlift. The city had been totally cut off. Depression was common. The predominant method for suicide was jumping out of windows. Private telephones were virtually non-existent; yet, the prevention service began as an effort to save lives. Even by 1967 most calls for help were made from public telephone boxes.

Upon my return from Europe, I came to the realization that something similar could be done in Canada. Numerous phone calls brought forth the impression that (1) nobody had ever heard of the concept and (2) very few seemed to care. Thus, I initiated a letter-writing campaign to anyone I thought *might* be interested. The result was, however, not particularly encouraging. However, Maritime Telephone in Halifax was concerned and provided its boardroom for a meeting. The date was 12 June 1968. Invitations were issued and, much to my surprise, twenty-two delegates from as many organizations showed up. I presented the idea of a telephone service, and the concept was accepted as a blueprint.

However, problems arose. A representative of an Atlantic association (of which I was not a member) offered himself as interim secretary. His offer was accepted, whereas I was frozen out. Nothing happened after the meeting in the Maritimes. (Of course, this is not unique to the Maritimes; this story has been repeated in many parts of this country.) Nothing, that is, until early in 1969, when I got a telephone call from the Student Union of Dalhousie University in Halifax. They had planned a 'teach-in' on suicide prevention. I was asked to be a speaker. In Halifax, I met with a group of students who wanted to start a suicide-prevention service. I addressed them for three hours before lunch, and for another three afterwards. None of the other speakers invited to the meeting showed up.

The group established a prevention service in the Student Union Building. The service has never stopped, and it is still the only 24-hour-a-day service in the Maritimes.

There were further efforts:

1 In 1969 I submitted a brief to the minister of justice (John Turner) that asked for removal of section 213 from the Canadian Criminal Code. Under the terms of the section, attempted suicide was punishable by six months in jail and/or a fine. In 1972 Minister of Justice Otto Lang phoned to say that section 213 had been removed from Criminal Code.
2 During 1969 I was invited by the National Institute for Mental Health in Bethesda, Maryland, to report on work done in this country.
3 In September 1969 I represented this country at the conference of the International Association for Suicide Prevention (IASP) in London, England. In 1970 I attended the IASP conference in Stockholm, primarily to tell the rest of the world that we had a working service – patchy, yes, but working nonetheless.

My trip to Stockholm in 1970 was my last main effort in the field. By 1973 I was in retirement.

Suicide Prevention and Distress Centre, Toronto (Winch and Letofsky)

'Passionately unselfish' was a phrase used by Knowlton Nash to pay tribute to Professor William Kilbourne, one of the founding members of Distress Centre, Toronto. This spirit of intense caring also informed the forty-eight trained lay workers, the board, and the church funders in 1967 as we reached out through this new telephone service to the lonely and suicidal on 1 November. This effort marked one of the first volunteer telephone lines in Canada. The first, to our knowledge, was started in Sudbury by Reverend Bruce McDougall, and was called Lifeline.

As the service began, we volunteers were concerned about the adequacy of our suicide-prevention skills. The first three calls were suicide threats. The Los Angeles Suicide Prevention Center and the Samaritans guided us, and our confidence increased through our experience with callers. Between 1967 and 1978 the number of suicidal calls increased each year. During that same period the Metro Toronto Coroner reported a rise in the number of suicidal deaths.

Using the telephone as a way to reach out for help in a crisis was a new idea. We were encouraged by grateful callers who reported feeling calmer and more hopeful after talking to us; some took the trouble to write to us in those critical first months of service: 'Dear Friends, I am writing this letter to thank you all very much for saving my life. My very special thanks to G——— for having such insight into helping me solve my problem and for persevering with me when it was hard. I remember hazily that if it wasn't for her, I wouldn't be here today ...'

The Service grew because of vital contacts with many people, most notably the following:

• Dr Graham Cotter. In 1964 Graham Cotter, after visiting branches in the United Kingdom and talking to the founder, Reverend Chad Varah, described the plan of the Samaritans. This document prompted the Anglican Social Service Council to form a committee that two years later, May 1967, became incorporated as the Board of Distress Centre.
• Reverend Chad Varah. A Canadian branch of the Samaritans was important to Chad and he visited Andrew Todd, the Distress Centre director, in October 1967, before the first call was taken. Varah had offered help to suicidal people in the early 1950s in London, England. The genius of Varah was in recognizing that caring people were able to ease suicidal feelings. Out of this vision of the lay person as a suicide-prevention worker came a formal structure that involved the recruitment of helpers, training, and running of telephone lines into a centre of operation in the church crypt.

Equally relevant at this time was publicity. The excitement of our work spread through the press. In 1968 Elizabeth Kilbourn wrote 'Life and Death on the Suicide Line' for *Saturday Night*. An article also appeared in *Reader's Digest* that carried our Toronto telephone number. (A family in Montreal was called day and night by suicidal people because they happened to have the same number.)

These early steps set a framework that included the following:

1 OATDC. Gordon Winch, the first author, invited the directors of newly emerging centres to meet on a weekend in November 1969. It was stimulat-

ing to hear of initiatives and insights from work in Scarborough, Niagara Falls, St Catharines, Ottawa, London, Sudbury, Collingwood, Belleville, and Oshawa as well as the Salvation Army Suicide Prevention Bureau. We called ourselves the Ontario Association of Telephone Distress Centres. Soon the word 'telephone' was omitted, and now the group is called Distress Centres Ontario. The Association held spring and fall conferences and set accreditation standards for its members early in the 1970s.

2 CCCC. Pat Delbridge hosted delegates from Canadian distress and crisis centres in Ottawa in the fall of 1972 for the first national conference. British Columbia and Ontario were well represented; other provinces whose centres were in various stages of growth were also present. The difficulties in establishing a national structure meant that we did not meet again until we invited the nearly one hundred centres to send delegates, in 1978 and in 1980 (Toronto) to what was to become the Canadian Council of Crisis Centres.

3 MADC. Metro and Area Distress Centres has held monthly meetings of support and learning since 1970 and has included twelve suicide and befriending centres in the Greater Toronto Area. One value of MADC has been maintaining consistency of response for young suicidal callers, who have often been highly manipulative in their intense usage of different centres.

To conclude from years of experience with crisis centres, we would like to quote Louis Dublin: 'The lay volunteer was the single most important discovery of the (suicide prevention) movement in this century. Nothing else of significance happened until he/she came into the picture' (1969: 45).

Psychiatric Developments (Sakinofsky)

Each of these vignettes presents a perception of the development of suicidology in Canada that is uniquely personal. My own is that of an immigrant who came to Canada from an English-speaking culture close to a generation ago, at a point where my interest in studying and working with suicidal people was well established and I had acquired the tools of a professional training in psychiatry. This had occurred both in my native South Africa and subsequently in Britain and necessarily reflected an Anglo-European perspective. Although my doctoral thesis in Cape Town had included a section on attempted suicide, my years in Britain reinforced the determination that my career in psychiatry would be wasted unless I chose to focus on one of the life-threatening mental-health problems. Suicide encompassed all of them, ergo this field was where I had to be. How foolhardy and arrogant are the young!

It was to McMaster University, Hamilton, and its cluster of teaching hospitals that I came in 1968, and fairly soon (with the help of an enlightened chief of medicine, Bill Goldberg) I was able to set up a special program for suicidal people at St Joseph's Hospital (site of the regional psychiatric emergency services) that was modelled on the unit created in Edinburgh by Norman Kreitman and Henry Mathew. Although I knew of the Los Angeles Suicide Prevention Center, I had only a hazy conception of how it worked. A few years later, when our unit was visited by Edwin Shneidman, I came to know more about it, and learned about programs in Oxford and Australia from other visitors (Keith Hawton and Bob Goldney). Our unit, which we euphemistically called the Liaison Unit (it had grown out of the hospital's psychiatric consultation-liaison service), took on a character of its own that, for the times, was untraditional. Although the team was led by its two psychiatrists (Emil Zamora and myself), the nurses functioned as primary therapists side by side with the psychiatric residents and medical students. The assessments of each case were comprehensive and included meetings with the family, judicious and protective contact with employers, and ongoing cooperation with the relevant social agencies, representatives of which were invited to the case conferences. Our goal was to do intensive crisis work and have the patient back in the community within seventy-two hours. We did not always achieve so tight a timetable, particularly with adolescents who had left home, but the goals of comprehensive evaluation and community orientation were always adhered to. Further details on the philosophy of the program may be gathered from presentations made at the 1979 IASP meeting held in Ottawa by Anne Howe (Howe and Sakinofsky, 1979), an early head nurse, and June Miller (Miller, Sakinofsky, and Streiner, 1979), a psychiatric social worker.

The Ottawa IASP meeting was a major early event in organized suicide prevention in Canada. Two important suicidologists who were mainly responsible for bringing this meeting to Canada should be mentioned: Jim Brown (of Winnipeg) and the then Diane Syer (who founded an innovative program based at the Toronto East General Hospital with some similarities to our own). Brown was at the time the national representative for Canada on IASP and his published work on suicide is first rate. Although some of us (including these two, as well as Gordon Winch of Toronto and Sol Hirsch from Halifax) had been attending international IASP meetings for years, there is no doubt that bringing the IASP meeting to Ottawa gave great impetus to the profile of the growing suicidology movement in Canada. It undoubtedly paved the way for the first attempt at a Canadian Association for Suicide Prevention. Until the first CASP was formed, suicidology was identified by two solitudes. On the one hand, a network of distress centres and telephone hot lines staffed by volunteers dotted the country, notably those centres in Toronto led by Gordon Winch and Pat Harnisch, and in Ottawa by Pat Delbridge. On the other hand, there were university- and hospital-based programs like ours in Hamilton, Jim Brown's unit in Winnipeg, Paul Termansen's SAFER program in Vancouver, and Diane Syer's program in Toronto (the last combined a professionally staffed in-patient unit with volunteers working in the emergency room). By the time of the Ottawa meeting, hospital-based SHARE (run by David Lippman and Rosemary Barnes) was well established at the Toronto General Hospital, and Barry Garfinkel was working with and writing about suicidal teenagers at the Toronto Hospital for Sick Children. At IASP (and later CASP) the two solitudes came together, as they have been doing at the American Association of Suicidology (AAS) in the United States.

By this time, an important development had occurred in Alberta: a sociologist, Menno Boldt, had chaired a provincial task force on suicide that led to the 'Alberta model' of suicide prevention and the appointment of Mark Solomon, an American, as the first provincial suicidologist (succeeded by Ron Dyck, who remains the only provincial suicidologist in Canada). It was quite natural that epidemiological studies would follow to determine the size of the problem in Alberta, and during the 1980s community surveys of suicidality were published out of Calgary (Ramsay and Bagley, 1985) and Edmonton (Dyck et al., 1988). Calgary had shown a strong interest in combating suicide even earlier. Keith Pearce, a leading psychiatrist there, had been much influenced by the work of Peter Sainsbury in England. This influence has possibly also permeated the education-based work there today of Bryan Tanney and Roger Tierney.

Indirectly, the Alberta task force and its report probably also inspired the federal government to set up its own task force on suicide, which so far has published two reports (National Task Force on Suicide in Canada, 1987, 1994). Meanwhile, the surge in suicide rates in Quebec carried its own public concern and led to the rapid growth of suicide-prevention centres and to much greater attention to suicide in medical and social research – too much to chronicle here and some of which I have detailed in the next chapter with reference to the work, among others, of Richard Boyer and Alain Lesage. Reference is also made there to the studies by Jarvis and colleagues in London, Ontario, by Hoening and co-workers in Newfoundland, and to the later work by Jon Ennis (who followed Lippman at SHARE and has himself been succeeded by Frances Newman) and Ken Adam (in attachment theory).

Insofar as organized suicidology is concerned, CASP did not long survive the emigration of Diane Syer-Solursh to the United States and the to-be-regretted departure from the field of Jim Brown. It was left to Antoon Leenaars, trained and mentored by Edwin Shneidman himself, to resuscitate a new CASP and to set it on its feet. Leenaars is also a prolific researcher and well complemented in his work in suicidology by his wife, Susanne Wenckstern.

For my own part, after some years in administration of a hospital department I moved to the Clarke Institute of Psychiatry in 1992, specifically to resume my clinical and research interests in suicide studies. At the Clarke I have established a High Risk Consultation Clinic that sees cases at a tertiary level, that is, referred by their treating psychiatrists and psychologists. These patients are systematically studied in the process of evaluating what might yet be added to the treatment of this hard-core, difficult clientele. The Suicide Studies Program at the Clarke Institute is involved in ongoing research studies that have so far included epidemiological studies (suicidality in the Ontario Health Survey; peacekeeping and suicide in the Canadian Armed Forces) and other clinical and biological research. Money is the major limitation. However, thanks to community workers led by Doris Sommer-Rotenberg, plans are afoot to establish at the Clarke a research chair in suicide studies in memory of her son Arthur before this century is out, which may alleviate some of the problem.

A Brief History of the Development of the Alberta Model of Suicide Prevention (Boldt)

The 'Alberta Model' for providing coordinated and comprehensive suicide-prevention services has already been fully described (see Boldt, 1985a). Therefore, my account here will be limited to providing a history of the *process* of establishing the 'Alberta Model,' and I do so from the personal perspective of my role in this process.

My involvement in suicide prevention came about quite by chance. Following my appointment at the University of Lethbridge in 1970, I undertook a collaborative venture with a student, Leroy Little Bear, to develop a proposal for a Native American Studies Department at our university. Our approach to this venture entailed broad consultation with native Indian elders, leaders, and educators. In early January 1973, Little Bear and I were returning from a visit with some elders of the Blood First Nation. Our route took us by the reserve cemetery. Just five days earlier the prairie landscape had been blanketed with a fresh fall of snow, so the six mounds of black earth marking new grave sites stood out starkly on the field of white. It troubled me that in such a small community six people had died in the space of five days. Upon returning to my office I made inquiries and discovered that only one of these six deaths was from natural causes. Of the remaining five deaths, two were traffic fatalities and three were suicides.

Convinced that the number of suicidal deaths signalled something seriously wrong, I felt compelled to write to the Honourable Neil Crawford, then Alberta's minister of social services and community health, informing him of what I had learned. At the same time, I urged that his department conduct a formal inquiry into the incidence of suicides in native communities in Alberta. Wondrously, this letter started a series of events that culminated, ultimately, in the 'Alberta Model' of suicide prevention. Some six weeks later I received a telephone call from the deputy minister of social services and community health informing me that the Government of Alberta was creating a special task force with a mandate to study suicides in Alberta. Subsequently, the minister appointed me to chair this task force.

The work of the task force involved extensive and intensive research and consultations. Our endeavours included a review and detailed analysis of the medical, psychological, social, and law-enforcement circumstances in 1147 suicidal deaths reported by the Alberta medical examiner over a five-year period. A related study comprised a survey and evaluation of existing suicide and self-injury services and staffing arrangements in all 184 helping agencies in Alberta's six urban communities. The data indicated that no agency defined itself or was recognized by other agencies as particularly qualified to deal with self-destructive behaviours. The findings from these two studies supported subsequent task-force recommendations for establishing training programs intended to develop effective suicide detection and treatment skills among 'gatekeepers' (front-line staff). Our data also provided the inspiration to organize local suicide-prevention services in a coordinated community interagency basis. Both of these concepts were subsequently implemented with significant results.

Another study focused on native Indian self-destructive deaths. This study revealed that native persons manifest different prodromal clues to suicide than other Canadians, and that few seek help from main-line agencies. This study supported task-force recommendations for a unique suicide-prevention service and training program for native gatekeepers designed for the social and cultural realities of native peoples.

During the period when the task force was doing its work, a provincial cabinet shuffle brought a different minister to the Department of Social Services and Community Health. My communications to the new minister requesting action on the report's recommendations were answered with polite excuses. On one occasion I was summoned to the minister's office in the legislature and reprimanded for my reported statements to the media criticizing the government for its inaction on the report's recommendations. It became clear to me that the task-force report was being relegated to the government's notorious 'shelf.' Perhaps it is a measure of my naiveté, but this was an outcome I had not anticipated, nor could I accept it. I determined to undertake a campaign intended to bring broad-based public pressure on the government to take action on the task-force recommendations.

Together with a colleague, Bob Arms, a psychologist at the University of Lethbridge, we mapped a strategy for an extensive and intensive province-wide campaign of public lobbying for government action on the report. We made it known to appropriate groups throughout Alberta that we were available to make a presentation on suicide and its prevention. There was considerable public interest in our offer, and we received more invitations than we could accept. We presented to schools, teachers conventions, nurses, social-welfare workers, community associations, church groups, service clubs, sororities, and so on. We addressed rural and urban groups ranging in size from fifteen to five hundred. The general response to our appeal was very encouraging and at times beyond our most optimistic expectations. One unforgettable event was a presentation we made to an annual convention of the women's auxiliary of the United Church. The attending delegates voted, there and then, to support our campaign of lobbying the government for meaningful action. Over 130 attending delegates returned to their respective churches and initiated a letter-writing campaign in their home congregations urging government action. This 'multiplier effect' produced a flood of letters to the legislature from various parts of Alberta demanding immediate action.

Throughout the period of our campaigning for public involvement and support, we also conducted an intensive lobbying initiative through the media. Television, radio, and print media all were uniformly interested and supportive of our goal. One of our media friends at the time was a popular reporter for CTV in Calgary, who later was elected mayor of Calgary, and subsequently became premier of the province of Alberta, the Honourable Ralph Klein. A great disappointment and hindrance in our efforts to spur the government to take action on the recommendations of the task-force report was the bizarre role played by the Alberta Medical Association. Despite repeated invitations the AMA had refused to participate or cooperate in the work of the task force, yet, subsequently, when the recommendations were submitted to the minister, the association forcefully opposed their implementation on the ground that the task force had failed to consult them. This opposition, expressed privately to the minister of social services and community health, was cited by the minister as justification for holding up action on the task-force recommendations.

Our public-lobbying efforts continued over a four-year period and began to yield some tangible results with the creation of the position of Provincial Suicidologist in 1978. This action had some symbolic significance, but truly meaningful action did not occur until 1981, following the installation of the Honourable Bob Bogle as minister of community health and services. By the time of Bogle's appointment the issue of suicide prevention had become politicized to such a degree that government officials had assumed a defensive position. In consequence, Bogle initially took a very discouraging posture when I first approached him to take action on the task-force recommendations.

At our first meeting, Bogle and I had a spirited debate. This confrontation turned out to be a pivotal event for suicide prevention in Alberta. Bogle proved he was a person of conscience, with a keen sense of 'rightness.' Following our debate, he made it his business to study the task-force report, and he came to the personal conclusion that, indeed, suicide and self-destructive behaviour constituted a significant human tragedy in Alberta, deserving of government intervention along the lines recommended in the task-force report.

Having reached this conclusion, Bogle took swift, imaginative, and decisive action. He established a citizen committee (the Suicide Prevention Provincial Advisory Committee) and invited me to serve as its chair. He gave the committee a broad mandate: to advise him on the development of programs for suicide prevention and intervention, to make recommendations for the funding of programs, training, and research, and to advise him on public-education needs. He then created a significant initial $800,000 annual budget for development of a suicide-prevention program in Alberta. Bogle arranged that the advisory committee would be responsible directly and only to himself for its decisions and actions. During my five-year tenure as chair of the committee, the minister, without a single exception, affirmed all of the committee's decisions. In effect, by locating decision making outside the multilayered bureaucratic maze, Bogle, calculatedly created a 'fast track' approach to establishing a suicide-prevention program in Alberta. This innovative approach proved to be efficient and cost-effective and, I believe, could advantageously be emulated in many spheres of government activity as an alternative and in preference to the current trend to privatize government services.

I want to close this account with a personal observation. My experience in the field of suicide-prevention has convinced me that if suicide prevention is to be effective we, the practitioners, must consider our work to be more than a career, a practice, or a field of academic study. People kill themselves because they find their life intolerable, and because they believe their future holds no hope for improvement. If we want to be effective in suicide-prevention we must do more than merely prevent people from killing themselves. We must act to make every life tolerable. We must act to change the coercive circumstances in the lives of individuals that impel them to seek an escape from life. In short, we must treat suicide prevention as a cause – the cause of enhancing human lives. This implies a need for a deep personal commitment to the promotion of the values of humanity and human dignity in our society. It is at this level that true prevention begins. Without this kind of prevention the growing burden of intervention, given the limited resources available, will soon overwhelm us.

In completing this account, it is appropriate that I acknowledge some special individuals who were a big part of the process of developing suicide prevention services in Alberta and who, I know, met the high standard of treating suicide prevention as a humanitarian 'cause.' For some this acknowledgment comes posthumously (p), but they deserve to be remembered for their selfless commitment: Walter Mackenzie (p), Sebastian Littmann (p), Hub Fish (p), Jean Collins, Tara Lavelle, Brenda Simpson, Pearl Wolfe, Kathy McKee, Judith Blythe, and Trevor Esau. The list would be wanting without acknowledging the assistance and inspiration provided to our 'cause' by Norman Farberow, Sam Heilig, and Margaret Kirpatrick, all from the Los Angeles Suicide Prevention Center. A list such as this is never exhaustive, and I extend sincere apologies to those deserving persons that have been omitted. To all who are committed to the cause, your reward will derive from the lives you save by helping to make them more tolerable.

The Canadian Association for Suicide Prevention (Leenaars)

Writing this piece on the history of suicidology is somewhat like a self-directed wish – calling a blessing on oneself.

The classical approach to the prevention of mental-health and public-health problems is that of Gerald Caplan, who in the book *Principles of Preventive Psychiatry* (1964) distinguished among primary, secondary, and tertiary prevention. The more commonly used concepts today for these three modes of prevention are *prevention*, *intervention*, and *postvention*, respectively. All have a place in the prevention (in the generic sense) of suicide.

Postvention – a term introduced by Edwin Shneidman in 1971 – refers to those things done after a dire event has occurred. Postvention deals with the traumatic aftershocks in the survivors of suicide.

Intervention relates to the treatment and care of a suicidal crisis or suicidal problem. Secondary prevention refers to doing something during the events. Intervention deals with the suicidal person.

Prevention relates to the principles of good mental hygiene in general. It consists of strategies to ameliorate the conditions that lead to suicide: 'to come before' (*prae-venire*) an event before it can occur. Primary prevention is education. This book itself is an example of 'something.' Associations for prevention are primary prevention. It is in this regard that I write this *autohistory*, namely about the Canadian Association for Suicide Prevention / L'Association canadienne pour la prévention du suicide (CASP/ACPS).

In June 1988, CASP was resurrected from its own suicide. That meeting was skilfully hosted by Suicide Action, Montreal. At that meeting, I was elected to be the first president of a viable CASP. A conscious decision was made by the newly elected board of directors to dissociate from the earlier attempt at an association and to develop a new CASP that would meet its objective: 'To promote within Canada activities designed to reduce the incidence and/or effects of suicide.'

The earlier attempt at CASP was started in 1985 with its incorporation. Much of the necessary paper work (with my thanks) was done by Diane Syer and Pat Harnisch. Yet, CASP had ceased to function shortly after 1986. Membership was problematic; for instance, members, especially from the West, had resigned, claiming that their needs were not met. No income-tax papers were filed (which later, through the kindness of a civil servant and hours of work by Marcia Krawll, was addressed). There was no annual general meeting, and so by its own bylaws CASP ceased to exist. Yet, the death was likely much more dynamic. At the top there was deep conflict. One side suggested that there was disrespect and aggression. The other blamed that side for avoidance. Regardless of what was the truth, such dynamics often lead to suicide in our patients – and, one can conclude, an association.

The real work to meet the objectives of the new CASP was undertaken within the peaceful and inspirational setting of Lake Louise. There was also an important meeting on a farm in St-Damien, Quebec. But it was especially Lake Louise that became the cornerstone for our development and fellowship in suicide prevention across Canada. As Aboriginal legends would predict, Lake Louise became CASP's spiritual home.

'The group of six' – I often called them 'the gang of six' – that first met at Lake Louise included Marcia Krawll, Brian Mishara, Linda Rosenfeld, Bob Sims, and Bryan Tanney. I was honoured to work with these bright – and dynamic – leaders in our field. These people are the true grandparents of our association. Yet, there was one other person who was my constant consultant in every step, namely Edwin Shneidman. Shneidman has been my guide throughout my suicidological career.

Of course, no association can function without day-to-day support. The first office of CASP was set up in my home. Susanne Wenckstern, my wife – and a respected suicidologist in Canada – worked as the office secretary. My children – Lindsey, Heather, and Kristen – stuffed the envelopes, mailed the letters, and so on. They were the earliest young volunteers of CASP. Subsequently, the Suicide Information and Education Centre (SIEC) became our office as CASP grew. CASP will always be grateful to their support.

Constructive plans were developed by 'the group of six' to meet our objective. A five-year plan was written by myself (and accepted by the board), focusing on the following initiatives: building membership; networking and

TABLE 1
CASP Five-Year Strategic Plan

The Canadian Association for Suicide Prevention's objective is 'To promote within Canada activities designed to reduce the incidence and/or effects of suicide.' To meet these objectives, the CASP Board of Directors accepted the following five-year plan of goals and objectives. The Board and committees are working on specific plans for accomplishing the following goals over the next five years:

1. Increase and Maintain Membership
    a) Substantially increase membership. 1989–1994
    b) Secure membership from across Canada. 1989–1994
    c) Ensure representation of all various Canadian groups involved in and concerned with suicide prevention. 1989–1994
    d) Maintain membership committee to biannually review membership. 1989–1994
2. Improve Networking via Communication
    a) Provide all communications in French and English. 1989
    b) Establish publication (CASP News). 1989
    c) Encourage submissions to publications. 1990
    d) Establish a list of resources. 1991
    e) Increase publications. 1992
    f) Maintain high standard of publication.
3. Establish Networking via Organizing Conferences, based on accepted principle of National and alternating Regional Conferences
    a) Organize first regional conference in Toronto. 1989
    b) Organize first national conference in Vancouver. 1990
    c) Organize regional conference in Atlantic region. 1991
    d) Organize national conference in Prairies. 1992
    e) Co-Sponsor conference of International Association for Suicide Prevention in Montreal. 1993
    f) Continue sponsorship of national and regional alternating conferences. 1994
4. Increase Awareness of Issues regarding Suicide
    a) Build media relationship. 1989–1994
    b) Request meeting with federal government. 1989
    c) Implement co-operative effort with federal government. 1990
    d) Enhance existing service. 1992
    e) Collaborate and expand resource center (i.e. SIEC) in providing up-to-date Canadian information.
5. Coordinate School Efforts
    a) Establish School Committee. 1989
    b) Assess needs for schools. 1989–1992
    c) Present first preliminary report to Board. 1990
    d) Develop draft recommendations. 1992
    e) Distribute information (e.g., resource). 1992–1993
    f) Maintain network. 1993–1994
6. Address Suicide in Native Canadians
    a) Meet with various Native groups. 1989–1992
    b) Convene Board meeting in Northern Canada. 1991

TABLE 1 (*continued*)

c) Assist in suggestions of native groups. 1992–1994

d) Develop options for printing and translation in Inuktitut.

7. Promote Research in Suicidology

a) Establish a research column in CASP News. 1990

b) Assess high risk groups. 1991

c) Provide findings through existing publications. 1992

d) Provide consultation to the federal government on research needs, in efforts to solicit their support. Ongoing

8. Improve Operational Structure

a) Obtain representation of Board members from across Canada. 1989

b) Improve participation of Board members. 1989–1990

c) Establish a central office. 1991

d) Hire an Executive Director and/or appropriate staff person to conduct Association business. 1991

e) Develop goal and objectives for next five-year plan. 1994

f) Develop fund raising strategies to diversify financial base to secure functioning of organization. Ongoing

October 21, 1989

Source: CASP News 1(2) (Jan. 1990): 3–4

communication; developing conferences; increasing awareness; establishing our first committee to address suicide in youth, the School Committee; addressing suicide among First Nations and Inuit Canadians; promoting research and improving operational structures.

Table 1 presents this plan as it appeared in 1990 in *CASP News*. This five-year plan, I believe, continues to serve as a blueprint for CASP's development as CASP moves through its second five-year plan.

There have been many activities; let me here highlight a few and then turn to the larger issue of advocacy.

1 *CASP News*. This national newsletter, first edited superbly by Bryan Tanney, was/is/will be designed to be a major link in suicide-prevention in Canada. It is professionally produced by the Suicide Information and Education Centre (SIEC) in Calgary.

2 Conferences. Our first regional conference, chaired by Isaac Sakinofsky, was held at St Michael's Hospital in Toronto in 1989. Our first national conference, chaired by Krawll, Rosenfeld, and Tanney (program chair), was held in Vancouver in 1990. Our keynote speaker was my dear friend Edwin Shneidman, the father of modern suicidology, who came as a personal favour to me. That event secured a firm place for CASP in Canada. There were sub-

sequent conferences in Moncton, Saskatoon, Montreal (in association with the International Association for Suicide Prevention), Iqaluit, and Banff. Future conferences will continue this means of primary prevention.

3 Awards. CASP in 1992 at its national conference in Saskatoon, chaired by Michael Kral and Bob Sims, handed out its first awards, both in research and service. Isaac Sakinofsky received the research award for his studies of suicide in Canada and Sheila Levy received the service award for her work in starting the crisis line in Baffin Island. The acknowledgment of the contributors to suicidology will be a continued reinforcement for excellence.

There have been efforts with our government to attempt *national* efforts in primary prevention. The most important event occurred in June 1990, when we met with the supportive Honourable Perrin Beatty, minister of health and welfare, in Ottawa. Having surveyed many people, we presented the people's ideas about suicide prevention in Canada. Let me here restate the leadership role that our government should take:

• Setting a realistic goal for a percentage reduction in the overall suicide rate for Canada by the year 2000
• Addressing the problem of unreliable reporting of suicide in Canada
• Establishing the means for surveillance of clinically treated suicide attempts
• Addressing the problem of Aboriginal suicide

Recommendations to the federal government were made in three areas that are within its domain:

1 *Health promotion.* We stressed the need for information for caregivers and the need for a publication for survivors. There is a need for Canadian information.
2 *Research.* We highlighted the need for Canadian research on attempters and called for a meeting for Canadian researchers to establish research priorities.
3 *Task-force report.* In 1987, the government released the report *Suicide in Canada.* This document contained many recommendations, but, as we formally questioned at its release in 1987: Have the recommendations been followed? What are Canadians doing? Or is the document only gathering dust? The important thing here is not the document or some revision, but what are we doing about suicide. We do not need more paper. We need to act on the report's recommendations (Leenaars et al. 1990; Tanney et al. 1987).

The recommendations to Perrin Beatty can be made again today. Regrettably, none of CASP's recommendations were followed, echoing the experiences of Menno Boldt in Alberta. In fact, CASP's advocacy at a national level resulted in disdain towards CASP from the bureaucratic maze. As an example of the price that we paid for advocacy, CASP, despite requests, was left off the list of participants in the second edition of the federal document *Suicide in Canada*. Because of fiscal constraints and government cutbacks, action will likely not occur in the near future, even if we would find someone like Alberta's Bogle in Canada. Maybe a suicidologist in 2090 will make CASP's recommendations again.

There have been many other activities in CASP. There are many people since 'the group of six' who deserve credit. There was and will be a lot of work to do in suicide prevention. There have been and will be struggles and frustrations. There will need to be new initiatives. CASP is alive, well, and now growing into its adolescence.

I left CASP in 1994, finishing my term as the first past president. I am honoured to have served in that capacity. I would like to conclude these reflections on our history with an induction (in the hypnotic sense) for well-being.

I once had the sterling pleasure of hearing Chief Dan George, one of Canada's most famous people, speak. He spoke about the importance of *dignity* for all people. That we need to *respect* all people. This is true for CASP and for all of us in Canada. This task, which should also be CASP's objective, is tantamount to preventing human misery. That would be true primary prevention.

'Lifting the Silence' Conference, 1990 (Krawll)

In 1990, the Canadian Association for Suicide Prevention (CASP/ACPS) sponsored the first national conference in Canada on suicide-prevention, entitled 'Lifting the Silence.' Because of the challenges inherent in trying to share information and exchange materials across our vast land and between cultures, this bilingual event was an important landmark in the area of suicide prevention. It proved the feasibility of such a conference and brought people together from all over Canada to develop strategies and approaches that reflect the diverse social fabric of Canada. Some five hundred people, mostly caregivers, clinicians, and researchers, came together for three days in Vancouver, British Columbia. This unique combination of participants connected people who would otherwise not have been able to trade viewpoints, professional expertise, and information.

Because of the diversity of the participants and their experiences, the highlights of the conference were different for different people. The welcoming reception was opened by the sounds of Uzume Taiko of Vancouver. Their lively performance, a dynamic fusion of old and new styles of drumming based on traditional Japanese taiko rhythms, was donated by the musicians.

Bea Shawanda, grief counsellor at the Stoney Medicine Lodge Treatment Centre in Alberta, rounded out the evening with a session on 'The Healing Power of Laughter and Play,' which celebrated the relationship of laughter and play to good health and stress management, and as a means for opening doors to connect people. The session set a tone for the conference that energized and encouraged participants to come together to learn and share.

The honourary co-chairmen of the conference were Edwin Shneidman, founder of the American Association of Suicidology and a pioneer in the field, and Phil C. Barter, senior partner from Price Waterhouse in Vancouver, and a committed community member. The chair of the program committee was Bryan Tanney; the co-chairs of the local conference committee were Marcia Krawll and Linda Rosenfeld; and the president of CASP/ACPS was Antoon Leenaars. The ability to plan and successfully launch this conference, however, was due to the assistance, efforts, and commitment of many more people, more than space will here permit.

Shneidman gave the keynote address at the opening plenary session, validating the Canadian experience and placing emphasis on grass-roots participation. In his address he distilled the essence of our work by reflecting on various approaches to the study of individual suicide and the suicide phenomenon.

The theme of the conference was captured in a painting donated by Sam English, a Native American artist from New Mexico. His visual image served to reinforce the truth that suicide crosses all lines – racial, ethnic, religious, and social – and emphasized the importance of people supporting one another.

In keeping with the theme, 'Lifting the Silence,' the conference was designed to offer a combination of clinical case studies, experiential workshops, and research paper presentations that reflected issues and factors specific to Canada. These varied presentations dealt with suicide prevention, intervention, and postvention. As a result, Canadians who were volunteers at crisis centres, clinicians, researchers, and survivors had the opportunity to participate.

The conference also sought to raise awareness about particular groups or populations that were at a higher risk for suicide in Canada. One such group are Aboriginal people. In response to raising such awareness, the conference featured workshops and discussions led primarily by Aboriginal presenters on the issues in Aboriginal communities. Isolation, unresolved multigenerational grief, cultural assimilation, and various forms of abuse were examined as factors in suicide.

The conference also offered ground-breaking sessions on suicide in gay and lesbian communities and, to a lesser extent, in diverse ethnic communities. The aim was to sensitize participants and the public to issues of suicide found in a variety of communities within Canada.

Youth suicide was very much in the public mind at the time of the conference. Materials for the conference covered youth issues, but, in addition, youth were given their own voice at the event. Workshops conducted by trained youth members of the Youth Suicide Prevention Team from Prince George, British Columbia, ensured that youth were listened to and that adults were not placed in the position of 'speaking for youth.'

A pre-conference public forum, 'No Longer Silent,' was held the day before the conference to allow interested members of the local community to attend and discuss suicide issues. The local conference committee felt that this opportunity would be of assistance to persons who had personal concerns related to suicide and who might want to talk about them or hear others talk about them. Furthermore, because of the publicity about the conference, the committee wanted to contain acting-out behaviours and prevent contagion. This public forum created the additional benefit that the media, members of the public, and members of the local coordinating committee for the conference (which included caregivers and representatives from government agencies and corporate sponsors) were brought together in ways that allowed for productive action both before and after the conference. In particular, for some weeks after the conference, CBC Radio featured sections of the 'No Longer Silent' forum as a nationwide radio broadcast on grief and loss issues related to suicide.

Throughout, the emphasis at the conference was on grass-roots work and action. The opening ceremony stressed how important it was for everyone to have opportunities at the gathering for expanding their networks, both for professional learning and for personal support. Suicide prevention work is highly stressful, and it attracts people who give it everything they have. Volunteers from the local suicide crisis centres provided an on-site reminder of this dedication, contributing their time before and during the conference to 'make it happen.'

Overall, the key value of the conference seemed to lie in its creation of the beginning of a process for action, both locally and nationally. When researchers are able to talk to practitioners and survivors, and vice versa, synergy starts to happen. Caregivers from the same geographical area were also able to network in ways that began or strengthened a process for more effective mutual activity in the future. The presentation of different viewpoints allowed for creative dialogue.

At the conclusion of the conference, CASP/ACPS had a database of people from across Canada who were working and interested in the field of suicide intervention. As a result of the excitement generated by the possibilities of mutual action, future conference planning became a priority for CASP/ACPS. An idea had taken form and created a process for Canadians to 'lift the silence.'

Notes on Community Suicide Prevention Initiatives in Toronto (Harnisch)

In December 1975, three years after attempted suicide was removed from the provisions of the Criminal Code of Canada (Lang, 1972), the Toronto Council on Suicide Prevention (COSP) was incorporated. The council consists of professional representatives from a variety of organizations concerned with the problem of suicide in the Metropolitan Toronto area. I joined this council in 1976 as a representative from Toronto's Distress Centre Two, a community-based crisis centre, and have been involved with its development ever since.

In the late 1970s, one of COSP's major challenges was to increase community awareness of suicide as a serious social and health problem. Council members undertook to provide public and professional information and suicide-prevention training events on a regular basis. While the majority of these events took place in the Toronto area, the expertise of individual council members was utilized by other local, national, and international organizations. These affiliations, in turn, provided linkages to other expertise from the wide variety of disciplines involved in the field.

Two events involving individual council members, which had later significance at a national level, were the second conference of the Canadian Council on Crisis Centres, held at the University of Toronto in 1978, and the tenth congress of the International Association on Suicide Prevention, held in Ottawa in 1979. The 1978 Canadian Council on Crisis Centres' conference attracted over 350 volunteers and staff from crisis centres across the country. The keynote speaker, Kjell Rudestam (COSP member), in a presentation on chronic callers to crisis centres, validated the need both for 24-hour crisis services and for ongoing education and support of telephone crisis workers. The tenth congress of the International Association for Suicide Prevention was a landmark event for suicide prevention in Canada. A steering committee was established under the chairmanship of Diane Syer-Solursh (COSP member) to investigate a co-operative approach to promote and facilitate action in the area of suicide prevention. Several years' work ensued, culminating in the incorporation of the Canadian Association for Suicide Prevention / L'Association canadienne pour la prévention du suicide (National Task Force on Suicide in Canada, 1987).

In April 1981, the council members were advised that the American Association of Suicidology had accepted their invitation to hold its 1985 annual meeting in Toronto. This was to be a portent for the very active decade that followed, highlights of which I will briefly describe.

Recognition of the need for support for those bereaved by suicide had escalated in the 1970s and spurred the establishment of many suicide survivor groups in the United States. At a 1979 meeting of the American Association of

Suicidology in Denver, Colorado, useful information was obtained on a survivor program in Marin County, California. This model was adapted by the joint committee of the Clarke Institute of Psychiatry and the distress centres of Toronto in planning and implementing the Survivor Support Programme of Toronto (Rogers et al., 1982). At the 1980 annual meeting of the Toronto Council on Suicide Prevention, Karen Letofsky, the program's director, presented a report on the pilot year of the program, the first of its kind in Canada.

In 1980, the council produced a report on suicide data in Ontario. Information arising from this report was later used by Canada's national task force for its report. Highlights of activities in 1981 included preparation of a tape on suicide prevention that was then recorded by Buffy Ste Marie, the native Canadian artist. During the year, several COSP members had assisted in the formation of a similar council in Hamilton, Ontario. Subsequently, similar groups were started in other cities (e.g., Ottawa, Windsor).

The major thrust of council members' efforts in 1984 was directed to the program and local arrangements for the 1985 American Association of Suicidology (AAS) meeting. The theme chosen, 'Suicide: A Critical Perspective,' was approved by the AAS board and the call for papers went out. This, eighteenth meeting of the AAS brought together the largest group of attendees in its history, with over 450 participants. The theme elicited widely diverse scholarly contributions, and a 'striking expansion of work in the areas of suicide survivors and prevention in schools, hospitals and other settings' was noted (Cohen-Sandler, 1985). The association of Canadians with AAS has benefited Canada in numerous ways. For example, a major contribution of AAS to community suicide prevention efforts in Canada continues to be its sharing of materials, including its organization's certification manual, which contains comprehensive standards for the operation of crisis centres and has, for example, been adapted by the network of distress centres in Ontario.

In the decade following this event, local developments occurred that had significant impact for the future of COSP. The Department of Health of the City of Toronto, recognizing the consistently high suicide rate in the city (17.6:100,000), formed a suicide prevention committee in 1986. A pilot project for the development of a network of agency representatives in the downtown core was implemented to allow these people to be trained in suicide prevention. In February 1987, people agreed to form what was to be known as the Downtown Suicide Prevention Network. Subsequently, three other networks were formed, using the same developmental model, to cover all geographic areas of the city. The Downtown Network undertook to provide training on a regular basis using the Alberta model (Ramsay et al., 1988), which resulted in several hundred people being trained during the following years.

Suicide prevention still remained a priority for the City of Toronto's Health Department in 1989, and that year the city's Public Affairs Department undertook to provide its professional help in organizing promotional efforts for Suicide Prevention Week. This resulted in a greater recognition of the problem. That year, COSP presented its annual Service Award to a Wardair first officer who, through his presence of mind and crisis-intervention skills, prevented a small-plane pilot from committing suicide by crashing into the CN Tower. As this incident had occurred just before Suicide Prevention Week, it attracted much public attention and excellent media coverage at the awards reception.

In 1992, the Ontario Psychological Foundation provided support to COSP to hold suicide prevention workshops for community agencies serving the increasingly diverse ethnocultural population of Metropolitan Toronto (Metropolitan Toronto Planning Department, 1992). These workshops were designed to provide current knowledge in critical aspects of suicide prevention together with the opportunity to identify ethnocultural factors essential to effective community suicide prevention efforts.

While COSP continued to fulfil its role during the 1980s, the Canadian Council on Crisis Centres fared differently. Two conferences, drawing volunteers and staff from across the country, took place during the 1980s. The 1987 conference, held at Ryerson Polytechnic Institute, was to be the council's last. Its demise might be attributed to many factors, not the least of which is the Canadian environment of the past few years. The Crisis Centre Committee of the Canadian Association for Suicide Prevention, together with provincial associations such as Distress Centres Ontario, would appear to be an avenue for future development of a national crisis-centre network.

As I review the comprehensive archives of the council, on which most of these notes are based, the productive work carried out over the years on a voluntary basis by this multidisciplinary group seems to have two common themes: suicide and voluntary action. Suicide still presents an enigmatic challenge as we approach the millennium (O'Brien, 1994). Voluntary action will no doubt continue to be a priority in its prevention.

Historical Overview of Suicide Information Retrieval in Canada (Kiddey, Harrington, and Ramsay)

When Canadians became cognizant of the escalating suicide rate in the mid-1970s, information about suicide prevention was scarce and difficult to attain. The impetus for change can be credited to initiatives made at the federal and provincial levels. These strategies became the catalysts for information retrieval and dissemination on suicidal behaviours in this country.

Federal Initiative

In 1974, a white paper by the federal minister of health, the Honourable Marc Lalonde, identified suicide as a major public-health concern in Canada and a significant cause of premature death for those under thirty-five (Lalonde, 1974). Five years later, Canada hosted the tenth congress of the International Association for Suicide Prevention (IASP) in Ottawa. Prompted by the growing interest in the problem of suicide, the government's first effort to define the knowledge-base on suicide was initiated by Health and Welfare Canada in 1980, when it commissioned the National Task Force on Suicide, resulting in the document *Suicide in Canada: Report of the National Task Force on Suicide in Canada* (National Task Force, 1987). The report became a reference guide for those wishing to understand the phenomenon of suicide, and for the first time, information on the epidemiology and aetiology of suicide and on high-risk groups in Canada were assembled in one text. Over 23,000 copies of the report have been distributed in both official languages.

The task force identified the lack of Canadian research as a major problem. Nine of the forty recommendations urged federal and provincial governments to work collaboratively to improve the level of Canadian-based research on suicide. Unfortunately, many of the recommendations have still not been addressed (Leenaars et al. 1990; Tanney et al. 1987). In 1991, an update of the report was commissioned by Health Canada's Mental Health Division and *Suicide in Canada: Update of the Report of the Task Force on Suicide in Canada* (National Task Force, 1994) was released in 1995.

The Ottawa meeting would become important historically for another reason. It was at this meeting that Canadian delegates first passed a resolution to form the Canadian Association for Suicide Prevention / L'Association canadienne pour la prévention du suicide (CASP/ACPS). The annual conferences of CASP/ACPS now provide a national forum for Canada's researchers, caregivers, and suicide survivors to share and disseminate current information about suicide prevention.

Provincial Initiatives

In 1974, the Government of Alberta divided the work of a larger provincial task force on highway accidents and suicides and established the Task Force on Suicide, to study and provide recommendations for the prevention of suicide in the province (Boldt, 1976). By 1978, the position of Provincial Suicidologist was established in the Division of Mental Health - the first of its kind in North America. The Alberta Medical Examiner system established in 1975 had greatly improved the collection of accurate, comprehensive mortality data on suicide (Boldt, 1982). In 1979, a volunteer task force struck by the Canadian Mental Health Association, Alberta South-Central Region, in Calgary concluded that 'a comprehensive and coordinated approach to suicide must be developed within a three-tier framework of preventive, interventive and postventive services' (Tanney, 1985). Both reports identified the priority need for a centralized information resource centre. The opportunity to synthesize the recommendations of these reports was realized in 1981, with the formation of a government-appointed Suicide Prevention Provincial Advisory Committee (SPPAC) chaired by Boldt. SPPAC, in cooperation with the provincial suicidologist, was mandated to expand suicide prevention efforts in the province. Four objectives of what is now known as the 'Alberta Model' were pursued: education and training, outreach services, an information resource centre, and a research centre (Ramsay, Cooke, and Lang, 1990). From these federal, provincial, and non-governmental-organization (NGO) initiatives, the concept of the Suicide Information and Education Centre (SIEC) grew as a central resource for all caregivers, researchers, and concerned members of the public. The other objectives, with the exception of the research objective, have continued to develop, with SIEC and the Suicide Prevention Training Programs (SPTP) gaining international recognition and acclaim.

Suicide Information and Education Centre (SIEC)

SIEC, funded by the Government of Alberta, opened its doors in 1982 as a program of the Canadian Mental Health Association, Alberta Division, and now operates as a unique Canadian public-access English-language library and database on suicidal behaviours. From its inception, SIEC's mandate has been 'to make available to gatekeepers, researchers, and the general public, a comprehensive information base on suicide' (Boldt, 1985b). SIEC's library collection policy is to identify, acquire, and catalogue all information written about suicide and suicidal behaviour in the English language since 1955. The idea of a centralized resource centre providing an essential information support is still an integral part of the government's province-wide coordinated approach to suicide prevention. This approach is based on the assumption that an informed and well-trained critical mass of caregivers will be prepared to reduce the incidence of suicidal behaviour in the general population. In 1993, the Alberta Model was reaffirmed and updated to include the following components: community coordination, education, training, research, evaluation, and public policy (White, 1993).

Before 1980, no effort had been made to centralize the existing information on suicide and make it readily available. Existing commercial databases contained clinical 'published' materials but lacked government reports, conference proceedings, training manuals, and a wide range of 'unpublished' materials. To help establish the initial collection of documents for the SIEC library, an agreement was reached with Norman Farberow of the Los Angeles Suicide Prevention Centre to duplicate an extensive collection of papers stemming from landmark bibliographies that were prepared for the National Institute of Mental Health (Farberow, 1972). A multidisciplinary group of clinicians, academics, and information specialists contributed their expertise to develop the concept and support materials for SIEC's remote-access multi-user computer database on suicidal behaviours. Another challenge was to design a classification system for cataloguing such a specialized collection. The *SIEC Hierarchy of Subject Terms*, the first of its kind for the suicide subject area, was created to provide a subject classification for database retrieval, and the *SIEC Thesaurus of Subject Terms* (Tanney, 1985) is an evolving lexicon of approximately nine hundred key words reflecting the literature of suicidology.

In 1995, SIEC library holdings numbered more than 21,000 print materials by over 16,000 authors. Journal articles, books, research studies, teaching materials, government documents, unpublished manuscripts, and dissertations constitute the greatest portion of documents cited on the bibliographic database, and about 1200 documents are added each year. In addition, SIEC has made a special effort to include all individual papers derived from the annual conference proceedings of the American Association of Suicidology (AAS). The centre provides over 60,000 documents annually to people and agencies working in the field, and new resources are developed to meet the demands of those working in the field. The SIEC *Current Awareness Bulletin* was initiated in 1984 to keep subscribers informed about current developments in suicidology and to provide a forum for the review of new print and audio-visual products. Since 1982 the SIEC database has been available electronically through public dialports across Canada. In 1995, SIEC established a home page on the World Wide Web. Internet users can now preview some of SIEC's resources and request on-line database searches and document delivery. In 1996, SIEC will produce a complete version of its database on CD-ROM, extending quick access to the database for institutions, libraries, and individual users.

National and International Links

As part of its mandate to make available local and international research on suicide, SPTP and SIEC have assisted with the organization of the annual Suicide Research Symposium, held in Calgary since 1982. In 1993, SIEC was one of several sponsors of an interregional experts meeting on the development of national suicide-prevention strategy guidelines, held in collaboration with the United Nations and the World Health Organization (Ramsay and Tanney, 1993).

Since 1989, SIEC has been the information arm for the Canadian Association for Suicide Prevention, and in 1993 was honoured with the CASP Service Award for its library and support service and the publication of the official newsletter, *CASP-ACPS News*. Staff and volunteers of SPTP and SIEC were selected to organize the sixth annual CASP/ACPS conference, October 1995, in Banff, Alberta.

Information about Suicide in Canada

In a literature review of Canada's trends in suicide research, the authors state: 'There are serious gaps in knowledge about suicidal behaviours, and this is particularly true of Canada' (Bagley and Ramsay, 1985). In 1995, a search for 'things Canadian' on the SIEC database still confirms their conclusion. Of the 21,000 primarily English-language documents on suicide listed on the database, roughly 1200 are Canadian. Of this group, a little more than 500 are published journal articles. Of these 1200 documents, the majority of the research in Canada focuses on epidemiology, hospital-based studies on suicide (particularly psychiatric disorders), community surveys on the attitudes and incidence of self-destructive behaviours, and studies of specific at-risk groups, including Aboriginal communities, older adults, university populations, and inmates.

In its short history, SIEC has become internationally recognized as a primary resource for English-language print materials on suicidal behaviours. This is not to say that other programs, individuals, and provinces do not produce and collect information on suicide. Government and NGO (most often initiated by the Canadian Mental Health Association) programs for suicide prevention are in effect in Alberta, Manitoba, New Brunswick, Northwest Territories, Ontario, Quebec, and Saskatchewan.

SIEC is a prototype for other regional and national governments to use. Instead of investing in the costs of developing additional information centres, other governments can share in the support of SIEC, and work in collaboration to establish links to the database and print collection in their own regions. SIEC is strategically poised to expand beyond its official mandate to provide the information support component for the Alberta Model of suicide prevention and become a similar support for Canada and other nations around the world.

In the field of suicide prevention, we are well aware that if we fail to take advantage of the information generated and gathered by our predecessors, we are destined to waste limited resources reinventing some of the same strategies and solutions.

REFERENCES

Bagley, C., and R. Ramsay. 1985. 'Problems and Priorities in Research on Suicidal Behaviours: An Overview with Canadian Implications.' *Canadian Journal of Community Mental Health* 4: 15–49.

Berry, J. 1990. 'Acculturation and Adaptation: Health Consequences of Cultural Contact among Circumpolar Peoples.' *Arctic Medical Research* 49: 142–50.

Boldt, M. 1976. *Report of the [Alberta] Task Force on Suicide to the Minister of Social Services and Community Health*. Edmonton: Department of Social Services and Community Health.

– 1982. 'A Model for Suicide Prevention, Intervention, and Postvention: The Alberta Task Force Proposals.' *Canada's Mental Health* (March): 12–15.

– 1985a. 'An Integrated Inter-Agency Model for Providing Coordinated and Comprehensive Suicide Prevention.' *Crisis* 6: 106–18.

– 1985b. 'Towards the Development of a Systematic Approach to Suicide Prevention: The Alberta Model.' *Canada's Mental Health* 33: 2–4.

Brant, C. 1987. 'Suicide in the North American Indian.' In J. Morgan, ed., *Suicide: Helping Those at Risk*, 175–84. London: King's College.

Canadian Mental Health Association [CMHA Alberta. South-Central Region] Task Force on Suicide 1981. *Task Force on Suicide Report*. Calgary: CMHA.

Cohen-Sandler, R., ed. (1985). *Proceedings of the Eighteenth Annual Conference of the American Association of Suicidology*. Denver: AAS.

Dublin, L. 1969. 'Suicide Prevention.' In E. Shneidman, ed., *On the Nature of Suicide*, 43–7. San Francisco: Jossey-Bass.

Dyck, R., R. Bland, S. Newman, et al. 1988. 'Suicide Attempts and Psychiatric Disorders in Edmonton.' *Acta Psychiatrica Scandinavica* 77 (Suppl. 338): 64–71.

Farberow, N. 1972. *Bibliography on Suicide and Suicide Prevention 1897–1957, 1958–1970*. Rockville, MD: National Institute of Mental Health.

Gawitrhá. 1991. *Dwanoha: One Earth, One Mind, One Path*. Hagersville, ON: Pine Tree Publishing Group.

Howe, A., and I. Sakinofsky. 1979. 'A Short-Stay Intensive Care Multi-Disciplinary Unit for Parasuicides.' *Proceedings 10th International Congress for Suicide Prevention and Crisis Intervention* 2: 34–8.

Kuhn, T. 1962. *The Structure of Scientific Revolution*. Chicago: University of Chicago Press.

Lalonde, M. 1974. *A New Perspective on the Health of Canadians: A Working Document*. Ottawa.

Lang, O. 1972. *House of Commons Debate, 28th Parliament, 4th Session*. Ottawa.

Leenaars, A. 1995. 'Suicide and the Continental Divide.' *Archives of Suicide Research* 1: 39–58.

Leenaars, A., ed. 1993. *Suicidology: Essays in Honor of Edwin Shneidman*. Northvale, NJ: Aronson.

Leenaars, A., and R. Diekstra. 1995. Editorial. *Archives of Suicide Research* 1: 1–2.

Leenaars, A., I. Sakinofsky, B. Tanney, and B. Mishara. 1990 (October). *Suicide in Canada*. Plenary panel presented at the Canadian Association for Suicide Prevention conference, Vancouver, BC.

Metropolitan Planning Department. Research and Special Studies Division. 1992. *Population Composition by Mother Tongue and Immigration*. Toronto: Author.

Miller, J., I. Sakinofsky, and D. Streiner. 1979. 'The Family and Social Dynamics of Adolescent Parasuicide.' *Proceedings 10th International Congress for Suicide Prevention and Crisis Intervention* 2: 122–34.

National Task Force on Suicide in Canada. 1987. *Suicide in Canada*. Ottawa: Author.

– 1994. *Suicide in Canada: Update of the Report of the Task Force on Suicide in Canada*. Ottawa: Author.

O'Brien, C. 1994. *On the Eve of the Millennium*. Concord, ON: House of Anansi Press.

Ramsay, R., and C. Bagley. 1985. 'The Prevalence of Suicidal Behaviors, Attitudes and Associated Social Experiences in an Urban Population.' *Suicide and Life-Threatening Behavior* 15: 151–67.

Ramsay, R., M. Cooke, and W. Lang. 1990. 'Alberta's Suicide Prevention Training Programs: A Retrospective Comparison with Rothman's Developmental Research Model.' *Suicide and Life-Threatening Behavior* 20: 335–51.

Ramsay, R., and B. Tanney. 1993 May. *Guidelines for the Formulation and Implementation of Comprehensive National Strategies for Prevention of Suicide and Provision of Supportive and Rehabilitative Services to Persons at Risk and to Other Affected Persons*. Formulated and adopted by the United Nations Interregional Expert Meeting, Calgary and Banff, Alberta, Canada.

Ramsay, R., B. Tanney, R. Tierney and W. Lang. 1988. 'A Suicide Prevention Training Program.' *Trainer's Handbook*. 3rd ed. Calgary: Authors.

Rogers, J., A. Sheldon, C. Barwick, K. Letofsky, and W. Lancee. 1982. 'Help for Families of Suicide: Survivors Support Group.' *Canadian Journal of Psychiatry* 27: 444–9.

Ross, R. 1992. *Dancing with a Ghost: Exploring Indian Reality*. Markham, ON: Octopus Publishing Group.

Shneidman, E., ed., 1973. *On the Nature of Suicide*. San Francisco: Jossey-Bass.

Solomon, A. 1994. *Eating Bitterness: A Vision beyond the Prison Walls*. Toronto: N.C. Press.

Tanney, B. 1985. 'Suicide Information and Education Centre.' Paper presented at the National Conference on Youth Suicide, Washington.

Tanney, B., C. Lakaski, A. Leenaars, and P. Syer-Solursh. 1987 May. *Canadian Perspectives: Suicide in Canada*. Release of report *Suicide in Canada*, presented at the American Association of Suicidology / International Association for Suicide Prevention Conference, San Francisco.

Westlake Van Winkle, N., and P. May. 1986. 'Native American Suicide in New Mexico, 1957–1979: A Comparative Study.' *Human Organizations* 45 (November): 4.

White, J. 1993. *Suicide Prevention in Alberta: Working towards Results*. Edmonton: Alberta Health, Mental Health Services Division.

PART II:
EPIDEMIOLOGY AND THE CANADIAN SCENE

Epidemiology is the study of the incidence and distribution of a phenomenon and, we would add, of its control and prediction.

Suicide data in Canada date back to 1924, but those statistics are incomplete. Data for Canada as a whole began to be compiled only from 1956 on. Today, however, despite questions about accuracy, mortality data provide many important findings, from identification of high-risk groups to gender differences to the positive impact of gun control to the various rates among different ethnic groups. Epidemiology can provide us with some snapshots of why suicide in Canada is, indeed, a major health problem and public-health problem.

Canada's suicide rates have been seen to shadow those of its neighbour, the United States. However, since the 1970s, Canadian rates appear to have been different from those of the United States. Epidemiology illuminates Canada's unique scene.

This section presents the epidemiology of suicide and aspects of the Canadian scene. It addresses the issues of cultural diversity, special Quebec issues, and more. It consists of four chapters: an overview of the epidemiology, a discussion of the Quebec studies about suicide in Canada's French-speaking people, a survey of immigration and ethnic factors, and a comparison of Canada and the United States to show how unique Canada's problem is.

2

The Epidemiology of Suicide in Canada

ISAAC SAKINOFSKY

This chapter reviews the epidemiology of suicide and non-fatal suicidal behaviour in Canada. Following an overall perspective of the field, it discusses the reasons why suicide has increased especially in young persons, cohort and longitudinal studies of suicide, methods of committing suicide, and some of the population groups who are at particular risk for suicide.

Suicide data for Canada go back to 1924, but those statistics are incomplete. Data for Canada as a whole start only from 1956. Quebec's figures were included after 1925, Newfoundland's from 1949, and the Yukon's and Northwest Territories' statistics since 1956 (National Task Force, 1994). Contrast this with the case of Sweden, which began collecting suicide data in 1749 (Murphy, 1982), and Switzerland, which began organized collection in 1876 (Jakob, 1979); Falret, in 1822, was already able to discuss comparative international statistics well before the better-known epidemiological studies of Morselli or Durkheim (Falret, 1822).

From their pattern of ebb and flow, Canada's suicide rates can be seen to shadow those of its neighbour to the south, but since the 1970s Canadian rates surpass those of the United States (Leenaars and Lester, 1990; Leenaars and Lester, 1992; Leenaars and Lester, 1994; Sakinofsky and Roberts, 1987; National Task Force, 1987). Whether this finding is significant has not been established, since their rates are not far apart and their population bases are hugely discrepant in size. Statistical artefact or errors arising out of different systems for data collecting might confound the observed differences. Estimates for both countries are likely to be understated (Brown, 1975; Speechley and Stavraky, 1991), and we cannot know whether that has occurred to the same extent. Intranational trends in suicide rates are more reliable than cross-national absolute differences (Sainsbury and Jenkins, 1982).

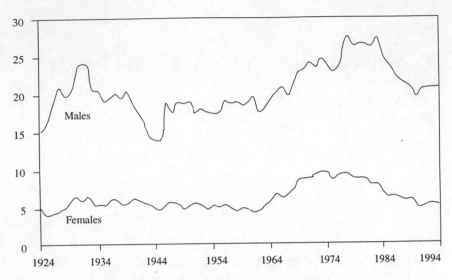

Data Source: Statistics Canada. Rates are per 100,000, 10 years and over.

Figure 1 Suicide rates in Canada, 1924–94

During the initial years of the Great Depression suicide rates in males rose and during the Second World War they fell, while rates for women seemed hardly to stir at all from their gently rolling, horizontal progression through the years (figure 1). These secular changes reflect the pressures and anxieties of particular age and gender sectors of the public. Before the beginning of the postwar period, suicide rates in both young males and females aged ten to nineteen hardly left the baseline. Young people appeared protected from the direct impact of the formidable social events that confronted their parents and older siblings, but following the end of the Second World War suicide rates in persons aged fifteen to thirty-four in Canada, males more than females, began to rise. They peaked during the late 1970s and plateaued at a new (higher) level only within the past decade. No one can confidently explain this prolonged upward movement of rates that lasted for a generation. It is part of a secular movement in suicide rates that caught in its grip young persons throughout North America and many regions of Europe, including the United Kingdom and Ireland, but spared other parts of the world such as Japan, Hong Kong, and parts of Latin America. In some countries rates in the elderly were dropping at the same time as they were rising in the young.

Why Has Suicide in Young People Increased?

Based on the findings of the NIMH Collaborative Program on the Psychobiology of Depression, Klerman (1988) associated the rise in suicide with increased rates of depression among young people. Data from the cross-sectional Epidemiologic Catchment Area (ECA) study in the United States, a community survey involving a very large sample, confirmed the greater lifetime prevalence among younger respondents – dramatically lower in the elderly – for major depression. This picture was also true for schizophrenia, anxiety disorders, and alcohol misuse (Simon and VonKorff, 1992). Since it is difficult to imagine an increased prevalence of depression and other mental disorders as related to augmented genetic presence, we must examine possible connections with changes in society over the period. After the Second World War Canada saw turbulent upheavals in long-standing norms and values within society, unprecedented attenuation of the bonds of the traditional nuclear family, a rise in the prevalence and misuse of illicit psychoactive substances, a revolution in the collective consciousness of the role of women, and a higher profile for minority groups such as gays. In addition, the postwar baby boom (ending in the early 1960s) generated a larger birth cohort than had preceded it, which had to be integrated into the institutions of society, the work force in particular.

Each of these factors has been blamed for increasing suicide. Farrow (1993) pointed out that economic recessions with subsequent unemployment had 'promoted the number of adolescents without a defined role in modern society ... [T]hese are our alienated youth.' The crisis was felt more in urban centres, where an increase in gang affiliation was the result. In other words, the tumultuous social changes that occurred have been associated with the anomic conditions that Durkheim thought were the primary causes of suicide (Rakoff, 1983).

In Canada increased divorce rates were related to rising suicide rates (Leenaars, Yang, and Lester, 1993; Trovato, 1986, 1987, 1992). Trovato (1992) associated the effects of divorce and disaffiliation from religion, less so economic stress, particularly with youth suicide. Similarly, Hasselback et al. (1991) looked at age-standardized suicide rates for 1980 to 1986 in 261 Canadian census divisions and related them to 21 population variables from the 1981 census in a stepwise linear regression. In the final model, suicide was related to homicides and to the proportions of native people, francophones, and persons disaffiliated from religious groups. A negative relationship was found with unemployment, not surprising as the study was cross-sectional; it is more usual to find a positive relationship in longitudinal studies (Platt, 1984). Previously, also in a cross-sectional ecological investigation, Sakinofsky et al. (1975)

related 1971 census data to age-standardized interprovincial suicide rates in a stepwise regression model. For male suicide 86 per cent of the variance was explained by the percentage of non-family households (persons living alone or separated from families), and for female suicide 89 per cent of the variance was explained by the percentage of foreign-born in the provinces. As in the Hasselback et al. (1991) study, negative correlations were found with unemployment, explained by the tradition in the Atlantic provinces of seasonal unemployment during the winters, which no longer carried a stigma and to which the communities had become habituated. Suicide was, however, positively correlated with other indices of social disorganization and mobility. The findings of these aggregate studies have yet to be confirmed at the individual level.

Easterlin suggested that suicide rates would be higher in a larger cohort that followed a smaller one when working age is reached: 'I shall show how those who first see the light of day in a low birth rate period may look forward to a buoyant job market when they reach working age. Job openings will be plentiful, wage rates relatively good, and advancement rapid. Conversely, high birth rates portend a relative labour market surplus and correspondingly unfavourable effects on one's economic life chances ... The experience of young men is placed in the foreground because of their primary breadwinner role, but that of young women is much the same, as we shall see. The early working period, however, is neither the first nor the last time that generation size makes its mark' (Easterlin, 1980).

Wisely, he warned that the actual size of the age sector in which the young person would have to function on reaching working age could be reduced by mortality within the cohort, but also inflated or diminished by the effects of internal or external migration. Using data for Canada and the United States, Leenaars and Lester (1994) were not able to find significant positive correlations between cohort sizes and suicide rates during 1969 to 1988 in young persons aged 15 to 24, finding them instead in age groups 25 to 34 and 45 to 54 and in the elderly as well. In the 35-to-44 age group they found significant negative correlations in both countries. These authors combined both genders in their analysis, which may have blurred a positive association in the 15-to-24 age group for males. In a subsequent study (1996) they calculated positive correlations between cohort size and suicide for males (but not females) aged 20 to 34. Ahlburg and Schapiro (1984), in the United States, did find significant positive associations between suicide and larger cohorts of both younger men and women aged 15 to 44 relative to smaller cohorts of older persons and in a recent reanalysis of their data dealing separately with data for both genders.

The 'employment bottleneck' theory of Easterlin (1980) was also supported by a longitudinal study of changes in interprovincial rates of suicide in Canadian provinces between 1969 and 1971 and 1979 and 1981 in relation to 122 ecological variables abstracted from the 1971 and 1981 censuses (Sakinofsky and Roberts, 1987). This study concluded that, over the decade, Canada experienced economic expansion and prosperity, despite which there was higher unemployment caused by the unprecedented entry into the workforce of women in large numbers in response to changed societal norms. Women were also the greater sufferers of this increased unemployment. A stepwise discriminant function analysis selected 'males not in the labour force' to explain suicide increase for both genders, followed (for suicide in females) by 'females not in the labour force.' The expanded economy had enticed 12.5 per cent more males over age fifteen into the labour market in the high male-suicide provinces (compared to 0.1 per cent in the low), but unemployment rates in males nevertheless rose by 16 per cent in the high, compared with 11 per cent in the low, provinces. Among women, unemployment rose by 86 per cent in the high-suicide provinces, compared to 47 per cent in the low provinces. Surprisingly, average and median incomes over the period rose more in the high than in the low-suicide provinces, suggesting that 'the inference cannot be avoided that the misery of the unemployed may have been compounded by the fact that they were living in the midst of a society enjoying unprecedented prosperity.'

In a study of data from eighteen industrialized nations, Lester (1988a) and Lester and Yang (1992) noted that time-series studies in the United States found that regional economic prosperity was beneficial to the elderly but detrimental for suicide rates in younger adults. Eyer (1977) implicated the fragmentation of community that occurs during periods of economic expansion. Pritchard (1990) examined the decades before and after the 1973 oil crisis (which gave rise to dramatic rises in unemployment in Western countries) in twenty-three nations including Canada. Significant positive correlations were found between percentage change in suicide during 1974 to 1986 but not for the earlier decade, confirming the contributory role of unemployment. It is noteworthy that at the end of the first decade Canada ranked first for the percentage of males unemployed (fourth for females), but fell to seventh (eleventh for females), during 1974 to 1986. Pritchard speculated about the possibility of a protective factor within English-speaking countries that might mitigate the impact of unemployment on women.

Reinfurt et al. (1991) used autoregressive integrated moving average (ARIMA) and structural time-series analysis in U.S. population data and did not find that the inclusion of unemployment data led to improved forecasting models for predicting rates of motor-vehicle fatalities, suicides, or homicides. However, their study used yearly data, and Wasserman (1984) has shown that it is difficult to determine the length of lag effect with required precision using annual data. Warr and Jackson, in an individual-based study of unemployed men in Britain, found that nine months of unemployment was necessary to produce despair and depression in men who had been made redundant, but as a group they tended to become adjusted to their predicament after two years (Jackson and Warr, 1984; Warr and Jackson, 1987). In another individual-based investigation of unemployed men, Moser et al. (1986) found increased mortality figures, including suicide. In Los Angeles, Dooley et al. (1989) combined aggregate and individual-level studies and showed that a contracting economy with unemployment lasting longer than six months appears linked to suicidal ideation. However, the correlation with suicide of shifts in the economy from quarter to quarter was weak, and not found in all subgroups of the population. None of these studies was designed to determine the degree of confounding by unemployment secondary to personality or psychiatric disorder, rather than from independent economic causes.

In Quebec, one of the regions where suicide rates in young men in particular have increased most, Cormier and Klerman (1985) showed a positive association between suicide in the 15-to-44 age group and the unemployment rate from 1966 to 1981 for both sexes. They noted the 'Quiet Revolution' beginning in the 1960s, which had led to greater modernism and secularism, a radical change in values, the abandonment of the former constraints of religion, and the encouragement of anomie. This striking cultural change has also been remarked upon by Krull and Trovato (1994).

Cohort and Other Longitudinal Studies

The increase of suicide in young persons in Canada stimulated a number of cohort and other time-series studies (Barnes et al., 1986; Dyck et al., 1988; Hellon and Solomon, 1980; Huchcroft and Tanney, 1988; Lester, 1988b; Mao et al., 1990; Newman and Dyck, 1988; Reed et al., 1985; Sakinofsky and Roberts, 1987; Solomon and Hellon, 1980; National Task Force, 1987, 1994; Trovato, 1988; Wasserman, 1989). The first of these studies (by Solomon and Hellon in Alberta) was replicated in the United States by Murphy and Wetzel (1980), and European and Australian workers also found cohort effects in suicide but not uniformly (Goldney and Katsikitis, 1983; Häfner and Schmidtke, 1985). Later cohort analyses concluded that the confounding effects of age and period could not be distinguished from those of cohort of birth, and all three factors were active in the rising trends in suicide (Newman and Dyck, 1988; Trovato, 1991). One study using data from both the United States and Canada found that age and cohort effects were stronger than period effect, and cohort effect was stronger in the United States than in Canada (Wasserman, 1989).

Interregional Differences

Newfoundland has traditionally enjoyed the status of having the lowest regional suicide rates in Canada, and the western provinces, chiefly Alberta and British Columbia, the highest rates (Sakinofsky et al., 1975). This picture changed after 1969 as Quebec began to move up the ladder. In a table of rank order for suicide among the provinces at the beginning of each decade, Quebec began in 1950 in ninth place for males (seventh for females) and finished in 1990 first for males (third for females) (National Task Force, 1994: 30–1).

Tables 1 and 2 and figures 2 and 3 (pp. 44–5, after National Task Force, 1994) demonstrate mean suicide rates for the provinces and territories for 1988 to 1992, with 95 per cent confidence intervals adjusted for age and gender. Table 1 and figure 2 (suicide in males) shows that the Northwest Territories topped the other regions, followed closely by Alberta and Quebec (not significantly different from each another). Newfoundland and Ontario tied for lowest rates.

Table 2 and figure 3 (suicide in females) shows a similar picture, with mean suicide rates highest for the Northwest Territories, Alberta, and Quebec, but the 95 per cent confidence intervals of these regions also overlap those of the remaining western provinces, so that it is unlikely that their true rates are significantly different. Newfoundland is last, this time not having to share that honour with Ontario. From time to time under-reporting has been questioned as responsible for Newfoundland's low ranking among the regions, but on each occasion careful scrutiny of death certificates and records confirms that, while suicide is understated, the province rightfully holds its claim to low suicide rates (Aldridge and St. John, 1991; Liberakis and Hoenig, 1978; Malla and Hoenig, 1979, 1983). Firearms have been shown to be the most important death factor for suicide in Newfoundland males, so that rates might be even lower if this means were prevented.

Methods Used in Suicide

Death factor is a term adopted by coroners for the method of suicide. Table 3 (p. 46) shows how death factors have changed for male suicides over the decade; table 4 shows the changes for females. Suicides by firearms and drug poisonings have fallen at the expense of hanging and gassing.

Huchcroft and Tanney (1989) analysed sex-specific suicide rates in Canada between 1971 and 1985 and commented on their divergence: male rates rose, while female rates fell. Ninety-two per cent of the variance in female suicide was explained by the declining rate for drug overdoses, while 65 per cent of the

TABLE 1
Mean-age adjusted suicide rates (males)* for Canada, provinces and territories, 1989–1992

| Province | No./year | Mean | Confidence intervals | |
			Lower	Upper
Canada	2792	20.16		
Newfoundland	38	13.28	9.03	17.53
Prince Edward Island	15	23.28	11.27	35.29
Nova Scotia	88	19.43	15.37	23.49
New Brunswick	74	20.20	15.59	24.82
Quebec	902	25.63	23.95	27.30
Ontario	766	14.87	13.81	15.92
Manitoba	112	20.63	16.80	24.46
Saskatchewan	109	22.44	18.19	26.68
Alberta	328	25.94	23.12	28.76
British Columbia	336	20.07	17.92	22.22
Yukon	4	23.64	0	49.20
Northwest Territories	19	54.80	29.38	80.22

*95% confidence intervals; direct standardization (1991 populations)

TABLE 2
Mean-age-adjusted suicide rates (females)* for Canada, provinces and territories, 1989–1992

| Province | No./year | Mean | Confidence intervals | |
			Lower	Upper
Canada	752	5.34		
Newfoundland	6	2.14	0.44	3.85
Prince Edward Island	1	1.98	0	5.46
Nova Scotia	17	3.73	1.96	5.50
New Brunswick	13	3.34	1.49	5.20
Quebec	226	6.18	5.38	6.99
Ontario	237	4.49	3.92	5.06
Manitoba	27	4.88	3.01	6.73
Saskatchewan	26	5.53	3.40	7.67
Alberta	97	7.81	6.24	9.38
British Columbia	98	5.80	4.66	6.95
Yukon	1	3.42	0	12.94
Northwest Territories	3	9.17	0	19.86

*95% confidence intervals; direct standardization (1991 populations)

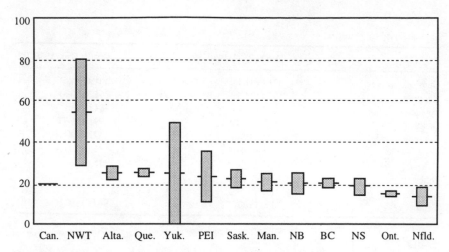

Note: Means and 95% confidence intervals. *Source:* Statistics Canada

Figure 2 Rank order of male suicide rates (1989–1992) for Canada, provinces and territories

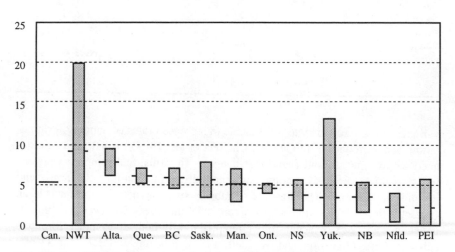

Note: Means and 95% confidence intervals. *Source:* Statistics Canada

Figure 3 Rank order of female suicide rates (1989–1992) for Canada, provinces and territories

TABLE 3
Methods used by males

	Deaths (%), 1980–82	Deaths (%), 1990–92
Guns, explosives	3218 (41.1)	3019 (35.6)
Hanging	1920 (24.5)	2612 (30.8)
Poisoning	844 (10.8)	811 (9.6)
Gases	843 (10.8)	991 (11.7)
Jumping	321 (4.1)	372 (4.4)
Drowning	333 (4.3)	266 (3.1)
Cutting	141 (1.8)	159 (1.9)
Other	210 (2.7)	241 (2.9)
Total	7830 (100)	8471 (100)

TABLE 4
Methods used by females

	Deaths (%), 1980–82	Deaths (%), 1990–92
Guns, explosives	277 (11.3)	195 (8.8)
Hanging	463 (18.9)	492 (22.3)
Poisoning	993 (40.5)	827 (37.4)
Gases	198 (8.1)	253 (11.5)
Jumping	157 (6.4)	150 (6.8)
Drowning	208 (8.5)	156 (7.1)
Cutting	43 (1.2)	37 (1.7)
Other	115 (4.7)	100 (4.5)
Total	2454 (100)	2210 (100)

variance in male suicide was attributable to increased rates of hanging, strangulation, and suffocation. In Quebec, Cheifetz et al. (1987) investigated suicides aged ten to nineteen and found that hanging, firearms, and jumping were the most common methods among boys, and drug intoxications, firearms, and jumping among girls. The presence of subway systems in some cities acts as an 'attractive hazard' for suicides. Between 1954 and 1980, 207 persons committed suicide and 223 unsuccessfully attempted to kill themselves under Toronto's subway trains (Johnston and Waddell, 1984). Shkrum and Johnston (1992) examined thirty-two deaths in Ontario from self-immolation between 1986 and 1988, of whom half had previously been diagnosed for psychiatric illness and many of whom had announced their intention.

Public controversy (Whitemore, 1995; Sakinofsky, 1995) and professional debate (Hung, 1993; Mundt, 1990, 1993) has been stirred up with the current new legislation for firearm registration and control. Rich et al. (1990) investigated suicide rates and methods in Toronto and Ontario as a whole for five years before and after the 1978 Canadian gun-control legislation. They compared these findings with similar ones in San Diego and concluded that in both centres substitution by jumping cancelled out the beneficial effects of fewer firearm suicides. Lester and Leenaars (1993) compared data for eight years before and after the 1978 legislation and found a slight reduction in the proportion of suicide deaths attributable to firearms. Regression analysis showed a significant negative trend during the post-legislation period for firearm suicide rates and non-significant trends for total suicide rates and for suicide by other methods.

Carrington and Moyer (1994a) compared firearm and non-firearm suicide rates in Ontario for 1965 to 1977 with those for 1979 to 1989. Unlike Rich et al. (1990) and Lester and Leenaars (1993), they used rates standardized for age. There was a decrease, both in absolute level and trend, for firearm and total rates without evidence of displacement. A regression analysis of suicide on regional gun ownership confirmed the association between gun availability and overall suicide rates (Carrington and Moyer, 1994b). The importance of guns as a death factor in the suicides of adolescents was underlined by Leonard (1994), who noted that guns were available in one-quarter of Canadian homes.

Special-Risk Groups

The federal task forces on suicide in Canada (National Task Force, 1987, 1994) and a comprehensive review of suicide prevention in Canada (McNamee and Offord, 1990) have highlighted the special groups at risk for suicide: persons with a mental disorder and/or substance abuse; youth; late-middle-aged and elderly people; Aboriginal communities; gays and lesbians; persons in custody; persons who have attempted suicide; and those newly diagnosed with acquired immune deficiency syndrome (AIDS) or other long-term painful or debilitating illness. Some of these categories are dealt with at length elsewhere in this book, and I will comment only on those on which there is significant Canadian literature.

Mental Disorder

In the world literature a number of retrospective studies of suicides and one or two prospective ones have found a prevalence of psychiatric diagnoses in 80 to 90 per cent of suicides. Patients diagnosed with mood disorders are generally considered to have a 15 per cent risk of eventual suicide; those with schizophrenia, alcoholism and other substance abuse, and borderline or antisocial personality disorders proportionately less. The psychological autopsy is a clinical epidemiological method for systematically studying cases of suicide in retrospect and comparing the findings with controls. In Canada, only one psychological autopsy study has been published to date, emanating from Quebec.

Lesage et al. (1994) collected 75 of 212 male suicides between the ages of 18 to 35 occurring during a fifteen-month period. A comparison group was matched for each case on neighbourhood, age, marital state, and occupation. For each suicide case and living control a key proxy was interviewed and given a number of standardized schedules to answer on behalf of the case or control. Because of the fairly high refusal rate among potential informants, the group of young suicides may not be representative of suicides in the general population of Greater Montreal and Quebec City. Nonetheless, the results obtained are consistent with other psychological autopsy studies of similar-aged suicides in the literature.

At least one DSM-III-R six-month axis I diagnosis was present in 88% of the suicides, but only in 37% of the controls; major depression was found in 39% versus 5%, alcohol dependence in 24% and 5%, and other substance abuse in 23% and 3%. Borderline personality disorder was found in 28% of the suicides and only 4% of the controls. Among the suicides, 24% (versus 9% of controls) had separated from a parent(s) before age fifteen on account of divorce or behavioural problems. The suicides had experienced more stressful life events such as separations, sexual difficulties, and moving during their last year than the controls. Notably, fewer than half of the suicides had been in contact with a mental-health professional over the year. The relatively low prevalence of mood disorder found in this study is in keeping with the caution that suicides may occur without manifest depression (Hirsch et al., 1978).

Aboriginal Suicide

Canada's Aboriginal peoples constitute 3.6 per cent of the total population and number about one million (Kirmayer, 1994). Suicide rates in Aboriginal communities are two to four times higher than in the rest of the country and even higher in some communities (Health and Welfare Canada, 1992; Kehoe and Abbott, 1975; Kirmayer, 1994; Larose, 1989; Mao et al., 1992; Sigurdson et al., 1994; National Task Force, 1994; Thompson, 1987). Abandonment of traditional values has been blamed by some, but it is clear that the roots of the problem are even more anomic and related to evidence of social disorganization.

Bagley (1991) replicated an American study in twenty-six native reservations in Alberta and found that in males aged fifteen to thirty-four poverty and suicide were closely correlated. Gotowiec and Beiser (1994) found that native children experience higher rates of school failure, encounter more risk of substance abuse and family violence, and are more likely to take their own lives than are children of the dominant culture. This bleak situation for native children living on reserves was corroborated by Gartrell et al. (1993), who studied children in the seventh to ninth grades and found frequent family disruption, often with a suicide already in the family; the children were depressed and their parasuicidal acts were more often fatal. One reason for the increased mortality is the frequent use of firearms in suicide among First Nations youngsters. The lethal combination of firearms and alcohol as death factors in adolescent suicide was noted by Spaulding (1986) among the Ojibway of Ontario and Tonkin (1984) in British Columbian natives. Sigurdson et al. (1994) in Manitoba found hanging and other substance abuse often present. Parasuicide in adolescent females using non-psychotropic agents has also been found prevalent in phenomenal proportions (Ross and Davis, 1986). Hardly any of the youngsters had previous contact with mental-health agencies.

Kirmayer (1994) emphasized the enduring family hardships, including frequent interpersonal conflict, prolonged or unresolved grief, chronic familial instability, depression, alcohol abuse or dependence, and unemployment. Half the deaths in thirty-five reserves investigated by Jarvis and Boldt (1982) resulted from accident, suicide, or homicide, and alcohol was a factor in the majority of violent deaths. Suicide rates among Aboriginal persons not living on reserves were similar to those of the general population, and compared to those with low rates, those reserves with high rates had markedly fewer healthy population characteristics (Cooper et al., 1992).

Although data are more difficult to obtain from Inuit communities, their suicide rates are reported to be as high as and the causes similar to those of First Nations peoples, including lack of social control, loss of dignity, changing lifestyles, alcohol abuse, depression, and family instability (National Task Force, 1994). Santé Québec has sponsored several studies of suicidal behaviour among Aboriginal people in that region (Boyer et al., 1994a, 1994b; Légaré et al., 1995). Some of this work is discussed in the succeeding chapter. *Choosing Life*, the report of the Royal Commission on Aboriginal Peoples (1995), emphasizes the suicidogenic effects of demoralization caused by the colonization of the Aboriginal peoples, and recommends widespread community redevelopment programs, together with improved crisis response and progress towards self-sufficiency and self-government.

Contagion

Suicide occurs sometimes in clusters or small epidemics within a relatively short time-span, usually in a small community such as a native village or a school. The event of the initial suicide has set off a chain reaction that may be fuelled by media coverage. Ward and Fox (1977) described eight native youngsters who had killed themselves in an Algoma village of two hundred within one year; Davies and Wilkes (1993) reported five teenage cases that occurred over a six-month period in a rural community in western Canada. And the royal commission report describes the outbreak at Big Cove, New Brunswick, in 1992. Kirmayer (1994), in his comprehensive review of Aboriginal suicide, 1955–94, commented that native communities were particularly vulnerable to contagious suicide. The Algoma cluster appeared related to family discord and alcohol misuse and to the youngsters being distressed by having to choose between traditional and mainstream Canadian cultural values. Five years later, Fox et al. (1984) were able to report that the suicide rate in the small community had diminished to one-tenth after measures were introduced controlling drinking and supporting traditional values.

Youth and Students

Suicidality in high school and CEGEP students were studied by a Quebec group. Pronovost et al. (1990a) and Côté et al. (1990) studied 2850 schoolchildren aged twelve to eighteen for the prevalence of suicidal thoughts and behaviour. The lifetime prevalence of suicidal ideation was 15.4 per cent and of attempts 3.5 per cent; the majority had considered it over the previous year. On the CES-D Dysphoria scale, 65.4 per cent were identified as depressed at the time of completion of the questionnaire (Côté et al., 1993). A case-control study identified more scholastic difficulties among the suicidal youngsters (Pronovost et al., 1990b).

There is little epidemiological knowledge of vulnerability to suicide in children younger than thirteen (Joffe and Offord, 1983). However, younger schoolchildren were studied by Normand and Mishara (1992), who found an increasingly age-dependent understanding of the relationship between death and suicide, so that 10 per cent of first graders, 50 per cent of third graders, and 95 per cent of fifth graders realized what suicide meant. The actual prevalence of suicidal thoughts among the group was not assessed. The Ontario Child Health Study interviewed 3294 children aged twelve to sixteen from 1869 families and found that 5 to 10 per cent of the male and 10 to 20 per cent of the female youth reported suicidal behaviour within a six-month period, related to psychiatric disorder, family dysfunction, and parental arrest (Joffe et al., 1988).

Bouchard and Morval (1988) surveyed 706 respondents among 1500 Montreal university students on the frequency and possible precipitants of suicidal behaviour. Adam et al. (1982) compared university students who had lost a parent(s) before age sixteen with those from intact families and found suicidal ideation and behaviour more often in those who had lost parents, maximally among those whose families had not restabilized. Family support and a confiding relationship with family were also found to be lacking among Quebec college and university students with suicidal ideation and attempt histories, but peer contacts were relatively intact (Hanigan et al., 1986; Tousignant et al., 1986, 1993; Tousignant and Hanigan, 1993).

Prisoners

Green et al. (1993) studied 133 penitentiary prisoners and found that suicide was predominantly a male phenomenon, committed by hanging soon after sentencing, and seemingly unrelated to the length of sentence or type of offence. Prison suicides more often had a previous history of psychiatric illness or suicide attempts. Bland et al. (1990) interviewed 180 male prisoners and found them, compared to same-aged male residents of Edmonton, less often married, more poorly educated, and with a higher proportion of native persons. They had significantly more mental illness and a seven times greater chance of having made suicide attempts. Similar findings were made in Quebec (Hodgins and Côté, 1990). The picture is true also for women prisoners. Rosenblatt and Greenland (1974) found a history of parasuicide more prevalent among women violent offenders than males, while Shaw (1992) studied 178 women prisoners and found that half reported parasuicidal experiences. Two-thirds had been sexually abused, more often among Aboriginal subjects. Most had little education and only one-third had received job training. Homelessness is a further disadvantage in 40 per cent of inmates, and mental illness and suicidal behaviour is commoner in homeless prisoners (Vitelli, 1993).

Canadian prisoners can thus be seen to embody complex social disadvantage and higher-than-average prevalences for psychiatric disturbance and suicidal behaviour. Implementation of large group training programs in one Alberta prison was shown to reduce the frequency of suicide (Ramsay et al., 1987). In addition, the importance of making special provision for the suicidal and mentally ill among prisoners has been recognized by policy planners and administrators in Canada (Conacher, 1993; Ogloff et al., 1994).

Refugees to Canada who have been detained in custody and submitted to forms of torture in their native lands have been found to have symptoms of post-traumatic stress disorder and increased frequency of suicide attempts (Allodi and Cowgill, 1982).

Murder-Suicide

Buteau et al. (1993) reviewed the epidemiology of homicides followed by suicide in the perpetrators and studied thirty-nine cases in Quebec that occurred between 1988 and 1990. The characteristics of the perpetrators more closely resembled suicide victims than murderers.

Non-Fatal Suicidality

It has been thirty years since attempted suicide was reportable in Canada, and even then the expectation was more honoured by omission than compliance. Specialized treatment programs based in general hospitals but reaching out into the community have been in existence for a generation (Barnes et al., 1979; Howe and Sakinofsky, 1979; Syer, 1975; Termansen and Bywater, 1975). The first of these is believed to be the Liaison Unit, a specialized eight-bed inpatient program for suicide attempters and ideators in Hamilton, Ontario, established in 1969 and modelled on the Edinburgh unit developed by Kreitman and Mathew (Sakinofsky, 1973a; Kreitman, 1977).

Treated Prevalence

A prospective study of treated prevalence of parasuicide (used interchangeably with attempted suicide) in London, Ontario, during 1969 to 1971 reported a crude rate of 730 per 100,000 per annum, several times that described elsewhere in North America (Jarvis et al., 1976, 1982; Whitehead et al., 1973). The study canvassed not only the general hospitals but general practitioners and community and legal agencies; its thoroughness may explain the unusually high frequencies. Rates were far higher among females and young persons, which is opposite from the picture in completed suicide. Sakinofsky et al. (1990) investigated all parasuicides who contacted one of the four hospitals in Hamilton, Ontario, during a three-month period and obtained an annual rate of 304 per 100,000, similar to figures from centres of Europe and the United States.

   Bland et al. (1994) examined the records of all parasuicides who attended University of Alberta hospitals over a six-month period. The peak age was 25-to-29 and the male-to-female ratio was 1:1.6. A previous act had occurred in 41 per cent of cases. The study was extended to include all Edmonton hospitals over one year and data sheets were prospectively completed (Bland et al.,

1995). The event incidence was 466 per 100,000 per year for persons aged fifteen and older, with a female-to-male ratio of 1.6:1. In the 15-to-24 age group these rates were higher than any of the European centres participating in the WHO/EURO Multicentre Study (Kerkhof et al., 1994).

Community-Based Surveys

However thorough surveys of clinical prevalence may be, they are still confounded by factors that select out persons who seek treatment and have facilities available to them. Community surveys investigating a representative sample stratified for possibly confounding covariates, are an improvement, and are more likely to obtain a truer reading of the actual prevalence of non-fatal suicidality (suicidal ideation or attempts) in the community.

In Calgary, Bagley and Ramsay (1985) studied the backgrounds of a sample of 679 adult respondents and related them to suicidal behaviour. They found the respondents more permissive towards suicide than expected (12% thought suicide was an acceptable solution for deeply depressed people and 4% considered it a 'normal' form of behaviour). More recently, Leenaars and Domino (1993) compared community attitudes in Los Angeles and Windsor, Ontario, using a suicide opinion questionnaire, and found that the Canadian subjects scored higher on scales indicating approval of the right to die and suicide as a cry for help, and lower on perception of the religious and moral prohibition of suicide. In Calgary the lifetime (one year) prevalences of suicidality were as follows: life not worth living, 37% (8.5%); seriously thought of or planned suicide, 13.4% (4%); parasuicide, 5.9% (1.3%); attempted suicide, 4.2% (0.8%) (Bagley and Ramsay, 1985; Ramsay and Bagley, 1985). An age-related analysis of their data that compared the groups aged eighteen to twenty-four to those older than sixty years showed that younger respondents reported a higher incidence of suicidal ideas and behaviour and were more unsure of themselves, were unattached to neighbourhoods, and had more stressful lives than the older group (Bagley and Ramsay, 1993).

A survey of the mental health of residents of Edmonton saw 3258 respondents interviewed using the Diagnostic Interview Schedule (DIS) and the General Health Questionnaire (GHQ) (Dyck et al., 1988). The lifetime prevalence of suicide attempts was 3.6% (males 1.8% and females 5.5%). Psychiatric disorder was present in 83% of the attempters, compared with 34% of the total sample, a risk ratio of 2.6. Mood and anxiety disorders were seven and four times as common, respectively, as among the total sample.

In Quebec, l'enquête Santé, not unexpectedly, revealed in those aged fifteen or more a high one-year period prevalence of non-fatal suicidality of 0.8%,

TABLE 5
Lifetime attempts*

Studies	N	%
Schwab et al. (1972)	1,645	2.7
Paykel et al. (1974)	720	1.1
Ramsey and Bagley (1985)	679	4.2
Velez and Cohen (1988)	724	3.5
Schepank (1987)	600	5.3
Dyck et al. (1988)	3,258	3.6
Moscicki et al. (1988)	18,571	2.9
Levy and Deykin (1989)	424	3.5
Breslau et al. (1991)	1,007	5.2
Wacker (1991)	470	4.7
Angst et al. (1992)	591	3.8
Bronisch et al. (1994)	481	4.1
Sakinofsky and Webster (1995)	9,943	3.3

*Modified from Angst et al. (1992)

equivalent to a rate of 840 per 100,000. This represents a non-fatal attempt to fatal suicide ratio of 49:1. Surprisingly, the one-year prevalence of ideation was only 3.9% (Emond et al., 1988). During 1990 to 1991 the Ontario Mental Health Supplement (OHMS) interviewed a representative sample of 9953 household residents. Clinical diagnoses were generated by means of the Composite International Diagnostic Instrument (CIDI) developed from the DIS for cross-national comparisons. The lifetime (one year) prevalence of suicidal ideation was 10.7% (3.4%) and of suicide attempts 3.3% (0.4%) (Sakinofsky and Webster, 1995). The attempted suicide to completed suicide ratio was 33:1 if compared with suicide data from Statistics Canada, and 26:1 if compared with data from the Chief Coroner of Ontario, lower than the Quebec estimate. The OHMS findings as a whole are similar to those of the Epidemiologic Catchment Area (ECA) study (Moscicki et al., 1988; Petronis et al., 1990) and those for lifetime suicide-attempt prevalence are within the international range shown in table 5 (modified from Angst et al., 1992).

Interestingly, the prevalence for any psychiatric diagnosis in the total population 15 to 64 (33.3%) was almost identical with that of the Edmonton study, but the prevalence among lifetime suicide ideators (61%) and attempters (66%) was lower. The risk of suicidality tripled in anyone who had a DSM-III-R diagnosis, and mood disorder was associated with the highest risk of lifetime ideation (41%), bulimia nervosa with the highest risk for lifetime attempts (19%). An adverse developmental environment – including parental conflict, physical and sexual abuse, and the necessity for child-welfare authorities to be involved – carried a powerful predictive risk of non-fatal suicidal behaviour. The presence of a confiding relationship with an adult was protective.

The most recent survey is the 1992–3 survey carried out by Santé Québec (Bellerose et al., 1994). Statistics for non-fatal suicidality were not significantly different from the earlier survey, which is comforting in light of the continuing high rates for completed suicide in Quebec (in 1992, 27.9 males and 7.5 females per 100,000).

Clinical Epidemiological Studies of the Environment of Non-Fatal Suicidality

Garfinkel et al. (1982) undertook a retrospective chart review with matched controls of 505 suicidal children and adolescents seen in the emergency room of a large children's hospital. They found higher rates of psychiatric illness (52% versus 16% in controls) and of suicide or attempted suicide (8% versus 1%) in the families of these youngsters. Fathers were twice as likely to be absent from the family. This accords with the finding of parental discord in 60% of suicide attempters under age 19, with 47% of such youngsters having stormy relationships with their fathers, 36% with their mothers (Miller et al., 1979). Grossi and Violato (1992) found that a single discriminant function (the lack of an emotionally significant other) differentiated adolescents with a history of suicide attempts from those who had not made an attempt. In Adam et al.'s study of 187 adolescents referred to outpatient services in three Canadian cities, evidence of 'affectionless control' by parents was found (Adam et al., 1994). In the London, Ontario, study by Jarvis et al. (1982), self-injury congregated more in the central areas of the city characterized by high population density, low socio-economic status, and single-person households.

Depressive Mood and Borderline Personality

There is a well-known association between borderline personality disorder (BPD) and self-injury. In DSM-IV 'recurrent suicidal behaviour, gestures, or threats of self-mutilating behaviour' continues to be one of the required characteristics for making the diagnosis. Paris noted the prominent feature of impulsivity in BPD and its relationship to repeated parasuicide. He suggested that when cultures change too rapidly, those without adaptive skills are left behind; youth suicide and parasuicide are epiphenomena of the social disintegration that accompanies rapid cultural transition (Paris, 1991, 1992). Paris and colleagues followed one hundred BPD patients for a mean of fifteen years and compared them with fourteen BPD patients who committed suicide (a rate of 8.5%) (Paris,

1990). The most significant predictors were previous attempts and higher education (Paris et al., 1989). At the fifteen-year follow-up time-point, 75 per cent of the hundred BPD patients of Paris were no longer diagnosable as borderline and had markedly improved in function (Paris 1987).

The relationship between mood disorder and BPD in suicide attempters is also of interest given the increased possibility of suicidal behaviour from both problems. Joffe and Regan (1989) found that mean borderline-personality scale scores on the Millon Clinical Multiaxial Inventory (MCMI) were significantly higher than controls among primary depressive-disorder patients who attempted suicide, but there was no increased frequency of formal BPD diagnoses. The authors concluded that persons with major depressive illness may develop borderline traits as a result of their illness and those who do so are more likely to attempt suicide. They followed up 80 per cent of the participants, and only ten of thirty-seven retained a BPD diagnosis on the MCMI after recovering from their depression. The corollary of this study was that of Levitt et al. (1990), who found a diagnosis of cyclothymia more often in BPD patients than in those with other personality disorders, but no increased frequency of other forms of mood disorders. It may be that cyclothymic borderlines are rendered more impulsive and therefore more at risk for parasuicide, but this remains to be investigated.

It is axiomatic that parasuicides are extremely distressed immediately before the act. Ennis et al. (1989) examined 71 consecutive admissions to the SHARE ward (a crisis unit for parasuicides) and found 80% with Beck Depression Inventory (BDI) scores on admission meeting criteria for moderate or severe depression. Within five days of admission only 59% scored within the moderate-to-severe range; only 31% of the total sample could be diagnosed as having a formal clinical depressive illness. This accords with Sakinofsky et al. (1990a), who found a diagnosis of affective disorder in 40% of 228 parasuicides and a further 47% with DSM-III adjustment disorders. Ennis et al. (1985), using the dexamethasone suppression test (DST) were unable to detect depressives likely to benefit from antidepressants because of the heterogeneity of types of depression in their parasuicide sample, confounding by alcohol abuse, and limitations in the biochemical test.

An international study on the prevalence of depressive disorder among parasuicides employed the Levine-Pilowsky Depression questionnaire, an instrument that differentiates 'endogenous' depression. This study was carried out in women attempters from Adelaide (Australia), Auckland (New Zealand), Hamilton (Ontario), and Vancouver (British Columbia), and depression scores were similar in all four centres. Depressive syndromes were variably prevalent in two-thirds to 90 per cent (Auckland) and 'endogenous depression' was diagnosed in one-third across centres (Goldney et al., 1981). Notwithstanding the finding in many studies that only a relative minority have formal diagnoses of depressive disorder, clinical studies of parasuicides in Canada have shown that as a whole they are an unhappy, dysfunctional group. Sakinofsky (1978) compared 106 suicide attempters with patients admitted to a family practice unit and found that the group scored significantly higher on depression (BDI), life-event stress, current problems facing them, and on externally and internally directed hostility. They were significantly lower on self-esteem. Their early family experience had been the precursor of continued social disorganization in their lives (Sakinofsky, 1979). Sakinofsky (1977) carried out a factor analysis of the 106 attempters and found three factors. The first factor (accounting for 40% of the variance) included the emotional and attitudinal variables, the second (18%) included the seriousness of the attempt, and the third (15%) incorporated age and social adjustment.

The frequent presence of hostility is clinically important in parasuicide patients; whether it is primarily intropunitive or externally directed may assist decisions on treatment and guide prognosis. Goldberg and Sakinofsky (1988) examined forty-eight parasuicidal in-patients and found that highly intropunitive patients benefited most from a cognitive therapeutic interview. Resolution of the problems that instigated the parasuicidal acts was associated with significant decreases in external and internal hostility, BDI scores, feelings of powerlessness, and increase in self-esteem at the three-month follow-up, but those who did not resolve problems were essentially unchanged on these parameters (Sakinofsky et al., 1990b). An earlier follow-up study that incorporated home visits showed that the majority of parasuicides admitted to various facilities in the city were coping within a year of discharge (Sakinofsky, 1973b).

Repetition

Barnes examined 163 suicide attempters and found that two-thirds had a previous history of self-harm. The male repeaters were more likely to have left school before grade nine, to be abusing alcohol, and to have family stress. Female repeaters were younger than first-time parasuicides and reported more difficulty with sexual adjustment and loneliness. Repeaters were more likely to have contacted distress centres or mental-health agencies (Barnes, 1979, 1986). Reynolds and Eaton (1986) also compared multiple with first-time attempters and found chronicity in 14 per cent. The multiple attempters showed poorer coping histories, more abuse of alcohol and drugs, higher lethality ratings, and more depression and hopelessness, *but less impulsivity*. In their one-year follow-up at three-month intervals of 228 suicide attempters, Sakinofsky and colleagues did not find higher lethality and less impulsivity associated with repetition (Sakinofsky and Roberts, 1990a, 1990b). In this study a subgroup of attempters was discovered who repeated in spite of resolving the problems that had precipitated their index attempts. The group manifested more severe problems, more external hostility, powerlessness, and 'normlessness,' which seemed trait- rather than state-related. A stepwise discriminant analysis at one year correctly classified 75 per cent of the non-repeaters and 62 per cent of the repeaters by greater number of previous episodes, normlessness, powerlessness, and severity of problems. Further analysis enabled correct identification of 70 per cent of the multiple (persistent) repeaters. In this study four (2%) of the sample group had killed themselves by the end of the year.

Conclusion

Since the 1970s epidemiological studies in Canada have helped us to understand the extent and distribution of its significant problem with suicide. Of concern are the high rates in young males and the elderly, the Aboriginal peoples, and those with a history of mental-health disorder or attempted suicide. The fundamental roots of the problem lie in the very cyto-architecture of the society, following tumultuous changes in structure and norms that occurred after the Second World War (witness the case of Quebec). In certain Aboriginal communities, but not others, there is rampant anomie, attributed by some experts to the diminution of their previously proud spirit that ensued after colonization of Canada's Aboriginal peoples. Increased prevalence of depression in the young (as measured by community prevalence studies) has been concomitant with increased suicide prevalence. It is tempting to conclude that the society has not kept pace with the needs of all its sections. Yet, is it really a less caring, less humane society than before, or is the increase in suicide merely apparent now that our attitudes towards suicide have become more accepting and legislative and religious sanctions have been relaxed? Such questions are difficult to answer, but it is unlikely that change in attitude alone accounts for all the increase. Society has changed very much as well, and some changes have been noxious to those who are vulnerable.

Looked at from the international perspective, suicide rates in Canada are too high, and suicide in youth and the other higher-risk groups needs to be targeted vigorously. One golden opportunity is the currently proposed Bill C-68, which aims at reducing firearm suicides by registration and restriction of both handguns and long guns in Canada.

Clearly, epidemiological studies alone are unlikely to find the solution to Canada's relatively high problem with suicide. Epidemiologists must work together with cognitive psychologists and neurobiological researchers to find some answers to a problem that intersects so many planes. The focus of epidemiological research must also now shift to studies that evaluate innovative treatments of suicidal people and that impact at any or several of these planes.

REFERENCES

Adam, K.S., A. Keller, M. West, S. Larose, and L.B. Goszer. 1994. 'Parental Representation in Suicidal Adolescents: A Controlled Study.' *Australian and New Zealand Journal of Psychiatry* 28(3): 418–25.

Adam, K.S., J.G. Lohrenz, D. Harper, and D. Streiner. 1982. 'Early Parental Loss and Suicidal Ideation in University Students.' *Canadian Journal of Psychiatry* 27(4): 275–81.

Ahlburg, D.A., and M.O. Schapiro. 1984. 'Socioeconomic Ramifications of Changing Cohort Size: An Analysis of U.S. Postwar Suicide Rates by Age and Sex,' *Demography* 21: 97–108.

Aldridge, D., and K. St. John. 1991. 'Adolescent and Pre-Adolescent Suicide in Newfoundland and Labrador.' *Canadian Journal of Psychiatry* 36(6): 432–6.

Allodi, F., and G. Cowgill. 1982. 'Ethical and Psychiatric Aspects of Torture: A Canadian Study.' *Canadian Journal of Psychiatry* 27(2): 98–102.

Angst, J., M. Degonda, and C. Ernst. 1992. 'The Zurich Study: XV. Suicide Attempts in a Cohort from Age 20 to 30.' *European Archives of Psychiatry and Clinical Neuroscience* 242: 135–41.

Bagley, C. 1991. 'Poverty and Suicide among Native Canadians: A Replication.' *Psychological Reports* 69: 149–50.

Bagley, C., and R. Ramsay. 1985. 'Psychosocial Correlates of Suicidal Behaviours in an Urban Population.' *Crisis* 6: 63–77.

– 1993. 'Suicidal Ideas and Behavior in Contrasted Generations: Evidence from a Community Mental Health Survey.' *Journal of Community Psychology* 21: 26–34.

Barnes, R.A. 1979. 'Characteristics of the Chronic Suicide Attempter.' *10th International Congress for Suicide Prevention and Crisis Intervention* (Ottawa) 1: 120–5.

– 1986. 'The Recurrent Self-Harm Patient.' *Suicide and Life-Threatening Behavior* 16(4): 399–408.

Barnes, R.A., C. Braseliten, D.H. Lippman, and L. Siegel. 1979. 'Team Approach to the Problem of Parasuicide in Downtown Toronto.' *Canadian Journal of Public Health* 70: 261–5.

Barnes, R.A., J. Ennis, and R. Schober. 1986. 'Cohort Analysis of Ontario Suicide Rates, 1877–1976.' *Canadian Journal of Psychiatry* 31(3): 208–13.

Bellerose, C., C. Lavallée, and J. Camirand, eds. 1994. *1992–1993 Health and Social Survey Highlights*. Montréal: Santé Quebec.

Bland, R.C., R.J. Dyck, S.C. Newman, and H. Orn. 1995. 'Parasuicide in Edmonton.' Canadian Academy of Psychiatric Epidemiology meeting, Victoria, BC, 19 September 1995.

Bland, R.C., S.C. Newman, and R.J. Dyck. 1994. 'The Epidemiology of Parasuicide in Edmonton.' *Canadian Journal of Psychiatry* 39: 391–6.

Bland, R.C., S.C. Newman, R.J. Dyck, and H. Orn. 1990. 'Prevalence of Psychiatric Disorders and Suicide Attempts in a Prison Population.' *Canadian Journal of Psychiatry* 35: 407–13.

Bouchard, L., and M. Morval. 1988. 'Enquête sur le vecu des étudiants et les comportements suicidaires à l'Université de Montréal.' *Canadian Journal of Community Mental Health* 7: 53–65.

Boyer, R., R. Dufour, M. Préville, and L. Bujold-Brown. 1994a. 'State of Mental Health.' In Santé Québec, ed., *A Health Profile of the Inuit. Report of the Santé Québec Health Survey among the*

Inuit of Nunavik, 1992, 117–44. Montréal: Ministère de la Santé et Service sociaux, Gouvernement du Québec.

Boyer, R., M. Préville, and G. Légaré. 1994b. 'Mental Health.' In Santé Québec, ed., *A Health Profile of the Cree. Report of the Santé Québec Health Survey of the James Bay Cree, 1991*, 161–73. Montréal: Ministère de la Santé et Service sociaux, Gouvernement du Québec.

Brown, J.H. 1975. 'Reporting of Suicide: Canadian Statistics.' *Suicide* 5(1): 21–8.

Buteau, J., A.D. Lesage, and M.C. Kiely. 1993. 'Homicide Followed by Suicide: A Quebec Case Series, 1988–1990.' *Canadian Journal of Psychiatry* 38(8): 552–6.

Carrington, P.J., and S. Moyer. 1994a. 'Gun Control and Suicide in Ontario.' *American Journal of Psychiatry* 151(4): 606–8.

– 1994b. 'Gun Availability and Suicide in Canada: Testing the Displacement Hypothesis.' *Studies on Crime and Crime Prevention* 3: 168–78.

Cheifetz, P.N., J.A. Posener, A. LaHaye, M. Zajdman, et al. 1987. 'An Epidemiological Study of Adolescent Suicide.' *Canadian Journal of Psychiatry* 32: 656–9.

Conacher, G.N. 1993. 'Issues in Psychiatric Care within a Prison Service.' *Canada's Mental Health* 41(1): 11–15.

Cooper, M., R. Corrado, A. Karlberg, and L.P. Adams. 1992. 'Aboriginal Suicide in British Columbia: An Overview.' *Canada's Mental Health* 40: 19–23.

Cormier, H., and G. Klerman. 1985. 'Unemployment and Male Labour Force Participation as Determinants of Changing Suicide Rates of Males and Females in Quebec.' *Social Psychiatry* 20: 109–14.

Côté, L., J. Pronovost, and L. Larochelle. 1993. 'Etude des composantes dépressives chez des adolescents à tendances suicidaires.' *Canadian Psychology* 34(3): 249–64.

Côté, L., J. Pronovost, and C. Ross. 1990. 'Comportements et idéations suicidaires chez les adolescents québécois.' *Psychologie Medicale* 22(5): 389–92.

Davies, D., and T.R. Wilkes. 1993. 'Cluster Suicide in Rural Western Canada.' *Canadian Journal of Psychiatry* 38(7): 515–19.

Dooley, D., R. Catalano, K. Rook, and S. Serxner. 1989. 'Economic Stress and Suicide: Multilevel Analyses. Part 2: Cross-Level Analyses of Economic Stress and Suicidal Ideation.' *Suicide and Life-Threatening Behavior* 19(4): 337–51.

Dyck, R.J., R.C. Bland, S.C. Newman, and H. Orn. 1988. 'Suicide Attempts and Psychiatric Disorder in Edmonton.' *Acta Psychiatrica Scandinavica* 77 (Supplement 338): 64–71.

Dyck, R.J., S.C. Newman, and A.H. Thompson. 1988. 'Suicide Trends in Canada, 1956–1981.' *Acta Psychiatrica Scandinavica* 77: 411–19.

Easterlin, R.A. 1980. *Birth and Fortune: The Impact of Numbers on Personal Welfare*. New York: Basic Books.

Emond, A., L. Guyon, F. Camirand, L. Chenard, R. Pineault, and Y. Robitaille. 1988. *Et La Santé, ça va? Rapport de l'enquête Santé Québec*. Montréal: Le Publications du Québec.

Ennis, J., R.A. Barnes, and S. Kennedy. 1985. 'The Dexamethasone Test and Suicidal Patients.' *British Journal of Psychiatry* 147: 419–23.

Ennis, J., R.A. Barnes, S. Kennedy, and D.D. Trachtenberg. 1989. 'Depression in Self-Harm Patients.' *British Journal of Psychiatry* 154: 41–7.

Eyer, J. 1977. 'Prosperity as a Cause of Death.' *International Journal of Health Services* 7: 125–50.

Falret, J.-P. 1822. *De l'hypochondrie et du suicide: Considérations sur les causes, sur le siège et le traitement de ces maladies, sur les moyens d'en arrêter les progrès et d'en prévenir le développement*. Paris: Chez Croullebois, Librairie de la Societé de Médecine.

Farrow, J.A. 1993. 'Youth Alienation as an Emerging Pediatric Health Care Issue: Update.' *American Journal of Diseases of Children* 147: 509.

Fox, J., D. Manitowabi, and J.A. Ward. 1984. 'An Indian Community with a High Suicide Rate: 5 Years After.' *Canadian Journal of Psychiatry* 29: 425–7.

Garfinkel, B.D., A. Froese, and J. Hood. 1982. 'Suicide Attempts in Children and Adolescents.' *American Journal of Psychiatry* 139(10): 1257–61.

Gartrell, J.W., G.K. Jarvis, and L. Derksen. 1993. 'Suicidality among Adolescent Alberta Indians.' *Suicide and Life-Threatening Behavior* 23(4): 366–73.

Goldberg, J., and I. Sakinofsky. 1988. 'Intropunitiveness and Parasuicide: Prediction of Interview Response.' *British Journal of Psychiatry* 153: 801–4.

Goldney, R.D., K.S. Adam, J.C. O'Brien, and P. Termansen. 1981. 'Depression in Young Women Who Have Attempted Suicide. An International Replication Study.' *Journal of Affective Disorders* 3(4): 327–37.

Goldney, R.D., and M. Katsikitis. 1983. 'Cohort Analysis of Suicide Rates in Australia.' *Archives of General Psychiatry* 40: 71–4.

Gotowiec, A., and M. Beiser. 1994. 'Aboriginal Children's Mental Health: Unique Challenges.' *Canada's Mental Health* 41(4): 7–11.

Green, C., K. Kendall, G. André, T. Looman, and N. Polvi. 1993. 'A Study of 133 Suicides among Canadian Federal Prisoners.' *Medicine Science and Law* 33: 121–7.

Grossi, V., and C. Violato. 1992. 'Attempted Suicide among Adolescents: A Stepwise Discriminant Analysis.' *Canadian Journal of Behavioural Science* 24: 410–13.

Häfner, H., and A. Schmidtke. 1985. 'Do Cohort Effects Influence Suicide Rates?' *Archives of General Psychiatry* 42: 926–7.

Hanigan, D., M.-F. Bastien, M. Tousignant, and S. Hamel. 1986. 'Le soutien social suite à un événement critique chez un groupe de cégépiens suicidaires: Etude comparative.' *Revue Québécoise de Psychologie* 7(3): 63–81.

Hasselback, P., K.I. Lee, Y. Mao, R. Nichol, and D.T. Wigle. 1991. 'The Relationship of Suicide Rates to Sociodemographic Factors in Canadian Census Divisions.' *Canadian Journal of Psychiatry* 36(9): 655–9.

Health and Welfare Canada. 1992. *Aboriginal Health in Canada*. Ottawa: Ministry of Supply and Services.

Hellon, C.P., M.I. Solomon. 1980. 'Suicide and Age in Alberta, Canada, 1951 to 1977: The Changing Profile.' *Archives of General Psychiatry* 37(5): 505–10.

Hirsch, S., M. Lowman, and R. Perry. 1978. 'Suicidal Behaviour in Halifax, Nova Scotia: With Some General Observations.' *Canadian Psychiatric Association Journal* 23: 309–16.

Hodgins, S., and G. Côté. 1990. 'Prevalence of Mental Disorders among Penitentiary Inmates in Quebec.' *Canada's Mental Health* 38(1): 1–4.

Howe, A., and I. Sakinofsky. 1979. 'A Short-Stay Intensive Care Multidisciplinary Unit for Parasuicide.' *10th International Congress for Suicide Prevention and Crisis Intervention* 2: 34–8.

Huchcroft, S.A., and B.L. Tanney. 1988. 'Sex-Specific Suicide Trends in Canada, 1971–1985.' *International Journal of Epidemiology* 17(4): 839–43.

– 1989. 'Sex-Specific Trends in Suicide Method, Canada, 1971–1985.' *Canadian Journal of Public Health* 80: 120–3.

Hung, C.K. 1993. 'Gun Control and Rates of Firearms Violence in Canada and the United States.' Comment. *Canadian Journal of Criminology* 35(1): 37–41.

Jackson, P.R., and P.B. Warr. 1984. 'Unemployment and Psychological Ill-Health: The Moderating Role of Duration and Age.' *Psychological Medicine* 14: 605–14.

Jakob, O. 1979. 'Analysis of the Swiss Death-Certificates, 1877–1977.' *10th International Congress for Suicide Prevention and Crisis Intervention* (Ottawa) 1: 32–9.

Jarvis, G.K., and M. Boldt. 1982. 'Death Styles among Canada's Indians.' *Social Science and Medicine* 16(14): 1345–52.

Jarvis, G.K., R.G. Ferrence, F.G. Johnson, and P.C. Whitehead, 1976. 'Sex and Age Patterns in Self-Injury.' *Journal of Health and Social Behavior* 17(2): 145–54.

Jarvis, G.K., R.G. Ferrence, P.C. Whitehead, and F.G. Johnson. 1982. 'The Ecology of Self-Injury: A Multivariate Approach.' *Suicide and Life-Threatening Behavior* 12: 90–102.

Joffe, R.T., and D.R. Offord. 1983. 'Suicidal Behaviour in Childhood.' *Canadian Journal of Psychiatry* 28(1): 57–63.

Joffe, R.T., D.R. Offord, and M.H. Boyle. 1988. 'Ontario Child Health Study: Suicidal Behavior in Youth Age 12–16 Years.' *American Journal of Psychiatry* 145(11): 1420–3.

Joffe, R.T., and J.J. Regan. 1989. 'Personality and Suicidal Behavior in Depressed Patients.' *Comprehensive Psychiatry* 30(2): 157–60.

Johnston, D.W., and J.P. Waddell. 1984. 'Death and Injury Patterns, Toronto Subway System 1954–1980.' *Journal of Trauma* 24(7): 619–22.

Kehoe, J.P., and A.P. Abbott. 1975. 'Suicide and Attempted Suicide in the Yukon Territory.' *Canadian Psychiatric Association Journal* 20(1): 15–23.

Kerkhof, A.J.F.M., A. Schmidtke, U. Bille-Brahe, D. De Leo, and J. Lönnqvist. 1994. *Attempted Suicide in Europe: Findings from the Multicentre Study on Parasuicide by the WHO Regional Office for Europe*. Leiden: Leiden University, DSWO Press, and World Health Organization.

Kirmayer, L.J. 1994. 'Suicide among Canadian Aboriginal Peoples.' *Transcultural Psychiatric Research Review* 31(1): 3–58.

Klerman, G.L. 1988. 'The Current Age of Youthful Melancholia.' *British Journal of Psychiatry* 152: 4–14.

Kreitman, N. 1977. *Parasuicide*, 7–9. London: John Wiley.

Krull, C., and F. Trovato. 1994. 'The Quiet Revolution and the Sex Differential in Quebec's Suicide Rates: 1931–1986.' *Social Forces* 72(4): 1121–47.

Larose, F. 1989. 'L'environnement des réserves Indiennes est-il pathogène? Réflexions sur le suicide et l'identification des facteurs de risque en milieu Amérindien Québécois.' *Revue Québécoise de Psychologie* 10(1): 31–44.

Leenaars, A.A., and G. Domino. 1993. 'A Comparison of Community Attitudes towards Suicide in Windsor and Los Angeles.' *Canadian Journal of Behavioural Science* 25: 253–66.

Leenaars, A.A., and D. Lester. 1990. 'Suicide in Adolescents: A Comparison of Canada and the United States.' *Psychological Reports* 67(3, pt 1): 867–73.

– 1992. 'Comparison of Rates and Patterns of Suicide in Canada and the United States, 1960–1988.' *Death Studies* 16(5): 417–30.

– 1994. 'Suicide and Homicide Rates in Canada and the United States.' *Suicide and Life-Threatening Behavior* 24(2): 184–91.

– 1996. 'Testing the Cohort Size Hypothesis of Suicide and Homicide Rates in Canada and the United States.' *Archives of Suicide Research* 2: 43–54.

Leenaars, A.A., B. Yang, and D. Lester. 1993. 'The Effect of Domestic and Economic Stress on Suicide Rates in Canada and the United States.' *Journal of Clinical Psychology* 49(6): 918–21.

Légaré, G., A. Lebeau, R. Boyer, and D. St-Laurent. 1995. 'Santé Mentale.' In Santé Québec, ed., *Et la santé, ça va. Rapport de l'Enquête sociale et de santé*, 217–55. Montréal: Ministère de la Santé et Service sociaux, Gouvernement du Québec.

Leonard, K.A. 1994. 'Firearm Deaths in Canadian Adolescents and Young Adults.' *Canadian Journal of Public Health* 85(2): 128–31.

Lesage, A.D., R. Boyer, F. Grunberg, C. Vanier, R. Morissette, C. Menard-Buteau, and M. Loyer.

1994. 'Suicide and Mental Disorders: A Case-Control Study of Young Men.' *American Journal of Psychiatry* 151(7): 1063–68.

Lester, D. 1988a. 'Economic Factors and Suicide.' *Journal of Social Psychology* 128(2): 245–8.

– 1988b. 'An Analysis of the Suicide Rates of Birth Cohorts in Canada.' *Suicide and Life-Threatening Behavior* 18(4): 372–8.

– 1990. 'Women in the Labor Force and Suicide.' *Psychological Reports* 66: 194.

Lester, D., and A. Leenaars. 1993. 'Suicide Rates in Canada before and after Tightening Firearm Control Laws.' *Psychological-Reports* 72(3, pt 1): 787–90.

Lester, D., and B. Yang. 1992. 'Social and Economic Correlates of the Elderly Suicide Rate.' *Suicide and Life-Threatening Behavior* 22(1): 36–47.

Levitt, A.J., R.T. Joffe, J. Ennis, C. MacDonald, and S.P. Kutcher, 1990. 'The Prevalence of Cyclothymia in Borderline Personality Disorder.' *Journal of Clinical Psychiatry* 51(8): 335–9.

Liberakis, E.A., and J. Hoenig. 1978. 'Recording of Suicide in Newfoundland.' *Psychiatric Journal of the University of Ottawa* 3(4): 254–9.

McNamee, J.E., and D.R. Offord. 1990. 'Prevention of Suicide.' *Canadian Medical Association Journal* 142(11): 1223–30.

Malla, A., and J. Hoenig. 1979. 'Suicide in Newfoundland and Labrador.' *Canadian Journal of Psychiatry* 24(2): 139–46.

– 1983. 'Differences in Suicide Rates: An Examination of Under-Reporting.' *Canadian Journal of Psychiatry* 28(4): 291–3.

Mao, Y., P. Hasselback, J.W. Davies, R. Nichol, and D.T. Wigle, 1990. 'Suicide in Canada: An Epidemiological Assessment.' *Canadian Journal of Public Health* 81(4): 324–8.

Mao, Y., B.W. Moloughney, and R.M. Semenciw. 1992. 'Indian Reserve and Registered Indian Mortality in Canada.' *Canadian Journal of Public Health* 83(5): 350–3.

Miller, J., I. Sakinofsky, and D.L. Streiner. 1979. 'The Family and Social Dynamics of Adolescent Parasuicide.' *10th International Congress of Suicide Prevention and Crisis Intervention* (Ottawa) 1: 122–34.

Moscicki, E., P. O'Carroll, D.S. Rae, B.Z. Locke, A. Roy, and D.A. Regier. 1988. 'Suicide Attempts in the Epidemiologic Catchment Area Study.' *Yale Journal of Biology and Medicine* 61: 259–68.

Moser, K.A., A.J. Fox, D.R. Jones, and P.O. Goldblatt. 1986. 'Unemployment and Mortality: Further Evidence from the OPCS Longitudinal Study 1971–81.' *Lancet* i, 365–6.

Mundt, R.J. 1990. 'Gun Control and Rates of Firearms Violence in Canada and the United States.' *Canadian Journal of Criminology* 32(1): 137–54.

– 1993. 'Gun Control and Rates of Firearms Violence in Canada and the United States': Rejoinder.' *Canadian Journal of Criminology* 35(1): 42–8.

Murphy, G.E., and R.D. Wetzel. 1980. 'Suicide Risk by Birth Cohort in the United States, 1949 to 1974.' *Archives of General Psychiatry* 37(5): 519–23.

Murphy, H.B.M. 1982. *Comparative Psychiatry: The International and Intercultural Distribution of Mental Illness.* Berlin, Heidelberg, New York: Springer-Verlag.

National Task Force. 1987. *Suicide in Canada: Report of the National Task Force on Suicide in Canada.* Ottawa: Minister of National Health and Welfare.

– 1994. *Suicide in Canada: Update of the Report of the Task Force on Suicide in Canada.* Ottawa: Minister of National Health and Welfare.

Newman, S.C., and R.J. Dyck. 1988. 'On the Age-Period-Cohort Analysis of Suicide Rates.' *Psychological Medicine* 18(3): 677–81.

Normand, C.L., and B.L. Mishara. 1992. 'The Development of the Concept of Suicide in Children.' *Omega Journal of Death and Dying* 25(3): 183–203.

Ogloff, J.R.P., R. Roesch, and S.D. Hart. 1994. 'Mental Health Services in Jails and Prisons: Legal, Clinical, and Policy Issues.' *Law and Psychology Review* 18: 109–36.

Paris, J. 1987. 'Long Term Follow Up of Borderline Patients in a General Hospital.' *Comprehensive Psychiatry* 28: 530–5.

– 1990. 'Completed Suicide in Borderline Personality Disorder.' *Psychiatric Annals* 20(1): 19–21.

– 1991. 'Personality Disorders, Parasuicide, and Culture.' *Transcultural Psychiatric Research Review* 28(1): 25–39.

– 1992. 'Social Risk Factors for Borderline Personality Disorder: A Review and Hypothesis.' '*Canadian Journal of Psychiatry* 37(7): 510–15.

Paris, J., D. Nowlis, and R. Brown. 1989. 'Predictors of Suicide in Borderline Personality Disorder.' *Canadian Journal of Psychiatry* 34(1): 8–9.

Petronis, K.R., J.F. Samuels, E.K. Moscicki, and J.C. Anthony. 1990. 'An Epidemiological Investigation of Potential Risk Factors for Suicide Attempts.' *Social Psychiatry and Psychiatric Epidemiology* 25: 193–9.

Platt, S. 1984. 'Unemployment and Suicidal Behaviour: A Review of the Literature.' *Social Science and Medicine* 19(2): 93–115.

Pritchard, C. 1990. 'Suicide, Unemployment and Gender Variations in the Western World 1964–1986.' *Social Psychiatry and Psychiatric Epidemiology* 25: 73–80.

Pronovost, J., J. Boucher, and L. Côté. 1990b. 'Fonctionnement scolaire chez les adolescents à tendances suicidaires.' *Apprentissage et Socialisation* 13(2): 111–20.

Pronovost, J., L. Côté, and C. Ross. 1990a. 'Epidemiological Study of Suicidal Behaviour among Secondary-School Students.' *Canada's Mental Health* 38: 9–14.

Rakoff, V.M. 1983. 'Anomic Suicide: The Persistence of a Problem.' *The Spectrum of Antidepressant Effect. Proceedings VII World Congress of Psychiatry.* Vienna.

Ramsay, R., and C. Bagley. 1985. 'The Prevalence of Suicidal Behaviors, Attitudes and Associated Social Experiences in an Urban Population.' *Suicide and Life-Threatening Behavior* 15: 151–67.

Ramsay, R., B. Tanney, C.A. Searle. 1987. 'Suicide Prevention in High-Risk Prison Populations.' *Canadian Journal of Criminology* 29(3): 295–307.

Reed, J., J. Camus, and J.M. Last. 1985. 'Suicide in Canada: Birth-Cohort Analysis.' *Canadian Journal of Public Health* 76(1): 43–7.

Reinfurt, D.W., J.R. Stewart, and N.L. Weaver. 1991. 'The Economy as a Factor in Motor Vehicle Fatalities, Suicides and Homicides.' *Accident Analysis and Prevention* 23(5): 453–62.

Reynolds, P., and P. Eaton. 1986. 'Multiple Attempters of Suicide Presenting at an Emergency Department.' *Canadian Journal of Psychiatry* 31(4): 328–30.

Rich, C.L., J.G. Young, R.C. Fowler, J. Wagner, and N.A. Black. 1990. 'Guns and Suicide: Possible Effects of Some Specific Legislation.' *American Journal of Psychiatry* 147(3): 342–46.

Rosenblatt, E., and C. Greenland. 1974. 'Female Crimes of Violence.' *Canadian Journal of Criminology and Corrections* 16(2): 173–80.

Ross, C.P., and B. Davis. 1986. 'Suicide and Parasuicide in a Northern Canadian Native Community.' *Canadian Journal of Psychiatry* 31: 331–4.

Royal Commission on Aboriginal Peoples. 1995. *Choosing Life. Special Report on Suicide among Aboriginal Peoples.* Ottawa: Minister of Supply and Services Canada.

Sainsbury, P., and J.S. Jenkins. 1982. 'The Accuracy of Officially Reported Suicide Statistics for the Purposes of Epidemiological Research.' *Journal of Epidemiology and Community Health* 36: 43–8.

Sakinofsky, I. 1973a. 'Experience of Comprehensive Care of Attempted Suicide within a General Hospital.' In A. Russell, ed., *Proceedings of the Suicide Symposium, Oxford Mental Health Centre*. Woodstock, Ontario.

– 1973b. 'A Domiciliary Follow-up of Suicide Attempters: Conclusions Regarding Prediction and Treatment.' In N. Speyer, R.F.W. Diekstra, and L. Van de Loo, eds, *Proceedings of the 7th International Congress on Suicide Prevention*. Amsterdam.

– 1977. 'An In-Depth Look at Suicide Attempters.' In P. Cantor, ed., *10th Annual Meeting of the American Association of Suicidology*. Boston.

– 1978. 'Life Situations and Lifestyles of Persons Who Attempt Suicide.' *11th Annual Meeting of the American Association of Suicidology*. New Orleans.

– 1979. 'Socioeconomic Implications of Early Family Disorganization in the Lives of Suicide Attempters.' *Royal College of Physicians and Surgeons of Canada Meeting*. Montreal, 9 February 1979.

– 1995. 'The risk that available guns pose.' Letter to *Globe and Mail*, 1 July 1995: D7.

Sakinofsky, I., and R. Roberts. 1987. 'The Ecology of Suicide in the Provinces of Canada, 1969–71 to 1979–81.' In B.Cooper, ed., *The Epidemiology of Psychiatric Disorders*, 27–42. Baltimore: Johns Hopkins University Press.

– 1990a. 'Why Parasuicides Repeat Despite Problem Resolution.' *British Journal of Psychiatry* 156: 399–405.

– 1990b. 'What Determines Repetition of Parasuicide?' In G. Ferrari, M. Bellini, and P. Crepet, eds, *Volumetto Estratto da: 3rd European Symposium Suicidal Behaviour and Risk Factors*, 951–4. Bologna: Monduzzi Editore.

Sakinofsky, I., R.S. Roberts, Y. Brown, C. Cooper, and P. James. 1990. 'Problem Resolution and Repetition of Parasuicide: A Prospective Study.' *British Journal of Psychiatry* 156: 395–9.

Sakinofsky, I., R. Roberts, and A. Van Houten. 1975. 'The End of the Journey: A Study of Suicide across Canada.' *8th International Congress on Suicide Prevention and Crisis Intervention*. Jerusalem.

Sakinofsky, I., and G. Webster. 1995. 'Major Risk Factors for Non-Fatal Suicidality in the Community.' *18th Congress of the International Association for Suicide Prevention and Crisis Intervention (IASP)*. Venice, Italy, 5 June 1995.

Shaw, M. 1992. 'Issues of Power and Control: Women in Prison and Their Defenders.' *British Journal of Criminology* 32(4): 438–52.

Shkrum, M.J., and K.A. Johnston. 1992. 'Fire and Suicide: A Three Year Study of Self Immolation Deaths.' *Journal of Forensic Sciences* 37: 208–21.

Sigurdson, E., D. Staley, M. Matas, K. Hildahl, and K. Squair. 1994. 'A Five Year Review of Youth Suicide in Manitoba.' *Canadian Journal of Psychiatry* 39(8): 397–403.

Simon, G., and M. VonKorff. 1992. 'Reevaluation of Secular Trends in Depression Rates.' *American Journal of Epidemiology* 135(12): 1411–22.

Solomon, M.I., and C.P. Hellon. 1980. 'Suicide and Age in Alberta, Canada, 1951 to 1977: A Cohort Analysis.' *Archives of General Psychiatry* 37(5): 511–13.

Spaulding, J.M. 1986. 'Recent Suicide Rates among Ten Ojibwa Indian Bands in Northwestern Ontario.' *Omega Journal of Death and Dying* 16(4): 347–54.

Speechley, M., and K.M. Stavraky. 1991. 'The Adequacy of Suicide Statistics for Use in Epidemiology and Public Health.' *Canadian Journal of Public Health* 82(1): 38–42.

Syer, D. 1975. 'Emergency Ward Treatment of Suicidal Patients.' *Ontario Psychologist* 7(2): 33–7.

Termansen, P.E., and C. Bywater. 1975. 'S.A.F.E.R.: A Follow-up Service for Attempted Suicide in Vancouver.' *Canadian Psychiatric Association Journal* 20(1): 29–34.

Thompson, T.R. 1987. 'Childhood and Adolescent Suicide in Manitoba: A Demographic Study.' *Canadian Journal of Psychiatry* 32(4): 264–9.

Tonkin, R.S. 1984. 'Suicide Methods in British Columbian Adolescents.' *Journal of Adolescent Health Care* 5(3): 172–7.

Tousignant, M., M.F. Bastien, and S. Hamel. 1993. 'Suicidal Attempts and Ideations among Adolescents and Young Adults. The Contribution of the Father's and Mother's Care and of Parental Separation.' *Social Psychiatry and Psychiatric Epidemiology* 28: 256–61.

Tousignant, M., M.-F. Bastien, S. Hamel, and D. Hanigan. 1986. 'Comportements et idéations suicidaires chez les cégépiens de Montréal: La part familiale.' *Apprentissage et Socialisation* 9(1): 17–25.

Tousignant, M., and D. Hanigan. 1993. 'Crisis Support among Suicidal Students Following a Loss Event.' *Journal of Community Psychology* 21(2): 83–96.

Trovato, F. 1986. 'The Relationship between Marital Dissolution and Suicide: The Canadian Case.' *Journal of Marriage and the Family* 48(2): 341–8.

– 1987. 'A Longitudinal Analysis of Divorce and Suicide in Canada.' *Journal of Marriage and the Family* 49(1): 193–203.

– 1988. 'Suicide in Canada: A Further Look at the Effects of Age, Period and Cohort.' *Canadian Journal of Public Health* 79: 37–44.

– 1991. 'Sex, Marital Status, and Suicide in Canada: 1951–1981.' *Sociological Perspectives* 34(4): 427–45.

– 1992. 'A Durkheimian Analysis of Youth Suicide: Canada, 1971 and 1981.' *Suicide and Life-Threatening Behavior* 22(4): 413–27.

Vitelli, R. 1993. 'The Homeless Inmate in a Maximum-Security Prison Setting.' *Canadian Journal of Criminology* 35(3): 323–31.

Ward, J.A., and J. Fox. 1977. 'A Suicide Epidemic on an Indian Reserve.' *Canadian Psychiatric Association Journal* 22(8): 423–6.

Warr, P.B., and P.R. Jackson. 1987. 'Adapting to the Unemployed Role. A Longitudinal Investigation.' *Social Science and Medicine* 25: 1219–24.

Wasserman, I.M. 1984. 'The Influence of Economic Business Cycles on United States Suicide Rates.' *Suicide and Life-Threatening Behavior* 14(3): 143–56.

– 1989. 'Age, Period and Cohort Effects in Suicide Behavior in the United States and Canada in the 20th Century.' *Journal of Aging Studies* 3(4): 295–311.

Whitehead, P., F.G. Johnson, and R. Ference. 1973. 'Measuring the Incidence of Self-Injury: Some Methodological and Design Considerations.' *American Journal of Orthopsychiatry* 43: 142–8.

Whitemore, L. 'Gun control.' Letter to *Globe and Mail*, 22 June 1995.

3

Epidemiology of Suicide, Parasuicide, and Suicidal Ideation in Quebec

RICHARD BOYER, GILLES LÉGARÉ,
DANIELLE ST-LAURENT, and MICHEL PRÉVILLE

This chapter lays out recent data on the incidence of suicide in Quebec and the major findings from a study of suicidal ideation and parasuicide[1] undertaken within the framework of the Quebec Health Survey (QHS). The QHS was conducted first in the general population of Quebec in 1987 and again in 1992–3 with a new sample. The native populations of Quebec, however, were excluded from these for reasons of feasibility. These populations, instead, were the object of two separate surveys, one conducted among the James Bay Cree in 1991 and the other among the Nunavik Inuit in 1992. A similar methodology and the same questions were employed throughout, thus rendering interpopulation comparisons possible.

The first part of the chapter describes briefly the evolution of suicide in Quebec and compares this picture with the trends identified elsewhere in Canada and the world. This is followed by a short outline of the methodology used in the QHS and a summary of its major findings, including the prevalence of suicidal ideation and parasuicide and a review of sociodemographic and psychosocial factors associated with these phenomena. Finally, the limitations of these studies are addressed and the results discussed within the context of the literature.

Incidence of Suicide in Quebec

Suicide is a major public-health issue in Quebec. In the span of two decades, the standardized suicide rate nearly doubled from 10.6 per 100,000 inhabitants in 1971 to 18.1 per 100,000 in 1993. The 1993 rate translates into 1313 cases (264 females and 1049 males). Suicide is the second leading cause of premature

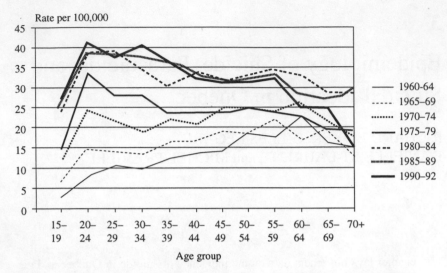

Figure 1   Average suicide rates per 100,000 among males aged 15 or over (Quebec, 1960–1992

death in the population after ischemic cardiopathy and the single leading cause of mortality among men aged twenty to thirty-nine.

Until 1970, suicide in Quebec involved primarily older men. Since then, however, a new trend has emerged, such that suicide is now much more frequent among younger males. Figure 1 shows that after 1974, incidence rates[2] for males aged fifteen to twenty-four increased very rapidly and have consistently surpassed those for age groups over twenty-four. The period 1990 to 1992 even witnessed a decline from the two previous periods in suicide among males aged fifty-five to fifty-nine. Since 1981, Quebec and the Prairies have registered the highest male suicide rates in Canada (St-Laurent, 1995). What sets Quebec apart more than all else from the other Canadian regions, however, is a marked uptrend in the incidence of overall male suicide.

For Quebec females, the age-specific rates by time period are lower than for males and do not exhibit the same accelerated growth among fifteen to twenty-four year olds (figure 2). The highest incidence was recorded by the thirty-five to fifty-four age group during the 1980–1992 periods. In 1990–1992, female incidence rates were down from the two previous periods for all age groups except the fifteen to nineteen bracket. Quebec statistics for females are in line with the trends observed in Ontario, the Prairies, and British Columbia, where suicide rates have been receding since 1981.

While the 1991 male suicide rate in Quebec was very high (26.5 per

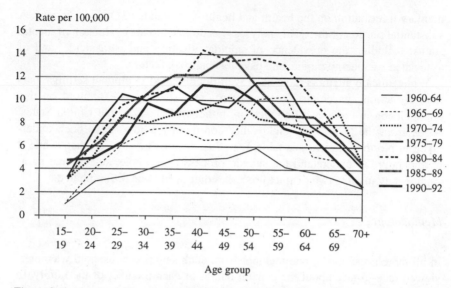

Figure 2   Average suicide rates per 100,000 among females aged 15 or over (Quebec, 1960–1992)

100,000), it was nevertheless lower than in many industrialized countries, including Hungary (59.8), Finland (49.3), Switzerland (33.0), France (29.6), Denmark (28.9), and Belgium (27.4). However, when the rate of potential number of years of life lost is considered, Quebec's premature male mortality by suicide (9.2 per 100,000) exceeds that of Italy (2.6), Spain (2.8), the Netherlands (4.0), Great Britain (4.3), Japan (5.2), the United States (6.6), Belgium (7.4), Australia (7.5), Denmark (8.1), and France (8.2). For Quebec females, instead, the 1991 rates of suicide and of potential number of years of life lost are among the lowest in the world. Quebec females had a rate of potential number of years lost of 2.0 per 100,000, compared with 3.4 in Finland, 3.1 in Denmark, 2.9 in Sweden, 2.7 in Switzerland and France, and 2.8 in Belgium (St-Laurent, 1995).

Quebec Health Surveys (QHS)

In the light of this serious public-health problem, Quebec authorities decided to investigate suicidal ideation and parasuicide and their repercussions on the population's physical and mental health, especially as suicide attempts are considered a predictor of reattempts and completions. The QHS provided a perfect opportunity for this effort. The object of these surveys was to gather complementary information on the health and health-care habits of Quebec citizens. A substantial portion of the QHS analyses was devoted to the evaluation of mental status, including the prevalence of suicidal ideation and parasuicide, and of associated sociodemographic and psychosocial risk factors.

While suicide attempts have been well documented in clinical settings, particularly among psychiatric patients, very few studies have focused on this phenomenon in the general population, either in Canada or the United States. Aside from the QHS, only eight other community studies have been undertaken in North America (see table 1, p. 79). It must be stressed that, while it is imperative to understand the suicide process as a whole, suicide and parasuicide may involve two distinct processes that need to be differentiated.

Methodology

In all three populations, one member from each sampled household was interviewed face-to-face about the general health of each member of the family. In the general population and among the Cree, a self-administered questionnaire was then left for each household member aged fifteen or over to complete. This instrument served to cull information on health behaviours, stressful life events, psychological distress, use of alcohol and illicit drugs, suicidal ideation, and parasuicide. With the Inuit, the same questions were administered verbally by an interviewer.

For the purposes of investigating suicidal ideation and parasuicide, three questions often employed in surveys of this type (Mościcki, 1989) were used: (1) 'Did you ever SERIOUSLY think about committing suicide (taking your life)?'; (2) 'Did you ever attempt suicide (try to take your life)?' An affirmative answer to either of these prompted a follow-up question: (3) 'Did this happen during the past twelve months?' The 1992–3 general-population survey contained an additional question concerning post-attempt recourse to professional and non-professional services.

The sampling frame of each survey ensured representativity despite different sampling strategies. For the 1987 and 1992–3 surveys of the Quebec general population, the frame of reference comprised all individuals aged fifteen or over, excluding those living in institutions or the nordic region, for a total of nearly five million. Over 13,000 residential units were randomly selected in both surveys. These produced more than 19,000 respondents to the self-administered questionnaire. Response rates for the 1987 and 1992–3 surveys were 81 per cent and 85 per cent, respectively (Santé Québec, 1988, 1995).

For the Cree survey, the reference frame was the private households in the nine Cree communities of James Bay, stratified by community. The sampling base consisted of nine lists obtained from the Housing Department, from which a systematic sample of four hundred households was drawn. Of these, 354 agreed to respond to the household interview. The sample size for the self-administered questionnaire was 1288 individuals aged 15 or over. The questionnaire was in English (Santé Québec, 1994a).

For the survey among the Inuit, a systematic sample was drawn using lists from the Conseil régional Kativik de la santé et des services sociaux and from the Housing Department. The population of reference consisted of 7078 Inuit aged 15 or over, from 14 villages in Nunavik. Four hundred households were selected, for a sample of 618 Inuit. Of these, 55.6 per cent completed the individual questionnaire serving to assess suicidal ideation and parasuicide. This figure reflects the fact that if an individual refused to complete the first questionnaire on the general health of the household, no member of that household was then eligible for the individual questionnaire. The response rate among eligible respondents was 69.6 per cent. The individual instrument was administered by an interviewer in either English or Inuktitut (Santé Québec, 1994b).

Results

The responses obtained yielded four prevalence estimates: lifetime and twelve-month prevalence of suicidal ideation and lifetime and twelve-month prevalence of parasuicides. In order to better differentiate individuals who attempted suicide from those who only thought seriously about suicide or never at all, individuals who reported a suicide attempt were excluded from the numerator and the denominator (population of reference) in calculating the prevalence of suicidal ideation. Likewise, calculation of the parasuicide rates excluded from the numerator and denominator individuals who reported suicidal ideation. These criteria resulted in somewhat lower ideation rates and a somewhat higher prevalence estimate of parasuicide, a point that should be kept in mind when comparing data from Quebec and other populations.[3]

Lifetime Prevalence of Suicidal Ideation and Parasuicide

Figure 3 gives the lifetime prevalence (crude rates) of suicidal ideation and parasuicide in the three populations targeted by Santé Québec. A 99 per cent confidence interval was used to determine the statistical significance of inter-rate differences.

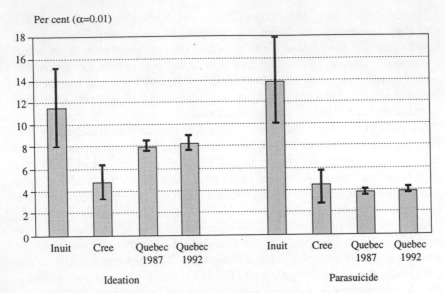

Figure 3 Lifetime prevalence of suicide ideation and parasuicide (crude rates)

Quebec General Population (1987 and 1992–93)

Where suicidal ideation is concerned, results from the two general-population surveys (figure 3) showed that about 8 per cent of respondents had thought seriously about suicide in their lifetime. The difference between males and females was not significant in either survey. The overall, sex-, age-, and sex-age-specific rates did not differ statistically from 1987 to 1992–3. In both surveys, the prevalence of suicidal ideation dropped with age.

Regarding parasuicides, both surveys found that almost 4% of the Quebec general population had attempted suicide. The prevalence of parasuicide did not differ between surveys. Contrary to 1987 results, lifetime rates for parasuicide in 1992–3 differed according to gender (2.8% and 4.5% for male and female, respectively). Parasuicide rates, too, were found to decline with age in both surveys. For example, the 1992–3 overall parasuicide rate was 6.0 per cent among respondents aged 15 to 24, compared with 0.7% among those aged 65 or over. The prevalence was 4.5% among males aged 15 to 24, and 0.4% among those 65 or over. Rates were 7.6% for females under 25, compared with 1.0% for those 65 or over.

Cree

Among the Cree, nearly 5 per cent (crude rate) had thought seriously about suicide and 4 per cent (crude rate) had attempted suicide (figure 3). The crude and age-standardized rates of suicidal ideation were significantly lower than for the Quebec general population in 1987 and 1992–3. No difference was observed between these populations regarding parasuicide. While the data did not support any significant gender or age differences in the prevalence of suicidal ideation and parasuicide among the Cree, parasuicides were reported only by respondents under the age of forty-five (Boyer, Préville, and Légaré, 1994).

Inuit

Over 10 per cent of Nunavik Inuit reported serious suicidal ideation in their lifetime and 14 per cent indicated having attempted suicide (crude rates). The crude rates for parasuicide were significantly different from those observed in the Quebec general population in 1987 and 1992–3 and among the Cree in 1991 (figure 3). However, given the notable age differences between the Inuit and the Quebec general population (i.e., the Inuit population was much younger), it was necessary to standardize the age structure of the two populations for purposes of comparison. After adjustment, suicidal ideation and parasuicides were, respectively, 1.5 (Standardized Mortality Ratio [SMR] = 1.5 [$CI_{99\%}$ = 1.03–2.0]) and 3.5 (SMR = 3.5 [$CI_{99\%}$ = 2.5–4.7]) times as frequent among the Nunavik Inuit as in the Quebec general population (Boyer, Dufour, Préville, and Bujold-Brown, 1994).

Suicidal ideation was seven times as prevalent among Inuit females under forty-five (21%) as among those aged forty-five or over (3%). However, when age and gender were considered together, no statistical difference emerged. Overall, Inuit aged 15 to 24 were twice as likely to have attempted suicide in their lifetime as those aged 25 to 44, and 33 times as likely as those over 44. This association, however, was more specific to women. Inuit females aged 15 to 24 were 18 times as likely to have attempted suicide as those over 44. The association between age and prevalence of parasuicide was not significant for males.

Twelve-Month Prevalence of Suicidal Ideation and Parasuicide

The findings on suicidal ideation, parasuicide, and associated risk factors for the twelve months preceding the surveys are epidemiologically more meaningful for two reasons: (1) the data collected were more recent and, consequently, more reliable; and (2) a respondent's sociodemographic and psychosocial char-

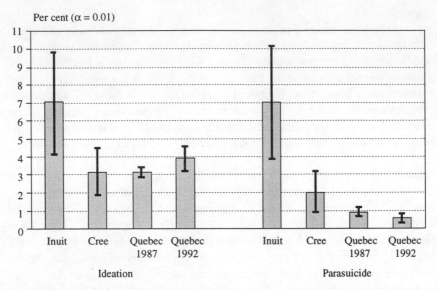

Figure 4 Twelve-month prevalence of suicide ideation and parasuicide (crude rates)

acteristics at the time of the survey were more likely to correspond to those at the time of ideation or parasuicide. Figure 4 gives the twelve-month prevalence (crude rates) of suicidal ideation and parasuicide in the three populations studied by Santé Québec. A 99 per cent confidence interval was used to determine whether the difference in prevalences between populations was significant.

Quebec General Population (1987 and 1992–3)
In 1992–3, nearly 4% of the general-population respondents reported serious suicidal ideation in the twelve months preceding the survey. No statistical difference was observed between genders (4.0% for males and 3.9% for females). The prevalence of suicidal ideation was found to be inversely related to age for the population as a whole as well as for each gender separately. For example, males aged 15 to 24 reported serious suicidal ideation 15 times as often as males over 64, and females in the 15 to 24 age group reported serious suicidal ideation 10 times as often as those over 64. Compared against the 1987 figures, these findings did not support the hypothesis of an increase in the prevalence of suicidal ideation in the population, even when sex, age, and sex by age group were considered separately. The 1987 global prevalence was 3.3% and the sex-specific prevalences were 3.1% and 3.5% for males and females, respectively (Légaré et al., 1995).

Analyses of the sociodemographic data gathered in 1992–3 revealed that suicidal ideation was more prevalent among single individuals (8%), individuals living in common law (5%), and individuals divorced or separated (5%) than among married individuals (2%). The survey also indicated that suicidal ideation was more common among students (9%) and the unemployed (7%), while the prevalence was 0.6% among the retired. This association with marital status and employment could be explained, at least in part, by the observed association of suicidal ideation with age. Ideation was also found to be associated with household income adjusted for household size. Twice as many individuals in the low-income group (i.e., below the poverty line) as those in the average or high-income group (i.e., above the poverty line) reported having thought seriously about suicide (7% vs 3%, respectively).

Regarding psychosocial factors, suicidal ideation was found to be more frequent among individuals with no one to confide in. Furthermore, there was almost three times as much suicidal ideation in the group of individuals with low social support (10%) as in the group with a high level of support (3%). In addition, individuals dissatisfied with their social life (as measured on a four-point scale) reported serious suicidal ideation over thirteen times as often as individuals very satisfied with their social life (16% vs 1.2%, respectively).

In all four surveys, psychological distress was investigated by means of the 'Indice de détresse psychologique de l'enquête Santé Québec' (IDPESQ) (Préville et al., 1991), an instrument similar to Ilfeld's Psychiatric Symptom Index (1976). Analyses of the general-population data revealed that psychological distress was strongly associated with suicidal ideation. Almost 12% of individuals with severe psychological distress reported suicidal ideation, compared with only 1.5% of those with a lower degree of distress. No difference emerged between 1987 and 1992–3 regarding the proportion of suicide ideators with severe psychological distress. The prevalence of severe psychological distress among male suicide ideators under twenty-five, however, increased 39% from 52.6% in 1987 to 73.1% in 1992–3. No significant change was noted for females over the two surveys.

The twelve-month prevalence of parasuicides for the Quebec general population was estimated at 0.6 per cent in 1992–3. This did not differ significantly from the 1987 rate of 0.9 per cent. Sex-specific prevalences were consistent over the two surveys, with no difference observed between genders. Unlike the 1987 survey, however, the 1992–3 survey revealed a significant link with age (see note 2). The percentage of overall respondents aged 15 to 24 who reported a suicide attempt (1.8%) was three times that for the 25 to 44 age group (0.6%) and nine times that for the 45 to 64 age group (0.2%). When each gender was considered separately, however, this relation remained significant only for males. No other association was found between parasuicide and sociodemographic characteristics.[4]

In 1992–3, 2.1 per cent of all respondents with severe psychological distress reported a parasuicide, a rate eleven times as high as for those with lower levels of distress (0.2%). No sex or sex-by-age difference could be confirmed in either survey. This represent an increase of 35 per cent as compared to the 1987 survey. The proportion of male attempters with severe distress increased between surveys from 55 per cent in 1987 to 81 per cent in 1992–3.

Regarding the use of professional and non-professional services following a parasuicide (1992–3), 68 per cent of females and 54 per cent of males indicated having consulted a person after an attempt. This difference was not statistically significant. Furthermore, the data suggested that attempters aged 15 to 24 (49%) underutilized available resources, compared with attempters aged 25 to 44 (64%) and those aged 45 to 64 (91%). The differences between age groups, too, did not reach significance.

Cree
Figure 4 shows that 3 per cent of the Cree had thought seriously about suicide and 2 per cent had attempted suicide in the twelve months before the survey. Even after age standardization, these rates were not statistically different from those observed in the Quebec general population. No sex or age difference was found for the twelve-month prevalence of suicidal ideation or parasuicide. This notwithstanding, suicide attempts were reported only by individuals under the age of forty-five. Psychological distress, as measured by the IDPESQ, was correlated with suicidal ideation and parasuicide. More than 8 per cent of the Cree with severe psychological distress had thought seriously about suicide, compared with 2 per cent of those without severe psychological distress. Cree respondents with severe distress were nearly thirteen times as likely to have reported a parasuicide (9%) in the year preceding the survey as were those without distress (0.7%). Owing to the small sample size, analyses of the relation between suicide phenomena and sociodemographic and psychosocial characteristics lack statistical power and do not yield a single significant difference. Post-attempt assistance from the community was not investigated among the Cree (Boyer, Préville, and Légaré, 1994).

Inuit
The crude twelve-month prevalence of suicidal ideation was 7 per cent among the Nunavik Inuit. While levels of suicidal ideation were comparable to those for the Cree, the suicide-attempt phenomenon seemed more serious in the Inuit

population (figure 4). In addition, even after age standardization, these phenomena were more prevalent among the Inuit than among the Quebec general population (1987): serious suicidal ideation was twice as frequent (SMR = 1.9 [$CI_{99\%}$ = 1.2–2.8]), and parasuicide seven times as high (SMR = 6.8 [$CI_{99\%}$ = 4.1–10.3]) (Boyer, Dufour, Préville, and Bujold-Brown, 1994).

Suicidal ideation did not vary by sex but was over six times as frequent among all those aged fifteen to twenty-four (11.1%) as among those over forty-four (1.7%). With a less stringent level of significance ($CI_{95\%}$), however, the data indicated that female Inuit under twenty-five (17.1%) contemplated suicide nearly 3.5 times as frequently as did those over twenty-four (5%).

The rate of parasuicide was 7 per cent among the Inuit. Nearly six times as many Inuit under twenty-five had attempted suicide (17.9%) as those over twenty-four (2.8%). As in the other two populations, parasuicide, but not suicidal ideation, was related to the level of psychological distress ($CI_{95\%}$). In this regard, three times as many Inuit suicide attempters presented a severe level of psychological distress (43%) in the two weeks before the survey as did Inuit respondents who reported neither ideation nor parasuicides. As was the case in the survey of the Crees, assistance from the community after an attempt was not investigated among the Inuit.

Discussion

Limitations of the Studies

The four studies summarized here all suffer from some methodological limitations. First, the retrospective nature of the surveys prohibits any causal interpretation of the data and, consequently, the independent variables considered are not 'risk factors' in the strict epidemiologic sense of the term. This limitation notwithstanding, the results presented did make it possible to identify segments of the populations where suicidal ideation and parasuicide are more prevalent.

Second, the exploratory approach employed in the analyses entailed a very high number of statistical comparisons, thereby increasing the chances of random artefacts being mistakenly identified as true differences (type I error). In order to attenuate the risk of such erroneous interpretations, a more conservative level of significance was used (α = 0.01)

Third, suicide completers were not included in the study. However, given the relative rarity of suicides compared with parasuicides, prevalence rates reported here are probably only slightly affected by the absence of such cases. Lifetime prevalences are probably the ones most affected, since the number of suicide casualties increases with the number of years taken into consideration. Between 1980 and 1993, Quebec registered 15,767 suicides in the population aged fif-teen or over (12,319 males and 3448 females); in 1993 alone, 1313 were recorded. Suicide completers may also have affected the association between parasuicides and some of the predictors considered.

Finally, a non-response bias may have diminished the accuracy of estimates. Reviewing the 1987 QHS data using logistic regression, Légaré et al. (1992) indicated that non-respondents to the question on suicidal ideation were usually men (OR = 1.35) either under twenty-five (Odds Ratio [OR] = 1.55) or over sixty-four and very poor (OR = 1.55), from urban areas (OR = 1.94), and with mental-health problems (OR = 1.14). Since these variables are generally associ-ated with greater suicidal ideation and attempts, the prevalences reported may have been underestimated and the lack of gender difference may have been masked by the greater propensity of males not to respond to the questions relat-ing to suicide.

While the studies provided information on lifetime and twelve-month esti-mates of suicidal ideation and parasuicide, bivariate analyses with the putative 'risk factors' were conducted only with the twelve-month prevalence data. This decision was motivated by the fact that longer prevalence periods carry a higher risk of recall bias. Older respondents have difficulty remembering whether they attempted suicide in their lifetime. Furthermore, the investigation of certain relations with independent variables becomes problematic with a longer refer-ence period, as there is a greater chance of the sociodemographic status of respondents changing since the time of a parasuicide.

It should also be stressed that, although the QHS program was based on a representative sample of households from the populations of reference, samples consisted solely of individuals aged fifteen or over and living in a household. Consequently, important segments of the population at high risk of attempted and completed suicide were not represented, including the homeless and the institutionalized (prisoners, general- and psychiatric-hospital patients, and nursing-home residents).

Quebec General Population

According to the 1992–3 QHS, the lifetime prevalence of parasuicide in the general population was 3.7% (table 1). General-population rates reported in the literature for the same time frame vary from 1.1% to 4.2%, with an average of 2.9%. For the twelve-month period, the QHS reported a parasuicide rate of 0.6%. This estimate is consistent with those reported in the literature by other community studies: Ramsay and Bagley (1985), 0.8%; Paykel et al. (1974),

TABLE 1

Prevalence of suicide ideation and parasuicide observed in community serveys conducted in North America

Authors	Location	N	Period	Prevalence
Suicide ideation				
Schwab et al. 1972	Florida	1,645	Lifetime	15.8
Paykel et al. 1974	New Haven	720	Lifetime	2.6
			12-month	1.5
Vandivort and Locke 1979	Kansas City and Washington, DC	3,921	6-month	5.4
Ramsay and Bagley 1985	Calgary	670	Lifetime	13.4
Mościcki et al. 1988	New Haven	5,020	Lifetime	10.2
	Baltimore	3,329	Lifetime	7.6
	St Louis	2,966	Lifetime	10.6
	Piedmont	3,821	Lifetime	10.0
	Los Angeles	3,105	Lifetime	14.6
Parasuicide				
Schwab et al. 1972	Florida	1,645	Lifetime	2.7
Paykel et al. 1974	New Haven	720	Lifetime	1.1
			12-month	0.6
Ramsay and Bagley 1985	Calgary	670	Lifetime	4.2
			12-month	0.8
Mościcki et al. 1988	New Haven	5,020	Lifetime	2.4
	Baltimore	3,329	Lifetime	3.4
	St Louis	2,966	Lifetime	3.1
	Piedmont	3,821	Lifetime	1.5
	Los Angeles	3,105	Lifetime	4.3
Dyck et al. 1988	Edmonton	3,258	Lifetime	3.6
Petronis et al. 1990	New Haven			
	Baltimore	13,670	12-month and 24-month	0.4
	St Louis		12-month and 24-month	0.4
	Piedmont			
	Los Angeles			

0.6%; and Petronis et al. 1990 (1990), 0.4%. The 1992–3 lifetime estimate of parasuicide in the Quebec general population translates into 188,281 individuals, and the twelve-month prevalence into nearly 30,000. Moreover, the 1992–3 QHS suggests that the severity of suicidal ideation and attempts increased, compared with 1987, as a greater number of ideators and attempters demonstrated high levels of psychological distress. This increase was concomitant with a 36% rise in severe psychological distress in the Quebec general population (Légaré et al., 1995).

The 1992–3 QHS data yielded parasuicide-to-suicide ratios of 34:1 for the general population, 21:1 for males and 80:1 for females. Based on these figures, it would appear that suicidal ideation and attempts are at best tenuous predictors of completed suicide. This would seem all the more salient in the case of female suicide.

In a review of the data on the relationship between attempted and completed suicide, Maris (1992) suggested that, on average, about 10 to 15 per cent of suicide attempters eventually do kill themselves, but that only 30 to 40 per cent of suicide completers had attempted suicide previously. These figures were based on a parasuicide-to-suicide ratio of approximately 8–10:1. The much larger ratios for Quebec mentioned above imply that a smaller proportion of suicide attempters will eventually complete the act. Maris also indicated that, because most suicide attempters make a relatively small number of attempts before succeeding, parasuicide was a poor predictor of suicide as it fails to predict about 75 to 90 per cent of all completed suicides. These speculations, however, may not hold in the case of Quebec, given the province's epidemiologic specificity vis-à-vis the United States where parasuicide is concerned. Further research is needed in Quebec in order to untangle the intricate relationship between attempted and completed suicide.

Like the Epidemiologic Catchment Area (ECA) study (Petronis et al. 1990), the QHS[4] revealed no association between gender and twelve-month prevalence of parasuicides. Both these community surveys had sufficient statistical power to detect such an association. This finding runs counter to that of numerous studies conducted in hospital emergencies (e.g., Bland et al., 1994). The discrepancy could be explained, however, by the fact that these non-community studies did not take into account the fact that females are more inclined to use health services after a suicide attempt, as they are with many other health problems. Data from the 1992–3 QHS suggests this likelihood. The tendency, however, is not statistically significant.

Results from the 1992–3 QHS indicated that suicidal ideation, but not parasuicide, was related to marital status. Single, divorced, or separated individuals reported thinking seriously about suicide more than twice as frequently as did married individuals. This relation, however, may be spurious since possibly confounded by age. In addition, Stravynski and Boyer (1995) found that perceived loneliness – not marital status or the presence of a friend in the individual's environment – was significantly correlated with these phenomena. In the twelve months preceding the 1987 survey, lonely individuals were eight times as likely to have had serious suicidal thoughts and twelve times as likely to have attempted suicide as those socially involved. These associations hold true in the face of conflicting objective circumstances (e.g., marriage and presence of a social network) and when controlled for age and sex. Indeed, it has been suggested that a sense of loneliness is experienced more keenly when a network of friends is available.

Cree

Few data are available on completed suicide among the native peoples of Canada. In their study of mortality on Canadian reserves between 1977 and 1982, Mao et al. (1986, 1992) reported that suicide was the third cause of death for males and the fifth for females. Suicide rates among the native populations were more than three times those for the Canadian general population, for both males and females. This higher risk held even when the native populations were compared with Canadian sub-populations living in isolated rural areas. Such higher mortality owing to suicide, however, was not observed among the James Bay Cree in the period 1975–81 (Robinson, 1985) and 1982–6 (Courteau, 1989).

The lifetime rate of suicide attempts among the Cree was not found to be different from that for the Quebec general population. However, when standardized, the lifetime rate of serious suicidal ideation was lower among the Cree. The twelve-month rates of ideation and parasuicide, too, were very close to those observed in the general population. There was some suggestion that these phenomena might be more common among native adolescents and young adults. Consistent with the 1987 and 1992–3 general-population findings, the data on the Cree did not support the hypothesis of a gender differential for either suicidal ideation or suicide attempts.

Inuit

The community survey conducted by Santé Québec on suicidal ideation and parasuicide among the Inuit was a Canadian first. The research afforded epidemiology and anthropology researchers an exceptional opportunity for collaboration. Although limited in scope, the study produced new and reliable information on suicidal phenomena. With the Inuit population, however, suicidal ideation and attempts are not a simple question of prevalence and risk factors. These must be understood within the specific context of Inuit culture. For this reason, much of the discussion in Santé Québec's (1994b) chapter on the mental health of the Inuit was devoted to a cultural interpretation of the results.[6]

Compared with the Quebec general population and the James Bay Cree, the Inuit situation is drastically alarming. Roughly 25 per cent of the Nunavik Inuit population reported serious suicidal ideation in their lifetime and 58 per cent reported a suicide attempt. The standardized twelve-month prevalence rate of suicide attempts was seven times as high in Nunavik as in the Quebec general population. The anguish seems to be more specific to younger females. These data bolster the clinical awareness of the epidemic nature of suicide attempts in this northern region of Quebec.

Conclusion

The QHS conducted in three separate populations corroborated the association already observed in many other studies that individuals with severe psychological distress are more prone to suicidal ideation and suicide attempts. Multivariate analysis of the 1987 QHS data controlling for sociodemographic variables, life events, alcohol abuse, and physical-health problems revealed that mental-health problems were significantly correlated to suicidal ideation (OR = 3.8) and suicide attempts (OR = 6.2) (Boyer, Préville, Perreault, and Légaré, 1992). These data were also congruent with the extensive literature on completed suicide based on psychological autopsies, which indicates that the majority of completers suffered from a mental disorder. Lesage et al. (1994) reached the same conclusion in a study of this kind conducted in Quebec.

NOTES

This work was partially supported by Health Canada (NHRDP #6605-3933-48) and the Fonds FCAR (#93-NC-1028).

1 Parasuicide designates all types of non-fatal suicide attempts.
2 Before 1980, suicide statistics for the younger age groups are probably less reliable and should be interpreted with caution.
3 For the purposes of comparison, the 1987 rates presented here were calculated according to the 1992–3 survey's definition of suicide ideation and parasuicide. Consequently, some 1987 prevalence estimates differ from those reported in the original report (Santé Québec, 1988).
4 Interestingly, based on the 1987 QHS data, Boyer et al. (1992) found that individuals living in urban areas were more likely to report lifetime and 12-month suicide attempts (OR = 1.38 and

1.39, respectively) and lifetime suicide ideation (OR = 1.13) than individuals living in rural and semi-rural regions.

5 The QHS data indicate that lifetime suicide attempts are almost twice as prevalent among females. These data, however, are tainted by a recall bias and the number of completed suicides over the period of reference and, consequently, should be interpreted with caution.

6 See the original publication for a detailed treatment of this highly complex issue.

REFERENCES

Bland, R.C., S.C. Newman, and R.J. Dyck. 1994. 'The Epidemiology of Parasuicide in Edmonton.' *Canadian Journal of Psychiatry* 39: 392–6.

Boyer, R., R. Dufour, M. Préville, and L. Bujold-Brown. 1994. 'State of Mental Health.' In Santé Québec, ed., 1994b. *A Health Profile of the Inuit. Report of the Santé Québec Health Survey Among the Inuit of Nunavik, 1992*, 117–44. Montréal: Ministère de la Santé et Service sociaux, Gouvernement du Québec.

Boyer, R., M. Préville, and G. Légaré. 1994. 'Mental Health.' In Santé Québec, ed., 1994a. *A Health Profile of the Cree. Report of the Santé Québec Health Survey of the James Bay Cree 1991*, 161–73. Montréal: Ministère de la Santé et Service sociaux, Gouvernement du Québec.

Boyer, R., M. Préville, C. Perreault, and G. Légaré. 1992. *L'épidémiologie des parasuicides et des idéations suicidaires*. Ministère de la Santé et Service sociaux, Gouvernement du Québec.

Courteau, J.-P. 1989. 'Mortality among the James Bay Cree of Northern Quebec: 1982–1986.' Unpublished M.A. thesis, McGill University, Montreal.

Dyck, R.J., R.C. Bland, S.C. Newman, and H. Orn. 1988. 'Suicide Attempts and Psychiatric Disorders in Edmonton.' *Acta Psychiatrica Scandinavica* suppl. 338: 64–71.

Légaré, G., R. Boyer, M. Préville, and P. Valois. 1992. 'Caractéristiques des non-répondants à une enquête sanitaire de santé mentale.' *Revue canadienne de santé publique* 83(4): 308–10.

Légaré, G., A. Lebeau, R. Boyer, and D. St-Laurent. 1995. 'Santé Mentale.' In Santé Québec, ed., 1995. *Et la santé, ça va en 1992–1993? Rapport de l'Enquête sociale et de santé 1992–1993*, 217–55. Montréal: Ministère de la Santé et Service sociaux, Gouvernement du Québec.

Lesage, A., R. Boyer, F. Grunberg, C. Vanier, R. Morissette, C. Ménard-Buteau, and M. Loyer. 1994. 'Suicide and Mental Disorders: A Case Control Study of Young Men.' *American Journal of Psychiatry* 151(7): 1063–8.

Mao, Y., B.W. Moloughney, R.M. Semenciw, and H.I. Morrison. 1992. 'Indian Reserve and Registered Indian Mortality in Canada.' *Revue Canadienne de Santé Publique* 83(5): 350–6.

Mao, Y., H.I. Morrison, R.M. Semenciw, and D. Wingle. 1986. 'Mortality on Canadian Indian Reserves 1977–1982.' *Revue Canadienne de Santé Publique* 77(4): 263–8.

Maris, R.W. 1992. 'The Relationship of Nonfatal Suicide Attempts to Completed Suicide.' In R.W. Maris, A.L. Berman, J.T. Maltsberger, and R.I. Yufit, eds, *Assessment and Prediction of Suicide*, 362–80. New York: Guilford Press.

Mościcki, E.K. 1989. 'Epidemiologic Surveys as Tools for Studying Suicidal Behavior: A Review.' *Suicide and Life-Threatening Behavior* 19(1): 131–46.

Mościcki, E.K., P. O'Carrol, D.S. Rae, B.Z. Locke, A. Roy, and D.A. Regier. 1988. 'Suicide Attempts in the Epidemiologic Catchment Area Study.' *Yale Journal of Biology and Medicine* 61: 259–68.

Paykel, E.S., E.S. Myers, J.J. Lindenthal, and J. Tanner. 1974. 'Suicide Feelings in the General Population: A Prevalence Study.' *British Journal of Psychiatry* 124: 460–9.

Perreault, C., G. Légaré, R. Boyer, and L. Blais. 1988. In Gouvernement du Québec, *Et la santé, ça va? Rapport de l'enquête Santé Québec*, 123–49. Québec: Les Publications du Québec.

Petronis, K.R., J.F. Samuels, E.K. Mościcki, and J.C. Anthony. 1990. 'An Epidemiologic Investigation of Potential Risk Factors for Suicide Attempts.' *Social Psychiatry and Psychiatric Epidemiology* 25: 193–99.

Préville, M., R. Boyer, L. Potvin, C. Perreault, and G. Légaré. 1991. *Détermination de la fiabilité et de la validité de la mesure utilisée dans l'enquête Santé Québec.* Québec: La direction des communication, Ministère de la Santé et Service sociaux.

Ramsay, R., and C. Bagley. 1985. 'The Prevalence of Suicidal Behaviors, Attitudes and Associated Social Experiences in an Urban Population.' *Suicide and Life-Threatening Behavior* 15(3): 151–67.

Robinson, L.N. 1985. 'Mortality mong the James Bay Cree, Quebec 1975–1982.' In R. Fortuine. ed., *Circumpolar Health 84*, 166–9. Seattle: Washington Press.

St-Laurent, D. 1995. 'Suicide.' In Ministère de la Santé et des Services sociaux, Gouvernement du Québec, ed., *Le Québec comparé: Indicateurs sanitaires, démographiques et économiques*, 199–205.

St-Laurent, D., and R. Boyer. 1995. 'Suicide Thoughts and Suicide Attempts among Young Quebecers.' Eighteenth Congress of the International Association for Suicide Prevention and Crisis Intervention (IASP), Venice, Italy.

Santé Québec. 1988. *Et la santé, ça va? Rapport de l'enquête Santé Québec.* Québec: Les Publications du Québec.

Santé Québec, ed., 1994a. *A Health Profile of the Cree. Report of the Santé Québec Health Survey of the James Bay Cree 1991.* Montréal: Ministère de la Santé et Service sociaux, Gouvernement du Québec.

– 1994b. *A Health Profile of the Inuit. Report of the Santé Québec Health Survey among the Inuit of Nunavik, 1992.* Montréal: Ministère de la Santé et Service sociaux, Gouvernement du Québec.

– 1995. *Et la santé, ça va en 1992–1993? Rapport de l'Enquête sociale et de santé 1992–1993.* Montréal: Ministère de la Santé et Service sociaux, Gouvernement du Québec.

Schwab, J.J., G.J. Warheit, and C.E. Holzer. 1972. 'Suicide Ideation and Behavior in a General Population.' *Diseases of the Nervous System* 33(11): 745–8.

Stravynski, A., and R. Boyer. 1995. The Link between Suicidal Ideation, Parasuicide and Loneliness.' Eighteenth Congress of the International Association for Suicide Prevention and Crisis Intervention (IASP), Venice, Italy.

Vandivort, D.S., and B.Z. Locke. 1979. 'Suicide Ideation: Its Relation to Depression, Suicide and Suicide Attempt.' *Suicide and Life-Threatening Behavior* 9(4): 205–18.

4

Immigrant Suicide in Canada

FRANK TROVATO

Immigrant Suicide in Host Nations

On the basis of the existing literature on this topic, four sets of factors can be identified as being relevant in explaining immigrant suicide in host nations: (1) factors associated with the country of origin; (2) factors associated with the country of destination; (3) selectivity; and (4) demographic compositional differences across groups.

Factors Associated with the Country of Origin

Studies conducted in Canada and in other immigrant societies, including the United States, Australia, France, and England, indicate that suicide is typically low among southern Europeans and is relatively high for persons from eastern and north-western Europe and, to a lesser extent, among migrants with Anglo-Saxon origins. For example, in Canada, Trovato and Jarvis (1986) observed that in relation to the Canadian-born, Portuguese and Italians have low rates of self-inflicted death, while persons from the United States, England and Wales, Scotland, and Germany were found to have relatively high suicide propensities. Cultural differences in how suicide is viewed and portrayed may explain some of these variations.

Cultures differ in their orientations to death. According to Aries (1985), death is a central aspect of collective identity, reflected in society's images and representations of it, such as in art, burial rituals, and tombs. The psychohistorian Howard Kushner (1984) has developed a thesis of suicide that elaborates in part on ideas surrounding death and social rituals associated with it. He has argued that differentials in suicide reflect variability in national culture pertaining to rituals of bereavement and their relationship to an unconscious motive in the individual for self-punishment when loved ones, such as parents, die.

Psychodynamic theory proposes that all humans have an unconscious desire to do away with persons of authority, including parents. However, for the individual, parents are also a source of love and affection. According to Kushner (1984), this is a source of conflict in the human psyche and represents the root cause of suicide. The cathartic effects of expressive mourning serve to alleviate the unconscious tendency for self-punishment when a loved one is lost. In fact, Kushner noted that in countries where expressive and exaggerated mourning rituals are not part of the culture, the suicide rate is typically high. Examples of this are the Scandinavian societies. In accordance with the theory, such world areas and their antipodes have high suicide propensities because individuals do not have access to an outward expression of guilt in the occasion of the death of a loved one. On the other hand, in countries where elaborate rituals prevail and exaggerated mourning is an accepted part of the culture, such as in southern European societies, the suicide rate has always been relatively low; and, correspondingly, the antipodes of such regions also possess low suicide predispositions.

Another dimension of culture and its relationship to suicide is the moral judgments embodied in the religion of a society concerning this act (Durkheim, 1951). For example, Catholic countries show lower suicide rates than Protestant nations because Catholicism has always viewed the taking of one's own life as sinful (ibid.). Therefore, all things being equal, persons socialized in predominantly Catholic societies would be less inclined to commit suicide, even in the presence of extreme psychological distress. With reference to Kushner's thesis, it may be that Catholicism and expressive mourning rituals are inseparable components of certain cultures, and that both contribute to reduce suicide propensities. The low suicide rates of southern European immigrants in Canada and in other host nations is perhaps a reflection of this possible link.

In Australia, Whitlock (1971) observed that southern European groups such as the Italians, the Greeks, and the Maltese commit suicide less frequently than persons born in the receiving society, whereas persons from eastern and northern Europe tend to suffer relatively high probabilities of self-murder. These observations have been confirmed more recently by Young (1987) and Burwill and associates (1982). In France, Brahimi (1980) noted similar tendencies for these migrant groups, as did Marmot and colleagues in England and Wales (1984).

In the early Australian studies (e.g., Burwill et al., 1973, 1982; Whitlock, 1971), the suicide rates of the total immigrant population tended to be higher than those of the Australian-born, yet the rates of most migrant groups exhibited suicide rates closer in magnitude to those prevailing in their home countries than to the Australian society. Authors have interpreted this pattern of differences in support of the proposition that background culture, tradition, and social attitude are common factors in both the home-based rates and those of the antipodes.

Thus, even for non–southern Europeans, suicide levels tend to be similar to their corresponding countries of origin. For example, migrants from Arabic countries have low rates of suicide in Australia, and their levels are similar to their home nations; and persons from eastern Europe and Germany show levels of suicide more akin to the levels in their home societies (Burwill et al., 1973, 1982; Whitlock, 1971; Young, 1987). Currently, Young (1987) has shown that overall the foreign-born in Australia now have lower rates than the Australian-born for most causes of death, including poisonings; and when the data are classified on the basis of nationality, the usual pattern emerges, with southern Europeans (Italians, Greeks, Maltese) having relatively low mortality, while migrants from eastern Europe (eg., Poland, Yugoslavia) and Germany show high death rates in relation to the total Australian population.

On the basis of this literature linking culture and social traditions to the incidence of suicide, the first hypothesis of this study is that migrants from southern European origins will show relatively low levels of suicide in Canada as compared to the Canadian-born and persons from other areas of the world, particularly from northern and eastern Europe. Furthermore, on the assumption that suicide risk in both migrant and origin populations is conditioned by their common culture, there should be close conformity between the suicide rates of immigrants and of their home countries.

Factors Associated with the Country of Destination

Some studies indicate that migrants tend to suffer high rates of psychiatric disorders and illness, which may be a consequence of the stresses associated with the migration experience (Burnam et al., 1987; King and Locke, 1987; Shuval, 1993; Vega 1991). It has also been reported that in some contexts immigrants may experience increased mortality not only from suicide, but also from homicide and accidents, which are to some extent associated with psychological stress and conflict (Shai and Rosenwaike, 1988; Trovato, 1992; Trovato and Clogg, 1991).

A mediating factor in these relationships is socio-economic status. All things being equal, groups that are relatively disadvantaged will suffer more stress and will therefore experience more suicide than groups that are economically advantaged. Thus, the second hypothesis of this study is that the higher the level of socio-economic well-being of a group, the lower the suicide risk in that group.

The ethnic community in the host country can provide an important integrative function for immigrants, as it can serve to buffer the psychological shocks associated with the migration experience through the provision of social support (Breton, 1964; Egolf et al., 1992; Trovato and Jarvis, 1986). Immigrants belonging to well-established and cohesive ethnic communities should have lower rates of suicide than those migrants for whom the degree of community cohesion is relatively low. The first part of this proposition applies closely to the case of the southern Europeans: beside Catholicism they have visible and well-established ethnic communities throughout the urban landscape of Canada (Trovato and Jarvis, 1986). For example, the Italians, the Portuguese, and the Greeks enjoy widespread access to dense networks of family, kin, and relatives in addition to both formal and informal institutions available to them within their ethnic communities (Breton, 1964). When there is a strong and viable ethnic community to welcome immigrants to the New World, the psychological shocks of resettlement can be reduced considerably. This proposition is consistent with the work of scholars in the area of social support and health, who assert that both social networks and social supports are essential elements in the explanation of disease and mortality (Berkman and Syme, 1979; House et al. 1988).

Groups lacking this important property tend to experience increased suicide rates, as exemplified by immigrants from the United States (Trovato and Jarvis, 1986). For the American-born, their cultural and geographic proximity to Canada obviates their need to establish a persisting and cohesive immigrant community in the same sense as the southern Europeans and other immigrants from other parts of the world, whose cultures are distinctly different from that of Canada. Therefore, a third hypothesis in this study is that the greater the level of ethnic-community cohesiveness of immigrant groups, the lower will be their suicide rates.

For immigrants, the duration of residence in the host society may represent another risk factor for suicide. If the shocks of migration are more intense during the initial years of resettlement, then the probability of suicide should be highest soon after the onset of arrival to the new country.

Some investigators have hypothesized that over time immigrants have the tendency to approximate the mortality patterns of the receiving population (McMichael et al., 1980; Stenhouse and McCall, 1970; Reed et al., 1982; Trovato and Clogg, 1991). Unfortunately, in most settings it is impossible to measure duration effects on mortality because the appropriate data are not readily available. To the knowledge of this writer, the only country that records such data is Australia; and the findings based on that country suggest only a weak, if any, association of duration with mortality convergence. For example, Young (1987) shows that many immigrant groups persist in exhibiting similar mortality rank orderings in Australia even after fifteen or more years of residence in the country.

Migration can affect health in a number of ways. In the immediate sense, it could result in extreme stress, leading to a greater susceptibility to immunological breakdown and thus a greater tendency to develop infectious illnesses. This may be true in the long term, as prolonged stress can often manifest itself in chronic conditions that take a long time to develop (e.g., heart disease and cancer). In the case of suicide, however, it would seem reasonable to assume that the risk would be greater near the early stages of relocation rather than later, since with increasing duration of stay in the host nation immigrants should be better adapted to their new environment. Therefore, a fourth hypothesis in this investigation is that the more recent the duration of residence in Canada for immigrants, the higher will be their risk of suicide.

Selection Effects

In relation to the society of origin, migrants are thought to be more adventurous and healthier, while in comparison to the society of destination they may be intermediate in human-capital characteristics, but healthier as a result of the stringent formal and medical screening procedures immigrants must undergo before entering a receiving nation (Trovato and Clogg, 1991; Young, 1987).

In the early stages of North American immigration history, especially before the Second World War, migrants tended to be negatively selected for health, and they often brought with them communicable diseases contracted in the old world (Evans, 1987). In fact, before the Second World War the foreign-born in the United States had higher overall mortality than native-born Americans (Kestenbaum, 1986). After the war, the situation has changed in the United States and also in other major immigrant-receiving societies, including England and Wales, France, Australia, and Canada (Marmot et al. 1978; Brahimi, 1980; Young, 1987). At present, foreigners have lower death rates overall and, as discussed earlier, certain groups have consistently low suicide rates when compared to their host nations.

It is extremely difficult to provide direct tests for the effect of health selection on mortality, as the appropriate data are not readily available. Indirect procedures are usually employed. In this study, the assumption is made that if selection is a factor in immigrant suicide, it should manifest itself more intensely in the early phases of relocation to the new society, before the possible occurrence of assimilation to the receiving society. Therefore, it is predicted that the more recent the period of immigration to Canada, the more pronounced should be the effects of positive health selection and hence the lower the risk of suicide among immigrants.

Demographic Factors

To the extent that social groups vary in their demographic composition, they will differ in their risk of suicide. Within any defined period of time, relatively young populations tend to have fewer deaths than older ones, while a preponderance of females is usually associated with reduced mortality; and the greater the proportion of the population married, the lower is the death rate. In this study these three variables are treated as statistical controls.

Data and Analysis

The data for this investigation were obtained from the Health Division at Statistics Canada in Ottawa. All the yearly deaths occurring in each province, classified by cause of death, age, sex, marital status, country of birth, province of occurrence, and many other variables of a medical nature are recorded in the Mortality Data Base at Statistics Canada. For the purpose of this study, data for 1985 to 1987 are used. This three-year period is conveniently centred around 1986, thus facilitating the use of census-based denominators in the computation of rates. At the time when the data were obtained this was the latest available information.

The suicide counts and corresponding populations were compiled as a multiway cross-tabulation by age, sex, marital status, and country of birth. These variables were coded as follows: age (15–24, 25–44, 45–64, 64–84, 85+), sex (male, female), marital status (single, married, other), country of birth (Canada, United States, Germany, Scotland, England–Wales–Northern Ireland, Greece, Italy, Portugal, Hungary, Poland, Czechoslovakia, Scandinavia, Asia, other).

The statistical analysis begins with an overview of age-sex and suicide distributions of the native-born and the foreign-born populations, with respect to five categories of suicide: poisonings with liquid or solid substances, other poisonings, hanging/strangulation, firearms/explosives, and 'other means.' The work proceeds with a breakdown of the immigrant population into fourteen unique nationalities (as listed above). For a subset of these groups it was also possible to relate their suicide rates to those of their corresponding home countries, based on data provided by the World Health Organization. The last part of the study concerns itself with a multivariate analysis of the data.

TABLE 1
Population distribution by age, sex, and nativity – Canada, 1986

Age	Canadian-born (%)			Foreign-born (%)		
	Males	Females	Total	Males	Females	Total
<15	12.6	12.0	24.6	2.6	2.5	5.1
15–24	9.0	8.8	17.7	5.5	5.3	10.8
25–34	9.2	9.2	18.4	7.5	8.2	15.7
35–44	6.7	6.7	13.3	10.4	10.3	20.7
45–64	8.4	8.8	17.2	15.7	15.3	30.9
65–84	3.6	4.7	8.3	6.8	8.5	15.2
85+	0.1	0.3	0.4	0.5	1.0	1.5
Total	10,444,065	10,644,615	21,084,680	1,914,765	1,996,010	3,910,775
(%)	(49.5)	(50.5)	(100.0)	(49.0)	(51.0)	(100.0)

Note: Based on 1986 Census of Canada.

Age-Sex Distributions

The demographic compositions of the two populations in 1986 are radically different. In table 1, the age-sex structure of the native-born is more akin to the usual pyramidal shape typically associated with national populations. The corresponding distribution for the immigrants resembles an inverted pyramid: there are relatively few persons under the age of twenty-five, particularly below age fifteen, where the proportion is only about 5 per cent; and at ages beyond thirty-five, the foreign-born percentages are larger than those of the receiving society's, such that in the post-retirement years migrants have proportionately almost two times (16.7%) the population of the Canadian-born.

Distribution of Suicide and Overall Rates

Table 2 shows the number of suicides by age, sex, and nativity, along with the corresponding percentage distributions and death rates per 100,000 population. Out of 10,537 suicides, 9027 were Canadian-born and 1510 came from the immigrant population. The overall suicide rates for these two groups are therefore 14.27 and 12.87, respectively. The proportion of native-born men committing suicide is greater than the corresponding proportion among immigrant men (78.9% vs 71.9%), and the associated rates are 22.75 and 18.91, respectively. Immigrant women show a higher suicide rate than their host counterparts (7.08 vs 5.96). In proportionate terms, immigrant females constitute 28.1 per cent of

TABLE 2
Distribution of suicides by age, sex, and nativity and Crude Death Rates per 100,000 population – Canada, 1985–1987

Age	Canadian-born			Foreign-born		
	Males	Females	Total	Males	Females	Total
<15	54 (0.8)	15 (0.8)	69 (0.8)	3 (0.3)	0 (0.0)	3 (0.2)
15–24	1586 (22.3)	272 (14.3)	1859 (20.6)	77 (7.1)	21 (5.0)	98 (6.5)
25–34	1890 (26.5)	448 (23.5)	2338 (25.9)	150 (13.8)	55 (13.0)	205 (13.6)
34–44	1254 (17.6)	406 (21.4)	1661 (18.4)	185 (17.0)	67 (15.7)	251 (16.6)
45–64	1610 (22.6)	540 (28.4)	2150 (23.8)	379 (34.9)	156 (36.8)	535 (35.4)
65–84	699 (9.8)	205 (10.8)	904 (10.0)	265 (24.4)	118 (27.8)	382 (25.3)
85+	30 (0.4)	16 (0.8)	46 (0.5)	28 (2.6)	7 (1.7)	35 (2.3)
Total (%)	7124 (78.9)	1902 (21.1)	9027 (100.0)	1086 (71.9)	424 (28.1)	1510 (100.0)
Rate per 100,000	22.75	5.96	14.27	18.91	7.08	12.87

Notes: Percentages in parentheses. Suicide counts exclude undetermined deaths.

all the migrant suicide cases, while women born in Canada make up 21.1 per cent of all native-born suicides.

Most suicides among the native-born occur between the ages of 25 and 64, with 25 to 34 year olds representing the modal category (25.9%). Among foreigners, most suicides occur between the ages of 45 and 84, and the modal class is age 45 to 64 (35.4%). Another interesting difference is that at age forty-five and above, the migrant percentages are larger than those corresponding to their host counterparts. On the other hand, there are very few suicides in this group at ages below fifteen.

There may be nativity differences with respect to the method used to commit suicide. Table 3 (p. 94) displays information for five categories of method: (1) poisonings with liquid/solid substances, (2) poisonings with other means, (3) hanging/strangulation/suffocation, (4) firearms/explosives, and (5) other means. The first two may be considered non-violent types, whereas the third and fourth imply the use of violent means. The 'undetermined' category of death is also included in the table because this class of mortality may in fact capture 'disguised' suicides.

In comparison to the Canadian-born, immigrants are more inclined to poison themselves using solid or liquid substances (17.5% vs 15.5%), hanging/strangulation/suffocation (31.8% vs 24.0%), and other means (20.0% vs 14.4%). The native-born die more as a result of poisonings with other means (12.4% vs 10.3%) and the use of firearms and explosives (33.7% vs 20.5%). With respect to 'undetermined' deaths, the distribution by sex does not vary across nativity groups, but the overwhelming majority of cases are Canadian-born (1198 vs 167).

Suicide in Specific Immigrant Groups

Table 4 (p. 95) lists Crude Suicide Death Rates (CDRs), and Standardized Suicide Mortality Ratios (SMRs) for the Canadian-born and fourteen specific immigrant groups. The SMRs were computed using the Canadian-born population in 1986 as the standard, thereby controlling for differences in age and sex compositions across groups.

There is a positive correlation between group CDRs and corresponding SMRs. The correlation coefficient between these measures is .995 for males and .997 for females; and that between male and female measures is .490 for the CDRs, and .500 for SMRs. Thus, the higher the male CDR or SMR, the higher the female CDR or SMR, respectively. But as can be judged from the magnitudes of the coefficients, this is not a perfect relationship.

The highest CDRs are associated with male and female migrants from east-

TABLE 3
Distribution of suicides by method used, sex, and nativity and total method-specific death rates per 100,000 population – Canada, 1985–1987

Nativity and sex	Poisonings, liquid/solid substances	Poisonings, other means	Hanging, strangulation, suffocation	Firearms/ explosives	Other means	Undetermined deaths
	N (%)	N (%)	N (%)	N (%)	N (%)	N (%)
Canadian-born						
Males	687 (49.2)	913 (81.6)	1814 (83.7)	2811 (92.4)	900 (69.1)	850 (71.0)
Females	708 (50.8)	206 (18.4)	354 (16.3)	231 (7.6)	403 (30.9)	348 (29.0)
Total	1395	1120	2168	3041	1302	1198
(Rate per 100,000)	(2.21)	(1.77)	(3.43)	(4.81)	(2.06)	(5.68)
Foreign-born						
Males	119 (45.2)	122 (77.8)	354 (73.8)	293 (94.7)	198 (66.0)	117 (70.1)
Females	145 (54.8)	35 (22.2)	126 (26.2)	16 (5.3)	102 (34.0)	50 (29.9)
Total	264	156	480	309	301	167
(Rate per 100,000)	(2.25)	(1.33)	(4.09)	(2.63)	(2.57)	(1.42)

Note: Data taken from mortality database at Statistics Canada, Health Division.

TABLE 4

Standardized Suicide Mortality Ratios (SMR) and Crude Suicide Death Rates (CDR) for the Canadian-born and various immigrant groups in Canada, 1985–1987 (ages 15+)

Group	Males		Females	
	CDR	SMR	CDR	SMR
Canadian-born	30.29	1.000	7.75	1.000
USA	27.69	.905	7.90	1.014
Germany	31.70	1.032	9.33	1.083
Scotland	23.86	.771	6.07	.751
England–Wales–N. Ireland	17.46	.569	6.83	.836
Greece	12.36	.404	3.34	.389
Italy	13.68	.443	4.47	.492
Portugal	13.83	.452	1.53	.213
Hungary	46.16	1.508	20.39	2.432
Poland	30.97	1.015	11.56	1.410
USSR	37.74	1.235	16.31	2.143
Czechoslovakia	40.23	1.300	18.04	2.230
Scandinavia	47.74	1.531	4.06	.495
Asia	11.46	.377	15.23	1.775
Other	20.93	.541	12.67	1.525

Correlations:
  Male–female CDR = .490
  Male–female SMR = .500

Notes: The crude rates are per 100,000 population. The Canadian-born is the standard population, and therefore their SMR is 1.000.

ern European and Scandinavian countries, while the lowest are associated with the southern Europeans, namely the Greeks, Italians, and Portuguese. Immigrants with Anglo-Saxon origins (USA, Scotland, England–Wales–Northern Ireland) appear to have intermediate levels of risk as measured by the crude rates as well as the standardized ratios. Among males, the Scandinavians and Hungarians commit suicide at a rate of 47.74 and 46.16 per 100,000 population, respectively. The corresponding SMRs for these two categories of immigrants are 1.531 and 1.508, which indicate that men from these two countries have approximately a 50 per cent greater chance of suicide that do Canadian-born men. The crude rates for men born in Asia, Greece, Italy, and Portugal are much lower: 11.46, 12.36, 13.68, and 13.83, respectively, as are their standardized ratios. Among females, those at high risk of suicide are the Hungarians (SMR = 2.432), the Czechs (SMR = 2.230), the Soviets (SMR = 2.143), Asians (SMR = 1.775), and other immigrants (SMR = 1.525). Women from Portugal, Greece, and Italy have the lowest CDRs and SMRs, respectively. Migrants with Anglo-Saxon origins (as well as the Canadian-born) share intermediate levels of risk.

Comparison of Migrant Rates with Those in the Countries of Origin

For ten of the fourteen immigrant groups in the preceding analysis there is corresponding suicide data for their home countries. This information allows for a partial test of the hypothesis of a close correspondence between the suicide rates of immigrants and their countries of origin. As was the case for the immigrants, the SMRs for the countries of origin were computed using the Canadian-born as the standard, thus establishing a common reference for the purposes of comparing across populations. In table 5 the correlations of male and female migrant CDR or SMRs with those of their corresponding counterparts in the home nations are all positive (shown at the bottom of the table). While the direction of correlations are consistent with the hypothesis that immigrants carry with them the suicide risk of their country of origin, the magnitude of the coefficients suggests that the relationship may not be very strong.

Some immigrant groups have SMRs that are very close to those of their home countries (e.g., males from the USA and Germany, and to some extent males from Poland and Czechoslovakia). Others show ratios that are substantially above or below those of their societies of origin. For example, among males, the Greeks, the Scottish, and the English have higher risks than their counterparts in their home nations, but Italian, Portuguese, and Hungarian men all show lower SMRs as compared to their original populations. Similar observations can be made in connection with female SMRs: those from the United States, England–Wales–Northern Ireland, Greece, Poland, and Czechoslovakia have notably higher suicide ratios in relation to women in their home countries, while women from Germany, Scotland, Italy, Portugal, and Hungary all demonstrate lower levels of risk.

Log-Linear Analysis

Native-born/Foreign-born Differences

Log-linear rate models were computed for each type of suicide indicated earlier in tables 2 and 3 (Clogg and Eliason, 1987). The question being investigated in this part of the analysis is whether nativity is of statistical importance in explaining suicide risk once age, sex, and marital-status differences have been taken into account simultaneously.

While in table 2 the foreign-born as a whole showed a higher tendency to

TABLE 5

Standardized Suicide Mortality Ratios (SMR) and Crude Suicide Death Rates (CSDR) for ten countries of origin, and corresponding differences in SMRs between immigrants and their countries of origin (ages 15+)

	Males			Females		
	Country of origin		Ratio Immigrant: Origin SMR	Country of origin		Ratio Immigrant: Origin SMR
	CSDR	SMR		CSDR	SMR	
Canadian-born	30.29	1.000	1.000	7.75	1.000	1.000
USA	26.48	.893	1.013	6.73	.862	1.176
Germany	31.52	1.034	1.001	13.89	1.765	.614
Scotland	20.78	.687	1.122	7.29	.937	.801
England–Wales–N. Ireland	14.80	.489	1.164	5.94	.763	1.096
Greece	7.59	.251	1.610	2.48	.311	1.251
Italy	14.69	.489	.913	5.76	.731	.673
Portugal	17.88	.592	.764	6.43	.823	.259
Hungary	85.31	2.817	.535	32.28	4.010	.606
Poland	29.69	.977	1.039	5.84	.735	1.918
Czechoslovakia	38.48	1.270	1.024	12.87	1.620	1.377

Notes: Data for countries of origin are for 1986, taken from World Health Organization computerized file, Geneva. CSDR is per 100,000 population. The Canadian-born is the standard population in the computation of both origin and immigrant SMRs and, therefore, their SMR is 1.000.

The correlation of immigrant with origin rates/ratios is as follows: male immigrant CSDR with male origin CSDR = .438; male immigrant SMR with male origin SMR = .466; female immigrant CSDR with female origin CSDR = .407; female immigrant SMR with female origin SMR = .395; total immigrant CSDR with total origin CSDR = .549; total immigrant SMR with total origin SMR = .428.

commit suicide, this is not the case in table 6, when all factors in the analyses are taken into account simultaneously. With the minor exceptions of two models – hanging/strangulation/suffocation and suicides by other means – where the effects of nativity are insignificant, it is the native-born who are more prone to commit self-murder. The strongest effect occurs in connection with suicide involving the use of firearms/explosives. Persons born in Canada have a 43 per cent higher chance of dying in this manner than do immigrants (exp (.386) = 1.433). In terms of overall suicide risk, the relative disadvantage for the Canadian-born is about 16 per cent (exp (.148) = 1.160). In connection with 'undetermined' deaths, the net excess risk for the native born is 29 per cent.

With the exception of suicide by poisonings, males have disproportionately higher odds than do females. This is particularly evident in connection with suicide with the use of firearms and explosives, where the relative risk is almost four times greater for men (exp (1.321) = 3.5).

Native-born/Immigrant Group Differences

Further multivariate analyses were executed pertaining to the Canadian-born and fourteen immigrant groups. Linear covariates for duration of residence in Canada, a proxy measure for ethnic cohesion, education, and country-of-origin suicide rate were also included in the equations.

In table 7, the parameters for sex are interpreted as the extent to which males or females increase or lower the overall risk of suicide (depending on the sign of the coefficient). For the country-of-birth terms, the coefficients are expressed as deviations from the Canadian-born's effects on suicide (therefore, this group will show a value of zero in the equations). To illustrate, in equation (1) the USA effect is .256; this means that immigrants from the United States share a relative risk of suicide that is .256 greater than that of the Canadian-born.

The interpretation of linear covariates is similar to usual multiple-regression coefficients. That is, they measure the effect of a unit change in X on raising or lowering the risk of suicide (i.e., the natural logarithm of the overall suicide death rate).

The duration variable measures the average period of immigration to Canada for each ijkl cell configuration in the multiway tabulation. This variable was computed with data contained in the Public Use Sample Tapes of the 1986 Census of Canada.[1] The higher the value of duration, the more recent the period of immigration. In accordance with the stress hypothesis, the more recent the period of immigration to Canada, the higher the risk of self-murder. Note, however, that the selectivity explanation makes the opposite prediction, postulating a lower level of suicide risk in the early phases of relocation on the assumption

TABLE 6
Log-rate parameters for the net effects of sex and nativity on suicide in Canada, 1985–1987

Effects	Known suicides	Suicide by poisonings with liquid/solid substances	Suicide by poisoning with other means	Suicide by hanging, strangulation, suffocation	Suicide by firearms/ explosives	Suicide by other means	Undetermined causes of death	Known suicides plus undetermined deaths
Sex								
Male	.682*	.027	.771	.805	1.321*	.454*	.534*	.664*
Female	-.682*	-.027	-.771*	-.805*	-1.321*	-.454*	-.534*	-.664*
Nativity								
CB	.148*	.113*	.239*	-.010	.386*	.005	.258*	.160*
FB	-.148*	-.113*	-.239*	.010	-.386*	-.005	-.258*	-.160*

*p < .05 (two-tailed test based on Z distribution).

Note: Nativity effects are net of age and marital status.

that immigrants constitute a group of people that are selected for overall good health.

The other two covariates, ethnic and education, were also based on Public Use Sample data. Ethnic is a proxy measure for ethnic cohesion, computed as a composite variable involving the proportion of individuals reporting a mother tongue other than English or French, plus the proportion indicating a home language other than English or French, and the proportion of respondents in the census giving an ethnicity other than British or French. These variables were factor analysed using Principal Components Extraction, and the resulting factor scores were then used as the education variable in the log-linear equations. The expectation is that the higher the level of ethnic cohesion, the greater is the ethnic-community integration and therefore the lower the suicide rate. Since in the log-linear models the Canadian-born is treated as the reference population, its corresponding ijkl cell configurations were assigned values of zero for both the duration and ethnic-cohesion covariates.

The variable of education represents the ijkl-specific average education level based on the coding of this variable in the Public Use Census Tapes. This variable is used as a proxy for socio-economic status; and consistent with the established suicide literature, the prediction is for an inverse relationship of this variable with suicide risk.[2]

In table 7, duration of residence exerts a negative effect on the expected risk of suicide, which means that the more recent the period of immigration, the lower the chance of committing this act. This result is also evident when the known suicides are combined with the 'undetermined' deaths. This finding is not consistent with the view that the early phase of relocation for immigrants is inherently stressful and suicidogenic. In an indirect way this provides support for the thesis that migrants are a select group in terms of robustness and psychological make-up, and are thus able to withstand the shocks of immigration and adjustment to the new society.

Ethnic cohesiveness (as operationalized in this study) is a protective factor against the chance of suicide, as indicated by the negative coefficient. The greater the degree of ethnic cohesion, the lower the risk of self-murder. This is true in both equations for known suicide alone, and for known suicides plus 'undetermined' deaths.

While in the known-suicides equation education fails to reach statistical significance, it becomes statistically important when entered in the explanation of known suicides plus 'undetermined,' as well as of 'undetermined' deaths alone. In general, the higher the education level, the lower the suicide death rate. Thus, socio-economic status, as measured by education, represents an additional source of suicide differences across immigrant groups.

TABLE 7

Net effects of sex, country of birth, and linear covariates on type of suicide – Canada, 1985–1987 (15 groups)

Effects	All suicides excluding undetermined deaths (1)		Poisonings (2)		Violent means (3)		Other means (4)		Undetermined deaths (5)		All suicides plus undetermined deaths (6)	
Sex												
Male	.776	(28.38)	.245	(3.03)*	1.155	(22.54)*	.563	(11.39)*	.531	(10.81)*	.732	(32.00)*
Female	-.776		-.245		1.155		-.563		-.531		-.732	
Country of birth												
USA	.256	(1.65)	.552	(1.82)	-1.92	(-.87)	.910	(2.71)*	.749	(1.75)	.293	(2.01)*
Germany	.618	(2.54)*	1.225	(2.51)*	-.024	(-.07)	1.427	(2.55)*	.811	(1.13)	.614	(2.67)*
Scotland	-.235	(-1.84)	.151	(.78)	-.368	(-1.92)	-.835	(-2.20)*	-.034	(-.12)	-.198	(-1.70)
E–W–N. Ire.	-.133	(-.95)	.535	(2.08)*	-.852	(-4.11)*	.488	(1.60)	-.033	(-.08)	-.141	(-1.07)
Greece	-.211	(-.61)	.362	(.50)	-1.159	(-2.44)*	1.282	(1.75)	-.462	(-.40)	-.248	(-.75)
Italy	-.111	(-.40)	.319	(.56)	-.816	(-2.19)*	.812	(1.30)	.273	(.35)	-.097	(-.37)
Portugal	-.169	(-.53)	.666	(1.03)	-.953	(-2.19)*	.312	(.38)	.260	(.28)	-.148	(-.49)
Hungary	.975	(3.61)*	1.857	(3.47)*	-.061	(-.16)	2.421	(4.11)*	.791	(.96)	.943	(3.68)*
Poland	.571	(2.22)*	.973	(1.81)	-.107	(-.30)	1.643	(2.85)*	.683	(.92)	.555	(2.29)*
USSR	.766	(3.01)*	1.537	(2.97)*	-.055	(-.16)	1.861	(3.31)*	.956	(1.35)	.758	(3.16)*
Czech.	.900	(3.02)*	1.421	(2.28)*	.091	(.22)	2.216	(3.38)*	1.041	(1.18)	.894	(3.17)*
Scand.	.485	(1.85)	.731	(1.27)	-.118	(-.34)	1.498	(2.52)*	1.111	(1.58)	.536	(2.19)*
Asia	-.032	(-.12)	.588	(1.12)	-.924	(-2.60)*	1.349	(2.38)*	-.086	(-.11)	-.057	(-.23)
Other	.073	(.35)	.592	(1.40)	-.589	(-2.04)*	.987	(2.10)*	.159	(.26)	.061	(.30)
Can.-born	.000		.000		.000		.000		.000		.000	
Linear covariates												
Duration	-.041	(-2.08)*	-.036	(-.95)	-.056	(-2.02)*	.028	(.64)	-.036	(-.61)	-.038	(-2.04)*
Ethnic	-1.183	(-1.88)*	-.479	(-2.47)*	.160	(1.20)	-.795	(-3.52)*	-.612	(-2.16)*	-.214	(-2.33)*
Education	-.049	(-1.53)	-.018	(-.32)	-.044	(-.93)	-.250	(-3.29)*	-.288	(-3.01)*	-.067	(-2.21)*
R^2_A	.927		.831		.931		.800		.819		.931	

*p < .01; **p < .05 (based on the Z test). All tests are two-tailed except for the linear covariates, which are one-tailed. (Z values are in parentheses.)

Notes: The sex and country-of-birth effects are net of age, marital status, and age-by-sex interactions. 'Poisonings' means the use of liquid/solid substances and other such means. 'Violent means' represents suicide using hanging, strangulation, suffocation, firearms, explosives, and piercing instruments. R^2_A is an analog measure of variance explained.

The use of poisons can be viewed as representing a less violent type of self-murder than the application of weapons such as knives or guns. Earlier, we saw that when the broad categories of Canadian-born/foreign-born were examined, the native-born exhibited an increased chance of suicide with the use of poisonous substances as well as the application of firearms/explosives. However, as shown in table 7, once age, sex, marital status, duration of residence, ethnic cohesion, and education are taken into account, all the immigrant groups now show higher probabilities of dying as a result of taking poisonous substances; but of the fourteen entities, only five actually exhibit significant deviations from the Canadian-born standard (Germans, English–Welsh–Northern Ireland, Hungarians, Soviets, and Czechs). Of the three linear covariates in this analysis, only the ethnic factor exerts a significant influence on this type of self-destruction; and its direction is negative, as anticipated by the hypothesis.

Although virtually all migrant groups show reduced chances of violent suicide (refer to note at bottom of table 7) in relation to the standard population, only five classes show significant differentials: the Greeks, Italians, Portuguese, Asians, 'Other' immigrants. While poisonings are more common amongst eastern Europeans and the English, violent self-murder is significantly less likely among southern Europeans and Asians.

For this type of suicide, the only significant covariate is duration of residence, indicating that recency of immigration is negatively linked with suicide. Thus, recency of relocation does not seem to be as problematic in Canada as is thought to be the case in the literature concerning immigrant stress in new environments. In fact, given the observed relationship, the risk of violent suicide rises with increased duration of stay in the host country. This result is consistent with the proposition that with the passage of time immigrants increase their risk of suicide and gradually approximate the risk prevailing in the host population.

With the exceptions of the English, the Scottish, the Greeks, the Italians, and the Portuguese, the remaining immigrant groups in table 8 demonstrate a greater likelihood than the Canadian-born in the use of 'other means' in the taking of one's own life. This effect tends to be particularly pronounced amongst eastern Europeans, the Scandinavians, the Germans, and the American-born. But Asians and 'Other' immigrants also show elevated chances of this type of suicide. The Scottish is the only group that exhibits a significant negative effect on this form of self-murder. Important differentiating factors in this cause of death are ethnic cohesion and education, indicating that those groups with higher levels of these two properties share reduced suicide propensities.

Country-of-Origin Effects on Immigrant Suicide

Earlier, in table 5, a positive association was observed between the suicide rates of immigrants and their corresponding populations of origin. This relationship is now explored further by incorporating into the statistical model a proxy for country-of-origin effects, measured as the suicide rate of the home country. The assumption behind this proxy is that both migrant and origin rates are determined to a large extent by their shared national culture, and that the socialization of the antipodes in the home country persists into the new world; therefore, there should be a positive association between the two rates due to their correlation with a common cause – in this case, the culture of origin.[3]

Table 8 provides confirmation of this thesis, specifically in the case of known suicides, as well as in connection with violent suicide and suicide using other means. In these equations, the coefficient for origin is consistently positive and statistically significant. This is also noted for the model containing known suicides plus 'undetermined' deaths.

An interesting change in these equations, as compared to the previous ones, is the loss of statistical significance for the duration effect. The substantive interpretation of this result may be cast in the light of the close association between recency of immigration, culture of origin, and these two variables' relationship with suicide. To a large extent, 'recency' captures the influence of origin factors because the influence of immigrants' national culture on suicide is bound to be more pronounced during the early phases of the immigration experience. Thus, when controlling for country of origin, the influence of duration disappears. It would seem, therefore, that selection is unimportant in explaining immigrant suicide. This, of course, does not disqualify the possibility that if measured differently or more directly, selectivity would be important; nor does it obviate its possible relevance with regard to other causes of death.

Concerning ethnic cohesion, with the exception of violent suicide, the effect of ethnic cohesion on the risk is quite consistent with what we saw earlier: the greater the level of ethnic cohesiveness, the lower the suicide rate. Similarly, the education variable continues to exert an important inverse influence on the likelihood of self-murder.

Net Effects of Group Membership on Suicide

Though the number of significant group terms is reduced in the case of known suicides, and also known suicides plus 'undetermined,' the net effects of group membership do not disappear once the country-of-origin factor has been introduced in the equations (tables 7 and 8). Immigrants from Germany and Czecho-

TABLE 8
Log-rate effects of sex, country of birth, and linear covariates on suicide by method used to commit suicide – Canada, 1985–1987 (11 groups)

Effects	Known suicides excluding undetermined deaths (1)		Poisonings (2)		Violent suicide (3)		Other means (4)		Undetermined deaths (5)		Known suicides plus undetermined deaths (6)	
Sex												
Male	.765	(24.95)*	.259	(3.14)*	1.192	(18.33)*	.503	(8.56)*	.497	(9.05)*	.718	(28.05)*
Female	−.765		−.259		1.192		−.503		−.497		−.718	
Country of birth												
USA	.104	(.52)	.797	(2.19)**	−.702	(−2.41)**	.961	(2.24)**	.663	(1.26)	.151	(.81)
Germany	.605	(2.13)**	1.651	(3.00)*	−.423	(−1.07)	1.692	(2.58)**	.867	(1.07)	.610	(2.28)*
Scotland	−.386	(−2.78)**	.173	(.79)	−.617	(−2.92)**	−1.088	(−2.80)**	−.274	(−.87)	−.357	(−2.81)
E–W–N. Ire.	−.210	(−1.24)	.746	(2.44)**	−1.201	(−4.77)*	.596	(1.59)	−.042	(−.09)	−.210	(−1.32)
Greece	−.219	(−.58)	.757	(.98)	−1.613	(−3.08)*	1.678	(2.04)**	−.285	(−.23)	−.238	(−.66)
Italy	−.144	(−.46)	.724	(1.16)	−1.297	(−3.01)*	1.131	(1.55)	.371	(.42)	−.118	(−.40)
Portugal	−.321	(−.87)	1.068	(1.50)	−1.661	(−3.26)*	.518	(.57)	.254	(.25)	−.284	(−.82)
Hungary	.585	(1.46)	2.443	(3.47)*	−1.166	(−1.93)	1.894	(2.22)**	.038	(.03)	.522	(1.39)
Poland	.562	(1.88)	1.407	(2.35)**	−.539	(−1.28)	1.947	(2.88)**	.751	(.91)	.553	(1.97)
Czech.	.808	(2.34)**	1.893	(2.75)**	−.492	(−1.02)	2.271	(2.96)*	.869	(.88)	.798	(2.45)**
Can.-born	.000		.000		.000		.000		.000		.000	
Covariates												
Origin	.006	(2.21)**	−.003	(−.53)	.009	(2.49)**	.011	(2.40)*	.010	(1.57)	.006	(2.56)*
Duration	−.001	(−.04)*	−.049	(−1.02)	.033	(.90)	.035	(.59)	−.023	(−.31)	−.001	(−.06)
Ethnic	−.334	(−3.11)**	−.630	(−2.97)**	.050	(.34)	−1.133	(−4.43)*	−.850	(−2.78)*	−.371	(−3.67)*
Education	−.141	(−3.75)	−.051	(−.77)	−.181	(−3.21)*	−.414	(−4.58)*	−.424	(−3.89)*	−.163	(−4.58)**
R^2_λ	.945		.853		.960		.838		.855		.947	

Notes: Refer to note at bottom of table 7.

slovakia continue to show elevated suicide probabilities, while the Scottish display reduced chances, net of other variables in the models. It may be concluded that for these immigrant categories there are unmeasured factors that contribute to raising or lowering the suicide rate. It seems clear, therefore, that while the origin factor contributes to a more complete understanding of immigrant suicide, it is also true that it fails to capture all of the complexities of the immigrant suicide phenomenon.

From the net group effects in table 8, the American-born are more likely to commit suicide by using poisons and 'other means,' but are less disposed to take their own lives in a violent manner. The English, the Hungarians, and the Poles also share an increased chance of applying poisons in the act of self-destruction. In general, violent means are used more by the Canadian-born than by immigrants, but within the latter population, only the Americans, the Scottish, the English, the Greeks, the Italians, and the Portuguese share significantly low probabilities of doing so. Six immigrant classes show relatively high chances of suicide using 'other methods': the American-born, the Germans, the Greeks, the Hungarians, the Poles, and those born in Czechoslovakia. The Scottish share low propensities for this form of self-murder.

Conclusions

Migrant suicide rates can be explained in part by differences in socio-economic status and background culture. Duration of residence seems to be relatively unimportant, because once a proxy for culture of origin was introduced into the analysis, its influence became statistically insignificant. This implies that immigrants transport to the new land the cultural 'baggage' of their home societies, and their home culture serves as a lasting source of either protection or susceptibility to committing suicide in the host country. Thus, immigrants from low-suicide regions of the world experience relatively low chances of self-destruction in Canada, while those from relatively high-suicide nations continue to suffer above-average levels of risk. The low suicide rates of southern European immigrants and the persisting high rates for eastern and northwestern Europeans provide support for this interpretation. An additional causal mechanism prevailing in the new environment of immigrants is the degree of ethnic cohesion. The more cohesive the group, the greater its level of community integration, and therefore the lower the incidence of suicide.

If immigrants do indeed experience high levels of psychological distress during the process of adaptation to their host environment, this does not translate into equal rates of suicide across groups. Some immigrants enjoy more 'protection' than others because they may have higher levels of socio-economic status, belong to cohesive ethnic communities, and come from societies where suicide rates are relatively low.

NOTES

This study was funded by Social Sciences and Humanities Research Council of Canada grant no. 410-91-1101. The assistance of the Council is gratefully acknowledged.

1 The Public Use Sample Tapes contain categorical information on the immigrants' period of immigration to Canada. In 1986, this variable was coded as follows: (1) before 1946, (2) 1946–50, (3) 1951–5, (4) 1956–7, (5) 1958–60, (6) 1961–2, (7) 1963–5, (8) 1966–7, (9) 1968–70, (10) 1971–2, (11) 1973–5, (12) 1976–7, (13) 1978–80, (14) 1981–3, (15) 1984–6. As the classification shows, the higher the value of this variable, the more recent the period of immigration.

2 Education in the 1986 Public Use Sample Tapes is coded into 11 categories of highest level of schooling, beginning with 'less than grade five' (code = 1) and ending with 'bachelor's degree or higher' (code = 11). Thus, the higher the value of this variable, the higher the completed education.

3 The suicide rate of the home countries is expressed as the ijkl-specific suicide rate in the country of origin of a given immigrant group. Note that the Canadian-born do not have a corresponding home country as such; therefore, a small constant value was assigned to each ijkl-specific configuration on the origin variable for this group in order to avoid complications in the estimation of the suicide equations.

REFERENCES

Aries, P. 1985. *Images of Man and Death*. Trans. J. Lloyd. Cambridge, MA: Harvard University Press.

Berkman, L., and L.S. Syme. 1979. 'Social Networks, Host Resistance and Mortality: A Nine-Year Follow-Up Study of Alameda County Residents.' *American Journal of Epidemiology* 115: 684–94.

Brahimi, M. 1980. 'La Mortalité des étrangers en France.' *Population* 35: 603–22.

Breton, R. 1964. 'Institutional Completeness of Ethnic Communities and the Personal Relations of Immigrants.' *American Journal of Sociology* 20: 193–205.

Burnam, A.M., R.L. Hough, M. Karno, J.I. Escobar, and C.L. Telles. 1987. 'Acculturation and Life-time Prevalence of Psychiatric Disorders among Mexican Americans in Los Angeles.' *Journal of Health and Social Behavior* 28: 89–102.

Burwill, P.W., M.G. McCall, N.S. Stenhouse, and T.A. Reid. 1982. 'Deaths from Suicide, Motor Vehicle Accidents and All Forms of Violent Death among Migrants in Australia, 1962–66.' *Acta Psychiatrica Scandinavica* 49: 28–50.

Burwill, P.W., T.T. Woodings, N.S. Stenhouse, and M.G. McCall. 1973. 'Suicide during 1961–70 of Migrants in Australia.' *Psychological Medicine* 12: 295–308.

Clogg, C.C., and S.R. Eliason. 1987. 'Some Common Problems in Log-Linear Analysis.' *Sociological Methods and Research* 16(1): 8–44.

Durkheim, E. 1951. 'Suicide.' Trans. J.S. Spaulding and G. Simpson. New York: Free Press.

Egolf, B., J. Lasker, S. Wolf, and L. Potvin. 1992. 'The Roseto Effect: A Fifty-Year Comparison of Mortality Rates.' *American Journal of Public Health* 82(8): 1089–92.

Evans, J. 1987. 'Introduction: Migration and Health.' *International Migration Review* (special issue) 21(3): 5–14.

House, J.S., K.R. Landis, and D. Umberson. 1988. 'Social Relationships and Health.' *Science* 241: 250–4.

Kestenbaum, B. 1986. 'Mortality by Nativity.' *Demography* 23(1): 87–90.

King, H., and F.B. Locke. 1987. 'Health Effects of Migration: U.S. Chinese in and outside the Chinatown.' *International Migration Review* 21(3): 555–7.

Kushner, H.I. 1984. 'Immigrant Suicide in the United States: Toward a Psycho-Social History.' *Journal of Social History* 18: 3–24.

McMichael, A.J., M.G. McCall, J.M. Hartshorne, and T.L. Woodings. 1980. 'Patterns of Gastro-intestinal Cancer in European Migrants to Australia: The Role of Dietary Change.' *International Journal of Cancer* 25: 431–7.

Marmot, M.G., A.M. Adelstein, and L. Bulusu. 1984. *Immigrant Mortality in England and Wales, 1970–78: Cause of Death by Place of Birth.* Studies on Medical and Population Sugjects no. 47. London: HMSO.

Reed, D., D. McGee, J. Cohen, K. Yano, S.L. Syme, and M. Feinleib. 1982. 'Acculturation and Coronary Heart Disease among Japanese Men in Hawaii.' *Journal of Epidemiology* 115(6): 894–905.

Shai, D., and I. Rosenwaike. 1988. 'Violent Deaths among Mexican, Puerto Rican and Cuban-born Migrants in the United States.' *Social Science and Medicine* 26(2): 269–76.

Shuval, J.T. 1993. 'Migration and Stress.' In L. Goldberger and S. Breznitz, eds, *Handbook of Stress: Theoretical and Clinical Aspects* (2nd ed.), 641–57. New York: Free Press.

Stenhouse, N.S., and M.G. McCall. 1970. 'Differential Mortality from Cardiovascular Disease in Migrants from England and Wales, Scotland and Italy and Native-Born Australians.' *Journal of Chronic Diseases* 23: 423–31.

Trovato, F. 1986. 'Suicide and Ethnic Factors in Canada.' *International Journal of Social Psychiatry* 32(3): 55–64.

– 1992. 'Violent and Accidental Mortality among Four Immigrant Groups in Canada, 1970–1972.' *Social Biology* 39(1–2): 82–101.

Trovato, F., and C.C. Clogg. 1991. 'General and Cause-Specific Adult Mortality among Immigrants in Canada, 1971 and 1981.' *Canadian Studies in Population* 19(1): 47–80.

Trovato, F., and G.K. Jarvis. 1986. 'Immigrant Suicide in Canada: 1971 and 1981.' *Social Forces* 65(2): 433–57.

Vega, W.A. 1987. 'Migration and Mental Health: An Empirical Test of Depression Risk Factors among Immigrant Mexican Women.' *International Migration Review* 21(3): 512–30.

– 1991. 'Ethnic Minorities and Mental Health.' *Annual Review of Sociology* 17: 351–83.

Whitlock, F.A. 1971. 'Migration and Suicide.' *Medical Journal of Australia* 2: 840–8.

World Health Organization. (n.d.). *Computerized Mortality File.* Geneva, Switzerland.

Young, C. 1987. 'Migration and Mortality: The Experience of Birthplace Groups in Australia.' *International Migration Review* 21(3): 531–54.

5

Suicide in Canada and the United States: A Societal Comparison

DAVID LESTER and ANTOON A. LEENAARS

It is often assumed that the behaviours of Canadians and Americans will be similar because Canada and the United States are in close proximity to each other and share similar languages and cultural backgrounds. However, despite a number of similarities, there is also a degree of divergence. For example, differences between Canada and the United States have been observed in such areas as recognition of authority, patterns of deviance, achievement motivation, and patterns of association and marriage (Spencer, 1985).

We do not mean to suggest that Canada and the United States are radically different countries because, of course, contrasts between Canada and the United States on a number of sociological issues are not as great when the comparison includes, for example, other nations of the world (Spencer, 1985). We wish only to stress that Canada and the United States are not identical, and that behavioural phenomena observed in one of the two nations will not necessarily be observed in the other.

Comparisons between Canada and the United States often highlight the fact that violence is more common in the United States than in Canada. Pierre Berton (1984), one of Canada's best-known historical commentators, has noted that Canadians have paid a heavy price for the 'best of all possible worlds' (that is, for order and security), namely authority, government control, and fewer civil liberties, whereas Americans have suffered more violence and sometimes anarchy for their liberty.

Suicide, a type of violence, is often assumed to be similar in Canada and the United States. Observations, literature, and even professional associations, evident for example in the close link between the American Association of Suicidology and the Canadian Association for Suicide Prevention, are often generalized across the border. Early comparisons of suicidal behaviour in Canada and the United States suggested no differences. Labovitz and Brinkerhoff (1977) are often cited as indicating that the countries' rates of suicide were highly similar in the 1970s. Lester (1985) has shown that suicide rates increase as one moves west in both countries. Similarities have been reported in both countries in the relationship between locus of control and suicide (Boor, 1976) and in the relationship between unemployment rates and suicide (Boor, 1980).

Leenaars (1989a) has recently questioned whether the suicide rates and patterns are similar today in Canada and the United States. We will examine this question by presenting our research examining the rates and patterns of suicide in Canada and the United States, the methods used, and the predictability of the suicide rates. Following this, we will offer some hypotheses to explain the findings.

Rates and Patterns of Suicide in Canada and the United States

Leenaars and Lester (1990, 1992) undertook an examination of the rates of suicide in both nations for the period of 1960 to 1988, a period for which comparative data are available, and they found important differences between the two nations. The data for Canada were obtained from the National Task Force's report *Suicide in Canada* (1987), supplemented with data from 1986, 1987, and 1988 from Statistics Canada. *Suicide in Canada* represents the final report of Canada's national task force on suicide. The data for the United States were obtained from the annual volumes published by the National Center for Health Statistics, *Vital Statistics of the United States*, from 1960 to 1988.

These data sources provide the official statistics on suicide in both countries. It has been argued that the use of such official data is problematic because data-collection and death-certification procedures in Canada and the United States may differ. There is, however, no evidence to date for or against this hypothesis. Moreover, time trends *within* each nation are less likely to be affected by differences in death certification between the nations.

A more general problem is the use of national mortality statistics themselves. Suicide statistics are collected, compiled, and published by governmental agencies. Although such suicide statistics have been criticized with respect to bias and under-reporting (Leenaars, 1989b; McIntosh, 1992), the evidence against their validity is not undisputed (for example, Sainsbury and Jenkins, 1982). It is likely that, although such governmental figures are not a totally accurate picture, they may be viewed at least as conservative estimates (McIntosh, 1992), and from a practical point of view they are the only systematically available data for Canada and the United States.

TABLE 1
Crude suicide rates (per 100,000 per year) in Canada and the United States

	Canada		United States	
	Men	Women	Men	Women
1960	12.0	3.0	16.5	4.9
1961	11.9	3.0	16.1	4.9
1962	11.2	3.1	16.5	5.4
1963	11.4	3.8	16.5	5.8
1964	12.3	4.1	16.1	5.6
1965	12.9	4.5	16.3	6.1
1966	12.8	4.3	16.1	5.9
1967	13.2	4.8	15.7	6.1
1968	14.2	5.2	15.8	5.9
1969	15.6	6.2	16.1	6.3
1970	16.2	6.4	16.8	6.6
1971	17.3	6.4	16.7	6.8
1972	17.2	6.9	17.5	6.8
1973	18.0	7.1	17.7	6.5
1974	18.7	7.1	18.1	6.5
1975	17.8	6.8	18.9	6.8
1976	18.4	7.2	18.7	6.7
1977	21.2	7.3	20.1	6.8
1978	22.4	7.3	19.0	6.3
1979	21.4	7.0	18.9	6.1
1980	21.3	6.8	18.6	5.5
1981	21.3	6.8	18.7	5.8
1982	22.3	6.4	19.2	5.6
1983	23.4	6.9	19.2	5.4
1984	21.4	6.1	19.7	5.4
1985	20.5	5.4	19.9	5.1
1986	22.8	6.4	20.6	5.4
1987	22.1	6.2	20.5	5.2
1988	21.4	5.9	20.1	5.0
1989	20.9	6.0	19.9	4.8
1990	20.4	5.2	n/a	n/a

n/a – not available

Suicide Rates by Year

The annual suicide rates for men and women for Canada and the United States show that, up to 1972, the reported suicide rates for both sexes were lower in Canada than the United States (see table 1). However, from 1977 on, the suicide rates in Canada were higher than those in the United States. It seems, therefore,

TABLE 2
Suicide rates (per 100,000 per year) by age

	Age						
	15–24	25–34	35–44	45–54	55–64	65–74	75+
Canada							
Men							
1970	15.6	20.1	26.6	27.9	31.9	28.0	24.6
1980	24.8	29.5	25.1	30.7	28.5	26.9	38.1
1988	26.9	29.2	26.1	24.2	28.0	26.2	30.6
Women							
1970	4.8	8.6	10.6	14.5	11.4	9.5	4.6
1980	5.4	8.1	8.8	13.7	12.1	9.5	5.9
1988	4.9	7.1	9.8	9.9	6.9	6.1	6.2
USA							
Men							
1970	13.5	19.6	22.2	27.8	32.8	36.5	41.8
1980	20.2	24.8	22.3	23.0	24.4	30.2	43.5
1988	21.9	25.0	22.9	21.7	25.0	33.0	57.8
Women							
1970	4.8	8.6	12.1	12.5	11.4	9.3	6.7
1980	4.3	7.0	8.4	9.4	8.4	6.5	5.4
1988	4.2	5.7	6.9	7.9	7.2	6.8	6.4

that Labovitz and Brinkerhoff's (1977) conclusion that the Canadian and American suicide rates are similar is dated. The rates of suicide in Canada are different from, and higher today than, those in the United States.

For men in both nations, the trend has been for an increasing suicide rate since 1960, with the suggestion of a recent decrease in Canada since 1983 (see table 1). For women, the suicide rates in both nations appear to have decreased during the 1980s. It would appear that predictions that the suicide rate of women would increase in recent years as women supposedly gained more equal social and economic equality with men (Lester, 1979) are not borne out by the data in either country.

Suicide Patterns by Age

One way of viewing the current patterns by chronological age is to use the age groupings commonly employed by national governments: 15–24, 25–34, and so on. The data are shown in table 2. It can be seen that, for Canada, suicide rates for men rose especially during the 1970s for those aged 15 to 24 and 25 to 34 and for those over the age of 75. The changes for women were less pronounced, but the suicide rates for women aged 45 to 54 and 55 to 64 did drop considerably during the 1980s.

The United States also witnessed a rise in suicide rates for those aged 15 to 24 and 25 to 34 in the 1970s and a rise in the suicide rates of those over the age of 75 in the 1980s, a little later than was observed in Canada. The decline in women's suicide rates, for those aged 35 to 44, 45 to 54, and 55 to 64 occurred in the 1970s in the United States rather than in the 1980s as in Canada.

These results concur with recent observations by McGinniss (1987) and Leenaars (1989a, 1991) that young adult males are a very high-risk group for suicide. Young adult males in Canada now have the highest rate of suicide across the lifespan. The data indicate that their suicide rate is continuing to rise, warranting greater prevention and service-delivery efforts.

However, despite the differences in the year when the changes occurred and the magnitude of the changes, the directions of the changes in Canada and the United States are reasonably similar, with a rise over the last twenty years in the suicide rates of young and elderly men and a decrease in the suicide rates of middle-aged women.

Interestingly, whereas the United States witnessed a drop in the suicide rate of people in late adulthood during the period, the Canadian rates for elderly men remained much the same. The observation itself is important because much recent attention has been paid to the declining rate of suicide in the elderly in the United States (e.g., McIntosh, 1988–9). It would appear that the same phenomenon is not occurring in Canada, suggesting an urgent increasing need to investigate and address suicide in the elderly in Canada.

Adolescents

Leenaars and Lester (1990) examined changes in the suicide rates of adolescents in Canada and the United States in greater detail from 1960 to 1985. As is clear from table 3, the suicide rates of fifteen to nineteen year olds rose in boys and girls in Canada and the United States, for example, from 5.3 per 100,000 per year in Canadian boys in 1960 to 18.4 in 1985.

There was also an increase in the suicide rates in those aged ten to fourteen during this period (see table 3), though part of the reason for this increase may have been the greater willingness for the governments to certify deaths as suicides in young adolescents. Nevertheless, the official suicide rates for those aged ten to fourteen rose, for example, from 0.6 per 100,000 per year in Canadian boys to 1.3.

TABLE 3
Suicide rates (per 100,000 per year) for adolescents

	Canada				USA			
	Boys		Girls		Boys		Girls	
	10–14	15–19	10–14	15–19	10–14	15–19	10–14	15–19
1960	0.6	0.3	0.1	0.2	0.9	5.6	0.2	1.6
1961	0.8	3.7	0.0	0.9	0.7	5.3	0.2	1.5
1962	1.0	5.1	0.2	1.4	1.0	5.5	0.1	2.0
1963	1.2	5.3	0.1	2.4	0.9	6.3	0.2	1.9
1964	1.2	5.3	0.1	1.7	0.9	6.3	0.1	1.7
1965	1.2	5.5	0.3	1.8	0.9	6.1	0.2	1.9
1966	1.7	6.0	0.1	1.3	0.9	6.5	0.2	2.1
1967	0.9	8.5	0.2	1.5	0.9	7.0	0.3	2.4
1968	1.2	7.8	0.3	1.3	0.9	7.8	0.2	2.2
1969	1.0	10.4	0.3	1.8	0.9	8.6	0.4	2.7
1970	1.2	10.1	0.3	3.8	0.9	8.8	0.3	2.9
1971	1.1	12.7	0.4	3.1	1.0	9.9	0.3	3.1
1972	1.4	14.2	0.5	4.3	0.7	10.9	0.4	2.8
1973	1.6	13.6	0.3	4.3	1.1	10.7	0.4	3.1
1974	1.1	18.0	0.3	3.2	1.4	11.0	0.4	3.2
1975	1.6	15.8	0.3	4.2	1.2	12.2	0.4	2.9
1976	1.5	16.8	0.4	4.3	1.2	11.4	0.4	3.2
1977	2.0	20.2	0.7	4.7	1.6	14.2	0.3	3.4
1978	2.2	19.4	0.5	4.4	1.2	12.8	0.4	3.1
1979	1.5	20.6	0.7	4.9	1.1	13.7	0.5	3.3
1980	1.5	19.4	0.6	3.8	1.2	13.8	0.3	3.0
1981	2.5	21.2	1.0	3.8	1.2	13.6	0.5	3.6
1982	2.4	21.5	0.4	3.2	1.7	14.1	0.4	3.2
1983	2.1	21.7	0.3	3.7	1.6	14.0	0.6	3.2
1984	2.4	21.0	0.4	3.2	1.9	14.3	0.6	3.5
1985	1.3	18.4	0.6	3.6	2.3	16.0	0.9	3.7
1986	2.1	20.2	0.6	4.5	2.3	16.4	0.7	3.8
1987	2.7	20.5	0.6	4.6	2.3	16.2	0.6	4.2
1988	2.5	21.7	0.5	3.2	2.1	18.0	0.8	4.4
1989	2.0	22.7	0.7	3.2	2.1	18.0	0.7	4.3
1990	2.5	19.1	0.7	4.7	n/a	n/a	n/a	n/a

n/a – not available

The Methods Used for Suicide

Lester (1990) examined the methods used for suicide in nations of the world
from 1960–4 to 1980 and found that the use of domestic gas decreased whereas

TABLE 4
Suicide rates (per 100,000 per year) by each method

	Canada		USA	
	1960–4	1980	1960–4	1980
Total	7.6	14.0	10.7	11.8
Solids/liquids	1.2	2.6	1.5	1.3
Domestic gas	0.0	0.0	0.1	0.0
Other gases (mainly car exhaust)	0.7	1.5	1.1	1.1
Hanging, strangulation, suffocation	1.7	3.1	1.7	1.6
Submersion (drowning)	0.6	0.8	0.3	0.2
Firearms, explosives	2.9	4.7	5.1	6.8
Cutting, piercing	0.2	0.2	0.2	0.2
Jumping	0.2	0.6	0.4	0.4
Other and unspecified	0.2	0.5	0.3	0.2

the use of car exhaust, hanging, firearms, and jumping increased. The data for Canada and the United States are shown in table 4. It can be seen that, for Canada, the rate of suicide using solids/liquids, hanging, and firearms increased during this twenty-year period. In the United States, only the rate of suicide using firearms increased. Thus, the increasing Canadian suicide rate during this period may reflect increases in a greater variety of methods than does the rising American suicide rate.

In the United States, the availability of firearms has been found to be strongly associated with the use of firearms for suicide (Clarke and Lester, 1989). Lester (1994) replicated this result in Canada, finding that the accidental death rate from firearms (a proxy measure for the availability of firearms [Cook, 1982]) in the Canadian provinces was associated with both the suicide rate using firearms and the percentage of suicides using firearms. The accidental death rate from firearms was associated with a lower rate of suicide by all methods other than firearms, suggesting that when firearms were less available, people switched to other methods for suicide. The possibility that such switching occurred is similar to findings from the United States (Clarke and Lester, 1989).

Incidentally, the percentage of homicides involving firearms (another possible proxy measure for firearm availability) was not associated with the use of firearms for suicide in Canada, whereas it was in the United States (Clarke and Lester, 1989).

Lester and Leenaars (1993) showed that the passage of stricter firearm-control laws in Canada in 1977 led to a decrease in the use of firearms for suicide, both in the firearm suicide rate and in the percentage of suicides using firearms, without there being an increase in the use of other methods for suicide. Such a study is not possible in the United States, since each state has its own firearm-control laws. However, regional studies *over the states of America* have indicated that stricter firearm-control laws are associated with a reduced use of firearms for suicide (Clarke and Lester, 1989).

Predicting the Suicide Rate

Several studies have compared the ability of social and economic variables to predict the time-series suicide rate in Canada and the United States (Leenaars and Lester, 1994a, 1994b, 1995, 1996; Leenaars, Yang, and Lester, 1993; Lester and Yang, 1992). This research has been guided by two theorists. Durkheim (1897) argued that suicide rates in societies would be affected by the level of social integration (that is, the degree to which people are bound together in social networks) and the level of social regulation (that is, the degree to which people's desires and behaviours are governed by social norms and rules). Thus, variables such as divorce, marriage, and birth rates should be associated with societal suicide rates. Second, Platt (1984) has documented that societal suicide rates are associated with the economic conditions in the society, and in particular with the unemployment rate.

Leenaars, Yang, and Lester (1993; see also Leenaars and Lester, 1994b) compared the time-series suicide rate in Canada and the United States from 1950 to 1985 and found that divorce rates were positively associated with suicide rates in both Canada and the United States, while birth rates were negatively associated with suicide rates in both nations, as predicted by Durkheim's theory. However, while marriage rates were negatively associated with suicide rates in the United States, as predicted by Durkheim's theory, the association was positive (though not statistically significant) in Canada. Thus, marriage did not appear to be beneficial as regards suicidal behaviour in Canada. In contrast to Platt's hypothesis, however, the unemployment rate did not play a role in predicting either the Canadian or the American suicide rate during this time period.

Atwood (1972), Lipsett (1990), and others have suggested that, indeed, marital and familial characteristics are viewed differently in Canada and the United States. In Canada, marriage and family are more often seen as a trap, while in the United States these are viewed as defining one's freedom. Clearly, more research is needed to throw light on this intriguing difference between Canada and the United States.

In a second study, Leenaars and Lester (1995) examined the predictors of the time-series suicide rate for individuals of different ages. In Canada, measures of domestic integration (divorce and birth rates) and the economy (the unemployment rate) predicted the suicide rate of youths (aged 15 to 24) more successfully than they did the suicide rates of older adults. This difference did not appear in the United States.

In a third study, Leenaars and Lester (1994a) examined the validity of Easterlin's (1980) hypothesis for Canada and the United States. Easterlin argued that, as the size of the youth cohort (those aged 15 to 24) in a nation increases, there is increasing competition for limited economic resources, resulting in relative deprivation for that generation. For the period 1969 to 1988, the correlation between the relative size of this youth cohort and the suicide rate was *negative* in Canada, opposite to the association predicted by Easterlin's hypothesis, while the association was not significantly different from zero (though still negative) in the United States. Thus, Easterlin's hypothesis did not appear to be relevant for Canada or the United States in this modern period.

Leenaars and Lester (1996) followed this study up by examining Easterlin's hypothesis for men and women of all ages. The suicide rates of men aged twenty to thirty-four were positively associated with their relative cohort size in both Canada and the United States. The hypothesis was not supported by the data for women and by the data for homicide. Leenaars and Lester employed several measures of relative cohort size in this study and found that the results depended in part upon the measure chosen for use.

Incidentally, suicide and homicide rates were positively associated in Canada, but were not associated in the United States. Neither of these associations are consistent with Henry and Short's (1954) hypothesis that suicide and homicide are alternative reactions to frustration, so that when one rate is higher, the other rate should be lower (Lester, 1987).

Discussion

The research conducted by Leenaars and Lester clearly shows that the rates and patterns of suicide in Canada and the United States are different. It appears that the suicide rate is currently higher in Canada than in the United States, with the shift occurring during the early 1970s. This finding suggests that much greater effort is warranted in Canada in research, prevention, and services, since these have been relatively neglected in the past (National Task Force, 1987). Furthermore, the question arises as to why the suicide rate is now higher in Canada than in the United States.

Suicide is probably best understood as a multidimensional malaise (Leenaars, 1988; Shneidman, 1985). It is an event with physiological, neuropsychological, sociocultural, interpersonal, psychological, and philosophical/ existential aspects. It is unlikely that any single theory can provide an explanation for the national differences between Canada and the United States. Although further research is needed, especially sociocultural (Leenaars, 1995), several factors may be seen to have contributed to the differences between Canadian and American suicide patterns, assuming that they are not the result of random variation in suicide rates.

1/ First, although there may be differences in the reliability of suicide certification from country to country (O'Carroll, 1989), are such differences that great between Canada and the United States today to account for the patterns? Clarke-Finnegan and Fahy (1983) reported that under-reporting of suicide was so extensive in Ireland that comparisons between Ireland and England were not valid. However, Sainsbury and Barraclough (1968), based on the finding that the rank order of suicide rates as a cause of death among immigrants in the United States was nearly identical to the rank order of suicide rates in their home countries, suggested that certification differences were not significant enough to invalidate cross-country comparisons. Sainsbury and Barraclough's observations have been replicated in Australia (Lester, 1972) and, though these studies did not include American and Canadian immigrants, they established the general principle that official suicide rates from national governments may validly be compared.

However, procedures and principles in certification may have changed radically in Canada or the United States over the time period under examination so as to account for the observed differences in rates and patterns. Researchers have, in fact, questioned the accuracy of the statistics in both countries (O'Carroll, 1989; Syer-Solursh, 1987). However, to our knowledge there is no research to suggest that Canadian certification has dramatically improved so to account for the reported increases in suicide rates. In addition, if there have been some changes, this would probably apply to all age groups, not just to the young adult males and the elderly. Nonetheless, Jobes, Berman, and Josselson (1987) in America and Leenaars (1989b) in Canada have called for investigations of certification procedures and for improvement in the medical certification of suicide.

2/ There was a major legal change regarding attempted suicide in the criminal code in Canada in 1972. Before 1972 it was illegal to attempt to kill oneself. Might this legal change account for the shift in Canadian suicide rates noted around the early to mid-seventies? Were medical examiners/coroners more willing to certify a death as suicide after this decriminalization?

Decriminalization of suicide attempts in Canada in 1972 may have had an effect on reporting practices, perhaps accounting for a percentage or maybe all of the 'increases' in suicides in the mid- to late 1970s. This would invalidate many of our other conclusions regarding relative rates across time between the two countries. However, we believe that we may be able to salvage the validity of these temporal trends by the following fact: suicide was fairly consistently on an upswing for males in Canada over the decade preceding the change in law. Furthermore, the impact of this legal change, if any, is likely to have disappeared by the 1980s.

To check on the impact of decriminalization of suicide in Canada in 1972, Lester (1992) documented that indeed the Canadian suicide rate increased from the period 1962–71 (9.3 per 100,000 per year) to 1973–82 (13.6 per 100,000 per year). However, he noted that the slope of the increasing suicide rate from 1962 to 1971 was 0.52, whereas the slope of the increasing suicide rate from 1973 to 1982 was only 0.22. Thus, the suicide rates rose at a slower pace *after* the decriminalization of suicide in Canada than before. Lester concluded that changing the legal status of suicide in Canada in 1972 was not associated with an increase in the suicide rate. However, more research on this issue would be welcome. In support of this conclusion, Lester (1993) found no impact from the decriminalization of suicide in New Zealand in 1961 on suicide rates in that nation.

3/ Despite the fact that these factors may account for our epidemiological findings, our research suggests alternatives. Research has shown differences in attitudes towards suicide (Domino and Leenaars, 1989, 1994; Leenaars and Domino, 1993), but not in levels of knowledge about suicide (Leenaars and Lester, 1992b) or in the psychological characteristics, such as psychopathology, which underlie suicide (Leenaars, 1992). These results, together with those presented here, seem to support Leenaars (1995), who suggested that sociocultural research may be the most profitable approach in accounting for the differences in the rates and patterns of suicide between Canada and the United States.

4/ One explanation for the Canadian–United States differences in suicidal behaviour is related to Trovato's hypothesis presented in this volume (chapter 4) that grieving rituals are different in different nations, with the more southern European nations being more expressive than the northern European nations. Americans may be more expressive and Canadians more conservative in their expression of emotion after the death of significant others, and this may create greater stress for the Canadians and a greater likelihood of suicidal behaviour.

5/ Although there are probably several models to explain the differences, a popular explanation for this divergence has been developed by S.D. Clark (Hiller, 1982). Clark speculated that divergence between Canada and the United States can best be explained by the different ways in which Canadians and Americans settled their respective frontiers. The Canadian moved westward under the organization of the British government, the influence of the military police, and the favour of the two predominant churches (the Church of England and the Roman Catholic Church). In contrast, America's frontier was settled independently rather than as an 'outpost of the empire.' Canada remained loyal to Britain, and the revolutionary attitude in the United States was very different from the more conservative attitude in Canada. Of course, empirical exploration is needed to examine which explanation best accounts for the divergence between Canadian and American behaviour, although it is unlikely that any single explanation will be found.

Whether S.D. Clark's or some other currently unknown explanation will account for the differences between the rates and patterns of suicide in Canada and the United States, it is clear that more research on suicide in Canada is warranted, since such studies have been relatively neglected in Canada as compared to the United States (Leenaars, 1995). We also believe that caution is warranted about generalizing research on suicide from one culture to another (as from the United States to Canada and vice versa). In addition, it should be noted that Canada and the United States are not homogeneous countries. Data presented in *Suicide in Canada* (National Task Force, 1987) shows considerable variation between provinces/territories (for example, Northwest Territories and Ontario). The data for the United States show a similar diversity. Even within both countries, there are high-risk groups (such as Aboriginal people). Yet, these considerations should not obscure the fact that comparisons between nations may be meaningful and stimulating for research.

Not only is there a need for further Canadian research, but there is also a greater need for prevention and service delivery in Canada (Leenaars, 1995). Awareness of the problem, we believe, is the first step. Canada has a serious suicide problem, one greater even than its closest neighbour, the United States. Equally important, there are different patterns, requiring each country to have its own unique response to the problem of suicidal behaviour. Suicide in Canada has its own uniqueness.

REFERENCES

Atwood, M. 1972. *Survival*. Toronto: Anansi.
Berton, P. 1984. *Why We Act Like Canadians*. Toronto: McClelland & Stewart.
Boor, M. 1976. 'Relationship of Internal-External Control and National Suicide Rates.' *Journal of Social Psychology* 100: 143–4.
– 1980. 'Relationships between Unemployment Rates and Suicide Rates in Eight Countries, 1962–1970.' *Psychological Reports* 47: 1095–1101.
Clark-Finnegan, M., and T. Fahy. 1983. 'Suicide Rates in Ireland.' *Psychological Medicine* 13: 385–91.
Clarke, R.V., and D. Lester. 1989. *Suicide: Closing the Exits*. New York: Springer-Verlag.
Cook, P.J. 1982. 'The Role of Firearms in Violent Crime.' In M.E. Wolfgang and N.A. Weiner, eds, *Criminal Violence*, 236–91. Beverly Hills, CA: Sage.

Domino, G., and A.A. Leenaars. 1989. 'Attitudes toward Suicide: A Comparison of Canadian and United States College Students.' *Suicide and Life-Threatening Behavior* 19: 160–72.
– 1994. 'Attitudes toward Suicide among English Speaking Urban Canadians.' In *Death Studies.* In press.
Durkheim, E. 1897. *Le suicide.* Paris: Félix Alcan.
Easterlin, R.A. 1980. *Birth and Fortune.* New York: Basic Books.
Henry, A.F., and J.F. Short. 1954. *Suicide and Homicide.* New York: Free Press.
Hiller, H. 1982. *Society and Change: S.D. Clark and the Development of Canadian Sociology.* Toronto: University of Toronto Press.
Jobes, D., A. Berman, and A. Josselson. (1987). 'Improving the Validity and Reliability of Medical-Legal Certification of Suicide.' *Suicide and Life-Threatening Behavior* 17: 310–25.
Labovitz, S., and M. Brinkerhoff. 1977. 'Structural Changes and Suicide in Canada.' *International Journal of Comparative Sociology* 18: 254–67.
Leenaars, A.A. 1988. *Suicide Notes.* New York: Human Sciences Press.
– 1989a. 'Are Young Adults' Suicides Psychologically Different from Those of Other Adults?' *Suicide and Life-Threatening Behavior* 19: 249–63.
– 1989b. 'Rates and Patterns of Suicide for Canada and the United States: Their Implications for Socio-Political Action.' Presidential address presented at the Canadian Association for Suicide Prevention conference, Toronto, Ontario.
– 1991. 'Suicide in the Young Adult.' In A.A. Leenaars, ed., *Lifespan Perspectives of Suicide,* 121–36. New York: Plenum.
– 1992. 'Suicide Notes in Canada and the United States.' *Perceptual and Motor Skills* 74: 278.
– 1995. 'Suicide and the Continental Divide.' *Archives of Suicide Research* 1: 39–58.
Leenaars, A.A., and G. Domino. 1993. 'A Comparison of Community Attitudes toward Suicide in Windsor and Los Angeles.' *Canadian Journal of Behavioural Science* 25: 253–66.
Leenaars, A.A., and D. Lester. 1990. 'Suicide in Adolescents: A Comparison of Canada and the United States.' *Psychological Reports* 67: 867–73.
– 1992a. 'Comparison of Rates and Patterns of Suicide in Canada and the United States, 1960–1988.' *Death Studies* 16: 417–30.
– 1992b. 'Facts and Myths of Suicide in Canada and the United States.' *Journal of Social Psychology* 132: 787–9.
– 1994a. 'Suicide and Homicide Rates in Canada and the United States.' *Suicide and Life-Threatening and Behavior* 24: 184–91.
– 1994b. 'Domestic and Economic Correlates of Personal Violence in Canada and the United States.' *Italian Journal of Suicidology* 4: 7–12.
– 1995. 'The Changing Suicide Pattern in Canadian Adolescents and Youth, Compared to Their American Counterparts.' *Adolescence* 30: 539–47.
– 1996. 'Testing the Cohort Size Hypothesis of Suicide and Homicide Rates in Canada and the United States.' *Archives of Suicide Research* 2: 43–54.
Leenaars, A.A., B. Yang, and D. Lester. 1993. 'The Effect of Domestic and Economic Stress on Suicide Rates in Canada and the United States.' *Journal of Clinical Psychology* 49: 918–21.
Lester, D. 1972. 'Migration and Suicide.' *Medical Journal of Australia* 1: 941–2.
– 1979. 'Sex Differences in Suicidal Behavior.' In E. Gomberg and V. Franks, eds, *Gender and Disordered Behavior,* 287–300. New York: Brunner/Mazel.
– 1985. 'Variation in Suicide and Homicide Rates by Latitude and Longitude in the United States, Canada and Australia.' *American Journal of Psychiatry* 142: 523–4.
– 1987. 'Murders and Suicide: Are They Polar Opposites?' *Behavioral Sciences and the Law* 5: 49–60.

- 1990. 'Changes in the Methods Used for Suicide in 16 Countries from 1960 to 1980.' *Acta Psychiatrica Scandinavica* 81: 260–1.
- 1992. 'Decriminalization of Suicide in Canada and Suicide Rates.' *Psychological Reports* 71: 738.
- 1993. 'Decriminalization of Suicide in New Zealand and Suicide Rates.' *Psychological Reports* 72: 1050.
- 1994. 'Use of Firearms for Suicide in Canada.' *Perceptual and Motor Skills* 79: 962.
Lester, D., and A.A. Leenaars. 1993. 'Suicide Rates in Canada before and after Tightening Firearm Control Laws.' *Psychological Reports* 72: 787–90.
Lester, D., and B. Yang. 1992. 'Social and Economic Correlates for the Elderly Suicide Rate.' *Suicide and Life-Threatening Behavior* 22: 36–47.
Lipsett, S.M. 1990. *Continental Divide*. New York: Routledge.
McGinnis, J. 1987. 'Suicide in America.' *Suicide and Life-Threatening Behavior* 17: 18–32.
McIntosh, J. 1988–9. 'Official U.S. Elderly Suicide Data Bases.' *Omega* 19: 337–50.
- 1992. 'Epidemiology of Suicide in the Elderly.' In A.A. Leenaars, R. Maris, J. McIntosh, and J. Richman, eds, *Suicide and the Older Adult*, 15–35. New York: Guilford Press.
National Task Force on Suicide in Canada. 1987. *Suicide in Canada*. Ottawa: Department of National Health and Welfare.
O'Carroll, P. 1989. 'A Consideration of the Validity and Reliability of Suicide Mortality Data.' *Suicide and Life-Threatening Behavior* 18: 1–16.
Platt, S.D. 1984. 'Unemployment and Suicidal Behavior.' *Social Science and Medicine* 10: 93–115.
Sainsbury, P., and B.M. Barraclough. 1968. 'Differences between Suicide Rates.' *Nature* 220: 1252.
Sainsbury, P., and J. Jenkins. 1982. 'The Accuracy of Officially Reported Suicide Statistics for Purposes of Epidemiological Research.' *Journal of Epidemiology and Community Health* 36: 43–8.
Shneidman, E.S. 1985. *Definitions of Suicide*. New York: Wiley.
Spencer, M. 1985. *Foundations of Modern Sociology*. Scarborough, Ont.: Prentice-Hall.
Syer-Solursh, D. 1987. 'The Canadian Suicide Reality.' In J. Morgan, ed., *Suicide: Helping Those at Risk*, 129–39. London, Ont.: King's College.

PART III: THEORY AND RESEARCH

Science means research. Research is the basis for sound knowledge in a particular scientific community, in this case suicidology. Research comprises the achievements that a scientific community acknowledges as its foundations. Research, we hope, not only reports the knowledge but also defines the problem. Although there is a great need for more research in suicidology, there are important endeavours in this field in Canada. We will present a small sample of these studies.

Research cannot only be tabular. It has to involve more. Theory must play a key role. It is only through theory that we can sort out the 'booming, buzzing mess of experience' (William James). The scientific study of suicide in Canada, in fact, has achieved its most important insight by descending below the level of familiar empirical phenomena.

This third section provides a sample of theory and research in Canada. It highlights current scholarly thoughts on suicide in three chapters: a discussion on pain, depression, and suicide; a summary of a series of psychiatric studies on mental-health issues and suicide; and an identification of stress, social supports, and personal variables in suicide.

6

Pain, Depression, and Suicide

PETER D. MCLEAN and STEVEN TAYLOR

Suicide, with the possible exception of euthanasia, is universally perceived as an irrational act that occurs under the influence of psychological problems such as clinical depression (e.g., major depression), problems of impulse control, substance abuse, or some combination of these factors. The most common antecedent to suicide is depression, which can be precipitated by circumstances that the person perceives to be highly aversive, disabling, and unrelenting. Many people who endure chronic pain find themselves in such circumstances. Accordingly, chronic pain is a risk factor for depression, which in turn is a risk factor for suicide. The relationship between chronic pain and depression has received surprisingly little attention by researchers and clinicians.

There has been a considerable amount of research into the relationship between clinical depression and suicide. Despite problems in accurately predicting suicide, clinical depression is a well-established risk factor (Davis and Schrueder, 1990; Hoffman and Dubovsky, 1991; Motto, 1992). The study of pain as a risk factor for suicide has evolved quite independently and rather slowly. Historically, pain has been viewed as a symptom of pathophysiology, rather than as a factor influencing mood and behaviour. More recently, clinicians and researchers have recognized that chronic pain and clinical depression are complex, multidimensional syndromes, with the capacity to influence one another. Chronic pain can lead to depression and suicide, and depression can influence pain. There are marked individual differences in the response to chronic pain; only some chronic-pain patients become depressed, and only some of the depressed become suicidal. Much remains to be learned about the ways in which pain, depression, and suicide interact with one another.

The purpose of this chapter is to examine the relationships among pain, depression, and suicide. Given the importance of cognitive and behavioural factors in the treatment of chronic pain and depression (e.g., Beck et al., 1979; Turk et al., 1983), chronic pain and clinical depression will be compared in terms of common cognitive styles and behavioural patterns. Finally, we will consider implications for the assessment and treatment of patients with these debilitating conditions.

Depression and Suicide

To understand the relationship between chronic pain and suicide we first need to consider the relationship between depression and suicide, because depression is typically an intervening variable between chronic pain and suicide. The prediction of suicide continues to be a significant challenge for health professionals (Leenaars, 1992). Part of the problem is that completed suicides are rare events, which make them difficult to predict (Maris et al., 1992). Another problem involves the inherent limitations in the development of predictive instruments. Motto (1992) noted the irony of being unable to develop a perfectly reliable and valid instrument to predict suicide because it would never be validated by its critical outcome criteria. That is, if suicide was predicted, we would be ethically obliged to do our utmost to prevent it.

There is broad agreement about the major risk factors for suicide (Motto, 1992). A diagnosable mental disorder is present in 85 to 90 per cent of those who commit suicide (Maltsberger, 1992). Schizophrenia, alcohol and drug dependence, and borderline personality disorder are frequently associated with suicide. However, the presence of clinical depression is the most important indicator of suicide risk (Guze and Robins, 1970; Jamison, 1986; Tanney, 1992).

Symptoms and syndromes of depression are frequently overlooked by clinicians. To illustrate, large-scale studies of family physicians (e.g., Wells et al., 1989) have found that up to 50 per cent of cases of depression are not detected during an office visit. Patients may not express their complaints in terms of depression and may present instead with somatic complaints (Hoffman and Dubovsky, 1991). According to the Canadian Task Force on the Periodic Health Examination (Feightner, 1994), clinical depression is a major health concern because of its potential for suicide. The task force recommended that Canadian physicians be sensitive to the possibility of depression in their patients, and carefully apply standardized clinical criteria to assess clinical depression. As many as 50 per cent of clinically depressed outpatients admit to suicidal ideation (McLean and Hakstian, 1979), underscoring the importance of early detection of this disorder. Once identified, most mood disorders respond well to treatment; the clinical challenge lies in the early detection of depressive symptoms.

Chronic Pain and Depression

Incidence and Interrelationship

Chronic pain often results in substantial impairments in social and occupational functioning, and substantial reductions in psychological well-being (International Association for the Study of Pain, 1986). There have been several attempts to estimate the incidence of depression in various pain populations. In a recent review, DeVellis (1993) estimated that approximately 30 per cent of all chronic-pain patients have clinically significant depression. The rates of clinical depression may be higher in some populations of pain patients compared to others. Potatin et al. (1992) found that 45 per cent of patients with chronic low-back pain had a current major depressive episode.

Given the aversiveness of the pain experience and its psychosocial consequences, it is not surprising that chronic pain is often associated with clinical depression. Psychosocial consequences of pain include the loss of one's important roles (e.g., occupational roles, family roles), reduced social contact, and demoralization and loss of hope when professional caregivers are unable to provide pain relief. Chronic pain occurring in the absence of an identifiable organic basis can cause significant others (including treating clinicians) to doubt the legitimacy of the patient's pain complaints. This can lead to reduced social support and further despondency on the part of the afflicted person.

Although pain can lead to depression, there is also evidence that a depressed mood can exacerbate pain. To illustrate, in an experimental study of forty-eight children who had undergone minor surgery (e.g., tonsillectomy or adenoidectomy), Johnson et al. (1994) manipulated the mood state by means of emotionally toned video clips. The children's rating of pain intensity increased when a negative mood was induced, and decreased when a positive mood was induced. Thus, mood influenced pain. In a longitudinal study, Magni et al. (1994) assessed 2324 people for the presence of muscle-skeletal pain and the presence of depression. The subjects then were reassessed seven years later. Depressive symptoms at time one significantly predicted the development of chronic muscle-skeletal pain seven years later (odds ratio = 2.14). Also, chronic pain at time one predicted the occurrence of depression seven years later (odds ratio = 2.85). These and other studies are consistent with the view that pain promotes depression and depression promotes pain.

It is now evident that depression is a frequent and dangerous consequence of chronic pain. For this reason the assessment of depression in chronic pain patients is a responsibility of the treating clinician.

Cognitive Factors

Cognitive mechanisms appear to play important roles in pain and depression. According to the gate-control theory of pain (Melzack and Casey, 1968; Melzack and Wall, 1965), pain is a product of two factors: pain intensity is influenced by the degree to which peripheral pain receptors activate central (brain) mechanisms, and by the extent to which central mechanisms influence (e.g., inhibit) the effects of peripheral receptors. Thus, the nature and intensity of pain is determined by the extent and severity of tissue injury, by cognitive mechanisms such as attention to the pain site, and by appraisal of the significance of the injury. Appraisals of the pain itself can also influence the pain experience. Thus, pain is likely to be experienced as more intense and more aversive when the person focuses his or her attention on it, and when he or she worries about its consequences. Feared consequences include death, profound disability, or the prospect of suffering years of intense pain.

According to Beck's cognitive theory of depression (Beck et al., 1979), depression can arise when stressful life events activate long-standing depressogenic beliefs. To illustrate, if a person believed that his or her worth depended entirely on gaining the approval of others, then the loss of such approval would cause the person to believe that he or she was worthless. Thus, a depressed mood would ensue.

Beliefs about pain can lead to depression, and cognitive (attentional) aspects of depression can exacerbate pain. Regardless of its source, pain is a stressful experience that can activate depressogenic beliefs. For example, if a person believed that only 'weak' people have chronic pain, then the occurrence of chronic pain would cause the person to blame him or herself, leading to guilt and depressed mood. Thus, pain-related beliefs can influence whether or not a person becomes depressed when chronic pain occurs. In turn, depression is associated with an inward-focused cognitive style, in which the person dwells on problems, including somatic problems such as pain. Selective attention to pain increases the perceived severity of pain (Craig, 1994). By these and related mechanisms, depression and pain interact with one another.

Behavioural Patterns Common to Chronic Pain and Depression

Avoidance and withdrawal behaviour are features common to clinical depression and chronic pain. In both cases the person avoids sources of aversive stimulation. The depressed person may avoid going to work or socializing because he or she expects to fail at tasks or expects to be rejected. In turn, this cuts the person off from potentially rewarding events (e.g., successful completion of tasks or enjoyable social interactions), which contributes to the maintenance of the depressed mood. A similar process occurs in chronic pain. The person with chronic pain may avoid physical activity because he or she expects that this will exacerbate pain. Thus, the person refrains from embarking on naturally distracting activities; instead he or she remains inactive and focused on his or her pain. This inactivity promotes the depressed mood (Williamson and Schulz, 1992).

In pain and depression, avoidance and withdrawal behaviours can be maintained by reinforcers in the person's environment (Keefe and Lefebvre, 1994; Lewinsohn, 1974). The sick role is often rewarding, especially when it is associated with desired attention from significant others. Other reinforcers include relief from onerous responsibilities (e.g., occupational demands) by remaining in the sick role. Thus, the affected person can be rewarded for avoidance and withdrawal. As we will discuss later, behavioural interventions are effective in treating chronic pain and clinical depression (Fordyce, 1976; McLean and Hakstian, 1979). These interventions reduce the extent to which avoidance and withdrawal are rewarding, and help the person seek more adaptive forms of reinforcement.

Chronic Pain and Suicide

Various lines of evidence show that people with chronic pain, compared to those without pain, are at an increased risk for suicide (Fishbain et al., 1991). However, published reports of the relationship between completed suicide and chronic pain are limited to case reports. On the basis of a small number of completed suicides in a chronic-pain sample, Fishbain et al. (1991) calculated that white males with worker's compensation claims owing to chronic pain were three times more likely to die by suicide, compared to their counterparts in the general population.

There is no reason to believe that the mechanisms responsible for depression are different when the stressor is chronic pain. Owing to its chronic and debilitating nature, such pain is a particularly potent stressor, especially for people who are vulnerable to depression. The latter include people with a pessimistic attributional style (e.g., as indicated by the tendency to blame oneself for aversive events) and with particular lifestyle factors (e.g., low levels of perceived social support and few interests or involvements). Other psychosocial mechanisms are also thought to be responsible for the development and maintenance of depression. These include negatively biased recall (i.e., the tendency to recall aversive experiences compared to pleasant events), somatic preoccupation, and catastrophic thinking (i.e., the tendency to magnify the aversiveness of unpleasant events). If the person believed that the pain was 'awful' or 'unendurable,' then he or she might contemplate suicide as a form of escape. Thus, chronic pain can increase the risk for suicide to the extent that pain causes the afflicted person to feel helpless and hopeless about ever recovering. Beliefs about one's inability to tolerate pain can also influence suicidal behaviour.

Euthanasia

Euthanasia deserves special consideration as a response to chronic pain because depression is not necessarily involved. Euthanasia has been described as a rational solution for individuals with chronic pain and terminal illness. This is in contrast to depressed individuals who are suicidal and assumed to be subject to irrational beliefs by virtue of being depressed. This is a critical distinction in the controversy over euthanasia and one that is likely to intensify owing to the aging of the Canadian population and the increase in prevalence of terminal illnesses such as AIDS.

Throughout history, suicide has been viewed either as senseless or as a rational act. Most frequently, suicide is seen as a senseless act arising from a temporarily unrealistic evaluation of one's life situation – that is, the temporary situation where the person sees his or her circumstances as being worse than they really are. In sharp contrast, there are cases of seemingly rational suicide, where people (e.g., in the final stages of terminal illness) recognize that death is imminent, and tolerate or support suicide as a dignified solution to unnecessary suffering.

The Senate of Canada (1995) recently recommended, by a narrow margin, that voluntary euthanasia remain a criminal offence, but that the criminal code be amended to allow for a reduced penalty 'in cases where there is the essential element of compassion or mercy' (p. xi). The issue of euthanasia is given further consideration elsewhere in this volume.

Implications for Assessment and Treatment

Major depression and dysthymia are the most common forms of clinical depression to be associated with chronic pain (Tanney, 1992). Accordingly, we confine our discussion to the treatment of these disorders. The management of suicide risk and suicidal behaviour is a standard component of depression treatments (e.g., Beck et al., 1979) and these aspects will be discussed together.

Assessment

Most clinicians regard the evaluation of suicide risk as mandatory in the assessment and treatment of depression. The gold standard for evaluating suicidal risk is the clinical interview, although there are several self-report inventories now available that have satisfactory psychometric properties (see Rothberg and Geer-Williams, 1992, for a review). Of necessity, such inventories are often used as screening tools to identify depression or suicide risk in general populations (e.g., schoolchildren) and in populations at risk for depression (e.g., patients attending their family physicians: Feightner, 1994).

Economy in screening for depression and suicide risk is achieved through a two-step process (Costello and Devins, 1988; Hakstian and McLean, 1989). The first step involves a brief psychometric rating scale that has a low-false negative classification rate, followed by a clinical interview of individuals thus identified. The two-stage screening process for the detection of significant depression is effective and efficient, and should be expanded to chronic pain populations as a matter of course. Early concerns that such instruments over-identified depression owing to the presence of somatic complaints common to both chronic pain and depression have been unjustified. For example, Turk and Okifuji (1994) assessed chronic-pain patients with the Centre for Epidemiological Studies depression scale (CES-D). The latter is a commonly used self-report measure that has been found to have satisfactory psychometric properties when used in non-pain populations. Turk and Okifuji found that the CES-D maintained its discriminatory ability in detecting depression in chronic-pain patients when the somatic items on this scale were removed.

Given the high prevalence of clinical depression and associated risk for suicide in chronic-pain populations, it is imperative that chronic-pain patients be assessed for the presence of depression. This is important because mood disorders are often missed when the assessment is narrowly focused on pain and pathophysiological processes (Doan and Wadden, 1989). Early detection of depression in chronic pain patients and triage to multidisciplinary health providers will reduce the incidence of severe depression and risk for suicide (Livengood and Parris, 1992; Wells et al., 1991). The treatment of depression is of further importance because it can facilitate improvement in chronic-pain management (Blanchard et al., 1992). Even subclinical levels of depression should be regarded seriously (Skevington, 1994) because of the dynamic time course of depression.

Individuals suffering from chronic pain who are significantly depressed may not recognize their depression as a disturbance of mood. Such people also may be reluctant to disclose suicidal thoughts or intentions, thus making it difficult to detect depression and suicide risk. Rapport and an empathic interview style are important means of eliciting vital information from reticent patients. Given that chronic pain is a risk factor for clinical depression, it would be useful to routinely assess chronic-pain patients for the presence of clinically significant depression. In addition to the obvious benefit of reduced suicide risk when depression is detected and treated, there is a further benefit in that reduced depression can result in a reduction in the severity of perceived pain.

Treatment

The use of antidepressant medication for the treatment of depression in chronic-pain patients is well documented (e.g., Sullivan et al., 1992; Teicher et al., 1993; Tollefson et al., 1993). Generally, these treatments have been found to be effective in reducing suicidal ideation and other symptoms of depression. However, psychosocial treatments also need to be considered, because a significant number of depressed patients do not improve on MAOI, multicyclic, or SSRI antidepressant medications, or are unwilling to accept these medications. In other cases, antidepressant medication is contraindicated on other grounds (e.g., tricyclic antidepressants may be contraindicated in people with cardiac disease).

There are numerous studies showing the efficacy of behavioural and cognitive-behavioural treatments for depression, suicidal crisis, and chronic pain (e.g., Fordyce, 1976; Keefe and Lefebvre, 1994; McLean and Hakstian, 1979; McLean and Taylor, 1992). The literatures on the psychosocial management of chronic pain and clinical depression bear remarkable similarities, undoubtedly because they address common mechanisms. It appears, for example, that catastrophic thinking mediates distress in both chronic pain and depressed patients (Geisser et al., 1994; Sullivan and D'Eton, 1990). There are several published therapy guides for restructuring maladaptive thinking styles in clinical depression (e.g., Beck et al., 1979; Fennell, 1989) and in chronic pain (e.g., Turk et al., 1983).

Behavioural treatment programs for chronic pain and clinical depression strive to promote goal setting and increasing the person's involvement in enjoyable, productive activities. Such interventions are effective (Fordyce, 1976; McLean and Hakstian, 1979; Turk et al., 1983). These programs also recognize the importance of social support. Accordingly, treatment protocols focus on increasing the rate and range of positive social support, while identifying and reducing social recognition for dysfunctional behaviour (Herr et al., 1993). When chronic-pain patients have serious suicidal intent, the treating clinician (and other caregivers) need to develop a structured treatment plan that emphasizes graduated goal attainment, social support, and cognitive self-control to minimize the risk of suicide attempts.

Conclusions

Chronic pain is a significant stressor that can contribute to the development of clinical depression and suicidal behaviour. In turn, depression can exacerbate pain. There is broad agreement that depressed chronic-pain patients are at substantial risk for suicide and that depression in this population is often underdiagnosed, frequently because patients minimize or fail to report their symptoms of depression. It is the collective responsibility of caregivers to evaluate chronic-pain patients for the presence of depression so that the possibility of suicide can be averted.

Chronic pain and depression appear to share common cognitive and behavioural mechanisms. Behavioural and cognitive-behavioural interventions, along with particular pharmacotherapies, are effective in reducing depression and alleviating chronic pain. However, much remains to be learned about the optimal combination of interventions in cases of comorbid depression and chronic pain. Advances in treatment efficacy will likely depend on advances in our understanding of the complex interplay of factors influencing chronic pain, clinical depression, and suicidal behaviour.

REFERENCES

Beck, A.T., A.J. Rush, B.F. Shaw, and G. Emery. 1979. *Cognitive Therapy of Depression*. New York: Guilford Press.
Blanchard, E.B., F. Andrasik, D. Neff, et al. 1982. 'Biofeedback and Relaxation Training with Three Kinds of Headaches: Treatment Effects and Their Prediction.' *Journal of Consulting and Clinical Psychology* 50: 562–5.
Costello, C., and G.M. Devins. 1988. 'Two-Stage Screening for Stressful Life Events and Chronic Difficulties.' *Canadian Journal of Behavioral Science* 20: 85–92.
Craig, K.D. 1994. 'Emotional Aspects of Pain.' In P.D. Wall and R. Melzack, eds, *Textbook of Pain*, 261–74. London: Churchill Livingston.
Davis, A.T., and C. Schrueder. 1990. 'The Predictors of Suicide.' *Medical Journal of Australia* 153: 552–4.
DeVellis, B.M.E. 1993. 'Depression in Rheumatological Diseases.' In S. Newman and M. Shipley, eds, *Psychological Aspects of Rheumatoid Disease: Ballieres' Clinical Rheumatology* 7: 241–57.
Doan, B.D., and N.P. Wadden. 1989. 'Relationship between Depressive Symptoms and Descriptions of Chronic Pain.' *Pain* 36: 75–84.
Feightner, J.W. 1994. 'Early Detection of Depression.' In Canadian Task Force on the Periodic Health Exam, eds, *The Canadian Guide to Clinical Preventive Health Care*, 450–4. Ottawa: Minister of Supply and Services Canada.

Fennell, M.J.V. 1989. 'Depression.' In K. Hawton, P.M. Salkovskis, J. Kirk, and D. M. Clark, eds, *Cognitive Behaviour Therapy for Psychiatric Problems*, 169–234. Oxford: Oxford University Press.

Fishbain, D.A., M. Goldberg, R.S. Rosomoff, and H. Rosomoff. 1991. 'Completed Suicide in Chronic Pain.' *Clinical Journal of Pain* 7: 29–36.

Fordyce, W.E. 1976. *Behavioral Methods for Chronic Pain and Illness*. St Louis, MO: Mosby.

Geisser, M.E., M.E. Robinson, F.J. Keefe, and M.L. Weiner. 1994. 'Catastrophizing, Depression, and the Sensory, Affective and Evaluative Aspects of Chronic Pain.' *Pain* 59: 79–83.

Guze, S.B., and E. Robins. 1970. 'Suicide and Primary Affective Disorders.' *British Journal of Psychiatry* 117: 437–8.

Hakstian, A.R., and P.D. McLean. 1989. 'Brief Screen for Depression.' *Psychological Assessment* 1: 139–41.

Herr, K.A., P.R. Mobily, and C. Smith. 1993. 'Depression and the Experience of Chronic Back Pain: A Study of Related Variables and Age Differences.' *Clinical Journal of Pain* 9: 104–14.

Hoffman, D.P., and S.L. Dubovsky. 1991. 'Depression and Suicide Assessment.' *Emergency Medicine Clinics of North America* 9: 107–21.

International Association for the Study of Pain. 1986. 'Classification of Chronic Pain: Descriptions of Chronic Pain Syndromes and Definitions of Pain Terms.' *Pain* (Suppl. 3): 1–222.

Jamison, K.R. 1986. 'Suicide and Bipolar Disorders.' *Annals of the New York Academy of Science* 487: 301–15.

Johnson, R., S.H. Spence, G.D. Champion, and Z.B. Ziegler. 1994. 'Pain, Affect and Cognition in Children: 1. The Influence of Affective State on Pain in Children.' In G.F. Gebhart, D.L. Hammond, and T.S. Jensen, eds, *Proceedings of the 7th World Congress on Pain, Progress in Pain Research and Management*, 2: 869–75. Seattle, WA: IASP Press.

Keefe, F.J., and J. Lefebvre. 1994. 'Pain Behavior Concepts: Controversies, Current Status, and Future Directions.' In G.F. Gebhart, D.L. Hammond, and T.S. Jensen, eds, *Proceedings of the 7th World Congress on Pain, Progress in Pain Research and Management*, 2: 127–47. Seattle, WA: IASP Press.

Leenaars, A.A. 1992. 'Suicide Notes, Communication, and Ideation.' In R.W. Maris, A.L. Berman, J.T. Maltsberger, and R.I. Yufit, eds, *Assessment and Prediction of Suicide*, 337–61. London: Guilford Press.

Lewinsohn, P.M. 1974. 'A Behavioral Approach to Depression.' In R.J. Friedman and M.M. Katz, eds, *The Psychology of Depression: Contemporary Theory and Research*. Washington: Winston/Wiley.

Livengood, J.M., and W.C.V. Parris. 1992. 'Early Detection Measures and Triage Procedures for Suicide Ideation in Chronic Pain Patients.' *Clinical Journal of Pain* 8: 164–9.

McLean, P., and A.R. Hakstian. 1979. 'Clinical Depression: Comparative Efficacy of Outpatient Treatments.' *Journal of Consulting and Clinical Psychology* 7: 818–36.

McLean, P., and S. Taylor. 1992. 'Severity of Unipolar Depression and Choice of Treatment.' *Behaviour Research and Therapy* 30: 443–51.

Magni, G., C. Moreschi, S. Rigatti-Luchini, and H.Merskey. 1994. 'Prospective Study on the Relationship between Depressive Symptoms and Chronic Musculoskeletal Pain.' *Pain* 56: 289–97.

Maltsberger, J.T. 1992. 'The Psychodynamic Formulation: An Aid in Assessing Suicide Risk.' In R.W. Maris, A. Berman, J.T. Maltsberger, and R.I. Yufit, eds, *Assessment and Prediction of Suicide*, 25–49. New York: Guilford Press.

Maris, R.W., A.L. Berman, and J.T. Maltsberger. 1992. 'What Have We Learned about Suicide Assessment and Prediction?' In R.W. Maris, A.L. Berman, J.T. Maltsberger, and R.I. Yufit, eds, *Assessment and Prediction of Suicide*, 640–72. New York: Guilford Press.

Melzack, R., and K.L. Casey. 1968. 'Sensory, Motivational and Central Control Determinants of Pain: A New Conceptual Model.' In D.L. Kenshalo, ed., *The Skin Senses*, 423. Springfield, IL: Charles C. Thomas.

Melzak, R., and P.D. Wall. 1965. 'Pain Mechanisms: A New Theory.' *Science* 150: 971–9.

Motto, J.A. 1992. 'An Integrated Approach to Estimating Suicide Risk.' In R.W. Maris, A.L. Berman, J.T. Maltsberger, and R.I. Yufit, eds, *Assessment and Prediction of Suicide*, 625–39. New York: Guilford Press.

Potatin, P.B., R.K. Kinney, R.J. Gatchel, M.A. Lillo, and T.G. Mayer. 1992. 'Psychiatric Illness and Chronic Low-Back Pain.' *Spine* 18: 66–71.

Rothberg, J.M., and C. Geer-Williams. 1992. 'A Comparison and Review of Suicide Prediction Scales.' In R.W. Marris, A.L. Berman, J.T. Maltsberger, and R.I. Yufit, eds, *Assessment and Prediction of Suicide*, 202–17. New York: Guilford Press.

Senate of Canada. 1995. *Of Life and Death: Report of the Special Senate Committee on Euthanasia and Assisted Suicide*. Ottawa: Ministry of Supply and Services Canada.

Skevington, S.M. 1994. 'The Relationship between Pain and Depression: A Longitudinal Study of Early Synovitis.' In G.F. Gebhart, D.L. Hammond, and T.S. Jensen, eds, *Proceedings of the 7th World Congress on Pain, Progress in Pain Research and Management*, 2: 201–10. Seattle, WA: IASP Press.

Sullivan, M.J.L., and J.L. D'Eton. 1990. 'Relation between Catastrophizing and Depression in Chronic Pain Patients.' *Journal of Abnormal Psychology* 99: 260–3.

Sullivan, M.J.L., K. Reesor, S. Mikail, and R. Fisher. 1992. 'The Treatment of Depression in Chronic Low Back Pain: Review and Recommendations.' *Pain* 50: 5–13.

Tanney, B.L. 1992. 'Mental Disorders, Psychiatric Patients, and Suicide.' In R.W. Maris, A. Berman, J.T. Maltsberger, and R.I. Yufit, eds, *Assessment and Prediction of Suicide*, 277–320. New York: Guilford Press.

Teicher, M.H., C.A. Glod, and J.O. Cole. 1993. 'Antidepressant Drugs and the Emergence of Suicidal Tendencies.' *Drug Safety* 8: 186–212.

Tollefson, G.D., J. Fawcett, G. Winokur, C.M. Beasley, Jr, J.H. Potvin, D.E. Faries, A.H. Rampey, Jr, and M.E. Sayler. 1993. 'Evaluation of Suicidality during Pharmacologic Treatment of Mood and Nonmood Disorders.' *Annals of Clinical Psychiatry* 5: 209–24.

Turk, D.C., D. Meichenbaum, and M. Genest. 1983. *Pain and Behavioral Medicine*. New York: Guilford Press.

Turk, D.C., and A. Okifuji. 1994. 'Detecting Depression in Chronic Pain Patients: Adequacy of Self-Reports.' *Behavior Research and Therapy* 32: 9–16.

Wells, K.B., W. Rogers, A. Burman, S. Greenfield, and J.E. Ware. 1991. 'How the Medical Co-morbidity of Depressed Patients Differs across Health Care Settings: Results from the Medical Outcomes Study.' *American Journal of Psychiatry* 148: 1688–96.

Wells, K.B., A. Stewart, R.D. Hays, M.A. Burnam, W. Rogers, M. Daniels, S. Berry, S. Greenfield, and J. Ware. 1989. 'The Functioning and Well-Being of Depressed Patients.' *Journal of American Medical Association* 262: 914–19.

Williamson, G.M., and R. Schulz. 1992. 'Pain, Activity Restriction, and Symptoms of Depression among Community-Residing Elderly Adults.' *Journal of Gerontology: Psychological Sciences* 47: 367–72.

7

Attempted Suicide in Edmonton

ROGER C. BLAND, RONALD J. DYCK,
STEPHEN C. NEWMAN, and HELENE ORN

Although the term 'attempted suicide' is commonly used, it is unsatisfactory, since the majority of patients designated in this way are not actually attempting suicide. Still, there is an association between the behaviours of 'attempted suicide' and suicide. Thus, the term 'parasuicide' was proposed (Kreitman et al., 1969). This encompasses a range of behaviours for which differing motives may be proposed from a failed suicide to a cry for help, to impulsive self-mutilation, all of which may be difficult to categorize in a practical manner.

The working group for the WHO/European multicentre study on parasuicide proposed the following definition: 'An act with a nonfatal outcome, in which an individual deliberately initiates a non-habitual behaviour that, without intervention from others, will cause self-harm, or deliberately ingests a substance in excess of the prescribed or generally recognized therapeutic dosage, and which is aimed at realizing changes which the subject desired via the actual or expected physical consequences' (WHO, 1986).

This definition would include a person rescued at the last minute from an act with anticipated fatal outcome, but would not include a person who, as a result of psychosis, felt they had special powers, such as flying from a high place, and was injured as a result. Accidental injury, for example, suffered while jay walking is not parasuicide, nor is the accidental taking of an overdose of licit or illicit drugs.

For the purposes of the study that we report here, we would also include as parasuicide a naive person who, for example, ingested a harmless quantity of medication in the expectation that it would be harmful. A person who sat in a car in a closed garage until the car ran out of gasoline, and suffered little more than nausea or headache, would be included as a case, since the outcome is dependent largely on the age of the vehicle and the integrity of its pollution-control equipment. We had difficulty in deciding how to classify persons who presented for treatment with the presenting complaint of suicidal thoughts or impulses, but had not actually performed an act. These were persons specifically presenting for treatment because they feared their own suicidal thoughts or impulses and believed that they would harm themselves without such intervention. Such cases differ from those who respond on a community survey to having at some time had suicidal thoughts; most of these people do not seek specific treatment. We decided to include such cases in the calculations of rates (but obviously not in the methods used), since this was regarded as a 'a non-habitual behaviour that, without intervention from others, will cause self harm.' There were 186 such persons who were Edmonton residents in the one-year period (1993–4). This represents 9.4 per cent of the total number of persons studied. Our calculated rates would be correspondingly lower were these cases not included. We are unclear how others would classify such cases. We did not encounter cases of habitual repetitive self-mutilators (e.g., wrist cutters) without suicidal intent. Such cases would not be classed as parasuicide. Mutilators with suicidal intent were, of course, included.

Weissman (1974) clearly described the typical profile of a suicide attempter as more likely to be female, with most taking an overdose and being young, with a peak age of twenty to twenty-four years. Others noted that they are frequently single, separated or divorced, and living alone (Bille-Brahe et al. 1985; Rygnestad, 1982; Wasserman, 1988; Willox, 1985). Weissman (1974) also noted increasing rates during the 1960s, continuing into the 1970s (Wexler et al., 1978).

The most recent and comprehensive study of parasuicide, the WHO/EURO multicentre project (Platt et al., 1992, Kerkhof et al., 1994), is used for comparisons with the Edmonton data. The purposes of the part of the Edmonton study reported here were to ascertain the rates of parasuicide for the city to describe the details (age- and sex-specific rates), demographics, and methods. We have used both the terms parasuicide and attempted suicide, with the definition given above of parasuicide, interchangeably.

Methods

For a one-year period, from mid-February 1993 to mid-February 1994, records of all persons attending the emergency departments of all Edmonton hospitals for a parasuicide were collected. Data sheets on each case were completed by staff of the medical-records departments at each hospital and faxed to the research staff several times each week. The data set was quite limited, but included age, sex, marital status, method of suicide attempt, whether admitted to hospital, and, if an overdose, what drugs were taken. Addresses and postal codes were part of the data, and thus persons who were Edmonton residents could be separated from those residing elsewhere but using Edmonton services. This permitted the calculation of age- and sex-specific rates based on the 1993 population of Edmonton, and also allowed comparison with other published studies. These are the data reported here. In addition, we interviewed in depth a sample of 508 parasuicides, conducted telephone contacts at intervals during the year following the parasuicide, and completed a follow-up interview at one year's time. For comparison of psychiatric and psychological profiles of the parasuicide cases, comparable interviews were conducted with a control group of age- and sex-matched emergency-room attenders. These later studies will be completed in the near future and will then be available for analysis.

In limiting our inception point for cases to those attending emergency departments we are inevitably missing some cases. Those who sought no help and those who, for example, saw their family physician, a therapist, or a crisis service and were treated without referral, and those who were treated out of the region are not included; thus, our rates are underestimates. Nevertheless, the usual pattern of service in the region is that such cases, if medical attention is required, would be directly seen in a hospital emergency department, or be referred there. There are no surrounding communities where substantial numbers of Edmonton residents are seen for clinical care.

It is usual when reporting the incidence of attempted suicide to use either or both of 'person' rates or 'event' rates. For the former, each person can only be an incident case once in the reporting period; for the latter, a single individual could make several attempts during the reporting period and thus contribute several incident events. Thus, event rates are higher than person rates. In this paper we report person incidence rates.

Results

Most results will be reported for Edmonton residents only. During the one year period 2264 persons were seen with 2780 attempts, of whom 1970 persons with 2436 attempts were city of Edmonton residents. The ratio of events to persons is 1.24:1, differing little by sex or age. Women accounted for 60.7 per cent of the persons, thus the female-to-male person ratio was 1.54:1. The female-to-male rate (persons) ratio was 1.42:1, and varied considerably by age. In those under age 15 years, the person rate was almost 3.5 times higher in females than males, falling to almost equal rates for the 30-to-34 year age group, followed by increasing female-to-male (person) rates, peaking at a person rate ratio of 2.11 in those age 45 to 49, and again falling to slightly below 1 after age 55.

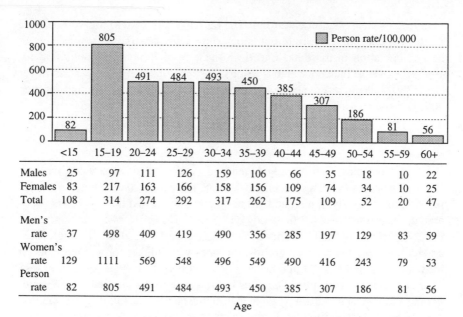

	<15	15–19	20–24	25–29	30–34	35–39	40–44	45–49	50–54	55–59	60+
Males	25	97	111	126	159	106	66	35	18	10	22
Females	83	217	163	166	158	156	109	74	34	10	25
Total	108	314	274	292	317	262	175	109	52	20	47
Men's rate	37	498	409	419	490	356	285	197	129	83	59
Women's rate	129	1111	569	548	496	549	490	416	243	79	53
Person rate	82	805	491	484	493	450	385	307	186	81	56

Age

Notes: Rates are based on Edmonton population data, 1993. Rates for age 15+: men, 309; women, 440; total, 376.

Figure 1   Edmonton parasuicides: Person rates/100,000/year, both sexes

Age

The five-year age group with the highest rate was those age 15 to 19 years (figure 1). Rates for both sexes combined remained fairly stable between ages 20 and 39, following which there was a progressive decline with each successive age group. The difference in rates by age is dramatic; those aged 15 to 19 years show fourteen times the rate of the over age 60. Those under age 15 (108 persons, 126 attempts) accounted for 5.5 per cent of all persons; thus, parasuicide in the young is not insignificant.

Sex

As mentioned above, the rates in women exceed those in men, except for persons aged 30 to 34 and after age 55, when the rates are virtually equal (figure 2). Rates in men begin declining after age 35, but it is almost a decade before female rates clearly start decreasing. The rate of 1111/100,000 for women aged 15 to 19 is exceptionally high, but is based on 217 cases and seems unlikely to be an abberation in the data. Based on the city of Edmonton population for 1993, the overall incidence rate (persons) for the population 15 years and over was 376/100,000/year; the corresponding rate for women was 440, and for men 309 (rate ratio 1.4).

Marital Status

Subjects were classified as single, married, widowed, or separated/divorced, and incidence rates were calculated by sex for each group. Figure 3 shows much higher rates (both men and women) in the single and the divorced or separated, than in the married or widowed, groups. However, of all persons, 59.5 per cent were single and 11.4 per cent separated or divorced. In the single, separated/divorced, and married groups, the rates were higher for women than for men, whereas in the small number of widowed persons (1.4 per cent of cases), the rate was higher for men. The rates in the single to the married are 4.9 times greater in males and 4.3 times greater in females. Similar ratios apply in comparing the separated/divorced to the married groups. Female-to-male ratios of rates vary from a low of 0.67 in the separated/divorced to a high of 1.7 in those who are married.

Disposition

Of the 1970 persons seen in the hospital emergency departments, only 398 (20.2 per cent) were admitted to an in-patient bed. In our pilot study in 1990–1, 30.2 per cent were admitted. This difference is significant (x^2 13.7, 1df, p < .001).

Methods Used in Attempts

Not surprisingly, the most-used method, in 74.5 per cent of all cases (figure 4, p. 142), was overdose of medication. Women were significantly more likely to overdose (80.3 per cent) than men (65.6 per cent) (x^2 8.2, 1df, p < .01).

Cutting, the second most-frequent method, was used by 14.7 per cent of men and 9.9 per cent of women. The difference was significant (x^2 10.0, 1df, p < .01). Hanging, although occurring in much smaller numbers, was more likely to be chosen by men.

The medications taken by those who took an overdose are shown in figure 5, which shows the percentage of overdose cases using each form of medication, an average of 1.4 medications per overdose. Analgesics (primarily acetami-

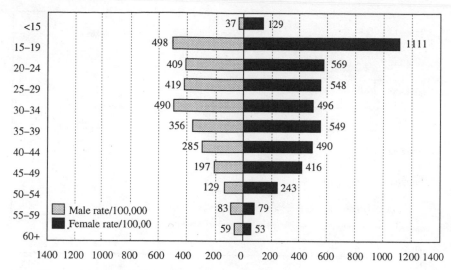

Note: Rates are based on Edmonton population data, 1993.

Figure 2 Edmonton parasuicides: Person rates/100,000/year, by age and sex

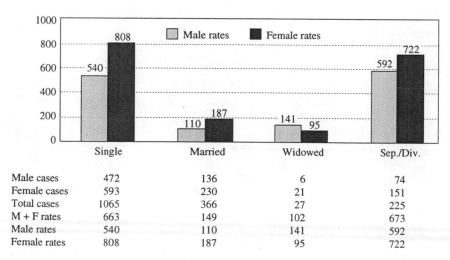

	Single	Married	Widowed	Sep./Div.
Male cases	472	136	6	74
Female cases	593	230	21	151
Total cases	1065	366	27	225
M + F rates	663	149	102	673
Male rates	540	110	141	592
Female rates	808	187	95	722

Note: Based on 1993 Edmonton census data.

Figure 3 Edmonton parasuicides (persons): Rates/100,000/year, by marital status and sex, age 15+

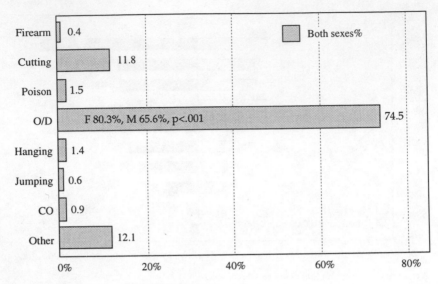

Note: 2029 methods were used by 1970 persons.

Figure 4 Parasuicide methods (percentage of cases using each method)

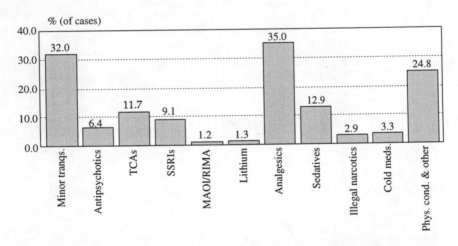

Note: A total of 2509 medications were taken in 1784 attempts (i.e., 1.4 per case). Percentages are of cases taking each medication and thus exceed 100%.

Figure 5   Edmonton parasuicides, overdose cases: percentage of cases taking each medication

nophen) are most commonly used, followed by minor tranquillizers. Sedatives (mostly of low lethal potential), accounted for 12.9 per cent. Among the antide-pressant overdose cases, 53 per cent used a potentially lethal tricyclic, and 47 per cent used a selective serotonin re-uptake inhibitor (SSRI) or monoamine oxidase inhibitor/reversible inhibitor monoamine oxidase A (MAOI/RIMA) (most by RIMA), of much lower lethal potential than tricyclics (figure 5).

Comparative and Standardized Data

The recent publication of results from the WHO/EURO multicentre study on parasuicide (Platt et al., 1992, Kerkhof et al., 1994) provides opportunities for comparison with the Edmonton data. The WHO/EURO study included sixteen centres, each of which collected parasuicide data in a defined population over several years (mostly 1989–92). Since the published data include age- and sex-specific rates, as well as the number of cases for most centres, detailed compar-isons are possible (Schmidtke et al., 1994; Platt, 1992). Although Schmidtke et al. (1994) provide standardized comparisons of the various European centres, this data is standardized to a European population structure. We used the 1988 post-censal population estimates provided by Statistics Canada to standardize by age and sex both the European-centres and Edmonton data to the Canadian population.

Overall Rates

Figure 6 shows the rates for Edmonton and the WHO/EURO centres for both sexes combined, age- and sex-standardized to the 1988 Canadian population, for ages 15 and over. Obviously, there is great variation in overall rates, and a 4.7 times difference between the highest (Edmonton) and lowest (Guipuzcoa). (Figure 7 shows the same data for each sex separately and arranged in order of overall rates.) Since in all centres, except Helsinki, rates for women are higher than for men, the female rates are more reflective of overall rates than are the male rates. Note that the rates given for Edmonton differ from those presented above, which were based on the Edmonton census population rather than the Canadian census population, and use the age bands available from the WHO/EURO publications.

Figure 8 shows the age-specific male and female rates for those aged 15 to 24 years. These are arranged in order of the overall, all-ages, and both-sexes rates. For both men and women the differences between highest and lowest rates vary 6.5 to 7 times, a larger variation than in the overall rates. Edmonton, with the highest overall rates, does however also have the highest rates for both men and

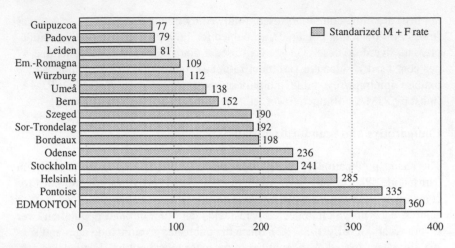

Notes: Data are from WHO/EURO multicentre study on parasuicide (Platt et al., 1992). Age and sex are standardized to 1988 population of Canada.

Figure 6 WHO/EURO parasuicide study and Edmonton: Rates/100,000/year, both sexes (persons), age 15+

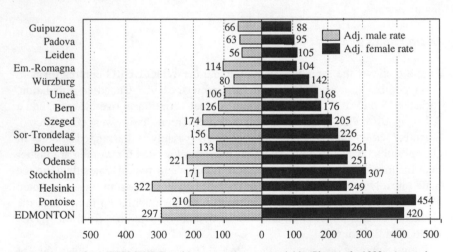

Notes: Data are from WHO/EURO multicentre study on parasuicide (Platt et al., 1992). Age and sex are standardized to 1988 population of Canada.

Figure 7 WHO/EURO parasuicide study and Edmonton: Rates/100,000/year, each sex (persons), age 15+ (ordered by overall rates)

women in this age group. This contrasts with rates found in the over-55 age group (figure 9), where Edmonton has lower-than-average rates for both men and women. Comparisons with age groups between 25 and 54 years shows higher rates in Edmonton persisting up to age 44, with some comparative decline between 45 and 54. Rates in Edmonton thus appear to be very high overall, especially high in young adults, and comparatively high in those born during and after the Second World War. Those born before this period have below-average rates compared to European centres.

Discussion

We previously reported a pilot study, with data collected in 1990–91 (Bland et al., 1994). The calculated parasuicide event rate was 448/100,000 per year. In this study our person rate was 376/100,000 per year. The event-to-person ratio was 1.2, which would give an event rate of 466, very close to that derived in the pilot study.

There are few studies in Canada where rates of attempted suicide are provided. The investigation in London, Ontario, in 1969–71 provided rates by age and sex that were somewhat lower than those that we report here for Edmonton (Jarvis et al., 1976). The overall rates in London were females 370, males 188/100,000/year. The pattern of high rates in young adults, and higher rates in women than in men, is consistent with the Edmonton study. Since the investigators in London went to considerable efforts to obtain case data from several sources (e.g., general practitioners), the rates may have been expected to be higher than those from hospital emergency departments only, as was the case in Edmonton.

Since we find very high parasuicide rates in Edmonton, methodological differences should be addressed. The Edmonton data derive solely from hospital emergency departments. No attempts were made to tap other possible treatment resources or to collect data on Edmonton residents treated outside Edmonton. The analyses of rates include only Edmonton residents. In the WHO/EURO study, inception methods for cases differed, and efforts were made to include all potential cases from different treatment resources depending on the local patterns of services. Thus, there may be a variable degree of under-reporting in all studies, despite attempts to overcome this, although the WHO/EURO centres consider that differences between centres do not result from methodological deficiencies.

The Edmonton findings of higher rates in women than in men are in general agreement with most other centres. The high rates found in the young are also found in other centres. Where Edmonton may differ is that exceptionally high

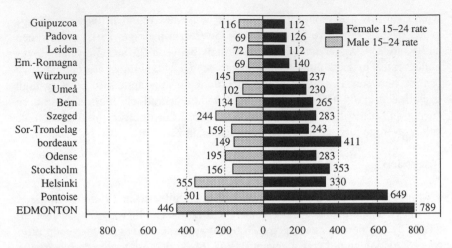

Note: Data is from WHO/EURO multicentre study on parasuicide (Platt S. et al., 1992; in order of overall rates).

Figure 8 WHO/EURO parasuicide study and Edmonton: Rates/100,000/year, each sex (persons), age 15–24

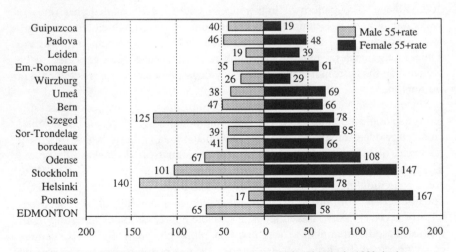

Note: Data is from WHO/EURO multicentre study on parasuicide (Platt et al., 1992; in descending order of overall rates).

Figure 9 WHO/EURO parasuicide study and Edmonton: Rates/100,000/year, each sex (persons), age 55+

rates are found in the young and only average comparative rates are found in older age groups. These findings cannot be explained on the basis of different population structures, since standardization does not much change the position of Edmonton as having exceptionally high overall rates.

There is no evidence of a decline in rates in the couple of years between the pilot study and the results reported here. Schmitdke et al. (1994) reported that in the WHO/EURO centres rates decreased between 1989 and 1991 by 14.4 per cent in females and 17.2 per cent in males, with all centres showing male decreases and 11 of 15 showing female decreases. Explanations for the decline in rates in European centres are not readily apparent.

The Edmonton findings on rates by marital status (figure 3), with much lower rates in the married and the widowed than in the single (never married) and divorced or separated groups, are quite similar to those from Oxford (Hawton et al., 1994), both in ranking and rates for each status. Most other centres (Hjelmeland and Bjerke, 1994; Bille-Brahe et al., 1994; Salander Renberg and Jacobsson, 1994; De Leo and Fantinato, 1994; Ostamo and Lonnqvist, 1994; Batt et al., 1994) do not show such a marked difference between the married and never married as do Oxford and Edmonton, but do show the highest rates in the divorced or separated.

Data on methods used for attempted suicide is provided for seven WHO/ EURO centres (Kerkhof, 1994). Overdose is the most frequent method in all centres, and is used by a low of 53 per cent of women in Bern and by a high of 90.9 per cent of men in Helsinki. Thus, the Edmonton proportions of 65.6 per cent of men and 80.3 per cent of women using this method fall well within the range. Cutting (using a sharp or blunt object) is the second-most-frequent method. With the exception of Umeå, higher rates are reported in men than in women, and vary from over 20 per cent of cases in Umeå (men and women) to 5.4 per cent of women in Sor Trondelag. Again, the Edmonton rates are mid-range. Rates of firearm use, hanging, and jumping are not reported separately for many centres. For all of these the rates are higher for men than for women, and such methods are used by fewer than 10 per cent of cases, except in Bern, where rates are higher. Combining these, Edmonton actually has fairly low rates of such 'hard methods.'

For the overdose cases (figure 4) there are some differences from the medication frequencies reported in our pilot study, with some decline in the use of analgesics and tricyclic antidepressants of high lethality, whereas the use of SSRI antidepressants, of low lethality, as a percentage of all cases has remained constant. The use of sedatives, minor tranquillizers, and illegal narcotics has changed little, but the frequency of antipsychotic use has declined by two-thirds. Also notable is that the number of medications taken by each overdose

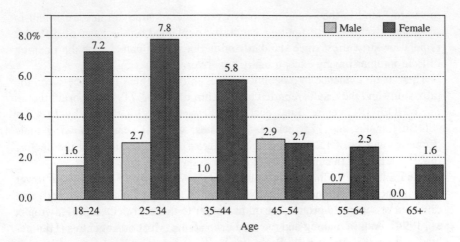

Source: Dyck et al., 1988

Figure 10 Lifetime prevalence of suicide attempts by age and sex

case shows a decline from 1.9 to 1.4. These changes, particularly the less-frequent use of more lethal substances and fewer medications per case, may be related to the lower admission rate to an in-patient bed, from 30.2 per cent of cases in our pilot study to 20.2 per cent in the present study.

The methods used by parasuicides must be contrasted with those used by persons who complete suicide. For Canada (1989) these methods were as follows: firearms 30.9 per cent, hanging 29.2 per cent, overdose 15.3 per cent, CO poisoning 10.2 per cent, and other methods 14.3 per cent. Obviously, overdose is not the predominant method in the completers. Probably owing to a lack of availability of barbiturates, overdose has dropped from 20 per cent in 1974–6 to 15 per cent in 1989–91.

High parasuicide rates in younger age groups found in Edmonton, compared to other centres, tend to be confirmed by an earlier population study in Edmonton (Dyck et al., 1988) (figure 10), in which lifetime rates for suicide attempts by age group for each sex showed, especially for women, higher rates in those aged 18 to 44 than in older ages. It should be noted that the Edmonton lifetime rate (both sexes) was 3.6 per cent, entirely consistent with the middle of the range reported from the ten studies reviewed by Angst et al. (1992). Since lifetime rates are cumulative, if the rates had remained constant as each age group ages, then the highest lifetime rates should be found in the elderly, which is clearly not the case, thus arguing for increasing rates in more recent birth cohorts.

Causes for particular concern in Edmonton include the high rates, especially among the young, an apparent increased rate in those who are young now compared to older persons when they were young, with no decline in recent years as experienced in most European centres. The apparent decrease in the number of medications taken by overdose cases, with more frequent use of less lethal versus more highly lethal substances, accompanied by a lower rate of admission to in-patient status, suggest that some changes may be occurring. It is difficult to interpret the apparent protected status of the married and widowed, compared to the single and separated/divorced. It may be speculated that those who maintain married status tend to have more stable personalities, and that the high rates in the single group are at least partly accounted for by the comparative youthfulness of this group, that is, there is an interaction between age and marital status.

The lack of simple epidemiological data on suicidal behaviour in Canada is difficult to understand. The costs of such behaviours are obviously high; the social, personal, and family disruption and distress may be even higher. The apparent trend towards increasing suicidal behaviours in late adolescence and early adulthood should be a major concern, since opportunities are available for preventive action at the population health level. The basic methodology to measure change over time or before and after a public-health intervention is clearly available, but is not being used.

ACKNOWLEDGMENTS

Alberta Mental Health Research Fund; National Health Research Development Program; Medical-Records and Emergency-Department staff of University of Alberta Hospitals, Royal Alexandra Hospital, Charles Camsell Hospital, Grey Nuns Hospital, and Misericordia Hospital.

REFERENCES

Angst, J., M. Degonda, and C. Ernst. 1992. 'The Zurich Study: XV Suicide Attempts in a Cohort from Age 20–30.' *European Archives of Psychiatry and Clinical Neuroscience* 242: 135–41.

Batt, A., C., Depoivre, F. Eudier, et al. 1994. 'The Epidemiology of Parasuicide in Brittany, 1990.' In Kerkhof, Schmidtke, Bille-Brahe, De Leo, and Lonnqvist, eds, *Attempted Suicide in Europe*, 245–52.

Bille-Brahe, U., W. Hanse, L. Kolmos, et al. 1985. 'Attempted Suicide in Denmark (I).' *Acta Psychiatrica Scandinavica* 71: 217–26.

Bille-Brahe, U., G. Jessen, E. Nielsen, et al. 1994. 'Attempted Suicide in a Danish Region, 1989–1992.' In Kerkhof, Schmidtke, Bille-Brahe, De Leo, and J. Lonnqvist, eds, *Attempted Suicide in Europe*, 35–51.

Bland, R.C., S.C. Newman, and R.J. Dyck. 1994. 'The Epidemiology of Parasuicide in Edmonton.' *Canadian Journal of Psychiatry* 39: 391–6.

De Leo, D., and S. Fantinato. 1994. 'The Epidemiology of Attempted Suicide in Padua, 1989–

1991.' In Kerkhof, Schmidtke, Bille-Brahe, De Leo, and Lonnqvist, eds, *Attempted Suicide in Europe*, 107–19.

Dyck, R.J., R.C. Bland, S.C. Newman, and H. Orn 1988. 'Suicide Attempts and Psychiatric Disorders in Edmonton.' *Acta Psychiatrica Scandinavica* 77 (Suppl. 338): 64–71.

Hawton, K., J. Fagg, S. Simkin, and J. Mills. 1994. 'The Epidemiology of Attempted Suicide in the Oxford Area, England 1989–1992.' In Kerkhof, Schmidtke, Bille-Brahe, De Leo, and Lonnqvist, eds, *Attempted Suicide in Europe*, 189–207.

Hjelmeland, H., and T. Bjerke 1994. 'The Epidemiology of Parasuicide in Sr-Trndelag, 1989–1991.' In Kerkhof, Schmidtke, Bille-Brahe, De Leo, and Lonnqvist, eds, *Attempted Suicide in Europe*, 17–33.

Jarvis, G. K., R.G. Ferrence, F.G. Johnson, and P.C. Whitehead. 1976. 'Sex and Age Patterns in Self-Injury.' *Journal of Health and Social Behaviour* 17: 146–55.

Kerkhof, A.J.F.M., A. Schmidtke, U. Bille-Brahe, D. De Leo, and J. Lonnquist, eds. 1994. *Attempted Suicide in Europe*. Leiden, Netherlands: WHO and DSWO Press.

Kreitman, N., A.E. Philip, S. Greer, and C.R. Bagley. 1969. 'Parasuicide.' *British Journal of Psychiatry* 115: 746–47.

Ostamo, A., and J. Lönnqvist. 1994. 'The Epidemiology of Attempted Suicide in Helsinki, 1989–1991.' In Kerkhof, Schmidtke, Bille-Brahe, De Leo, and J. Lonnqvist, eds, *Attempted Suicide in Europe*, 137–58.

Platt, S., U. Bille-Brahe, A. Kerkhof, et al. 1992. 'Parasuicide in Europe: The WHO/EURO Multicentre Study on Parasuicide. I. Introduction and Preliminary Analysis for 1989.' *Acta Psychiatrica Scandinavica* 85: 97–104.

Rygnestad, T.K. 1982. 'Prospective Study of Social and Psychiatric Aspects in Self-Poisoned Patients.' *Acta Psychiatrica Scandinavica* 66: 139–53.

Salander Renberg, E., and L. Jacobsson 1994. 'Parasuicide in Västerbotten County, Umeå, 1989–1991.' In Kerkhof, Schmidtke, Bille-Brahe, De Leo, Lonnqvist, eds, *Attempted Suicide in Europe,* 87–105.

Schmidtke, A., U. Bille-Brahe, D. De Leo, and A. Kerkhof et al. 1994. 'Rates and Trends of Attempted Suicide in Europe 1989–1992.' In Kerkhof, Schmidtke, Bille-Brahe, D. De Leo, and Lonnqvist, eds, *Attempted Suicide in Europe,* 209–29.

Wasserman, D. 1988. 'Separation: An Important Factor in Suicidal Actions.' *Crisis* 9: 49–63.

Weissman, M.M. 1974. 'The Epidemiology of Suicide Attempts, 1960 to 1971.' *Archives of General Psychiatry* 30: 737–46.

Wexler, L., M.M. Weissman, and S.V. Kasl. 1978. 'Suicide Attempts 1970–75: Updating a United States Study and Comparisons with International Trends.' *British Journal of Psychiatry* 132: 180–5.

WHO Summary Report, Working Group on Preventive Practices in Suicide and Attempted Suicide. 1986. York, England. September, 22–6.

Willox, D.G.A. 1985. 'Self Poisoning: A Review of Patients Seen in the Victoria Infirmary, Glasgow.' *Scottish Medical Journal* 30: 220–4.

8

Correlates of Suicidal Ideation: Personal Variables, Stress, and Social Support

ANTON F. DE MAN

There is but one true philosophical problem and this is suicide: Judging whether life is or is not worth living amounts to answering the fundamental question of philosophy.

Camus, 1960: 11

Scope of the Problem

It appears that many youths and adults in Canada would agree with Camus's observation. Over the past decades there has been a significant rise in the number of suicides to the extent that suicide now ranks among the major causes of death.

A particularly perplexing development has been the alarming increase in suicides among young adults, adolescents, and even children. It has been estimated that each year in Canada some seven hundred young people between the ages of fifteen and twenty-four, and some twenty-five to thirty children under the age of fifteen take their lives (Canadian Association for Suicide Prevention, 1994).

At the other end of the lifespan, the suicide rates for the elderly, which remained fairly stable between 1960 and 1980, have since been on the increase. The rate of completed suicides among seniors between the ages of seventy-five and eighty is now as high as that for young adults in the twenty to twenty-four age bracket (National Task Force, 1987; Statistics Canada, 1990).

Official statistics already indicate that suicide is a problem, but the problem may in fact be greater than is suggested by these figures. The numbers probably underestimate the actual incidence of suicide, because only obvious self-inflicted deaths are included. Many apparent accidental deaths (e.g., drug overdoses, car accidents, drownings, etc.) may in fact be concealed suicides that consequently will not appear in the official statistics.

The seriousness of the problem of suicidal behaviour becomes even more apparent when one considers suicide attempts and suicidal ideation. Conservative estimates suggest that for every completed suicide there are four to ten unsuccessful attempts (Charron, 1981; Morisette, 1984). Health and Welfare Canada (National Task Force, 1987) proposed ratios of 12:1 for men and 45:1 for women. The Canadian Association for Suicide Prevention (1994) reported that per year some 70,000 to 100,000 young people attempt suicide to varying degrees. Besides the people who successfully commit suicide and those who make unsuccessful attempts, there are countless others who are troubled by suicidal thoughts. For instance, suicide has been found to be a personal concern for many high school and college students (e.g., Côté et al., 1989; Tousignant et al., 1988). In fact, the suicidal-ideation rates for fifteen to twenty-four year olds are almost double those of other age groups (Emond et al., 1988). But it is not only the younger ones who entertain suicidal thoughts; the elderly also often think about and carefully plan their demise (Achte, 1988).

Community Concern and Need for Information

In light of these alarming statistics, many mental-health professionals, teachers, parents, and others who deal with suicide and the circumstances that lead to it wish to know what can be done to counter these developments. They want information about antecedent factors and about what actions they can take in terms of primary prevention. Professionals and community volunteers involved in intervention and postvention similarly want to know on what aspects they should focus when a person is in a suicidal crisis or what they should do to effect a change in the individual's attitude towards life and death once the crisis has passed.

Farberow and Litman (1970) noted that suicidal people are not a homogeneous group, but may in fact be classified in three categories. Each of these categories reflects a different level of suicidal intent and requires a different type of intervention.

The first category comprises a relatively small group of people who seemingly wish to die. They generally do not communicate their distress and give little or no warning of their intention. The means they use to commit suicide tend to be more violent, and they arrange the situation in such a way that intervention is not really possible. Any assistance one might hope to give these individuals in dealing with suicide and the factors that contribute to it has to be provided at the prevention level.

The second, and larger, category includes those who appear to be ambivalent about dying and seem to leave the question of life and death to chance. Their attitude seems to be, 'If I die, the conflict is settled, but if I am rescued that is what is meant to be' (Carson and Butcher, 1992). They usually talk about their troubles, and generally use methods that, though often dangerous, are slow acting, thereby allowing the possibility of intervention.

The third and largest group involves people who do not really want to die, but instead wish to communicate their distress in a dramatic way. They generally choose non-lethal methods and arrange the attempt in such a way that intervention by others is almost inevitable.

The individuals in categories two and three, unlike those in category one, communicate their distress and their ambivalence about death, and at the same time are soliciting the help of others. Because they do not keep their intentions to themselves but rather send out warning messages, intervention may be possible. In order to be able to successfully provide assistance in those cases, a good understanding of suicidal ideation and associated risk factors and warning signs is needed.

Factors in Suicidal Ideation

Because suicide attempts and completed suicides logically are preceded by suicidal ideation (Beck et al., 1979), one may assume that an identification of true predictors of suicidal ideation may lead to a better understanding of suicidal intent and risk. Such an understanding in turn may lead to better approaches to prevention, intervention, and postvention.

Charron (1981) suggested that suicidal ideation is a function of *personal characteristics*, *negative life experiences*, and *social support*. Her suggestion integrates demographic, sociocultural, sociological, and psychological factors. She postulated that certain personal characteristics by themselves or in combination with stressful life events may increase the risk of suicide. These factors may lead to an existential crisis where the individual questions the purpose of his or her existence and the meaning of life. The outcome of this crisis depends to a large extent on the person's social support network: if the individual receives adequate support, the crisis may be resolved; if support is not available, inadequate, or not sought, the person may contemplate suicide.

Personal Characteristics

Over the years, research has identified many personal characteristics that appear to be directly or indirectly related to suicidal behaviour. What follows is a review of some of the more salient ones; a more extensive account may be found in David Lester's (1992) book *Why People Kill Themselves*.

Statistics indicate that suicidal behaviour varies with age. Even allowing for systematic under-reporting, suicide is still uncommon in children under the age of sixteen (Brooksbank, 1985); however, as adolescents get older there is an increase in suicidal ideation (De Man, Leduc, and Labrèche-Gauthier, 1993b; Emond et al., 1988). Among adults, the highest suicide rates are found among young adult males and males over the age of sixty-five (Statistics Canada, 1990).

Furthermore, there are gender differences. Men and women differ in terms of suicidal ideation, the number of attempted and completed suicides, and the manner in which they commit suicide. During adolescence, suicidal thinking seems to be more prevalent among girls (Côté et al., 1989; De Man, Leduc, and Labrèche-Gauthier, 1993a); moreover, girls make attempts more often (Corbeil, 1984; Côté et al., 1989; Tousignant et al., 1988). Boys, by contrast, lead in the number of completed suicides (Sommer, 1984). These gender differences continue throughout the lifespan: adult women have more suicidal ideation and make more attempts, whereas men tend to complete suicide more often (Charron, 1981; National Task Force, 1987; Statistics Canada, 1990). Men and women also differ in terms of the method they choose to commit suicide. Men generally select highly lethal methods such as firearms, whereas women tend to opt for poisonous substances.

Variation in suicidal behaviour has been found to be associated with religious affiliation and perceived level of religiousness. Religious taboos with respect to suicide undoubtedly play an important role in suicidal thinking. Indeed, there is a lower incidence of suicide among people whose religion emphatically disapproves of suicide (Carson and Butcher, 1992). With respect to relative religiousness, De Man et al. (1987) noted that people who perceive themselves as less religious than others report greater suicidal ideation.

Several mental-health variables have been found to be related to suicidal tendencies. Many suicidal people have problems in terms of their perception of self. Individuals who threaten or attempt suicide usually have a negative self-image and low self-esteem (Cole et al., 1993; Dukes and Lorch, 1989). Adolescents and adult men and women with suicidal ideation often report feelings of self-depreciation and low self-esteem (De Man, Leduc, and Labrèche-Gauthier, 1993a; De Man et al., 1987; Bagley, 1975). In the elderly, changes in social status and roles due to retirement, and age-related changes in physical ability and appearance, may lead to a decrease in self-esteem and an increase in suicidal tendency (Achte, 1988; Osgood, 1992).

The belief that one lacks control over the outcomes of one's life (external locus of control) has also been cited as a correlate of suicidal thinking (e.g., Lester, 1989). Adolescents in particular, who feel that they cannot personally influence what happens to them and who believe that life is determined by chance, luck, or powerful others, tend to report greater suicidal ideation (De Man, Leduc, and Labrèche-Gauthier, 1993a). Similarly, young adults with suicidal ideation tend to be more external in locus of control than those without such thoughts (Goldney et al., 1989).

People who think about committing suicide generally suffer from relatively greater anxiety and tend to psychologically turn away from the external world. Colson (1972), Irfani (1978), and Lester (1987) found that suicide ideators are more neurotic and introverted than their peers who are free of such thoughts.

Compared to the general population, a higher percentage of depressed people who die do so from suicide (Guze and Robins, 1970). Many investigations have found a relationship between depression and suicidal behaviour in adolescents (e.g., Côté et al., 1989; Davidson and Choquet, 1981; De Man, Leduc, and Labrèche-Gauthier, 1993a; Lamontagne et al., 1986; Sommer, 1984), although the reported percentage of affected adolescents varies from study to study. Vandivort and Locker (1979) found higher levels of depression among urban adults who reported suicidal ideation. In the elderly, the culmination of losses and changes as a result of retirement and aging frequently results in depression that, if severe enough, may place them at risk for suicide (Atchley, 1991). Depression is more common among the elderly than among any other age group (Kirsling, 1986); it appears to be the underlying cause for the majority of late-life suicides (Bongar, 1992).

Alcohol and other drug use are often cited as correlates of adolescent suicidal behaviour (e.g., Corbeil, 1984; Simon, 1991; Tousignant et al., 1988). Dukes and Lorch (1989) found that suicidal ideation in adolescents is related to alcohol use, but not to drug use, whereas De Man, Leduc, and Labrèche-Gauthier (1993a) reported associations between suicidal ideation and alcohol and drug use. Alcohol abuse is considered to be a major precipitating factor in geriatric suicide (Osgood, 1992); the elderly who abuse alcohol are more likely to attempt suicide compared to those who consume little or no alcohol (Templer and Cappelletty, 1986).

Negative Life Experiences

In life there are many unusual and threatening experiences that place stress on the individual. The conditions that cause stress may be of a physical, social, or psychological nature. However, for most people, the principal causes of stress are – disregarding medical problems for the moment – socio-psychological in nature.

The actual degree of stress one experiences depends in part on (1) the characteristics of the conditions that cause the stress (e.g., perceived importance and severity, predictability, duration, multiplicity of demands), (2) the characteristics of the person (i.e., situations that one person finds highly stressful may be only mildly stressful or non-stressful to another), and (3) the context in which the stress occurs (i.e., if one lacks personal or material support, stress may be experienced as more severe).

If stress is too severe for a person's coping ability, or if the individual believes this to be the case, then it can be damaging. Because stress is a state of body and mind, the effects may be physiological and/or psychological in nature. Suicidal ideation is an example of the latter.

Several studies have found that suicidal ideation in adolescents is related to recent stressful events (e.g., De Man, Leduc, and Labrèche-Gauthier, 1993a; Dubow et al., 1989). Some of these stressful experiences have their origin in the structure and functioning of the youngsters' families. Suicidal behaviour has been observed in children from single-parent families where one of the elders is absent because of death, divorce, or separation (e.g., Davidson and Choquet, 1981; Garfinkel et al., 1982; Husain and Vandimer, 1984; Lamontagne et al., 1986; Simon, 1991; Tousignant et al., 1988). Furthermore, suicidal ideation has been found to be related to disturbed, hostile intra-familial relationships (Kosky et al., 1986), and to child abuse (Brooksbank, 1985; De Man, Leduc, and Labrèche-Gauthier, 1993a; Hendin, 1987).

Suicidal adolescents usually have problems at school (Husain and Vandimer, 1984; Pronovost et al., 1990). Their academic performance often is poor (Gispert et al., 1985) and their level of absenteeism higher than average (Garfinkel and Golombek, 1983). Although these youngsters frequently are above average in intelligence, they underachieve academically because of problems in their personal lives (Husain and Vandimer, 1984).

Barraclough (1971) suggested that medical problems play a role in precipitating suicidal behaviour. Hypochondriasis, chronic illness, recent surgery, and even childbirth are associated to risk. The psychological factor that appears to be shared by those facing such stressors is a sense of hopelessness. Many feel that there is no solution to the medical problem and that suicide is the only way out. Chronic severe pain, debilitating disease, and diagnosis of terminal illness have been associated with suicidal behaviour among the elderly (Horton-Deutsch et al., 1992; McIntosh, 1985). Zantra et al. (1989) noted that elderly men and women who report health problems also suffer from higher levels of anxiety, psychological distress, and suicidal ideation than their peers with fewer health concerns.

Late-life suicide is often traced to several negative occurrences and circumstances rather than one isolated problem (Templer and Cappelletty, 1986). Stressors commonly experienced by the elderly include changes in financial situation brought about by retirement (McIntosh, 1985; Osgood, 1992) and the expectation of nursing-home placement, especially if it involves separation from a spouse (Loebel et al., 1981). Bereavement also increases the risk of suicide in this age group, particularly among men (Kirsling, 1986; Templer and Cappelletty, 1986).

Social Support

Charron (1981) noted that suicide is not so much the outcome of pressure, as of pressure without social support. Indeed, lack of support makes a given stress more severe and undermines a person's coping ability. Negative life events are experienced as more debilitating if one is left feeling alone than if one is surrounded by people who genuinely care. It is therefore not surprising that individuals who are exposed to stressful situations tend to turn to others for support. Unfortunately, some people have no family or friends, or they do have family and friends, but the latter are unwilling to help, or reject them. In cases where communication between the stressed individual and others has been broken off or does not really exist, the potential for suicidal behaviour will increase.

Social support is often found within the family. This may explain the fact that suicide has been shown to be inversely related to family size. People with children generally have lower rates of completed suicides than those who are childless (Danigelis and Pope, 1979). Family structure is also associated with suicidal behaviour. Suicide rates for widowed, separated, divorced, or single men and women are higher than for married people (Danigelis and Pope, 1979). The highest rates are found among those who are separated or divorced. The rates for singles are higher than those for married individuals, but considerably lower than those for the separated, divorced, or widowed. Among the widowed, elderly men in particular are a high-risk group (Glass and Reed, 1993; Templer and Cappelletty, 1986).

Suicidal ideation in adolescents has been found to be associated with the feeling that there is no one to whom one can turn for help (Bagley, 1975). They perceive the support they receive from their parents as insufficient (De Man, Labrèche-Gauthier, and Leduc, 1993). They often feel lonely (Kirkpatrick-Smith et al., 1989) and experience a sense of anomie (De Man, Leduc, and Labrèche-Gauthier, 1993a). Adult suicide attempters are less likely to be married and more likely to be socially isolated, interpersonally alienated (Humphrey et al., 1971), and less socially involved (Nelson et al., 1977). Elderly male suicides are less likely to have a person they can confide in, and visit friends and relatives less often (Miller, 1978). Elderly men tend to rely solely on their spouse for emotional support, whereas elderly women seek support from their spouse, children, or friends. It has been found that the proportion of elderly men who report that they will not seek support from anyone is more than twice as high as that found for women (McDaniel, 1993).

Concluding Comments

The first task of an integrated theory of suicidal ideation is to identify the variables that play a role in the evolution of the problem. Although this is still an ongoing process at present, progress has been made in this respect. Research findings reported in the literature suggest that Charron's (1981) assumption that suicidal thinking is a function of personal characteristics, negative life experiences, and social support has merit. Many personal, stress, and social-support variables have been identified as potential predictors of suicidal ideation. These include demographic factors (e.g., age, gender, religion), internal factors that may be found in the personality or physical circumstances of suicidal ideators (e.g., identity, self-image, self-esteem, locus of control, anxiety, introversion, depression, threat perception, coping ability, drug use, physical health), and external factors that exist in the person's own milieu (e.g., family, school, friends) or in society in general (e.g., the status of seniors). Few, if any, of these variables operate independently; rather, they form a conglomerate of factors that interact and contribute to suicidal thinking; hence, suicidal ideation is a multivariate phenomenon.

Because suicidal people are not a homogeneous group, many paths leading to suicidal ideation may be identified within this conglomerate of factors. However, although each person will follow his or her own path, it may be possible to distinguish routes that are followed more often, thereby bringing some structure to the network of factors. To discover these main routes is the second task of an integrated theory.

Some progress has been made in this respect too. For instance, De Man, Leduc, and Labrèche-Gauthier (1992) have reported that suicidal ideation in adolescents appears to be primarily related to low self-esteem, depression, negative stress, and dissatisfaction with social support, whereas in adults the emphasis seems to be on low self-esteem and negative stress. The authors have suggested that suicide-intervention programs may have to focus on different aspects when they are dealing with adolescent and adult ideators.

Notwithstanding such promising initial findings, it must be concluded that suicidal-ideation theory is still in its infancy as far as the discovery and description of the more salient features are concerned.

REFERENCES

Achte, K. 1988. 'Suicide Tendencies in the Elderly.' *Suicide and Life-Threatening Behavior* 18: 55–65.

Atchley, R.C. 1991. *Social Forces and Aging: An Introduction to Social Gerontology.* Belmont, CA: Wadsworth.

Bagley, C. 1975. 'Suicidal Behaviour and Suicidal Ideation in Adolescents.' *British Journal of Guidance and Counseling* 3: 190–208.

Barraclough, B. 1971. 'Suicide in the Elderly.' In D. Kay and A. Walk, eds, *Recent Developments in Psychogeriatrics*, 87–97. London: RMPA.

Beck, A.T., M. Kovacs, and A. Weissman. 1979. 'Assessment of Suicidal Intention: The Scale for Suicide Ideation.' *Journal of Consulting and Clinical Psychology* 47: 343–52.

Bongar, B. 1992. *Suicide: Guidelines for Assessment, Management and Treatment.* New York: Oxford University Press.

Brooksbank, D.J. 1985. 'Suicide and Parasuicide in Childhood and Early Adolescence.' *British Journal of Psychiatry* 146: 459–63.

Camus, A. 1960. *The Myth of Sisyphus.* London: Hamish Hamilton.

Canadian Association for Suicide Prevention. 1994. *Recommendations for Suicide Prevention in Schools.* Calgary: CASP.

Carson, R.C., and J.N. Butcher. 1992. *Abnormal Psychology and Modern Life.* New York: Harper-Collins.

Charron, M.F. 1981. *Le suicide au Québec, analyse statistique.* Québec: Ministère des Affaires Sociales.

Cole, D.E., H.O. Protinsky, and L.H. Cross. 1993. 'An Empirical Investigation of Adolescent Suicidal Ideation.' *Adolescence* 27: 813–18.

Colson, C. 1972. 'Neuroticism, Extraversion and Repression-Sensitization in Suicidal College Students.' *British Journal of Social and Clinical Psychology* 11: 88–99.

Corbeil, S. 1984. 'Suicide et adolescence.' In P. Morisette, ed., *Le suicide, démystification, intervention, prévention*, 272–306. Québec: Garotex.

Côté, L., J. Pronovost, and C. Ross. 1989. *Etude sur la prévalence des comportements suicidaires chez les adolescents de la région 04: Faits saillants.* Shawinigan, PQ: Département de santé communautaire.

Danigelis, N., and W. Pope. 1979. 'Durkheim's Theory of Suicide as Applied to the Family.' *Social Forces* 57: 1081–1106.

Davidson, F., and M. Choquet. 1981. *Le suicide de l'adolescent, étude épidémiologique.* Paris: Les Editions ESF.

De Man, A.F., S. Balkou, and R.I. Iglesias. 1987. 'Social Support and Suicidal Ideation in French-Canadians.' *Canadian Journal of Behavioural Science* 19: 342–6.

De Man, A.F., L. Labrèche-Gauthier, and C.P. Leduc. 1993. 'Parent-Child Relationships and Suicidal Ideation in French-Canadian Adolescents. *Journal of Genetic Psychology* 154: 17–23.

De Man, A.F., C.P. Leduc, and L. Labrèche-Gauthier. 1992. 'Correlates of Suicide Ideation in French-Canadian Adults and Adolescents.' *Journal of Clinical Psychology* 48: 811–16.

– 1993a. 'Correlates of Suicidal Ideation in French-Canadian Adolescents: Personal Variables, Stress, and Social Support.' *Adolescence* 28: 819–30.

– 1993b. 'A French-Canadian Scale for Suicide Ideation for Use with Adolescents.' *Canadian Journal of Behavioural Science* 25: 126–34.

Dubow, E.F., D.F. Kausch, M.C. Blum, and J. Reed. 1989. 'Correlates of Suicidal Ideation and

Attempts in a Community Sample of Junior High and High School Students.' *Journal of Clinical Child Psychology* 18: 158–66.

Dukes, R.L., and B.D. Lorch. 1989. 'The Effects of School, Family, Self-Concept, and Deviant Behaviour on Adolescent Suicide.' *Journal of Adolescence* 12: 239–51.

Emond, A., L. Guyon, T. Camirand, L. Shenard, R. Pineault, and Y. Robitaille. 1988. *Et la santé, ça va? Rapport de l'enquête Santé Québec* vol. 1. Québec: Les Publications du Québec.

Farberow, N.L., and R.E. Litman. 1970. *A Comprehensive Suicide Prevention Program*. Suicide Prevention Center of Los Angeles, 1958–69. Unpublished final report, DHEW NIMH grants no. MH 14946 & MH 00128. Los Angeles.

Garfinkel, B.D., A. Froese, and J. Hood. 1982. 'Suicide Attempts in Children and Adolescents.' *American Journal of Psychiatry* 139: 1257–61.

Garfinkel, B.D., and G.H. Golombek. 1983. 'Suicidal Behaviour in Adolescence.' In B.D. Garfinkel, and G.H. Golombek, eds, *The Adolescent and Mood Disturbance*, 189–217. New York: International University Press.

Gispert, M., K. Wheeler, L. Marsh, and M.S. Davis. 1985. 'Suicidal Adolescents: Factors in Evaluation.' *Adolescence* 20: 753–62.

Glass, J.C., and S.E. Reed. 1993. 'To Live or Die: A Look at Elderly Suicide.' *Educational Gerontology* 19: 767–78.

Goldney, R.D., A.H. Winefield, M. Tiggeman, H. Winefield, and S. Smith. 1989. 'Suicidal Ideation in a Young Adult Population.' *Acta Psychiatrica Scandinavica* 79: 481–9.

Guze, S.B., and E. Robins. 1970. 'Suicide and Primary Affective Disorders.' *British Journal of Psychiatry* 117: 437–83.

Hendin, H. 1987. 'Youth Suicide: A Psychosocial Perspective.' *Suicide and Life-Threatening Behaviour* 17: 151–65.

Horton-Deutsch, S., D. Clark, and C. Farran. 1992. 'Chronic Dyspnea and Suicide in Elderly Men.' *Hospital and Community Psychiatry* 43: 1198–1203.

Humphrey, J., D. Niswander, and T. Casey. 1971. 'A Comparison of Suicide Thinkers and Attempters.' *Diseases of the Nervous System* 32: 825–30.

Husain, S.A., and T. Vandimer. 1984. *Suicide in Children and Adolescents*. New York: Medical and Scientific Books.

Irfani, S. 1978. 'Personality Correlates of Suicidal Tendencies among Iranian and Turkish Students.' *Journal of Psychology* 99: 151–3.

Kirkpatrick-Smith, K., A. Rich, R. Bonner, and F. Jans. 1989. 'Substance Abuse and Suicidal Ideation among Adolescents.' In D. Lester, ed., *Suicide '89*, 90–1. Denver, CO: AAS.

Kirsling, R.A. 1986. 'Review of Suicide among Elderly Persons.' *Psychological Reports* 59: 359–66.

Kosky, R., S. Silburn, and S. Zubrick. 1986. 'Symptomatic Depression and Suicidal Ideation: A Comparative Study with 628 Children.' *Journal of Nervous and Mental Disease* 174: 523–8.

Lamontagne, Y., R. Elie, M. Belisle, A. Duchastel, M. Marseille, and G. Mercure. 1986. 'Suicide et dépression chez les étudiants de cégep.' *Union Médicale du Canada* 115: 522–7.

Lester, D. 1987. 'Suicidal Preoccupation and Dysthemia in College Students.' *Psychological Reports* 61: 762.

– 1989. 'Locus of Control, Depression and Suicidal Ideation.' *Perceptual and Motor Skills* 69: 1158.

– 1992. *Why People Kill Themselves*. Springfield, IL: Charles C. Thomas.

Loebel, J.P., J.S. Loebel, S. Dager, B. Centerwall, and D. Reay. 1981. 'Anticipation of Nursing Home Placement May Be a Precipitant of Suicide among the Elderly.' *Journal of American Geriatrics Society* 39: 407–8.

McDaniel, S. 1993. 'Emotional Support and Family Contacts of Older Canadians.' *Canadian Social Trends* (Spring): 30–3.

McIntosh, J. 1985. 'Suicide among the Elderly: Levels and Trends.' *American Journal of Orthopsychiatry* 55: 288–93.

Miller, M. 1978. 'Geriatric Suicide.' *Gerontology* 18: 488–95.

Morisette, P. 1984. *Le suicide: Démystification, intervention, prévention.* Québec: Garotex.

National Task Force on Suicide. 1987. *Suicide in Canada: Report of the National Task Force on Suicide in Canada.* Ottawa: Department of National Health and Welfare.

Nelson, V., E. Nielsen, and K. Chicketts. 1977. 'Interpersonal Attitudes of Suicidal Individuals.' *Psychological Reports* 40: 983–9.

Osgood, N. 1992. 'Suicide in the Elderly: Etiology and Assessment.' *International Review of Psychiatry* 4: 217–23.

Pronovost, J., J. Boucher, and L. Côté. 1990. 'Fonctionnement scolaire chez les adolescents à tendances suicidaires.' *Apprentissage et Socialisation* 13: 111–20.

Simon, R. 1991. *Enquête sur les comportements et idéations suicidaires des élèves de 3e, 4e et 5e secondaire de la région 02.* Chicoutimi, PQ: Centre de Prévention du Suicide 02.

Sommer, B. 1984. 'The Troubled Teen: Suicide, Drug Use, and Running Away.' *Women and Health* 9: 117–41.

Statistics Canada. 1990. *Health Reports. Mortality: Summary List of Causes in 1988.* Ottawa: Author.

Templer, D., and G. Cappelletty. 1986. 'Suicide in the Elderly: Assessment and Intervention.' *Clinical Gerontologist* 5: 475–87.

Tousignant, M., S. Hamel and M. Bastien. 1988. 'Structure familiale, relations parents-enfants et conduites suicidaires à l'école secondaire.' *Santé Mentale au Québec* 13: 70–93.

Vandivort, D.S., and B.Z. Locker. 1979. 'Suicide Ideation.' *Suicide and Life-Threatening Behavior* 9: 205–18.

Zantra, A.J., B.M. Maxwell, and J.W. Reich. 1989. 'Relationship among Physical Impairment, Distress and Well-Being in Older Adults.' *Journal of Behavioral Medicine* 12: 543–57.

PART IV: FIRST NATIONS AND INUIT

Suicide rates among the Aboriginal population in some areas of Canada run six to seven times the national average. Rates are particularly high among males fifteen to twenty-four years of age. But the tabular data reveal only part of the overall picture. Related to these data are multiple issues. There is, for example, a tremendous amount of social pain. There was/is, as an even more traumatic event, a cultural genocide. When people are long oppressed, their response often turns to suicide.

The Inuit have a particularly high rate of suicide among Aboriginal people. There are limited epidemiological data; yet the data that exist reveal a tragic malaise in the North. Beyond the epidemiology, narrative accounts – a common pathway among the Inuit to knowledge – reveal stories of the people's deep unbearable pain. These personal documents illuminate such themes as childhood separation and loss, accessibility to firearms, alcohol abuse, past sexual or physical abuse, and, for youth in particular, delinquent behaviour, interpersonal and intrafamilial conflict, and having friends or relations who have completed or attempted suicide. Yet, the stories are also a way to healing and wellness. Like all Aboriginal people, the Inuit have an extremely long tradition of wisdom. Aboriginal people have initiated many traditional and Western approaches to coping with suicide, especially Aboriginal youth suicide. We present some of this insight and the ways to healing.

This section presents a special focus on suicide in the First Nations and Inuit. It outlines the tragedy and integrates that tragedy within the larger Canadian scene. It consists of four chapters: a discussion of suicide in First Nations people, highlighting the process of acculturation; a reflection of Inuit elders on traditional healing in suicide prevention; a special focus on suicide in the Inuit; and a discussion of treatment issues in Aboriginal mental health.

9

Suicide in First Nations People*

C. MURRAY SINCLAIR

While it is with great appreciation that I acknowledge and thank the organizers of the 1992 conference of the Canadian Association for Suicide Prevention for inviting me to attend and address the assembly, it was also with a great deal of sadness that I prepared this talk, for in doing so I was compelled to contemplate one of the great tragedies of our society – the act of self-destruction.

Suicide and internal violent crime rates among the Aboriginal population in some areas run at six to ten times the national average. Suicide rates for the ten-year period 1973–82 for Manitoba Indians were 2.9 times that for non-Indians. Rates are particularly high among males fifteen to twenty-four years of age, where the national rate of 130 per 100,000 is fully six times higher than the overall rates in that age group. Attempted suicides, particularly by young girls, are estimated to be more than fifteen times more common than completed suicides. With increasing recognition being given to the connection between suicide attempts and preceding episodes of sexual abuse, one has to have great concern for the potential for increased numbers given the identification of high rates of family violence and child abuse in some communities. The 1989 study by the Ontario Native Women's Association reported that 80 per cent of Aboriginal women have experienced abuse. In some of the women's shelters and crisis centres in Manitoba, 70 to 100 per cent of the clientele are Aboriginal. But statistics concerning suicide show only part of the overall picture. Related to those data are a whole host of other issues.

Leaving the issue of systemic racism within the legal system aside for the

---

*This chapter is based on the keynote address delivered at the 1992 annual conference of the Canadian Association for Suicide Prevention, Saskatoon.

moment, it is clear that Aboriginal people in Manitoba and throughout Canada are experiencing tremendous and disproportionate amounts of social conflict. We see that every day in our court system, where Aboriginal youth represent more than 60 per cent of all youth charged with criminal offences and more than 70 per cent of youth incarcerated in Manitoba – despite the fact that Aboriginal people represent only 12 per cent of the provincial population. In some parts of the country, Aboriginal people are incarcerated over ten times their presence in the population. In provincial systems, Aboriginal women make up 70 to 90 per cent of all women incarcerated. In western Canada, 40 to 70 per cent of all men incarcerated are Aboriginal. The majority of the current Aboriginal inmate population is under the age of thirty and the majority of youth in the youth courts of western Canada are Aboriginal. In many provinces, particularly in western Canada, Aboriginal people represent the single largest identifiable group of accused who will appear in the court systems.

It would appear as well that with the greater rate of growth among Aboriginal people, there is a good chance that those numbers will increase. In Manitoba, approximately 45 per cent of the Aboriginal population is under the age of fifteen. Over 50 per cent is under the age of eighteen. Manitoba's statistics would appear to hold true for other provinces. Two out of every three Aboriginal persons in Canada are under the age of twenty-five. Frankly, without significant steps being taken to alter the situation, the numbers of Aboriginal accused charged by the police, appearing in our courts, and incarcerated in our jails will increase in the future rather than decrease. But statistics only give a hint of the sense of despair and desperation prevalent among too many of our people.

The attention of the country has recently been focused upon the tragic events taking place in the community of Shamattawa in my province, but many of us realize that what is going on in that community is only a microcosm of events that occur in too many others. The sad truth of the matter is that Aboriginal people today are doing a great deal to complete the cycle of genocide started by government administrators and missionary leaders over a century ago. Far too many of our people are attacking and killing each other and themselves.

Franz Fanon, in his text *The Wretched of the Earth* (1988), writes that when a people have long been oppressed their reaction quickly becomes one of violence. First, he says, violence is turned inward, towards the self and towards one's immediate family. Next, it is turned against a larger circle of friends and family, and against the community where one resides. Finally, he writes, the violence will take the form of action against the oppressor and his institutions. We have seen a great deal of the first, something less of the second, and a little of the last. However, if there are no significant developments in the future for

Aboriginal people in this country, I believe that it is inevitable that we will eventually see all three forms of Aboriginal violence, probably in inverse proportion to what we are now witnessing. Why is this so? More important, what can or should we do about it? I would like to discuss some issues with you that may suggest some answers to those questions.

How We Got Here

Growing up Aboriginal in Canada is, and has been, a difficult and sometimes traumatic experience. Our lives as Aboriginal youth are filled with images and expectations that sometimes have little basis in, or are at odds with, our individual realities. We have to reconcile all of the pulls and pushes acting upon us within the confines of our own sense of identity. Yet the development of our sense of identity often comes about only after a long period of being or feeling lost. I do not know an Aboriginal person today with a good grasp of who he or she is, or where he or she fits into the overall scheme of things. All youth, I suppose, have to struggle with that sort of conflict, but for Aboriginal youth it is particularly more difficult. I would like to discuss why this is so.

People have described the manner in which Aboriginal people have been treated by Canadian governments and Canadian society as cultural genocide. It is a rather dramatic phrase, but it does convey a certain concept – which is that past government policies and efforts were aimed at 'killing' the cultures of Aboriginal people. That is what genocide means – the killing of a people – and cultural genocide is the killing of a culture. Other writers have coined the term 'ethnocide' to better capture the flavour of what went on, but the two phrases mean the same thing: that the cultures of Aboriginal people were to be annihilated. Genocidists believe that a people must be destroyed. The ethnocidist believed that the people could be saved, but that the inferior cultures to which Aboriginal people belonged had to be destroyed in order to save them from a life of barbarism, paganism, and backwardness.

It is hard to envision the possibility that the genocidist could be motivated by anything other than malice or evil, or at the very least cold-heartedness. With cultural genocide, however, the motivation was not an evil one. Almost always, it involved a belief that what the practitioner was in fact doing was in the best interests of the people. Acts of cultural genocide were perceived by both the practitioner and others as being acts of kindness. It was, we are told, unfortunately, a case of having to take strong medicine to overcome a terrible condition. The legal and political efforts and policies of the institutions of government – including those of justice – insofar as Indian people are concerned, in the past and to a certain extent even today, were motivated by a belief that what needed to be and was being done, in the long run, was the best thing for Indians: their gradual civilization.

Cultural genocide has largely been eliminated from our thinking in modern times, but its strong role in historical times has given rise to policies, programs, and laws over the years and generations that are still with us. The result is that much of what we think and do today concerning Aboriginal people and Aboriginal issues is permeated with inherent biases. Cultural bias is the problem that we must begin to address. It is important to recognize and come to understand how the phenomenon of ethnocide or cultural genocide has been implemented if we are to protect our present and future decisions from it. We must, however, begin with one very important thought. There is no cure within the assertion of the superiority of one culture's beliefs and values over another. The sad truth is, as we are now discovering – and as Indian people have known all along – that the intended cures of the past have only worsened the condition.

While I was growing up in the community I come from, I was always struck by the fact that as Aboriginal people we appeared not to have a history. The beginning of our history as Canadians started with European explorers such as Christopher Columbus, Jacques Cartier, John Cabot, Henry Hudson, La Vérendrye, and Samuel de Champlain. It continued with colonizing figures such as Talbot, Montcalm, Wolfe, and Lord Selkirk, and with the growth of European settlements at Montreal, Ottawa, and Toronto, and at the forks of the Red and the Assiniboine Rivers.

As Aboriginal people, however, we apparently never had a history worth discussing. We were, literally and figuratively, irrelevant. That can and does have a dramatic effect upon one's sense of identity and self-worth. Yet the absence of such history in the public schools I attended was the result of many deliberate acts over the years, a few of which I would like to discuss. In doing so, however, I wish to make it clear that I am not trying to make anyone feel guilty. (I recognize that guilt can be a great motivator, but I have no interest in relating what you are about to read simply in order to make anyone feel guilty.) Rather, I want to show you how history has fashioned the problems that we face and, in turn, how history can teach us how to develop better solutions. I want to help you understand why we have what we have so that to the extent that you have a role to play in shaping the course of the future, whether of an individual or of society, you will be able to take action in a manner that shows appreciation and respect for Aboriginal aspirations and needs.

The Indian Act of Canada

It is a wise person who said that if you do not know your history, then you are doomed to repeat it. It is time to stop repeating the historical mistakes of this country. The Indian Act was a remarkable tool of assimilation designed not to protect the Indian people in their lands and rights, but to facilitate the government's plans to abolish their special rights and to integrate them fully into Canadian society. The premise and promise of the Act was to assist in the eventual extinguishment and extinction of Indians as Indians, and to overcome whatever legal obstacles might lie in the way of that goal. Thus, the initial provisions of the Act granted powers to the minister of Indian affairs to enfranchise Indians and entire bands, to remove traditional chiefs from office, and to prevent Indians from engaging in economic activities on their lands that could compete successfully with local white businesses. Indian farmers were prohibited from selling their grain and farm produce; by official government policy they were prevented from establishing anything more than subsistence farms. Indians could not sell or lease any of their natural resources from their lands. Businesses could not locate on an Indian reserve unless the minister's permission was given. It rarely was.

When Indian people of the prairies signed treaties with the Queen's representative, they did so knowing that they were being asked to surrender their rights to exclusive use of large parcels of land. However, it was also clear that they wanted lands for their exclusive use as tribal homelands – a concept the government understood but that it took advantage of and perverted into a policy to corral and control Indian movement and growth. In the 1880s, the government of Canada enacted special amendments to the Indian Act of Canada at the request of missionary societies who had been mandated by the government to educate Indians. These amendments became known as the Potlatch and Sundance laws. They made it an offence for any Indian person to participate in any traditional Indian ceremony or to wear traditional Indian costume or dress. The intent was to remove tribal traditions from their positions of importance in the lives of Aboriginal people. Many of those who were prosecuted under these laws were the traditional leaders of the tribe, and upon conviction they were invariably sentenced to hard labour. The statistical evidence (such as it is) available for Stony Mountain Penitentiary in Manitoba at the turn of the century shows that many of the Indian people incarcerated at that time were sentenced under these laws. In this way as well, the influence of those leaders within the tribe was reduced both by their removal from the community and by the fact that the government could show Indians that it had the power to lock up their most influential people.

There is ample evidence from Canadian and provincial archives of ministerial and departmental directives issued both before and for some time after the turn of the century to prosecutors, judges, and magistrates in western Canada exhorting and, in some cases, demanding that they sentence Indian offenders harshly so as to make it clear to their fellow tribesmen that they must abide by the laws of Canada. It was easy for the government to get its way on this point. At that time magistrates did not enjoy any type of judicial independence, holding office 'at pleasure' of the government. In addition, most of the magistrates in the Northwest Territories (before the western provinces were created) were employees of the federal government, foremost among them being Indian agents and RCMP (NWPM) officers.

In the 1880s, the federal government enacted amendments to the Indian Act by which Indian children were legally required to attend schools established or arranged by the minister of Indian affairs. This was, interestingly, some time before compulsory education existed for the rest of Canada. The only schools established by the minister at that time were residential schools patterned on the industrial-school model then popular in the United States for Indian children and juvenile delinquents. Pursuant to these policies, Indian children were taken from their parents (and from their influence), the minister was appointed their legal guardian, and they were educated in schools run sometimes by the department but generally by missionary societies. This policy coincidentally facilitated the Christianization of the Indians – and fit neatly into government policy that Indian people needed to be saved from their pagan existence through Christianity.

At the same time, the Department of Indian Affairs inaugurated what came to be called the 'pass system,' whereby Indian people were not allowed to leave their reserves without the written permission of the local Indian agent. The system was designed and requested by the Canadian military following the Saskatchewan Rebellion of 1885 in order to control Indian movement in western Canada (then the Northwest Territories) and prevent another Aboriginal insurgency. Though never legally mandated or sanctioned, the system was primarily used to prevent Indian parents from travelling to where their children were attending schools and 'interfering' with them, or attempting to remove them. Not only could Indians not leave their reserves to see their children, but the pass system was also sometimes invoked to prevent Indians from seeking employment outside of their reserves. There is considerable evidence that it was abused in many other ways to enhance the power of the local Indian agents over the lives of the band members.

In the 1890s the minister was empowered by further amendment to the Indian Act to declare that traditional leaders and chiefs of the band no longer held any authority in the tribe and that only chiefs elected under the supervision of the local Indian agent were allowed to represent the tribe. Only men could run for chief and only men could vote for them. This rule greatly interfered with the traditional role of women in such strongly matriarchal societies as the Ojibway and the Mohawk. The amendment also required that any time the newly elected chief wished to hold a council meeting he had to notify the Indian agent. The Indian agent was, automatically and by law, the presiding officer of the council meeting. Any legislation enacted by the tribe could also be disallowed by the minister of indian affairs. These amendments were, ironically, entitled 'The Indian Advancement Act.'

Amendments to the Indian Act at around the same time made it an offence for a lawyer to represent an Indian or a band in action against the government unless the consent of the minister of Indian affairs was first obtained. Needless to say, many perfectly valid legal claims against the government languished for decades – nobody ever got the minister's permission. As an example, the famous case of *St Catherines Milling*, which decided the nature of Aboriginal title in Canada, was decided not only without Aboriginal representation in the form of council, but also without any evidence from Aboriginal people about how they understood their rights. Finally, the Indian Act was amended at around this time to include a definition: 'person' was defined to mean 'anyone other than an Indian' – the ultimate reflection of government thinking.

For the most part, the children who were removed from their families and sent to residential schools suffered emotional and psychological harm that had differing degrees of impact upon their own coping and parenting skills. Often, the result was a belief on their part that what was 'Indian' was bad – their languages, their ceremonies, their beliefs, their rituals, their religion, their Elders, and other traditional Indian people. When these children became adults, they sometimes carried on the culturally destructive attitudes and attacks of the missionary people with whom they had grown up. In addition, children returning from residential schools generally lacked the skills necessary to cope with life on the reservation. Hunting, fishing, trapping, hide tanning, food preparation, beadwork, and other traditional pursuits that had formed an integral part of Aboriginal lifestyle, not simply for economic but also for social reasons, were activities that many did not know how to perform and were not inclined to learn. Despite the promise of the residential school system, most who were sent there did not receive any training in an employment-related field beyond physical labour. Reliance upon government handouts or social assistance subsequently became commonplace. None had received instruction in how to raise children, so that when they had families they experienced coping problems.

Because of the legal ban on Indian ceremonies and rituals, traditional Indian men and women were harassed and persecuted. The public display that had always accompanied such practices became dangerous, and so the practices went underground. They were never effectively wiped out – many Indian people still practised their traditional ways and customs but they had to do so clandestinely. This secrecy reduced the effectiveness of those customs as tools of societal bonding, for the numbers of those who could attend such ceremonial gatherings and teaching sessions – for that is what they are – were necessarily limited. In addition, with the advent of new religions among many of the tribes, some tribal members became agents for the 'white man's churches' and for the Indian agents who were bent on destroying Aboriginal practices. Such Indians actively assisted in the discovery and destruction of ceremonial gathering places and symbols, which occasioned considerable distrust between the older traditional people and the younger ones returning from the missionary schools. It further prevented the public transmission of the cultural values inherent to the tribes that the traditions and ceremonies were designed to promote.

Although traditional ceremonies and rituals continued to be practised by a number of tribal members, the utility of the tribe's beliefs and practices as a social tool was limited to older people and to those who were outside the influence of the missionary societies. In addition, the churches could not replace what was lost, for in losing the right to publicly and regularly engage in their traditional practices and customs large numbers of Indian people lost contact not only with their religious rituals but with an entire lifestyle. While many Indian people did gravitate to other religions, these practices did not gain as important a foothold in the lives of Indian tribes as those that had been removed.

The enforcement of the kinds of laws I have mentioned created distrust of the white man's laws and legal systems on the part of Indians, as one can well understand. During the course of the hearings of the Aboriginal Justice Inquiry we heard considerable evidence of that distrust, which has clearly contributed to the fact that Aboriginal people are up to five times more likely to plead guilty than non-Aboriginal accused persons. There is considerable evidence to show that they often plead guilty to offences of which they are in fact not guilty. For the most part, the inordinate numbers of Aboriginal people we now see in the justice system did not begin to occur until the mid-1950s. Until then, it would appear that the representation of Aboriginal people in our court system was about equivalent to their numbers in society – in other words, there was little if any evidence of over-representation.

In Manitoba, elders point out that the increase in police contacts and court appearances by Aboriginal people coincides with the change in liquor laws allowing Indian people to drink beer in parlours – a 'right' hitherto denied them in most provincial legislation. There is no doubt that there is a high incidence of alcohol-related crime among Aboriginal people today, and that the beginning of the rise of those numbers starts at around the same time. One must be careful of drawing conclusions from the relationship in time between the rise in Aboriginal-justice-system contacts and liquor-law changes, however. It seems clear that rather than being a cause of an increase in Aboriginal crime, alcohol abuse along with school drop-outs, suicides, and crime are all strong indicators of something even more significant at work on the Aboriginal psyche.

The rise in criminal charges involving Aboriginal people in the 1950s also coincides with an increase in the numbers of RCMP officers working in our provinces owing to new federal-provincial policing agreements, and with a policy by the Department of Indian Affairs to encourage the migration of Indian people from their reserves to cities. In Manitoba, as in most provinces, most Aboriginal people appear in and are incarcerated by urban courts. It is fair to say that Aboriginal people have generally regarded the schools and courts of our country as tools of oppression. They do not see our courts as vehicles of dispute resolution or as a positive influence. The vast majority of Aboriginal contacts with the justice system even today involve appearances in our criminal courts as accused, as parents of a young person charged with an offence, or as parents in our family courts fighting some child-welfare agency that wishes to remove their children from the home. Aboriginal people do not go to our court system for relief of their civil and domestic problems. We are not providing the same type of service to them that other members of society receive. Civil and family disputes are resolved informally or not at all. Interestingly, geography has nothing to do with it; Aboriginal people in urban areas are just as unlikely to make claims for relief in our civil and family courts as are Aboriginal people in remote isolated communities.

Interestingly, despite the early belief on the part of those involved in the administration of justice as to its educational utility, there was generally little effort outside of larger remote communities to establish courts on Indian reserves until the 1960s and 1970s. Indian people charged with offences were generally transported, or were required to travel on their own, to larger urban centres for court appearances. Though this practice was perhaps cost effective, the absence of a connection between the community and the process of dispute resolution undoubtedly led to further misunderstanding and perhaps even mystery. We encountered several elderly people in our hearings in remote communities in Manitoba who asked us to find out what happened to their children who had been arrested and taken away years ago. They had not seen them again.

The absence of traditional leadership, the removal of tribal institutions, and the lack of appropriate replacement with Canadian models or institutions led almost invariably in some places to situations bordering on social chaos. To list the kinds of things that can go on in communities in which there are few effective social controls would be too depressing, but I am sure that you can well imagine what I am alluding to. In a strange sort of way, this state of affairs – an almost direct result of the ethnocidal policies mentioned – reinforced the unspoken belief that Indian people were inherently inferior. The result of the practice confirmed its premise – a true self-fulfilling prophesy.

Finally, there is one other effect I want to mention, which I would call a collective social depression. Many Aboriginal people came to believe what society was telling them, that there was no hope in being an Indian. The fact that the government of Canada was officially opposed to aspects of Indian culture so basic to their continued survival as a unique people was the catalyst for a pervasive belief among the rest of Canadian society that it was best for all Aboriginal people to assimilate and surrender their 'Indianness.' Any attempt on the part of Indian people to resist doing so was dealt with harshly. All Aboriginal people were affected by this belief – Métis, Indian, and Inuit – for Canadian society could not distinguish between the variety of Aboriginal groups in society. Some Aboriginal people who were the object of such policies actually came to believe the propaganda. Others, even if they did not believe it, would have at least sensed the futility of resistance and thereby sought passivity. Resistance very quickly led to punishment, and any person who felt inclined to speak out would have very quickly found out that discretion was the better part of valour.

There was silence for the most part from Indian people to the oppression they were under, at least until very recently. From the perspective of Aboriginal people, for the past few generations governments have essentially 'had their way' with us. If one were to try to describe the Indian attitude to what was going on, one could easily describe it as individual passive resistance – a dropping out resulting from an unwillingness to be co-opted as part of the system. The impact upon us as Aboriginal people has been devastating. Our people have been terribly, horribly, and sometimes brutally oppressed. It is very hard to articulate in a meaningful and accurate manner what that has done to us – to our grandmothers and grandfathers, to our parents, to our aunties and uncles, to our brothers and sisters, to our very souls. I hope you can sense even a small flavour of what I am talking about.

There was historically, and still exists, a generally unspoken belief that Aboriginal people, because of their cultures, their beliefs, and their customs, are just not capable of dealing with the complicated and complex social problems of the day. Aboriginal values, beliefs, traditions, and practices have for too long been rejected as a means of resolving serious social and community problems for Aboriginal and Canadian societies. The perception and belief that Western civilization, with its basic tenets and roots firmly founded in Christianity and its

fixation on education, training, and specialization, held the answers and is a better road to travel on than the Aboriginal one is now being challenged not only
by Aboriginal people but by governments as well.

The Aboriginal Road

The problem is that many people do not know what the Aboriginal road is all
about. There is still a great deal of misunderstanding and even ignorance about
Aboriginal people, their cultures, and beliefs prevalent within Canadian society,
and to a certain extent among Aboriginal people themselves. This latter problem is one that must be addressed quickly. From my own experience as an
Aboriginal person, this experience was strongly reinforced during my work as
co-commissioner of Manitoba's Aboriginal Justice Inquiry. One thing remains
abundantly clear to me. So long as Canadian society and governments lack the
willingness to look to Aboriginal societies for some answers, the problems that
Canadian and Aboriginal people face not only with the administration of justice, but in society generally, will be perpetuated. The violence we see today
among and between Aboriginal people will evolve, perhaps as Fanon (1988)
predicted, but with a disenchanted and disenfranchised Aboriginal youth. There
is a great deal to be concerned about. So long as we believe that European-
based values and systems hold the only sure answer, then Canadian society will
remain ineffective in coping with the major issues that give rise to the situation
we are facing.

Equality has not always been the hallmark of Indian life in this country. The
result of this reality has been the social and spiritual desperation that we now
observe in the lives of too many Indian people. As Slapin and Seale have stated:
'Educated people are likely to have acquired most of their attitudes towards
Indians from the writings of anthropologists, for whom Native societies are
considered worthy of study insofar as they have preserved aspects of pre-con-
quest cultures. For them, contemporary Indians are, by and large, degenerate
survivors of a more glorious past. The idea that such people may have meaningful contributions to make ... is one that is received with scorn. At the same time,
to be educated is to somehow become less "Indian"; to be successful is to find
oneself dismissed as no longer "authentic" ' (1988: 14).

That is part of the very real dilemma that Aboriginal people, particularly
Aboriginal youth, face. I can remember, as an Aboriginal student, and as an
adult I have observed, that Aboriginal youth are burdened with anxieties and
vulnerabilities in addition to those that burden the average white youth. The
accusation that Aboriginal young people have always had to live with, from
early childhood and throughout the course of growing up, is that they are infe-

rior. Inferior simply because they are Aboriginal. This accusation has been so uniform that it has become ingrained in the cultural imagery of this country. It has been enforced by law, by custom, and by every form of power at play in Canadian society. As a result, it has left its mark.

Aboriginal inferiority was a precept not merely accepted, but encouraged by the European settlers of this nation. It was a principle of social organization that relegated Aboriginal people to the sidelines of Canadian life and regarded them as irrelevant. When young Aboriginal students move from their home communities on reserves to schools and universities in urban environments, they find themselves surrounded by people who historically have claimed to be superior. They are surrounded by the myth of their own inferiority because they are surrounded by people who believe in the myth of their own superiority. This is so both inside and outside of educational institutions, but for Indian students within educational institutions the stress and pressures can have particularly devastating consequences. Not only are our educational institutions the shapers and moulders of the thinking of our youth, but it is in those institutions that future leaders of our societies make their most fundamental career choices. That is why it is important for all people to understand what has happened to Aboriginal people and why.

The irony is that, because of our history, of fewer opportunities made available to us, and of racism, we as Aboriginal people *are* in a sense inferior, but our inferiority has to do with the inferiority of the position to which we have legally, politically, and socially been relegated and with the limited opportunities to overcome that status made available to us. What has been done to our parents is the problem, not any *inherent* inferiority. The problems we face in achieving our rightful place within society must therefore be seen as a challenge rather than a mark of shame. To a certain extent, for Aboriginal people there is some truth to what Martin Luther King Jr. once said: 'When you are behind in a foot race the only way to get ahead is to run faster than the guy in front of you.'

The Road Ahead

There is much that needs to be done. To begin with, it must be seen that the problems Aboriginal peoples face arise from their unique histories. As well, it should be apparent that solutions to the problems faced by Aboriginal youth will arise partially at least in their ability to approach those problems with a stronger sense of self-determination and identity. In many places, medical and other professionals are beginning to recognize that there is merit in the utilization of traditional Aboriginal methods of healing. The use of the sweat lodge, the naming ceremony, the clan dances, the sun-dances, lodge gatherings, and so

forth are some methods of addressing the despair of those who contemplate sur-
rendering their lives. It is an issue that needs to be given greater acceptance.
Those Elders with whom I am associated tell me that the spirit of the people
needs to be healed. From a medical perspective, I have encountered some professionals who ask, 'What can we do about that?' The answer is, 'Whatever you
can.' If you give a man a fish you feed him for a day, but if you teach him how
to fish you feed him for a lifetime.

Aboriginal people, individually and collectively, must – if they are to come to
terms with the tremendous problems they face – take control of who they are to
be, and they will have to feel and to believe that they are in control of their destiny. If the Serenity Prayer is to have any meaning for us as Aboriginal people –
'God grant me the *serenity* to accept things I cannot change, the *courage* to
change the things I can, and the *wisdom* to know the difference' – then Aboriginal people will first have to believe that they have the power to change or to
accept. They will have to have faith that whatever they do, right or wrong, is
part of this great mystery we call life. We do not have that faith now. The people
of Shamattawa and other communities have not felt they had it. Their despair
and frustration over that feeling of powerlessness and hopelessness is evident.

It is clear that ideas shape the course of history. This is true of the future more
so than of the past or the present, and this notion has particular implications for
Aboriginal people in this country. If their future is to include controlling their
Aboriginal destiny, then that future requires an Aboriginal academia. We need
to begin to speak and write about some of the issues facing us in the future. No
culture or society of people has ever evolved without debate and the discussion
of ideas. We need some of our own people to begin to present some of their
ideas about the future direction we should be following as Aboriginal people.
We can no longer restrict ourselves to writings intended only to educate white
people about who we are. We need that type of writing, but we need more. We
need Aboriginal people to write about twentieth-century Aboriginality; about
what it means and where it is going and, most important, about where it should
be going. As Aboriginal people we need to begin to think about issues that we
would have been thinking about if we had had control of our lives to this point.

This is the role and the challenge that I see for the future Aboriginal leaders
of this country. The temptation to train our children to be only technicians and
tradespeople must be resisted. Those are worthy professions, but no society has
ever existed which did not recognize and develop its dreamers and thinkers. We
need to develop our philosophers, thinkers, and writers – our people of wisdom
and foresight. Our educators must look for those abilities in all our children and,
when discovered, nurture and feed them. We have those people now. I've met
many of them. They are the ones who still have the spark of life within their

eyes, who have not yet had the ability to think or dream or believe in their dreams taken from them.

In my father's generation, those abilities were snuffed out when Aboriginal children crossed the thresholds of the residential schools to which they had been sentenced. In my generation those abilities were denied to us from the time we were born because our parents tried to live an artificial life constructed for them. But some of our parents and grandparents never did lose those abilities, and some of my generation has learned to think and dream once again. We need those thinkers and we need those dreamers, for we are a people in need of ideas and dreams.

REFERENCES

Fanon, F. 1988. *Wretched of the Earth*. New York: Grove/Atlantic.
Slapin, B., and D. Seale, eds. 1988. *Books without Bias: Through Indian Eyes*. Berkeley, CA: Oyate Press.

10

Stories of Distress and Healing: Inuit Elders on Suicide

MICHAEL J. KRAL with MEEKA ARNAKAQ,
NAKI EKHO, OKEE KUNUK, ELISAPEE OOTOOVA,
MALAYA PAPATSIE, and LUCIEN TAPARTI

A Background

The Inuit people of Canada live primarily in the eastern Arctic, as well as in northern Quebec and Labrador. Approximately 80 per cent of the people of the eastern Arctic are Inuit. Literature tells us that the present-day Inuit people stem from the Thule whale-hunting culture that dates back to about AD 900 and overlapped with the Dorset people (approx. 1700 BC – AD 1100), who in turn overlapped with the pre-Dorset and Denbigh people (approx. 3000 BC – 500 BC). Archaeologists have found evidence that people resided in what is now Igloolik four thousand years ago (Purich, 1992). Canadian Aboriginal people, including the Inuit, Dene, and Métis of the north, are a culture long of this land.

In her book *Issumatuq* ('wise person'), Kit Minor (1992) shares her knowing of the Inuit people after spending a decade living with them. She describes the Inuit as having traditionally been a collectivist culture. Collectivist cultures have different views of the self than individualist (e.g., Euro-Western) ones (see Markus and Kitayama, 1991; Triandis, 1995). Collective 'selves' see group membership as central to their identity, whereas individualist selves are more autonomous from any particular group and may value 'individuation' quite highly. Because the Inuit have been in the north for a very long time, it behooves all to respect their accounts of both how they have survived well and how they have experienced their lives over time. Minor notes that relationships among the Inuit have consisted of three basic features related to mutual interdependence: collaborative partnerships, extended-family kinship patterns, and dyadic relations within the nuclear family. Elders have held the role of providing guidance and wisdom within their communities. Important concepts in heal-

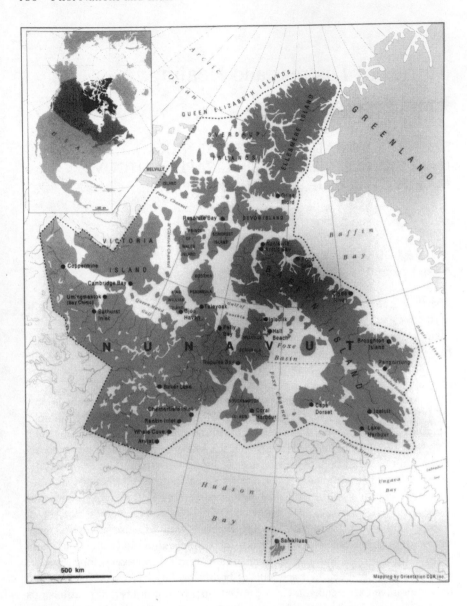

Figure 1 Nunavut will become an independent territory of Canada in 1999 (photo courtesy of Nunavut Tunngavik Inc.).

ing and wellness have included *ajurnarmat* or the acceptance of things that cannot be changed, respect for the privacy of silence, and seeking advice when change is viewed as possible. Such values and practices guided the Inuit for many centuries before foreigners came to their lands.

Northern Aboriginal people had foreign visitors or *qallunaat* (Inuktitut for non-Inuit) long ago, such as Scandinavian Vikings around 1008 and British or European fishing ships after 1400. Related to these early visits were tensions around the kidnapping of some of these northern people. Martin Frobisher, for example, took a man and his kayak from Baffin Island back to England to be exhibited by Queen Elizabeth I 'hunting royal swans on the palace pond' (Crowe, 1991: 65). The *qallunaat* did not begin to have a major impact on northern Aboriginal life, however, until the whaling expeditions and fur trade of the nineteenth century. Both friendships and hostilities were common between the Aboriginals and Europeans. Great diseases for which the Aboriginal people's immune systems were unprepared, brought by the Europeans, took tens of thousands of lives; by 1900, only about one-third of the Inuit population was left alive. These epidemics continued during the first half of the twentieth century, and it has been estimated that by 1950 one-fifth of the Inuit population had tuberculosis. As the fur trade declined and ultimately collapsed in the 1930s, the Canadian welfare state underwent many changes, resulting in significant involvement of the federal government in the lives of the Inuit. The presence of the military and of missionaries, and large-scale community relocations during the 1940s and 1950s of the Inuit, in the context of attempts at assimilation into Canadian society, changed northern life enormously (Tester and Kulchyski, 1994). Food and other important resources changed for the people; some communities had to alter their diets from caribou to fish and their lifestyles from extended-family kinship and nomadic hunting practices to a modern economy and the establishment of new settlements.

Oil exploration and wells began on Melville Island in 1959, further affecting life in the north. However, concerns related to self-government were already beginning. All social services were transferred to the territorial government by 1967, and Aboriginal concerns were now being addressed even more directly. The discovery of gas fields in the 1980s prompted the federal government to settle a major land claim in 1984 in the western Arctic named Inuvialut. Inuktitut, the language of the Inuit, is increasingly being spoken in the territorial government, and towns with English names are being given names in Inuktitut. A new Inuit territory called Nunavut, first proposed in 1976, is planned to come into official existence in the eastern Arctic in 1999 (see figure 1).

Against this brief historical background, the demographics of Canada's northern people remain quite different from those living in the south. In terms of assimilation, Purich (1992) indicates that while 80 per cent of the Canadian population completes grade 9, only 34 per cent of Inuit children do so. Comparisons for high-school graduation are 52 versus 15 per cent, respectively. Unemployment rates range from 15 to 72 per cent across the eastern Arctic, and a larger proportion of people in the Northwest Territories work for the government (46%) than do nationally (21%). Eighty per cent of the territorial budget comes from the federal government.

The Inuit continue to experience social distress in many of their communities. They have one of the highest birth rates globally, and the proportion of Inuit youth under the age of fourteen is almost double that for Canada. Infant mortality is 3.5 times higher than it is nationally, and life expectancy is up to fifteen years lower. There is also a significant housing shortage in the Arctic (Purich, 1992). A cautionary note may be heard in the words of During (1993): 'In a paradox that helps us understand certain problems at work at the heart of the social democratic power bloc, those who are most vulnerable to market forces respond most positively to its cultural products' (p. 9). Colonial stress has impacted upon each living cohort of Inuit in different ways in the context of the strong and rapid social changes in the Arctic (O'Neil, 1986).

The Inuit, like many Aboriginal people living in Canada and elsewhere, have been impacted by suicide in recent years. Reports from Health Canada (National Task Force, 1987, 1995), a recent Royal Commission publication (1995), and other research (see Kirmayer, 1994) indicate that in spite of wide variability across their communities, Canadian Aboriginal people have a suicide rate that far exceeds the average Canadian rate. This holds true especially for males in the fifteen to thirty age range, where youth suicide follows a pattern similar to the national one but is greatly magnified among Aboriginals. Although the proportion of Inuit suicides (63%) is close to their population in the Northwest Territories (60%), the suicide rate among northern Aboriginal people is very high. The suicide rate in the Northwest Territories for the years 1989 to 1992 per 100,000 was 32.58, whereas for the country it was 12.69. For males and females in the NWT, compared to the rest of the country, these rates were 54.8 versus 20.16 and 9.17 versus 5.34, respectively. Issues of identity, anomie, and powerlessness in the changing social context of Aboriginals' lives are recurring themes in discussions of why this dire situation exists (e.g., Kirmayer, 1994; Minore et al., 1991; O'Neil, 1986).

It is now well documented that the Canadian government, beginning in particular in the late nineteenth century, systematically suppressed traditional Aboriginal beliefs and lifestyles through treaties, the Indian Act, residential schools and reservations, and the outlawing of spiritual ceremonies and persecution of those who were caught practising (Dickason, 1992; Sinclair, this volume; York, 1989). However, York (1989) notes that the fifth-generation prophesy is coming true in the national revival of Aboriginal culture. The prophesy comes from demoralized Prairie Indian Chiefs in the 1870s who, signing the treaties in which they gave up their land, often made reference to their 'children's children's children's children's children.' The fifth generation is now with us.

Oral Narratives as Cultural Documents

Narrative accounts are becoming increasingly common in the human sciences, supplementing the importance of a multidisciplinary perspective in the understanding of human experience. While numerical indices are meaningful summaries of various communities, regions, or countries, we are often left wondering what the individuals representing these numbers might say, if asked, about the topic in question. Humans live richly storied lives, and are able to tell of them. Listening to another's account of particular experiences, of enduring themes, of personal transformations punctuated by joy or terror, or of edifying encounters and lessons learned, is being taken at face value as serious business in fields from psychoanalysis (Shafer, 1992, Spence, 1982), philosophy (Toulmin, 1988), and psychology (McAdams, 1993; Polkinghorne, 1994; Sarbin, 1986) to research methodology (Denzin, 1989; Langness and Frank, 1981) and even literary works on 'the poetics of self-creation' (Randall, 1995: 4). In a recent book in which Yukon Elders talk about their lives, Cruikshank (1990) makes the point about 'taking seriously what people say about their lives rather than treating their words simply as an illustration of some other process' (p. 1). She refers to these stories as *cultural documents*, as explanatory ways 'in which much is implicit, in which metaphor and symbol play a role in how ideas are presented' (p. 3).

It is hoped that this chapter will be such a supplement to others in this book that portray suicide from a variety of perspectives, many of them representing the more quantitative or summative approaches and insights into others' shared experiences and beliefs. Suicide has many shared experiences. Those who cause themselves death share not only the fact of what they do but the conscious decision to carry it out. They share ideas about the means by which they commit this act and to some extent its timing in their lives (Colt, 1991; La Fontaine, 1975). Furthermore, those 'left behind' and currently referred to as survivors share the anguish and other long-lasting states when a loved one suddenly takes her or his life (Farberow, 1993; Bailley, 1994). We must listen closely to individuals tell their stories in order to augment our understanding of their lives and of the phenomenon of suicide itself. Narratives of distress such as William Sty-

ron's (1990) vivid account of his experience that almost ended in suicide cannot
but further this understanding. Fortunately, a focus on the local, on the particular, and on individual lives in the north in the context of suicide is already
appearing (Leenaars, 1995). The words of Inuit Elders are extended here
beyond the public forum at which they spoke. Their stories had a powerful
effect on those who listened, and the intention here is to gain some understanding of suicide in the north from them.

Aboriginal Elders have an extremely long tradition as purveyors of wisdom
and healing (e.g., Knudson and Suzuki, 1992). At the conference of the Canadian Association for Suicide Prevention held in Iqaluit in 1994, these Elders
gathered together on a panel: Meeka Arnakaq, Naki Ekho, Okee Kunuk, Elisapee Ootoova, Malaya Papatsie, and Lucien Taparti. Their stories of pain and
healing were compelling and all had had first-hand experience with suicide,
having lost their children, husbands, or close friends. They shared their personal
journeys and offered wisdom to others along the way. In the north, one does not
have to look far to see love and caring up close. A strength endures, and a spirit
of self-determination and hope is very much alive.

A sampling of the stories the Elders shared with their audience is presented
here. The only intention in doing this is to give a sense of their presence, one they
willingly shared in order to be of help to others. They spoke in their native language of Inuktitut, so their words are from the simultaneous translation. As only
excerpts of their many statements, what is presented here may appear slightly out
of context. No misrepresentation whatsoever is intended. It was an honour to hear
them, and it is hoped that the larger context for these narratives is one of both the
northern Aboriginal experience and universal human experience.

Readers expecting a thematic interpretation following the narratives may be
disappointed; none is provided. There is an advantage to letting the words stand
alone. The reader is invited, as was the northern audience, to hear the stories.
Themes will emerge as they always do. But the reader is respected for being
able to discern these. There are times when it is ours to listen.

Unikkaartuit / The Sharing

I have been deeply affected. Suicide affects the whole community. I am old, I am more
open, but I still have things from the past that come up. I lost two children to hanging and
to shooting. It is hard to open up, because you feel shame and guilt. We have to break the
silence, overcome our shyness and our shame. I now have to help other people who are
going through the same situation.

There is a lack of communication in the present day, even among our children. When we were young we didn't contemplate suicide because life was precious. My husband committed suicide. In order to cope I had to think of what my parents would do. This is the worst thing I have ever experienced – twenty-three years ago – I go back to that experience. Because of that experience some of my own children have contemplated suicide. Being blamed is the biggest problem – you are alone, guilty, lonely. There is nothing like that feeling, when you are blamed, ignored. Because I have gone through that experience I can now help others.

I didn't think that I was going to comment. I have lost grandchildren and my own children to suicide. I can help because I still need help. No wonder that our children are committing suicide – we're not talking to them. I feel grateful that I have the opportunity to talk to you. Our people have gone through changes over the years. Things are different now. It is a state of bewilderment we go through. It seems we cannot talk to anybody, and it is good that we are here to talk about it.

I lived in three outpost camps. Our grandmothers used to tell us what it was going to be like. Our mothers and grandmothers are no longer around, but what they said is still around. It is true, what they told me was going to happen. I'm now going through those experiences. We were told not to talk back to our elders. I felt very ashamed because my father was a white man. Others didn't mind – it was I who was going through that. He didn't have any relations with the community. When I was growing up I was told that 'your father's relatives are not your relatives.' I used to go to church with my mother. She used to tell me, 'You're not going to understand now, but when you grow up and have your own children you will understand.' A lot of things were going on in the community. There was alcohol when I was growing up. My mother said that when you live in the community, 'you should keep your ears closed and your mouth closed. You're going to see a lot of things you don't like.' That's what it was like when I was growing up as a child. A lot of things were going on in the community. It seems we're talking about it now. If we know where our roots are ...

Alcohol is not the only problem in the community. When you're mentally burdened as a child, growing up in a single-parent environment, you have a harder time coping with men. I had a grandfather, but I don't remember what he looked like. I grew up with my mother. I didn't know I had a problem until I started talking about it. It was like peeling off layer after layer. Only when you open up can you start peeling the layers. Nobody grows up on this earth without having pain or trauma. There has to be openness in communication in order to cope, and to pave the way for our children and grandchildren. I can't speak to my grandchildren in English – I think they should learn Inuktitut first in order to know their language, their roots. My first education was learning the Inuktitut syllabics. We have different dialects, but this shouldn't make a difference. We are all equal. The advice given to us by our parents and grandparents is coming back. I thank you for giving us this opportunity.

I lost two children – one who shot himself, one who hanged himself. Because of that I now want to help. At that time, I was not able to help anyone. I was totally in the black. We had a hard life when we were growing up. When my father died, my mother brought me up and I used to be envious of the children who could talk to their fathers and ask them for their advice. You have to go back to your childhood in order to get back on your feet today. We had two children born in an igloo when I was still a hunter. My first-born shot himself in Rankin Inlet. I lost all hope when I lost my son. My wife was gone at that time. I didn't even feel for my other children at the time. I had to be drugged and put to sleep for a while, and my daughter – we couldn't cope. My wife was back when I woke up. Things got better when she came back. All those things on my mind started coming back. I had lots of problems when I was married. I was considering separating. The only way we stayed together was because we had our children. All those things that are trivial are going on inside you and are building up, and you don't feel it.

In sadness, when it starts getting bigger and bigger, it is very hard to open up at that time. Lots of people out there become hopeless because they've been like that for a long time. You can tell. It is up to every individual to help.

Our language is eroding. I don't know if I should say that to people here. It would be like cheating. But we have to preserve our language. We are still using our writing system and are still using our language. My son, he's seventeen. When he goes to the media, I tell him to say it properly. It is up to us to preserve what we have, our language and our culture.

When you have a problem, don't be shy. Come forward. That's why you have the problem. It's the only way you can deal with it. It starts building up ... If you have personal problems, start talking to someone before it builds up. If you don't, there are going to be more and more layers building up.

We can live together. I have forgiven myself. I've lost two children to suicide. When I wake up, my two sons are the first thing that comes to my head and I try to be okay. Prayer has a lot to do with coping with your life. We talk about youth but they're not the only ones that have problems. We are the ones who can be their guiding hands. At times we have to carry them in order to keep them going.

A lot of Elders don't say anything, but that doesn't mean they don't want to help. They're just there waiting.

NOTE

The people of Iqaluit are thanked for hosting the 1994 conference of the Canadian Association for Suicide Prevention. They provided a forum for the exchange of concerns, ideas, tears, and laughter, and shared their wonderful food and warm company. Gratitude is expressed in particular to Sheila Levy, Errol Fletcher, Monica Ittusardjuat, Kate McDermott, Rhoda Ungalaq, Lena Autut, Jodi Payant, Josh Teemotee, Ian Smith, Angus Mackay, and Jack Anawak. Appreciation and thanks are extended to Mary Ekho Wilman and Sheila Levy for their assistance in continued contact with the Elders during the preparation of this chapter. Most important, the Elders who shared their experiences and whose words appear here are thanked for their modelling of courage and hope.

REFERENCES

Bailley, S.E. 1994. 'Impact of Mode of Death on the Bereavement Experience: Suicide, Accident, and Natural Death Survivors Compared.' Unpublished MA thesis, University of Windsor.
Colt, G.H. 1991. *The Enigma of Suicide*. New York: Simon and Schuster.
Crowe, K.J. 1991. *A History of Original Peoples of Northern Canada*. Rev. ed. Montreal and Kingston: McGill-Queen's University Press.
Cruikshank, J. 1990. *Life Lived Like a Story*. Vancouver: University of British Columbia Press.
Denzin, N.K. 1989. *Interpretive Interactionism*. Newbury Park, CA: Sage.
Dickason, O.P. 1992. *Canada's First Nations: A History of Founding Peoples from Earliest Times*. Toronto: McClelland & Stewart.
During, S., ed. 1993. 'Introduction.' In S. During, ed., *The Cultural Studies Reader*, 1–25. London: Routledge.
Farberow, N.L. 1993. 'Bereavement after Suicide.' In A.A. Leenaars, ed., *Suicidology: Essays in Honor of Edwin Shneidman*, 337–45. Northvale, NJ: Jason Aronson.
Kirmayer, L.J. 1994. 'Suicide among Canadian Aboriginal Peoples.' *Transcultural Psychiatric Research Review* 31: 3–58.
Knudson, P., and D. Suzuki. 1992. *Wisdom of the Elders*. Toronto: Stoddart.
La Fontaine, J. 1975. 'Anthropology.' In S. Perlin, ed., *A Handbook for the Study of Suicide*, 77–91. New York: Oxford University Press.
Langness, L.L., and G. Frank. 1981. *Lives: An Anthropological Approach to Biography*. Novato, CA: Chandler & Sharp.
Leenaars, A.A. 1995. 'Suicide in the Arctic: A Few Stories.' *Archives of Suicide Research* 1: 131–9.
McAdams, D.P. 1993. *Stories We Live By: Personal Myths and the Making of the Self*. New York: William Morrow.
Marcus, H., and S. Kitayama. 1991. 'Culture and the Self: Implications for Cognition, Motivation, and Emotion. *Psychological Review* 98: 224–53.
Minor, K. 1992. *Issumatuq: Learning from the Traditional Healing Wisdom of the Canadian Inuit*. Halifax: Fernwood.
Minore, B., M. Boone, M. Katt, and P. Kinch. 1991. 'Looking in, Looking out: Coping with Adolescent Suicide in the Cree and Ojibway Communities of Northern Ontario.' *Canadian Journal of Native Studies* 11: 1–24.
National Task Force on Suicide. 1987. *Suicide in Canada: Report of the Task Force on Suicide in Canada*. Ottawa: Minister of Supply and Services Canada.

– 1995. *Suicide in Canada: Update of the Report of the Task Force on Suicide in Canada.* Ottawa: Minister of Supply and Servies Canada.

O'Neil, J.D. 1986. 'Colonial Stress in the Canadian Arctic: An Ethnography of Young Adults Changing.' In C.R. Janes, R. Stall, and S.M. Gifford, eds, *Anthropology and Epidemiology*, 249–74). Dordrecht: D. Reigel.

Polkinghorne, D.E. 1994. 'Narrative Approaches in Psychology: Theories, Methods, and Applications.' *History and Philosophy of Psychology Bulletin* 6(2): 12–18.

Purich, D. 1992. *The Inuit and Their Land: The Story of Nunavut.* Toronto: James Lorimer & Company.

Randall, W.L. 1995. *The Stories We Are: An Essay on Self-Creation.* Toronto: University of Toronto Press.

Royal Commission on Aboriginal Peoples. 1995. *Choosing Life: Special Report on Suicide among Aboriginal People.* Ottawa: Minister of Supply and Services Canada.

Sarbin, T.R., ed. 1986. *Narrative Psychology: The Storied Nature of Human Conduct.* New York: Praeger.

Schafer, R. 1992. *Retelling a Life: Narration and Dialogue in Psychoanalysis.* New York: Basic Books.

Spence, D.P. 1982. *Narrative Truth and Historical Truth: Meaning and Interpretation in Psychoanalysis.* New York: Norton.

Styron, W. 1990. *Darkness Visible.* New York: Random House.

Tester, F.J., and P. Kulchyski. 1994. *Tammarniit (Mistakes): Inuit Relocation in the Eastern Arctic, 1939–1963.* Vancouver: University of British Columbia Press.

Triandis, H.C. 1995. *Individualism and Collectivism.* Boulder, CO: Westview Press.

Toulmin, S. 1988. 'The Recovery of Practical Philosophy.' *American Scholar* 57: 337–52.

York, G. 1989. *The Dispossessed: Life and Death in Native Canada.* Toronto: Lester & Orpen Dennys.

11

Suicide among the Inuit of Canada

LAURENCE J. KIRMAYER, CHRISTOPHER FLETCHER,
and LUCY J. BOOTHROYD

Across Canada, Aboriginal people suffer from suicide rates two to three times
that of the general Canadian population (Royal Commission on Aboriginal
Peoples, 1995). Many reasons have been advanced for this disparity, including
socio-economic disadvantage, geographic isolation, rapid culture change with
attendant acculturation stress, and the oppressive effects of a long history of
internal colonialism (Kirmayer, 1994).

In this chapter, we will focus on the Inuit, who have had particularly high
rates of suicide in recent years (Dickason, 1992; Petawabano et al., 1994;
Young, 1994). The 1991 census recorded some 43,000 Canadians with Inuit origins (Waldram et al., 1995). Most Inuit live in communities of 200 to 1000 or
more, across the coastal regions of the Canadian north. Across all regions, the
rate of completed suicide among Inuit is currently estimated at about 3.9 times
that of the Canadian average; among Inuit young people, the suicide rate is
about 5.1 times that of non-Aboriginal youth, based on data from 1987 to 1991
(Royal Commission, 1995).

The Inuit of Canada share culture and history with Inuit across the Arctic and
subarctic from Siberia to Greenland. While there are regional variations in dia-
lect, beliefs, and practices, underlying this diversity is a remarkable consistency
in language, mythology, and lifestyle. Accordingly, we will draw on data from
Alaska and Greenland to supplement Canadian studies. In the first section, we
summarize what is known about the epidemiology of suicide among the Inuit
and review studies that have examined risk and protective factors. The second
section takes an excursion through the ethnographic literature to reconsider the
historical stereotype of 'easy' or altruistic suicide. This ethnographic history
then provides a basis for considering the impact of culture change in the third

section. Finally, we consider current initiatives to reduce the high prevalence of Inuit suicide.

Epidemiology of Suicide among the Inuit

There are limited epidemiological data on completed and attempted suicide among the Inuit of northern Canada. Suicide statistics on Aboriginal peoples at the national level have lacked in representativeness, including only Inuit living in the Northwest Territories (NWT) and registered Indians (Royal Commission, 1995). However, despite wide variations across communities, a number of studies of Inuit and Eskimo suicide in Canada, Alaska, and Greenland have noted a dramatic increase in suicide rates over the past thirty years, with young males constituting the group at highest risk (Bjerregaard, 1991; Blum et al., 1992; Petawabano et al., 1994; Rodgers, 1982; Thorslund, 1990).

Among Alaskan Natives, suicide rates per 100,000 increased from 14 in 1960 to 44.2 in 1983/84 (Kettl and Bixler, 1991). This increase was not seen among all Alaskan Native groups; the greatest rise occurred among the Inupiat Eskimo in a region developed by oil companies in the 1970s, for whom the rate increased from no reported deaths in 1960 to 106/100,000 in 1980 (Travis, 1984). These increases were significantly greater than those experienced by other U.S. Aboriginals outside of Alaska in the same time period (Kettl and Bixler, 1991). Suicides in the Greenland-born population began to increase in the early 1970s and rose over tenfold from 9.4/100,000 in 1962–6 to 114.1/100,000 in 1982–6, with the highest rates among young men 15 to 24 years old (Thorslund, 1990).

The overall suicide rate among Inuit in the NWT was 44/100,000 in 1979–86, compared to an overall Canadian rate in 1978 of 14/100,000. In the Baffin region, suicide rates averaged 34.1/100,000 from 1975 to 1986 and reached 54.5 to 74.3/100,000 in some communities (Abbey et al., 1993). Statistics for the NWT reveal an increasing rate of suicide for males from 1965–9 to 1985–6; this trend was not observed for females (Young et al., 1992). Among males the age group with the highest rate has dropped from 45 to 64 years in 1961–70 to 20 to 24 in 1971–80, and 15 to 19 in 1981–6.

Suicide rates per 100,000 among Inuit in Nunavik (northern Québec) increased from 5.2 in 1944–68 to 80 in 1979–83, with a dip in the rate during 1974–8 to 16.2 (Thorslund, 1990). From 1979 to 1983 the rate in Labrador was also 80/100,000 and reached 295/100,000 among 15 to 24 year olds (Wotton, 1985). In Québec, the number of Inuit suicides from 1989 to 1992 ($N = 24$) was nearly double that over the preceding eight years (13). From one to nine suicide deaths per year were reported from 1981 to 1992, yielding an average rate of 51.4/100,000.

These high community rates are reflected in the few published clinical epidemiological studies. Data from psychiatric consultations with 296 Inuit women in the Baffin Island region (1986–9) showed that the second most common reason for referral, after depression, was suicidal ideation or attempt (20.6 per cent) (Abbey et al., 1993). Suicide was a significantly more common reason for referral among men during the same time period (32.8 per cent of consultations). There was no gender difference in the use of more violent methods of suicide (shooting or hanging).

There are few data on rates of attempted suicide among the Inuit and most studies are limited to clinical samples or police records. For the 14 Inuit communities of Nunavik, records compiled by Sureté Québec over the period 1989–92 show 39 suicide attempts and 24 suicide deaths, resulting in a suicide attempted/completed ratio of 38 per cent (Petawabano et al., 1994). This is about three times higher than that expected based on the suicide literature, and probably reflects under-reporting of suicide attempts in this region.

In 1992, Santé Québec conducted a large-scale survey of the Inuit communities of Nunavik and found a lifetime prevalence of attempted suicide of 14 per cent, using self-report questionnaires from 618 respondents aged fifteen years and older (Boyer et al., 1994). When adjusted for age distribution, the frequency of attempted suicide was 3.5 times that observed in a general-population survey of Québec in 1987. Seven per cent of respondents reported a suicide attempt in the year previous to the survey. Among young people 15 to 24 years old the frequency of lifetime attempted suicide was 27.6% for males and 25.3% for females; in the previous 12 months, 19.8% of young males and 15.8% of young females had attempted suicide.

The 1992 Nunavik survey also collected data on suicidal ideation. The lifetime frequency of suicidal thoughts was 12% overall, with reported frequencies of 11.6 and 20.7% among young males and females, respectively, aged 15 to 24 years. In the previous 12 months these figures were 7% overall, and 5.1 and 17.1% among young males and females, respectively. The observed prevalence of suicidal ideation was close to that of suicide attempts; many respondents may have interpreted the question 'Have you ever *seriously* thought of committing suicide (killing yourself)?' to be the same as having actually attempted suicide.

In a survey of Inuit youth aged 14 to 25 years, conducted by us in a single Nunavik community in 1992, 34% of respondents reported an attempt of suicide in their lifetime (Kirmayer et al., 1996). For 32% of attempters, the attempt was serious enough to have resulted in some injury. Twenty per cent of respondents reported more than one suicide attempt. The proportion of young people who reported thoughts of suicide in their lifetime was 43%, and 26% of the sample had suicidal ideation in the previous month. Estimates of rates of suicidal ideation may be more meaningful in this survey than in that of Santé Québec owing to a question that did not use the qualifier 'seriously.' While the very high rates of attempts and ideation from our survey are reflective of only one community that had experienced a cluster of completed and attempted suicides before the time of the study, there are indications of similar rates in other Inuit communities. A recent study of 163 Inuit living in a Baffin region community used clinical interview measures to assess psychiatric morbidity and level of suicidal ideation (Haggerty et al., work in progress). Fully 45% of respondents reported some suicidal ideation in the past week and 6% reported suicidal ideation 'often' or 'most of the time' in the past week.

Risk and Protective Factors

Research on risk factors for completed and attempted suicide among Aboriginal populations has identified multiple factors, including familial instability, childhood separation and loss, poverty, accessibility to firearms, alcohol abuse and dependence, history of personal or familial mental health problems, past sexual or physical abuse, and, for youth in particular, delinquent behaviour, interpersonal and intrafamilial conflict, having friends or relatives who have completed or attempted suicide, and poor self-perception of health (Bachman, 1992; Bagley, 1991; Earls et al., 1991; Grossman et al., 1991; National Task Force, 1994; Kettl and Bixler, 1991; Kirmayer et al., 1996; Rodgers, 1982; Royal Commission, 1995; Thorslund, 1990).

There are limited data on the prevalence of psychiatric disorders among the Inuit, so it is not possible to determine what proportion of suicides are associated with major psychiatric disorders. Experiences with psychiatric consultation in Aboriginal communities indicate high rates of major depression, dysthymia, and substance abuse in many communities (Abbey et al., 1993; Armstrong, 1993; Hood et al., 1985; Kirmayer et al., 1993; Sampath, 1974, 1990). The Baffin region community survey, conducted by Haggerty and colleagues (work in progress), found that among those with suicidal ideation, 27% had high levels of depressive symptomatology, 24% had high levels of anxiety symptoms, and 64% had evidence of alcohol abuse. Individuals with depression or other psychiatric disorders may be more vulnerable to the demoralizing effects of social problems. However, social problems may cause or contribute to suicide even in the absence of diagnosable psychiatric disorders.

A study of Greenland Inuit 15 to 30 years old who died by suicide between 1977 and 1986 showed wide variation in suicide rate by district despite high rates in general (25–600/100,000) (Thorslund, 1991). Eighty per cent of cases had evidence of a personal problem before death, 44% had attempted or spoken of suicide previously, and 90% of those with information (data for half the cases) were intoxicated at the time of the suicide.

In a case-control study of Inuit suicide victims on the east coast of Hudson Bay from 1982 to 1992, data were collected from medical and social-service charts on sociodemographics, medical and psychiatric history, family history, childhood events, substance use, and use of medical and social services (Kirmayer et al., in progress). Of the 21 suicide cases, 17 (81%) were between the ages of 15 and 25 at death, one was younger than 15 years, and three (14%) were older than 25 years. Fully 91% of cases were male; 17 cases (81%) were single and had never married. A previous suicide attempt was recorded for 19% of cases (two had attempted suicide more than once) compared to none of the controls. Only one case was recorded as having seen a nurse at a health clinic in the two weeks before his/her death. In the year before death, 18 suicide cases (86%) had visited a health clinic and three cases (14%) had been hospitalized. Seventeen cases (81%) had been hospitalized in their lifetime and five (24%) had had contact with a psychiatrist (compared to 91% and 14% respectively for the controls). Five cases (24%) had received a lifetime diagnosis of depression, conduct disorder, or personality disorder, compared to 10% of the controls.

A case-control study of thirty-three suicides in Alaska who died between 1979 and 1984 identified previous attempts and alcohol abuse as important risk factors (Kettl and Bixler, 1991). Among Greenlandic Eskimos, a comparison of suicides and attempters with hospital controls found a higher risk among those with personal or familial alcohol abuse, interpersonal conflict within the home and with close contacts, and problems with job stability and crime (Grove and Lynge, 1979).

In the Santé Québec Inuit survey, factors associated with suicide attempt in bivariate statistical analyses included younger age, higher level of education, exposure to a higher level of stress, severe psychological distress, and lifetime use of drugs (including cocaine, solvents, marijuana, or hashish) (Boyer et al., 1994). No association was observed between suicidal ideation and age group or lifetime use of drugs. No results were reported for the possible correlation of levels of education, stress, or psychological distress with suicidal ideation. Multivariate analyses to assess the independent contributions of factors were not carried out.

Risk factors for suicide attempts and suicidal ideation were examined in more detail in our own community survey of Inuit young people (Kirmayer et

al., 1996). At the bivariate level, risk factors for suicide attempt included parental history of an alcohol or drug problem, friend(s) having attempted or completed suicide, solvent (inhalant) abuse, a personal or mental health problem in
the past year, and feelings of alienation from the family and community. Protective factors included doing well in school and regular church attendance. A similar pattern of risk and protective factors was observed for suicidal ideation.
Logistic regression analysis was used to test a series of models of potential risk
factors for suicide attempt. Results indicated that the odds of an attempt were
increased by four to eight times for males, by four to five times for victims of
physical abuse, and by three to six times for those with a friend who had
attempted suicide. Use of solvents in the past was associated with eight-fold
greater odds of suicide attempt, while having a parent with a drinking or drug
problem increased the odds by six times. Treatment of a psychiatric problem in
a family member decreased the odds of attempt by a factor of about 1/10, and
younger age was associated with a decrease in odds by 1.3 times/year.

There is a need for more epidemiological research among the Inuit, despite
its intrusiveness, since basic data are lacking. In particular, most studies have
only addressed factors at the level of individuals. Further consideration of
social structural factors would require study of multiple communities in the
same time frame. The same methods can be used to assess the impact of intervention programs.

Ethnographic Research on Suicide among the Inuit:
The Myth of Easy Suicide

Suicide has become one of the emblematic cultural traits of the 'Eskimo.'
Nearly every popular film with Inuit content contains a scene in which a dutiful
and wise elder ends his or her own existence for the good of the group, usually
with remarkable equanimity. This 'altruistic' suicide is viewed as a distinctively
Inuit practice, albeit one that demonstrates the harsh exigencies of life in the
Arctic. As one early ethnographer put it, 'life sometimes seems harder than
death, and so is regarded as a little thing to give' (Weyer, 1962/1932: 248), and
'when he [an Inuk] commits suicide he has the composure and assurance of a
civilized man who purchases a railroad ticket to another city' (248–9). In this
section, we trace the history of this portrait of Inuit suicide through the ethnographic literature to consider its validity.

Nearly all of the turn-of-the-century ethnographic literature discusses suicide
to some extent (Boas, 1964; Jenness, 1922; Rasmussen, 1929, 1930, 1931,
1932; Turner, 1888; Weyer, 1962/1932). However, most of these accounts use
the term 'suicide' loosely, collecting together incidents of abandonment, mur-

der, family obligations to assist in kin death, group obligations to assist in an individual's death, self-determined and achieved death, group-determined but individually achieved death, and so on. Clearly, we are dealing with a number of different issues and ideas.

How prevalent – and how casual – was suicide in the past? Franz Boas, an ardent cultural relativist, treated suicide tangentially in a discussion of the Inuit conception of the afterlife. Suicide was 'not of rare occurrence' (Boas, 1964: 207) and was generally accomplished through hanging. Boas sought to demonstrate the logic of suicide by describing its social and spiritual context. Although Boas found suicide relatively frequent among the central Inuit, it was not considered lightly. Kin, affinal relations, and others had extensive responsibilities towards the old, young, crippled, and ill. Men were obliged to feed relatives who had no one to provide for them. Men with no relatives or dogs would be adopted into a family. Further, ritual proscriptions, taboos, and mourning customs made suicide a socially significant event. A violent death – including one by suicide – was preferable to a lingering one. Through violent release the soul could travel freely to '*Qudlivun*, the happy land,' something also remarked on by others (Hall, 1865; Hawkes, 1916; Rink, 1875). While men had the right to kill their elderly parents, they did so infrequently. Family groups regularly consisted of adopted children, widows, and old people who were well cared for. Elders and children were occasionally left behind at the fish weirs while the adults went inland for caribou, but they were well able to feed themselves and had no fear of permanent abandonment. In a footnote, Boas (p. 261) described the deaths of two elders: one case was evidently a murder with group sanction; the second was an assisted suicide in which an elderly woman asked her son to kill her so that she could spare him the ritual obligation of having to destroy all of his clothing, an obligation he would incur if she died a natural death.

Writing of the Labrador Inuit, Hawkes (1916) was considerably more explicit on the subject of suicide and the burden of the elderly: 'Aged people who have outlived their usefulness and whose life is a burden both to themselves and their relatives are put to death by stabbing or strangulation. This is customarily done at the request of the individual concerned, but not always so. Aged people who are a hindrance on the trail are abandoned' (109).

This apparent indifference towards the fate of the elderly was tempered by other observations concerning their social importance. 'The aged are treated with great respect, and the word of the old men and women is final. The Eskimo say that they have lived a long time and understand things in general better. They also feel that in the aged is embodied the wisdom of their ancestors. This does not prevent them however from putting the old folks out of the way, when life has become a burden to them, but the act is usually done in accordance with the wishes of the persons concerned and is thought to be proof of devotion' (Hawkes, 117).

As with Boas's description, murder and voluntary death are confounded in Hawkes's account. His central concern was with the place of the elderly in society, rather than with suicide as a category of behaviour.

Weyer (1962/1932) claimed that for the Inuit violent death was simply part of their experience as a hunting culture. Suicide was most commonly caused by remorse over the loss of a loved one and frustration in relationships. Weyer remarked that passive suicide occurred as a reaction to an influenza epidemic among Alaskan Eskimos. The apparent ease of suicide was supported by a conception of the soul in which the recently deceased are reborn through naming of newborns (cf. Guemple, 1965, 1994). Weyer's arguments, while certainly ethnocentric, clearly made the link between reincarnation and ease of death.

Jenness's (1922) account of Copper Inuit life marked a departure from other descriptions of this period. He found this group, unlike most others, to be quite free of European-introduced diseases, such as measles, tuberculosis, and influenza, and also found suicide extremely rare. Elders were well treated among the Copper Inuit and 'under ordinary conditions the aged and infirm are never abandoned' (236). Jenness cited two cases in which elders who were unable to care for themselves were protected, and he had knowledge of only one case of suicide. This was preceded by the victim's terror of revenge for a crime he had committed rather than by any 'morbid weariness of life.' Death among the Copper Inuit was nearly always due to old age, accident, or occasionally murder (42).

Knud Rasmussen's (1929, 1930, 1931, 1932) accounts of early-twentieth-century Inuit life are remarkable for their detail. Rasmussen found that the death of elders by suicide was commonplace among the Iglulik Inuit. He heard of 'many' old men and women who had hung themselves. They did this in part because the moon-spirit legend suggested that the transition from life to death and from the present world to the spirit world was a brief and painless experience marked only by slight dizziness. By ensuring they died a violent death, Inuit elders purified the soul for its journey to the afterworld. Rasmussen's first winter in the Arctic was marked by the suicide of three elderly people. He also recounted the story of a woman who completed suicide with the help of her son. She was provoked to kill herself when she began to spit blood due to 'consumption.'

Among the Iglulik, there were explicit links between forms of death and conceptions of the afterworld. During sleep, spirits of the living and the dead were in close contact and it was possible for someone to slip between worlds. Shamans had more direct and conscious control over movement between the world. The souls of the dead were reincarnated into living bodies through the birth name, while their spirits went to one of three places to live among the *Udlormiut*[1] (people of the day), the *Qimiujârmiut* (a narrow strip of land under the sea), or the 'Sea Spirit *Takánakapsâlik*' (Rasmussen, 1929: 94).[2] The *Udlormiut* were generally people who had died violent deaths or those few who had lived exemplary lives without breaking taboos. They inhabited the sky and lived a comfortable life. People who had died natural deaths, and those who had broken some taboos in their lifetimes went to the *Qimiujârmiut*. People who had committed antisocial acts, or who had ignored ritual prescriptions, dwelt in the house of the Sea Spirit in the water. From there the spirit could send them to the other places or keep them captive. While the dead who made up both the *Udlormiut* and the *Qimiujârmiut* lived without hardship, most living people preferred to go to the former. The living would seek to rejoin relatives here and avoided the *Qimiujârmiut* by having their corpse disposed of in a specific manner. If the body was laid out on the ice, instead of on the land, the spirit would travel to the people of the day. Someone who wished to be certain to go to the people of the day could arrange his or her own death. In one example given by Rasmussen, an old woman drowned herself in the winter on hearing of the death of her son in a kayak accident. She 'could not be certain that others would comply with her wishes when once she was dead' (95) and hence killed herself.

Contrary to his findings among the Iglulik, Rasmussen (1931) found among the Netsilik, even after 'exhaustive enquiries as to the treatment of the aged' (143), only one case in which the burden posed by an elder suggested coercion to suicide. In this case, an unlucky and poorly equipped family left an elderly woman behind when they moved camp in search of food in the winter. Rasmussen's discussions with other Inuit about this case elicited a rationalization for the woman's treatment: the impoverishment of the family – they had only two dogs and a poor sledge – along with the lack of game during that winter, made the elderly woman's plight understandable to his informants. It was a choice between helping a woman who was 'at death's door anyhow' (144) or feeding a wife and child.

Leighton and Hughes (1955) published the first systematic examination of Inuit suicide, focusing on Alaskan and to a lesser extent Siberian Eskimo populations. Data were collected in 1940 at St Lawrence Island and were indicative of turn-of-the-century conditions. Indirect but relatively complete accounts of fifteen suicides were supplemented by partial reconstruction of another twenty-nine. Family-assisted suicide had stopped shortly after the arrival of a missionary in the region, although at least one later attempt was made by a man suffering from measles (p. 330).

Hanging, shooting, and stabbing were the methods used for suicide. People seeking assistance in their suicide made three consecutive requests to relatives for help. Family members would attempt to dissuade the individual at each suggestion, but the third request became obligatory. In some cases, a suicide vow was retracted and dogs were sacrificed instead. The actual suicide was a publicly acknowledged and attended event. Once the suicide had been agreed to, the victim would dress him or herself as the dead are clothed, in this case with the clothing turned inside out. The death occurred at a specific place, where the material possessions of deceased people were brought to be destroyed. After the death, the executioners were confined for twenty days. During this time, they wore their clothes inside out as if they too were dead and were not permitted to work, touch food directly, or change clothes. Hangings were accomplished by a number of people, who were not obliged to observe any ritual afterward.

In Leighton and Hughes's sample, it was primarily elderly men who completed suicide. There was no evidence of the abandonment of elders. The most common reasons given for suicide were illness, grief over the death of someone close, or depressive symptoms. Acts of suicide associated with illness were supported by a folk model in which the spread of disease to other living people could be arrested through suicide of the afflicted.

In some cases, men in their prime killed themselves. Leighton and Hughes suggested that this allowed them to preserve the social status of their family rather than having it decline as they aged. Again, the act was supported by a belief system that saw violent death as leading to a pleasant afterlife. Death brought relief from suffering and might confer prestige on the family, enhancing their ability to survive and prosper.

Leighton and Hughes's article marks one of the first attempts to link ethnographic data on suicide to larger theoretical considerations of the phenomenon. They explicitly interpreted the social repercussions of suicide from a functionalist perspective: suicide removes people who are potentially destabilizing forces in society. In Durkheim's (1897/1951) categorization, the Eskimo displayed *altruistic suicide*, characterized by individual sacrifice for group benefit in a society with high social integration. Leighton and Hughes ended their article with a summary of 'latent functions' of suicide: reinforcement of the power of spiritual belief; demonstration of worthiness of the individual in society; and reinforcement of the importance of elders' knowledge through their final statements before death. Despite these potential benefits, suicide seemed dysfunctional for the group when it was the most productive members of society who killed themselves.

Balikci (1961) followed Leighton and Hughes's approach and reconstructed Netsilik suicide data for the first half of the twentieth century. Until about 1920, the Netsilik lived a 'fully aboriginal life' (576). Rifles were introduced at the turn of the century and there was no starvation at this time, although caribou were limited. Netsilik Inuit converted to Christianity in 1936 and, while the young were no longer aware of traditional religion, the elderly remained knowledgeable at the time of Balikci's study.

Balikci's data were highly structured compared to previous accounts. In the fifty years preceding his interviews, informants recollected thirty-five cases of completed suicide, four attempted, and eleven intended but not carried out. Men completed suicide more frequently than women. The distribution by age for all categories of suicidal behaviour was 12% under 20 years of age, 48% in the 20 to 55 age group, 12% in the 55 to 60 age group, and 24% over 60 years of age. Married people predominated: 34 were married men with children. These data suggest that the demographic profile had changed for this population; in all previous studies, it was the elderly who committed suicide most often.

A variety of methods were used: guns ($N = 11$), hanging (23), strangulations (3), and drowning (2). The majority (34/35) of people interacted with others regarding their suicide: 11 stated their desire to suicide, 6 asked to be killed by others, 2 asked for help to kill themselves, 18 consulted with a relative, and 9 were stopped from killing themselves by relatives. About half the cases were initiated by 'preoccupation with another person,' or reaction to an unfortunate event (p. 579). Twenty people decided on suicide after the loss of a relative, often a descendant, sixteen because of illness, and six owing to marital dissatisfaction. In only four cases was suicide attributed to old age.

Balikci discounted ecological or social-burden explanations of Inuit suicide. These did not apply to the Netsilik data as there were only four elderly suicides (out of twelve attempts in people over sixty years of age) and one case of assisted suicide of a young person (who was incapacitated by frozen knees). The sick were discouraged from ending their lives, nor was suicide a result of group consensus. Balikci also discounted Weyer's view that death was simply commonplace. Balikci's Netsilik informants denied any spiritual beliefs that supported suicide. Ultimately, Balikci advanced the hypothesis that Netsilik suicide met Durkheim's criteria for *egoistic suicide*. Given the great dependence on collaborative hunting techniques and a limited number of closely associated relations, the death of a relative resulted in sudden isolation, followed by a rapid descent into desperation and suicide. The individual was easily detached from his or her social network and marginalized owing to a lack of social cohesion. There are problems, however, with this argument. The people most likely to commit suicide were men with wives and children, who were surely among the less isolated members of the group. As well, most people discussed their suicidal intentions with others before acting and, presumably, had some social recourse.

In a later book, Balikci (1989) re-examined his data in the light of sociobiological arguments for the adaptive value of suicide (p. 248). He argued that traditional conflict-management techniques (drum duelling, wife exchange, joking relationships) contributed to disintegrative tendencies within the group and exacerbated interpersonal conflict. The social tensions that resulted encouraged suicide, which acted as a mechanism to remove socially unproductive or maladapted people from the group. Balikci cautioned that this interpretation is hypothetical and unproven. Traditional methods of conflict management could just as plausibly be interpreted as cohesive elements of society, relieving interpersonal tension, increasing group solidarity and hence the ability to survive.

In the same chapter, Balikci expanded the egoistic hypothesis of suicide to include social breakdown owing to acculturation. Traditional practices that encouraged group cohesion were altered by the presence of traders and new technologies: the availability of high-powered rifles reduced the necessity for cooperation in hunting; family groups fractured for migration to other regions with trading posts. According to Balikci, these changes isolated individuals and increased their likelihood to commit suicide.

Relatively little ethnographic work has directly addressed Inuit suicide since Balikci's publication. In Canada, the reduction of sociological and anthropological interest in Inuit suicide corresponds to an increase in government-sponsored health care initiatives with growing use of epidemiological surveys and clinical assessments of mental health (Boag, 1970; Rodgers, 1982; Sampath, 1974; Willis, 1962). Suicide along with other forms of psychological distress or deviant behaviour came to be considered a symptom of larger social problems faced by Aboriginal peoples, especially political powerlessness and economic disadvantage (Armstrong, 1993; Atcheson and Malcolmson, 1976).

Despite this political contextualization of suicide as a pathological outcome of powerlessness and economic inequity, we also find a claim, in some accounts, that contemporary Inuit suicide is representative of traditional cultural norms. For example, Minor (1992: 83) states: 'In the case of the young Inuit, it may be that the victims were making an effort to return to a traditionally accepted and respected death. Or the burden of life may have been so great and the confusion of cultural transition so frustrating that they acted irrationally. One could argue either that suicide expresses traditional attitudes or is a result of their collapse. I am firmly convinced that there is a traditional component in most of the suicides among the youth.'

This style of thinking is echoed in a recent epidemiological survey of the Nunavik Inuit. In a section discussing the cultural and historical context of the Inuit relevant to understanding the survey results, we find the following interpretation (Boyer et al., 1994: 140): 'Suicide could be considered a culturally

adapted behaviour because it is associated with an ancient ritual which was performed by the elderly, resourceless people who relieved the community of the
burden created by their dependence. Is it not true that current suicides by young
people bespeak of Inuit identity and a sense of community belonging? In that
sense, could suicide among young Inuit be perceived as the statement of a double paradox, namely the merging with Inuit culture and identity, and the necessity of severing the merging process? In the Inuit cosmogony, violent death
enables the soul to reach a better world (Boas, 1964).'

Clearly, our review of the ethnographic literature does not support the idea
that youth suicide was in any way a traditional norm or value; it was in fact
extremely rare. There is also no evidence that youth suicide was viewed as
acceptable or respected in any traditional context. Whether violent death
remains a route to a better afterlife in the thinking of contemporary Inuit youth
is not known, but it seems unlikely given the widespread influence of Christian
teaching. If Inuit youth themselves are influenced by cinematic portrayals of
'altruistic' or 'easy' suicide as part of their heritage, they are involved in a mis-
interpretation of historical events.

Traditional spirituality among the Inuit has been supplanted by Christianity
in various forms. However, this does not mean that Inuit understandings of life
and death are not culturally modulated, or that they can be understood in an
explicitly Western model. Almost all the early ethnography provides details of
the spiritual context of death among the Inuit and the importance of soul and
spirit transfer in determining the afterlife (Merkur, 1985, 1991; Rasmussen,
1931). The multiple realms of the spirits of the dead, and their interaction with
the living through the shaman, are certainly important notions in Inuit concepts
of self and person (Balikci, 1989; Hultkrantz, 1992; Saladin d'Anglure, 1986).
However, these beliefs and rituals are not specific to suicide; they apply to all
the dead. By separating suicide as a category of death and looking for cultural
mechanisms to explain its internal logic, the importance and relevance of death
rituals may be misconstrued.

There is an allure to 'culturalist' arguments that make sense of seemingly
senseless suicide by imputing a collective meaning and value to the act. However, drawing an analogy between the burden of the elderly in the past and the
disaffection of youth in the present is a tenuous argument at best. Youth are not
a burden in the sense used to explain suicide among the elderly, nor do they
constitute a risk to group survival. Ultimately, this view of suicide as a form of
cultural resistance may deflect attention from the social conditions that generate
hopelessness, and could lead Inuit to internalize blame for the very conditions
that oppress them.

Through the ethnographic literature we can see a process of demographic change in who commits suicide. The earliest accounts clearly show that suicide occurred among the elderly, ill, and disabled. As contact with non-Inuit intensified and lifestyles changed, suicide became more prevalent among the healthy adult population. As we approach the present, suicide becomes the domain of the young. This transition in the demographics of Inuit suicide involves multiple historical factors that make the current situation discontinuous with the traditional past. Indeed, we would argue, it is this very discontinuity that underlies the elevated rates of suicide seen at present.

The Predicament of Culture Change:
Suicide Clusters, Social Structure, and the Mass Media

Testimony given to the Royal Commission on Aboriginal Peoples (1995) and our own ethnographic study among the Inuit of Nunavik (Kirmayer et al., 1994) indicate that suicide is recognized to be a serious problem in most Inuit communities. Informants link suicide among young people to interpersonal conflicts, particularly problems with anger and dependency. The most frequent precipitants mentioned were the break-up of relationships or other frustrations with family, school, or friends. Such angry suicide attempts, though, were often described as gestures: 'Frustrated young people, for the most part. Young people that feel that their parents don't give a damn. Or just don't understand their problems, are unsympathetic. Ah ... people who fail at things that they, they want to accomplish. Ah, lover's quarrels. That's a very big one. Disagreements between boyfriend, girlfriend, or common-law spouse. For the most part they threaten to do so when there is someone there to stop them – knowing full well that they're going to be stopped from doing it.'

In more serious attempts, suicide was preceded by silence, withdrawal, and self-isolation. 'Other times, you don't know how things began. Like if someone begins to close their door in their room, lock themselves up, you don't ... at first you don't notice that. That's the time when you begin to see that something is wrong with the person. That they are depressed. And creating some kind of imaginary stuff in their mind.' Many informants noted, however, that it was very difficult to tell that someone was going to commit suicide, even among close friends or relatives.

Several informants introduced historical awareness of recent social and cultural changes as important causes of mental-health problems, especially substance abuse, suicide, family violence, and child abuse and neglect. This awareness did not take the form of a vague nostalgia for times past, but involved explicit links between mental health, child rearing, life circumstances, and changes in the scale and configuration of the community, the family, and the economic and educational systems. The history of contact between the Inuit and Canadians of European descent parallels that of most Aboriginal communities in this country, but the time frame is greatly compressed (Brody, 1975; Crowe, 1991; Dickason, 1992; Duffy, 1988). The Inuit have experienced profound changes in their life-ways in just two generations. This sort of rapid culture change, and the specific demands that have come with it, have contributed to the range of mental health problems.

Traditionally, Inuit lived in small migratory bands composed of one or a few extended families. They congregated at certain times of the year in larger camps, but spent much time in relative isolation. In camp life, children naturally gravitated to watch parents' activities and learn by modelling and imitation. Periodic larger gatherings were times of celebration and conflict would be solved by elders' mediation and, ultimately, by dispersing again into smaller groups back on the land (Boas, 1964).

Along with other Aboriginal groups, Inuit have experienced a high frequency of separations owing to education in boarding schools, prolonged hospitalization out of their communities for tuberculosis and other chronic illness, and forced relocations (Kleinfeld and Bloom, 1977; Manson et al., 1989; Tester and Kulchyski, 1994). The residential-school system exposed Aboriginal children to prolonged separations from family and kin, physical and sexual abuse, and active suppression of their cultural identity (Haig-Brown, 1988; Knockwood, 1992). While their parents often went to residential schools, contemporary Inuit youth are more likely to be educated in their communities. This difference accentuates the generation gap.

In current communities, children are sent to school – which parents may expect to replace much of their own socialization efforts – or else wander about the community freely, in continuation of the laissez-faire approach that fit camp life but that now seems to some community members to border on neglect. While camp life still allows families to enjoy some of their traditional solidarity, some disaffected youth choose not to accompany their parents out on the land during the summer months. The new arrangements of settlement life make peers more important than family for many Inuit adolescents (Condon, 1988; O'Neil, 1986). The multiple losses brought on by disruption of families, communities, and traditions may lead youth to cling to each other in adolescent love relationships. The intensity of this dependence increases vulnerability for interpersonal conflict, abuse, and catastrophic reactions when relationships founder.

Culture change has probably had more drastic effects on the roles of men than women. There has been some historical continuity in the tasks of home-making and childcare, and women's social skills transfer well to available jobs in human services and the helping professions (McElroy, 1975). The shift from hunting and a subsistence-based economy to a status hierarchy based on wage-earning and ability to successfully negotiate with local and distant bureaucracies has left many men, young and old, feeling marginalized and ineffective. There are, in fact, few wage-earning jobs and it takes truly exceptional ability to succeed with the limited opportunities available.

The change in the nature of youth culture is of concern to many people who view it as an intrusion of non-Inuit values through the various media and a source of suffering for young people and parents alike: 'Before 40 years ago, nobody in our community thought of committing suicide. I guess people were respecting themselves, they were respecting each other. But today it's a different story. Young people are committing suicide – I guess the cause would be neglect. They are neglected by their family. They're doing their own things. Listening to rock and roll music. I think it has to do with our way of life now. Some people are not looking after their children' (Kirmayer et al., 1994: 80).

Alcohol, drug, and solvent abuse were among the most common problems raised spontaneously by informants in connection with youth suicide and violence. In our survey of Inuit youth in one Inuit community in Québec, 37 per cent reported having used solvents at one time and 5 per cent had used them within the last month (Kirmayer et al., 1996).

Suicide clusters pose a special problem for many Inuit communities in which many individuals are closely related and share the same predicaments, so that the impact of one suicide is deeply felt within the whole community and has strong reverberations. This close connection between many individuals and sense of a shared predicament increases the risk of a cascade effect, giving rise to a cluster of suicides. It appears these suicide clusters involve individuals who were previously at risk. However, the choice of methods, time, and place for the attempt may be strongly influenced by exposure to other suicides.

The prominent display of a suicide in the newspaper, television, or other mass media leads to a predictable increase in deaths over a one- to two-week period following the display (Eisenberg, 1986; Gould et al., 1990; Phillips and Carstensen, 1986). The relationship is dose responsive; that is, the more intense the media coverage, the greater the increase in the suicide rate (Phillips et al., 1992). This adverse effect of media attention has been noted in recent Native American suicide clusters (Tower, 1989). Sensationalized newspaper and radio accounts probably have played a role in exacerbating recent clusters of suicide among Inuit and other Canadian Aboriginal youth. There is an urgent need for media to adopt a more thoughtful and responsible approach to the reporting of suicide and related social problems.

From Clinical Intervention to Community Action

Clearly, there is a need to provide ongoing counselling and socialization programs for youth with histories of solvent abuse, mental health problems, and friends who have attempted or completed suicide. The epidemiological data discussed in the first section also suggest that identifying and treating mental-health problems in other family members may help to prevent youth suicide. A broader emphasis on family health may be more effective than an exclusive focus on troubled youth, who may otherwise feel blamed for problems that arise, at least in part, from their parents' difficulties.

A variety of initiatives are under way in many communities to respond to the high rate of Inuit suicide. These include a telephone hotline based in Iqaluit, school education programs, community education using local FM radio, additional training of community workers, the development of a crisis intervention team, 'half-way' houses where youth in crisis may be brought for support in a non-medical setting, peer-counselling groups in which youth help each other, and heritage camps that teach traditional skills of living on the land.

Inuit must be provided with ready access to culturally sensitive mental health care. In the case of individuals with major psychiatric disorders, who comprise a large proportion of suicidal individuals, this includes comprehensive psychiatric care with access to evaluation and the full range of treatment modalities. Serious attention must be given to validating assessment methods and adapting treatments to Inuit social and cultural realities. Traditional values of non-interference (Minor, 1992) that are used to justify non-intervention and lead to avoidance of problems must be counteracted with education on appropriate help-seeking for specific problems.

However, the problems of many suicidal adolescents are inextricably intertwined with problems in the family and the social order. Consequently, youth need programs aimed at helping them to negotiate and master the chaotic social situations they face. Family therapy or social-network interventions aimed at uncovering abuse, resolving conflicts, and ensuring the emotional support of youth may be more useful than an individually centred approach. For suicidal adolescents who are withdrawn 'outsiders' vis-à-vis the community, interventions aimed at social reintegration may be most effective, but these must avoid further stigmatizing individuals. For adolescents who are outward success stories, but who inwardly harbour perfectionistic strivings and an inability to share pain and self-doubt, it may prove helpful to identify some of the burdensome community expectations they receive, and develop relationships in which they can confide their concerns and receive support.

One type of program that may be particularly effective at the level of cultural transmission, enhancing self-esteem, and promoting social integration is the development of heritage camps that bring together youth and elders. Under skilful leadership and design, these programs can integrate troubled youth without singling them out for further labelling or ostracism.

The issue of cultural identity appears only sporadically in the suicide-prevention literature. Grossman and colleagues (1991) found alienation from culture and community to be an important risk factor in a survey of suicide attempts among Navajo youth. Elders in an Inuit community on Hudson Bay – the site of a suicide cluster in 1991–2 – reported, 'We don't know what to teach the children any more' (M. Malus, personal communication). This breakdown in cultural transmission points to the importance of community interventions grounded in the culture and customs of the community. The challenge, then, is to encourage and support local initiatives that build on traditional values to provide renewed community solidarity and integration that reach alienated youth. Grass-roots development programs have been undertaken in the NWT and elsewhere in Canada, but these programs have not been systematically evaluated.

Conclusion

While suicide certainly existed among the Inuit at the turn of the century, not all groups were equally affected. In his account of the Copper Inuit, Jenness (1922) remarked on the infrequency of suicide, the absence of epidemic disease, and the traditionality of their lifestyle. Rasmussen found suicide commonplace among the Iglulik Inuit (Rasmussen, 1929), but not among their neighbours the Netsilik (Rasmussen, 1931). Leighton and Hughes (1955) mention influenza and Christian conversion in conjunction with suicide on St Lawrence Island. Finally, Balikci (1961) discussed population movements to trading posts and the changing demographic profiles of Netsilik Inuit who committed suicide. Taken together, these studies suggest that suicide was less representative of traditional life than it was a response to contact and change. They also point to the possibility that suicide was in part a response to losses suffered as a result of contagious diseases carried by Euroamericans for which the Inuit had little resistance.[3]

A careful reading of the literature suggests that early accounts of the striking nature of senilicide and apparently 'easy' suicide may have contributed to ethnocentric bias in subsequent reporting. This bias resulted in 'easy' or altruistic suicide occupying a large place in the academic literature and popular imagination about the Inuit. In the earlier material, the adaptive value of 'easy' suicide was understood to mean the role suicide played in eliminating the weak and permitting the group to survive under harsh physical conditions. In more recent accounts, this has been restated as the adaptive role suicide plays in response to a bleak and harsh emotional and social environment. In both cases, the burden of the individual on society determines the outcome. The individual remains subordinate to the social good and the social consciousness. Surely, it is time to look at how the individual determines social reality rather than the reverse (Cohen, 1994).

Both Aboriginal and non-Aboriginal rates of adolescent suicide have increased in Canada since 1945 (Sigurdson et al., 1994). Possible risk factors for youth suicide in general, including family disruption, unemployment, alcohol and substance abuse, and ready availability of firearms, have higher prevalence in many Inuit communities. Of greatest importance, the effects of rapid social, cultural, and economic change on Inuit peoples in the Canadian north have contributed to the increasing rates of destructive behaviour through their impact on personal and community identity and sense of wellness (Brody, 1975; Dickason, 1992; Duffy, 1988; Matthiasson, 1992; Stieb and Davies, 1993).

Suicide is almost always an effort to escape intense frustration, grief, and psychic pain (Shneidman, 1993). The prevention of suicide must therefore counteract frustration, hopelessness, and unbearable pain in all of their toxic forms and provide other means of changing or escaping intolerable circumstances. In many cases, this may involve psychotherapy, medication, or other forms of healing that renew the individual's sense of power, self-efficacy, and self-worth. Where the loss of hope affects whole communities, however, this individualized approach may be woefully inadequate. Rather than turning Inuit and other Aboriginal communities into 'therapeutic milieus,' where everyone is preoccupied with mental health issues, it may be more effective to address directly the social problems of economic development, the transmission of cultural tradition and identity, and political empowerment.

NOTES

Portions of this chapter are adapted from Kirmayer (1994). Preparation of this chapter and the research on which it is based was supported by grants from the Fonds de la recherche en santé du Québec, Conseil québécois de la recherche sociale, the Royal Commission on Aboriginal Peoples, and the Kativik Regional Board of Health and Social Services. However, the authors alone are responsible for the contents.

1 We follow Rasmussen's orthography throughout this section.
2 The Sea Spirit is known under various names among different Inuit groups, but is most commonly referred to by Boas's appellation 'Sedna.'
3 Recently, questions have been raised about the role of disease in pre-historical culture change among the Inuit (McGhee, 1994). Archaeological evidence indicates that significant culture change among the Inuit, as shown in changing assemblages of material remains, predates direct European contact and, further, that epidemic diseases of European origin reached the Inuit much

earlier than previously thought, through contact with other Aboriginal groups. The havoc
wreaked by epidemic disease may then have driven the culture change of the Inuit shown in the
archaeological record, as it did among other Amerindians (Thornton, 1987). Whether this scenario is true or not, it raises questions about conventional explanations of suicide among the
Inuit. We must reconsider whether the accounts of Inuit culture constructed out of the earliest
record are 'traditional,' in the sense of being timeless and unaffected by outsiders, or simply represent one particular historical moment in an ongoing process of change. We also must consider
whether epidemic disease, mentioned tangentially in many of the texts, should be given greater
importance in explaining Inuit suicide. Restated as a research question: Was turn-of-the-century
Inuit suicide a response to inevitable death owing to epidemic disease for which the Inuit carried
little or no resistance?

REFERENCES

Abbey, S.E., E. Hood, L.T. Young, and S.A. Malcolmson. 1993. 'Psychiatric Consultation in the
    Eastern Canadian Arctic: III. Mental Health Issues in Inuit Women in the Eastern Arctic.'
    Canadian Journal of Psychiatry 38: 32–5.
Armstrong, H. 1993. 'Depression in Canadian Native Indians.' In P. Cappeliez and R.J. Flynn,
    eds, *Depression and the Social Environment*, 218–34. Montreal: McGill-Queen's University
    Press.
Atcheson, J.D., and S.A. Malcolmson. 1976. 'Psychiatric Consultation in the Eastern Canadian
    Arctic Communities.' In R.J. Shepard and S. Itoh, eds, *Circumpolar Health*, 539–42. Toronto:
    University of Toronto Press.
Bachman, R. 1992. *Death and Violence on the Reservation: Homicide, Family Violence, and
    Suicide in American Indian Populations*. New York: Auburn House.
Bagley, C. 1991. 'Poverty and Suicide among Native Canadians: A Replication.' *Psychological
    Reports* 69: 149–50.
Balikci, A. 1961. 'Suicidal Behaviour among the Netsilik Eskimos.' In B. Blishen, ed., *Canadian
    Society: Sociological Perspectives*. Chicago: Free Press of Glencoe.
– 1989. *The Netsilik Eskimo*. 2nd ed. Prospect Heights, Il: Waveland Press.
Bjerregaard, P. 1991. 'Disease Pattern in Greenland: Studies on Morbidity in Upernavik 1970–
    1980.' *Arctic Medical Research* 50 (Suppl. 4): 1–62.
Blum, R.W., B. Harmon, L. Harris, L. Bergeisen, and M.D. Resnick. 1992. 'American Indian–
    Alaska Native Youth Health.' *Journal of the American Medical Association* 267(12): 1637–44.
Boag, T.J. 1970. 'Mental Health of Native Peoples of the Arctic.' *Canadian Psychiatric Association
    Journal* 15(2): 115–20.
Boas, F. 1964. *The Central Eskimo*. Lincoln: University of Nebraska Press.
Boyer, R., R. Dufour, M. Préville, and L. Bujold-Brown. 1994. 'State of Mental Health.' In M.
    Jetté, ed., *A Health Profile of the Inuit: Report of the Santé Québec Health Survey among the
    Inuit of Nunavik, 1992*, 2: 117–44. Montréal: Ministère de la santé et des services sociaux, Gou-
    vernement du Québec.
Brody, H. 1975. *The People's Land: Eskimos and Whites in the Eastern Arctic*. Middlesex: Penguin
    Books.
Cohen, A.P. 1994. *Self Consciousness: An Alternative Anthropology of Identity*. London: Routledge.
Condon, R.G. 1988. *Inuit Youth: Growth and Change in the Canadian Arctic*. New Brunswick, NJ:
    Rutgers University Press.

Crowe, K.J. 1991. *A History of the Original Peoples of Northern Canada*. Rev. ed. Montreal: McGill-Queen's University Press.

Dickason, O.P. 1992. *Canada's First Nations: A History of Founding Peoples from Earliest Times*. Toronto: McClelland & Stewart.

Duffy, R.Q. 1988. *The Road to Nunavut: The Progress of the Eastern Arctic Inuit since the Second World War*. Kingston: McGill-Queen's University Press.

Durkheim, E. 1897/1951. *Suicide: A Study in Sociology*. Glencoe, IL: Free Press.

Earls, F., J.I. Escobar, and S.M. Manson. 1991. 'Suicide in Minority Groups: Epidemiologic and Cultural Perspectives.' In S.J. Blumenthal and D.J. Kupfer, eds, *Suicide over the Life Cycle*, 571–98. Washington, DC: American Psychiatric Press.

Eisenberg, L. 1986. 'Does Bad News about Suicide Beget Bad News?' *New England Journal of Medicine* 315(11): 705–7.

Gould, M.S., S. Wallenstein, and M. Kleinman. 1990. 'Time Space Clustering of Teenage Suicide.' *American Journal of Epidemiology* 131: 71–8.

Grossman, D.C., B.C. Milligan, and R.A. Deyo. 1991. 'Risk Factors for Suicide Attempts among Navajo Adolescents.' *American Journal of Public Health* 81(7): 870–4.

Grove, O., and J. Lynge. 1979. 'Suicide and Attempted Suicide in Greenland: A Controlled Study in Nuuk (Godthaab).' *Acta Psychiatrica Scandinavica* 60(8): 375–91.

Guemple, D.L. 1965. 'Saunik: Name Sharing as a Factor Governing Eskimo Kinship Terms.' *Ethnology* 4: 323–35.

Guemple, L. 1994. 'Born Again Pagans: The Inuit Cycle of Spirits.' In A. Mills and R. Slobodin, eds, *Amerindian Rebirth: Reincarnation Belief among North American Indians and Inuit*. Toronto: University of Toronto Press.

Haggerty, J., H. Merskey, P. Kermeen, Z. Cernovsky, and L. Holliday. Work in progress. 'Psychiatric Symptoms in an Arctic Community: A Validation Study of Two Screening Tools.' Department of Psychiatry, University of Western Ontario, London, Ontario.

Haig-Brown, C. 1988. *Resistance and Renewal: Surviving the Indian Residential School*. Vancouver: Tillacum Library.

Hall, C.F. 1865. *Life with the Eskimaux: A Narrative of Arctic Experience in Search of Survivors of Sir John Franklin's Expedition*. London: Sampson Low & Son.

Hawkes, E.W. 1916. *The Labrador Eskimo*. Geological Survey Memoir 91. Ottawa: Department of Mines.

Hood, E., S.A. Malcolmson, J.D. Atcheson, and R. Glennie. 1985. 'Patterns of Psychiatric Referral and Consultation in an Eastern Arctic Region.' In R. Fortuine, ed., *Circumpolar Health 84*, 517–18. Seattle: University of Washington Press.

Hultkrantz, A. 1992. *Shamanic Healing and Ritual Drama: Health and Medicine in Native North American Religious Traditions*. New York: Crossroad.

Irwin, C. 1989. 'Lords of the Arctic: Wards of the State.' *Northern Perspectives* 17(1): 2–12.

Jenness, D. 1922. *The Life of the Copper Eskimo: Report of the Canadian Arctic Expedition, 1913–1918*. Vol. 12, pt. A. Ottawa: Department of Naval Service.

Kettl, P.A., and E.O. Bixler. 1991. 'Suicide in Alaska Natives, 1979–1984.' *Psychiatry* 54: 55–63.

Kirmayer, L.J. 1994. 'Suicide among Canadian Aboriginal Peoples.' *Transcultural Psychiatric Research Review* 31(1): 3–58.

Kirmayer, L.J., E. Corin, A. Corriveau, and C. Fletcher. 1993. 'Culture et maladie mentale chez les inuit du Québec.' *Santé mentale au Québec* 18(1): 53–70.

Kirmayer, L.J., C. Fletcher, E. Corin, and L. Boothroyd. 1994. *Inuit Concepts of Mental Health and Illness: An Ethnographic Study*. Working paper 4. Montreal: Culture and Mental Health

Research Unit, Institute of Community and Family Psychiatry, Sir Mortimer B. Davis–Jewish General Hospital.

Kirmayer, L.J., M. Malus, and L. Boothroyd. 1996. 'Suicide Attempts among Inuit Youth: A Community Survey of Prevalence and Risk Factors.' *Acta Psychiatrica Scandinavica* 94: 8–17.

Kirmayer, L.J., M. Malus, M. Delage, and L. Boothroyd. In progress. *Characteristics of Completed Suicides among the Inuit of Nunavik, 1981–1996: A Case-Control Study.* Working paper 5. Montreal: Culture and Mental Health Research Unit, Institute of Community and Family Psychiatry, Sir Mortimer B. Davis–Jewish General Hospital.

Kleinfeld, J., and J. Bloom. 1977. 'Boarding Schools: Effects on the Mental Health of Eskimo Adolescents.' *American Journal of Psychiatry* 134(4): 411–77.

Knockwood, I. 1992. *Out of the Depths: The Experiences of Mi'kmaw Children at the Indian Residential School at Shubenacadie, Nova Scotia.* Lockeport, NS: Roseway Publishing.

Leighton, A., and C.C. Hughes. 1955. 'Notes on Eskimo Patterns of Suicide.' *Southwestern Journal of Anthropology* 11(4): 327–38.

McElroy, A. 1975. 'Canadian Arctic Modernization and Change in Female Inuit Role Identification.' *American Ethnologist* 24: 662–86.

McGhee, R. 1994. 'Disease and the Development of Inuit Culture.' *Current Anthropology* 35(5): 565–94.

Manson, S.M., J. Beals, R.W. Dick, and C. Duclos. 1989. 'Risk Factors for Suicide among Indian Adolescents at a Boarding School.' *Public Health Reports* 104: 609–14.

Matthiasson, J.S. 1992. *Living on the Land: Change among the Inuit of Baffin Island.* Peterborough, ON: Broadview Press.

Merkur, D. 1985. *Becoming Half Hidden: Shamanism and Initiation among the Inuit.* Stockholm: Almqvist & Wiksell.

– 1991. *Powers Which We Do Not Know: The Gods and Spirits of the Inuit.* Moscow, ID: University of Idaho Press.

Minor, K. 1992. *Issumatuq: Learning from the Traditional Healing Wisdom of the Canadian Inuit.* Halifax: Fernwood Publishing.

National Task Force on Suicide in Canada. 1994. *Suicide in Canada: Update of the Report of the Task Force on Suicide in Canada.* Ottawa: Minister of National Health and Welfare.

O'Neil, J.D. 1986. 'Colonial Stress in the Canadian Arctic: An Ethnography of Young Adults Changing.' In C.R. Janes, R. Stall, and S.M. Gifford, eds, *Anthropology and Epidemiology*, 249–74. Dordrecht: D. Reidel.

Petawabano, B., E. Gourdeau, F. Jourdain, A. Palliser-Tulugak, and J. Cossette. 1994. *Mental Health and Aboriginal People of Québec.* Montréal: Gaëtan Morin Éditeur.

Phillips, D.P., and L.L. Carstensen. 1986. 'Clustering of Teenage Suicides after Television News Stories about Suicide.' *New England Journal of Medicine* 315(11): 685–9.

Phillips, D.P., K. Lesyna, and D.J. Paight. 1992. 'Suicide and the Media.' In R.W. Maris, A.L. Berman, J.T. Maltsberger, and R.I. Yufit, eds, *Assessment and Prediction of Suicide*, 499–519. New York: Guilford Press.

Rasmussen, K. 1929. *Intellectual Culture of the Iglulik Eskimos.* Report of the Fifth Thule Expedition, 1921–24, VII, no. 1. Copenhagen: Gyldendalske Boghandel, Nordisk Forlag.

– 1930. *Observations on the Intellectual Culture of the Caribou Eskimos.* Report of the Fifth Thule Expedition, 1921–24, VII, no. 2. Copenhagen: Gyldendalske Boghandel, Nordisk Forlag.

– 1931. *The Netsilik Eskimos: Social Life and Spiritual Culture.* Report of the Fifth Thule Expedition, 1921–24, VIII, no. 1–2. Copenhagen: Gyldendalske Boghandel, Nordisk Forlag.

– 1932. *Intellectual Culture of the Copper Eskimos.* Report of the Fifth Thule Expedition, 1921–24, IX. Copenhagen: Gyldendalske Boghandel, Nordisk Forlag.

Rink, H. 1875. *Tales and Traditions of the Eskimo*. London: William Blackwood & Sons.
Rodgers, D.D. 1982. 'Suicide in the Canadian Northwest Territories 1970–1980.' In R. Harvald and J.P. Hart-Hansen, eds, *Circumpolar Health 81*, 492–5. Nordic Council for Arctic Medical Research Report.
Royal Commission on Aboriginal Peoples. 1995. *Choosing Life: Special Report on Suicide among Aboriginal People*. Ottawa.
Ryland, D.H., and M.J.P. Kruesi. 1992. 'Suicide among Adolescents.' *International Review of Psychiatry* 4: 185–95.
Saladin d'Anglure, B. 1986. 'Du foetus au chamane: La construction d'un "troisième sexe" inuit.' *Etudes/Inuit/Studies* 10(1–2): 25–113.
Sampath, H.M. 1974. 'Prevalence of Psychiatric Disorders in a Southern Baffin Island Eskimo Settlement.' *Canadian Psychiatric Association Journal* 19: 363–7.
– 1990. 'The Changing Pattern of Inuit Suicide and Attempted Suicide.' Paper presented at the Papers from the Seventh Inuit Studies Conference, Fairbanks, Alaska.
Shneidman, E.S. 1993. 'Suicide as Psychache.' *Journal of Nervous and Mental Disease* 181(3): 145–7.
Sigurdson, E., D. Staley, M. Matas, K. Hildahl, and K. Squair. 1994. 'A Five Year Review of Youth Suicide in Manitoba.' *Canadian Journal of Psychiatry* 39: 397–403.
Stieb, D., and K. Davies. 1993. *Health Effects of Development in the Hudson Bay / James Bay Region*. Report prepared for the Hudson Bay Programme. Ottawa: Canadian Arctic Resources Committee.
Tester, F.J., and P. Kulchyski. 1994. *Tammarniit (Mistakes): Inuit Relocation in the Eastern Arctic 1939–63*. Vancouver: University of British Columbia Press.
Thornton, R. 1987. *American Indian Holocaust and Survival: A Population History since 1492*. Norman: University of Oklahoma Press.
Thorslund, J. 1990. 'Inuit Suicides in Greenland.' *Arctic Medical Research* 49: 25–34.
– 1991. 'Suicide among Inuit Youth in Greenland 1974–86.' In B.D. Postl, P. Gilbert, J. Goodwill, M.E.K. Moffatt, J.D. O'Neil, P.A. Sarsfield, and T.K. Young, eds, *Circumpolar Health 90*, 299–302. Winnipeg: University of Manitoba Press.
Tower, M. 1989. 'A Suicide Epidemic in an American Indian Community.' *American Indian and Alaska Native Mental Health Research* 3(1): 34–44.
Travis, R. 1984. 'Suicide and Economic Development among the Inupiat Eskimo.' *White Cloud Journal* 3(3): 14–21.
Turner, L.M. 1888. 'Ethnology of the Ungava District, Hudson Bay Territory.' In J. Murdoch, ed., *11th Annual Report of the Bureau of American Ethnology for the Years 1889–1890*. Washington: Bureau of American Ethnology.
Waldram, J.B., D.A. Herring, and T.K. Young. 1995. *Aboriginal Health in Canada: Historical, Cultural, and Epidemiological Perspectives*. Toronto: University of Toronto Press.
Weyer, E.M., Jr. 1962/1932. *The Eskimos: Their Environment and Folkways*. Hamden, CN: Archon Books.
Willis, J. 1962. *Mental Health in Canada's North*. Ottawa: Department of Health and Welfare.
Wotton, K. 1985. 'Labrador Mortality.' In R. Fortuine, ed., *Circumpolar Health 1984*, 139–42. Seattle: University of Washington Press.
Young, T.K. 1994. *The Health of Native Americans: Toward a Biocultural Epidemiology*. New York: Oxford University Press.
Young, T.K., M.E. Moffat, and J.D. O'Neill. 1992. 'An Epidemiological Perspective of Injuries in the Northwest Territories.' *Arctic Medical Research* 52 (Suppl. 7): 27–36.

12

Coping with Northern Aboriginal Youths' Suicides

MAE KATT, PEGGY KINCH, MARGARET BOONE,
and BRUCE MINORE

As is the case, tragically, throughout Canada's provincial and territorial north, youth suicides are a frequent occurrence in the Aboriginal communities of northwestern Ontario. In the past year alone, twenty-two young Nishnawbek from the Sioux Lookout Zone took their own lives. The magnitude of their loss is underscored by the fact that, at the time (1994), only 13,389 Cree and Ojibway people lived in the twenty-eight Nishnawbe-Aski First Nations of the region. As further evidence of the extent of the problem, the Zone hospital that serves the area reported treating 447 youth who had attempted suicide in the same period. The sheer frequency of suicides and suicidal behaviour means that health and other human-service providers in these communities work in a continual state of crisis management. In the event of a suicide or an attempt, their performances are subject to intense scrutiny and often criticism by anguished residents. Moreover, the victim is always someone familiar or, occasionally, even related to the caregivers. The situation is similar in isolated Aboriginal communities across the Canadian north.

Knowing how health-care and service providers cope – or fail to cope – in such emotion-laden circumstances is essential for fully understanding the suicide epidemic that currently is ravaging Canada's First Nations. It is the authors' belief that such knowledge is also key to ensuring that services for northern Aboriginal youth in mental distress are both adequate and appropriate. Particularly critical is an appreciation of the factors or challenges that enhance or impede the workers' functioning as an integrated team, since mental-health care in these remote places depends upon collaboration among professionals and paraprofessionals with widely different training and backgrounds.

Awareness of the importance of this topic is a direct result of the experiences of two of the authors as First Nations people and health professionals working for the Nishnawbe-Aski Nation (NAN). On the one hand, as staff of this Ontario non-profit corporation responsible for representing the health interests of Aboriginal people across the provincial north, they know that there are successes in treatment and prevention at the local level. But, on the other hand, NAN also receives both complaints and anecdotal accounts that call into question the adequacy of some front-line health teams' handling of suicide cases. The observations included in this chapter derive from a number of sources: (1) a community consultation on youth suicide, undertaken in 1990 for NAN; (2) the Nishnawbe-Aski Nation's 1992 Aboriginal Health Policy Consultation; (3) a national survey on the preparation for northern health practice, done in 1992; (4) in-depth interviews with Aboriginal health paraprofessionals from the region, conducted in 1993; (5) an exploratory 1994 case study of the multidisciplinary human-service team working in one community; and (6) the on-going NAN Forum on Youth Suicide.

Matthew's Story: A Case Study of Suicide Crisis Management

The main issues in suicide crisis management are evident in the story of Matthew. That is not his real name, but this is a real story; one that is all too familiar to those who work with the survivors of suicide in Canada's northern First Nations. The authors' pieced Matthew's story together from the accounts of a 'critical incident' told by members of the multidisciplinary human-service team during interviews done in one of the small Cree communities of the Sioux Lookout Zone. The intent of this enquiry was to gain a better understanding of the practices of mental-health care teams, *as teams*, in managing suicide-related events.

Matthew has had a troubled life. His father drowned when he was still young, leaving his mother to raise four young children. According to various reports, alcohol abuse and violence – including that on Matthew's part – have been a problem for the family. The critical sequence of events discussed by the informants had occurred the previous fall, when he was still seventeen. To the extent possible, quotes from the interviews are used here to tell the story.

One of his teachers told of a pattern of suicide ideation in Matthew's school work. 'He mentioned a couple of times that he wants to die, that he doesn't want to be here. He drew a picture of daggers and the words that go with it are 'kill' or 'death.' He's also [drawn] a picture of a boy hanging – the message was [that] drugs are bad for you, but just the picture of the boy hanging would be kind of like crying out.' Another teacher quoted a poem that Matthew wrote, which included the words 'don't tell me you know what I'm going through when you have no idea what I'm going through. All you say is that you're going to help, but you can't help me.' The same teacher expressed surprise, since Matthew was a good student, although he allowed that he thought the boy was 'using school to escape his problems, keeping himself busy and trying to get away [from his problems at home].' Once 'those problems caught up with him and he no longer saw school as an escape,' he started to skip school. The community leaders sent Matthew to a conference on self-destructive behaviour. When he came back the teacher reports, 'He was more confrontational, more difficult to get along with and he made it a point to miss school more often.' Eventually the principal sent a letter to Matthew deregistering him because of poor attendance. The letter angered Matthew since, as he pointed out, others who miss a lot of school are still allowed to attend. It also precipitated a series of violent events.

The band constable was called to Matthew's home where the teenager, drunk and enraged, had cornered members of his family in the crawl space under the house. Matthew was arrested for disturbing the peace and taken to the lock-up. While there Matthew tried to hang himself repeatedly. 'We had to cut him down about eight times in a period of four hours. He was cutting his t-shirt and his shirt [to use] and his socks and shoelaces so we finally just said "that's it" and we took his clothes off him.' The police contacted the nurse, who attended to him in the lock-up and then put the wheels in motion to have Matthew sent out of the community for a psychiatric assessment.

This did not occur before Matthew's next attempt, however. He was back at home a week later when the nurse received a call from the community health representative (CHR), an experienced paraprofessional from the community. A family member had to cut Matthew down from a wooden hook that he had rigged to the ceiling of his room. They had confiscated everything lethal from his room and then called the CHR, as well as another paraprofessional worker and the nurse for help. The other paraprofessional, a National Native Alcohol and Drug Addiction Program (NNADAP) worker, credits himself with calming Matthew by 'sitting him down, talking to him and counselling him spiritually.' The nurse meanwhile arranged for an emergency evacuation and took his mother to the nursing station for respite care. It took 12 hours to arrange for Matthew to be flown 465 nautical miles south to the psychiatric hospital in Thunder Bay. There were problems in arranging to have a physician at the Zone Hospital in Sioux Lookout sign the required form, and for a police escort to arrive from Thunder Bay. Matthew survived his ordeal and is now back in the community.

There is a particular lesson in the details of this case that may help to understand the stories of other youth as well. In this community, as in most northern

Aboriginal communities, there are several individuals who are human-service providers – the nurses, CHRs, NNADAP workers, band constables, teachers – who should be functioning as a team. All of these individuals dealt with Matthew, but they did so within the confines of their own professional roles, not as a coordinated team. In other words, they had not yet adopted a case-management approach, which would have ensured collaboration across discipline boundaries and included not just health, but all human-service providers. To a very large extent, the professionals did what they could, as set out in their job descriptions, and then disengaged. They assumed, in the words of one, that Matthew 'was going to be alright.'

Consider some examples of disengagement in the story. Matthew's teacher, commenting about the principal's action, said: 'I think it was necessary, looking at the mandate of the school, to deregister him, but I wish there were other things for him as well. If I was here next year, I would do my best to see him get on board in September and stay with it for the whole year.' (Unfortunately this man intended to leave the community at the end of the school year.) Another teacher noted: 'He was going to this conference and I thought other people knew about his problem ... He was actually recommended by certain people in the band office to go on this and I think it was funded by them. [So] I thought in order to preserve the relationship he had ... with me, I would just pretend to be oblivious to it.' Although the band constable admitted that Matthew's attempts while in lock-up were potentially lethal, he says: 'It was more or less looking for attention from us or just to be a trouble maker.' As for follow-up by the police during the week leading up to Matthew's attempted hanging, the constable said: 'The nurse, I think, at that time had talked to the mother so she ... kept a closer eye on him and I let them know that they can contact me right away if he does try to do something.'

In addition to the 'disengagement' phenomenon, the outline of Matthew's story illustrates several factors that determine how health and other human-service providers respond to suicide incidents and, consequently, the nature and scope of the help they offer. Perhaps the most outstanding feature of the story is the lack of coordination in the response by individuals who were responsible, each in various ways, for dealing with Matthew. This fact testifies to a lack of awareness of one another's roles, and the lack of preparation for their own role as a member of the response team. Also apparent in the events reported is the impact of geographic isolation on the delivery of mental-health care in northern Aboriginal communities. To fully appreciate the way in which team members cope with suicide behaviour it is necessary to understand the environment and health-care delivery system of the Sioux Lookout Zone.

A Challenging Health-Care Setting

The Nishnawbe-Aski First Nations in the Sioux Lookout Zone are scattered across a vast subarctic area of boreal forest that stretches some seven hundred miles north of the fiftieth parallel and extends four hundred miles west from the Hudson Bay coast to the Manitoba border. The twenty-eight communities, which range in size from between 30 and 1600 people, are all relatively isolated places. Most are accessible only by airplane – often float planes that can land on nearby lakes. Thus, transport to many communities is actually cut off for at least a month during both fall 'freeze up' and spring 'break up' because conditions make water landings impossible.

In terms of their size and remoteness, these Nishnawbek settlements are typical of northern Aboriginal communities across Canada. Also typical are the prefabricated, poorly insulated houses in which people live, frequently under crowded conditions, without running water or safe sewage systems. These living conditions are usually blamed for the high occurrence of tuberculosis, gastroenteritis, skin infections, and pneumonia that the people experience. Various demographic characteristics indicate that the population of the Sioux Lookout Zone is also at high risk for certain mental-health problems. As is the case in terms of their environment, the age, education, and economic profile of the Nishnawbek parallels that of other northern First Nation people: 67 per cent are under thirty years of age; the average level of education attained is less than grade nine; community unemployment rates are never less than 65 per cent and may be as high as 95 per cent; and social-assistance payments are the principal source of income. It almost seems like a recipe for suicide: the convergence of youth living in isolation, without education, without jobs, without much to do – and without hope.

To a large extent, the region's fragile health-care system reflects the fact that so few people live scattered over such a vast land mass. Given a low population density, even reasonably high levels of investment do not translate into levels of service equivalent to those found in southern Canada. Rather, one finds an over-extended system, marked by variably – sometimes inappropriately – equipped facilities, heavy case loads, and astonishingly high rates of staff turnover. In the larger communities, two or three nurses and CHRs work in the nursing station when the staff compliment is full (which is not often). The satellite nursing stations in smaller places only have a resident CHR, who works under the guidance of the fly-in nurse or doctor. Physicians visit the communities, usually once a month, from the Sioux Lookout Zone hospital, and patients – like Matthew – who require advanced levels of treatment are 'medivaced' (medical evacuation) out to the hospital or another tertiary-care centre in the south. For the most part, both human and physical resources are provided by the Medical Services Branch (MSB) of the Department of Health and Welfare Canada. Health professionals are hired to work in the communities, either directly by MSB or by the First Nations themselves using transfer payments from the federal government. Paraprofessionals, such as mental health workers (MHWs), CHRs, and NNADAP workers, are recruited locally under various federal programs. As indicated, these health-care workers are part of a larger network of individuals who provide human services to the Nishnawbek-Aski First Nations.

Professional Challenges to Meeting Mental-Health Care Needs

The decade-long epidemic of youth suicides in northern communities has resulted in calls for a close examination of the working relationships within community-based multidisciplinary teams of human-service providers (Nishnawbe-Aski Nation, 1990; Minor, 1992), and between team members and the communities they serve (Minore et al., 1991). These calls echo the demand for collaborative practice embedded in the Primary Health Care declaration, which was proclaimed by the World Health Organization in 1978 and accepted as a planning model by NAN. Germain (1984) defines collaborative practice as a 'cooperative process of exchange involving communication, planning, and action on the part of two or more disciplines (or, in some instances, on the part of two or more individuals from the same discipline). Its purpose is to achieve specific goals and tasks related to health care that cannot be achieved, or achieved as well, by one discipline (or individual) alone' (p. 199). Germain points out that the ability to undertake collaborative practice requires not only specific knowledge, skills, and attitudes about clinical practice, but also knowledge and attitudes about co-workers as well.

   Consider what happened in the case of Matthew. Members of the multidisciplinary team had a clear sense of professional-role boundaries and the context in which they apply. Even the communication between professions was within proscribed bounds. Individual team members expressed respect for the skills and knowledge possessed by others on the team. But they seemed to lack a full understanding of one another's roles in a time of crisis, or of the root causes of the suicide epidemic that they were amidst. All too often this allowed them to rationalize working within the limits of their own specialization or discipline. So, for example, the nurse explained that when she was called to the house, 'I certainly didn't take charge because to me [the situation] had already been taken charge of' by the CHR, 'because she's kind of like a family member to those people.' The NNADAP worker also put his involvement in the incident into a broader role context: 'Usually what happens is that when the person attempting suicide is drunk the first person [called] is the police, and when they (the victims) are not drunk it's usually me.' Individuals expressed admiration for the skills of other workers. What they did not see was the professional isolation from one another in which they worked.

Failure to understand one another's roles results in attitudinal barriers that partially explain the lack of cooperation among workers. Gregory's (1992) study of nursing practice in northern Aboriginal communities, which identifies the lack of role clarity as a barrier to team cohesion, lends support to this position. He found that professionals often fail to understand or fully appreciate the role of the paraprofessionals with whom they work. Subsequent interviews with several current and former paraprofessionals in northwestern Ontario confirmed this view (Kinch et al., 1994). One CHR reported: 'I am unable to complete my tasks [because the nurses] expect me to translate all the time.' In these interviews evidence of role incongruence standing in the way of collaborative practice was sometimes quite pointed. Asked to rate the relationship among human-service providers, a CHR from one of the largest First Nations said: 'On a scale of 1 to 10, I'd say about 3 due to lack of communication.' And another admitted: 'We really [don't] get along. Everybody does their own thing [except] when problems arise – and that's when you get criticism!'

Writing in reference to psychiatric care in underserviced areas, DuBois, Nugent, and Broder (1991) argue that it is important for members of the team to have confidence in one another and to recognize that individuals have 'equal but different expertise' (p. 459). Professionals and paraprofessionals providing mental-health services in northern Aboriginal communities often fail to understand that they must deal with two cultures, not only the obvious Native culture of the community, but also the culture of the health- and social-care system. The latter culture has both informal and formal role expectations, failure to understand either of which can become a barrier to effective team work. For example, individuals may assume that membership in a certain profession automatically makes a person the leader of the team or the decision maker for all health-related community issues. On the one hand, a person may take charge based on their professional role, mindless of the fact that the community expects someone else to lead. On the other hand, the community may expect leadership from professionals when they, for their part, do not see themselves in that capacity. In either case, the team's ability to function is compromised, and the clients' care is jeopardized. Hertzberger (1993), who was concerned about such 'predetermined expectations' of team members, points out that most disciplines 'have little or no background or education in interdisciplinary team functioning and may tend to favour discipline specific priorities over team goals' (47). In sum: while recognizing the importance of discipline-specific skills and knowledge, these authors stress the need for mutual respect for the preparation and abilities of all disciplines by each team member. The issue may be clouded, however, if community members do not fully understand the skills and limitations of the workers.

In the latter regard, the Scott-McKay-Bain Health Panel (1989) noted the particular dilemma faced by Aboriginal caregivers in the Sioux Lookout Zone who found themselves caught between community expectations that are 'extremely high, often unrealistic and sometimes in conflict with the expectations of the nurses and doctors' (39). One former CHR interviewed by the authors remembers that '[s]ome nurses didn't understand the native culture or what my role was and so they didn't provide me with much help.' The strains, then, derive from both the vertical divisions of professional knowledge and the lateral divisions in cultural knowledge. Yet it is the mix of knowledge, skills, and judgment of professionals and paraprofessionals, natives and non-natives alike, that best meets the needs of the community. This has been recognized for a long while in the case of other minority groups; nonetheless, similar problems have arisen. Schindler and Brawley (1987) and Austin (1978) found that it was common for health and social-service paraprofessionals from minority groups to have to balance the importance of familiarity with a given culture and language against the importance of effective teamwork within their discipline.

A major underpinning of effective teamwork is the sharing of information and the ability of the team to set common goals for action. In small isolated First Nation communities, where health workers are closely connected through family and friendship ties with the majority of residents, the flow of information may be seriously constrained in two ways. First, community members are often unwilling to confide in local workers, turning instead to 'seek help from knowledgeable strangers,' the professionals from outside the community (Rogers et al., 1994: 488). And, second, because many community-based workers struggle with their ethical responsibility to the client regarding confidentiality, the 'value of confidentiality may need reexamination in a team context. When a social worker [or any worker] says to team members, 'I don't have the patient's permission to tell you that,' the statement may be construed by other team members as a power play – information is power. Or it can lead to the setting of clear and overt group norms regarding the use of information: All team members will tell all patients and families that whatever is told to an individual team member has to be shared with the team. The team's information, however, is confidential to the team' (Germain, 1984: 222). For the most part, concern about client confidentiality makes both the professional and paraprofessional staff reluctant to share information about their clients. Consequently, they do not meet with members of other disciplines to discuss clients whom they have in common.

In preparing teams to work in the Nishnawbe-Aski First Nations, it is now recognized that a distinction must be made between the workers' responsibilities not to discuss the details of the case informally outside the context of helping and the need to maximize the use of information in the client's interest. To maintain client confidentiality and yet to ensure that all community-based workers are aware of, and can contribute to, effective case management, the use of *informed consent* is essential. *Informed consent* provides written confirmation from clients that they understand and approve the sharing of information with others on the team, across discipline boundaries. This type of consent allows workers to feel comfortable sharing information, knowing that they are not breaking their personal oaths of confidentiality, but are, rather, contributing the best possible care through a case-management process.

Personal Challenges to Meeting Mental-Health Care Needs

Many people from the communities do not accept an Aboriginal person as being fully competent in a provider role. This is not too surprising, perhaps, since these positions have been filled by non-Aboriginal outsiders for so long. The present authors' study of Aboriginal suicide in northern Ontario identified some of the difficulties inherent in these roles. '[Native] front-line workers must deal with the expectations and criticisms of their communities ... [On the one hand,] some people think that one front-line worker can solve the community's suicide problem ... [but] others are unwilling to trust service providers, or challenge them by reminding them of their own past' (Minore et al., 1991: 16).

Human-service providers take personally the social isolation and lack of support from the community that often accompany suicide occurrences. Not only must workers deal with their own sense of loss and failure with every suicide or parasuicide, they must also, at times, face up to hostile communities. However, these problems are grounded most often in the communities' expectations of the role, rather than of the individual in the role. In similar circumstances, Wodarski (1983) notes that mental-health social workers whose reception in a rural community was guarded, 'respond to this coldness on the part of the community with a tendency to be behaviorally defensive and to maintain a professional distance which, at times, will have a negative bearing on the community's acceptance of services and programs' (7).

Both Aboriginal and non-Aboriginal service providers who work in First Nation communities report isolation and loneliness as a general condition. In the case of Aboriginal nurses, Goodwill (1984) found that this was due, in part, to the policies of their employers, which discourage social visits with community members. Compounding the problem, workers may perceive that there is a need to be somewhat aloof in order to maintain control (O'Neil, 1989). In the case of Matthew, for example, team members report finding their support outside the community. For example, the nurse indicated: 'I would talk to my ZNO [Zone Nursing Officer] if I had to talk to someone in a big hurry.'

Preparing Caregivers to Cope with Suicide

The lack of basic or adequate ongoing training, coupled with the lack of preparation for collaborative teamwork are major factors accounting for the inadequate response to mental-health conditions in the communities. This is partly due to the fact that the majority of mental-health and social services in the Nishnawbe-Aski area are provided by First Nation paraprofessionals, very few of whom receive extensive prior training. Of necessity, the paraprofessionals hired often work for a period of time without training; because of personnel shortages and immediate crises they are thrust into front-line positions. However, inadequate preparation for teamwork is a common failing among human-service providers, professionals and paraprofessionals alike, according to Diller (1990): 'Most of us have been introduced to the team approach by circumstance rather than by formal training. The tendency is, therefore, to learn entirely by experience, rather than profit from accumulated knowledge or principle' (278).

Matthew's story emphasizes the importance of adequate preparation for those charged with meeting the mental-health needs of First Nation people in a small community setting. Not only must these individuals possess appropriate technical skills, they must also learn to work with others as part of a multidisciplinary team. Professionals and paraprofessionals all too often find themselves well prepared to deal with individual clients, but lacking the knowledge and interpersonal skills necessary to work cooperatively with one another. Their challenge is to find ways to maintain their discipline specialties while still functioning effectively as members of a coordinated team. One participant, at a conference on rural and northern health care, summed up the problem well by saying that 'disciplines are educated in separate silos, but no one gets together on the farm to see what's really going on' (Pallen and Boone, 1995: 639). While it is important to have a thorough grounding in one's own discipline, it is also necessary to understand and respect the knowledge and skills of other team members: in other words, to be less discipline-bound and more discipline-based.

Findings from the authors' Canada-wide survey of programs that prepare health workers for northern practice showed that every program recognized the need for community development and the assessment of a community's health status. However, each discipline presented the topic differently and as lying exclusively within the domain of that profession. For instance, schools of social work concentrated on social policy and legal issues, nursing schools stressed community-assessment strategies, and medical schools emphasized the role of the physician in the community. No program included an interdisciplinary basis to planning services or to allocating resources. Moreover, although there was recognition that professionals working in northern Aboriginal communities require specific preparation for cross-cultural communications, it was with their clients not their paraprofessional colleagues, in mind. While a few programs addressed the issue of coping with professional/personal isolation, it should be noted that they did so by emphasizing the importance of maintaining professional and personal contacts outside of the community. Of all the programs that responded to the survey, only one, a paraprofessional program, addressed the issue of the 'self' in the community. Other programs recognized, at most, the importance of understanding and working within the community, but did not address the personal role (Boone et al., 1994).

Meeting the Challenges

In 1990, after four years of staggering suicide statistics in the Sioux Lookout Zone, the communities came together to tell one another their stories – and to try to answer some difficult and tormenting questions. The views expressed in that community consultation formed the basis for a number of subsequent interventions. Although the crisis has not abated, five years later it is worthwhile looking at the approaches adopted to meet the challenges of dealing with youth suicides, because these are based on the suggestions of the Nishnawbek themselves.

The key recommendations relevant to human services from the consultation focused on the need to build *community capacity*. At present, through integrated service agreements (federal-government funding arrangements), each First Nation can develop community work plans to be implemented by service providers as a team. For this to occur, however, special attention must be paid to interagency networking, so that there is better coordination of human resources within each First Nation. It is then possible to have a unified approach to community education about the root causes of suicide, and to promote collegial relationships so workers have emotional support, especially in times of high stress.

Team support makes it easier to confront families and victims when sexual-abuse disclosures are made or when unhealthy and damaging relationships are apparent. Community-development efforts, family rebuilding, and self-esteem building for all sectors of the community are ways to challenge widespread denial, so that sexual abuse and battering emotional or physical assaults can be confronted. The team members can decide who is most skilful or most trusted by the family or victim and can initiate early intervention strategies and counselling, before situations develop into extreme behaviours – violence, suicidal behaviours, or suicides.

Many ideas from the 1990 consultation were incorporated into the planning and operations of the on-going Youth Forum on Suicide. This region-wide enquiry, jointly funded by the federal and provincial governments and coordinated by the Nishnawbe-Aski Nation, commenced in the summer of 1993. Responding to the realization that young people needed to give voice to their stories *in their home communities* – and to be heard, supported, and safe when doing so – NAN developed a careful, reflective process for the public and private hearings, which take place at the invitation of the communities.

To date, hearings have been held in thirteen communities. Each week-long hearing involves a visit by a panel of youth forum commissioners, the majority of whom are youth nominated for this role by one of the Nishnawbe-Aski First Nations. The panel is made up of three youth and one adult commissioners, all of who have had extensive training in suicide prevention, postvention, crisis intervention, the handling of disclosures, and stress and anger management.

A multi-stage process is involved in preparing for and conducting hearings. Once a community has made contact with NAN, a planning session is scheduled with the leadership and front-line workers to present factual information about the initiative and to select dates for the advance preparation work necessary, as well as the hearing dates. Following these decisions, the forum's communications coordinator works with the community to deliver information about the Forum to members of the community. Meetings are held with different groups: youth, Elders, front-line workers, schools, natural helpers, and volunteers. The nature of the preparation done varies from community to community, depending on initial responses to the announcement of the up-coming hearings. For example, if the initial community meeting is not well attended, then a visit is made to each home, in order to ensure that everyone has background material, written in both syllabics and English, and an opportunity to express their concerns and questions. On average, the community-preparation phase has taken two weeks; but it has proved to be the vital link in the implementation process.

Recognizing that the hearing process will place considerable emotional strain on participants, and may trigger critical incidents, all front-line workers in the community receive one week of intensive training before the forum's hearings. This training is provided by the team of highly experienced and skilled counsellors in the mobile training unit, which travels to each community to prepare not only with front-line workers, but also with volunteers, crisis-team members, and other interested community members. On the training curriculum are team building, crisis management, crisis intervention, crisis-team functions, basic assessment and counselling skills, case conferencing, debriefing procedures, and service-referral protocols. If a community does not have an established crisis team, one is organized during the training sessions. So far, the special training has been carried out in sixteen communities.

The forum commissioners are accompanied into the community for the days of the hearing by an Elder, who serves as support for the commissioners, the youth forum director, and a three-member assessment team, made up of a psychologist, a nurse, and a social worker who have extensive counselling and assessment skills. After taking an oath of confidentiality, the commissioners listen to the concerns, ideas, problems, and recommendations of the community members in public presentations. If an individual requests a private hearing, this is done with a commissioner and an assessment-team member present. All public presentations are documented for the purposes of drafting community-specific recommendations, which are then fed back to the leadership, front-line workers, and other community members before the forum delegation leaves the community. Of course, the recommendations do not contain any details that might identify individual presenters. As well, a summary from the assessment team identifies healing interventions that may be required.

Members of the assessment team, who are present during public and private presentations, ensure that the presenters are supported during what is, often, a stressful ordeal. They also work closely with front-line workers from the community to ensure continuing support for the presenters following the hearing process. The psychologist is the team leader and all assessments and clinical findings are reported to him. Each case is handled on an individual basis, with referrals being made to front-line workers or to out-of-community services as deemed necessary. The assessment team participates in case-management meetings and assists with the development of treatment plans and goals for individuals who are traumatized by the hearing process. The team is involved with debriefing sessions for staff and commissioners during and following a youth forum. As well, the clinician completes a follow-up of clients from previous hearings and clients from the community who have been assessed as 'high risk.' He is responsible for communicating with referral agencies and front-line workers after the fact, to ensure that vital information is shared and that there is a timely response to client needs.

The final stage in the youth-forum process involves acting on the recommendations brought forward by the youth and other community members. This requires mobilizing those community members who are committed to working together as a committee to implement the short-term recommendations. Their purpose is to help their community to continue the process of identifying and implementing solutions to issues that, in the past, would have generated a sense of frustration, hopelessness, and despair among Nishnawbek youth.

A Few Final Thoughts

Some sources of conflict relating to suicide in the Nishnawbe-Aski First Nations are to be found within communities, while others are seen as rooted in the larger society. Research and public inquiries are moving us towards a fuller understanding of causative factors. However, as we become more knowledgeable about the causes we must also search for new approaches to meet the challenges of front-line workers coping with the crisis – to find ways for them to maintain their discipline specialty while still working effectively as members of a coordinated team. In other words, to be less discipline-bound while still being discipline-based. The challenge is to transform knowledge into action – so that service providers are not dealing with youth like Matthew separately, but together.

NOTES

The authors wish to acknowledge the financial support provided for their research by the Ontario Ministry of Health. The results and conclusions are the authors' alone, however; no official endorsement by the ministry is intended or should be inferred.

REFERENCES

Austin, M. 1978. *Professionals and Paraprofessionals.* New York: Human Sciences Press.
Boone, M., B. Minore, M. Katt, and P. Kinch. 1994. 'Preparing Health Care Workers for Northern Practice: Towards a Solution for Retention Problems in the Nishnawbe-Aski First Nations of Northern Ontario, Canada.' In L. Heininen, ed., *The Changing Circumpolar North: Opportunites for Academic Development. Third Circumpolar Universities Cooperative Conference*, 54–64. Rovaniemi, Finland: Arctic Centre Publications.
Diller, L. 1990. 'Fostering the Interdisciplinary Team, Fostering Research in a Society in Transition.' *Archives of Physical Medicine and Rehabilitation* 71: 275–8.
Dubois, J., K. Nugent, and E. Broder. 1991. 'Psychiatric Consultation with Children in Underserviced Areas: Lessons from Experiences in Northen Ontario.' *Canadian Journal of Psychiatry* 36: 456–61.
Germain, C. 1984. *Social Work Practice in Health Care: An Ecological Perspective.* New York: Collier Macmillan.
Goodwill, J. 1984. *Barriers to Employment and Retention of Native Nurses.* Ottawa: Indian and Inuit Nurses of Canada.

Gregory, D. 1992. 'Nursing Practice in Native Communities.' In A. Baumgart and J. Larsen, eds, *Canadian Nursing Faces the Future*, 181–98. St Louis: Mosby Year Book.

Hertzberger, D. 1993. 'The Interdisciplinary Team: The Experience in the Armenia Pediatric Rehabilitation Program.' *Holistic Nursing Practice* 7(4): 42–8.

Kinch, P., M. Katt, M. Boone, and B. Minore. 1994. 'On Being Everything and Nothing: The Retention of Native Health Care Workers in Northern Communities.' In G. Petursdottir, S. Sigurdsson, M. Karlsson, and J. Axelson, eds, *Circumpolar Health 93: Proceedings of the 9th International Congress on Circumpolar Health, Arctic Medical Research* 53 (supp. 2): 92–7.

Minor, K. 1992. *Issumatuq: Learning from the Traditional Healing Wisdom of the Canadian Inuit.* Halifax: Fernwood Press.

Minore, B., M. Boone, M. Katt, and P. Kinch. 1991. 'Looking in, Looking out: Coping with Adolescent Suicide in the Cree and Ojibway Communities of Northern Ontario. *Canadian Journal of Native Studies* 11(1): 1–24.

Nishnawbe-Aski Nation. 1990. *Community Response to Suicide: A Model for Caring and Sharing ... for Our Young.* Thunder Bay.

O'Neill, J. 1989. 'The Politics of Health in the Fourth World: A Northern Canadian Example.' In K. Coates and W. Morrison, eds, *Interpreting Canada's North: Selected Readings.* Toronto: Copp, Clark, Pittman.

Pallen, D., and M. Boone. 1995. 'Translating Issues into Action: A Synopsis of Group Discussions.' In B. Minore and C. Hartviksen, eds, *Redressing the Imbalance: Health Human Resources in Rural and Northern Communities.* Thunder Bay: Centre for Northern Studies, Occasional Paper Series no. 16.

Rogers, J., S.J.J. Freeman, J. Cochrane, and P. Goering. 1994. 'The Northern Mental Health Outreach Project: Evaluation Results, Issues and Recommendations.' In G. Petursdottir, S. Sigurdsson, M. Karlsson, and J. Axelson, eds, *Circumpolar Health 93: Proceedings of the 9th International Congress on Circumpolar Health, Arctic Medical Research* 53 (supp. 2): 483–90.

Schindler, R., and E. Brawley. 1987. *Social Care at the Front Line: Paraprofessional Worldwide.* New York: Tavistock Press.

Scott-McKay-Bain Health Panel. 1989. *From Here to There: Achieving Health for All in the Sioux Lookout Zone.* Toronto.

Wodarski, J. 1983. *Rural Mental Health Practice.* Toronto: University Park Press.

PART V: FAMILY, COMMUNITY, AND GOVERNMENT APPROACHES

Canada's vast geographical domain and its different ethnic mix calls for a multi-divergent approach. Family, community, and government are three systems that are progressive steps in the movement towards suicide prevention.

The theme of the family is common in the suicide literature. Data for Canada offer some hints as to how suicide correlates with familial variables. Divorce, for example, is highly correlated, whereas marriage, unlike in the United States where it is a protective factor, is not correlated with suicide in Canada. Beyond the family is the role of the larger community, a fact that is especially true in rural areas. Suicide among farmers, public education, and community coordination are just a sample of issues addressed in these communities. Overall, the family and community are impactful on suicide and suicidal behaviour, and ultimately will have to play a key role in its prevention in Canada.

Beyond the family and community is the government. Across Canada, numerous provinces, territories, and municipalities have initiated a variety of prevention programs. One of the most promising approaches to reducing the rate of suicide is an overall guiding framework. The World Health Organization, for example, has provided clear guidelines that are applicable worldwide. Yet, any review of the current efforts in Canada will reveal that much work needs to be done at the level of the government.

The fifth section addresses Canada's unique need to respond divergently at various levels. An outline of family, community, and government approaches is presented. The section consists of three chapters: a review of the role of the family with its unique Canadian findings, an outline of suicide prevention in rural and isolated communities, and discussion of the role provincial and territorial governments have played (and should play) in prevention.

13

Suicide and the Family in Canada

MICHEL TOUSIGNANT

The theme of the family is ubiquitous in the suicide literature and Canada has not stood apart in this respect. Its contribution has been significant, both in the field of epidemiology and in that of intervention. Researchers have regularly discovered new paths of enquiry and intervention programs have been innovative, thanks to the fact that suicide, especially among young people, has been rapidly recognized as a public-health priority and that provincial as well as country-wide preventive efforts have been undertaken.

The scope of this chapter is to cover epidemiological data, studies of impact on the family, as well as assessed interventions. The content is all Canadian but certainly sums up at the same time conclusions of the international literature from industrialized countries.[1] Publications concerning Aboriginal nations are covered by other chapters of this book.

Suicide and Divorce

Aggregate data for provinces and territories offer some hints as to how suicide correlates with family variables. The advantage of such analyses is to take into account several variables. The limits are that such analyses only apply to populations and not to individual cases. This caution is even more important with low-probability events such as suicide. Besides, greater weights should be given to categories with more observations, which is usually not the case when data are divided by province.[2]

The number of divorces almost quadrupled, from 53 to 191 per 100,000, between the sixties and the seventies while the suicide rate jumped from 8.5 to 13.0. In Canada, between 1950 and 1985, the rate of divorce correlated positively and the birth rate negatively with that of suicide (Leenaars et al., 1993). The provincial rates of divorce have been associated with the rates of suicide during the seventies, but this association has been smaller in 1978 than in 1971, the two years compared by Trovato (1986). The likely explanation is that the differences in the rates of divorce and of suicide between the provinces have narrowed over the years, leaving less room for covariation. A later analysis, on thirty years' data at the pan-Canadian level, still revealed some association between divorce and suicide (Trovato, 1987). This time, though, the association was inverse for females in the fifteen-to-thirty-four age group and non-significant for young adults. A more recent analysis on the 1981 data later found, in contrast, a positive contribution of marital break-up on suicide rates among young people of both sexes and concluded to a link to the increase of suicide in this group (Trovato, 1992). In recent years, the picture has been complicated further by the fact that fewer Canadians, especially in Quebec, become formally married, a fact that will require reconsideration of data on divorce in the future.

Large surveys, unlike aggregate data, focus on individuals rather than collectivities, but their conclusions are restricted to suicide attempts and ideations. This type of information is equally important for prevention. The 1987 survey of Santé Québec included nearly 20,000 informants. Despite the fact that non-married informants in all categories (divorced/separated, widowed, and single) had reported twice the rate of suicidal attempts as married informants, marital status was non-significant in a regression analysis when twelve other factors were simultaneously taken into account (Boyer and Langelier-Biron, 1991). Non-married people had higher rates of attempts mainly because they were more likely to have a psychiatric diagnosis and a lower education.

A crucial test as to how divorce acts on suicide will in part come from an in-depth analysis of events and difficulties preceding suicide. A team led by Alain Lesage has been working on this theme at the Centre de recherche Fernand-Séguin of the Louis-H. Lafontaine Hospital in Montreal. A pilot study was conducted in 1994–5 with a series of eleven cases of homicide-suicide and sorted out the main events preceding suicide. Six of the victims had just lived a separation initiated by their partner, sometimes within twenty-four hours; in two other cases, the separation had probably taken place or was imminent. Considering that data were missing for two cases, feeling rejected after a marital separation appears to be a powerful provoking agent for suicide. There was a high psychiatric vulnerability in this small sample and the decision of the partner was certainly related to the victim's behaviour. Nevertheless, we can still bring the question as to whether the suicide could have been prevented in the absence of a less-threatening separation. These tentative conclusions, based on a small series of homicide-suicides, certainly need to be substantiated on larger samples of suicides.

Family Changes

With the rise in divorce, a child can also be subjected to various family changes following the separation of his biological parents, which can even be more detrimental than the divorce itself.

A community study based on a personal interview covered two cohorts of 14 to 17 year olds and of 18 to 24 year olds (Hamel and Tousignant, 1993), compared suicidal youths, approximately two-thirds of whom had made a suicide attempt and one-third had had serious ideations, to non-suicidal youths. Almost all subjects had a high score of lack of attention from at least one parent as assessed by the Parker scale, so the factor of negligence was similar in the two groups. Surprisingly, in the two comparisons, parents of the suicidal group had separated *less* often than the parents of the non-suicidal group reporting a lack of attention (below the twentieth percentile of the general population). Nevertheless, more than two-thirds of the suicidal group in the 14 to 17 year olds had experienced a change of family arrangement following a parental separation, a death, a placement, or other causes. Considering now only the portion of this 14-to-17 sample with more than one family arrangement during their lifetime, the suicidal group reported more family arrangements than the non-suicidal group with a lack of parental attention, that is five compared to four. Besides, their mothers entered a new union much quicker than was the case in the control group. They took only eighteen months to find a partner, compared to forty-six months for the other group. The rate of failure of this second union was 88 per cent for the suicidal group and 69 per cent for the non-suicidal group. There was also a large gap in the duration of the second union, which lasted only thirty months on average for the mothers of the suicidal group, compared to fifty months in the case of the non-suicidal group. Another contextual factor is the period of development at which these changes took place. In the suicidal group, the child was six at the start of the second union and had not reached nine by the time of the second separation. The non-suicidal child not only had more time with his or her mother alone, but was already eight at the time of the second union and already twelve when it failed. This research also analysed the types of caretaking arrangements after separation. Both groups had a similar profile, except that the non-suicidal group tended to more often report that the father had stopped visiting at one point ($p < 0.10$). The interpretation may be that, when there is a serious conflict, it may be better for the father to stay away to quiet down the family climate.

Parent-Child Relationships

Parental Separation and Quality of Care

The consequences of parental divorce on children's suicidal behaviour are difficult to identify, considering that divorce is part of a longer process of parental conflict still going on years after the divorce has taken place.

There is no doubt that children coming from divorced families have been largely over-represented in suicidal groups, generally by a factor of two to three times. The samples include the Toronto clinical group (Garfinkel et al., 1982), a clinical group of university students at McGill (Adam et al., 1982), and various francophone-community samples from Quebec, either of college (Tousignant et al., 1984) or high-school level (Tousignant et al., 1988). The McGill study showed that the shock of parental separation was almost universal. But if the climate had settled down a few months after the separation, the risks of suicidal behaviour were less than in a comparison group of students from intact families with a negative climate.

Two studies on large francophone-community samples confirmed that the negative assessment of the parent-child relationship was a much more important risk factor than a parental divorce or separation (Tousignant et al., 1993). The first sample included 2300 high-school students from fourteen to seventeen years of age and belonging to six institutions with a wide socio-economical and cultural range. The second random sample included seven hundred young adults, aged eighteen to twenty-four, and was reached by phone. The parental attitude was measured with an adapted version of the Quality of Care scale of the Parental Bonding Instrument (Parker, 1983). This instrument correlated at .80 with a question assessing the quality of the relationship with the parent during childhood.

A hierarchical logit analysis showed that 'mother low care' and 'separation/ divorce' had a significant contribution for the 14 to 17 year olds, but that 'father low care' was much stronger. In the 18-to-24-year-old sample, only 'father low care' came out significant. In fact, there were four times more subjects in this second sample who reported a bad relation with the father only ($N = 82$) than with the mother only ($N = 20$). Interestingly, the girls in the high-school sample reported twice as many suicidal attempts and ideations as the boys (17.3% vs 8.7%), contrary to the young-adult sample (13.4% vs 14.5%). This distribution paralleled a 1.7:1 ratio of girls:boys with a negative relation with their father, a difference that disappeared in the 18-to-24 group. The sexual asymmetry in the 14-to-17 sample was also reflected in demographics. Girls had a significantly lower probability of coming from an intact family (66.6% vs 70.8%; $X^2 = 5.6$;

df = 1, p < .02), and especially when there was an only child. The amount of intact families among girls from one-child families was only 50 per cent, as compared to 65 per cent among boys from one-child families ($X^2 = 5.6$; df = 1; p < .02).

This survey was repeated in the Saguenay–Lac-St-Jean area of Central Northern Quebec on a sample of 2546 high-school students from 23 schools (Simon, 1991). Both negligence of the parent and divorce were strongly associated to suicidal behaviour in separate analyses. Other results showed that the rate of suicidal behaviour increased not only with the level of disharmony and the frequency of arguments, but with the level of children's involvement in the family and with the presence of physical abuse and injury. For instance, when there had been some injury following a domestic fight, the rate of suicidal behaviour was 43 per cent compared to 19.5 per cent for the whole sample.

Another high-school survey done in the La Mauricie area found that students who had attempted suicide came more often from non-intact families than those who had made plans or who had merely thought about suicide, but the difference was not statistically significant (Côté et al., 1990).

To summarize, we cannot conclude that parental separation is a risk factor independently of the family climate. In extreme chaotic situations, divorce may even be the better solution for some children.

Separation from Parents

The theory of attachment proposes that separation from parents at an early age disturbs normal growth. This separation generally occurs in a context where the child feels rejected or abandoned. Trauma or maltreatment suffered before or after the separation or from the foster parents often increase the child's vulnerability. Concerning separation, a psychological autopsy was recently completed in Montreal on seventy-five cases of adult male suicides victims. The two control groups included road-accident victims and a general-population sample paired on many socio-demographic variables, such as social class and marital status (Lesage et al., 1993). The experience of separation between birth and fifteen years of age was twice as high in the suicide group (24%) as in the road-accident (13%) or general-population groups (9%). The difference was highest in the six-to-ten-years-old period. The suicide victims with a diagnosis of borderline personality or of substance dependence reported the highest number of separations.

A high incidence of separation from both parents was also found at an emergency service of a Toronto hospital, looking at the files of about five hundred children and adolescents who had attempted suicide (Garfinkel et al., 1982).

More than 25 per cent of suicidal teenagers were separated from both biological parents, compared to 13 per cent among non-suicidal psychiatric patients of the same age.

In the two-cohorts study conducted in Montreal, the rate of separation was much lower in this community suicidal group than in the above clinical group. Around 9 per cent of the suicidal group, as against 4 per cent of the non-suicidal group, had reported a separation of longer than six months. The main result, though, was that eight suicidal informants reported a separation associated with serious family problems before the age of twelve; there were none in the comparison group ($X^2 = 6.85$, p < .01). The interviews showed a high level of maltreatment and negligence, associated with alcohol, prostitution, and son-mother incest. The number of foster homes was, respectively, four, five, and fourteen in three of the cases, and some instances of bad treatment came from foster homes. One foster home hosted as many as fourteen children.

In Boyer and Langelier-Biron's analysis (1991), those who had been in a foster home before the age of twelve had an odds ratio of 2.4 in a multivariate analysis of having ever committed a suicidal attempt.

A Toronto survey interviewed a sample of 145 homeless and 'street' youth, 83 per cent of whom were between sixteen and twenty-one years old (Smart and Walsh, 1993). Only seventeen had not experienced a foster home, a group home, a detention centre, or a placement with relatives, and most would therefore be classified as having been separated from both parents during childhood and adolescence. The percentage of those who reported having ever attempted suicide was 42 per cent, which is six to seven times the rate of the same age group in the general population. One-third also reported chronic symptoms of depression and two-thirds had at least one drug problem.

Separation from one parent following death has sometimes been identified as a risk factor. Suicidal students seen at a university clinic reported more often the death of their father than those who were not suicidal (Adam et al., 1982). But in one large survey, college students whose father had died when the parents were still living together reported less suicidal behaviour than those still living in an intact family, showing that this type of separation is not necessarily a risk factor (Tousignant et al., 1984). The death of a parent was also not associated in the Montreal high-school survey (Tousignant et al., 1988).

One small study done at the Clarke Institute of Toronto found manic-depressive patients ($N = 13$) who committed suicide to have experienced more often early parental loss through death or definitive separation of the parents as compared to patients with the same diagnosis ($N = 13$) who were alive (Roy, 1984). The suicide group tended to be more often single (five vs one) and was living alone significantly more often (seven vs two).

Negligence and Abuse

Parental rejection or the syndrome of the 'expendable child' is a recurring theme in the youth-suicide literature. In a Quebec study including 210 adolescents from refugee families, of seven adolescents who had reported a suicide attempt over one year, four had experienced a serious rejection from at least one parent in their lifetime, an event extremely rare in the rest of the sample. In the homicide-suicide study mentioned above, rejection from the father was found in four cases. In one example of rejection, a mother left home while her two boys were fighting with a knife and said, 'You can kill yourselves, I don't give a damn.' Not surprisingly, other indicators of bad treatment were astonishingly high in this small sample. Negligence by both parents was found in five cases, high control in six, physical abuse in six, psychological abuse in six, and high family discord in all seven. Note that in six of these seven cases, the maximum score was attributed by the consensus team, which is used rather infrequently, even among deviant families.

An Ontario study investigated the presence of child abuse among adolescent offenders in a correctional institution who had committed single or multiple acts of self-mutilation, a behaviour by definition different from a suicide attempt but also having some similarities with it (Ross, 1980). Nearly half of those with multiple acts of scarification had been victims of violence from parents or surrogates, 19 per cent of those with a single act of scarification and only 2 per cent of the offenders with no previous act of self-mutilation.

The Ontario Child Health Study analysed suicidal behaviour in the twelve to sixteen age group (Joffe et al., 1988). Suicidal behaviour was defined as any thinking about killing oneself or trying to hurt or kill oneself. A logistic regression analysis confirmed the independent contribution of family dysfunction and parental arrest. Family dysfunction was measured with the McMaster Family Assessment Device, a psychometric instrument covering various dimensions of family processes at cognitive, emotional, and behavioural levels.

In Côté, Pronovost, and Ross's survey (1990), family problems were by far the most frequent difficulty identified as the provoking agent by young suicide attempters. This category, mentioned by 46 per cent, was twice as frequent as love problem, the next category in importance.

Sociodemographic Factors

In the Montreal high-school study (Tousignant et al., 1988), there was no association between suicidal behaviour and the socio-economic status of the parent assessed with the three indicators: parents' education, profession, and employment status. Though higher-status fathers tended to have a more positive relation with their adolescents, they also had a higher rate of divorce/separation. However, in another high-school survey, fathers of students who had attempted suicide had significantly less education than the fathers of those who had only ideations (Côté et al., 1990).

In the Montreal study, suicidal behaviour was less prevalent among immigrants (Tousignant et al., 1991). Rates were 8.2 per cent in the two schools with more than 50 per cent allophones, compared to 15.0 per cent in the four francophone schools. The authors perceived a lower degree of negligence in the immigrant families but more extreme forms of control, which may be more conducive to rebellion and acting out than to suicide attempt.

In the two-cohorts study of Montreal (Tousignant et al., 1994), a precise history was made of all the geographical moves up to seventeen years of age. Analyses on residential mobility were conducted in two steps, first on the whole samples, and then excluding those without any family break-up before the age of seventeen. Results showed that, among informants with a family break-up, the suicidal group reported more mobility than the non-suicidal group, but only among the eighteen to twenty-four years olds. A multivariate analysis indicated, however, that family instability predicted suicidal behaviour better than residential mobility. The results suggest that residential mobility is not acting independently of family instability.

Leaving the Family

One distinctive feature of suicidal adolescents is that they try to cut early the emotional or physical links with the family. In a Montreal survey with college students aged seventeen and eighteen, those who were suicidal had a high rate of running away during the last year, that is, 13 per cent as compared to only 1 per cent in the non-suicidal group (Tousignant and Hanigan, 1993a).

One strategy to sever emotional ties from parents is to become deeply involved in a love relationship, with the consequent risk of pregnancy. In the above college survey, 27 per cent of those who feared being pregnant during the last year were suicidal, as compared to only 10 per cent in the non-suicidal group. The fear of becoming pregnant was probably not a provoking agent of suicide as much as the risk of getting strongly attached to a boyfriend.

When asked to describe recent break-up experiences, the suicidal group had longer-lasting relationships and projects of cohabitation were occasionally mentioned (Tousignant and Hanigan, 1993b). In contrast, the non-suicidal students had been going out for shorter periods and had set a higher priority on career plans.

Another characteristic of suicidal youths is that they are more likely to invest in relationships with adults even when they are compared with a non-suicidal group with family problems (Tousignant et al., 1994). Their personal network also includes a higher proportion of adults. In school, they have more conflicts with teachers and school administrators. Of particular interest for prevention is the fact that a majority of suicidal girls named an adult over twenty years old as their boyfriend, as compared to only one in the comparison group.

Suicide Accompanied by Infanticide

The phenomenon of a parent killing one of his or her children and committing suicide simultaneously is still rare in Canada but certainly not insignificant (Rodenburg, 1971). An analysis of the Dominion Bureau of Statistics during the five years between 1964 and 1968 showed a total number of 1379 homicide victims, 141 or 11 per cent of whom were children below age seventeen. Of this total, 114 were killed by a parent, almost equally as often by mothers (41) as by fathers (35). Fathers though were twice as likely as mothers (24 vs 12) to commit suicide, while seven other parents attempted suicide. About half of the infanticide parents committed suicide at the same time. In total, nearly 4 per cent of all homicides in Canada during that 1964–8 period, which is grossly half of the 114 children killed by a parent, were in the category of infanticide-suicide.

Bereavement in the Family

The bereavement of family members following a suicide is highly distressful. One study used Lesage's sample to analyse the grief reactions among thirty family survivors of suicide and thirty family survivors of car accidents (Séguin et al., 1995a). The victims in both groups were between eighteen and thirty-five years old. The survivors of suicide were more depressed than the control group six months after the death but the difference had disappeared nine months after, though the average in both groups stayed above the clinical level. There was no difference in the level of grief reactions at both periods. The survivors of suicide also expressed more shame, with an odds ratio of 4. One-third of the survivors of suicide reported a positive impact, saying that they felt relieved at not having to worry any more. In most cases the victim was a son with a mental illness or a substance-abuse problem. The suicide group reported less support from the immediate family and mentioned fewer persons as being helpful. In conclusion, the results proposed a grief model more complex than originally expected because it needed to take into account the survivors' life history. For instance, mothers in the suicide group reported more early parental losses (five out of sixteen) than the comparison group, which may increase vulnerability to bereavement (Séguin et al., in 1995b).

There are many helping groups for family survivors of suicide in Canada, but only one has been assessed. This project took place at the School of Social Work, McGill University (Hopmeyer and Werk, 1994). Compared to other bereaved groups, the family survivors of suicide were looking more to finding ways of avoiding loneliness than to sharing and support. Sometimes, their social network didn't know about the suicide. Other forms of gain were casting the blame away and enhancing self-worth by helping another member of the group.

Family Treatment

Treating suicidal adolescents present a big challenge to professionals. The Shawbridge Youth Centre, in collaboration with the Montreal Children's Hospital and the Ville Marie Social Service Centre, has conceived a program oriented towards a population with needs for long-term institutional care (Lothian, 1991). Nearly two-thirds of these adolescents manifest suicidal ideations. The clientele is described as being unpredictable and taxing the confidence of their helpers. The main problem in the family was the incapacity of parents to exercise authority and a fear of change. The intervention was geared towards forming an alliance with the parents, supporting them whatever their interpretation of the problem was, and communicating that they needed very special skills to manage their difficult child. In the residential unit, adolescents were asked to make the program their own by taking responsibilities according to a principle of seniority. The more experienced residents were held accountable for the inappropriate behaviour of the most newly arrived, such as self-mutilation or running away. The hierarchical structure was aimed at sharing responsibilities with the group and at diminishing the narcissistic dynamic learned in the family. In so doing, the program forced the adolescents to cope with anxiety-producing behaviour among their peers and to get insight in the state of helplessness that they created in others through their own suicidal behaviour. At the same time, this shared responsibility took some pressure off the helpers. The residence period terminated with a graduation ceremony to which the network of friends and relatives were invited. Of the twenty-two graduates followed up, only one had been readmitted and all but one of the others were either in school or employed.

Short-term intervention in an emergency clinic has been proved effective for avoiding hospitalization without a consequent increase in the use of psychiatric services (Greenfield et al., 1991). Hospitalization was in fact reduced by 16 per cent in a group of 150 treated patients. The approach relied on a rapid and intensive program of consultations over a short period of time, using various treatment stategies. The other characteristic was a focus on the problems of the parents and siblings. Patients and family members were also referred to community resources for further support.

Conclusion

The Canadian scene has certainly witnessed a great contribution concerning the role of the family in suicide in the fields both of research and of treatment. In this chapter, we have somewhat overextended the mission to include the impact of suicide on the family, keeping in mind that family processes continue to go on after the death of one member. We hope that the lessons learned from the data will help in the near future to bolster the efforts of prevention and to finally bring down suicide rates to a more acceptable level.

NOTES

1   We would like to thank the Suicide Information and Education Centre for its help with the reference list. We have tried to include all published material. Some research data are in the process of being published and most manuscripts have undergone a peer review process. Readers will excuse the bias of the author's personal network in the coverage of non-published manuscripts.
2   This criticism invalidates to some extent the work of Cumming and Lazar (1981) and of Cumming, Lazar, and Chisholm (1975) according to Ornstein (1983), and, for this reason, we are omitting their work.

REFERENCES

Adam, K.S., J.G. Lohrenz, D. Harper, and D. Streiner. 1982. 'Early Parental Loss and Suicidal Ideation in University Students.' *Canadian Journal of Psychiatry* 27: 275–81.
Boyer, R., and L. Langelier-Biron. 1991. 'Actes de violence: Suicides, parasuicides, homicides et voies de fait.' In G. Baulne, ed., *Traumatismes: Comprendre pour prévenir*, 231–64. Québec: Les Publications du Québec.
Côté, L., J. Pronovost, and C. Ross. 1990. 'Étude des tendances suicidaires chez des adolescents de niveau secondaire.' *Santé mentale au Québec* 15(1): 29–45.
Cumming, E., and C. Lazar, 1981. 'Kinship Structure and Suicide: A Theoretical Link.' *Canadian Review of Sociology and Anthropology* 18(3): 271–82.
Cumming, E., C. Lazar, and L. Chisholm. 1975. 'Suicide as an Index of Role Strain among Employed and Not Employed Married Women in British Columbia.' *Canadian Review of Sociology and Anthropology* 12(4, part 1): 462–70.
Garfinkel, B.D., A. Froese, and J. Hood. 1982. 'Suicide Attempts in Children and Adolescents.' *American Journal of Psychiatry* 138(1): 35–40.

Greenfield, B., L. Hechtman, and C. Tremblay. 1991. 'Short-Term Efficacy of Interventions by a Youth Crisis Team.' Poster presented at the American Academy of Child and Adolescent Psychiatry annual meeting, 6 October.

Hamel, S., M. Tousignant, and M.F. Bastien. 1993. 'Comportements suicidaires et placement hors foyer avant 12 ans.' *Prismes* 3: 517–24.

Hopmeyer, E., and A. Werk. 1994. 'A Comparative Study of Family Bereavement Groups.' *Death Studies* 18: 243–56.

Joffe, T., D.R. Offord, and M.H. Boyle. 1988. 'Ontario Child Health Study: Suicidal Behavior in Youth Age 12–16 years.' *American Journal of Psychiatry* 145(11): 1420–3.

Leenaars, A.A., B. Yang, and D. Lester. 1993. 'The Effect of Domestic and Economic Stress on Suicide Rates in Canada and the United States.' *Journal of Clinical Psychology* 49(6): 918–21.

Lesage, A.D., R. Boyer, F. Grunberg, C. Vanier, R. Morissette, C. Ménard-Buteau, and M. Loyer. 1993. 'Childhood Separations, Axis II and Suicide.' Paper presented at the American Psychiatric Association meeting, San Francisco, May.

Lothian, D. 1991. 'Working with Suicidal Adolescents and Their Families within a Specialized Group Home.' *Intervention* 87: 33–9.

Ornstein, M.D. 1983. 'The Impact of Marital Status, Age, and Employment on Female Suicide in British Columbia.' *Canadian Review of Sociology and Anthropology* 20(1): 96–100.

Parker, G. 1983. *Parental Overprotection: A Risk Factor in Psychosocial Development.* New York: Grune and Stratton.

Rodenburg, M. 1971. 'Child Murder by Depressed Parents.' *Canadian Psychiatric Association Journal* 16: 41–7.

Ross, R.R. 1980. 'Violence in, Violence out: Child-Abuse and Self-Mutilation in Adolescent Offenders.' *Canadian Journal of Criminology* 22(3): 273–87.

Roy, A. 1984. 'Suicide in Recurrent Affective Disorder Patients.' *Canadian Journal of Psychiatry* 29: 319–22.

Séguin, M., A. Lesage, and M.C. Kiely. 1995a. 'History of Early Loss among a Group of Suicide Survivors.' *Crisis* 16(3): 121–5.

– In 1995b. 'Parental Bereavement after Suicide and Accident: A Comparative Study.' *Suicide and Life-Threatening Behavior* 25(4): 489–99.

Simon, R. 1991. 'Family Factors and Suicidal Behavior.' Paper presented at the 24th Annual Conference of the American Association of Suicidology, 17–21 April, Boston.

Smart, R.G., and G.W. Walsh. 1993. 'Predictors of Depression in Street Youth.' *Adolescence* 28(109): 41–53.

Tousignant, M., and D. Hanigan. 1993a. 'Suicidal Behavior and Depression in Youth.' In P. Cappeliez and R.S. Flynn, eds, *Depression and the Social Environment,* 93–120. Montreal and Kingston: McGill-Queen's University Press.

– 1993b. 'Crisis Support among Suicidal Students Following a Loss Event.' *Journal of Community Psychology* 21: 83–96.

Tousignant, M., M.F. Bastien, and S. Hamel. 1991. 'Le suicide et les communautés culturelles: Le cas des jeunes au Québec.' *Frontières* 3(3): 11–17.

– 1993. 'Suicidal Attempts and Ideations among Adolescents and Young Adults: The Role of Father and Mother Care and Parents Separation.' *Social Psychiatry and Psychiatric Epidemiology* 28: 256–61.

– 1994. 'Ecologie de la famille. Réseau social et comportements suicidaires en milieu scolaire.' *Santé mentale au Québec* 19(2): 41–62.

Tousignant, M., S. Hamel, and M.F. Bastien. 1988. 'Structure familiale, relations parents-enfants et conduites suicidaires à l'école secondaire.' *Santé mentale au Québec* 13: 79–93.

Tousignant, M., D. Hanigan, and L. Bergeron. 1984. 'Le mal de vivre: Comportements et idéations suicidaires chez les cégépiens de Montréal.' *Santé mentale au Québec* 9(2): 122–33.

Trovato, F. 1986. 'The Relationship between Marital Dissolution and Suicide: The Canadian Case.' *Journal of Marriage and the Family* 48: 341–8.

– 1987. 'A Longitudinal Analysis of Divorce and Suicide in Canada.' *Journal of Marriage and the Family* 49: 193–203.

– 1992. 'A Durkheimian Analysis of Youth Suicide: Canada, 1971 and 1981.' *Suicide and Life-Threatening Behavior* 22(4): 413–27.

14

Suicide Prevention in Rural Communities: 'Designing a Way Forward'

DAVID MASECAR

The Current Situation

Research on the problem of suicide in Canada has received little attention over the years (Leenaars, 1995; Tanney, 1995). The impact of suicide on rural communities has received even less attention in the general literature. On-line searches of many databases (Suicide Information and Education Centre, Psychlit, Wilson Social Sciences, ERIC) produced 107 articles on suicide on any aspect of rurality since the 1950s. Twenty of the 107 articles are from Canada. Of these twenty articles, those that represent actual publications address such issues as community coordination and service-delivery issues (Boldt, 1985; Duplessis and McCrea, 1993; Elliot, 1992), public education among teens in a rural community (Carter, 1988), the development of a crisis line (Moore, 1992), the description of a suicide cluster (Davies and Wilkes, 1993), and suicide among farmers (Pickett and Davidson, 1993).

There are two additional sources that relate indirectly to suicide prevention in rural areas. The first involves several articles on the Alberta experience that discuss various components of what has come to be called the 'Alberta Model' (Boldt, 1982, 1985; Ramsay et al., 1990; Tanney, 1995). A number of these components, particularly the CISPP (Community Inter-Agency Suicide Prevention Program) are located within rural communities, and by 1995 those involved have several years' experience in dealing with the problem of suicide within rural settings. The second source involves the experiences of a number of First Nations communities with high suicide rates within rural areas. Many of these communities have shared experiences and a growing body of expertise in responding to suicide clusters within their respective communities (Hollow

Lake, Big Cove, etc.). Within the literature on suicide and First Nations communities, factors such as acculturation and economic deprivation (Connors, 1994) rather than 'ruralness' are cited as contributing to high rates.

Many of the problems identified by Tanney (1995) inherent in dealing with suicide on a national level (cultural diversity, lack of a widely accepted prevention model, etc.) can also be applied to the issue of suicide prevention within rural communities. Several authors have identified significant barriers to providing prevention programs for a variety of social problems within rural communities. These barriers include factors such as geography, distance between communities, population density, lack of services, insider-outsider dynamics, inappropriate government policies, cultural differences, and educational opportunities (Bushy, 1994; Farie and Cowen, 1986; MacDonald, 1990; Parlour, 1992; Sullivan, 1990).

With respect to suicide prevention within Canada, the 1994 updated report *Suicide in Canada* adopts a very broad view, including many strategies such as self-injury prevention, health promotion, amelioration of negative societal conditions, suicide-prevention education, and the reduction of availability of many lethal means (National Task Force, 1994). Widening the scope of what constitutes suicide-prevention strategies by expanding our collective involvement in other areas of prevention is a theme found in more recent contributions by Silverman and Maris (1995) and Dyck (1995).

A Different Perspective

The paucity of rural suicide-prevention programs across Canada, the lack of research into suicide-prevention efforts within rural areas, and the general problems inherent in the field of prevention make it difficult to present to the reader anything more than a summary of problems in prevention and/or rural service-delivery issues that are well documented in many other publications. Perhaps the dearth of information and research specific to suicide prevention for rural communities provides an opportunity to examine the issue from a different perspective. While many of the above obstacles do reflect current and past realities for rural communities, more than likely the greatest barrier has to do with how we continue to *think* about the problem and the potential solutions.

For the purpose of illustration consider the following scenario.

A rural town of 6000 people experiences two suicides each year for the past three years. A number of service providers become concerned and decide to form a suicide-prevention committee to consider what can be done. From their contacts and follow-up calls they receive a wealth of information about determining high-risk groups and organizing public meetings and intervention workshops, as well as advice on how to involve the key stakeholders in the community. A survey is distributed to all gatekeepers regarding their experience with suicidal individuals, the amount of education they received on suicide, and what they believe the community needs for suicide prevention.

For the next meeting several representatives from the local school board, counselling agency, hospital, churches, police force, and ambulance services are invited and eagerly become part of the committee. They review the information they have gathered and conclude that while young people presented with more incidents of ideation and unsuccessful attempts, middle-aged adults and particularly men constitute the highest-risk group. After much discussion they agree that, although the higher incidence of suicide completions is among middle-aged men, attention to all age groups is warranted. They decide that a suicide-prevention awareness program is needed for their community.

Based on the information the committee received, their program will consist of information (i.e., brochures), a story in the local paper, a radio interview on the station in a nearby town, a public-education night, provision of a two-day suicide-intervention workshop, promotion of services (guidance counsellors at school, the Employee Assistance Program at the local mill, the medical centre, etc.), and production of a show on the local cable channel consisting of a film on suicide followed by a discussion. In addition, they decide to form a tragic-events response team to deal with the aftermath of a suicide. A workshop on postvention services and bereavement counselling is arranged.

From everything that the committee members have read and heard, many of the components cited as part of a suicide-prevention program (education, development of intervention skills, and a tragic-events response team) exist within their efforts and are quite reasonable for a rural community of 6000 people with limited financial resources. After approximately four months the program is in full operation. Information has been distributed, the two-day training went extremely well, and both the newspaper article and local cable show received much praise. The local counselling agency reports that they have experienced an increase in referrals. This increase has necessitated a waiting list for clients in which indications of suicidal risk were not present, but overall this situation is preferable to the possibility of more suicides.

In the following year there are no suicides. The members of the suicide prevention committee are ecstatic. They recognize that there may be some other forces at work that could also account for the decrease; however, they are quite proud of their efforts. In order to err on the side of caution, and recognizing that this is only the first year, they decide to continue their program.

In the next year one suicide is recorded. The tragic-events response team becomes involved and does a good job in supporting those who are affected, conducting risk assessments and providing follow-up. The committee members decide that perhaps they should repeat some of the training and redistribute the brochures. Since two of the victims in the past were high-school students, the school decides to provide a class on suicide awareness as part of the health/physical-education curriculum.

In the first month of the following year a student from the local high school suicides. In the next eleven months two more suicides occur, bringing the total for the year to three suicides. The committee is beginning to express concern. What is it that they are not doing right? Why was the first year so successful? Is their suicide-prevention program contributing to the problem, and if so, should they discontinue it? After consulting with several professionals in the field, they learn that fluctuations in the suicide rate do occur. After some reassurance they decide to continue their program and, furthermore, to repeat the training component and concentrate further on identification and early intervention with those identified high-risk groups (young people, middle-aged men, those with mental illness, etc.).

In the following year two suicides occur. Questions are again raised by the committee about any relationship between their program and the numbers of suicides. After considerable discussion and consultation they decide that more than likely they are doing the best they can and that suicide is indeed a complex and challenging problem. Perhaps a further increase in education, information, and skills training would allow for earlier intervention. A decision is made to continue the prevention program and an attempt is made to find those gaps that may account for the continuing suicides and to lobby the government for additional funds through the various ministries. However, each committee member secretly questions if their efforts are in fact working. In addition, interest in the committee begins to wane with several members citing increased work demands in other prevention areas.

What happened? Given the fact that this was a rural community with limited funds and resources, the committee did as well as anyone could expect. They consulted, gathered information, and provided education and intervention, and yet, while the problem abated in the first year, over the long term they came to question if they were making any progress with respect to the suicide rate. In spite of some of this questioning, they responded with many of the same efforts and actually increased some of these efforts. At this point many readers may find themselves suggesting activities such as more research, expanding education, increasing resources within the community, and so on.

Perhaps the best way of illustrating what happened, which reflects a simple and often-repeated pattern, can be found in figure 1.

Essentially, what our suicide-prevention committee did was to create a pattern based on information and suggestions that were offered to them. These suggestions included the distribution of published information, public-education opportunities, training workshops, and so on. When an event such as suicide is present a great deal of anxiety occurs. In order to reduce this problem and manage the anxiety, many activities are initiated that reflect a perception as to how a serious problem should be prevented. It's not that these activities or beliefs are incorrect. The problem is that it is easy to get caught up in a pattern that becomes self-organizing and self-reinforcing. This pattern of events and actions may not contribute to the number of suicides a community experiences (as in creating an iatrogenic effect). However, the pattern limits the potential number of responses and therefore the potential number of solutions.

Review any number of articles on suicide prevention over the past ten years, and you soon realize that they essentially make the same suggestions. While they contain some variations, it is questionable as to whether they are saying anything new or different. When many of the issues and recommendations were originally introduced, they were quite innovative and represented an important historical step in the field of suicide prevention. However, much of the 'pattern' in suicide prevention is well established and it is this 'pattern' that potentially impacts on the problem of suicide within rural communities. This pattern becomes easily adopted, as rural communities often turn to larger urban centres for advice, guidance, and models on dealing with complex problems. The motivation for modelling from larger urban centres stems from the perception that rural communities lack the requisite resources and information.

Developing the Pattern

How these patterned responses to suicide and other complex problems become established relates to how we *think* about these problems. To further understand this process requires a short diversion. Our approach to thinking about complex problems in Western civilization is influenced in large part by 'critical thinking." Edward deBono (1994) suggests that 'Western' approaches often view analysis, judgment, and argument as sufficient in understanding and solving many problems. DeBono goes on to state that while judgment thinking has its place, it often lacks or sacrifices generative, productive, creative, and design aspects of thinking that are vital. 'Many of the present problems around the world persist because traditional education has mistakenly believed that analysis, judgement and argument are enough. Our success in science and technology

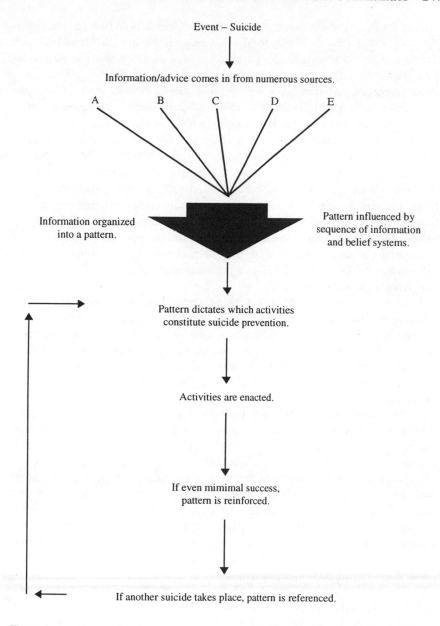

Figure 1   A self-organizing pattern

comes not from critical thinking but from the "possibility" system. The possibility system moves ahead of our information to create hypotheses and visions. These give us a framework through which to look at things and also something to work towards' (15).

An important part of thinking is perception, that is, how we look at the world. Perception, as deBono describes it, is a 'self-organizing information system.' Self-organizing systems pattern information in such a way that thinking becomes trapped within these patterns. This 'entrapment' produces a number of errors in thinking, the greatest error being partialism (deBono, 1976), whereby the 'thinker' looks at only part of the situation and bases his/her conclusions on this part. This error often leads to fragmented and potentially ineffective solutions. For our suicide-prevention committee, their error existed in the perception that the problem was a lack of information, education, and skills necessary to prevent suicides. Once these 'truths' were addressed, the problem should have decreased, and in fact it did during the first year, which further reinforced this perception. When suicides once again started to occur, this thinking pattern was referenced and repeated.

A second error consisted of confusing knowledge and action. Many who work in the field of psychotherapy recognize that 'insight' is generally not enough to guarantee change, although that was a strongly held belief for many years. Furthermore, many people are unaware of the genesis of their difficulties and yet are able to make changes in order to live a more satisfying life. Knowing what causes something and actually doing something about it are not necessarily synonymous.

A third error often attributable to 'partialism' concerns how communities are involved. Communities are not fragmentary in nature. They are complex ecological systems that are intrinsically interdependent. Furthermore, like many organisms (used in the broadest sense of the word) they evolve. Social, political, economic, and technological realities are continually impacting, changing, and developing into something else. In spite of a collective endorsement that suicide is a complex 'multidimensional malaise' (Shneidman, 1985) and that communities are complex, intrinsically interdependent ecological systems, we continue to think in reductionistic and fragmentary terms. This leads to the development of a template 'pattern' that is then applied to many situations (and particularly to rural communities).

A fourth error concerns the element of time and its relationship to the problem. With a problem that has existed for centuries, what is a reasonable amount of time to expect improvement? Furthermore, although it makes sense that a reduction in the number of suicides is a reasonable criterion for the success of any prevention effort, is it the only criterion? Although the outcomes to the risk of being suicidal is that one remains alive or has died, is this outcome the same as preventing the entire problem of suicide? To date, the most successful efforts in preventing suicides have been on an individual level. By 1997 we have acquired considerable expertise and developed training opportunities in how to intervene with someone who is at risk for suicide. In fact, if one were to follow the efforts of many individuals involved in this area, one would conclude that they have been extremely successful in preventing suicides.

How we currently think about suicide prevention and even 'prevention' is going through a transformation. Part of this transformation stems from a number of identified problems in the field of 'primary prevention.' These include the lack of a common definition of primary prevention (Gullotta, 1994), confusion in separating normative behaviours and diagnosable mental-health problems, lack of recognition of diverse strategies (Weissberg et al., 1991), a focus on micro issues at the expense of macro issues (Bennett, 1992), confusion between primary prevention and health promotion (Bushy, 1994), a lack of a code of ethics for those involved in primary prevention activities (Pope, 1990), and problems in evaluation and in connecting between prevention activities and future indicators of success (Rae-Grant, 1994; Connor, 1990).

On a much larger scale, this transformation is not separate from the enormous economic, political, social, and technological changes taking place in the world. Peters (1994) points out that, owing to technological advances, we are going through the biggest changes in two centuries. The last major technological advance (the Industrial Revolution) required, as Peters states, 'six generations, transformation of age old societies and two world wars to realize the full impact.' Peters proposes that the 'impact of the new technology tools will be settled in the next twenty five years, however the social readjustment will require another century.'

These changes will have tremendous implications for the field of prevention, including suicide prevention. For one, many rural communities are single-industry towns (fishing, mining, pulp and paper, agriculture). Many who are employed in these industries have a high-school education or less, with a heavy emphasis on labour-intensive skills. The loss of these industries (e.g., fishing in Newfoundland, mining in Northern Ontario) is resulting not only in a loss of jobs, but in the dissolution of entire communities. Furthermore, given that an information- and knowledge-based economy requires different skills, the possibility that a large number of individuals in these communities can be retrained to compete for a smaller number of jobs is low. Therefore, what may once have been experienced as a cycle of seasonal employment (e.g., fishing, agriculture) or as fluctuations such as 'lay-offs' and 'recalls' will no longer take place. For a large number of individuals and families, it will no longer be that 'I am unemployed,' but that 'I am unemployable.' Therefore, what has worked as a prevention strategy in a relatively stable economy, even five to ten years ago and including a major recession, will have to evolve. It will require what Dyck (1995) refers to as 'opening the borders' between suicide prevention and other prevention efforts. It will no longer be sufficient that suicide preventionists only provide information, education, and skills training in suicide. They will need to become involved in an integral way in many social problems and in overall community development.

Designing a Way Forward

Recognizing (1) that suicide prevention, like many other preventative efforts, can become self-organizing and self-reinforcing, (2) that communities are complex ecological systems that are intrinsically interdependent, and (3) that there are tremendous transformations taking place on many levels (social, political, economic, technological) that affect communities and will determine how we view 'prevention,' how do we begin to approach the issue of suicide prevention within rural communities? We collectively, as deBono terms it, 'design a way forward.' 'Designing a way forward' relies on other aspects of thinking that are generative and usually overlooked when initiating conventional approaches to prevention. It relies on changing and widening perceptions, incorporating creativity and energy into the design of the response, rather than relying only on a critique of the problem.

The point is that rural communities do not have to rely primarily on an established pattern in order to become involved in suicide prevention. Nor do they have to throw out all that has been learned, for there is a lot of valuable information and skills available. Those who live and work within rural communities must be willing to constantly develop new perceptions and new patterns – not because the old ones work or don't work, or because we have not yet achieved a level of sophistication to determine if they do work. We must develop new patterns and perceptions because rural communities and the forces that affect them are constantly changing. To continue to not acknowledge these changes and to respond to any problem in the same way is to invite stagnation. Thus, those who are involved in prevention must continually develop new perceptions, new hypotheses, and new designs that can then be tested. In addition, there are appreciable differences between rural and urban centres, and in many areas of prevention the need for rural models is increasingly being recognized. It is no longer sufficient to 'borrow' a template from another program and merely apply it. Rural communities must be willing to develop their own programs and their own models of prevention. The use of 'possibility' thinking, rather than 'critical' thinking, may fit in better with the character of many rural communities.

Perhaps there are parallel lessons in other areas as to how problems can be addressed through the 'possibility' approach – whether in business, science, or technology – from which the field of suicide prevention could also benefit. Yes, suicide is a very complex problem and there are many dilemmas in evaluating effectiveness for prevention programs (Lester, 1993). Yet we need to ask ourselves how many times the 'complexity' argument becomes an excuse rather than a valid reason for not doing something. There are many complex problems for which individuals have designed innovative products and services.

A page can be taken from the suicide-prevention book in this respect. Of all the strategies that have been developed over the years, one of the more effective, and yet least explored with respect to suicide-prevention programs, has been attention to 'environmental prevention' – that is, focusing on the methods used in suicide by, for example, replacing coal gas with natural gas (Britain), building barriers to popular jump sites such as bridges (Clarke and Lester, 1989), and enacting gun-control legislation (Lester and Leenaars, 1993). It was estimated that the lowering of automotive emissions through installation of catalytic converters in the United States helped to prevent 1200 accidental deaths and 1400 suicide deaths (Shelef, 1992). While the ambivalence associated with suicidal behaviour is part of a complex phenomenon, these activities for the most part recognize the role of ambivalence and represent simple technological achievements that can have profound impacts.

A small native community experiences a number of suicides by hanging. Many of these hangings involve young people taking electrical cords, tying them to closet rods, and leaning forward. One of the crisis workers suggests (again, understanding the relationship between suicide, ambivalence, and time) installing or developing 'breakaway' closet rods. The benefits of this are far-reaching. The first is that the time available for intervention could be increased. The second is that this measure does not require any degree of expertise to enact and therefore can provide many more people with the feeling that they are actively involved in addressing the problem of suicide.

These examples demonstrate that one's perception about the problem can be expanded and that indeed the problem can be approached from a different angle. The prevention of suicide need not rely on just public education, skills development, and counselling; technology can now be an important component.

While many of these strategies rely on technological innovations, what of the social precursors to suicidal behaviour? For example, the relationship between 'needs' and suicide has been identified by Shneidman (1985) as an important commonality (one of ten) across suicides. Shneidman states: 'The common stressor in suicide is frustrated psychological needs' (126); furthermore, 'The clinical rule is: Address the frustrated psychological needs and the suicide will not occur' (127).

It is not a huge leap from considering the needs of individuals to considering the needs of communities. What would a list of 'community needs' contain? Would this list be consistent between communities? In assessing community *needs*, five techniques are often used. These techniques involve community forums, rates-under-treatment, social and health indicators, field surveys, and key informants (Rhodes and Jason, 1991).

In addition to the techniques listed above, there is a large volume of literature that focuses on a number of contributing factors to suicidal behaviour. Much of the research examines the relationship between several factors and suicide, and attention to these factors is often cited as an important part of prevention. The assumption is that if we can intervene early in these conditions we can prevent suicide over the long term. We can easily forget that there are many individuals who experience these problems and never make a suicide attempt.

If the same rule of thumb for preventing suicide (address the frustrated psychological needs) exists for communities as for individuals, then part of the needs assessment involves the identification of community needs and of those factors that are frustrating the attainment of these needs. Consider the following situation.

In 1994, a First Nations community of approximately 1200 people in northwestern Ontario experienced seven suicides. This situation received considerable media attention across Canada and one prominent Canadian news show produced a documentary. As the crisis continued and pressure increased on the government to respond, the minister for indian affairs travelled to this community. After a five-hour visit one of his concluding remarks was that the community needed more crisis workers; building additional housing would not solve the suicide problem. His statement reflected the fundamental dilemma. It wasn't that he was entirely incorrect; the community did require more crisis workers. The error (reflecting partialism) was in failing to consider if 'housing' (the need for shelter in addition to many other psychological needs) was at all connected to suicidal behaviour.

In this community, the birth rate is one of the highest in the world and housing is in short supply, a factor also influenced in part by a steady migration from a nearby community. It is not uncommon that a small home has ten to twenty people residing there at night. Also, there is some degree of 'homelessness.' One family developed many fears about their home after the suicide of their child, and were forced to find other shelter. In a remote community of 1200 with limited housing, one less house – forcing the relocation of ten individuals represents – a further strain on the resources of the community and threatens the needs of others (for shelter, privacy, etc.). Furthermore, as inadequate as this house may have been to shelter its occupants comfortably, moving represents another loss in addition to the loss of their family member.

The government's failure to acknowledge the continued request of the chief and band council for additional funding for housing, as well as their need to be understood and validated, their need for some control of their fate, and their need for achievement in managing undermined the political affairs of their community.

The challenge then in addressing such frustrated or thwarted needs is to 'design' ways in which they can be met. For example, the need for affiliation is the opposite of isolation, which is consistently identified as a high-risk sign for suicide (Ramsay et al., 1994). A number of caregivers within the community described above developed a community patrol to deal with the problem of solvent abuse, which was closely tied to suicidal behaviour. Essentially, this patrol would search through the community at night, and once they located someone who was 'high' would escort them to the nursing station, where they could be monitored. Some of the members of this patrol were youth from the community who had been involved in substance abuse themselves, and knew where all the 'hot spots' were located. Furthermore, as this patrol continued (with such paraphernalia as walkie-talkies, a patrol 'office,' and the provision of refreshments), other 'at-risk' youth became involved. Their needs for affiliation and group identification (so important during adolescence) were now being met and they became less of a risk for suicide. While the patrol was not originally designed to increase affiliation and feelings of usefulness, these became important features for a high-risk group.

The above example represents a common-sense solution to a very real problem that was part of the larger problem, influenced not by 'critical thinking' but by the possibility system. Furthermore, this approach contained activities that were possible within their respective communities. They didn't solve the entire problem (remember the time element); but they did allow the community to become involved on some level.

In the end, we need to recognize that communities (both urban and rural) and the field of suicide prevention are continually facing new challenges. The challenges require that those of us who work in prevention in rural communities – in order that we not continue to adopt template models – must be prepared to change not only some of our strategies to meet these challenges, but also our approach to thinking about these problems. One important change will need to be the recognition of rural communities as possessing different skills, resources, and strengths from which creative solutions can be designed, rather than as being communities that lack urban qualities.

REFERENCES

Bennett, E.M. 1992. 'Community-Based Economic Development: A Strategy for Primary Prevention.' *Canadian Journal of Mental Health* 11(2): 11–31.
Boldt, M. 1982. 'A Model for Suicide Prevention, Intervention and Postvention: The Alberta Task Force Proposals.' *Canada's Mental Health*, March.
– 1985. 'A Systematic and Integrated Interagency Model for Providing Coordinated and Comprehensive Suicide Prevention Services.' *Crisis* 6(2): 106–18.
Bushy, A. 1994. 'Implementing Primary Prevention Programs for Adolescents in Rural Environments.' *Journal of Primary Prevention* 14(3): 209–29.
Carter, G. 1988. 'Suicide Prevention in Rural Areas: Survey of Hinton Teens Regarding Suicide.' *Research and Information (Mental Health Newsletter)* 3(1): 2–3.
Clarke, R.V., and D. Lester. 1989. *Suicide: Closing the Exits*. New York: Springer-Verlag.
Connor, R.F. 1990. 'Ethical Issues in Evaluating the Effectiveness of Primary Prevention Programs.' *Prevention in Human Services* 8(2): 43–64.
Connors, E. (1994). Appendix Three: First Nations and Inuit Communities. *Suicide in Canada – Update of the Report on the Task Force on Suicide in Canada*. Mental Health Division, Health Programs and Services Branch, Health Canada.
Davies, D., and T.C.R. Wilkes. 1993. 'Cluster Suicide in Rural Western Canada.' *Canadian Journal of Psychiatry* 38(7): 515–19.
deBono, E. 1976. *Teaching Thinking*. Toronto: Penguin Books.
– 1994. *deBono's Thinking Course*. London, England: BBC Books.
Duplessis, G., and M. McCrea. 1993. *What Works! Innovation in Community Mental Health and Addiction Treatment Programs*. Toronto: Canadian Scholars' Press.
Dyck, R. 1995. 'Suicide Prevention: Opening the Borders.' Keynote address, annual meeting of the Canadian Association for Suicide Prevention, 11–14 October, Banff, Alberta.
Elliot, C. 1992. *Sexually and Physically Abused Native Youth: Intricacies of Service and Delivery*, 61–2. Annual meeting (25th) of the American Association of Suicidology, Chicago.
Farie, A.M., and E.L. Cowen. 1986. 'The Development and Implementation of a Rural Consortium Program to Provide Early, Preventive School Mental Health Services.' *Community Mental Health Journal* 22(2): 94–103.
Gullota, T.P. 1994. 'The What, Who, Why, Where, When, and How of Primary Prevention.' *Journal of Primary Prevention* 15(1): 5–14.
Leenaars, A. 1995. 'Suicide and the Continental Divide.' *Archives of Suicide Research* 1: 39–58.
Lester, D. 1993. 'The Effectiveness of Suicide Prevention Centres.' *Suicide and Life-Threatening Behavior* 24(3): 263–7.
Lester, D., and A. Leenaars. 1993. 'Suicide Rates in Canada before and after Tightening Firearm Control Laws.' *Psychological Reports* 72: 789–90.
MacDonald, F.F. 1990. 'A Case Study of Insider-Outsider Dynamics in Rural Community Development.' *Human Services in the Rural Environment* 14(3): 15–20.
Moore, L. 1992. 'Sarnia Features Non-Traditional Programs.' *Focus on Listening* 1(3): 2.
National Task Force. 1994. *Suicide in Canada: Update of the Report of the Task Force on Suicide in Canada*. Ottawa: Health Canada.
Parlour, S. 1992. 'The Retention of Children's Mental Health Workers in Northern Ontario.' In D. Masecar, ed., *Northern Lifelines: A Suicide Information and Resource Manual*. Sault Ste Marie: Algoma Child and Youth Services.
Peters, T. 1994. *The Tom Peters Seminar: Crazy Times Call for Crazy Organizations*. New York: Vintage Books.

Picket, W., and J.R. Davidson. 1993. 'Suicides on Ontario Farms.' *Canadian Journal of Public Health* 84(4): 226–30.

Pope, K.S. 1990. 'Identifying and Implementing Ethical Standards for Primary Prevention.' *Prevention in Human Services* 8(2): 43–64.

Rae-Grant, N.I. 1994. 'Preventive Interventions for Children and Adolescents: Where Are We Now and How Far Have We Come?' *Canadian Journal of Community Mental Health* 13(2): 17–36.

Ramsay, R.F., M.A. Cooke, and W.A. Lang. 1990. 'Alberta's Suicide Prevention Training Programs: A Retrospective Comparison with Rothman's Developmental Research Model.' *Suicide and Life-Threatening Behavior* 20(4): 335–51.

Ramsay, R., B.L. Tanney, R.J. Tierney, and W.A. Lang. 1994. *Suicide Intervention Training Program: Trainers Manual.* Calgary: Living Works Education, Inc.

Rhodes, J.E., and L.A. Jason. 1991. 'Community Needs Assessment.' In H.E. Schroeder, ed., *New Directions in Health Psychology Assessment.* New York: Hemisphere Publishing Corp.

Shelef, M. 1992. 'Unanticipated Benefits of Automotive Emission Control: Reduction in Fatalities by Motor Vehicle Exhaust Gas.' *SAE Technical Paper Series* 922335.

Shneidman, E. 1985. *Definition of Suicide.* New York: John Wiley & Sons.

Silverman, M.M., and R.W. Maris. 1995. 'The Prevention of Suicidal Behaviours: An Overview.' *Suicide and Life-Threatening Behavior* 25(3): 10–21.

Sullivan, W.P. 1990. 'Technical Assistance Consultation with Community Support Programs in Rural Settings.' *Human Services in the Rural Environment* 14(2): 23–8.

Tanney, B. 1995. 'Suicide Prevention in Canada: A National Perspective Highlighting Progress and Problems.' *Suicide and Life-Threatening Behavior* 25(3): 105–22.

Weissberg, R.P., M. Caplan, and R.L. Harwood. 1991. 'Promoting Competent Young People in Competence-Enhancing Environments: A Systems-Based Perspective on Primary Prevention.' *Journal of Consulting and Clinical Psychology* 59(6): 830–41.

15

Suicide Prevention in Canada: Work in Progress

RONALD J. DYCK and JENNIFER WHITE

Across Canada numerous provinces, territories, municipalities, organizations, and agencies have initiated, or are considering developing, a variety of suicide-prevention programs and activities. These efforts and interests have arisen in response to the mounting evidence that suicidal behaviour is a major public health issue. Indeed, task-force reports (Boldt, 1976; National Task Force, 1987; 1994; Royal Commission, 1995) have not only provided a good deal of evidence highlighting the magnitude of the problem of suicide, specifying the major risk factors and suggesting future directions, but have also stimulated widespread interest in expanding and improving current suicide-prevention efforts. This interest, however, has been expressed somewhat differently from one province and territory to the next. Some provinces/territories have well-developed programs in place that have endured over time; others are in the process of developing province-wide or regional approaches; and other provinces could best be described as engaging in a variety of suicide-prevention-specific activities, without necessarily having a provincial structure to guide them.

The purpose of this chapter, therefore, is to review what is taking place across the country in suicide prevention by examining provincial and territorial efforts according to specific, predetermined criteria. It is our belief that the most promising approach to reducing the rate of suicide and suicidal behaviour is through the development and implementation of an overall guiding framework. The provincial and territorial review that follows is organized around five key criteria that we believe to be fundamental to any comprehensive approach.

General versus Issue-specific Frameworks

Various frameworks have been developed to conceptualize and guide interven-

tion strategies for a range of health issues and social problems, including suicide. Some of these models, like the PRECEDE/PROCEED health-promotion
planning framework (Green and Kreuter, 1991), the Healthy Communities
Project (National Task Force, 1987); the American Public Health Association
(APHA) Criteria for the Development of Health Promotion and Education Programs (APHA, 1987), and the Ottawa Charter for Health Promotion (World
Health Organization, 1986) are more 'generic,' allowing one to apply the framework at a broad community level, depending on the particular health issue or
current concern. Despite their unique orientations, what many of these frameworks appear to have in common is their emphasis on community involvement /
target-group participation, supportive environments, decision making based on
sound evidence and research, and the importance of evaluation.

Several suicide-prevention-specific frameworks and guidelines have also
been developed recently (Dyck, 1995; Centers for Disease Control and Prevention, 1992; Royal Commission, 1995; White et al., 1993), with each highlighting various broad-level strategies for responding to the problem of suicide. For
example, the CDC *Youth Suicide Prevention Programs: A Resource Guide*
highlights very specific interventions that appear to hold the most promise for
reducing youth suicide: school gatekeeper training, community gatekeeper
training, general suicide education, screening programs, peer support programs,
crisis centres, and means restriction (CDC, 1992). Dyck's (1995) guidelines
distinguish between essential services – prevention, mental health promotion,
early identification and crisis intervention, treatment, and postvention – and
structural supports – research, training, and information dissemination.

Choosing Life: A Special Report on Suicide among Aboriginal People (Royal
Commission on Aboriginal People, 1995) describes three levels of intervention
that could be described as more general in scope: (a) those that focus on building direct suicide crisis services; (b) those that focus on promoting broadly preventive action through community development; and (c) those that focus on the
long-term needs of Aboriginal people for self-determination, self-sufficiency,
healing, and reconciliation within Canada. Alberta's most recent framework for
suicide prevention (White et al., 1993) outlines six broad strategies that need to
be included in any comprehensive suicide-prevention effort: community coordination, education, training, research, evaluation, and healthy public policy.

By bringing together the important and common elements from both the
general and suicide-specific frameworks a set of criteria for suicide-prevention
program development can be articulated. In addition to suggesting several of
issues and questions that require consideration during the process of program
development, these criteria can serve to guide program priority specification
and resource allocation. Therefore, the proposed criteria suggest that a provin-
cial/territorial suicide-prevention framework should

1 Include a statement of purpose, results-oriented goals, carefully designed measures or indicators of goal achievement or outcome, a standard or benchmark level for each goal, and general strategies that will lead to goal achievement;

2 Delineate clear areas of responsibility for the provincial/territorial levels as well as for the community or local program levels;

3 Highlight a wide range of interventions, based on sound research, that have a high degree of potential in effectively reducing the influence of risk factors or enhancing protective factors;

4 Be organized, planned, and implemented in such a way that its operation and effects can be evaluated; and

5 Be based upon community participation and key stakeholder involvement, collaborative efforts and partnerships, and be oriented towards long-term sustainability.

Given that these criteria reflect the foundation for comprehensive suicide-prevention program development, our intent now is to review the current state of suicide prevention in the provinces and territories using these framework criteria as a guide.

Provincial/Territorial Review Using Framework Criteria

How do the provincial/territorial suicide-prevention approaches measure up against the above criteria for a comprehensive suicide-prevention approach? Six provinces and one territory will be discussed in light of these criteria. They include British Columbia, Alberta, Saskatchewan, Ontario, Quebec, New Brunswick, and the Northwest Territories. These examples have been selected for case analysis on the basis of availability and completeness of information. While the other provinces and territory do not appear to have a specific focus on suicide-prevention, they include suicide prevention in the activities of either local organizations and agencies or the mental health system in general.

1 A suicide-prevention framework should include a statement of purpose, results-oriented goals, carefully designed measures or indicators of goal achievement or outcome, a standard or benchmark level for each goal, and general strategies that will lead to goal achievement.

British Columbia
Through the Ministry of Health (Mental Health Division, Child and Youth Mental Health Services), British Columbia has recently initiated a process to

develop a provincial suicide-prevention model in collaboration with mental health specialists throughout the province and in western Canada. Informing the process is research on the epidemiology of suicide, other frameworks and models for comprehensive suicide-prevention programs, and experts working in a variety of areas within the domain of suicide prevention.

Following on Alberta's experience and development, British Columbia has proposed a framework that specifies three directional goals: to reduce fatal and non-fatal suicidal behaviour; to reduce the impact of fatal and non-fatal suicidal behaviour on individuals, families, and communities; and to improve access to, and the availability and response capacity of, appropriate services for at-risk and vulnerable persons. Moreover, five strategies have been proposed for goal achievement: (1) increase the number of people responsible for, and skilled at, assessing and intervening with those at risk for suicide; (2) increase the knowledge of the people of British Columbia about suicide and related issues; (3) increase community representation and collaboration for healthy public policies that serve to increase protective factors against suicide; (4) increase community coordination at every level for a full range of suicide prevention, intervention, and postvention activities and services; and (5) develop and implement evaluation strategies to measure the effectiveness of suicide prevention, intervention, and postvention activities and services, increase the amount of research relevant to suicidal behaviour, its prevention, and treatment, and coordinate research activities. No mention has been made of the specific indicators to be used in measuring goal achievement or of the benchmark or target level within a given time-frame of goal achievement for each goal.

Alberta

This is the province with the longest-standing provincial suicide-prevention program in the country. Beginning with the Task Force Report on Suicide in Alberta (Boldt, 1976), the province began to initiate its comprehensive strategy by the creation of, and appointment to, the Office of the Provincial Suicidologist in 1978 and the establishment of the Suicide Prevention Provincial Advisory Committee in 1981.

The goals established for this program were as follows: (1) to reduce the number of suicides; (2) to reduce the number of attempted suicides; and (3) to reduce the impact of suicide and suicidal behaviours on individuals, families, and communities. To accomplish these goals, the framework proposed four general strategies: (1) community outreach through interagency coordination; (2) suicide-awareness education; (3) training in suicide intervention; and (4) research. At this time, no formal consideration was given to specifying what the indicators or measures would be for each of the goals or the targeted decreases for each of the goals within a given time-frame that would be acceptable.

In 1993, a provincial review of the program was conducted. This stakeholder consultation process – involving senior government officials, community-based suicide-prevention-program staff and their respective board members, consumers, mental health directors, other government departments, and others interested in the area – resulted in a reaffirmation of the general direction of the program and a document, *Suicide Prevention in Alberta: Working towards Results* (White et al., 1993), that updated the program and provided it with some new directions. Specifically, the goals were changed to: (1) to prevent fatal and non-fatal suicidal behaviour; (2) to reduce the impact of fatal and non-fatal suicidal behaviour on individuals, families, and communities; and (3) to improve access to and availability of appropriate services for at-risk and vulnerable persons. In addition to establishing clear measures for each goal, six province-wide strategies were established: (1) community coordination of a full range of suicide-prevention services; (2) suicide-awareness education; (3) training in suicide intervention and suicide bereavement; (4) research; (5) evaluation of suicide-prevention activities and program overall; and (6) advocacy for healthy public policy. Specific targets were established later for goal 1.

Saskatchewan

In this province, suicide prevention appears to be organized within the context of local communities or in partnership with several organizations who wish to focus directly on suicide prevention within a particular population. For example, the City of Regina began its efforts in the prevention of youth suicide in 1990 in response to the increase in the number of suicidal youth being referred to agencies. Through an extensive community consultation process and being informed by analyses of suicide-related data, the Adolescent Suicide Awareness and Prevention (ASAP) project was established in 1990 by Saskatchewan Health in cooperation with the Departments of Social Services, Education, and the Family Foundation.

This project sets out the following framework. The stated goals are: (1) to improve the health and well-being of youth, adults, families, and communities within the Regina Health District by providing a coordinated district-wide approach to suicide prevention, intervention, and postvention; (2) to reduce the number of suicides within the Regina Health District; (3) to reduce the number of attempted suicides; and (4) to reduce the negative impact of suicides and attempted suicides on individuals, families, and communities. To accomplish these goals, the model suggests the following general strategies: (1) training; (2) information dissemination; (3) networking; and (4) suicide response activities.

The other major example in Saskatchewan is a joint-partnership project between Saskatchewan Power and the Canadian Mental Health Association. This project is included in the review because it reflects an example of a non-traditional partnership in a strategy for reducing youth suicide. This partnership has resulted in a framework entitled 'Friends for Life,' with the single goal being to prevent fatal and non-fatal youth suicidal behaviour. In the strategic-framework document, six strategies are proposed for goal achievement, including public awareness, public education, community development, youth involvement, research and evaluation, and development of a resource centre.

In neither of these projects were measures of goal achievement or benchmarks for goal achievement identified.

Ontario

Like Saskatchewan, Ontario does not have an articulated provincial suicide-prevention framework supported by the provincial government. What Ontario does have can be divided into two categories. The first can be described as communities with a suicide-prevention committee whose tasks involve sponsoring the occasional workshop, distributing information about suicide, and providing public education on suicide and its prevention.

The second category consists of Councils on Suicide Prevention (COSP), which were funded or continue to be funded at least in part by the provincial government. In addition to undertaking many of the activities of communities with a suicide-prevention committee, these councils coordinate such activities as suicide-prevention weeks and the development of relevant and appropriate policies in schools. Some also develop and promote other local suicide-prevention activities and collaborate with distress centres, crisis lines, or each other.

There are also a variety of other activities, some occurring through the Canadian Mental Health Association, others through First Nations communities. Again, there is no provincial or even regional framework to guide the suicide-prevention effort in Ontario.

Quebec

Suicide-prevention efforts have been in place for many years in Quebec. Not until 1992, however, did the government paper 'Policies for Health and Well-being' tentatively talk about suicide prevention and set a provincial target of a 15 per cent reduction in the rate of suicide by the year 2002. Unfortunately, no resources were allocated to this activity nor was there any provincial suicide-prevention framework development work undertaken that could guide the achievement of the target.

As a result, the suicide-prevention movement in Quebec is essentially community-oriented and has been operating in this manner since 1978. The suicide-prevention centre, much like those operating in the United States, appears to be the primary model or framework that gives guidance to the suicide-prevention strategy in communities. While the goals and strategies generally are consistent with other provincial approaches, what can actually be accomplished is very much dependent upon the resources available within each community. Nonetheless, the community movement in suicide prevention remains ever-present.

New Brunswick

This eastern province initiated a province-wide suicide-prevention program in 1990. Under the auspices of the Mental Health Commission, a Provincial Interdisciplinary Suicide Prevention Committee was established to oversee the implementation of the Provincial Suicide Prevention Program and to make adjustments as required. The provincial framework has a clear direction-oriented goal (to reduce the incidence and impact of suicidal behaviour) and specific activities under the general strategies of prevention, intervention, and postvention. No mention is made of the indicators of goal achievement or of the benchmark of that achievement.

Northwest Territories

The government of the Northwest Territories, in consultation with a variety of stakeholders, has developed a framework for suicide prevention. In the document 'Working Together: A Strategy for Suicide Prevention in the Northwest Territories' (1991), three primary goals are identified (to reduce the number of suicides; to reduce the number of attempted suicides; to reduce the impact of suicides and attempted suicides on individuals, families, and communities), along with strategies that encompass both supportive elements for suicide (e.g., research, training, and information and education for all groups within communities) and service elements (e.g., prevention, mental health promotion, early identification and intervention, treatment, postvention). All strategies are to be carried out within a community context in cooperation and coordination with community agencies, organizations, and leaders.

It is important to note that much of the suicide-prevention work is now being rolled into a more general framework, entitled 'Working Together for Community Wellness.'

2 A suicide-prevention program framework should delineate clear roles and responsibilities for the provincial/territorial levels as well as for the community or local program levels.

British Columbia
The suicide-prevention effort in British Columbia is currently organized at the provincial level as well as within communities. Broadly defined roles and responsibilities for the various levels have been articulated. At the provincial level, the Ministry of Health, in cooperation with the Suicide Prevention Program of CUPPL (Cooperative University-Provincial Psychiatric Liaison), Department of Psychiatry, University of British Columbia, is responsible for motivating and enabling current developmental efforts.

Interministerial and regional committee development is also being planned, with the intent of coordinating services and establishing a collective responsibility for suicide prevention. A system is being planned to ensure that communication and collaboration between the ministry and community representatives is maintained.

A set of principles has also been developed to guide local suicide-prevention efforts, based on the developmental tasks of community organization.

Alberta
In Alberta, roles and responsibilities are defined for the provincial-level efforts, including the Office of the Provincial Suicidologist (Alberta Health) and two provincial programs: Suicide Information and Education Centre (SIEC) and Suicide Prevention Training Programs (SPTP). Among other things, the provincial government (through Alberta Health) is responsible for the provision of leadership, advocacy, advice, and assistance, and of funding to suicide-prevention programs. SIEC and SPTP are responsible for suicide-prevention information and training needs throughout the province.

Areas of responsibility are also defined for the community/local level. There are currently nine community-based outreach programs operating throughout the province that are responsible for ensuring the availability of a full range of suicide-prevention services in their communities, including mental health promotion, prevention / early intervention, crisis intervention, treatment, and postvention/bereavement services.

Saskatchewan
In November 1994, the Adolescent Suicide Awareness Program (ASAP) proposed to expand its program district-wide under the auspices of the Regina

Health District. The role of the regional suicide-prevention effort would be to expand current administrative and community coordination responsibilities.

Through an existing interagency committee structure, program leadership would be maintained and an identification of needs would be undertaken in order to expand the effort to address other target groups. A full-time coordinator would be required for program administration, organization, and coordination of program activities, including networking, community development, training, and resource development.

Ontario and Quebec

Neither Ontario nor Quebec have a well-articulated suicide-prevention approach at the provincial level. Community-based initiatives exist throughout both provinces, but roles and responsibilities vary from region to region. The suicide-prevention efforts in both Quebec and Ontario are essentially community-oriented, involving various non-profit organizations, and are maintained to a large degree through the goodwill and strength of conviction of the community members. With the exception of one-time-only grants for the development of specific projects, there are no provincial-government funds earmarked for provincial suicide-prevention efforts in either province.

New Brunswick

Roles and responsibilities for the suicide-prevention effort in New Brunswick have been identified. The Mental Health Commission of New Brunswick established a Provincial Interdisciplinary Suicide Prevention Committee, which is responsible for overseeing the implementation of the Provincial Suicide Prevention Program and making adjustments as required.

Recognizing the need to involve people at the local level, community suicide prevention committees were established throughout the province to ensure that suicide prevention, intervention, and postvention programs are being developed to meet the needs within their respective areas.

Northwest Territories

The suicide-prevention effort in the Northwest Territories is undertaken through the involvement of all levels of government, Aboriginal organizations, community groups, and individuals to deal with the underlying causes of suicide. Through the Department of Health and Social Services, a Suicide Prevention Consultant is responsible for the provision of strategic planning, program development, and advice and assistance to all regions.

Another newly created position within the department, Training Officer, is responsible for the overall coordination and implementation of the Suicide Prevention Program across each region of the Northwest Territories. In addition, a Mental Health Specialist located in each region is responsible for working with communities in the development of action plans.

3 A suicide-prevention program should highlight a wide range of interventions, based on sound research, that have a high degree of potential in effectively reducing the influence of risk factors or enhancing protective factors.

All six provinces and one territory have undertaken research projects, including reviews and epidemiological analyses of suicide mortality data, that provide information about prevalence and incidence rates for suicidal behaviour (mostly completed suicide). In addition, these endeavours examined age and gender variations, with some studies pursuing the assessment of specific contributing factors. From the material provided by the provinces, it is not always clear to what extent this research played a role in deciding on what strategies or activities to pursue.

British Columbia
British Columbia's suicide-prevention framework outlines a series of specific services that the communities will be encouraged to make available. These include mental health promotion – to increase protective factors through environmental, family, or individual change; prevention and early intervention – to increase specific interventions before a crisis situation arises; crisis intervention – to decrease imminent risk during a crisis; treatment – to enhance coping efforts and provide ongoing support; and bereavement and postvention – to reduce further suicidal behaviour among survivors. These are closely linked to the goals and strategies set out in the suicide-prevention framework.

Alberta
Alberta's framework is explicit about the coordination of a wide range of interventions. In its documentation, the coordination at the local level of interventions in the areas of mental health promotion, prevention and early intervention, crisis intervention, treatment, and bereavement and postvention are essential. In the broadest sense, each of these areas has the potential for being effective in goal achievement.

Saskatchewan
In Regina's Adolescent Suicide Awareness and Prevention Project, the inter-

ventions put into place to date include the training of gatekeepers in suicide intervention; the training trainers to deliver the Suicide Intervention Workshop; the coordination of workshops in such areas as suicide awareness, intervention, advanced clinical intervention, and agency suicide-prevention protocol development; identification and distribution of resource material; and the development of suicide-response guidelines, describing the roles and responsibilities of agencies responding immediately following a suicide and the coordination of community response activities.

The Friends For Life project in Saskatchewan is proposing to engage in a variety of interventions and activities that flow from its policy framework. These include stimulating public interest in improving youth suicide-prevention services, increasing community knowledge about suicide in youth and improving the level of intervention skills, assisting communities to develop a comprehensive range of youth suicide-prevention programs, involving youth in prevention activities, and establishing a comprehensive collection of print and non-print resources supporting youth suicide-prevention activities.

Ontario

A variety of interventions are in place throughout the province that have the potential of making a significant impact. These include crisis intervention centres and/or crisis lines; suicide intervention training; public education regarding suicide and its prevention; treatment and bereavement services; suicide-prevention education and training-material development for use in northern communities (Northern Lifelines Manual); and school-based protocol development for suicide-prevention education and postvention.

Quebec

Suicide-prevention interventions in the province of Quebec take place primarily through the suicide-prevention centres located in various communities. These centres focus on providing crisis-intervention services, suicide intervention training to community gatekeepers, and bereavement and postvention counselling. Like Ontario, there does not appear to be a provincial model for suicide-prevention into which the work of these suicide-prevention centres fit. However, it is noteworthy that Quebec has Canada's only provincial organization, the Association Québécoise de Suicidologie, that brings together researchers, care providers, and suicide-prevention centres for mutual support, dialogue, learning, and direction setting.

New Brunswick

New Brunswick has embarked upon a series of interventions that emerge specifically from the provincial framework. Specifically, the government has implemented suicide-awareness sessions; is working through the Department of Education to effect changes in curricula that are relevant to suicide prevention; developed guidelines for help lines; produced media kits for directors of community mental health centres; produced pamphlets on suicide; facilitated suicide-intervention workshops as well as 'training for trainers' workshops; provided advanced clinical workshops for members of the mental health system; promoted workshops in counselling the bereaved; and is involved in psychological autopsies and tragic-events response.

Northwest Territories
The suicide-prevention effort in the Northwest Territories is guided by a very ambitious set of interventions. Not only are crisis-line services offered, but the approach to reaching into the remote communities through a community-wellness approach is indeed innovative. While training for community gatekeepers in suicide-prevention is taking place, emphasis is being given to community empowerment for the creation of community wellness. Because this effort is now at a very early stage, it is not possible to identify how it will unfold.

4 A suicide-prevention framework should be organized, planned, and implemented in such a way that its operation and effects can be evaluated.

Despite the indication that the suicide-prevention approach and the individual interventions will be evaluated, there is little documented evidence at present to indicate that this has been done, planned, or in process in many of the provinces. It is true that most of what has been described is in development; nonetheless, there should be some supporting explicit evidence that evaluation is being planned and is taking place.

Alberta is one of the few provinces to have documented its evaluation efforts in suicide prevention. In the late 1980s, Alberta undertook a major process evaluation of the suicide-prevention program that resulted in affirmation for the basic model, but with some recommendations put forth regarding the overall provincial coordination of the program (LaFleur, 1989).

The two-day suicide-intervention workshop for community gatekeepers, offered throughout the province through the Suicide Prevention Training Program (SPTP), has also been evaluated, with positive results. Results indicate that people retain the skills they were taught for up to six months following the completion of the workshop (Tierney, 1988).

More recently, following the re-examination of the model and some subsequent redesign in 1993, there has been considerable emphasis placed on process and outcome monitoring, and clear mechanisms for evaluation have been put into place. Not only are the community-based outreach, training, and information programs required to assess whether their specific interventions are having the desired effects (e.g., following a suicide-awareness presentation, do the participants have more knowledge about suicide, and what to do and where to turn for assistance, than they did before?), but programs also have set specific suicide-rate (or frequency) targets to the year 2000. In this way each program will know whether its interventions are having the desired effect and whether or not the program is on track for reaching its targets, measured through rates of suicide.

5 A suicide-prevention framework should be based upon community participation and key stakeholder involvement, collaborative efforts, and partnerships, and be oriented towards long-term sustainability.

British Columbia
In British Columbia, much of the work is being undertaken within the mental health system, with consultation from a number of agencies, organizations, and experts throughout western Canada. It is proposed that the general implementation of the approach will take place within a community-development model. Specifically, the framework outlines a set of principles to guide local efforts. These principles highlight the importance of community representation, community collaboration, community responsibility, multilevel coordination, long-term planning, community outreach, a continuum of care services, and accountability and evaluation. Thus, implementation of the program fits the above criterion quite well.

Alberta
Alberta's most recently developed framework for suicide prevention was developed through a process of stakeholder consultation. Over eighty individuals were invited to attend a two-day consultation meeting to review the provincial suicide-prevention program and make recommendations for its future. At the community level, Community Interagency Suicide Prevention Program (CISPP) councils exist to guide the efforts of many of the community-outreach programs.

Saskatchewan
Regina's ASAP project was developed to address the problem of youth suicide and was established on the premise that suicide prevention is a community concern requiring community action. Project activities are supported by an exten-

sive network of caregivers and volunteers. Several working committees, with representation from over thirty human-service agencies, guide the project.

Ontario
Most of the individual suicide-prevention programs in Ontario are guided by the efforts of a community-based suicide-prevention committee, typically made up of representatives from several service agencies. Councils on Suicide Prevention (COSP) also exist in various communities throughout southern Ontario. Within Ottawa-Carleton specifically, there is a well-organized suicide-prevention program, guided by the input of various service providers.

Quebec
With very few financial resources provided by the provincial government for suicide prevention, Quebec's suicide-prevention programs survive primarily because of the high level of support and commitment from community members and non-profit organizations for these programs.

New Brunswick
Thirteen community suicide-prevention committees throughout the province have been established to ensure that suicide prevention, intervention, and postvention programs are in place to meet local needs.

Northwest Territories
By situating suicide prevention within the larger framework of community wellness, there is a strong emphasis on community involvement and participation. By defining a shared vision for healthy communities and highlighting a process for government departments and communities to work together, the foundation for working together in a collaborative manner is well established in the Northwest Territories.

Observations and Recommendations

An Overall Framework versus Suicide Prevention Activities

For the purposes of this chapter, we can make a distinction between those provinces/territories that have developed a provincial/territorial *framework* for suicide prevention and those that are engaged in very specific suicide prevention *activities*. While it is clear that many actions are being undertaken across the country in an effort to reduce the rate of completed suicide, the sheer volume of suicide-prevention activities alone is by no means a useful criterion for judging the effectiveness or quality of program efforts.

Based on these reviews, British Columbia, Alberta, New Brunswick, and the Northwest Territories have fairly well-defined, provincial/territorial framework approaches, with an overall purpose and a set of defined goals and strategies. Of notable significance is the fact that each of these provinces has government funding and support for the development and implementation of suicide-prevention efforts.

While Saskatchewan, Ontario, and Quebec do not have a provincial model or government-endorsed framework for suicide prevention, they have undertaken suicide-prevention efforts within parts of their respective provinces. The difficulty for each of these three provinces is that even though there are pockets of suicide-prevention activity taking place in various regions, there is no overall unifying model or framework to provide communities with the sense that they are 'pulling in the same direction.' Such random program planning and isolated delivery efforts lead to a loss of comprehensiveness at the provincial level as well as potential fragmentation and duplication of efforts.

Maximizing the Impact of Suicide-Prevention Efforts

Unfortunately, current scientific evidence is insufficient to support the effectiveness of any one intervention in reducing suicidal behaviour (Potter et al., 1995). Perhaps common practice, political expediency and funding, and availability of particular resources or interventions, combined with good clinical and common sense, play the most important role in the decision to follow a specific course of action in tackling the problem of suicide.

Given this reality, paralleled with a sense of urgency to deal with suicide, it is our contention that the most promising and systematic approach to addressing the issue of suicide is to develop an overall guiding framework, which could be adopted at a provincial/territorial level. Such an approach enhances the likelihood that efforts will be better coordinated throughout the region or province and more comprehensive, improving the opportunity for all the players and contributing partners to move in the same direction. Compared with the suicide-prevention 'activity approach,' a 'framework approach' to suicide prevention, organized around multiple intervention points and based on good information and sound evidence, will often be more amenable to evaluation efforts and yield more meaningful data, because clear measures for success are made explicit at the outset for each of the framework components. Ultimately, the framework approach will lead to a more systematic, consolidated, and strategic effort in dealing with suicidal behaviour.

REFERENCES

American Public Health Association. 1987. 'Criteria for the Development of Health Promotion and Education Programs.' *American Journal of Public Health* 77(1): 89–92.

Boldt, M. 1976. *Report of the Alberta Task Force on Suicide.* Edmonton, AB: Government of Alberta.

Centers for Disease Control and Prevention 1992. *Youth Suicide Prevention Programs: A Resource Guide.* Atlanta: U.S. Department of Health and Human Services.

Dyck, R.J. 1995. 'Guidelines for the Development and Organization of Suicide Prevention Programs.' In R. Diekstra, W. Gulbinat, I. Kienhorst, and D. De Leo, eds, *Preventive Strategies on Suicide*, 51–75. Leiden: E.J. Brill.

Green, L., and M. Kreuter. 1991. *Health Promotion Planning: An Educational and Environmental Approach.* Mountain View, CA: Mayfield Publishing.

Health and Welfare Canada. 1989. *Challenge: The Newsletter of the Canadian Healthy Communities Project.* Ottawa: Health and Welfare Canada.

La Fleur, R. 1989. *Evaluation of Alberta's Suicide Prevention Program.* Edmonton, AB: Alberta Community and Occupational Health.

National Task Force on Suicide in Canada. 1987. *Suicide in Canada: Report of the National Task Force on Suicide in Canada.* Ottawa: Health and Welfare Canada.

– 1994. *Suicide in Canada: Update of the Report of the Task Force on Suicide in Canada.* Ottawa: Health Canada.

Potter, L., K. Powell, and S. Kachur. 1995. 'Suicide Prevention from a Public Health Perspective.' *Suicide and Life-Threatening Behaviour* 25(1): 82–91.

Royal Commission Report on Aboriginal Peoples. 1995. *Choosing Life: A Special Report on Suicide among Aboriginal People.*

Tierney, R. 1988. "Comprehensive Evaluation for Suicide Intervention Training." Unpublished doctoral dissertation. University of Calgary, Calgary, Alberta.

White, J., R.J. Dyck, G. Harrington, F. Auburn, and S. Meurin. 1993. *Suicide Prevention in Alberta: Working towards Results.* Edmonton, AB: Alberta Health.

World Health Organization. 1986. *Ottawa Charter for Health Promotion.* International Conference on Health Promotion, Ottawa.

Canada's youth have high rate of suicide: for example, in boys aged fifteen to nineteen, the rate of suicide in Canada today is 60 per cent higher than in the United States. Canada's rates have drastically increased since statistics were first compiled in 1956. To illustrate, suicide among males aged fifteen to nineteen in 1992 was 20.1 per 100,000, compared to 5.1 thirty years ago. For Canadian females aged fifteen to nineteen, the rate of suicide in 1992 was 5.4 per 100,000, whereas in 1962 it was 1.3. Suicide in youth is truly tragic, because their life expectancy is greatest in terms of both the interval of years ahead and the diversity of experience that would await these youth.

An array of services, educational programs, and public-awareness programs have been developed to tackle the problem of youth suicide. Many different factors account for the rates of suicide, and thus the services must be multifarious. A model of 'prevention,' consisting of prevention, intervention, and postvention, will be needed.

Schools especially have been and will be in the foreground of preventing suicide in youth. Everyone in our schools needs to be informed of ways to detect and identify suicidal risk. Schools and the communities need to provide intervention services, often of a long-term nature. Simple solutions like short-term therapy are of little value. Province-wide health programs are needed. Yet, it is likely that postvention will be the most critical approach. Postvention refers to those things done after the dire event has occurred that serve to mollify its aftershocks. Such programs, for example, address the contagion effect that is quite powerful in youth. Schools and communities must play a key role in postvention and in all efforts of prevention.

The sixth section outlines suicide in youth and the response to suicide in communities and schools. It consists of three chapters addressing suicide in youth: an overview of suicide in youth in Canada, an outline of suicide-prevention programs in schools and communities, and a special discussion on cultural issues in suicide postvention.

16

Comprehensive Youth Suicide Prevention: A Model for Understanding

JENNIFER WHITE

Youth suicide is a troubling fact of our contemporary society, striking a discordant note among those who would like to believe that adolescence is a carefree time, characterized by great expectations and hope for the future. When our youth, who have 'the whole world ahead of them,' become so hopeless and desperate and wilfully act to bring about their own deaths, many of our fundamental beliefs about the world get challenged. Death by suicide among adolescents is a collective concern, confronting all of us with many unanswered questions, but also providing the impetus for the development of a range of preventive programs and strategies. This chapter presents a conceptual model for understanding and responding to the very grave and urgent problem of youth suicide in the 1990s.

Magnitude of the Problem

In the last thirty years, the rates of suicide among Canadian youth aged fifteen to nineteen have risen considerably, with the period between 1960 and 1980 showing a particularly dramatic increase. To illustrate, the rate of suicide among males of this age group was 5.1 per 100,000 in 1962, 13.8 in 1972, and 20.9 in 1982. Since the 1980s, rates for this age group appear to have levelled out; in 1992 the rate of completed suicide among males aged fifteen to nineteen was 20.1 per 100,000 (National Task Force, 1994). For Canadian females aged fifteen to nineteen the rate of suicide was 5.4 per 100,000 in 1992, in contrast to rates of 1.3 in 1962, 4.2 in 1972, and 3.1 in 1982 (National Task Force, 1994).

Among twenty- to twenty-four-year-old males, the rate of suicide in 1992 was 29.0 per 100,000, while the rate among females of this age group was 6.6. In 1992, the overall rate of suicide among all Canadians of both sexes was 13.0.

Of further note, rates of completed suicide among older Canadian male teen-agers are higher than their American counterparts. Leenaars and Lester (1990) observed a clear and constant difference in suicide rates between Canadian and American males aged fifteen to nineteen for the period 1969 to 1985.

Clearly the problem is serious, and if we estimate, as others have done (Smith and Crawford, 1986), that fifty to one hundred attempts occur for every youth death by suicide, and that many youngsters contemplate suicide in times of stress and crisis, we can only then begin to appreciate the true magnitude of the problem. It is imperative that we begin to develop preventive programs that specifically target young people, their families, and the communities and cul-tural contexts within which they live.

Approaches to the Problem of Youth Suicide

Information Dissemination

An array of services, educational programs, and public-awareness campaigns have been developed to tackle the problem of youth suicide. Traditionally, the bulk of suicide-prevention work has been devoted to heightening awareness about how to recognize and assist a suicidal person. Target groups to receive these educational efforts generally include students, peer counsellors, school faculty and staff, and parents.

These programs are typically designed to increase the likelihood that suicidal persons will be identified early and offered the necessary help, ultimately resulting in fewer completed suicides. Such an approach depends almost exclu-sively on the process of information dissemination as the primary mechanism by which such outcomes are to be achieved.

In the field of suicide prevention, where much of our collective energy has been devoted to this task of heightening awareness about the issue of youth sui-cide, it is becoming increasingly evident that we need to begin to critically examine the assumptions underlying our efforts and systematically evaluate our activities. We must also determine whether this particular approach to youth suicide prevention is the best direction to maintain in order to achieve results.

Crisis Intervention

In addition, many suicide-prevention programs have typically been considered synonymous with the provision of crisis-intervention activities. For example, when people think about the term 'suicide prevention,' what often is conjured up in their minds is the image of a person who is 'on the edge,' threatening to commit suicide, while another person 'talks him or her down.' Such a view offers us a very narrow understanding of the scope of suicide-prevention activities, which in turn limits our chances to effect widespread, long-lasting change.

We must avoid the danger of being too restrictive in our understanding of what suicide prevention means. Teaching people how to intervene in a crisis, ensuring the existence of twenty-four-hour distress lines, and providing training in risk assessment are all important aspects in preventing suicides. However, all of these activities are designed to be initiated only following the emergence of a crisis. We need to determine whether this is the best level to direct most of our time and energy towards and what the underlying logic governing such a decision would entail.

Without question, we need to be focused and strategic in our aims, identifying clearly who the intended targets are for our interventions and what the desired outcomes are to be. Being specific in our focus is not, however, the same as being narrow in our vision. We must envision the 'work of suicide prevention' as encompassing a broad array of activities occurring across multiple contexts, but with very specific targets for change identified at each level and for each activity. In the absence of such specificity, our efforts become diffused and scattered. Given the current climate of economic restraint, it is more imperative than ever that energy is concentrated in those areas where the greatest impact can be achieved.

Development of a Model for Understanding Youth Suicidal Behaviour

Guiding Questions

Some of the questions that this chapter will address include: (a) How can we conceptualize youth suicidal behaviour in such a way as to capture its multifaceted complexity? (b) How can we utilize such a conceptualization to organize the findings from the literature regarding risk and protective factors for youth suicidal behaviour? (c) How can we integrate the theory and the evidence to develop a comprehensive preventive program? (d) What are the essential service-delivery components for tackling the problem of youth suicide in the most effective manner? and (e) How might we translate these theoretical ideas into broad-based action?

Developmental Considerations

Understanding the nature of suicidal processes in young people requires an appreciation of the different developmental changes and life-cycle tasks facing youngsters in general. Successfully resolving the challenges that are inherent in the normative developmental stages of youth, such as identity formation, gaining peer acceptance and approval, and separating from parents and families, can be a stressful and tumultuous experience for many adolescents (Egan and Cowan, 1979). For those young people who might be vulnerable to suicide because of other factors, facing these age-appropriate developmental tasks might be enough to precipitate a serious crisis, including suicide.

These developmental considerations need to be taken into account when trying to understand youth behaviour in general, and in particular suicidal behaviour. Moreover, the different types of factors that might heighten the risk for suicide and the way in which such factors might interact across various contexts to produce a suicidal outcome clearly need to be better understood.

An Ecosystemic Perspective

Like the ecosystem that exists in the natural world, where different properties and organisms of the earth interact with and reciprocally influence a range of other living things, the 'human ecosystem' concept offers a model for understanding human behaviour that captures much of its complexity. An ecosystemic perspective acknowledges the interaction among various intrapsychic and interpersonal factors in the emergence of a range of human behaviours (Jasnoski, 1984). The model can be seen in figure 1, where it is graphically depicted by layers of concentric circles, starting with the individual at the centre.

For the purposes of this model, layers of influence have been defined as self, family, peers, school, community, culture, society, and the physical environment. Other layers could also be defined and highlighted. Even though they are not directly adjacent to each other in the one-dimensional representation, all of the layers are capable of reciprocally influencing and interacting with one another. This human-ecosystem model will provide a backdrop for the framework for understanding youth suicidal behaviour to be developed here.

Factors of Influence

In addition to acknowledging the context within which suicidal behaviour occurs, it is necessary to give consideration to certain types of influencing factors. Adam (1990) offered a model for understanding suicidal behaviour that emphasized the role of interacting psychosocial and environmental factors in the development of suicidal behaviour. He described three different types of factors that could lead to suicidal behaviour in an individual: (a) 'predisposing' factors, which leave an individual vulnerable; (b) 'precipitating' factors, which

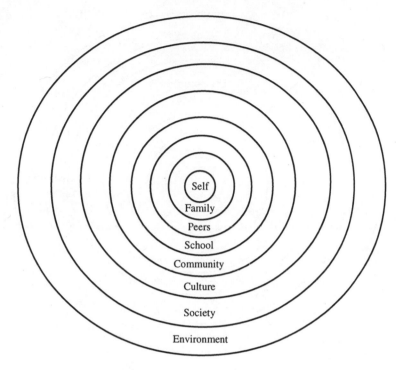

Figure 1 The human ecosystem

can act as a trigger for predisposed persons; and (c) 'contributing' factors, which act to increase the exposure of individuals to other predisposing or precipitating conditions. In addition to Adam's three factors, a fourth category, 'protective factors,' has been identified that will be incorporated into the model of youth suicidal behaviour, describing those conditions that act to mitigate the risk for suicide.

Each of these factors tends to emerge along a dimension of time and will have different degrees of intensity. Predisposing factors are understood to be generally more historical in nature or tend to have an enduring quality. Precipitating factors are understood to be typically more acute, with a fairly sudden onset. Contributing factors can be either acute or ongoing, but they will serve to exacerbate the other factors. Protective factors are most likely to be more stable over time, but fluctuations and shifts would be expected. Specific findings from the youth-suicide-prevention literature, organized according to these four factors of influence, will be presented in a later section.

In order to integrate the foregoing ideas into a conceptual model for under-

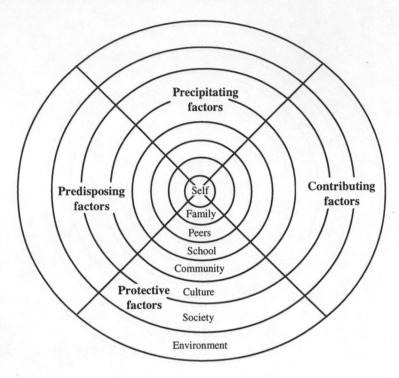

Figure 2 Factors of influence

standing youth suicidal behaviour and its prevention, one must first consider how these four influencing factors can be understood to be embedded across the various levels represented by the ecosystemic perspective. An example of how this might be conceptualized is shown in figure 2.

Risk and Protective Factors

Through research efforts, epidemiological studies, and clinical observations, certain variables and conditions have been identified as being associated with suicidal behaviour, and many of these factors have become widely accepted as reliable indicators of suicide risk. It is important to clarify that while we may be able to predict which members of a population will be at heightened *risk* for suicide, we cannot determine with sufficient reliability who will actually *die* by suicide.

In other words, even though a number of these factors for suicide have been identified, it is not known for certain which combinations of factors must be present and what the relative weights of each of these factors must be before a suicidal outcome can be reliably predicted.

Of further note, we cannot fully understand the complex dynamics that lead young people to take their own lives by focusing exclusively on risk factors. We must also take into account the presence or absence of protective factors and the processes by which such factors might serve to circumvent a suicidal outcome.

Thus, the model that has been developed here provides an extensive overview of the known risk and protective factors that influence youth suicidal behaviour and conceptualizes these factors in such a way that allows for the development of a population-focused, comprehensive, youth-suicide prevention and intervention program. In contrast to an approach that targets the individual, this model reflects more of a population-health approach, because, as Silverman and Felner (1995) point out, 'prevention efforts are by definition *mass or population focused*' (73).

Focus on the Interaction

It is the reciprocal and dynamic interaction among the four factors of influence across layers of the human ecosystem that will create the conditions out of which self-destructive or adaptive behaviours will emerge. Precisely how these factors interact with each other to create a suicidal condition is legitimately the subject of much research and ongoing debate. The purpose of this chapter is not to develop a precise formula or equation for determining who will die by suicide, but rather to highlight the interaction between those contextual conditions and those intrapsychic and interpersonal variables that create a vulnerability to suicidal behaviour among youth.

The next section will provide an overview of some of the findings regarding what has been defined here as 'factors of influence,' in particular, how these different types of factors manifest themselves across layers of the ecosystem. While the section that follows is not intended to be an exhaustive review of the literature on youth suicidal behaviour, it is hoped that the highlighted findings and the organization of the material itself will offer some fresh insight into how to understand the issue of suicidal behaviour among youth and assist with the development of broad strategy areas designed to reduce the overall risk.

Findings from the Literature

Predisposing Factors

To restate, predisposing factors are those that are typically historical in nature, setting the stage for a vulnerability to suicidal behaviour. At the *intra*personal level of the self or the individual, there are some fairly well-established conditions that are thought to predispose a youngster to suicide, including a history of previous attempts (Davidson et al., 1989; Pfeffer et al., 1991; Shaffer et al., 1988) and a diagnosis of mental illness or depression (Brent et al., 1988; Pfeffer, 1990; Shaffer, 1988; Spirito et al., 1989).

Predisposing factors at the level of the family have also been studied extensively. Evidence indicates that young people can be predisposed to suicidal behaviour when the following familial characteristics are present: abuse by family (Bayatpour et al., 1992; Riggs et al., 1990; van der Kolk et al., 1991) parental mental illness (Adam, 1990; Pfeffer, 1990), early loss – especially of a loved one (Adam, 1990; Pfeffer, 1990; Spirito et al., 1989), attachment pathology (Adam, 1990; Richman, 1986; van der Kolk et al., 1991), and a family history of suicide (Garfinkel et al., 1982; Spirito et al., 1989).

Long-term difficulties with peer relationships and a history of antisocial behaviour and isolation have also been considered to be predisposing factors to youth suicidal behaviour (Marttunen et al., 1992; Shafii et al., 1985; Spirito et al., 1989), as has a history of school problems (Hoberman and Garfinkel, 1988).

For those youngsters who have experienced frequent moves in the community, a predisposing vulnerability to suicidal behaviour may be implicated (Cantor, 1989; Davidson et al., 1989). Culturally, societally, and environmentally, adolescents are facing tremendous change and social pressure, which has led some Canadian researchers to suggest that such instability and loss of social integration could be considered a predisposing factor for suicide (Bagley, 1992; Sakinofsky and Roberts, 1985; Trovato, 1992).

Precipitating Factors

Precipitating factors generally referred to as 'trigger events,' are those that are sudden in their onset. At the level of the individual, these factors can include such things as a health crisis, pregnancy, a developmental crisis, or a sudden loss in esteem (Spirito et al., 1989).

More commonly, precipitants to adolescent suicidal behaviour evolve out of an interpersonal context, often involving conflict with others or the loss of a valued relationship. Within the family system, such precipitants can take the form of conflict with a family member, death or divorce of parents, or perceived rejection by one's family (Brent et al., 1988; Graham and Burvill, 1992; Garfinkel and Hoberman, 1988).

Peer relationships are very significant and influential in the lives of young people. A conflict between friends or the break-up of a relationship can often be the trigger event for the emergence of a suicidal crisis in young people (Brent et al., 1988; Davidson et al., 1989; Graham and Burvill, 1992; Hoberman and Garfinkel, 1988). Experiencing the loss of a friend through death, in particular suicide, should also be considered a possible precipitant to youth suicide (Davidson et al., 1989).

Problems at school have also been cited as common precipitants to youth suicidal behaviour; specifically these have included: failure, expulsion, school transition, and overwhelming pressure to succeed (Brent et al. 1988; Hoberman and Garfinkel, 1988; McGibben et al., 1992).

At the level of the community, precipitating factors have included such things as conflict with the law and legal problems (Brent et al., 1988; Davidson et al., 1989; Graham and Burvill, 1992; Hoberman and Garfinkel, 1988).

Precipitating events that could be understood to be taking place within the specific contexts of the culture, society, or the environment include events like a sudden loss of status within one's own cultural group, becoming alienated from one's religion, or financial difficulties arising because of economic conditions (Cantor, 1989).

Contributing Factors

Contributing factors are those that serve to exacerbate the existing risk for suicidal behaviour caused by either predisposing or precipitating factors, and they can be either sudden in their onset or more historical in nature. At the level of the individual, contributing factors to suicidal behaviour might include such things as substance abuse (Adcock et al., 1991; Hoberman and Garfinkel, 1988; Marttunen et al., 1992; Pfeffer et al., 1991; Spirito et al., 1989), risk-taking or self-destructive behaviour (Adcock et al., 1991; Marttunen et al., 1992), attitudes about the acceptability of suicide (Kienhorst et al., 1992), physical illness (Hoberman and Garfinkel, 1988; Spirito et al., 1989), impulsivity (Cantor, 1989; Hoberman and Garfinkel, 1988), sexual-identity issues (Gibson, 1989), and learning disability or cognitive deficits (Kienhorst et al., 1992; Rourke et al., 1989; Spirito et al., 1989).

For those children who are growing up in a family where members are abusing alcohol or drugs, where relationships between family members are unstable and communication could be characterized as dysfunctional, and where running away from home is commonplace, the risk for suicidal behaviour may be exacerbated (Davidson et al., 1989; Graham and Burvill, 1992; Kienhorst et al., 1992).

Having a friend die by suicide does not necessarily predispose a youngster to suicide, and such an event will not, in and of itself, precipitate a suicide among those close to the deceased, but given the existence of other vulnerabilities and acute stressors, the suicide death of a peer may have a contributing effect in the emergence of suicidal behaviour among other youngsters (Davidson et al., 1989; Gould et al., 1990).

Within the context of the school system, an example of a contributing factor to suicide might include an unreasonable emphasis on academic performance leading to competition and stress (Cantor, 1989; McGibben et al., 1992). For young people living in communities where there is little or no access to appropriate resources, creating an increased risk for social isolation, the risk for suicide might be enhanced (Cantor, 1989).

From a cultural, societal, and environmental perspective, the following conditions can be considered as contributing factors that heighten the risk for youth suicidal behaviour: media influences, increased violence in general, access to firearms and other lethal methods, the rapid rate of technological advances, and cohort effects, like growing up in a baby-boom population where competition is high (Brent et al., 1988; Cantor, 1989; Spirito et al., 1989).

Protective Factors

Protective factors are those that appear to reduce the risk for suicide among youngsters. The following factors could be considered protective factors across a range of contexts: personal resilience, including a capacity to tolerate frustration, prior experience with self-mastery, adaptive coping skills, having positive expectations for the future, creative problem solving, a sense of humour, at least one positive and healthy family relationship, consistent family discipline, and positive peer modelling (Benard, 1991; Brooks, 1994; Rubenstein et al., 1989; Werner, 1989); believing that school is relevant and establishing a healthy school climate (Felner and Adam, 1988; Weissberg et al., 1991); feeling part of a community and having access to appropriate resources (Benard, 1991); and legislative action such as restricting access to firearms (Centers for Disease Control, 1992).

Translating Ideas into Action

Many different factors of influence have been identified at each level and it now becomes possible to plan interventions in very context-specific ways. The outermost ring of figure 3 illustrates how many suicide-prevention-program service-delivery components identified by Dyck (1995) can easily correspond with the four types of influencing factors described here.

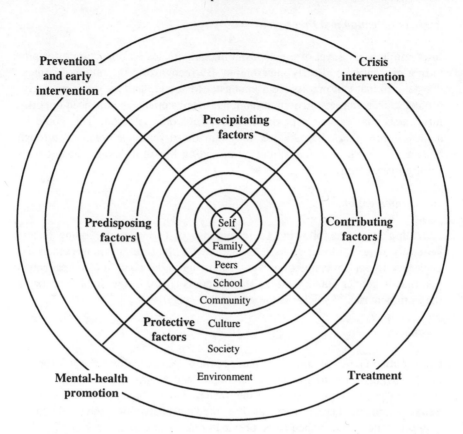

Figure 3 Service-delivery components

Mental-Health Promotion

One extremely important aspect of youth suicide prevention includes identifying and enhancing the effects of certain protective factors as they are present across the various contexts of a youngster's life. It makes sense to conceptualize the process of enhancing protective factors as mental-health-promotion activities. This level of activity would include intervening with a generally healthy population by promoting positive and adaptive health behaviours where a risk for suicide has not yet been established.

Early Intervention and Prevention

Intervening at the level of predisposing factors creates an opportunity for providing prevention and early intervention. By recognizing the range of contextual factors that can predispose a youngster to suicide and by targeting at-risk groups to receive preventive interventions before a crisis, an enhanced opportunity exists for averting a possible suicidal outcome later on. This could be achieved through the introduction of systematic surveillance practices, through enhanced referral procedures, and by providing life-skill development groups for high-risk youth.

Crisis Intervention

Providing a service following the emergence of certain precipitating factors generally requires doing crisis intervention. By the time a young person has been faced with a precipitating event, occurring in the context of other factors that may engender vulnerability, a state of crisis is almost inevitable. Reducing the imminent risk of suicide is the goal at this stage.

Treatment

Contributing factors as conceived here are those that exacerbate the risk for suicide. Providing long-term treatment strategies and programs that seek to reduce the prevalence of these contributing factors would be appropriate service-delivery strategies here. It should also be noted that postvention and bereavement support strategies, designed to be provided *after* a suicide has taken place, are equally important elements in the development of any overall suicide-prevention effort.

Any overall suicide-prevention strategy must be considered multilevel in its scope, requiring the concerted efforts of a multiplicity of disciplines. In addition, we must become much more purposeful and strategic in our aim, less reactive in our actions, and ever cognizant of the ongoing need to evaluate our efforts. As the school setting and the community represent two key contexts within which youth-suicide-prevention programs are planned and implemented, these two levels will be highlighted briefly below in an effort to exemplify how broad-level service-delivery strategies can be integrated into a comprehensive approach.

School-based Efforts

As the school setting constitutes a logical site for delivering services to youth, many suicide-prevention efforts have been developed within the school context (Leenaars and Wenckstern, 1991). The key components necessary for the development of a comprehensive approach to youth suicide prevention within the school context have been well articulated by Tierney et al. (1991). These authors suggest that a comprehensive approach should include system-wide policy, a full range of prevention, intervention, and postvention approaches including education and awareness for students, staff, and parents; internal and external resources and staff support; a systematic training program; evaluation; and follow-up, including refresher courses.

In addition to the development of suicide-awareness education, gatekeeper training, and policies to support suicide-prevention activities, explicit emphasis should also be given to developing primary prevention programs for the purposes of enhancing youth competencies and improving skills in specific areas like problem solving, help seeking, and coping with distress (Garland and Zigler, 1993; Klingman and Hochdorf, 1993; Weissberg et al., 1991).

We should ensure that what we are doing at one level is being reinforced and supported at other levels. If, for example, community mental-health professionals are providing follow-up treatment to a student who has attempted suicide, then the parents of the attempter, friends, and classmates, as well as key school personnel, should each be considered potential service recipients when planning and coordinating a comprehensive postvention response (White, 1994).

Community-Level Efforts

At this level, consideration needs to be given to ensuring that a full range of coordinated and appropriate services, as well as opportunities, are available to youth and their families. These would include health-promotion initiatives, youth volunteer opportunities, development of mechanisms for ensuring youth input in community decision making, leisure and work-experience opportunities for youth, as well as twenty-four-hour crisis services and a range of treatment options.

Many community-based prevention programs for youth, including substance-abuse prevention and school-drop-out prevention programs, for example, can also make significant contributions to the overall suicide-prevention effort. The task of youth-suicide-prevention program planners should be to build on the existing community infrastructure whenever possible and to make explicit the links between these other preventive programs and youth suicide prevention. Community-gatekeeper training and general suicide education are also important strategies for building a knowledgeable community that can recognize and respond appropriately to suicidal youth. In addition, systematic education and policy efforts designed to reduce access to the means for committing suicide are community-level strategies that have a high potential for success in reducing youth suicide (CDC, 1992).

Summary

This chapter has focused on the identification of specific types of influencing factors that interact across contexts to produce youth suicidal behaviour and has highlighted the importance of developing comprehensive preventive programs that reflect the complexity of youth suicidal behaviour. Intervening with specific target groups across a range of contexts, with the specific purpose and the means for evaluating progress made clear at the outset, is the approach most likely to yield favourable results. In the absence of such a proactive and systematic approach to this very serious problem, our prevention efforts will remain limited, both in their potency and in their breadth.

REFERENCES

Adam, K. 1990. 'Environmental, Psychosocial, and Psychoanalytic Aspects of Suicidal Behavior.' In S. Blumenthal and D. Kupfer, eds, *Suicide over the Life Cycle: Risk Factors, Assessment and Treatment of Suicidal Patients*, 39–96. Washington: APA Press.

Adcock, A., and S. Nagy. 1991. 'Selected Risk Factors in Adolescent Suicide Attempts.' *Adolescence* 26(104): 817–28.

Bagley, C. 1992. 'Changing Profiles of a Typology of Youth Suicide in Canada.' *Canadian Journal of Public Health* 83(2): 169–70.

Bayatpour, M., R. Wells, and S. Holford. 1992. 'Physical and Sexual Abuse as Predictors of Substance Use and Suicide among Pregnant Teenagers.' *Journal of Adolescent Health* 13: 128–32.

Benard, B. 1991. *Fostering Resiliency in Kids: Protective Factors in the Family, School, and Community.* Portland, OR: Western Regional Centre for Drug-Free Schools and Communities.

Brent, D., J. Perper, C. Goldstein, D. Kolko, M. Allan, C. Allman, and J. Zelenak. 1988. 'Risk Factors for Adolescent Suicide.' *Archives of General Psychiatry* 45: 581–8.

Brooks, R.B. 1994. 'Children at Risk: Fostering Resilience and Hope.' *American Journal of Orthopsychiatry* 64(4): 545–53.

Cantor, P. 1989. 'Intervention Strategies: Environmental Risk Reduction for Youth Suicide.' *Report of the Secretary's Task Force on Youth Suicide.* Washington: U.S. Department of Health and Human Services.

Centers for Disease Control. 1992. *Youth Suicide Prevention Programs: A Resource Guide.* Atlanta, GA: Department of Health and Human Services.

Davidson, L., M. Rosenberg, J. Mercy, V. Franklin, and S.V. Simmon. 1989. 'An Epidemiologic Study of Risk Factors in Two Teenage Suicide Clusters.' *Journal of the American Medical Association* 262(19): 2687–92.

Dyck, R. 1995. 'Guidelines for the Development and Organization of Suicide Prevention

Programs.' In R. Diekstra, W. Gulbinat, S. Platt, and A. Schmidtke, eds, *Identification of Preventive Strategies on Suicidal Behaviour*, 51–75. Leiden: Brill.

Egan, G., and M. Cowan. 1979. *People in Systems: A Model for Development in the Human-Service Professions and Education*. Monterey, CA: Brooks/Cole.

Felner, R., and A. Adam. 1988. 'The School Transitional Environment Project: An Ecological Intervention and Evaluation.' In R. Price, E. Cowen, R. Lorion, and J. Ramos-McKay, eds, *Fourteen Ounces of Prevention: A Casebook for Practitioners*, 111–22. Washington: American Psychological Association.

Garfinkel, B., A. Froese, and J. Hood. 1982. 'Suicide Attempts in Children and Adolescents.' *American Journal of Psychiatry* 139: 1257–61.

Garland, A., and E. Zigler. 1993. 'Adolescent Suicide Prevention: Current Research and Social Policy Implications.' *American Psychologist* 48(2): 169–82.

Gibson, P. 1989. 'Gay Male and Lesbian Youth Suicide.' *Report of the Secretary's Task Force on Youth Suicide*. Washington: U.S. Department of Health and Human Services.

Gould, M., S. Wallenstein, M. Kleinman, P. O'Carroll, and V. Mercy. 1990. 'Suicide Clusters: An Examination of Age-Specific Effects.' *American Journal of Public Health* 80(2): 211–12.

Graham, C., and P. Burvill. 1992. 'A Study of Coroner's Records of Suicide in Young People, 1986–88 in Western Australia.' *Australian and New Zealand Journal of Psychiatry* 26: 30–9.

Hoberman, H., and B. Garfinkel. 1988. 'Completed Suicide in Youth.' *Canadian Journal of Psychiatry* 33: 494–502.

Jasnoski, M. 1984. 'The Ecosystemic Perspective in Clinical Assessment and Intervention.' In W. O'Connor and B. Lubin, eds, *Ecological Approaches to Clinical and Community Psychology*, 41–56. Toronto: John Wiley & Sons.

Kienhorst, C., E. de Wilde, R. Diekstra, and W. Wolters. 1992. 'Differences between Adolescent Suicide Attempters and Depressed Adolescents.' *Acta Psychiatrica Scandinavica* 85: 222–8.

Klingman, A., and Z. Hochdorf. 1993. 'Coping with Distress and Self Harm: The Impact of a Primary Prevention Program among Adolescents.' *Journal of Adolescence* 16: 121–40.

Leenaars, A., and D. Lester. 1990. 'Suicide in Adolescents: A Comparison of Canada and the United States.' *Psychological Reports* 67: 867–73.

Leenaars, A., and S. Wenckstern, eds. 1991. *Suicide Prevention in Schools*. New York: Hemisphere Publishing Corp.

McGibben, L., C. Ballard, S. Handy, and W. Silveira. 1992. 'School Attendance as a Factor in Deliberate Self-Poisoning by 12–15 Year Old Adolescents.' *British Medical Journal* 304: 28.

Marttunen, M., H. Aro, and J. Lonnqvist. 1992. 'Adolescent Suicide: Endpoint of Long-Term Difficulties.' *Journal of the American Academy of Child and Adolescent Psychiatry* 31(4): 649–54.

National Task Force on Suicide in Canada. 1994. *Suicide in Canada: Update of the Report of the Task Force on Suicide in Canada*. Ottawa: Health Canada.

Pfeffer, C. 1990. 'Suicidal Behaviour in Children and Adolescents: A Clinical and Research Perspective.' *Yale Journal of Biology and Medicine* 63: 325–32.

Pfeffer, C., G. Klerman, S. Hurt, M. Lesser, J. Peskin, and C. Siefker, C. 1991. 'Suicidal Children Grow Up: Demographic and Clinical Risk Factors for Adolescent Suicide Attempts.' *Journal of the American Academy of Child and Adolescent Psychiatry* 30(4): 609–16.

Richman, J. 1986. *Family Therapy for Suicidal People*. New York: Springer Publishing.

Riggs, S., A. Alario, and C. McHorney. 1990. 'Health Risk Behavior and Attempted Suicide in Adolescents Who Report Prior Maltreatment.' *Journal of Pediatrics* 116: 815–21.

Rourke, B., G. Young, and A. Leenaars. 1989. 'A Childhood Learning Disability that Predisposes those Afflicted to Adolescent and Adult Depression and Suicide Risk.' *Journal of Learning Disabilities* 22: 169–75.

Rubenstein, J., T. Heeren, D. Housman, C. Rubin, and G. Stechler. 1989. 'Suicidal Behavior in "Normal" Adolescents: Risk and Protective Factors.' *American Journal of Orthopsychiatry* 59: 59–71.

Sakinofsky, I., and R. Roberts. 1985. 'The Ecology of Suicide in Canada, 1971–81.' Presentation to the Epidemiology and Community Psychiatry Section, Symposium on the Future of Psychiatric Epidemiology, Edinburgh.

Shaffer, D. 1988. 'The Epidemiology of Teen Suicide: An Examination of Risk Factors.' *Journal of Clinical Psychiatry* 49: 36–41.

Shaffer, D., A. Garland, M. Gould, P. Fisher, and P. Trautman. 1988. 'Preventing Teenage Suicide: A Critical Review.' *Journal of the American Academy of Child and Adolescent Psychiatry* 27: 675–87.

Shafii, M., S. Carrigan, J. Whittinghill, and A. Derrick. 1985. 'Psychological Autopsy of Completed Suicide in Children and Adolescents.' *American Journal of Psychiatry* 142(9): 1061–4.

Silverman, M., and R. Felner. 1995. 'The Place of Suicide Prevention in the Spectrum of Intervention: Definitions of Critical Terms and Constructs.' *Suicide and Life-Threatening Behaviour* 25(1): 70–81.

Smith, K., and S. Crawford. 1986. 'Suicidal Behaviour among "Normal" High School Students.' *Suicide and Life-Threatening Behavior* 16(3): 313–25.

Spirito, A., L. Brown, J. Overholser, and G. Fritz. 1989. 'Attempted Suicide in Adolescence: A Review and Critique of the Literature.' *Clinical Psychology Review* 9: 335–63.

Tierney, R., R. Ramsay, B. Tanney, and W. Lang. 1991. 'Comprehensive School Suicide Prevention Programs.' In A. Leenaars and S. Wenckstern, eds, *Suicide Prevention in Schools*, 83–98. New York: Hemisphere Publishing Corp.

Trovato, F. 1992. 'A Durkheimian Analysis of Youth Suicide: Canada, 1971 and 1981.' *Suicide and Life-Threatening Behavior*, 22(4): 413–27.

van der Kolk, B., C. Perry, and J. Herman. 1991. 'Childhood Origins of Self-Destructive Behavior.' *American Journal of Psychiatry* 148(12): 1665–71.

Weissberg, R., M. Caplan, and R. Harwood. 1991. 'Promoting Competent Young People in Competence-Enhancing Environments: A Systems-Based Perspective on Primary Prevention.' *Journal of Consulting and Clinical Psychology* 59(6): 830–41.

Werner, E. 1989. 'High-Risk Children in Young Adulthood: A Longitudinal Study from Birth to 32 Years.' *American Journal of Orthopsychiatry* 59(1): 72–81.

White, J. 1994. 'After the Crisis: Facilitating the Suicidal Student's Return to School.' *Guidance and Counselling* 10(1): 10–13.

17

Youth Suicide Prevention in Schools and Community: A Progress Report

ROGER J. TIERNEY

The United Nations through UNICEF published a report in 1994 which stated that Canada had the third-highest rate of suicide in the world for those fifteen to nineteen years of age and that the increase in the rate for this group from 1970 through 1991 was very high. The UNICEF publication compared rates of suicide for those fifteen to nineteen years of age in 1970 and 1991 for a number of countries. Canada's 15-to-19 rate went from 7.0 to 13.5 persons per 100,000 over this period. The 1991 figure is the third largest, following behind New Zealand at 15.7 and Finland at 15.0 (UNICEF, 1994).

While suicide among youth is most certainly a problem in Canada, there are two major limitations in this data. First, figures from various countries are not necessarily comparable in that data-collection methods differ so widely and, second, UNICEF is comparing two specific years and not examining the trend of data over that time. As such, the information is misleading. The greatest part of the increase in youth rates in Canada took place in the 1970s. Rates for those fifteen to nineteen increased 68 per cent between 1970 and 1980. They increased a much more moderate 2.5 per cent in the 1980s.

While the UN publication focused on figures for youth fifteen to nineteen, it should be noted that youth suicide should also focus on the behaviour of children and young adolescents (ten to fourteen years of age) and young adults (twenty to twenty-four). The rate of child and young-adolescent suicide (10–14 years) in Canada increased 57 per cent between 1970 and 1980 and 36 per cent between 1980 and 1990. The rate of young-adult suicides (20–24 years) increased 34 per cent between 1970 and 1980 and actually decreased 6 per cent between 1980 and 1990. There are strong connections between the 10-to-14, the 15-to-19, and the 20-to-24 age groups in terms of siblings and friends, and

TABLE 1
Five-year rate of completed suicide per 100,000 persons, 1988–1992

Age	Female	Male	Both genders
10–14	0.8	2.4	1.6
15–19	4.2	21.5	13.1
20–24	5.8	30.7	18.4
All ages	6.6	24.9	13.5

strong cohort effects. That is, suicide risk does not end at one age level, but may build and develop throughout childhood and adolescence especially among those with the early onset of major depression (Rao et al., 1993). It is important to note also that the effects and benefits of prevention programs may also last throughout childhood and adolescence. This aspect will be discussed later.

The rates for completed suicide in the Canadian population have levelled off at the current time. An examination of Statistics Canada data for the years 1988 through 1992 showed there were no appreciable increases or decreases. Variability was small. Thus, a five-year rate was calculated from this data for each of the age groups to demonstrate the current picture for completed and reported suicide. As can be seen in table 1, suicide is rare in children and young adolescents under fourteen. It increases for adolescents between fifteen and nineteen and rises strikingly in young adults aged twenty to twenty-four. Males demonstrate higher rates of completed suicide than do females at all ages.

It is important to note that official suicide statistics only reflect a small part of the problem of suicidal behaviour. Suicide data are not always accurate. Underreporting is common (Jobes et al., 1986). Also, what are actually suicide deaths may be misclassified as some other type of death, especially for groups with low official suicide rates (Phillips and Ruth, 1993), such as children and adolescents. Thus, there are likely more completions than are recorded.

Non-fatal suicidal behaviour is a sign of severe pain that requires attention for the ultimate well-being and survival of the individual. Females demonstrate higher rates of attempted suicide behaviour than do males. Non-fatal suicidal behaviours are estimated to occur at one hundred times the rates of completed suicide over all ages and three hundred times the completion rates for adolescents (Jarvis et al., 1976; Ramsay and Bagley, 1985). Thus, there is a tremendous amount of non-fatal suicidal behaviour occurring.

Ideation is also a sign of psychological pain. Survey results indicate that some 40 to 50 per cent of all high-school students report having had thoughts of suicide and some 10 per cent have exhibited at least one non-fatal suicidal behaviour (Cohen and Poland, 1988; Ross, 1985; Smith and Crawford, 1986).

Thus, thoughts of suicide are frighteningly common among young people. They need help in dealing with the pain that brings on these thoughts and the possible behaviour that may result from them. That help needs to come from peers, family, the schools, and the community.

Suicide among young people is a very serious problem, but the level of increase in the rate has slowed, and it remains slightly lower than the overall rate for all people in the population. Canada's increased rate in the 1970s for youth suicide was not unique. The dramatic increase in rates was experienced by most countries in the Western world. Many people in Canada became aware of the problem of suicide among its young people and have been doing something about it, which is one possible reason why the level of increase has diminished.

In 1987 Canada had a national task force, sponsored by Health and Welfare Canada, report on matters related to suicide (National Task Force, 1987). Of forty recommendations, five dealt specifically with youth suicide and two of these with schools. These recommendations were as follows:

8. Teachers should be informed, either through initial training or professional development, of techniques in the detection and assessment of suicidal risk in students, and of the available counselling services in the community.
   ...
19. Provincial Ministers of Education should consider the feasibility of developing province-wide mental health programs for adolescent students focusing on factors crucial to the development of self-confidence and self-esteem, strategies in problem solving and decision making, and interpersonal skills.
20. The treatment of young people who are at risk to suicide should recognise and account for vulnerability factors and environmental influences.
21. There should be a coordinated effort to identify gaps in counselling and psychiatric services for young people, and to establish programs based on a comprehensive approach to the family and the problems of the young.
22. All deliberately self-inflicted injuries and threats of suicide on the part of young people should be taken seriously, and involve professional assessment and appropriate therapeutic follow-up. (pp. 43, 52)

No national body, governmental or otherwise, has taken on the challenge of developing and initiating a national policy based on the task force's recommendations. It has been left to provinces, agencies, associations, and institutions to do what they will within their own mandates and capabilities. An update of this national report has reiterated and reinforced the recommendations and reported on some of the more recent developments regarding suicide in Canada (National Task Force, 1994).

This chapter will look at and report on the current nature of efforts in Canada to deal with youth-suicide issues in schools and in the community.

Suicide Prevention in the Schools

Schools present a most logical environment for providing suicide-prevention activities and services for young people. Schools are one of the first major long-term community involvements outside of the family that children and adolescents come into contact with. Schools are staffed by adults who are more objective, detached observers than parents, are trained in working with young people and assisting in their development, and are experts in teaching and assisting young people in gaining skills for living. It is only logical that they assist in helping young people who are experiencing pain and considering dying to get over it. Indeed, the increase in suicide-prevention activities in schools throughout the eighties and nineties may account in part for the slowing of rates for young people over this time period.

An essential factor in providing assistance for young people is meaningful connection (Berkovitz, 1985; Motto, 1985; Slaby and Garfinkel, 1994): with helpful peers; with caring adults who do not need to be experts, but who do need to be able to help; and, in many situations, with professional helping resources. Such meaningful connections are developed, encouraged, and implemented in comprehensive suicide-prevention programs.

The need for comprehensive, systematic school suicide prevention programs is well documented (Dyck, 1990; Poland, 1989; Ross, 1985; Ryerson, 1991; Tierney et al., 1991). School programs for suicide prevention have been debated, discussed, developed, and implemented throughout the seventies and eighties.

The content for such programs and the principles behind them have been well documented elsewhere. Complete discussions of implementation issues and what should be involved in school policy and practice may be found in Leenaars and Wenckstern's book *Suicide Prevention in Schools* (1991). This resource has numerous chapters that deal with school prevention issues in detail. Poland (1989) is a good resource and is itself a source of further resources. The Suicide Information and Education Centre in Calgary is also an excellent resource as it is a clearing house of information on suicide and related issues and has numerous sample programs available.

The Canadian Association for Suicide Prevention (CASP) recently published recommendations for school suicide-prevention programs (1994a) that outline the major elements necessary for comprehensive school initiatives. These guidelines were developed by the Schools Committee of CASP on the basis of reviews of the literature, discussion with school personnel, and expert consultation. They have been distributed to all ministries of education in Canada and are available to whomever wishes to have them.

The overall general recommendation is as follows: 'The Canadian Association for Suicide Prevention recommends that all school jurisdictions have guidelines and procedures relating to suicide prevention, and that each school within the jurisdiction be prepared to deal with this important issue' (CASP, 1994a, 2). Because of the prevalence of adolescents experiencing emotional pain and difficult problems in their development, no school jurisdiction can afford not to be doing something to provide help for students who might be suicidal.

There are a wide range of things that school jurisdictions might do to meet this need. The CASP document makes specific recommendations regarding (a) the need for system-wide policy, (b) the scope and content of activities that may be included in policies, (c) resources that may be developed and utilized, (d) training needs, (e) evaluation, and (f) follow-up. Each of these recommendations will be discussed briefly, as more in-depth information regarding the elements is available elsewhere (Berkovitz, 1985; Dyck, 1991; Ryerson and Kalafat, 1994; Tierney et al., 1991).

System-wide Policy

The CASP recommendations stress that policies need to be designed by all constituencies in the system as a shared effort, need to be written to provide clear and concise goals, objectives, and mandates, and need to be approved by those responsible for leadership in the system. System-wide policy indicates a commitment to prevention efforts and makes the mandate clear to staff, parents, and students. School jurisdictions that do not have such policies leave themselves open to criticism and are unprepared for assisting those who are suicidal and for dealing with staff and students when suicidal behaviour occurs.

Scope and Content

The scope of school prevention efforts should include activities and procedures involved with Caplan's (1964) basic span of prevention activities as applied by Shneidman (1970) to suicide prevention and named prevention, intervention, and postvention. As the CASP (1994a) recommendation defines them:

a) Prevention includes mandatory education and awareness elements for students, staff, and parents.

b) Intervention includes immediate crisis intervention as well as longer-term follow-up elements.

c) Postvention includes written protocols and the resources and mandate to implement them. (p. 3)

Schools excel at prevention work. Much of what they do for young people is a form of prevention for various difficulties that people can encounter. The climate of a school in terms of providing appropriate psychological/social support for young people is crucial. Curricular components regarding suicide for delivery to students are very important, as are programs to increase staff and student awareness and cooperation in this area.

Staff must be prepared to intervene and provide or arrange for counsel, referral, and parental consultation as appropriate. It is crucial that there be procedures and policies that mandate and guide interventions, referrals, and consultations with other resources and with parents or guardians. Staff require the support and assistance that such policies and procedures provide.

Schools must be prepared to deal with crisis and tragedy when it occurs in order to preserve and assist students and staff affected by suicide or non-fatal suicidal behaviour that has major impact.

Resources

It is recommended that schools provide resources in terms of staff for providing immediate assistance, and that connections be established for consultation and assistance from professional resources in the community. This applies to all aspects of a prevention program in terms of prevention, intervention, and postvention. In-house resources are mandatory for dealing immediately with students in situations involving their own suicidality, or for situations that involve dealing with the suicide of another student. Community resources need to be available for enhanced or further assistance and links must be developed with such resources so that they will be available when needed.

Training

Appropriate training must be provided to relevant system staff for preparing them to (a) deliver suicide curricula, (b) deliver awareness presentations (for staff and parents, (c) conduct interventions, and (d) carry out postvention protocols. Staff can only be effective to the extent that they are comfortable with dealing with issues of suicide. Training is the key to developing relevant skills and confidence.

Evaluation

Programs need to be monitored to ensure that they have been implemented according to their design, and to ensure that they are not harming anyone and indeed are achieving that for which they were designed.

Follow-up

It is recommended that systems follow up with (a) suicidal students, (b) referrals, (c) the immediate families of suicidal students, and (d) staff and students after suicidal events. Follow-up in terms of refresher training for staff who provide the suicide curriculum and staff who are responsible for interventions is recommended as well. Follow-up provides for better, more focused service, allows for corrections in terms of procedures and policies, and keeps relevant staff trained and refreshed in the important work that they do. It is a necessary form of support.

These recommendations are supported by the work of the Centers for Disease Control (CDC) in the United States. CDC published a guide based on the input of suicide-prevention experts in the United States and Canada as to what existing suicide-prevention programs were likely to be effective in reducing suicidal behaviour in youth (Centers for Disease Control and Prevention, 1992). These programs were then examined in detail and further exemplary programs were identified. The programs so identified were categorized into eight strategies for youth suicide prevention and model programs that incorporated one or more of the strategies were identified. These strategies are described by O'Carroll et al. (1994) as follows:

School gatekeeper training. This type of program is designed to help school staff (e.g., teachers, counsellors, and coaches) identify and refer students at risk for suicide. These programs also teach staff how to respond to suicide or other crises in the school.

Community gatekeeper training. These programs train community members (e.g., clergy, police, merchants, and recreation staff) and clinical health-care providers who see adolescent and young adult patients (e.g., physicians and nurses) to identify and refer persons in this age group who are at risk for suicide.

General suicide education. Students learn about suicide, its warning signs, and how to seek help for themselves or others. These programs often incorporate a variety of activities that develop self-esteem and social competency.

Screening programs. A questionnaire or other screening instrument is used to identify high-risk adolescents and young adults and provide further assessment and treatment. Repeated assessment can be used to measure changes in attitudes or behaviors over time, to test the effectiveness of a prevention strategy, and to detect potential suicidal behavior.

Peer support programs. These programs, which can be conducted in or outside of school, are designed to foster peer relationships and competency in social skills among high-risk adolescents and young adults.

Crisis centres and hotlines. Trained volunteers and paid staff provide telephone counselling and other services for suicidal persons. Such programs also may offer a 'drop-in' crisis center and referral to mental health services.

Restriction of access to lethal means. Activities are designed to restrict access to handguns, drugs, and other common means of suicide.

Intervention after a suicide. These programs focus on friends and relatives of persons who have committed suicide. They are partially designed to help prevent or contain suicide clusters and to help adolescents and young adults cope effectively with the feelings of loss that follow the sudden death or suicide of a peer. (p. 4)

The CASP recommendations reflect the first, third, and eighth of the CDC identified strategies. The fourth, related to screening, is not a common strategy in Canadian schools and is a matter for discussion and debate in the field of suicide prevention. The fifth strategy, related to peer support groups, is part of school-climate efforts in some schools. It involves prevention and intervention recommendations in the programs. The other strategies are more commonly considered as part of broader community efforts in suicide prevention.

Schools' Progress

It is exceedingly difficult to determine how many school-based programs are in existence, as such programs are not usually written about and there is no central, agreed-upon clearing house for these. A recent survey of provincial and territorial ministers of education by CASP indicated that there were many school programs across Canada but that they are mainly under the purview of individual boards of education.

Most education ministries could not provide a complete picture of what was happening in the provinces and referred CASP to the actual school jurisdictions in addition to providing a contact person for further departmental consultation. CASP is attempting to bring these contact people together to network and discuss the issues. CASP has taken on this initiative as it is currently the only national body in Canada focusing on suicide in general and youth suicide in particular.

Some provinces did provide information regarding some aspects of prevention efforts. It is apparent that provincial and territorial education ministries provide varying degrees of leadership and support in relation to suicide-prevention programs within their jurisdictions. There is no overall policy or plan in Canada, and little or no overall policy or plan in many of the provinces regarding suicide-prevention programs, in the schools or otherwise (Tanney, 1995). There are benefits and costs to leaving it to local jurisdictions to determine policy and procedures. On the one hand, local jurisdictions have a more accurate sense of their own needs, strengths, and weaknesses. On the other hand, leadership and support, financial and otherwise, from higher-level policy makers provides more influence and act both as a catalyst and support for local efforts.

The education ministries in the provinces of Alberta, New Brunswick, Saskatchewan, and the Northwest Territories have active programs in terms of curriculum and interdepartmental involvement, usually with departments of health and or social services, regarding the issue of suicide. British Columbia and Manitoba (see also Sigurdson et al., 1994) are considering departmental initiatives. Education departments in Newfoundland, Nova Scotia, Prince Edward Island, Quebec, and the Yukon encourage and have provided some training for school personnel. Ontario responded with a contact name only and provided no information regarding provincial efforts.

Many school systems have developed policy in the case of postvention situations. Schools have recognized the importance of dealing with major trauma stemming from the impact of the suicidal behaviour of students and staff and the severe emotional impact of other sources such as accidental and homicidal death and criminal acts. Most systems have designed some response to such matters that is either provided by the individual school or, more commonly, by system response teams that include people from various schools and functions. The impetus for such programs often comes from hard, often tragic, experience.

The truth of the matter in regards to having comprehensive system-wide policy and procedures regarding school suicide prevention programs is that some do, but many don't at the system or board mandated level. Many individual schools have their own policies and procedures, usually developed due to the interest and experience of particular staff, and/or due to learning the hard way through difficult experiences with suicidal students.

While many school suicide-prevention programs have been developed and conducted over the past fifteen to twenty years, implementation has not been as broad as many have hoped. Concerns have been expressed regarding the efficacy of certain elements of such programming.

Reasons for Concern

Among the reasons for limited implementation are that suicide remains a controversial subject and that suicide-prevention efforts have often been fragmented, have suffered from a lack of evaluation, and have not received reasonable funding to support system-wide comprehensive programs, research, and evaluative efforts (Berman and Jobes, 1995; National Task Force, 1994; Tanney, 1995). The issue of suicide has not truly gained widespread attention in the public consciousness. This is due in part to the low incidence of completions in relation to other issues (attempts and ideation have not been brought to the public's attention) and in part to the discomfort that surrounds the issue of suicide. Most frequently efforts have had to be funded with existing budgets and limited resources. These are easily redirected as other needs come to the fore and the suicide-prevention agenda has failed to demonstrate the full range of desired effects.

A major factor hindering support for school efforts has been concern regarding the effectiveness of suicide-prevention programming. The main concern has been raised regarding the prevention portion of programs involved with suicide-prevention curriculum that is presented to students. There is much debate among the experts regarding the effects of such programs and there has been a large degree of polarization and much controversy surrounding the issue. David Shaffer has become one of the most vocal critics of such school presentations. Shaffer et al. (1990), in an evaluation of three suicide-prevention programs, found limited positive effects overall and a negative effect in terms of students who had attempted suicide being upset by the program. They reported that students already had favourable knowledge about suicide and favourable help-seeking attitudes. They concluded that programs did not affect knowledge or attitude variables. Concerns have been raised that programs might increase suicidal behaviour in students (Shaffer, 1993) and otherwise 'undermine protective attitudes about suicide' (Shaffer, 1993: 4), and that these types of primary prevention efforts are not cost-effective (Shaffer et al., 1988).

It would appear that Shaffer's work has tapped into an attitudinal and/or philosophical issue, as the arguments in support of and in opposition to his views have become heated and appear to have created more discussion than the data support. The truth of the matter is that the Shaffer et al. study (1990) that engendered much of the concern is seriously limited in terms of its scope, sample, instrumentation, and conclusions (Tierney and Lang, 1991).

Other studies using pre-post measures have shown the positive effects of suicide-awareness curriculum programs (Overholser et al., 1989; Ciffone, 1993; and Kalafat and Elias, 1994). Orbach and Bar-Joseph (1993) also demonstrated positive effects with a seven-week introspective program designed for and applied to increasing coping abilities related to suicidal tendencies.

Garland and Zigler (1993) and Kalafat and Elias (1995) have written articles that discuss the debate and cite the results of studies related to the issues in much detail. What the results suggest is that we need to be clear about what we are doing and why we are doing it. And efforts need to be evaluated.

Being clear about what we are doing in part relates to a controversy between stress and mental-disorder theories about the causes of suicide as expressed in awareness curriculum. Many suicide-prevention programs offer the impression that suicide is most commonly a result of stressors occurring in the lives of adolescents and young adults. Data suggest that completed suicides are more accurately a result of pre-existing mental disorders largely represented by depressive and substance-abuse disorders (Garland and Zigler, 1993). Those who believe in the overwhelming-stress theory design programs that talk about stress and how to cope with it. In part this is also done because of the stigma of mental disorders. Many educators wish to avoid the term in dealing with young people, as their own level of acceptance and understanding of the concept of mental disorder, and that of their students, is low. Some of those who recognize the involvement of mental disorder feel that programs targeted at everyone (i.e., both normal teenagers and suicidal or disordered ones) are a waste. Measures such as screening for disorder and referral for treatment are proposed instead (Shaffer, 1994).

It is interesting to note that many young people do recognize the role of depression and substance abuse, but they don't classify these as mental-illness issues.

The relationship of factors is a complex one. The role of life events – what are termed precipitating conditions – in suicidal behaviour is known, but these alone are generally considered insufficient for causing suicide (Adams et al., 1994; Heikkinen et al., 1993). Mental disorders and/or developmental vulnerabilities such as experiences of early separation, loss, and emotional deprivation are predisposing conditions. It is the interaction of major stressors with pre-existing conditions and vulnerabilities that may lead to suicide (Silverman and Felner, 1995). Too often, among students, the press, teachers, and sometimes family, it is only the precipitating stresses that are known or recognized. It is an error to blame the proximate event. Of course, as Silverman and Felner (1995) point out, the complexity is heightened because the majority of people who experience both predisposing conditions and precipitating events do not suicide.

The stress–mental illness debate does not have to be polarized. Both factors have a relationship to the problem under discussion. Ciffone (1993) has shown that the role of mental illness can be included in curricular presentations without affecting positive outcomes. Garland and Zigler (1993) would support this argument and offer a broader perspective yet: 'Schools provide an appropriate setting for potentially useful primary prevention programs, including social competence building programs, problem-solving skills training, and basic mental health education. After thoroughly investigating the psychopathology of adolescent suicide, Cole (1989) concluded that problem-solving skill training and self-efficacy enhancement for adolescents may be the most effective suicide prevention effort. In addition, programs that include general mental health education, health promotion, and help-seeking encouragement might be very beneficial. The destigmatization and demystification of mental illness and the mental health system could encourage troubled youth to seek help' (177).

This broader perspective is supported by authors who point out that the single-focus educational program (i.e., suicide) is inappropriate (Berman and Jobes, 1995; Millstein et al., 1993; Silverman and Felner, 1995; Silverman and Maris, 1995), as the public-health model (Potter et al., 1995) is only one of many models for prevention that are available to us. Suicide has many antecedent factors. These factors are also related to other problems experienced by youth. School curriculum that can focus on the broad range of antecedent factors may have a far better chance of being supported as it may achieve multiple outcomes. As Silverman and Felner (1995) point out, 'There is little to apologise for in reducing the incidence of school failure, increasing attachment and adaptive behaviours in school, and reducing depression and the range of associated health problems, while also attempting to reduce the suicide rate' (99).

This is not to say that suicide curriculum should be lost in more general human-development primary-prevention efforts. There is a role for some specific awareness programming. If we wait for some ultimate proof that such programs work or lose them in larger efforts, we are making a grave (the pun is fully intended) mistake. Young people want to talk about suicide. They are very familiar with it from both print and the electronic media (Ryerson, 1991). They are talking about it. We, as educators, helpers, and concerned people, need to be talking about it with them. If we don't, we rob them of opportunities for learning, understanding, and getting help. Specific suicide content needs to relate students as peers. Troubled young people turn most frequently to other young people for help as opposed to their family or outside professionals (Kalafat and Elias, 1995; White, 1993, 1994). Thus, young people need to know about warning signs, how to make connections, and how to get help. It is a first-aid lesson aimed at helpers to encourage those suffering to get help and to show them where they might find it.

Unfortunately, our ability to offer prevention programming as well as other sources of help is being sorely tested in the economic environment of the nineties. Major reductions in the funding of education and social services in North America create severe pressure on these systems. Service beyond basic mandates, and for those in trouble, is itself in trouble. While the advantages of educators' involvement and networking with social agencies have been clearly demonstrated (Dryfoos, 1993; O'Carroll et al., 1994; Shulman and Athey, 1993), these agencies have been hard hit as well. Referral to outside social and mental-health resources is becoming problematic.

Demands will increase on those who work at the grass-roots level with youth, that is, individual caregivers such as teachers, friends, family, school counsellors, social workers, police, corrections personnel, ministers, and others. Care at the grass-roots level is crucial if we are to connect with suicidal people and have any chance at assisting them and involving other resources as appropriate. Fortunately, major strides have been made related to caregiver/gatekeeper training. One of the major historical concerns regarding suicide was in finding people, both professional and otherwise, who were prepared to deal with it and offer assistance (Boldt, 1976; Royal, 1979; and Tanney, 1989). This situation has applied both within and outside of schools. As the CDC guide has demonstrated, two major strategies have involved school and community gatekeeper training. This training has been shown to have favourable results with caregivers (Garland and Zigler, 1993; Klingman, 1990; Tierney, 1994). Resources have also been published that assist caregivers in dealing with the issue. Berman and Jobes (1991) have provided an excellent text for professional caregivers regarding intervention with adolescents, and Ramsay et al. (1994) have provided a basic handbook on suicide intervention for both non-professional and professional caregivers. Texts by Bongar (1991) and Leenaars et al. (1995) provide in-depth discussion for professionals on matters of treatment with the suicidal person in school or community contexts.

Youth Suicide Prevention in the Community

If we are truly to affect youth suicide we must look to the broader community as well to support and supplement the work of the schools and to carry it on after school attendance is over or when it is not applicable. Many young people are in post-secondary education, jail, hospitals, and the military. Lipschitz (1995) suggests that comprehensive prevention programs can be applied in these settings as well, and should involve the following:

- The promotion of a facilitywide awareness of suicide as a real and preventable hazard, so that all staff members recognise a personal responsibility for detecting and referring suicidal prisoners, students, soldiers, sailors, and airmen and women
- The identification of high-risk groups who are given special monitoring and prevention services
- The provision of intensive interventions at times of special risk, with psychiatric evaluation and hospitalisation readily available

- The preparation of postvention plans that are actuated after a suicide occurs, in order to prevent contagion (p. 167)

Lipshitz's recommendations involve the strategies of gatekeeper training, general suicide education, screening programs, and intervention after a suicide. Peer support programs could be added to this list, as these can be highly useful in the contexts to which Lipshitz refers.

What of those young people who are not in any type of institutional context? One strategy for this group is training community caregivers, which could include police, social-agency personnel, and employment-agency personnel.

The more people trained in a community, the more recognition, intervention, and referral can occur. A Canadian Royal Commission on Aboriginal Peoples (1995) studying the issue of suicide among Aboriginal people made whole-community involvement a major recommendation. Suicide is a major concern for Aboriginal peoples as their rates, especially for the young, are exceedingly high (Medical Services, 1991). Kirmayer (1994) notes that in native communities family and social-network approaches have more likelihood of success as they are more consistent with native values and realities than are psychological approaches based on psychotherapeutic models.

Another way of reaching people in the community is through the use of the media. Advertising for crisis centres and hotlines can inform people of a valuable resource, while also drawing attention to the issue. General suicide awareness needs to be promoted in the media both when tragedies occur and at other times. It is a popular subject for the media, and media resources such as the CASP media resource book (CASP, 1994b) need to be made available to assist the media in their work. Public-health promotions dealing with wellness, effective parenting, substance-abuse issues, and mental illness also can have positive effects.

The strategy of controlling access to the means of suicide as a preventive measure has been an underutilized strategy in the community. Controlling access to firearms, for example, is a community strategy that would reduce suicidal behaviour (Berman and Jobes, 1995; Lester and Leenaars, 1993; Mishara, 1995; O'Carroll et al., 1994; Silverman and Maris, 1995).

Summary

There are many strategies for youth suicide prevention that can be applied in schools and in the broader community. And many are working. Rates of completed suicide have stabilized in young people. Moreover, many of the strategies and recommendations can have effects with people of all ages, not just youth. We have achieved some progress in this serious human issue, but we need to build upon the successes and learn more from our evaluative efforts as we continue to work in this difficult area. We must continue those things that help us connect with the human pain that, as Shneidman (1993) reminds us forcefully, simply, and most of all humanly, underlies all suicidal thought and behaviour.

REFERENCES

Adams, D.M., J.C. Overholser, and A.S. Spirato. 1994. 'Stressful Life Events Associated with Adolescent Suicide Attempts.' *Canadian Journal of Psychiatry* 39(1): 43–7.
Berkovitz, I.H. 1985. 'The Role of Schools in Child, Adolescent, and Youth Suicide Prevention.' In M.L. Peck, N.L. Farberow, and R.E. Litman, eds, *Youth Suicide*, 170–90. New York: Springer.
Berman A.L., and D.A. Jobes. 1991. *Adolescent Suicide: Assessment and Intervention*. Washington: American Psychological Association.
– 1995. 'Suicide Prevention in Adolescents (Age 12–18).' *Suicide and Life-Threatening Behavior* 25(1): 143–54.
Boldt, M. 1976. *Report of the Task Force on Suicide to the Minister of Social Services and Community Health*. Edmonton: Government of the Province of Alberta.
Bongar, B. 1991. *The Suicidal Patient: Clinical and Legal Standards of Care*. Washington: American Psychological Association.
Canadian Association for Suicide Prevention. 1994a. *Recommendations for Suicide Prevention in Schools*. Calgary, AB: CASP.
Canadian Association for Suicide Prevention. 1994b. *Suicide: A Media Resource Book*. Calgary, AB: CASP.
Caplan, G.R. 1964. *Principles in Preventive Psychiatry*. New York: Basic Books.
Centers for Disease Control and Prevention. 1992. *Youth Suicide Prevention Programs: A Resource Guide*. Atlanta: CDC.
Ciffone, J. 1993. 'Suicide Prevention: A Classroom Presentation for Adolescents.' *Social Work* 38(2): 197–203.
Cohen, D., and S. Poland. 1988. Suicide survey results. Unpublished raw data.
Cole, D. 1989. 'Psychopathology of Adolescent Suicide: Hopelessness, Coping, Beliefs and Depression.' *Journal of Abnormal Psychology* 98: 248–55.
Dryfoos, J.G. 1993. 'Schools as Places for Health, Mental, Health, and Social Services.' *Teachers College Record* 94(3): 540–65.
Dyck, R.J. 1990. 'Suicide in the Young: Implications for Policy and Programming.' In R.J. McMahon and R. DeV. Peters, eds, *Behavior Disorders of Adolescence: Research, Intervention, and Policy in Clinical and School Settings*, 125–38. New York: Plenum.
– 1991. 'System-Entry Issues in School Suicide Prevention Education Programs.' In Leenaars and Wenckstern, eds, *Suicide Prevention in Schools*, 41–50.
Ferguson, W.W. 1981. 'Gifted Adolescents, Stress and Life Changes.' *Adolescence* 16: 973–85.
Garland, A.F., and E. Zigler. 1993. 'Adolescent Suicide Prevention: Current Research and Social Policy Implications.' *American Psychologist* 48(2): 169–82.
Heikkinen, M., H. Aro, and J. Lonnqvist. 1993. 'Life Events and Social Support in Suicide.' *Suicide and Life-Threatening Behavior* 23(4): 343–58.

Jarvis, G.K., R. Ference, F.G. Johnson, and P.C. Whitehead. 1976. 'Sex and Age Patterns in Self-Injury.' *Journal of Health and Social Behavior* 17: 145–55.

Jobes, D.A., A.L. Berman, and A.R. Josselsen. 1986. 'The Impact of Psychological Autopsies on Medical Examiners' Determination of Manner of Death.' *Journal of Forensic Science* 31(1): 177–89.

Kalafat, J., and M. Elias. 1994. 'An Evaluation of a School-Based Suicide Awareness Intervention.' *Suicide and Life-Threatening Behavior* 24(3): 224–33.

– 1995. 'Suicide Prevention in an Educational Context: Broad and Narrow Foci.' *Suicide and Life-Threatening Behavior* 25(1): 123–33.

Kirmayer, L.K. 1994. 'Suicide among Canadian Aboriginal Peoples.' *Transcultural Psychiatric Research Review* 31: 3–58.

Klingman, A. 1990. 'Action Research Notes on Developing School Staff Suicide Awareness Training.' *School Psychology International* 11: 133–42.

Leenaars, A.A., J.T. Maltsberger, and R.A. Neimeyer. 1995. *Treatment of Suicidal People*. Bristol, PA: Taylor & Francis.

Leenaars, A.A., and S. Wenckstern. 1991. *Suicide Prevention in Schools*. New York: Hemisphere Publishing Corp.

Lester, D., and A.A. Leenaars. 1993. 'Suicide Rates in Canada before and after Tightening Firearm Control Laws.' *Psychological Reports* 72: 787–90.

Lipschitz, A. 1995. 'Suicide Prevention in Young Adults (Age 18–30).' *Suicide and Life-Threatening Behavior* 25(1): 155–70.

Medical Services Branch Steering Committee on Native Mental Health (1991). *Agenda for First Nations and Inuit Mental Health*. Ottawa: Health and Welfare Canada.

Millstein, S.G., E.O. Nightingale, A.C. Petersen, A.M. Mortimer, and D.A. Hamburg. 1993. 'Promoting the Healthy Development of Adolescents.' *Journal of the American Medical Association* 269(11): 1413–15.

Mishara, B. 1995. 'Canadian Association for Suicide Prevention Position on Gun Registration in Canada.' Presentation to Commons subcommittee on gun registration.

Motto, J.A. 1985. 'Treatment Concerns in Preventing Youth Suicide.' In M.L. Peck, N.L. Farberow, and R.E. Litman, eds, *Youth Suicide*, 91–111. New York: Springer.

National Task Force. 1987. *Suicide in Canada: Report of the National Task Force on Suicide*. Ottawa: Health and Welfare Canada.

– 1994. *Suicide in Canada: Update of the Report of the Task Force on Suicide in Canada*. Ottawa: Health Canada.

O'Carroll P.W., L.B. Potter, and J.A. Mercy. 1994. 'Programs for the Prevention of Suicide among Adolescents and Young Adults.' *Centers for Disease Control and Prevention, Morbidity and Mortality Weekly Report* 43(RR-6): 3–7.

Orbach, I., and H. Bar-Joseph. 1993. 'The Impact of a Suicide Prevention Program for Adolescents on Suicidal Tendencies, Hopelessness, Ego Identity, and Coping.' *Suicide and Life-Threatening Behavior* 23(2): 120–9.

Overholser, J., A. Hemstreet, A. Spirato, and S. Vyse. 1989. 'Suicide Awareness Programs in the Schools: Effects of Gender and Personal Experience.' *Journal of the American Academy of Child and Adolescent Psychiatry* 28: 225–30.

Phillips, D.P., and T.E. Ruth. 1993. 'Adequacy of Official Suicide Statistics for Scientific Research and Public Policy.' *Suicide and Life-Threatening Behavior* 23(4): 307–19.

Poland, S. 1989. *Suicide Intervention in the Schools*. New York: Guilford Press.

Potter, L.B., K.E. Powell, and S.P. Kachur. 1995. 'Suicide Prevention from a Public Health Perspective.' *Suicide and Life-Threatening Behavior* 25(1): 82–91.

Ramsay, R.F., and C. Bagley. 1985. 'The Prevalence of Suicidal Behaviors, Attitudes, and Associated Social Experiences in an Urban Population.' *Suicide and Life-Threatening Behavior* 15(3):
151–67.

Ramsay, R.F., B.L. Tanney, R.J. Tierney, and W.A. Lang. 1994. *Suicide Intervention Handbook.*
Calgary, AB: LivingWorks Education.

Rao, U., M.M. Weissman, J.A. Martin, and R.W. Hammond. 1993. 'Childhood Depression and Risk
of Suicide: A Preliminary Report of a Longitudinal Study.' *Journal of the American Academy of
Child and Adolescent Psychiatry* 32(1): 21–7.

Ross, C. 1985. 'Teaching Children the Facts of Life and Death: Suicide Prevention in the Schools.'
In M. Peck, N. Farberow, and R. Litman, eds, *Youth Suicide*, 147–69. New York: Springer.

Royal, P. 1979. *Report of the Committee on the Nature of, and Response to Personal and Family
Crisis in the Province of Alberta.* Edmonton: Government of the Province of Alberta.

Royal Commission on Aboriginal Peoples. 1995. *Choosing Life: Special Report on Suicide among
Aboriginal People.* Ottawa: Canada Communication Group.

Ryerson, D. 1991. 'Suicide Awareness Education in Schools: The Development of a Core Program
and Subsequent Modifications for Special Populations or Institutions.' In Leenaars and
Wenckstern, eds, *Suicide Prevention in Schools*, 99–112.

Ryerson, D., and J. Kalafat. 1994. 'The Crisis of Youth Suicide.' In R.G. Stevenson, ed., *What Will
We Do: Preparing a School Community to Cope with Crises*, 79–94. Amityville, NY: Baywood.

Shaffer, D. 1993. 'Advances in Youth Suicide Research Update.' *Lifesavers* 5(4): 1, 3–4.

Shaffer, D., A. Garland, M. Gould, P. Fisher, and P. Trautman. 1988. 'Preventing Teen Suicide:
A Critical Review.' *Journal of the American Academy of Child and Adolescent Psychiatry* 27:
675–87.

Shaffer, D., V. Vieland, A. Garland, M. Rojas, M. Underwood, and C. Busner. 1990. 'Adolescent
Suicide Attempters: Response to Suicide Prevention Programs.' *Journal of the American Medical Association* 264: 3151–5.

Shneidman, E.S. 1970. 'Recent Developments in Suicide Prevention.' In E.S. Shneidman, N.L.
Farberow, and R.E. Litman, eds, *The Pychology of Suicide*, 145–55. New York: Aronson.

– 1993. 'Controversies in Suicidology.' *Suicide and Life-Threatening Behavior* 23(4): 292–8.

Shulman, D.A., and M. Athey. 1993. 'Youth Emergency Services: Total Community Effort, a
Multisystem Approach.' *Child Welfare* 72(2): 171–9.

Sigurdson, E., D. Staley, M. Matas, K. Hildahl, and K. Squair. 1994. 'A Five Year Review of Youth
Suicide in Manitoba.' *Canadian Journal of Psychiatry* 39: 397–403.

Silverman, M.M., and R.D. Felner. 1995. 'Suicide Prevention Programs: Issues of Design, Implementation, Feasibility, and Developmental Appropriateness.' *Suicide and Life-Threatening
Behavior* 25(1): 92–104.

Silverman, M.M., and R.W. Maris. 1995. 'The Prevention of Suicidal Behaviors: An Overview.'
Suicide and Life-Threatening Behavior 25(1): 10–21.

Slaby, A.E., and L.F. Garfinkel. 1994. *No One Saw My Pain: Why Teens Kill Themselves.* New
York: W.W. Norton.

Smith, K., and S. Crawford. 1986. 'Suicidal Behavior among "Normal" High School Students.'
Suicide and Life-Threatening Behavior 16: 313–25.

Tanney, B.L. 1989. 'Preventing Suicide by Improving the Competency of Caregivers.' In *Report of
the Secretary's Task Force on Youth Suicide, volume 3: Preventions and Interventions in Youth
Suicide.* Washington: U.S. Department of Health and Human Services, Alcohol, Drug Abuse and
Mental Health Administration.

– 1995. 'Suicide Prevention in Canada: A National Perspective Highlighting Progress and Problems.' *Suicide and Life-Threatening Behavior* 25(1): 105–22.

Tierney, R.J. 1994. 'Suicide Intervention Training Evaluation: A Preliminary Report.' *Crisis* 15(2):
    69–76.
Tierney, R.J., and W.A. Lang. 1991. 'Cutting Suicide Prevention Programs in Schools.' *SIEC
    Current Awareness Bulletin.*
Tierney, R.J., R.F. Ramsay, B.L. Tanney, and W.A. Lang. 1991. 'Comprehensive School Suicide
    Prevention Programs.' In Leenaars and Wenckstern, eds, *Suicide Prevention in Schools*, 83–98.
UNICEF. 1994. *Progress of Nations.* New York: UNICEF.
White, J. 1993. 'School-Based Suicide Awareness in Alberta.' *Alberta Mental Health Research
    Review* 2(2): 5–6.
–   1994. 'Youth Suicide Awareness about Suicide.' *Injury Prevention Centre News* 7(1): 18–19, 27.

18

Suicide Postvention: Cultural Issues

SUSANNE WENCKSTERN and ANTOON A. LEENAARS

Suicide is experienced as traumatic by its survivors. Suicide is 'a psychologically traumatic event that is generally outside the range of usual human experience' (American Psychiatric Association [APA], 1987: 238). A post-traumatic response develops after the event. For a few survivors, but at alarming rates, post-traumatic stress disorder (PTSD) occurs (ibid.). Although even fewer, for some survivors, suicide becomes their option. Figley (1985) defined such post-traumatic responses as 'a set of conscious and unconscious behaviors and emotions associated with dealing with the memories of the stressors of the catastrophe and immediately afterwards' (p. xix). In addition to a recognized stressor, these tramatized people experience recurrent recollections, dreams, and associations, a numbing of responsiveness or a reduced involvement with their world, and persistent symptoms of arousal and grief (Leenaars and Wenckstern, 1990b).

Our own experience with survivors of suicide would suggest that much of the aftershock has to do with some basic assumptions that people hold about the operation of the world (Leenaars and Wenckstern, 1990 a,b). Most people (in the Western world) believe that 'Johnny, the ten year old, doesn't kill himself.' With a suicide, say Johnny's, our view of the world may be shattered, resulting in a possible post-traumatic response. Such reactions may differ for a host of reasons, ranging from psychological to biological to cultural. The intent of this chapter is to examine cultural factors, utilizing East Asian Canadian examples.

Postvention: Preliminary Observations

Postvention refers to 'things done' to address and alleviate possible reactions to trauma, such as a suicide, homicide, or terrorist attack. The term was first introduced by Shneidman (1973, 1981a, 1983). Shneidman defined postvention as follows: 'Those things done after the dire event has occurred that serve to mollify the aftereffects of the event in a person who has attempted suicide, or to deal with the adverse effects as the survivor-victims of a person who has committed suicide'(1973: 385). Postvention includes services to all survivors of such a dire event who are in need (e.g., children, parents, teachers, and friends), not just the immediate family members. When a tragic, unusual event occurs – such as a student's suicide – schools must play a key role in postvention.

School suicide postvention programs represent an 'organized response of a caring humanistic institution in addressing the traumatic loss of a student in such a way that the emotional needs of those remaining are dealt with effectively' (Pelej and Scholzen, 1987). These programs are designed specifically to address the traumatic loss. One thrust of such programs is addressing the contagion or 'copycat' effect (Leenaars and Wenckstern, 1986; Phillips and Carstensen, 1986) by preventing, for example, suicide role modelling (Lamartine-Anderson and Sattem, 1986). As we noted clinically almost two decades ago (Leenaars and Wenckstern, 1986, 1990a) it seems that such processes are especially true in people who themselves have a history of being traumatized, suicidal, and/or depressed (Brent, 1992).

Our postvention efforts essentially represent a synthesis of educational strategies largely gleaned from the American Association of Suicidology and the Canadian Association for Suicide Prevention; consultative intervention acquired in part from Goodstein (1978) and Watzlawick, Beavin, and Jackson (1967); crisis intervention from Farberow (1967), Hoff (1984), Leenaars, Maltsberger, and Neimeyer (1994), Leenaars and Wenckstern (1994), Parad (1965) and Shneidman (1981b, 1985); a few strategies related to trauma response, for example, Figley (1985), Lifton (1969), and Lindemann (1944); and, especially, postvention strategies from Shneidman (1981a).

Postvention programs include some specific generic aspects, although modifications will be necessary depending on such factors as time, situation, and the nature of the suicide. The issue of cultural difference or variation, as an example of these factors, will be the major focus of this paper. Cultural differences require awareness, sensitivity, and program modifications, as highlighted in an idiographic (single case) study of an East Asian Canadian death.

Culture and Ethnicity

Culture and related terms such as ethnicity, subculture, multicultural, ethnic identity, and minority group are frequently encountered terms, but they are difficult to define. Devore and Schlesinger (1987), noting the simplicity of dictionary definitions, propose that culture 'refers to the fact that human groups are distinguishable by the manner in which they guide and structure behavior and the meanings they ascribe to it' (14).

Ethnicity is a key element in culture. The ethnic group refers to 'those who conceive of themselves as alike by virtue of their common ancestry, real or fictitious, and who are so regarded by others' (Shibutani and Kwan, 1965: 23). Superseding race, religion, and national and geographic origin (McGoldrick, 1982), ethnic values and identification are retained for many generations after immigration to a new country – so also the rate of suicide (Sainsbury and Barraclough, 1968). Extensive evidence (Greeley, 1969) has shown that ethnicity is a powerful influence in one's development and may well be a basic psychological need (McGoldrick, 1982). Simply stated, people need culture.

Our own understanding and, hence, usage of these terms and their underlying concepts are limited or maybe even ethnocentric. Cultural 'filters' or 'blinders' are ubiquitous. Sensitivity to cultural issues is imperative.

As an example, East Asians show considerable variation from our Western culture. Shon and Ja (1982) note that, given the long history of civilization, philosophical approaches to life, based primarily on traditional systems, are strikingly divergent. In these Asian systems of thought the individual is often superseded by the family. The concept of the family extends both backwards and forwards. Rituals and customs (e.g., keeping of family record books and ancestor worship) are reinforced. Personal decisions and actions, then, reflect not only upon the individual, but also on the extended family.

Some characteristics of the 'model Asian personality' have been proposed by Toupin (1980): many Asians are likely to express deference to others, to devalue themselves and their families to others, and to avoid confrontation. *Shame* is emphasized in Asian socialization practices. Family honour is preserved, for example, by not discussing personal problems outside the family. The expression of emotion, even in trauma, reflects negatively on the family.

In view of these perceived similar characteristics, differences between East Asian groups (even within a country) may seem minimal to the Western observer, yet they are critical, as seen in the obvious difference of language and most importantly in the historical, social, and economic developments of these distinct nations.

To illustrate, the senior author was asked at a school interview to provide information from an English as a Second Language (ESL) report on a ten-year-old Vietnamese boy who was not progressing academically as well as might be expected. The family had been in Canada for three years. The father came to the interview as the traditional representative of the family. As the father spoke very little English, the school obtained the services of a well-spoken Vietnamese woman to translate. Despite what we felt to be a well-organized information feedback session, it was readily apparent that there was an awkwardness/discomfort in the session. In retrospect, it seems very likely that this father may have experienced shame on the family regarding his son's academic progress. Yet, what is equally, if not more important culturally, the awkwardness in the session was more likely related to the fact that the translator was ethnic Chinese, although she and her family had lived in Vietnam for several generations, whereas the father was ethnic Vietnamese. Class or status distinctions remain in Vietnam. As we stated, sensitivity to cultural issues is imperative.

In light of the above brief discussion of culture and ethnicity, a complex event such as suicide, as understood primarily within our Western cultural framework, becomes even more complex when viewed within a multicultural or from a cross-cultural perspective.

Postvention Strategies

Before addressing the issue of postvention and culture we wish to outline briefly some basic postvention strategies; more comprehensive discussion is presented elsewhere (Leenaars, 1985; Leenaars and Wenckstern, 1986, 1990a and b, 1991, 1995; Wenckstern, 1990; Wenckstern and Leenaars, 1990, 1993).

1. Consultation. Discussion, coordination, and planning are undertaken at every phase, beginning with the school administration and followed by school staff and other involved individuals, such as students and parents, under the direction of the postvention coordinator, that is, a mental-health expert who takes charge and provides structure. Concurrent peer consultation and review among professional staff who are involved in the postvention program (postvention team) are undertaken to review the plans that were implemented and to plan or coordinate further action.

2. Crisis intervention. Emergency or crisis response is provided, using basic problem-solving strategies.

3. Community linkage. Since it is imperative that survivors of suicide be provided with the appropriate support, we assist these individuals to obtain such services. Educational systems need to develop a linkage system or network to aid in making referrrals, exchanging information, and coordinating services with appropriate community services. Being familiar with and updating local community resources before a traumatic event is highly recommended. In the case of culturally different students, having a directory on hand listing local cultural centres and the names of translators, with pre-established communications, may be not only very helpful but a necessity.

4. Assessment and counselling. Evaluation and therapy are provided as

needed or requested by the school administrator, for example, the principal or his/her designate. Here, especially, cultural awareness and sensitivity are crucial (Ishikawa, 1994).

As an aside, the signs or markers we commonly utilize to tell us whether someone is having psychological problems, or is suffering from a possible post-traumatic reaction may be misleading and even wrong within the context of other ethnic groups (Kashiwaga, 1994). For example, East Asians' non-verbal communication/cues may differ significantly from our North American cues; for instance, many of the Southeast Asian students seen for therapy present as soft-spoken, quiet, and engage in minimal eye contact.

5. Education. Information about suicide and its prevention (e.g., clues, myths, causes, what to do, where to go for help) is provided through discussion, seminars, and workshops at the school and within the community. We may especially need to 'reach out' more to culturally different students and their families. Some may argue, for example, that since Koreans are often referred to as 'silent immigrants', one should not intrude upon their silence or 'privacy.' Such a view, however, likely represents rationalization as a defence against our discomfort with suicide and against our own fears and anxieties.

6. Liaison with the media. Information about suicide in the form of publicity, especially that which tends to sensationalize or glamorize the suicide, should be avoided. However, our experience has shown us that (a) a media spokesperson for the school must be appointed at the outset of the crisis, and (b) this role should be filled by the postvention coordinator and not by a school administrator (e.g., the principal). Not only does this function ensure the accuracy and consistency of information being given out, but, most important, it ensures that the procedures being enacted and their positive impact are emphasized to the media.

7. Follow-up. Periodic follow-ups are undertaken with school administrators, school staff, and mental-health professionals. A formal final consultation is provided several months after the suicide to facilitate a formal closure to the program. However, every attempt is made to let all concerned know that we are available on request for follow-up if the need arises.

Suicide and Culture

The father of contemporary suicidology, Edwin Shneidman, has embedded his widely accepted definition of suicide within a cultural framework. Shneidman writes: 'Currently *in the Western world*, suicide is a conscious act of self-induced annihilation, best understood as a multidimensional malaise in a needful individual who defines an issue for which the suicide is perceived as the best solution' (1985: 203; italics ours). Shneidman (1985, 1991) stated that his proposed definition is applicable only to the Western world and noted that this caution needed to be given 'so that cross-cultural comparisons do not make the error of assuming that a suicide is a suicide' (1985: 203).

The views of suicide commonly held in Western cultures (e.g., as portrayed in the media) are likely not shared by the individual, family, or community outside the Western hemisphere and perhaps even within (e.g., by Aboriginal peoples). Here we will illustrate our views with some examples, mainly from East Asian peoples.

In Japan, for example, according to Iga (1993), suicide, though not welcomed, has traditionally been accepted. It is seen as a personal problem, not the government's (Iga, 1993; Takahashi, 1993). To understand suicide in Japan, one must especially understand Japanese views of death, which include the following: death (even if by suicide) is a philosophical concept based on the idea of mujo, the sense of eternal change and the ephemeral nature of all things; death is welcomed as an emancipation; death allows one to identify with family, to have a continuing life through one's children and their children; and (with deep devotion) the dead continue to communicate with family members at the butsudan (miniature household temple).

This view of death and, by implication, of suicide, within the larger Japanese cultural framework helps us to understand Japanese suicide better as for example, in the well-publicized case of Fumiko K. This was a case of oyako shinju, only one aspect of the diversity of basic assumptions about suicide in Japan (Takahashi, 1994). Fumiko K., a dedicated mother, who was about to be divorced, walked into the Pacific Ocean off Santa Monica, California, with her infant daughter and four-year-old son. Passers-by intervened and Fumiko K. survived, although her children died. Fumiko K. was charged with their murder. It seemed incomprehensible to many Westerners that this woman, who had lived in America for fourteen years, had not become socialized to American attitudes towards divorce, infanticide, and social services. How could she have killed her children? Why would she have tried to kill herself?

To understand Fumiko K.'s actions, it is necessary to appreciate not only the Japanese concept of death but also other Japanese cultural norms and rules. To illustrate, Iga (1993) has argued that in Japan divorce robs women of their family. Familial failure is blamed primarily on the woman. In Japan, there is also a prejudice against orphans, and prejudice is a strong force in Japan (Iga and Sneden, 1994). Japanese peoples' sense of shame is strong. There is a reluctance to take problems to others. After all, suicide and death are personal-familial problems. This outlook left Fumiko K. with limited ability to avail herself of social services and outside resources. Therefore, by her homicide-suicide, Fumiko K. would traditionally be viewed as having acted in the best interest of her children.

As a further illustration of the diversity in even one group – in this case, East Asians – Carter and Brooks (1991) present the case of fourteen-year-old Lee, who immigrated to the United States from Cambodia at age eight. He was reported to be a serious, driven youngster, and just before his suicide was involved in an uncharacteristic prank. He scared some girls at school with a garter snake. Following school disciplinary action, which included a severe reprimand and a note to his father threatening suspension, Lee later that night hanged himself from a tree in front of his house. His shame was deep. In some Cambodian villages, when a person is ostracized from the community or otherwise dishonoured, 'he or she is expected to stand by a tree, where some type of winged mythic creature takes the individual up into the branches and "takes him or her away" through something equivalent to hanging' (203).

Ritualistic expectations are not rare in East Asia, as was documented earlier this century (Zilboorg, 1936). Recently, Japan became alarmed by the successive suicides of two thirteen-year-old school boys; both cases involved bullying, dishonour, and shame (*Globe and Mail*, 1994). Iga and Sneden (1994) have, in fact, suggested that Japanese traditions would promote self-destruction in such situations to preserve absolute adherence to the group. Obviously, such suicides are a complex expression, even in their cultural aspects. Our discussion is only a brief note on this complexity.

Other cultures have different meanings. Even within North America, there is a great diversity of peoples – Aboriginal peoples, Inuit people, French Canadians, African-Canadians, and so on. Our examples of East Asian Canadians are meant to be heuristic. It is erroneous to assume that there is one commonly held definition or understanding of suicide (or even of death and life) (Nakagawa, 1994; Ohi, 1994). Suicide is a multidimensional concept that one needs to understand within the general heuristic framework of the dominant culture/society, while appreciating and being sensitive to the specific meanings of suicide held by cultures within the varied North American mosaic. To be insensitive to these cultural issues in postvention will likely result in problems, not only in the program but also in cultural relations. By implication, we should not make the error of assuming that postvention is postvention. Since we cannot isolate all cultures here, we hope that an example will serve as a useful mnemonic.

An Idiographic Illustration

We illustrate a few of these cultural issues and postvention program modifications by way of the following suicide case, using a time-sequence format.

The postvention coordinator was notified of the suicide of Tim, a seventeen-year-old boy, by the boy's secondary-school principal, the morning following his suicide. Tim had immigrated to Canada from Korea, with his parents and older sister, six years before his suicide. His parents were hard-working members of the community, spending long hours every day at their small family-owned business. Tim was described by many of his classmates and friends as a diligent, serious-minded student. Everyone expressed initial shock and utter disbelief that this quiet, likeable student, who received good grades at school, had hanged himself.

1. When Tim's sister (who had discovered her brother hanging) and her girl-friend were found sitting in the school guidance office even before school began, immediate basic support was provided to them. His sister expressed many confused and contradictory feelings: among them shock, guilt, and shame, coupled with a questioning of her decision to say anything at school against what she perceived her family's wishes might be. She was clearly experiencing the pressures of two divergent cultures. Once the suicide 'secret' is 'out in the open,' Tim's sister seemed to experience some, though slight, immediate relief. She and her friend were given assurances that immediate follow-up by mental-health professionals would occur.

2. The postvention team (which included mental-health professionals, key school personnel, and community people) then met for the school planning meeting. Cultural issues surfaced immediately. For example, it was discussed whether or not the family should be contacted, and if so, who should contact the family and when. We believe it is helpful to discuss the 'usual' way such a communication would be handled in relation to any student death. As was his norm, the principal informed the deceased student's parents of planned postvention efforts.

When the culture of the deceased is not well understood, the best route may be to state honestly and frankly to the family that one is trying to be sensitive but one is unsure about what to say or do. The message that might be given is one of offering help, now and/or in the future, coupled with providing the family (from an acknowledged Western perspective) with the courtesy of informing them about the school's postvention efforts and what they might expect to be occurring both within the next few days and in the foreseeable future.

It is recommended that before communication with the home, a suitable translator for this difficult and sensitive task be obtained, if needed. Further, discussing in advance with the translator the reason for the contact and what will be conveyed may provide valuable insights into how to approach the family. Equally, consulting with a person from the deceased person's cultural group can be extremely helpful in allowing one to get a glimpse of the meaning of suicide for that culture.

Another cultural issue that arose in this instance was how the Korean community would perceive our postvention efforts. Would our efforts be seen as overly intrusive? Aside from information on parental employment, school personnel knew nothing else about Tim or his family. Assistance was actively sought from the Korean community, which was not only imperative but also increased opportunities for networking.

3. A school staff meeting was called at the end of the first day, targeting in particular Tim's eight classroom teachers. Cultural issues surfaced at this meeting, primarily cultural stereotypes: Tim was seen as a 'typical' East Asian student – a very quiet, hard-working, polite, and respectful student. School staff shared their perceptions that there were absolutely no warning signs given out by Tim in the last days and/or weeks before his suicide. Weeks later, however, following staff in-servicing on suicide prevention (including what signs to look for), it became apparent that, indeed, there had been some classic signs. A few staff members talked about their having been 'blind' to the possibility that Tim could kill himself, in light of his perceived attributes.

4. It was necessary to modify the second day's planned postvention efforts to accommodate to that day's funeral memorial services (Tim was cremated), as arranged by the immediate family with little advance notice to the school/community (i.e., forty hours after Tim's death). In Western Christian culture it is generally anticipated by mourners that there is a three-day (or 72-hour) waiting period before the actual funeral service, with expected customs or rituals during that time, such as funeral-home visitation. This seemingly small change catapulted the school, especially many of the students, into great distress and overwhelming confusion. Almost all the non–East Asian survivors expressed shock, confusion, and anger at the timing of the funeral; this reaction was most pronounced among Tim's close friends and peers, who, mere hours before, had just learned of his death and felt unprepared for the funeral. Six of Tim's closest friends broke down in tears and anger (yelling and screaming) in the school hallway upon learning this information. Intensive small-group support was provided to them. Other postvention team members carried on with the modified postvention plans for the day with the rest of the school.

5. Basic support and information on how and where to obtain help were provided in all eight of Tim's classes during regularly scheduled class time.

6. We believe it important in post-traumatic situations for the postvention team to meet frequently in the days following the event with key people within the school and community in order to process ongoing efforts, to continue to clarify facts as they emerge, and to provide support to one another. These fre-

quent meetings proved critical for the postvention team itself, several of whom expressed an even greater sense of anxiety and lack of confidence in their efforts in light of the many cultural issues that had arisen.

7. Throughout the initial days following the suicide, and subsequently, a number of 'at risk' students were identified, a very few of whom were East Asian. In a school with a significant multicultural profile, notwithstanding very careful risk assessment, even greater care in assessment and counselling needs to be undertaken, by taking into account, as much as possible, the cultural meaning/context within which any 'at-risk' individual presents.

8. As a crucial part of the postvention program, suicide-prevention workshops, including a mandatory staff program, and workshops for students and parents were conducted several weeks after the suicide, during which cultural questions were often being raised.

9. In the following weeks, periodic follow-ups with involved school personnel, as well as community contacts, were undertaken. A more formal wrap-up was undertaken several months later to provide a sense of closure to these postvention efforts and included an academic 'autopsy' to aid in future refinements of the program. The doors were 'left open' to the school, as we believe that the potential for contact over indefinite periods should be included in any crisis-intervention program designed to address possible traumatic reactions. After all, postvention is not simplistic debriefing.

10. Five years following Tim's suicide, those school administrators, teachers, and members of the postvention team who were involved with this case, and were available, were interviewed. Comments centred around how emotionally difficult, draining, and anxiety-provoking this experience was for all involved, regardless of role or position.

One of the mental-health team members, for example, recalled that although there was not a 'flood' of subsequent referrals, there were some. She clearly recalled one specific referral for counselling: a fifteen-year-old Korean-Canadian girl, a friend of Tim's, made two suicide attempts following his death. She was referred following the second attempt. This girl was subsequently hospitalized for evaluation and treatment planning within the community. The counsellor further recalled the concern of the girl's mother that the family's problems (there were other problems with another child) not be made known in the Korean community. Yet, guidance staff reported that even several years later, friends of Tim had come in to talk, asking that it be kept confidential.

Concluding Remarks on Culture and Postvention

Doing postvention work is difficult, complex, and often emotionally exhausting. It can become even more complex when one encounters cultural issues, not only with regard to postvention, but also relating to suicide prevention and intervention and other critical issues (such as system-entry issues and resistances).

We agree with Ryerson (1990) when she stated, 'The need to modify a basic suicide awareness-prevention program effectively, making it appropriate and acceptable to a school community, cannot be overemphasized' (107). This is equally true for postvention. Service delivery includes a priori steps of asking and learning about the structural and demographic make-up (e.g., socio-economic, ethnic, and religious profile) of the school before implementation of the program. Even in the haste of crisis, some sensitivity is a must! This process assures educators and parents that the program coordinator(s) recognize the unique characteristics of the school/community and allays fears that a 'packaged program' will be forced on them.

As suicide-prevention efforts (prevention, intervention, and postvention) continue to grow in North America, perhaps the time has come for us to become more introspective, more self-critical about our interventions and our programs. Research is sparse, and often that which exists (e.g., Hazell and Lewin, 1994) is dangerously simplistic. Do our interventions and programs work? If not, why not? If so, what is it that works? Embedded within this process is an important question that we should be asking ourselves; namely, how can we be more aware of, and sensitive to, cultural issues when delivering programs? How do we translate this sensitivity into appropriate program modifications so that our interventions truly meet the needs of all people involved?

REFERENCES

American Psychiatric Association. 1987. *Diagnostic and Statistical Manual of Mental Disorders.* 3rd ed., rev. Washington: APA.
Brent, D. 1992. 'Psychiatric Effects of Exposure to Suicide among Friends and Acquaintances.' Paper presented at the American Association of Suicidology conference. Chicago, April.
Carter, B.F. and A. Brooks. 1991. 'Clinical Opportunities in Suicide Postvention.' In A. Leenaars and S. Wenckstern, eds, *Suicide Prevention in Schools*, 197–210. Washington: Hemisphere Publishing Corp.
Devore, and W., E.F. Schlesinger. 1987. *Ethnic-Sensitive Social Work Practice.* 2nd ed. Columbus, OH: Merrill Publishing.
Farberow, N. 1967. 'Crisis, Disaster and Suicide: Theory and Therapy.' In E. Shneidman, ed., *Essays in Self-Destruction*, 373–98. New York: Science House.
Figley, C. 1985. 'Introduction.' In C. Figley, ed., *Trauma and Its Wake*, xvii–xxvi. New York: Brunner/Mazel.
Globe and Mail. 'Second Japanese pupil hangs himself.' 14 December: A10.
Goodstein, L. 1978. *Consulting with Human Services Systems.* Menlo Park, CA: Addison-Wesley.

Greeley, A.M. 1969. *Why Can't They Be Like Us?* New York: Institute of Human Relations Press.
Hazell, P., and T. Lewin. 1994. 'An Evaluation of Postvention Following Adolescent Suicide.' *Suicide and Life-Threatening Behavior* 23: 101–9.
Hoff, L. 1984. *People in Crisis.* 2nd ed. Menlo Park, CA: Addison-Wesley.
Iga, M. 1993. 'Japanese Suicide: A Personological and Contextualist View.' In A. Leenaars, ed., *Suicidology: Essays in Honor of Edwin S. Shneidman*, 301–23. Northvale, NJ: Jason Aronson.
Iga, M. and L. Sneden. 1994. *Japanese Egoism.* Needham Heights, MA: Ginn Press.
Ishikawa, Y. 1994. 'Principles of Crisis Intervention.' Paper presented at the conference 'Life and Death,' Tokyo Institute of Psychiatry, Tokyo, October.
Kashiwaga, T. 1994. 'Psychiatric Issues in Terminal Care.' Paper presented at the conference 'Life and Death,' Tokyo Institute of Psychiatry, Tokyo, October.
Lamartine-Anderson, C., and L. Sattem. 1986. 'After a Suicide in an Educational Setting.' Paper presented at the conference of the American Association of Suicidology, Atlanta, April.
Leenaars, A. 1985. 'Suicide Postvention in a School System.' *Canada's Mental Health* 33: 29–30.
Leenaars, A., J. Maltsberger, and R. Neimeyer, eds. 1994. *Treatment of Suicidal People.* London: Taylor & Francis.
Leenaars, A., and S. Wenckstern. 1986. 'Suicide Postvention in a School System.' Paper presented at the conference of the American Association of Suicidology, Atlanta, April.
– 1990a. 'Suicide Postvention in School Systems: A Model.' In J. Morgan, ed., *The Dying and the Bereaved Teenager*, 140–59. Philadelphia: Charles Press.
– 1990b. 'Post-Traumatic Stress Disorder: A Conceptual Model for Postvention.' In A. Leenaars and S. Wenckstern, eds, *Suicide Prevention in Schools*, 173–80. Washington: Hemisphere Publishing Corp.
– 1991. 'Suicide Prevention in Schools.' Presidential Address/Keynote workshop presented at the Canadian Association for Suicide Prevention conference, Moncton, NB, October.
– 1994. 'Helping Lethal Suicidal Adolescents.' Workshop presented at the Canadian Association for Suicide Prevention conference, Iqaluit, Nunavut/NWT, May.
– 1996. 'Postvention with Elementary School Children.' In C. Corr and D. Corr, eds, *Handbook of Childhood Death and Bereavement*, 265–83. New York: Springer.
Lifton, R. 1969. *Death in Life: Survivors of Hiroshima.* New York: Vintage.
Lindemann, E. 1944. 'Symptomatology and Management of Acute Grief.' *American Journal of Psychiatry* 101: 141–8.
McGoldrick, M. 1982. 'Ethnicity and Family Therapy: An Overview.' In M. McGoldrick, J. Pearce, and J. Giordano, eds, *Ethnicity and Family Therapy*, 3–30. New York: Guilford Press.
Nakagawa, Y. 1994. 'Death and Dignity in Japanese Culture.' Paper presented at the conference 'Life and Death,' Tokyo Institute of Psychiatry, Tokyo, October.
Ohi, G. 1994. 'Ethical Orientations and Dignified Death.' Paper presented at the conference 'Life and Death,' Tokyo Institute of Psychiatry, Tokyo, October.
Parad, H., ed. 1965. *Crisis Intervention: Selected Readings.* New York: Family Service Association of America.
Pelej, J.P., and K.C. Scholzen 1987. 'Postvention: A School's Response to a Suicide.' Paper presented at the conference of the American Association of Suicidology, San Francisco, May.
Phillips, D., and M. Carstensen. 1986. 'Clustering of Teenage Suicides after Television News Stories about Suicide.' *New England Journal of Medicine* 315: 685–9.
Ryerson, D. 1990. 'Sucide Awareness Education in Schools: The Development of a Core Program and Subsequent Modifications for Special Populations or Institutions.' In A. Leenaars and S. Wenckstern, eds, *Suicide Prevention in Schools*, 99–111. Washington: Hemisphere Publishing Corp.

Sainsbury, P., and B. Barraclough. 1968. 'Differences Between Suicide Rates.' *Nature* 220: 1252.
Shibutani, T., and K.M. Kwan. 1965. *Ethnic Stratification*. New York: Macmillan.
Shneidman, E. 1973. 'Suicide.' *Encyclopedia Britannica*. Chicago: Benton.
– 1981a. 'Postvention: The Care of the Bereaved.' In E. Shneidman, ed., *Suicide Thoughts and Reflections, 1960–1980*, 157–67. New York: Human Sciences Press.
– 1981b. 'Psychotherapy with Suicidal Patients.' In E. Shneidman, ed., *Suicide Thoughts and Reflections, 1960–1980*, 149–56. New York: Human Sciences Press.
– 1983. 'Postvention and the Survivor-Victim.' In *Deaths of Man*, 33–41. New York: Aronson.
– 1985. *Definition of Suicide*. New York: Wiley.
– 1991. 'The Commonalities of Suicide across the Life Span.' In A. Leenaars, ed., *Life Span Perspectives of Suicide*, 39–52. New York: Plenum.
Shon, S.P., and D.Y. Ja. 1982. 'Asian Families.' In M. McGoldrick, J. Pearce, and J. Giordano, eds, *Ethnicity and Family Therapy*, 208–28. New York: Guilford Press.
Takahashi, Y. 1993. 'Some Perspectives on Recent Trends of Suicide and Its Prevention in Japan.' In A. Leenaars ed., *Suicidology: Essays in Honor of Edwin S. Shneidman*, 324–34. Northvale, NJ: Jason Aronson.
– 1994. 'Recent Trends in Suicidal Behavior.' Paper presented at the conference 'Life and Death,' Tokyo Institute of Psychiatry, Tokyo, October.
Toupin, E. 1980. 'Counseling Asians: Psychotherapy in the Context of Racism and Asian American History.' *American Journal of Orthopsychiatry* 50: 76–86.
Watzlawick, P., J. Beavin, and D. Jackson 1967. *Pragmatics of Human Communication*. New York: W.W. Norton.
Wenckstern, S. 1990. 'Suicide Postvention in Schools.' In R. Tierney (chair), S. Davidson, D. Ferguson, S. Vangolen, and S. Wenckstern, *Suicide Postvention in the Schools: Prevention, Intervention, Postvention, Evaluation*. Plenary panel presented at the Canadian Association for Suicide Prevention conference, Vancouver, October.
Wenckstern, S., and A. Leenaars. 1990. 'Suicide Postvention: A Case Illustration in a Secondary School.' In A. Leenaars and S. Wenckstern, eds, *Suicide Prevention in Schools*, 181–94. Washington: Hemisphere Publishing Corp.
– 1993. 'Trauma and Suicide in Our Schools.' *Death Studies* 17: 151–71.
Zilboorg, G. 1936. 'Suicide among Civilized and Primitive Races.' *American Journal of Psychiatry* 92: 1347–69.

PART VII: DISTRESS CENTRES

Suicide and crisis intervention are linked. Since the 1970s there has been a massive effort to reduce suicide mortality in Canada through the establishment of suicide-prevention centres. Today, distress centres play a major role in the community in the delivery of mental-health crisis services. They offer immediate and accessible intervention, predominantly by the telephone, often through trained volunteers. Volunteers play a major role in preventing suicide.

Numerous issues are, however, facing the crisis lines. One of the most current is telephone technology and confidentiality. The telephone debate has expanded to include the Internet, a means of communication that has not only Canadian, but also global implications. There are other questions as well about their effectiveness and the appropriate role for community-based intervention. Yet, despite the need to address these issues, intervention is needed now. The need is especially high, for example, in the Arctic to address the suicidal behaviour of the Inuit.

The seventh section outlines the role that distress centres have played in preventing suicide in Canada. This section consists of three chapters: an outline of risk assessment and crisis intervention, a discussion of the current issue of telephone technology and confidentiality at centres; and a discussion of a community approach in Canada's vast arctic region, the Baffin Island Crisis Line.

19

Crisis Intervention: Distress-Centre Model

JOAN WRIGHT and SUSAN PATENAUDE

Distress centres play a major role in the community in the delivery of mental-health crisis services (Helig et al., 1968). They offer immediate and accessible crisis-intervention services, predominantly by telephone and often through trained volunteers with the support of qualified staff. Besides suicide there are a number of serious social issues to which staff and volunteers must be prepared to respond on a distress line: family violence, child abuse, and sexual assault. A distress centre, or crisis centre as some are called, may also incorporate other programs such as suicide prevention, crisis counselling, and mobile outreach as an extension of their role in crisis intervention.

In exploring a distress centre's role in crisis intervention the meaning of the term 'crisis' must first be defined. A common definition refers to crisis as a time when the level of stress an individual is experiencing exceeds the adaptive capacities of that individual. A crisis is sudden, unpredictable, and stressful and there is potential for danger to self or others. The individual's perception is critical in defining a crisis. Some of the major features of a crisis are as follows:

- An acute, rather than chronic, state of four to six weeks or less.
- The individual generally undergoes marked changes in behaviour.
- The individual experiences one or more of the following feelings: anger, anxiety, helplessness, shame, ambivalence, and ineffectiveness in solving a pressing problem.

If help can be effectively given when most needed, the first step in the recovery process – namely, a decision towards action – can take place. One of the results of obtaining help should be the development of new coping skills. This development will have serious implications for the future of the individual experiencing the crisis.

Crisis intervention is an active but temporary entry into the life situation of an individual, a family, or a group during a period of stress in order to supply support until equilibrium is restored (Hoff, 1984; Hoff and Miller, 1987). The minimum goal of crisis intervention is resolution of the immediate crisis and restoration to the level of functioning that existed before the crisis period. The maximum goal is an improvement in functioning above the pre-crisis level.

The goals of crisis intervention for a distress centre are specifically to provide information and support in order to mobilize the individual to take protective action; to assist in mobilizing resources; or, when responding to an offender, to provide support in seeking help to stop the inappropriate behaviour (Grollman, 1988; Slaiken, 1984).

According to Callahan (1994), there is a difference between crisis intervention and emergency intervention. He states that telephone crisis lines and crisis centres actually do more emergency intervention than crisis intervention. They respond to real mental-health emergencies such as potential suicide, potential violence, and acute psychosis. These are, in his opinion, the only situations that require immediate assessment and intervention.

Finally, a crisis should be viewed as an opportunity for change and growth by distress-centre staff and volunteers. Their job is not to label or diagnose a psychiatric illness, but to assess and manage the crisis experience. This philosophy differentiates the role of a crisis centre and a centre or service offered within a medical framework.

Infrastructure

The quality of service delivered by a distress centre is ultimately a reflection of its human resources and its development and enforcement of clear policies and procedures regarding crisis response (Wells and Hoff, 1984). Staff and volunteers involved in the service delivery of crisis intervention must be selected, trained, supported, and evaluated to enable them to offer this critical service. Selection must be thorough and appropriate to the stressful role that the individual is to perform. According to research done in the field of human resource management (Werther et al., 1990), realistic job previews, that is, prior knowledge of the basic requirements and expectations of a job, show positive results in the retention of staff. A candidate's understanding of his or her role and work environment encourages early self-selection for inclusion to occur before both parties actually invest in training time and effort.

If an individual does crisis-intervention work, she or he is referred to as a 'crisis worker' or 'crisis counsellor.' Volunteer crisis workers are the mainstay of crisis centres throughout most countries, including Canada. In a high-quality centre, they should be treated as 'professionals' because of their training and expertise in the crisis field.

Implicit in the standards set by distress centres are the prevailing attitudes towards volunteers and the value placed on voluntarism. A service delivered by people who are 'just volunteers' will, in all likelihood, neither respect nor cultivate its potential for quality, thereby diminishing the true potential of the distress centre. The pressure to keep the telephone lines open at all costs, combined with a perception that one must have limited expectations of volunteers, can result in the 'warm body syndrome'; screening criteria are minimal, training is simplistic, volunteer skill is neither demanded nor evaluated, but the lines are open. The question ultimately becomes, 'What service do we provide and why is it being provided?'

Screening

A credible screening and training process for human resources is a necessary building block in a distress centre's infrastructure if it is to offer crisis-intervention services. The screening of potential volunteers through individual interviews is a first step in clarifying the unusual and stressful nature of this commitment.

The screening interview should explore the candidate's experience with suicide, physical and sexual violence, addictions, mental illness, and child abuse, with the intent of understanding how those experiences, or lack thereof, may affect his or her performance, either positively or negatively. An agency policy may exist regarding recovery time following traumatic events. For example, Edmonton's Support Network (1995) does not accept a candidate who has lost a significant other to suicide within the last year because experience has shown that those volunteers, however well intentioned, are further traumatized by the frequency and intensity of suicide calls this particular phone line receives. Another recommendation would be to strongly discourage anyone who is actively receiving treatment for mental-health issues. Given that relapses are frequently triggered by stress and the demand to respond to continually changing needs (Schizophrenia Society, 1995), the environment of a crisis centre could be unhealthy for such individuals. The perception that one's own healing can be promoted by helping others, in the context of a distress line, might prove faulty and undo much of the progress an individual has previously achieved.

The candidate should also be able to readily identify personal stress reactions and coping styles. The volunteer who heeds early warning signs and is typically able to use coping strategies effectively to recover quickly has a greater potential for maintaining stability on the job. Resiliency is an important characteristic of a successful distress-centre volunteer. The interview process also explores the candidate's appreciation of both his/her own strengths and vulnerabilities. The candidate's honesty and clarity of understanding is reflective of a knowledge of personal limits, increasing the likelihood she or he will appreciate agency policies and comfortably seek the knowledge and support of staff and peers.

Other topics for discussion during screening include time commitment, standards for the successful completion of training, legal issues, and moral issues. A volunteer should never be placed in a position of contravening his or her own morality. Open discussion of policies regarding abortion and homosexuality affords the candidate the opportunity to consult spiritual and moral advisers in exploring his or her comfort level with the agency's position.

The candidate should leave the interview with a keen awareness of the intellectual and emotional challenges of the role, coupled with an appreciation for the seriousness of the commitment required. She or he should also be aware of any concern felt by the interviewer, thus allowing the opportunity to reconsider his or her readiness for the position. The interviewer should leave the interview with a strong sense of the candidate's emotional health, strengths, and vulnerabilities. At least two reference checks should be conducted to explore helping styles, stress-management issues, and reliability. On occasion, a second interview may be important to clarify concerns of either the candidate or program personnel.

Training

Training for volunteers builds on their basic helping skills and characteristics. Prospective volunteers often have abilities and natural helping techniques that can be developed to deal with acute crisis situations. Training or education in crisis intervention needs to follow accepted adult learning techniques to be successful.

The ideal training will balance theory, practical knowledge, and role-play opportunities to develop and enhance the knowledge and skills of the candidate. Training components should be constantly reviewed to maintain a current, interesting, and challenging program.

The model followed by the Support Network (1995) includes the following components, but it would be expected that training needs would vary from one area to another based on the types of calls received, community issues, the availability of specialized crisis services, and even the source of volunteers.

Communication Skills
Our emphasis is on understanding the role of a listener which is essentially that

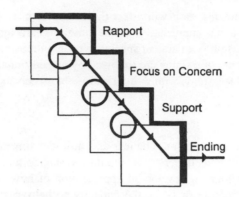

Figure 1 Listening Model (The Support Network)

of a non-judgmental facilitator for callers. Strategies for effective communication are explored. This segment involves seven hours of training, followed by four hours of facilitated role-play experience in which volunteers are given verbal and written feedback on their communication skills.

Listening Model
The training package would not be complete without outlining a 'Listening Model' (figure 1) to add structure and provide guidelines to listeners when responding to distress calls. All distress/crisis calls or interviews must be 'structured' to move through different stages. The stages overlap and movement is circular, allowing for backtracking. There are many other models available to assist distress centres when training staff and volunteers in a consistent approach to callers.

Special Issues
Coping strategies are taught for dealing with difficult callers who are angry, drunk, seductive, chatty, or silent. As well, policies for the handling of threatening callers or those using the line for their own sexual gratification are discussed. Volunteers are given a basic appreciation of the issues and challenges facing callers living with mental illness. Stabilizing techniques are explored and intervention procedures explained. Approximately three hours of training are required.

Loss
Through exercises, small group work, and lectures, volunteers develop an understanding of loss as reflective of change and accompanied by a grief process. Death and dying are discussed in terms of the past learning and life expe-

riences of the candidates, as it will affect their behaviour as listeners. Special attention is given to an appreciation of the unique characteristics of suicide bereavement, because it is an area of speciality programming within the centre. Three and a half hours of training are followed by an additional three and a half hours of facilitated role-play, with written and verbal feedback again presented to the candidates.

Suicide Intervention

Candidates explore their personal beliefs and attitudes towards both a potential suicide that is seen as understandable and the suicide threat that is seen as manipulative behaviour, to develop an appreciation of how one's life experiences can either promote or block the capacity to help. Strategies for overcoming blocks are discussed. Although the knowledge and appreciation of one's personal limits are discussed in the screening interview, volunteers now come to terms with the limits placed on them by agency policy, their role, and the fact they are working on a telephone. Considerable time is spent discussing the realities of one person's responsibility for the life of another. Additional teaching focuses on appreciating the characteristics of suicidal thought in terms of ambivalence and perceived isolation. Considerable time is spent teaching in fine detail the risk-assessment tools volunteers are expected to use. They are expected to develop an understanding of how the information gleaned can be interpreted and the strategies they are required to employ in stabilizing and supporting suicidal callers. Agency policies and procedures are explained in detail as they are applied to levels of risk up to and including helping a caller whose suicide attempt is already in progress. Candidates are given a clear understanding of the risk factors relating to murder-suicides as well. Finally, in teaching our expectations for volunteers' approach to helping third-party callers, it becomes clear that they are expected to achieve a high level of skill and knowledge in a relatively short period in the agency. This training component includes seven hours of lecture and discussion as well as three and a half hours of facilitated role-play. Feedback is provided, as noted earlier.

Crisis Intervention

This training component focuses on criminal activity and our reporting responsibilities, threatened homicide, domestic violence, sexual assault, and child abuse. The risk-assessment model applied to suicide is adapted for use in assessing risk relating to violence, and specific intervention strategies are taught that are appropriate to the nature of the threat. Three and a half hours of training is followed by three and a half hours of facilitated role-play.

Community Resources
Given a computerized referral base, volunteers are provided with an opportunity to increase their awareness of resources through exercises and role-plays. Practical application accounts for three and a half hours of training.

Finally, the candidates are given another role-play opportunity of three and a half hours during which each individual determines the focus needed to supplement their learning. A two-hour exam is delivered on the final evening of training as an objective source of information about the knowledge level of the candidates.

Successful candidates will have scored at least 75 per cent on the exam and will have demonstrated the following in role-play:

1 a consistently developing ability to apply the material taught
2 an understanding of agency policies and procedures
3 an ability to accept and incorporate feedback
4 an ability to express non-judgmental, genuine empathy for the caller
5 an appreciation for the value of empowerment

In addition, the three-person selection committee considers the candidates' behaviour during training in terms of punctuality, relevance of questions, participation in discussions, and respect for the knowledge and skills of others. Successful candidates are interviewed again for the purpose of putting closure to the training as well as to clarify the strengths and vulnerabilities identified through training.

The probation period includes a minimum of twenty-four hours of service followed by a direct evaluation of the volunteers' work with a cross-section of callers. Throughout their volunteer experience every call is evaluated through the documentation provided and the volunteers' discussion with on-call staff. Volunteers receive written feedback on a monthly basis, usually supplemented by verbal feedback, as appropriate.

Advanced training and in-services are offered throughout the year to enhance the volunteers' basic skills and continue their learning process.

Without a similar structure for training, screening, and evaluating, the quality of the crisis interventions conducted will be in question (Wells and Hoff, 1984).

Risk Assessment

Conducting a complete and appropriate risk assessment is fundamental to crisis-intervention work and requires explicit training and practice.

The purpose of conducting a risk assessment is to determine immediacy (how soon an attempt might occur) and lethality (the risk of that attempt resulting in death). When risk-assessment components are tied to the philosophy of the centre, it serves to stabilize the caller while providing the volunteer with a structured process allowing consistency of application. This consistency, in turn, translates into positive relationships with other crisis response services such as the police, ambulance services, and mobile mental-health teams.

Volunteers are expected to be able to identify and respond to clues to suicidal thought within tight time-frames. They quickly learn to appreciate the caller who is able to state directly his or her intent to commit suicide. Because the fear of judgment or other inappropriate responses prevents most suicidal callers from offering anything more than soft signs, the onus is placed on the volunteer to establish rapport and listen carefully to what is said, as well as for what is not spoken. The symptoms of the caller's fear and isolation become the clues prompting the volunteer to ask directly, but with genuine concern and caring, about the client's intent to commit suicide.

Given an affirmative response, the volunteer begins assessing risk by exploring the degree of planning, the caller's previous related experience, and his or her resources – the three primary components of risk assessment. Our experience has shown that detailed forms which include appropriate questions and reminders of procedural requirements serve to maintain consistency and quality of response. Volunteers are expected to explore each of the three components, as follows, using as many open questions as possible. Because the risk assessment can sound like an interrogation coming from an unskilled or anxious volunteer, it is vital that good communication skills be taught in combination with an understanding of important factors such as voice tone and pace.

1. Planning

The initial question asked in risk assessment is, 'Have you thought about how you would commit suicide?'

Caller's Response:
  Ideation: Defined for our purposes as not having chosen a specific plan.
  Threat: Caller has selected a plan even if not all details are worked out.

The nature of the threat is explored by posing relevant questions, the elements of which are detailed in table 1 (pp. 334–5).

It is important to note that, when working on a telephone, one can never assume the suicide is not in progress already. It is vital, in determining potential helpers, to explore whether others are present with the caller or expected. In addition, a volunteer needs to ascertain the presence of anyone who would be at risk if the caller died and was not found immediately, for instance, a baby; or whether someone is at risk because the caller intends to commit a murder-suicide.

Volunteers are educated about the refinements commonly made to these plans by knowledgeable callers.

The suicide plan becomes the foundation for determining the present level of risk, but the potential level of risk is determined by exploring the caller's prior experience and resources.

2. Prior experience

Next, one asks about previous experience:

- Have you ever thought about suicide in the past? If so, when? What was happening in your life then? How did you cope with these feelings?
- Have you ever attempted suicide in the past? If so, when? What was happening in your life then? What attempt did you make? How did you survive that attempt?
- Has anyone you know attempted or completed suicide? When? How has that affected you? What support have you had to cope with that experience?

Understanding how the caller survived previous experiences emotionally and physically can often be identified as a strength that the caller can possibly use to survive this experience.

3. Resources

It has been our experience that a thorough exploration of resources can often reduce the level of risk. Choices other than suicide are identified by the caller and his or her self-esteem is bolstered by time spent exploring their strengths and resiliency.

a. Internal Resources
   • What coping skills does the caller usually use to handle his or her situation? Are they presently being used? If not, can they be? Can past strategies be adapted to suit the present circumstances?
   • Draw upon survival and recovery strategies discovered through exploration of prior experience and examine their application now.

TABLE 1

Method	Questions to ask
Gun	– Gun available? where?
	– Bullets available? where?
	– Type of weapon?
	– Familiarity with weapon?
	– Intended location of attempt?
	– When do you plan to attempt?
	– Are other people present?
	– Are you expecting anyone?
	– Is substance abuse a factor?
Hanging	– With what?
	– From what?
	– Intended location of attempt?
	– When do you plan to attempt?
	– Are other people present?
	– Are you expecting anyone?
	– Is substance abuse a factor?
Carbon monoxide	– Source of carbon monoxide intended?
	– Location of attempt?
	– Access to the means?
	– When do you plan to attempt?
	– Are other people present?
	– Are you expecting anyone?
	– Is substance abuse a factor?
Jumping	– From what?
	– Anticipated landing if jumping from a bridge?
	– Access to the means?
	– When do you plan to attempt?
	– Are other people present now?
	– Are you expecting anyone?
	– Is substance abuse a factor?
Overdose	– Have you started?
	– If not, what do you intend to take?
	– Is it available?
	– Quantity available?
	– Prescription medication?
	– Normal dose?
	– Intended location of attempt?
	– When do you plan to attempt?
	– Are other people present?
	– Are you expecting anyone?
	– Is substance abuse a factor?

TABLE 1 (*Concluded*)

Method	Questions to ask
Slash/stab	– Have you started? – If not, what do you intend to use? – Is it available? – How do you intend to use the weapon? – Intended location of attempt? – When do you intend to attempt? – Are other people present? – Are you expecting anyone? – Is substance abuse a factor?

• What other life experiences has the caller had that were difficult to overcome? How did she or he do that? Identify the strength and courage required to cope, and discuss their application now.

Note: Internal resources are often not explored in favour of developing external referrals and giving referrals. The Support Network takes the position that building on what already exists lays a strong foundation for adding external resources and reduces client dependency.

b. External Resources
• Includes the people the caller trusts with his or her issues; e.g., family, friends, neighbours, co-workers, teachers, and counsellors.
• When the client does not see people as a resource, some alternative sources of non-judgmental support include pets and teddy bears.

c. Referrals
• Referrals should be carefully selected to fill gaps identified either by the caller or through the exploration of internal and external resources.
• Referrals must also be respectful of the client's readiness to access various types of service. As noted by Gandy et al. (1978) callers to a distress line are often apprehensive about face-to-face or professional contacts. They use the line not only because it is readily accessible but also because it is the least-threatening source of support available. Faced with a reluctance to accept professional help, it can be beneficial for a volunteer to offer a support group as a stepping stone to the professional care they may ultimately require.
• Whenever possible, multiple referrals to similar programs are recommended as a means of enhancing the client's control over who she or he uses as helpers.

Procedures Related to Levels of Risk

Once the risk-assessment information has been collected, the distress centre can use required procedures to ensure consistency of response while also evaluating and supporting the volunteer.

One way of accomplishing this end is to develop clear definitions of broad levels of present and potential risk that require the volunteer to consult with staff at specific stages in the conversation with the caller. The purpose of the consultation is as follows:

− To establish that all relevant information has been gathered.
− To confirm the level of risk as assessed by the volunteer.
− To determine the necessity of activating crisis responses (as indicated by agency procedures).
− To ensure referrals are accurate and appropriate.
− To support the volunteer, who may be emotionally challenged by the nature or intensity of the call.
− To develop potential short- and long-term action plans with the volunteer, based on the caller's identified resources.
− To ensure that a contract (verbal agreement with the caller) is established with respect to his or her suicidal feelings.

The immediate support and evaluation could be supplemented by monitoring the documentation of each call. This process can be made easier by developing detailed risk-assessment forms that serve to guide volunteers through the issues to be explored and identify when staff consultation must occur. Comparison of the information initially shared with staff and documented information can serve to evaluate volunteer skill. In our experience, volunteers have welcomed the consultation process because it offered them reassurance that they were doing everything possible to assist the caller, while giving them an opportunity to debrief quickly in difficult situations. The expectation that volunteers will use staff to debrief gives the volunteers the freedom to be vulnerable without fear of being seen as unable to cope. Ongoing in-servicing and dedication to ensuring that volunteers are supported emotionally are important components of ensuring a crisis service is able to provide consistent, credible responses to callers in need. Table 2 demonstrates risk assessment in the context of the complete call.

Other Services

Motto (1979) describes the natural maturation of a distress centre providing

TABLE 2
Anatomy of a suicide call

Stage 1. Rapport
- Establish a bond with the caller.
- Put the caller at ease.
- Communicate empathy.
- Gather clues and information; look for indicators of potential suicide.
- Ask directly about intent to commit suicide.

Stage 2. Focus on concern (understand/assess)
- Assess lethality:
  - plan   • prior attempts
  - resources   • stressors
- Exploration of resources is the bridge to Stage 3.

Stage 3. Support and Stabilization
- Dispose of available means.
- Give positive reinforcement, identifying caller's own strengths and coping strategies.
- Connect the caller to own resources and refer to community resources, as needed.
- Activate crisis response procedures (police, ambulance, etc.) as appropriate for agency policy.

Stage 4. Consultation with Designated Staff
For purposes outlined previously

Stage 5. Closure
- Facilitate client's development of an action plan for the next few hours and then the next few days. Focus is on self-care, reducing stressors, and connecting with resources.
- Contract (a verbal agreement) a call-back if situation worsens or action plan is unsuccessful (as determined by agency policy).

---

both lay and professional programs. This expansion 'tends to take shape as skills are developed in the day-to-day telephone counselling and crisis work, becomes firmer with face-to-face encounters in a drop-in room or outreach activity, and finally emerges in the form of a more experienced staff feeling a need to provide still another dimension of service' (47).

Distress centres, as they mature (as stated by Motto) or as funding becomes available, are able to expand their services while still fulfilling their mandate and maintaining their principles of operation. Policies and procedures previously described are easily transferred to apply to the expanded services. A centre's mission to support and empower people to discover and develop their own resources should not be lost as the centre moves to different formats for the work of crisis intervention.

An additional focus for some distress centres is to offer specialized crisis lines for teens or youth such as the Youth Help Line in Halifax, Nova Scotia, and Teen Touch in Winnipeg, Manitoba. Information and referral lines also complement services offered by a distress centre, such as the Need Crisis and Information Line in Victoria and the Lifeline Crisis and Information Centre, Coquitlam, British Columbia.

Suicide-prevention programs have often become an integral part of the delivery of crisis-intervention service within a centre such as Some Other Solutions suicide-prevention program in Fort McMurray, Alberta. The linkages between a distress line and a suicide-prevention program are easily defined. The crisis line often acts as an access point for individuals who are suicidal or concerned about someone. The suicide-prevention program, through volunteers, is then in a position to follow up with support and information. The other components, education and training and suicide bereavement, are appropriate additions to the distress-centre model. Volunteers and staff supporting this program should receive similar screening, training, and evaluation as stated earlier.

According to Frank Campbell, executive director of the Baton Rouge Crisis Intervention Centre in Louisiana, USA (personal communication), crisis centres can play a unique role in the area of problem gambling because of their training and resources already developed in the mental-health field. An elevated rate of suicide attempts among persons in treatment for pathological gambling was reported in *When Luck Runs Out: Help for Compulsive Gamblers and Their Families* (Custer and Milt, 1985). Distress centres should be informed about the psychological risks that accompany compulsive gambling. Some centres, like the Calgary, Alberta, Distress Centre, operate an 800 line for problem gambling. Centres can play a leadership role by networking with existing resources and establishing services where none exist, especially in provinces where gambling has been legalized.

A mental-health crisis-intervention service is another good example of program expansion compatible with the distress-centre model of crisis intervention. Such a program offers community outreach and emergency response to persons in psychiatric crisis. Although the crisis workers in these programs are usually professional caregivers, that is, psychiatric nurses or social workers, the screening, training, and evaluation should still follow a basic distress-centre model. This process then builds on their formal training and previous experience to allow for a more comprehensive service.

The distress centres in Edmonton, Alberta, and Victoria, BC, currently operate such programs as part of the mental-health service community. The functions of the team are to triage, provide initial stabilization, offer consultation and support to caregivers, and coordinate support services required at the time of the crisis. For purposes of this program, a person is considered to be experiencing a psychiatric crisis when he or she poses a risk to themselves and/or others owing to psychiatric symptomatology. The distress line again can be used as the main access point for the community, but a separate consultation line for caregiver access is recommended. A risk assessment for this crisis-intervention service must also include a psychiatric assessment as well an assessment of the psychosocial issues involved in the crisis situation.

Counselling services, especially crisis counselling, offer another dimension to a distress centre. Clinical support, either through a drop-in service or an appointment system, completes the continuum of support for individuals in crisis. For example, the Distress Centre / Drug Centre, Calgary, Alberta, and the Sarnia, Ontario, Distress Centre offer counselling as part of their services. Although the clinical training of a therapist needs to be complete before hiring, the clinician should, upon employment, become aware of how crisis intervention is implemented through the centre and have an understanding of the policies and procedures of the agency.

Regularly scheduled clinical supervision and debriefings are as important for mental-health staff as they are for volunteers on a crisis line.

It is important to create a supportive working climate for both staff and volunteers engaged in this high-stress business. This can be achieved by allowing opportunities not only for debriefings, but also for necessary paperwork and for ongoing training and education. Crisis work, especially at the entry level, like the work done by telephone crisis workers and mobile outreach workers, is characterized frequently by not knowing the outcome or resolution of the crisis experience. Therefore, the need for consultation and open communication with an experienced supervisor is as necessary for the crisis worker as it is to the caller in crisis. Paid staff and supervisors also need similar treatment and support. Without adequate training, in-servicing, holidays, and clinical support, they will be unable to empower others.

Evaluation

Distress and suicide-prevention centres are increasingly being challenged to prove their effectiveness by measuring outcomes. According to research completed recently by Leenaars and Lester (1995), 'the density of suicide prevention and crisis centres in Canadian provinces in 1985 was associated with a preventive effect on suicide rates from 1985 to 1991' (39). Crisis centres do make a difference, as shown by this and other research, in preventing suicidal behaviour.

Evaluation of all programs is essential to the ongoing credibility of distress centres and their future development and funding. The certification process offered by the American Association of Suicidology (AAS) is an excellent avenue for distress centres to measure the quality of their service delivery against national standards. The AAS Certification Standards Manual (Wells and Hoff, 1984) gives criteria for systematic, ongoing self-evaluation.

Various evaluation techniques have been developed by individual distress centres across Canada. A *Directory of Suicide Prevention and Crisis Centres in Canada*, published by the Canadian Association for Suicide Prevention, includes contact numbers and is available through the Suicide Information and Education Centre (#217-1615 10th Avenue S.W., Calgary, Alberta, T3C 0J7). Some evaluation techniques used by distress centres include file reviews, evaluation questionnaires for clients and referral agencies, 'listening posts' (a dedicated telephone that would allow an evaluator to listen in on conversations between a distress-line caller and the distress-line operator) for crisis lines, and review of statistics and service costs.

Conclusion

Distress centres play many roles; one of their most important ones is to act as agents of social or community change. They may promote an environment in which community groups, schools, and individuals feel empowered to participate in suicide prevention and crisis intervention. Distress centres need to be more proactive in broadcasting their worth ... that they do makè a difference.

As stated throughout this chapter, crisis-intervention services, as offered by various programs compatible with the distress-centres model, must have a well-developed risk-assessment procedure and training program. Although distress centres also offer basic supportive listening and often counselling services, their role in the community is usually seen as providing crisis and suicide intervention services. A distress centre's mission statement, values, and operating principles should continue to be the base guideline for future program additions and development. The board, staff, and volunteers must come together to enhance and protect a centre's role in the community as the entry-level service for mental-health crisis intervention.

REFERENCES

Callahan, J. 1994. 'Defining Crisis and Emergency.' *Crisis* 15: 164–71.
Custer, R.L., M.D., and H. Milt. 1985. *When Luck Runs Out: Help for Compulsive Gamblers and Their Families*. New York: Facts on File.
Gandy, J., J. Campbell, J. Filipowski, and E. Kruk. 1978. 'A Study of Volunteers at Distress Centre One.' Mimeo. University of Toronto, Faculty of Social Work.

Grollman, C. 1988. *Suicide: Prevention, Intervention, Postvention*. Boston: Beacon Press.

Helig, S., N. Farberow, R. Litman, and E. Shneidman. 1968. 'The Role of Nonprofessional Volunteers in a Suicide Prevention Centre.' *Community Mental Health Journal* 4(4).

Hoff, L.A. 1984. *People in Crisis: Understanding and Helping*. Menlo Park, CA: Addison-Wesley.

Hoff, L.A., and N. Miller. 1987. *Programs for People in Crisis*. Boston: Northeastern University Custom Book Program.

Leenaars, A.A., and D. Lester. 1995. 'The Impact of Suicide Prevention Counselling on Suicide in Canada.' *Crisis* 15: 39.

Motto, J. 1979. 'Starting a Therapy Group in a Suicide Prevention and Crisis Centre.' *Suicide and Life-Threatening Behavior* 9: 47–56.

Schizophrenia Society of Alberta (Edmonton Chapter). 1995. *Preventing Schizophrenia Relapse: Seeking Common Ground*. Edmonton, AB.

Slaiken, K. 1984. *Crisis Intervention: A Handbook for Practice and Research*. Boston: Allyn & Bacon.

The Support Network, Edmonton's Distress Centre. 'Training Manual.' Revised 1995. Edmonton, AB.

Wells, J.O., and Hoff, L.A. 1984. *Organization Certification Standards Manual*. Denver: American Association of Suicidology.

Werther, W., K. Davis, H. Schwind, and H. Das. 1990. *Canadian Human Resource Management*. Toronto: McGraw-Hill Ryerson.

20

Crisis Lines, Telephone Technology, and Confidentiality

NEVILLE TWINE and NADA BARRACLOUGH

The interrelationship between crisis lines, telephone technology, and confidentiality has been the basis of crisis-intervention work begun in the 1960s in North America. Where does that relationship stand now, and are there basic changes to be made to crisis work in the 1990s?

Telephone technology serves as the 'change icon' in the crisis centre's visionary window. Technological change involving the telephone has an impact on consumers of the service, the crisis line, and the environment in which the crisis line works. The challenge is not about incremental tinkering, but, as Senge writes in *The Fifth Discipline* (1990), about 'the nature of systems/ services, their culture, and structure.'

The Issues Involved

The phenomenon of people in crisis is not a recent occurrence. Crisis is 'self-defined' (McGee, 1974). It occurs when a person feels unable to cope with the situation as it presents itself. Crisis is non-discriminatory and does not reside in any one geographic location. It is worldwide. The conditions giving rise to a crisis are often unique, always personal. A crisis is not an event, but a behavioural response to one. Shneidman (1987) has stated that 'life is often a choice among many unpleasant possibilities, and the goal is to select the least unpleasant one.' He also believes that 'we should do almost anything to resolve the caller's pain' (ibid.). The words are clear. The truth is indisputable. The response is not always easy.

Suicide and Crisis Intervention

Suicide and crisis intervention are inextricably linked (Leenaars and Lester 1995). Crisis lines respond to people 'who are at greater risk for suicidal behavior (not just suicide) than the general population' (Diekstra 1992). A critical aspect of some centres' response to suicidal behaviour is the use of call-trace technology. This response assumes first that the technology is available to the worker, caller, police, and phone company. A second assumption is that, the centre has determined that, notwithstanding the underpinnings of self-determination, call-trace will be implemented. Does the caller wish to be rescued? Should the centre respond regardless?

The crisis-intervention models as described by Hoff, McGee, and others are generally non-medical and assume that crisis is a point of both danger and opportunity. The intervention approach requires conditions of a therapeutic relationship and demands a belief in the capabilities and desires of people to help themselves. People in crisis need support that begins with telephone communication and a clear understanding that it is help and not rescuing that is important and that the degree of information to be shared will be decided by the caller within the context of the supportive and secure relationship of the listener. In 1995, 99 per cent of Canadian households had a telephone (private communication). As Marshall McLuhan (1964) astutely observed 'we have extended our central nervous system itself in a global embrace, abolishing both space and time as far as our planet is concerned.' There are few people in this country who cannot now 'reach out and touch someone.'

The telephone-technology debate is spurred on not only by the complexity of crisis response but also by the opportunities provided by other new technologies for clients and service providers. 'The Internet is a global revolution ... perhaps even more far reaching than the invention of the telephone' (Broadhead and Carroll, 1994). The Canadian Association for Suicide Prevention, in 1995, identified some of the challenges related to suicide and the Internet and the need for an effective strategy to respond to the raw expressions of pain, confusion, and crisis played out in a medium found useful for some in our crisis-lined communities.

Confidentiality brings into focus the emerging conflict of individual versus collective rights. 'Care givers have a moral and professional obligation not to reveal any information without the caller's knowledge and authorization unless it is in the client's interest to do so' (Shaw, 1970). A critical component in the expression of confidentiality and in the relentless production of manuals to address this practice is one of caller/worker trust. It is this trust that defines the expectations and secures the confidence of those in distress (Hill, 1993).

The Emergence of Crisis Lines

While crisis centres have been described as diverse in their client base, their services, and their role in the community, they are consistent in their belief and knowledge that listening helps and that being there for another person is the first step in helping, whether in an information, support, or crisis-intervention situation. Their evolution can be traced to three significant influences that acted as catalysts for the growth of crisis-intervention centres in North America.

The first significant ingredient was a *dissatisfaction* with existing services (Echterling and Wylie, 1981). In 1961, a five-year study by the Joint Commission on Mental Illness and Health in the United States reported that 'people were not getting the help they needed, when they needed it and where they needed it, close to their natural social settings' (Hoff, 1995). The second major development was the dramatic shift in service delivery in the mid-1960s, started to a significant degree by the Normalization Movement with its emphasis on community development, deinstitutionalization, and self-help. Within this environment, crisis-intervention centres became attractive alternatives responding at low cost, with less red tape, requiring low threshold, and emphasizing self-determination and self-help. Distress centres were the *response to a need* (Simmons, 1990). The third factor was the *popularization of the telephone*. The magic of listening and the simplicity of the phone created what Marshall McLuhan (1964) said was the 'extension of the ear and voice that is a kind of extra sensory perception.' The telephone erased or diminished the issues of geographic boundaries and of physical and emotional impediments. It was easy to use, reliable, and allowed self-determination. A caller could reveal much or little, and even remain anonymous (Rosenbaum and Calhoun, 1977). The telephone greatly facilitated the notion of a first point of entry into the health-care system.

Crisis Lines: The Canadian Development

In a National Survey of Canadian Crisis Centres, undertaken in 1976, it was noted that centres came into being 'because of a strongly felt need for immediately available, accessible and appropriate help. They operated under the principles of anonymity, confidentiality and client (or caller) initiative' (Powicke, 1976). The essence of crisis-intervention services today is the ability to provide each community with a safety net and, in this age of alliances and partnerships, to maintain a 'vital commonality in relationships between the caller and the volunteer and between the center and other community agencies' (Fitchette, 1993; Stroul, 1987).

In Canada the first recorded centre, traditionally, was Telecare National in Sudbury, Ontario, in 1964, followed closely by Distress Centre Toronto. Since that beginning three decades ago, distress centres have developed in every province in Canada. In Ontario, centres resulted from a recognized need by the community for their services, some as a direct response to suicide. In British Columbia, centres developed mainly in the late 1960s and early 1970s from a need for services because of the drug problems of that era. In Alberta, drug issues and consumer needs again necessitated the creation of the centres, some in the 1960s and 1970s, but mainly in the 1980s. In the early 1990s two of the original centres combined to form the Support Network, with mobile outreach and direct connections to other service providers. Saskatchewan's centres arose in the late 1970s and early 1980s to fill service gaps and deal with the issue of sexual assault. One of these centres developed a mobile unit. Manitoba's centres arose because of general needs and, unlike most other centres, used no volunteers. Quebec's centres arose mainly in the 1980s specifically to deal with suicide. New Brunswick developed centres very locally, all in the early 1990s, as a result of too many calls being received by police, local hospitals, and mental-health providers. Prince Edward Island's centres developed from a concern by hospital and mental-health service providers. In Nova Scotia, one centre emerged in 1969 from a pilot project in problem solving started by students; another came about in the 1980s as a result of need for support and crisis intervention and, in one case, to provide support to military personnel. Centres in Newfoundland and the Northwest Territories developed as a response to suicide, all in the early 1990s.

The Canadian Council of Crisis Centres' 1978 survey identified 92 centres across Canada using 4500 volunteers and providing service to approximately 450,000 callers annually. A second survey completed in 1995 by the Distress Centres Ontario reaffirmed the impact that centres continue to have in the initial and sometimes ongoing provision of crisis services.

Telephone Technology and Crisis Intervention

The person in crisis needs support and that support begins with communication. The telephone works because it is a 'cool medium or one of low definition, because the ear is given a meager amount of information. Speech is *also* a cool medium ..., because so little is given and so much has to be filled in by the listener ... Cool media are high in participation or completion by the audience' (McLuhan, 1964).

Communication involves listening. At crisis centres that means 'active listening,' involving 'paraphrasing, clarifying and identifying feelings all in the concept of acceptance. That acceptance is synonymous with respect and is non-judgmental' (Hinson, 1982). This is the basis of crisis-centre philosophy, which is rooted in the theoretical constructs of Rogerian non-directive therapy. It is also influenced by counselling theories from Caplan, Glasser's Reality Therapy, Transactional Analysis, and Carkhuff's work designed to assist the helper maintain effective progress in addressing the dynamic range of crisis.

The telephone allows the client anonymity and immediacy twenty-four hours a day (Rosenbaum and Calhoun, 1977). It provides non-threatening, easy access to help without the stigma of welfare or charity. It gives the caller total control of present and future actions; there is no forced need to be hooked into any other unwanted helping system. The telephone allows self-determination to rule. One has only to hang up the receiver (Fulford, 1995). It is an acceptable form of help to persons who would not ordinarily come into a helping agency. While it is difficult to 'attribute a causal relationship to a single activity' (Mishara and Daigle, 1992), 'telephone counseling has an established place among the various modalities for delivering mental health care in the community' (Hornblow, 1986).

Confidentiality and Privacy

'Canadians have a basic right to live their lives in privacy *and* as technology develops and becomes more complex, many Canadians believe that their personal privacy is being threatened' (Bell Canada, 1994). For crisis centres the very mention of privacy conjures up visions of an invasive technology vulnerable to considerable misuse. The issues inherent in the technology range from loss of caller anonymity and all of the risks involved in this loss to the increased costs of addressing life-threatening situations (Nelson et al., 1975). The continuously developing technological complexities consume scarce time and create what seem to be endless new procedural guidelines.

Confidentiality is understood as a critical component for callers wanting assurance that their personal crisis thoughts or needs will be kept private. It plays a significant role in the shaping of the ethical practices of client-information management in crisis centres. Confidentiality permeates the culture of crisis lines in several ways: as a *word* that appears in manuals, in forms, and in the code of ethics in many centres, it is defined as being entrusted with secrets, spoken or written in firm trust; as a *procedure* it infiltrates the various organizational systems touching on the management of client information; as a *legal entity* it is used to ensure that the rights of the callers as well as of the organization are addressed in the various protocols of the organization.

Confidentiality is a practice that crisis centres introduced at the outset of their services. It is a concept to which they have tenaciously adhered. It is also an area in which centres have procedural guidelines, but for which centres often have no formal written policy, perhaps because of a difficulty in discovering a legal basis or definition. Many of the mandatory reporting provisions in both the legal and medical professions have been determined by their provincial or federal associations, not necessarily by legal statutes. Many social-services policies with respect to confidentiality have been based on the Guidelines on Confidentiality of the American Psychological Association.

A conference presented by the Canadian Bar Association, titled 'I've Got a Secret: The Duty of Confidentiality in the Private Sector,' in March 1994, noted that a confidence of a personal nature, communicated outside of a professional relationship, is protected provided that it has the requisite characteristics of confidential information. To be 'confidential at law,' three characteristics of information, whether of a personal, financial, or commercial nature, must exist. These are: (1) information must be of a confidential nature, that is, not generally available in the public domain; (2) information must have been disclosed in circumstances that impose an obligation on the confidant to respect the confidentiality of the information given; (3) confidential information must have been disclosed by the recipient for another and improper purpose without the consent, either expressed or implied, of the confider. The basis for protecting confidences is often as much to foster a relationship as it is to safeguard the integrity of the confidential process. This viewpoint fits in with the present expectations of callers to a crisis line.

A Layered Practice

Confidentiality is used to recognize both the caller's legal right and the organization's responsibility to respond to a need within the context of the law (Harper and Mickelson, 1990). The implementation of confidentiality within a centre can be a layered practice. This is a practice that is given expression at many levels within an organization. 'What you tell me stops with me.' At another level, some callers present challenges that require that information or an instructional file be kept to assist other phone workers to stay focused on the provision of support, intervention, information, or referral within the context of the immediate problem. Understanding key information pieces related to family dynamics or mental and physical health allows the worker to enhance the repeat caller's request for help to secure information. The information collected, then, is justified on the basis of the provision of support to the worker to maximize the service delivered. Case files tend to be restricted to a small percentage of callers whose psychosocial environment tends to aggravate them in crisis, and an informed worker frequently can provide appropriate response. The files are identified by first name and rarely contain a full name or address or other identifying information. Exceptions can be found where call-trace has been used or, in warm lines, where call-backs form a part of the service. Here crisis lines are organizationally connected to other mainstream services and referrals have been made as a natural part of an integrated service-delivery model. It is clear, then, that the expression of confidentiality has many divergencies and depends on a crisis line's history, geography, and organizational structure (Tate and Greenfield, 1972).

'Many "hot-lines" state their commitment to confidentiality explicitly' (Mayo, 1984). Most counsellors and therapists explain to their client that confidentiality does not apply to information that, if kept confidential, can potentially contribute to the client's death, for example, a lethal suicide plan. What happens to the caller's right to self-determination and the crisis line's mission that directs an intervention when there is a life-threatening situation or when child abuse has occurred or is occurring (Hoff 1995)? One strategic approach has been the differentiation, at the implementation level, between crisis intervention (support) and emergencies, with the latter defined as 'a state of helplessness which requires rescue by an outside agency.' Many interventionists believe that 'since the caller has initiated the intervention of the service' (Brockopp and Oughterson, 1973), there is an implied request for help. Centres surveyed in 1995 follow this philosophy ardently, but often have no written policy because of the complexity of the issues.

The moral dilemma for crisis interventionists is well outlined by David Mayo. He describes the conflict between two of our culture's most fundamental ethical values, concern for the client's right to anonymity and confidentiality and concern for the caller's welfare. These two competing values set the stage for conflict that 'goes beyond the crisis lines.' Mayo's description of the philosophical dilemma concludes that there is no universally accepted standard for right and wrong in this area.

Anonymity is a related principle also entrenched in crisis-line work. While confidentiality refers to the management of information, anonymity refers to the client's right to remain nameless. Some callers, even at a high level of distress or crisis, may nevertheless remain anonymous until they are assured of the counsellor's 'degree of caring' (Syer and Scott 1978). While callers correctly assume that the line respects their anonymity and treats their information as confidential, each organization must begin to address the issues not only from the perspective of the caller's right to self-determination but also from the perspective of the needs of caller and organization. The centre must ensure that services are fully promoted in the community. They must also consider the perceived need for volunteer anonymity along with secrecy of crisis-centre knowledge, information, location, and services.

In exploring the application of privacy in Canada we discover that it is not explicitly guaranteed under the Charter of Rights and Freedoms. In many ways, the common understanding of privacy has come to mean being alone and undisturbed. Communications Canada (Wright, 1992) presents privacy first as protection against unwanted intrusion and second as the ability to control information about oneself and one's activities.

The Consumer and Telephone Technology

What is important to a person in crisis calling a crisis line is not so much that there are more regularly defined, philosophically explored, and legally washed definitions, but rather that there are adequate responses to the questions: (1) Do I have a choice in revealing what I am comfortable with and will you respect my choice? (2) Will you help me if I am desperate? (3) Can I assume that you will not share my information with those who need not know? These questions have implications for community planning, volunteer training, and case management.

Crisis lines operate not in a vacuum, but in the context of neighbour helping neighbour in communities that bring their own strengths and challenges to the business of responding to crisis (Bomford, 1981). It is with this context in mind that some clarity begins to emerge regarding telephone technology and confidentiality. There are many deployment options related to call management and these are directly related to the line's perception of its mission, caller need, geography, history, and current demands. Above all, it is assumed that the organization has made its decision within the context of well-researched and evaluated practices in the art and science of meeting the needs of those calling crisis lines (Lester, 1993). Diversity is needed. The line's sensitivity to local needs and its ability to respond to those needs is its strength, and thus there is a diversity between communities. The challenge is to be clear about whom the crisis line serves. The word caller is frequently used to define the client population and to define the services and practices. But calling is a means. Crisis-centre clients are not just callers. People in crisis have chosen this means to address their crisis and their immediate needs. The services provided must relate to the needs of those calling, and crisis centres must avoid the institutionalization of calling.

Our research indicates that there is a paradigm shift affecting the way crisis lines do business and the environment of consumers of crisis line services. Our challenge is to understand and utilize the technology to respond to our collective understanding of emerging need. What to do with call management and confidentiality? The person in crisis will determine the direction. Respect, trust, clarity of action, and an understanding of the community are sufficient criteria to manage our actions.

Conclusion: Focus on Listening

This paper argues that the mid-1990s have witnessed significant expansions and change in interactive technologies that can only be compared to the impact that manufacturing technologies once had on Western culture. The depth of this change and the related environmental impacts have necessitated a close examination of the way we do business and consideration of whether the consumer's needs continue to be met. The challenge of mixing adaptation and flexibility with established practices creates questions related to relevance and survival. Have we become institutionalized to the point where means and ends are confused or have the changing needs of consumers bypassed the service of crisis lines? The Distress Centres Ontario survey clearly confirms the relevance of crisis lines in meeting the needs for intervention, support, information, and referral. However, with the plethora of hot and warm lines and crisis-intervention programs there is increasing evidence that crisis lines want to meet the new demands inherent in the change in the demographic, technological, and social areas. The management of technological change and confidentiality can become immobilized in policy manuals that aptly reflect the spirit of service but may risk becoming strident predeterminants of how that service is provided. The changing environment is proving to be more creative technically, more diverse culturally, and more demanding of services. This environment will tease out the critical issues of consumers' needs and force us to determine how technology can best serve those needs. In addition, market share, or lack thereof, will also provide strategic fodder to the organization's debate on the interrelationship between the telephone, technology, and the application of the principles of confidentiality and anonymity. Crisis lines may be at risk of losing their relevance, in a rapidly changing world, in which there is risk of a social-service meltdown. 'All Alone by the Telephone has come full circle. It will soon be the telephone that is "all alone and feeling blue"' (McLuhan, 1964).

The emerging discussions on confidentiality will be raised to a vigorous debate fuelled by the technological opportunities available to the public, by the complexity of crisis response, and by consumer demand for relevant services.

REFERENCES

Bell Canada. 1994. *Privacy and Your Telephone Service: A Guide for Bell Canada Customers.* Brochure, Bell Canada Public Affairs. Toronto.

Bomford, J.P. 1981. 'The Crisis Interview.' In J.P. Soubrier and J. Vedrinne, eds, *Depression and Suicide*, 736–41. Paris: Pergamon Press.

Broadhead R., and J. Carroll. 1994. *Canadian Internet Handbook.* Scarborough: Prentice-Hall Canada.

Brockopp, G.W., and E.D. Oughterson. 1973. 'Legal and Procedural Aspects of Telephone Emergency Services.' In D. Lester and G. Brockopp, eds, *Crisis Intervention and Counseling by Telephone*, 117–31. Springfield, IL: Charles C. Thomas.

Diekstra, R.F. 1992. 'The Prevention of Suicidal Behavior: Evidence for the Efficacy of Clinical and Community-Based Programs.' *International Journal of Mental Health* 21(3): 69–87.

Distress Centres Ontario. 1995. 'A Survey of Canadian Crisis Centres.' Unpublished report. Toronto.

Echterling, L., and M. Wylie. 1981. 'Crisis Centers: A Social Movement Perspective.' *Journal of Community Psychology* 4: 342–6.

Fitchette, B. 1993. 'The Role of Distress Centres in Ontario Mental Health Reform Planning Toronto.' Unpublished.

Fulford, R. 1995. 'Reach Out and Snub Someone.' *Saturday Night*, May 1995, 29–33.

Harper, J.M., and D.J. Mickelson. 1990. *Working with Suicide: A Discussion of Legal and Ethical Aspects.* Marinette, WI: Alpha-Omega Venture.

Hill, C. 1993. 'Bell Canada's Call Management and Its Impact on the Ontario Distress Centre.' Unpublished report.

Hinson, J. 1982. 'Strategies for Suicide Intervention by Telephone.' *Suicide and Life-Threatening Behavior* 12(3): 176–84.

Hoff, L.A. 1995. *People in Crisis: Understanding and Helping.* 4th ed. Redwood City, CA: Addison-Wesley.

Hornblow, A.R. 1986. 'The Evolution and Effectiveness of Telephone Counseling Services.' *Hospital and Community Psychiatry* 37(7): 731–3.

Leenaars, A.A., and D. Lester. 1995. 'Impact of Suicide Prevention Centres on Suicide in Canada.' *Crisis* 16: 39.

Lester, D. 1993. 'The Effectiveness of Suicide Prevention Centres.' *Suicide and Life-Threatening Behavior* 23: 263–7.

Lester, D., and G. Brockopp, eds. 1973. *Crisis Intervention and Counseling by Telephone.* Springfield, IL: Charles C. Thomas.

McGee, R.K. 1974. *Crisis Intervention in the Community.* Baltimore: University Park Press.

McLuhan, M. 1964. *Understanding Media: The Extensions of Man.* New York: McGraw-Hill Book Co.

Mayo, D.J. 1984. 'Confidentiality in Crisis Counseling: A Philsophical Perspective.' *Suicide and Life-Threatening Behavior* 14(2): 96–112.

Mishara, B.L., and M. Daigle. 1992. 'The Effectiveness of Telephone Interventions by Suicide Prevention Centres.' *Canada's Mental Health* 40(3): 24–9.

Nelson, G., J. McKenna, M. Koperno, J. Chatterson, and J.H. Brown. 1975. 'The Role of Anonymity in Suicide Contacts with a Crisis Intervention Centre.' *Canadian Psychiatric Association Journal* 20(6): 455–9.

Powicke, H. 1976. 'The Canadian Directory of Crisis Intervention Centres.' In D. Syer and S. Scott, 'A National Survey of Canadian Crisis Centres.' Unpublished report.

Rosenbaum, A., and J.F. Calhoun. 1977. 'The Use of the Telephone Hotline in Crisis Intervention: A Review.' *Journal of Community Psychology* 5: 325–39.

Senge, P.M. 1990. *The Fifth Discipline: The Art and Practice of the Learning Organization.* New York: Bantam Doubleday Dell.

Shaw, S. 1970. 'Privileged Communications, Confidentiality and Privacy.' *Professional Psychology* 1(2). Reprinted in J.M. Harper and D.J. Mickelson, *Working with Suicide: A Discussion of Legal and Ethical Aspects.* Marinette, WI: Alpha-Omega Venture, 1990.

Shneidman, E. 1987. 'At the Point of No Return.' *Psychology Today* 21: 54–8.

Simmons, H. 1990. *Unbalanced: Mental Health Policy in Ontario, 1930–1989*, 197–208. Toronto: Wall & Thompson.

Stroul, B. 1987. *Crisis Residential Services in a Community Support System.* Rockville, MD: National Institute of Mental Health.

Syer, D., and S. Scott. 1978. 'A National Survey of Canadian Crisis Centres.' Unpublished report.

Tate, P., and C. Greenfield. 1972. Legal Considerations in Crisis Centre Operations. In U. Delworth, E.H. Rudow, and J. Taub, eds, *Crisis Center / Hotline: A Guidebook to Beginning and Operating*, 55–61. Springfield, IL: Charles C. Thomas.

Wright, T. (Commissioner). 1992. *Privacy and Telecommunications* (brochure). Submission to the Ontario Telephone Service Commission, 18 September 1992. Toronto: Information and Privacy Commissioner / Ontario.

21

Kamatsiaqtut, Baffin Crisis Line: Community Ownership of Support in a Small Town

SHEILA LEVY and ERROL FLETCHER

The foremost responsibility of any society is to nurture and protect its citizens, especially its children. In the Canadian North today, one of the most serious threats to the health and well-being of its citizens, especially its young people, is suicide.

This chapter will discuss a program that was initiated in Iqaluit, a small community in Canada's Arctic. We believe that sharing our experiences and ideas on community ownership of problems and solutions has relevance for other Aboriginal settlements and small towns experiencing extensive social problems. Specifically, it outlines the development of the first successful northern crisis telephone line.

The programs and ideas that are discussed in this chapter are the result of the authors' own experiences in Nunavut, the new Inuit region that will become a separate Canadian territory in 1999. It is a cross-cultural setting, where the population is mainly Inuit whose first language is Inuktitut, connected to the rest of Canada only by air and the occasional summer supply ship. Iqaluit itself, where the crisis line originated, is a community of approximately 3700 people – about two-thirds Inuit, the balance a mix of anglophone and francophone non-Aboriginals – in the southern part of Baffin Island. Over half the population of Nunavut (comprising Baffin, Keewatin, and Kitikmeot Regions) is under twenty-five years of age (GNWT Bureau of Statistics, 1993), with those in the fifteen-to-twenty-four age group being at highest risk of suicide in this culture-in-transition.

The Northern Setting

Most of us living above the sixtieth parallel know of at least one person who has committed suicide, and of many who have tried. Some of us have lost personal friends and relatives; others have had to wrestle with their own suicidal thoughts. One suicide can set an entire community reeling in shock, and with a whole region feeling the effects. In 1971 the Northwest Territories (NWT) suicide rate was about the same as the Canadian average of 10 per 100,000, but this figure rose to 35 per 100,000 by 1978 (Anawak and Cook, 1988). This alarming trend has continued: in the past ten to fifteen years, rates among Aboriginals have been approximately three times higher than the national average. According to the Special Report on Suicide among Aboriginal People, current statistics place the suicide rate for registered 'Indians' at 3.3 times, and for Inuit at 3.9 times, the national average (Royal Commission on Aboriginal Peoples, 1995). According to the 1995 royal commission, the figures are even more alarming for Aboriginal youth, whose suicide rate is five to six times higher than that of their non-Aboriginal peers. Comparatively, northern Canada has one of the highest suicide rates in the world (National Task Force on Suicide in Canada, 1987): in 1994, up to 45 per cent of registered deaths in the Northwest Territories have been attributed to suicide, and it was the leading cause of death in 1990.

The chronic self-destructive behaviours among northerners, especially among the Inuit young people, who are by far at the highest risk of suicide, have been attributed to several environmental factors. These can be broadly categorized as psycho-biological factors, life-history or situational factors, and socio-economic factors. Irwin (1985), Tsai (1989), Anawak and Cook (1988), and other researchers list a host of contributing factors such as the breakdown of cultural values and traditions, a lack of effective role models and leadership, the breakdown of the family unit, a lack of parenting and interpersonal skills, inability to express feelings, failure of the school system to address needs, unemployment, misuse of alcohol, and loss of or blurred identity. Several studies (including O'Neil, 1986; Armstrong et al., 1978; Dacks, 1981) discuss the negative effects of 'internal colonialism' in the North and the acculturation and dependency that it fosters. All the preceding factors have contributed to a host of social problems such as high rates of criminal prosecutions and school dropouts; the highest birth rate in Canada (Stoesz and Lopatka 1990); and the chronic depression, intense and unmanageable jealousy, anger, and violence being experienced by the young people of the North. This reality has spawned numerous studies, surveys, and research projects.

A variety of solutions have been proposed: banning alcohol, teaching interpersonal and parenting skills, hiring more professional counsellors and mental-health workers, cultural programs, community-development projects, and a variety of socio-economic political solutions. Although these approaches to the problems have merit, the authors nevertheless believe that a good starting point is the community itself: community ownership of the problems and community responsibility for their solution. Though governments and other organizations may share the responsibility for creating some of these problems, the community ought not to sit passively and wait for hired professionals and government bodies to solve the problems for them. Community responsibility involves awareness, open talk, skill building, and *action*: local individuals, groups, and communities must work collectively to penetrate the wall of despair behind which many northerners, especially young people, live.

Rationale for the Creation of Kamatsiaqtut

The development of Kamatsiaqtut, Baffin Crisis Line was a community response to the cries of hopelessness and helplessness that had been vibrating through the North. The Inuktitut name *Kamatsiaqtut* means 'thoughtful people who care.' Kamatsiaqtut is still young, only six years old at the time of this writing; but the fact that it has survived and grown in an area where many programs and initiatives die quick deaths is a sign that it is doing something right. We believe that its successful survival stems from the fact that it was a service initiated not by government intervention, nor as a result of studies or surveys, but by a caring, concerned group of Iqaluit's citizens who not only talked about the problems but were committed to action and willing to put in time, energy, and knowledge.

Kamatsiaqtut provides a telephone counselling and contact service for those who may be in crisis, or just need a listener. Given that our present traditionally accepted psychology of the person rests mainly on a model of the self as a thing that exists in isolation, valuing self-fulfilment – and realization – as opposed to traditional Inuit culture, which takes the individual beyond himself, beyond his own isolated island of experience, feelings, and reflections, and grounds him in the wider context of life within relationships to others and nature – it may be questioned why a service that is so obviously based on 'Western' beliefs and assumptions that permeate the notion of 'help' would be chosen and accepted in a society whose traditional world-view is somewhat in conflict with these accepted practices. Community ownership played an enormous role in the development of the service. The concept of a northern crisis line was initiated by native northerners who had heard of and perhaps used this type of service while visiting or residing in the south. They felt that providing such a service in the north, delivered by northerners who hopefully better understood the culture, setting, and problems, with as many Inuktitut speakers as possible manning the lines, would give northerners in distress another outlet and opportunity to discuss, process, and work towards resolving their concerns. The concepts of confidentiality and anonymity, although foreign to the traditional cultural beliefs, were viewed as a bonus by the Inuit who worked with us on establishing this service. It was felt that many people in distress, for a variety of reasons, were internalizing their problems, and the direct impact of this was increased depression, violence, and suicide. There are few helping resources available in the North, and some of these are seen as counterproductive. Talking to friends, relatives, or the limited number of overworked community professionals was clearly not enough. As well, in the small northern communities, privacy has been compared to living in a fishbowl, and confidentiality is a scarce commodity. Many callers in fact have expressed that they are glad that they do not know the volunteer helpers, and they feel freer discussing their problems with 'someone they are not going to have tea with the next day.' Thus, the anonymity (of both caller and volunteer) and confidentiality of the phone service are viewed as attractive: callers appreciate the opportunity to talk openly with a 'stranger' whom they do not have to face the next day. For many, this is the first time they have shared their pain. It is often said that in traditional Inuit culture it was not considered acceptable to openly express feelings, especially negative emotions (Anawak and Cook, 1988). This was apparently necessary for survival, because the Inuit lived in small family groups under very harsh conditions. In such conditions, it is said, one silently accepts one's fate since it would be futile, unproductive, and destructive to the necessary attitude to complain (Briggs, 1970; Minor, 1992). Considering such a cultural factor, a telephone service where people discuss their problems with others, especially strangers, might seem to be an alien, unacceptable alternative. Paradoxically, the Rogerian notion of 'unconditional acceptance' that many Western crisis lines use as a basis for their interaction with callers does fit with traditional Inuit cultural beliefs in patience, the ability to accept realities beyond one's control, and non-interference (Pauktuutit, 1991). Nevertheless, whether it is because of cultural change or the fact of being given permission to discuss feelings for the first time, people use the service regularly and make an average of three calls per night. It is worth noting that they usually, openly and without prompting, discuss the most painful details and problems of their lives, for they know they safely can.

History of Kamatsiaqtut

During the winter of 1989, there was a disturbing increase in suicides on Baffin Island, especially among young people. A conference was organized, with participants from many of the affected communities: Iqaluit, Pangnirtung, Broughton Island, Clyde River, and Pond Inlet. The problem and possible solutions were explored. One idea put forth was the establishment of the first northern crisis line, staffed by trained volunteers. In the spring of 1989, a group of CBC employees in Iqaluit sponsored a Curl-a-thon to raise funds for start-up costs. This event provided the impetus for a group of like-minded citizens, representing the cultural and language make-up of Iqaluit, to form the first working committee.

Over the summer, the trainers donated their time to develop a relevant training program for volunteers. We did not reinvent the wheel; the trainers were most familiar with training models from crisis lines in the south, so we borrowed ideas from them. Our challenge, however, was to make the model culturally relevant, so we had to take into account the local culture, climate, languages, and community make-up in order to make the service appropriate. In the fall of that year we trained the first group of volunteers. With the generous assistance of community organizations, businesses, and individuals, the line began operation on 15 January 1990 with two Iqaluit phone lines.

It quickly became evident that this was a necessary, relevant, and well-used service. During the first year of operation, the line received over four hundred calls, an astonishing number considering the small population base and the fact that this service had never been offered in an area where telephone service itself was in its infancy.

Communities from all over the North, including the Nunavik region of Arctic Quebec, asked if they could use the service for free, as the need in their communities was great but the population was not large enough to provide the necessary number of volunteers for establishing individual-community services. In January 1991, with contributions from the Nunavut and Nunavik hamlet councils, from the social-services departments in Quebec and the NWT, and a special deal from Bell Canada, we were able to install an 800 line that allows individuals living within the entire 819 area code to call us toll-free. Yellowknife and Rankin Inlet eventually set up their own lines, basing their service and training on the Kamatsiaqtut model.

The operation began with fourteen volunteers. Training consists of twenty intensive hours over three days, and more than one hundred people have now taken training. We currently have forty-five active volunteers, working seven days a week from 9:00 p.m. to midnight. Calls average three a night. Service is offered in three languages (Inuktitut, English, and French) as often as possible, although it cannot be ensured at this point that service in all three languages is available every night. As with most crisis lines, people call about a variety of problems, but a significant number of the calls focus on losses related to relationships, friends, families, or relatives. Suicidal phenomena play a part in a large portion of the calls. This is not surprising in a region where suicidal behaviour has become somewhat of a norm. As the focus though is on preventing suicide, we encourage people to call whenever they need a listening ear, in the hope that they will be able to work through issues before suicide becomes the only seemingly viable option.

Necessary funding for operating expenses such as space, phone lines, and utilities are contributed through community businesses, individuals, service clubs and agencies, and fund-raising events such as an annual dinner-and-local-entertainment evening (which has become an important event in Iqaluit's social calendar and serves also to encourage new volunteer involvement). In the beginning, space was donated, but now adequate funds allow rental of an appropriate office.

Kamatsiaqtut's motto is 'Helping Others to Help Themselves,' and the mandate is simple, as it must be for a volunteer service to operate successfully. The mission statement is 'To set up and maintain a crisis line in Iqaluit.' From that flow the following objectives:

1 To meet regularly, coordinate, and train volunteers for the line.
2 To maintain the line and coordinate on-going training.
3 To develop sufficient resources to maintain the line.
4 To promote community awareness.
5 To recruit volunteers.
6 To establish and maintain an effective board of directors.
7 To maintain records of all meetings and calls.
8 To maintain anonymity and confidentiality.

The Kamatsiaqtut line is now known both nationally and internationally and has become involved in many initiatives such as hosting the 1994 annual conference of the Canadian Association for Suicide Prevention (CASP). This conference in turn led to more community initiatives: local radio talk shows, self-help groups, mini-conferences, and so forth.

Uniqueness of Kamatsiaqtut

There are many distress centres and crisis lines throughout the country. What makes our unique? We see several differences.

First, we service what is probably the largest geographical area of any centre: we include three time zones, half the Northwest Territories, and a large portion of Quebec.

Second, we are specifically designed to service three distinct groups: approximately 80 per cent Inuit, 15% anglophones, and 5% francophones. In attempting to provide service to a community, one must understand the dynamics of the group and have a certain understanding of what characteristics are held in esteem by the people and what values they are expected to live by. Our training model focuses on the culture, values, beliefs, problems, and concerns, and subsequent most-effective helping styles, of these three groups in relationship with themselves, each other, and the unique environment in which they all reside.

Third, the service is run entirely on volunteer effort; it has no paid employees. For this region, this in itself is an anomaly. In the past, much money poured into the North, and the government felt an enormous responsibility to 'take care of' native northerners. As a result, it has sometimes seemed that everyone expected payment for any service, and that government was the expected source of change. Although organized volunteerism is a new concept, informal sharing and helping each other are acknowledged as being traditionally very important values in Inuit culture (Pauktuutit, 1991). This back-to-our-roots aspect of the service seems to be in tune with the community spirit, and increasing numbers of Inuit are becoming involved.

Next, this is the first line in the North, and its success is perhaps the result of starting small and not trying to do more than is realistic and manageable. Instead of offering longer hours, we have kept to a schedule that meets a need without overtaxing volunteers, who all have job and family responsibilities. Volunteer burn-out and drop-outs are therefore minimized.

Finally, we have a very small population base from which to draw volunteers. All volunteers are from Iqaluit, but of a population of about 3700 at least half are children. The 100-plus people who have taken training are a significant proportion of the adult population, indicating the enthusiasm with which the community has embraced the opportunity to help. Apart from the volunteers who work the line, there is vigorous approval and support from local private businesses, governments officials, local organizations, and other individuals who give in whatever way they are able. This strong community support and ownership is, we feel, the essential ingredient of Kamatsiaqtut's success, and deserves further mention.

Community Support and Ownership

We cannot speak about Kamatsiaqtut without speaking in terms of the community. Nothing can be accomplished in isolation from the people who are to be served. The community must be involved. In *Choosing Life: Special Report on Suicide among Aboriginal People* (1995), the royal commission reports that the staff and organizers of Rainbow Lodge (a non-medical alcohol and drug treatment and prevention facility on Manitoulin Island in Lake Huron) took the position that suicide prevention was a whole-community responsibility and that involvement of the whole community was essential for success. We completely agree with this position. This theme is repeated by all the successful programs that the commission studied. Northerners all know of many wonderful, well-meaning programs that have been brought to communities, but which have failed. These may not and often do not produce the results desired and expected by the funding bodies, politicians, mental-health workers, and community members themselves, if they do not have the support and involvement of the communities in which they are initiated. Support and involvement mean more than simply agreeing to the programs. Individuals and groups within the community must take *ownership* and ensure that enough time and effort are given to achieve lasting positive effects. Community members must be intimately involved at every stage of the planning and implementation of any project. The following quote from the royal commission supports our position: 'Commissioners believe that if the ideas for suicide prevention and supportive community change come from a careful process in which the community looks into its heart for its direction, they are almost never wrong. This is because the act of looking into the heart – the act of thinking deeply about how things are in a community, and making plans to move a little piece of the mountain that blocks community well-being – is empowering. It is an announcement that the community cares – about itself, about its children, about its future – and it is part of suicide prevention' (64).

It is possible to make a difference as individuals; but when we work in conjunction with others in our community, the effects are more likely to be long-lasting, and the weight of problems and efforts is distributed onto many shoulders. A truly effective program must receive community sanction, must have participation from community leaders, and must include aspects of that community's attitudes and beliefs.

In addition to understanding healing, loss, abuse, grief, and death, effective caregivers must understand the dynamics of the community within which they are trying to effect change. What are the prevalent belief systems? How do people work and play together? How does the community function when faced with challenges and problems? How much does the community trust those who are trying to help? Communities sometimes react to outside workers with the attitude, 'I don't care how much you know until I know how much you care.' Credibility and trust must be established, and this takes time.

Kamatsiaqtut is an example of how true community ownership works to make a program successful. This support was evident from its inception, which was the result of creative community brainstorming. It continues to be a service that all, regardless of title or qualifications or experience, can join, and in which they can integrate personal and community knowledge with new 'helping' knowledge and skill, in order to contribute to the health of their community and region.

Community-Development Beliefs

We believe that communities can develop capacities to deal with their own issues. Community members must participate in making, adjusting, and controlling change in their respective communities. Changes and programs that are self-developed and self-imposed have meaning and permanence, whereas imposed outside change draws both outspoken and hidden resistance. It is probably apparent by now that the authors share a certain bias about external control and responsibility versus internal control and responsibility. We are aware that our values are influenced by our culture and profession and that a common desirable belief in Western culture and the profession of counselling in particular is the concept of empowerment and taking control of one's life. We believe that although these concepts are usually applied to individuals, they also hold true for a community as a whole. It is entirely possible that a community in general, for whatever reason, can feel collectively that it has no control over its fate. This is particularly true if dependency was nurtured in the community over a long period of time. Research indicates that dominated or minority groups often feel that they have no control over their lives. The following quote from Belkin 1988: 82 supports this idea: 'Many studies investigating the relationship among ethnicity, socioeconomic level, sex, and the locus of control conclude that ethnic-group members (Hsieh, Shybut & Lotsof, 1969; Levenson, 1975; Strickland, 1973; Tulkin, 1968; Wolfgang, 1973), lower-class people (Battle & Rotter, 1963; Crandall, Katkovsky & Crandall, 1965; Garcia & Levenson, 1975; Lefcourt, 1966; Strickland, 1971), and women (Sanger & Aker, 1972) tend to be more external' in terms of locus of control.

Frideres (1988), Dacks (1981), Armstrong et al. (1978), and others believe that northern native groups have been colonized by the Canadian government and, as a result, grew dependent on it. The government and its officials assumed the role of major authority figures and, in many ways undermined the role of elders and native leaders. They made many decisions for native groups, often without consultation. Under such a system, people eventually learn to become dependent and expect others to be in control of their lives. We believe that such values as respect for elders and other authority figures are compatible with taking control of one's life and responsibility for one's decisions.

Ownership, control, and responsibility are our thesis statement and motivating belief. These beliefs and values are the philosophical foundation on which

Kamatsiaqtut is built. However, planning a project such as Kamatsiaqtut is a complex matter, and a simple set of guiding principles is not enough. The most well-meaning plan can end in bitter disappointment if all important factors are not taken into consideration. Therefore, in the next section we offer some recommendations for any group or community wanting to implement a program. Implicit in these points is the understanding that they be adapted in a culturally appropriate manner.

Recommendations

Most organizations have an individual or group of individuals (board of directors) who have the primary responsibility for planning and maintaining its operation. We have found that the make-up of this essential group, especially if the organization is voluntary, is crucial for the success of the program and services it expects to disseminate. Our experience has proved that in order for a program to get off the ground there needs to exist a few extremely committed and energetic individuals who 'live and breathe' the project until it can stand better on its own and has become a 'community institution.' We recommend the following ideas for the board of directors or people responsible for planning and running a program to consider. The list is not comprehensive, or in any particular order of importance.

1 Recruit other members whom you believe are able to cooperate, are committed, responsible, and willing to work hard. Figureheads, people with personal agendas, people with highly conflicting styles, or reluctant members are not likely to ensure the continuing success of the program.
2 Form relationships that bring together the best thinking and knowledge of all cultures in the targeted community and region, for problems are not unique to any one group. Network! Share information, knowledge, skills, success stories, and so on, among communities, agencies, and individuals. Ensure community empowerment and control of all initiatives: community leaders must endorse and participate in programs.
3 Belief in the ability of people to change is essential. It is not always true that, because a person's formative relationships were dysfunctional or painful, he or she will forever be bound by those experiences and condemned to repeat patterns. People want to and can change. A holistic approach to healing rather than a fragmented one is necessary. This viewpoint takes into account the whole person within his environment. Sound mental health means balance and harmony within and among the four aspects of human nature: physical, emotional, intellectual, and spiritual. Include appropriate cultural and

traditional healing methods and practices in program's development and implementation. Both the old and the new are important, and their combination can provide the most effective help for the most people.

4 Foster co-reliance, not dependence, in individuals and within families, groups, and communities. Assisting people, not rescuing them, is the objective. An effective program involves the people for whom it is developed. Encourage the development of group support programs in communities. Even those returning from outside professional treatment situations need ongoing, sometimes long-term, support and encouragement within their home communities. This support must be institutionalized so that it kicks in immediately. Survivors' groups are especially useful, as they help people come to terms with their grief and loss, and can deter copycat or contagion suicides.

5 Be willing to identify and talk openly about the problems and potential solutions within the community. Use outside help, if necessary, to get started. In the past, there has often been a tendency to think, 'It's not my business,' or to believe that talking will aggravate a problem. Within each group there are also the inevitable personality conflicts, so a willingness to talk and work out problems must be practised by the 'helping' group as well. Role modelling on all levels is important!

6 Train local people, within the community if at all possible, and set up a support system. The support system may have to be outside the community, but access should be easily available. Make training available to anyone in the community who wants it, not only those who commit themselves as volunteers. Having community-based training available has benefits for non-volunteers and those who approach them. It is known that suicidal people will often seek help from those they know: a teacher, a community drug and alcohol counsellor, a friend or relative, someone they trust. If these people have basic training, they then become more aware and knowledgeable friends, colleagues, and family members, able to offer more relevant and effective intervention and support.

7 Any government involvement must be balanced by an equal partnership with the community. Self-reliance, empowerment, and ownership lead to self-worth and competence.

8 When planning, look not at what *doesn't* work, but find the successes and explore what *did* work, even partially. Build these ingredients into projects and programs. Local community-based research should be done, as what worked in one community may not have worked in another. Look for creative solutions to resource-allocation problems. Too often, good ideas are shelved because 'we can't find the money,' and services and programs compete for

the few dollars that are available. Look for ways to cooperate, check out sources of freebies, build good will. Creative preventive efforts that address multiple problems are necessary.

Concerns and Changes

Success for Kamatsiaqtut was not without rough spots. Although there was much expressed support in the planning stages, it took the hard work and intense commitment of a few individuals to get it running, and to ensure that it took on a life of its own, strong enough to survive even if the initiators left.

The volunteer pool was small at first, so burn-out was a risk, but many of those who started are still with us – if they are still in town. Iqaluit is basically a town of people who come from somewhere else, and resident turnover is an everyday fact of life: southern Canadians and Inuit alike often return to their original home communities.

As mentioned above, the concept of organized volunteerism is new to Inuit, and the number of Inuit volunteers was initially low. As the primary target population was Inuit, the dearth of Inuktitut-speaking workers was a problem we were sensitive to. (Inuktitut is not easily learned by a non-native adult, so we did not have access to fluent non-Inuit, nor was that our ideal. We wanted to provide a service where Inuit could help Inuit.) Because Inuit had been involved in the planning from the beginning, however, the word spread that this was not just a *qallunaaq* (colloquially, 'white man') organization. As respected members of the Inuit community took an active part, the number of Inuit increased. An Inuktitut-speaking volunteer trained as a trainer, thus making it possible for even unilingual Inuktitut-speakers to become volunteers. Of the over one hundred who have undertaken training, approximately a third have been Inuit; the same percentage is true of our current forty-five active volunteers.

Our hours of service are limited, and communities have mentioned that they would like us to be open overnight, but, as mentioned above, we cannot afford to stretch our volunteer resources to the breaking point. Given the size of the population, we may not be able to acquire the volunteers necessary for longer hours. We have therefore tried to pick those hours during which community members felt people were most at risk.

Anonymity and confidentiality are crucial, yet secrets are hard to keep in a small town. We seem to have been successful, however. The location of the service's quarters is not made public (for both anonymity and volunteer safety reasons) and volunteers (who use pseudonyms on the line) are enjoined not to publicize the fact that they are involved. They are proud of their work, but understand that the neighbour in whom they may confide might then feel awkward about calling. Most important, we have never received complaints that a caller's issues have been 'spread around,' or that we have overstepped our mandate and boundaries.

Conclusion

The reality of suicide in the North raises continuous questions and anxieties. Professionally, institutionally, locally in communities, and interpersonally in families and among friends, people still often feel reluctant or awkward about discussing and dealing with suicide. It is a deeply private – and, to some, incomprehensible – act that raises emotional questions both about our ways of living and the meanings we attribute to life.

The rapid social changes that have taken place in the Canadian Arctic in the past twenty or thirty years have created a host of challenges and dilemmas for Inuit and non-Inuit alike. Inuit have adapted from a small-group hunter-gatherer culture to modern high-tech Western society in less than two generations, and with this transition have come intense social and personal problems.

Kamatsiaqtut, Baffin Crisis Line has worked hard to involve the people themselves in combating and overcoming those problems. It is difficult to evaluate empirically the effectiveness of organizations like crisis lines: whether they save lives, decrease violence, improve community life, and so forth. We nevertheless celebrate our sixth year of service. Most important, we see the creation and continuing existence of the line as a symbol that a community can and will take charge of its own problems and solutions, and that the community is sending out a signal to those most in need of its service that it does care.

REFERENCES

Anawak, C., and M. Cook. 1986. *Keewatin Suicide Prevention and Intervention Study*. Rankin Inlet: Keewatin Regional Council.
Armstrong, T., et al. 1978. *The Circumpolar North*. London: Methuen.
Belkin, G. 1984. *Introduction to Counseling*. Iowa: C. Brown Publishers.
Briggs, J. 1970. *Never in Anger: Portrait of an Eskimo Family*. Cambridge, MA: Harvard University Press.
Dacks, G. 1981. *A Choice of Futures: Politics in the Canadian North*. Toronto: Methuen Publications.
Frideres, J. 1988. *Native Peoples in Canada: Contemporary Conflicts*. 3rd ed. Scarborough, ON: Prentice-Hall.
GNWT Bureau of Statistics. 1993. *Statistics Quarterly*. Yellowknife: Department of Public Works and Services.

Irwin, C. 1985. *Lords of the Arctic, Wards of the State*. Ottawa: Department of Health and Welfare.

Minor, K. 1992. *Issumatuq: Learning from the Traditional Helping Wisdom of the Canadian Inuit*. Halifax, NS: Fernwood Publishing.

National Task Force on Suicide. 1987. *Suicide in Canada*. Ottawa: Health and Welfare Canada.

O'Neil, J. 1986. 'Colonial Stress in the Canadian Arctic: An Ethnography of Young Adults Changing.' In C. Janes, R. Stall, and S. Gifford, eds, *Anthropology and Epidemiology*. Boston: D. Reidel Publishing.

Pauktuutit. 1991. *The Inuit Way: A Guide to Inuit Culture*. Ottawa: Inuit Women's Association.

Royal Commission on Aboriginal Peoples. 1995. *Choosing Life: Special Report on Suicide among Aboriginal People*. Ottawa: Canada Communication Group, Publishing.

Stoesz, R., and S. Lopatka 1990. *NWT Data Book*. Yellowknife: Outcrop Publishers.

Tsai, L. 1989. *The Problem of Suicide among Inuit Youth*. Ottawa: Pauktuutit (Inuit Women's Association).

PART VIII: SURVIVORS

Suicide puts the emotional pain of the suicide in the minds and hearts of survivors. During the 1980s, survivors of suicide began to receive the professional concern and self-help and empowerment attention in Canada that their difficult emotional experience warrants.

A survivor is anyone left behind. Although the worst has happened, the pain rages. As one of our authors, a survivor, writes in this section, 'I will never forget that Tuesday evening, June 15, 1982.' The old etched-in-stone stages of grief have, however, been left behind. This is necessary because each person goes through her or his own process of mourning. Often people take a lifetime in their mourning. Post-traumatic stress disorder develops in some, and for a few the pain becomes so unbearable that suicide becomes their solution. There are aftershocks – some, such an another suicide, adding to the emotional pain of others.

Yet, postvention heals, even in children and youth. Survivors need to be respected in their healing, especially in bereavement counselling. We need to understand survivors better. We need to respond to survivors in a more compassionate and humane manner.

The eighth section turns to survivors of suicide, and presents four essays: a story from a survivor's experiences, an overview on survivorship from various perspectives, a discussion on surviving, and an outline of postvention with women as survivors.

22

My Story: Thoughts of a Survivor

ANNE EDMUNDS

My Story

I will never forget that Tuesday evening, June 15, 1982, when the phone rang about eleven o'clock. I came rushing downstairs fearful of who might be calling so late at night. Forever seared in my memory are those words my husband spoke, 'Anne, sit down. Richard is dead!' Our worst fears had taken place – our oldest son, twenty-seven years old, had been discovered dead by suicide, hanging in a closet in his new residence in Calgary, Alberta.

I remember wandering around the main floor of our large home wailing inconsolably. Hours later I discovered our tiny, beloved poodle shivering beneath a chair. He, too, felt the terrible pain his family was suffering. Immediately, friends gathered at our home to offer comfort and support. This was our first step in reaching out to others who could accept suicide and the anguish we were experiencing. We left the next day for Calgary to make arrangements to bring Richard's body home. We also began a journey of trying to understand his suicide and all the unanswered questions that surrounded the event.

My brother and his wife met us as our flight west changed planes in Winnipeg. Their eyes reflected the pain and horror of what had taken place. As we neared our destination, I remembered how ecstatic we had been that day when our first son had been born in Calgary. As we wept on the plane everyone around ignored us, something I would experience over and over again in the future.

That evening we were taken to the condominium where Richard had died. Standing outside was the young man who had discovered his body, but the look of despair on his face stopped me from going over to him. There was also the feeling for me that our son had done something unacceptable that should not be talked about. It was also an indication of the burden people carry when they discover the body and of their need to replay this scene over and over until they can cope with their horror.

When I insisted that I, too, wanted to see the room and the closet where the suicide had taken place, everyone tried to stop me. I felt that I had borne Richard in pain and I wanted to see where he had died. Little did I know that this was the beginning of my search for answers to this awful event. I had not worked so hard in my life to be stopped now in my need to know 'Why?'

While in Calgary we visited his place of employment, where he had been a chemical engineer. People were very kind to us. His supervisor told us how talented he was; the business office explained in detail about his insurance and other matters. It was very painful to be there as the reality of his death began to set in.

The visit to his psychologist, who had insisted on seeing us, was also very painful. Although my immediate reaction to Richard's suicide had been to say that I wanted to sue this man, I did not feel this way after we talked to him. His description of Richard's depression was almost more than I could bear. I felt that as a mother I had abandoned him to this illness so far from home and his loved ones. It would be many years before I could visit Calgary without feeling utter despair about the suicide.

Richard was the second of our five children, born very quickly with little pain into a family that was so excited to have a healthy boy. He was a placid baby, ate well, gained weight rapidly, and loved to sit and watch the world go by.

When we moved to Saskatoon from Calgary he was a handsome blonde little boy who enjoyed digging and building in the sand. He always listened carefully to what I said, and usually did what he was told to do, but if he disagreed he was very, very stubborn.

Richard was the one who helped me when it was time to shovel topsoil, light the campfire, or take care of his active younger brother. He became a superb long-distance runner, gold-medal scholar, and a respected engineer in the oil and gas industry. I knew he was a gentle man. I worried about him. I wanted to protect him, to save him, but I couldn't.

He phoned us November 15, 1981, and began to weep. He said he was very anxious and sad and thought that he had buried all his emotions throughout the past ten years. When he came home for Christmas we talked a great deal and he purchased all the books he could find on depression at the university bookstore.

After Richard returned to Alberta the phone calls from him became increasingly tense. He was not sleeping, he was depressed, and he wanted to quit his job. One night in March he called us from a hotel room in Calgary and his conversation was so strange that my journal for that day says, 'Please somebody! HELP!'

As the days progressed, we were in a constant state of anxiety and made many phone calls to Alberta. In May we received a disturbing letter from Richard in which he stated that he had constant thoughts of suicide. We immediately phoned his psychologist, who said that he had hope for Richard's recovery from depression. But a week later another sad letter arrived.

On June 14 I sat outside by the river enjoying the beautiful evening and thinking of Richard. He was probably in a great deal of anxiety at that time and for years I punished myself for not calling him that fateful evening. After his death I read Richard's journal, which his psychologist had encouraged him to keep. It covered the period from January to his death in June. It was very painful to read about his efforts to combat the depression – all of the people he talked with and all of the things he did to feel better. I can never forget those words written in May, 'I was born and bred to be frustrated. I cannot stand the pain any longer. I negate the past, and I have negated all of the future.'

Talking about Suicide

After Richard's funeral our daughters stayed with us a few extra days and I began to talk to our children about the suicide. I felt as if I was going to explode with all this terrible pain inside. They were able to listen to me and to express a little of their grief. I went through my address book, writing to everyone I had known in all our moves throughout western Canada. The tears poured down my face as I sat writing, and one of our sons asked me why I would do this when it upset me so much. I knew it was something that I was compelled to do. I now realize that I was beginning to deal with the word 'suicide.'

One Saturday a young friend came to visit, and although she had never had any children she sat with me for hours, never saying a word as I poured out my grief. I tell her now that she gave me a gift by allowing me to express all of my painful thoughts and to cry without giving me advice or trying to stop me. A week later I wanted to blame everyone for Richard's suicide. Survivors have such strong and conflicting emotions.

The next door neighbours' young daughter had died of leukemia many years before. I relied on them and spent many hours with them talking and crying. I talked to anyone who would listen to me. At a baptismal party someone pointed out a young psychologist who was doing research into suicide notes. I rushed over to him, gripped his arm and asked him to please help me. We arranged a meeting, where he was most helpful because he talked about suicide. He advised me to go to libraries and to read about suicide.

I met Mary, who worked at the meat market I shopped at every week. Her young son had completed suicide a few years before. What a relief it was to talk to someone who really knew what it was like to try and live and function after a suicide. We spent hours together, and when I thanked her, she, in turn, thanked me for giving her the opportunity to talk about her son's suicide. This was the beginning of my realization that survivors often need to hear other people talk about their despair, how they began to cope with the pain, how to try to understand suicide, and how to attain some peace of mind.

Searching for an Answer

In July we travelled again to Calgary to settle Richard's affairs and to dispose of his possessions. This was one of the most difficult things I have ever done in my life. While there we talked again with his psychologist, as well as his aunt and uncle, who had dinner with him that last evening of his life. Being in the house where he had stayed during his time of severe depression made for sleepless nights. Why couldn't we help him? I kept trying to imagine what had happened during those last hours and what it was like to die by hanging. Since his body was not discovered for about a day after his death I kept asking people who might know if he had suffered. I did not realize that in the future I would need to replay these events and suppositions until I could put them to rest.

We called his dear friend in Peace River many times. She had been with him the weekend before he moved to Calgary and completed suicide there. She needed to talk also, and throughout the next year we continued to phone her and to review over and over the events before his death.

A detailed autopsy report arrived from Calgary, but this only added to my confusion. His body was in excellent condition except for the injuries suffered during the hanging. He had not ingested any drugs or alcohol. I wanted to know why he had completed suicide!

In August, I began to read about suicide. In my search of the public library I found a book, *After Suicide*, that helped me very much (Hewitt and Oates, 1980). When I travelled to Toronto, I phoned the Canadian Mental Health Association national office, searching for a group of survivors or for information about surviving a suicide. In 1982 they could not help me. I was so relentless in my searching that other survivors called it my 'research project.' Throughout the fall I continued to talk with a bereavement specialist every two weeks, and over and over I recorded in my diary that it helped so much. As Richard's grave was across the road from the school where I taught I visited it often. When I returned from these trips shaken and weeping, the crossing guard and staff just ignored me. I needed to talk to Richard at his grave, but I also needed some loving human contact – a hug, an acknowledgment that I was hurting.

All that winter I suffered sleepless nights, and headaches and my stomach hurt. In fact, I described the grey days of November as trudging through a grey world carrying a heavy pack on my back.

Suicide Bereavement Group

In January 1983, the Canadian Mental Health Association, Windsor/Essex Branch, Bereavement Resources Program decided, after much prodding from myself and others, to begin a group for survivors. I was apprehensive about meeting strangers, but this feeling soon left me as people began to tell about the suicides of their loved ones. A couple told me after the first meeting that my story was so similar to theirs they thought their hearts would break again. Later the facilitators of the group told us that they went home and had a drink after listening to so much anguish in one room. The survivors were exhausted and went home and slept soundly.

I thought that at these meetings I did nothing but cry, but during the weeks between meetings I would remember what people had said and I would be comforted. When I met group members in public places I would greet them as close and loving members of a special family. Lifelong friendships have been made in these group situations.

Some of the members of the original group and myself took the volunteer and bereavement training necessary to become facilitators. Survivors decided that group sessions should be open so that grieving people could participate in meetings at any time. We did not want survivors to be on a 'waiting list' before they could learn and share with others. The group has functioned continuously since January 1983, with funding and supervision from the Bereavement Resources Program.

As a group member, volunteer facilitator, and staff member I have been involved with this group from its very beginnings. We accept referrals from community professionals and from survivors. These individuals are interviewed in the office or a home visit/presentation is made. Usually they are encouraged to attend the Suicide Bereavement Group meetings.

Representing the Canadian Mental Health Association and as a survivor I have given presentations both locally and at national conferences in Canada. It is my strong conviction that survivors, if they are able to, should speak publicly about the suicide and about the need for acceptance of the intensity of their emotions and of the length of time needed to attain a sense of peace. I know from meeting and supporting many survivors in Essex County that a suicide may occur in any family in any situation. In 1990 three of us attended a 'Healing after Suicide' conference sponsored by the American Association of Suicidology. At the conclusion of the conference a candlelight service was held. We found this to be a great emotional release and a fitting tribute to our loved ones. In 1993 I organized the first of our annual candlelight services, which also proved to be a healing experience. The number of people attending has increased each year and we have remembered and honoured many of those in our area who have completed suicide. As survivors we want to remember our loved ones with dignity and to remove the stigma associated with a death by suicide. Although years have passed since Richard's suicide, there are still occasions when I am overwhelmed by the realization that he is not a part of an expanding family of spouses and grandchildren. The death of a loved one is painful, but death by suicide may be the hardest to bear.

I have been fortunate to share my story with many people in Essex County and across Canada. Survivors need opportunities to talk or write about suicide. We need people who are able to accept the word suicide, friends who will listen to the same stories, recriminations, the endless 'Whys?' We must be allowed to weep or to shout out our pain. Often other survivors are the recipients of all this emotion.

If we seek information after the suicide from officials and professionals, we should be given this with speed, respect, and understanding. With so many unanswered questions we are often driven to search for the meaning and for acceptance of the death. I did not find any conclusive answers, but I needed to gather as much information as possible and to ponder it for years.

During the past two decades professionals and researchers have begun to examine the myriad factors that may lead to a suicide. The study of these characteristics and family dynamics has led to the development of programs on such issues as suicide prevention, crisis lines, and support and under-standing for people who are experiencing depression. But there is still much that needs to be identified and provided for those who are grieving after a suicide.

We must remove the subtle stigma that surrounds these deaths. Survivors will then be free to use the word suicide, to talk about their loss, and to remember their loved one with the honour and respect he or she deserves.

I mourn for Richard and for all those other individuals who sought a release from their pain by completing suicide. I now treasure my family, my friends, my health, my faith. I intend to continue to help in suicide prevention and in support for survivors in any way I can.

SELECTED BIBLIOGRAPHY

I have found these books to be particularly helpful in suicide-bereavement activities.
Bolton, Iris. 1983. *My Son ... My Son ...* Atlanta: Bolton Press.
Chance, Sue, M.D. 1992. *Stronger than Death: When Suicide Touches Your Life*. New York: W.W. Norton
Dunne, Edward J., J.L. MacIntosh, and Karen Dunne-Maxim, eds. 1987. *Suicide and Its Aftermath: Understanding and Counselling the Survivors*. New York: W.W. Norton
Hewitt, J.H., and W.E. Oates, eds. 1980. *After Suicide*. Philadelphia: Westminster Press

23

'I Can't Hear the Music'

LINDA ROSENFELD

'I feel as if I'm in a crowded room watching everyone around me dance, but I can't hear the music,' said Claire, a survivor who lost both her father and sister to suicide.

When a loved one dies by suicide, family members in mourning are left alive, left behind, left alone. They do feel left, abandoned to experience pain and loss, and they feel that this is a solitary experience, one that cannot be understood by anyone else.

In the past fifteen to twenty years, mental-health professionals and volunteer caregivers working in the field of suicidology have learned much about the impact that the trauma of a suicide death has on family members. Therapists, educators, and researchers still, however, have a long way to go to be really helpful during this unique bereavement process. Sometimes with professional help and sometimes without, survivors themselves have found original and complex ways to rebound from being a victim of trauma to being a survivor of trauma.

Development of the Survivor Movement

If there was a hallmark year for survivors of suicide, it was 1972. In the United States Albert Cain edited the first book exploring the problems of survivors. That year, Edwin Shneidman recognized survivors as the true victims of the suicidal act and called 'postvention' (a term he had coined a few years earlier) the greatest area for potential aid (Shneidman, 1972). Here in Canada, suicide legally ceased to be a criminal offence. It now became easier to study survivors and their needs. As a result, there was an increasing awareness that suicide survivors have a higher risk for suicide themselves. Postvention is intervention after a death. It facilitates the mourning process by helping survivors to reach their own personally acceptable conceptualization of the suicide while eliciting and reinforcing their most effective modes of coping (Cain, 1972). Postvention indeed seems to be an effective tool in suicide prevention.

But if North Americans are to respond to survivors in a more compassionate and humane manner, it will come through a better understanding of both suicide and the multitude of issues it leaves for those left behind. For hundreds of years, stigmatization of survivors has existed throughout Western civilization. While suicide is no longer a crime and property is no longer confiscated as it was in the eighteenth century, punishment still exists in many forms today. Many life-insurance policies do not pay the grieving family if the suicide occurred within two years of taking out the policy. Some religious institutions do not bury a suicide in consecrated ground unless mental illness is used as a reason for the suicide. In spite of this stigma, survivors began to search each other out, break the barriers of solitary mourning, and address their own issues.

In 1980, two hundred survivors from more than thirty states and Canada attended a National Survivors' Conference in Iowa City (Colt, 1987). About the same time, mental-health professionals in Canada began working, studying, and writing about this new area of concern. Toronto's Survivor Support Program, begun in 1979, was the first of its kind in Canada. It was developed by liaison between the Clarke Institute of Psychiatry and local distress centres under the guidance of Karen Letofsky, its director. S.A.F.E.R. (Suicide Attempt Follow-up, Education, and Research), in Vancouver, is a multifaceted suicide-intervention agency that incorporated a suicide-bereavement program among its services. Since 1980, this program has used professional counsellors to work with suicide survivors both in individual grief counselling and in therapy groups, as well as to provide postvention in schools and communities. In addition, education and training in suicide bereavement for both professionals and lay people has become an integral part of the service mandate. In Alberta, Mark Solomon, the first provincial suicidologist in Canada, published 'The Bereaved and the Stigma of Suicide' (1982–3) and started a group for survivors in Edmonton. In Windsor, Ontario, bereavement groups for survivors of suicide began under the auspices of Canadian Mental Health. In Peterborough, Ontario, crisis-centre organizer Barbara Moffat recognized that often volunteers in training were survivors themselves and arranged a meeting between survivors and concerned professionals. In Quebec City in 1982 Linda Delisle started the first survivor groups, and in Montreal a short time later groups were developed at Suicide Action, a crisis centre. Atlantic Canada was also aware of this development. First Nations survivors of suicide bereavement groups were developing in small communities and on reserves as mutual support for the high numbers of native Canadians who were mourning suicide deaths.

The survivor movement in Canada had begun and was spurred on by need. The stigma of suicide was slowly changing as the silence was lifted. The time was right and the need for help was being filled spontaneously across the country.

Specific Issues of Suicide Bereavement

Suicide death evokes different reactions in the mourning process of the bereaved, which is complicated by its tragic circumstances and traumatic aftermath.

In suicide bereavement, throughout the process of grieving, recovery is impeded because social supports are either non-existent or pull back after a short time, and the survivor must deal with his or her feelings in isolation. After a suicide death, cards and condolences are often not sent, obituaries do not mention the cause of death, the usual conversations do not take place. Instead, families hear whispers. They feel they are being condemned for something or silently accused of something. There is a vague feeling that they were at fault as a family, and so somehow responsible. They hear implications that there is mental illness in the family. If the suicide victim was mentally ill, it is another stigma the family must face; and it raises even more concerns. Does this family harbour some genetic defect that caused the death? If so, will it affect others in the family? A woman whose husband had shot himself four months earlier said, 'It felt like being quarantined ... I was afraid to go out because people were always looking at me strangely and almost no one phoned or came over anymore. Friends who did call never talked about it. Soon I began to wonder if I imagined people were looking at me strangely. If so, maybe I was going crazy.'

In North America we are generally fearful of death. We study suicide, but we are not certain what causes it or what can prevent it. At the same time, we are surrounded by suicide. It permeates our culture through art, literature, music, and the media. We also know that as individuals we harbour self-destructive impulses that can emerge in times of despair, and we each wonder what would constitute unendurable psychic pain for us. Because of the fear of death and uncertainty about whether we are safe from our own self-destructive impulses, we imagine a kind of contamination by contact. So, tragically, survivors feel the withdrawing of, or avoidance by, friends that leaves them confused, angry, and isolated with their overwhelming emotions. The family members also feel they have been abandoned by the one who chose to die. When family members are grieving – feeling rejected, abandoned, lonely, sad, and now isolated – they often feel suicidal themselves (Rosenfeld and Prupas, 1984).

Feeling suicidal, the survivor feels ashamed and cannot share these feelings with other family members. Each family member also questions his own responsibility for the death and blames both himself and other family members. This is done silently. The undeclared blame then becomes covert, concealed from the rest of the family. This veil of secrecy makes it difficult for the mourner to make any sense of the death and forces him to search for answers within himself endlessly. Also, he believes that feelings triggered by the suicide death, especially anger and relief, are not acceptable to have and certainly not to talk about. A young man, whose fiancée killed herself, said, 'What I feel and what I present to the world can be so different that I am confused about myself and what I really feel.'

So the community imposes a stigma and isolates the bereaved because of fear: fear of death, fear of mental illness, and fear of contamination by suicide. The mourner reinforces this isolation because he hides from the world, or does not reach out for support because he has fears of inheriting suicide, fears of being blamed, or fears of admitting, or expressing, forbidden feelings. Stigma, then, is externally imposed by society for an unacceptable act and internally imposed by oneself for unacceptable feelings.

The endless questions that can never be answered lead the survivor always back to 'If only I had noticed ... paid more attention ... been more caring ... been different ... this might not have happened.' The survivor continues to blame himself for things he should or should not have done.

Perhaps the most difficult feeling to cope with is guilt. It certainly appears to be the most intense and last the longest. Its savage hold seizes the heart and burrows in, never completely leaving the survivor at peace. The word guilt itself is so emotionally laden that survivors will talk about regret, remorse, responsibility, or blame more easily.

Winch and Letofsky (1981) found that it is important to know about the survivor's relationship to the deceased before the suicide when looking at suicidal feelings, anger, and guilt. Through studying case notes and anecdotal material, they found that suicide survivors who anticipated the suicide, and had therefore already disengaged from other family members, had no suicidal feelings and less guilt and anger than suicide survivors who were not anticipatory grievers. The sudden unexpected death experience, rather than the suicide itself, appeared to be a major factor in the amount of guilt and anger.

Beth's husband overdosed on medication prescribed for an illness. Beth talked about her guilt after her husband's death:

My guilt was first for that day: things I shouldn't have done that day. Then it spread like a blanket to encompass everything. It goes backwards in time, into the relationship; all through our lives from the time we first met until his death. As I work further backwards it gets wider in perspective as well. The emotional state I was in before Dave's death has a lot to do with how much guilt I felt after. I was in a desperate state myself. I felt guilty: for being angry, for not wanting to change my lifestyle, for being tired of caretaking. Dave was sick and the responsibility for his well-being was given to me by his employer, other family members, and his doctors. They put him in my care but didn't say what to look for, how to care for him. I absorbed expectation from outside sources and added that to my own need to care for him; and I took responsibility for his life. So now I have to take responsibility for his death. Somehow I failed. I didn't make the right decisions.

When asked what helped to alleviate her guilt, Beth said, 'Gradually I came to terms with aspects of the guilt, but whether I'll come to terms with all of it I don't know. I have optimism that one day I may reconcile it. I also need to come to terms with my humanness. I'm not infallible, I can't do everything, I can't get it right all the time. Its just as simple as that!'

Feeling responsible and guilty and grief-stricken, the bereaved search for clues as to why the victim committed suicide, for answers to unanswerable questions. At the same time as they are feeling guilty, the bereaved are often angry at themselves, at other family members, and at the person who died. If the anger is buried along with the deceased, the ghost of anger stalks the mourner who tries to deny its existence. 'How can I be angry at someone who died because he suffered?' But he did abandon his family to pain, to living without him, to family responsibilities, and to a lifetime of stigma.

When the survivor feels angry, he blames himself for the death. When he is angry and blaming towards himself, he feels guilty and searches the relationship he had with the loved one who died by suicide. In his search he needs to accept responsibility for words or acts that may have influenced the thought processes or behaviours of the family member who died, but he cannot take the blame or responsibility when it is not rightfully his. Anger erodes self-esteem as much as guilt does. Low self-esteem and anger turned inward can cause depression. This anger not outwardly expressed then can exhibit itself as sadness. Sadness is much easier for others to tolerate. Also, survivors would often rather show sadness than anger, because anger expressed further isolates the bereaved. But constant self-blame can become intolerable. Anger then may shift and the survivor begins to look outside himself and condemn others. The 'other' that is the recipient of anger may be the school, church, friends, employer, co-workers, hospital, other family members, or professional helper. Sometimes this anger may be justified, and sometimes it is a way of trying to avoid blaming oneself. Anger directed outward, however, often creates frustration in trying to battle the 'system,' not relief. Also, if the survivor isolates himself even more by accusing others, he ends up with another reason for feeling angry (Rosenfeld and Prupas, 1984).

The most difficult anger to uncover is the rage at the suicide victim. This feeling, like guilt, will depend on what was taking place in the relationship before the death. But anger is a natural response to feelings of loneliness, abandonment, sadness, responsibility, and shame – as well as a life that is irrevocably changed. When talking about the effect anger has on how she views the world since her husband's death, a young woman said, 'I'm always expecting the unexpected. I'm bewildered by the unpredictability of life.'

Anger during grieving also affects how the bereaved views 'suicide.' A mother of a young man who died in his car by carbon monoxide said, 'When I'm angry, I think of suicide as a coward's choice. At other times I think of it as a cry of despair or as a final desperate plea for peace.'

When a person is mourning the loss of someone with whom there has been a loving relationship, bereavement can include physical, mental, and emotional reactions. This discussion has focused primarily on the emotional ones. However, all reactions are interwoven. Physical reactions are commonly seen in doctors' offices that are related to grief. Many pre-existing conditions such as migraines, hypertension, or aching of joints and muscles tend to become exacerbated during the grief process, and symptoms of new stress-related illnesses may surface. Because suicide is so often not discussed, it may not occur to either the physician or patient that the symptoms are related to grief. Mental confusion and inability to concentrate or focus on work are also a normal part of the grief experience, but survivors, not knowing this, may worry about themselves and wonder what is happening to them, concerned that they may be 'losing their minds.' This inability to concentrate can be related to an increase in accidents. Many survivors talk about having car accidents after visiting the cemetery.

So suicide bereavement is unique, not in the amount of pain and the intensity of feeling, but because

1 it seems preventable,
2 there is anger and guilt and stigma,
3 the family member *chose* to die, and
4 there is a search for reasons.

'Dave's suicide is a measure of my interior life: for the rest of my life, everything is in relationship to it,' said Dave's widow.

Suicide deaths, then, do not usually bring families closer together. Stigma, isolation, guilt, and anger tend to isolate family members from each other. Initially, families may come together to deal with the impact of the death and perform rituals that guide them through the impact of the trauma, but survivors, friends, and professional helpers need to be aware of the importance of open communication and loving support throughout the whole process. Sharing the pain, while recognizing the differences in the way family members grieve, can enable families to accept their mutual loss and appreciate each other more fully. Much later, when the ferocious fingers of pain have loosened their grasp, survivors will be able to recognize some positive change in themselves or in the way they are with people around them. Molly's husband jumped to his death after twenty years of marriage. As part of her therapy Molly did a lot of writing. In a letter to her dead husband Molly said, 'I'm no longer angry at you, dear Jesse. In fact, I've become a more compassionate person. That is what your death has taught me.'

What Helps?

While denial and a freezing of emotional response appear to be a necessary stage during which personal resources are assembled and mobilized to face the reality of the death, this is generally not the time for outside intervention. As survivors move out of the cushion of shock and begin to experience the emotional spectrum of the next dimension of grieving, they may become intellectually and emotionally available to the positive influence of postvention.

For some, individual counselling is important. This is especially true if there is a scarcity of social support. Therapists and counsellors need to understand the difficulties of suicide bereavement. Then mourners can be provided with the time, place, and relationship that will enable them to reconcile the death within their own belief system about who they are now. Beth, who was quoted earlier about guilt over her husband's suicide, was in individual counselling for a period of time. She felt it was helpful and described the counselling process: 'Looking back over the past ten months I can recall so many instances where a quiet word or sentence, judiciously placed, helped me to take things one step further and see them in a new light.' This therapeutic setting can become a sanctuary that relaxes the body, renews the spirit, and revives the soul.

For many, groups are important. Schneiderman et al. (1994) have stated that social class, pre-death family functioning, social support, the age of the deceased family member and survivors, as well as the nature of the death (sudden death, suicide, etc.), have as much to do with individual and family functioning during the bereavement period as any intervention that might be provided. It appears that suicide death, then, is one factor that does influence the bereavement process. Studies have shown that a group experience for bereavement and especially for suicide bereavement can be beneficial.

Hopmeyer and Werk (1994) studied support groups of peers for different kinds of bereavement. The benefits could be summarized as commonality, normalization, solidarity, reciprocity, and control. The survivors-of-suicide groups' most common reasons for forming were (1) sharing similar experiences, (2) gaining comfort and reassurance, and (3) learning new skills for coping. The most valuable thing gained was, for all group members, a belief that they benefited from the opportunity to share with others. The survivors-of-suicide group members especially felt it was important not to feel alone. These authors stated that disenfranchised mourners need the validation and acceptance they receive from other group members.

Survivors have repeatedly told their counsellors that they need information in their search for answers about why suicide was a choice for their loved one. They may contact teachers, employers, friends, or coroners. They may also seek this information from the doctor or therapist who may have been treating the suicide victim. Even when they have the courage to reach out in this way, family members are often denied this vital information on the grounds it is still confidential. What is often denied them as well is empathy or concern for their well-being, which would help immensely with their grief. In a study done by Dr Michael Brownstein in conjunction with S.A.F.E.R. (Brownstein, 1992) in Vancouver, only one out of twelve families studied were contacted by the treating psychiatrist after the death of a family member. The eleven others all said it would have been greatly appreciated and believed it would have modified their grief process.

Therapist's and counsellors' own feelings of shock, grief, and responsibility, and subsequent feelings of professional worthlessness, can affect how they respond to survivors. The bereaved need comfort and support from the caregiver at a time when it may be very difficult for the caregiver to be objective. It can be devastating for a 'helper,' whether professional or volunteer, to feel 'helpless' in his or her chosen role. If the caregiver cannot help the suicidal person, he begins to question not only his competence, but also his value or worth in relation to his work. In this shaken state, caregivers are not ready to deal with the survivors' needs. They must do their own grief work in order to become available to respond to the mourning family.

In Canada, then, a survivor of suicide may be able to get individual counselling or group support or therapy. But Canada is a country that, while fluid in compassion, is divided into boundaries by its vastness. Pockets of people are isolated from one another and from traditional sources of help available in larger centres. This country's bilingual heritage also contributes to the boundaries with which it continually struggles. It is also a multicultural nation whose many different groups view death, suicide, and grief from many different belief systems. These issues are a challenge for all Canadians.

Conclusion

While survivors differ on nearly all demographic measures, they are united in their feelings of grief, anger, shame, and guilt; by their experiences of stigma and isolation; and by their search for answers as to why their family member died by suicide. So survivors form self-help groups where change is rooted in the principle that group support around a shared condition opens up the potential for a critical alteration in the perception of self.

Professionals have developed and use depression scales, helplessness scales, bereavement scales, distress-symptom checklists, self-esteem questionnaires, and so on in an attempt at understanding the differences between suicide bereavement and other forms of bereavement. While these studies are helpful, clinical interviews over a long period and grief counselling with individuals going through the process also continue to give new insights into this unique form of pain.

Thus, researchers and clinicians need to walk hand-in-hand and travel together with survivors along pathways that go forward in understanding. Then the survivor of suicide will be better able to cope with, adjust to, and live with the changes that death has wrought.

After two years of grief counselling, Claire said, 'I'm in that same room and I can now hear the music. Maybe some day, I'll be able to dance to it.'

REFERENCES

Brownstein, M. 1992. 'Contacting the Family after a Suicide.' *Canadian Journal of Psychiatry* 37 (April): 208–12.
Cain, A. (ed.) 1972. *Survivors of Suicide*. Springfield, IL: Charles C. Thomas.
Colt, G.H. 1987. 'The History of the Suicide Survivor.' In E.J. Dunne, J.L. McIntosh, and K. Dunne-Maxwell, eds, *Suicide and Its Aftermath*, 15. New York: W.W. Norton.
Hopmeyer, E., and A. Werk. 1994. 'A Comparative Study of Family Bereavement Groups.' *Death Studies* 18(3): 243–56.
Rosenfeld, L., and M. Prupas. 1984. *Left Alive: After a Suicide Death in the Family*. Springfield, IL: Charles C. Thomas.
Schneiderman, G., P. Winders, S. Tallett, and W. Feldman. 1994. 'Do Child and/or Parent Bereavement Groups Work?' *Canadian Journal of Psychiatry* 39 (May): 494–9.
Shneidman, E. 1972. 'Foreword.' In A. Cain, ed., *Survivors of Suicide*. Springfield, IL: Charles C. Thomas.
Solomon, M. 1982–3. 'The Bereaved and the Stigma of Suicide.' *Omega* 13: 377–87.
Winch, G., and K. Letofsky. 1981. 'The Nature of the Suicidal Death as a Factor in Understanding Reactions of Surviving Family Members.' In *Depression and Suicide*, 523–32. Paris: Pergamon Press.

24

After Suicide: Reweaving the Web

JEANNETTE A. AMBROSE

Suicide is not just a type of death. It is a human act – a willful annihilation of self. The 'other' who committed suicide leaves a complicated legacy of grief for those who were emotionally attached.

Rynearson, 1981: 84

Suicide delivers a triple whammy: survivors must deal not only with the trauma of the suicide death and the personal conceptualization of the suicide act, but also with the psychosocial context in which it occurs. Consequently, assisting those bereaved by suicide involves attending to intrapsychic issues of bereavement, including those that may distinguish it from other types of bereavement, as well as responding to survivors within the context of family and social relationships.

Since Cain's (1972) seminal study of suicide survivors, suicide bereavement has been defined as unique and difficult (Dunne et al., 1987; Henley, 1984), but research is by no means equivocal regarding the severity or distinctiveness of its symptoms compared to other types of bereavement. Current research suggests that survivor reactions can be extremely complex (Henley, 1984; McIntosh, 1993; Rando, 1993) and are characterized by a high degree of individual variability (Rudestam, 1992). While suicide bereavement is likely more similar to than different from other forms of bereavement, there are quantitative and qualitative differences (Brent et al., 1992; Silverman et al., 1994–5). It may be helpful to understand survivor reactions as an accretion of four distinct types of grief reactions experienced to some degree in other forms of bereavement, but unique in their constellation for suicide survivors (Barrett and Scott, 1990). The reactions include common grief reactions resulting from the loss of a loved one, other-than-natural grief reactions to a traumatic death perceived as avoidable, grief reactions resulting from sudden death, and reactions resulting from the additional trauma of dealing with the suicidal nature of the death.

In addition, suicide appears to have more in common with other forms of sudden death (in terms of bereavement) than with normal death (Rando, 1993; Reed, 1993; Reed and Greenwald, 1991; van der Wal, 1989–90), and while not the defining feature, the manner of death is a significant factor (Cleiren et al., 1994; Rudestam, 1992). Researchers and clinicians are identifying other factors that predispose suicide survivors towards a more or less difficult course of mourning. Various sub-populations believed to be at risk for greater difficulty include adolescents (Valente et al., 1988), those who discover the body of the victim (Andress and Corey, 1978; Brent et al., 1992), parents (Klass, 1988; Rando, 1986), and those survivors who experience post-traumatic stress reactions (Rynearson, 1987; Zisook, 1987).

Many survivors will resolve their grief with family and community support. Others will not. Those who do not – those whose needs are more intense or complex, or whose experiences put them at greater risk for bereavement complications – are the survivors for whom After Suicide grief therapy groups were developed. After Suicide is a non-profit organization dedicated to meeting the needs of survivors through outreach, community awareness, and support groups as well as the therapy groups that are the subject of this chapter.

After Suicide: Assisting Suicide Survivors

Rationale for Group Therapy for Survivors

'I borrow myself from others; man is a mirror for man' – Merleau Ponty

Suicide bereavement is often accompanied by many risk factors associated with complicated bereavement as well as some of the features commonly associated with trauma and post-traumatic stress reactions (Leenaars and Wenckstern, eds, 1991; Rando, 1993). Counselling and support services are beneficial for survivors experiencing 'normal' grief, with no significant blocks to the tasks of bereavement. While the support and nurturance provided by bereavement support groups are essential, they may sometimes be insufficient to deal with the intense and overwhelming nature of survivor grief. Many survivors require more intensive, focused intervention and a greater degree of intensity and commitment (Parkes, 1980) than most support groups can provide.

Grief therapy refers to the specialized techniques used to assist people with complicated grief reactions (Worden, 1982), where the circumstances of the loss are unusual (such as AIDS and suicide). It implies the need for significant emotional and cognitive changes to resolve underlying issues so that grief can proceed. Grief therapy is psychotherapy intertwined with grief work.

Groups have long been the 'treatment' of choice for survivors of suicide (Appel and Wrobleski, 1987; Hopmeyer and Werk, 1994; Winch and Letofsky, 1981), and are frequently recommended for survivors of other trauma (Borman and Lieberman, 1979; Everstine and Everstine, 1993; van der Kolk, 1987). The role of a group for suicide and trauma survivors may be even more important than it is in many other bereavement situations. Though family and social support are widely recognized as the most important factors in healing (Figley, 1986; Rando, 1993; Scurfield; 1986; Solomon, 1986), suicide and trauma are frequently accompanied by impoverished social relationships and a loss of autonomy. A therapy group may act as a temporary community that reduces isolation and provides the interim support necessary for survivors to regain previous, or to establish new, supportive relationships.

Groups are bound together by the sharing of the trauma experience. They validate and normalize participants' reactions that may seem aberrant, and decrease the stigma often experienced by suicide survivors. Groups afford participants the reassurance that healing will occur in a 'protected space in which not only can the current self be seen with clarity in the psychological mirror, but the possibilities of new selves can be glimpsed' (Nichols and Jenkinson, 1991: 6). The ideal therapeutic group includes the creation of 'community,' the power of its members to help each other, and an emphasis on interaction and growth rather than loss, pain, and emotional catharsis.

Curative Factors

After Suicide utilizes the basic curative factors of groups as described by Yalom (1975), but emphasizes those that add to the impact of the group as a *forum for change*. The first of these factors is the recapitulation of the primary family group. 'Group interaction can give members the chance to understand their families of origin, explore their consequent adaptive style, and learn how this helps or hinders the grieving process (Cook and Dworkin, 1992: 95). The second factor is the emphasis on interpersonal learning and socializing techniques. Participants can tap into the inherent healing powers of the group, which provides opportunities to clarify insights, correct distortions, and offer support within a new, more generous framework. Groups facilitate change by bringing collective motivation for change, a challenge to entrenched thoughts and perceptions, and mutual encouragement.

Finally, the third curative factor of therapy groups concerns the opportunity to examine the existential questions that present a particularly powerful challenge to those bereaved by suicide (Dunn and Morrish-Vidners, 1987–8; Rynearson, 1981) or trauma (Everstine and Everstine, 1993; Horowitz, 1986). Such experiences force us to examine our sense of meaning in life, the limits of our power and control, and the recognition that life can be unfair and unjust and that, ultimately, there is no escape from life's pain.

After Suicide: Structure and Process

After Suicide therapy groups are closed groups that afford the best opportunity to develop the trust, cohesion, and commitment necessary to meet the goals of group therapy. The group of eight adult members meets weekly for sixteen to thirty sessions depending on the degree of complexity and trauma experienced by the group members. While there is no time limit imposed regarding length of time since the suicide, usually survivors do not join the group before the second month following the death. Group members who have experienced a suicide many years ago and 'new' survivors generally work well together. Couples and family groups may participate following careful assessment to ensure that the needs of individual members can be met within the group.

Leadership

While members bring themselves as the key ingredients, the therapist leaders play an important role. They guide, model, shape, and preserve safety, serving as catalysts for personal change. In After Suicide, we are guided by the core belief that people have a continuing ability to change and grow. We believe in a process of therapy in which there are no experts prescribing or assuming, and we adopt the perspective that all human beings walk the same paths. The atmosphere created as a result is one of positive acceptance, lack of judgment, and support, coupled with information and gentle challenge.

Since groups serve highly vulnerable and frequently traumatized participants, leaders must be well-qualified professionals, experienced in group dynamics and crisis intervention. They must be skilled in assessing and treating both complicated grief and trauma, in assessing and monitoring each member's progress and barriers to progress, and in the art of knowing when to take the lead and when not. Leaders must be comfortable in challenging group members to approach, not avoid, painful feelings in a timely manner. In addition, at least one leader must also be a survivor of suicide. Good group therapists must also understand how personal issues will affect their leadership style and decisions.

With death-related issues, client-therapist dynamics are very complex. Working with survivors requires not only that we listen to and accept the telling of graphic and horrific stories, but that we share the pain of the survivor while maintaining our own health and balance.

Therapeutic Assessment Interview

Assessment is an ongoing process, beginning with an in-depth screening interview. A therapeutic interview is also an introductory step in facilitating the bereavement process (Raphael, 1977). Questions should be designed to indicate comfort in speaking about any aspect of the client's experiences around death and to assess for possible risk factors and difficulties, as well as for the necessary match between client and group. Because many of our group members are at higher risk for complicated bereavement, and frequently experience post-traumatic stress reactions, our assessment framework is fairly extensive and includes at least an initial assessment of complicated risk factors and trauma reactions (Everstine and Everstine, 1993; Matsakis, 1994; Rando, 1993).

Our assessment framework includes the following factors: (1) the grieving context, including the death and previous relationship with the deceased; (2) previous loss history; (3) the client's present coping style and developmental status; (4) family support and communication system, and role of the deceased member; (5) the nature and degree of social support and the client's ability to gain access to it; (6) the role of spiritual, religious, and cultural issues; (7) post-traumatic stress reactions; (8) physical condition and symptoms; and (9) suicide risk.

Preparing Group Members

An important element to ensuring the success of the group is to assess the client's expectations and ideas about, and prepare the client for, the group (Nichols and Jenkinson, 1991). Preparation commences with our first contact with prospective members and proceeds on levels of both structure and process. We describe to them the structure and composition, content, and expectations of the group. Since grieving and traumatized people are frequently flooded with information and emotion, written information about the group is also provided. On a process level, we recognize the bereaved's inner pain, emotions, and common fears, as well as the difficulty in expressing them. We are clear that while we can provide a safe atmosphere and a map for the grief process, we cannot take away their pain.

Techniques

After Suicide utilizes a wide variety of interventions and techniques. These are not formulas or recipes for grief therapy and are only as useful as the person using them. Techniques may be seen as tools that stimulate and facilitate the processes of growth, change, and healing. We strongly recommend that these interventions be used only by qualified therapists with specialized training in grief work.

Evocative techniques are designed for those who are experiencing difficulty recognizing and expressing grief reactions. They rely on re-establishing emotional links with perceptual experiences. Such techniques include verbal approaches, guided imagery, role-play or Gestalt techniques, letter writing, the use of significant articles or pictures, and visiting the cemetery. Learning to tolerate emotional pain and decrease avoidance are the desired goals. More cognitive techniques such as shared reminiscence also facilitate the exploration and sharing of the legacy of the deceased. Cognitive techniques such as bibliotherapy, storytelling, letter and journal writing, and reframing promote understanding and acceptance of the grief reactions.

Techniques employing the therapeutic use of symbols and multiple levels of meaning and senses facilitate the exploration of the history of the deceased and of the former relationship. They involve multiple forms of artwork and the use of poetry, music, and metaphors. Poems, songs, and other artistic creations serve as concrete reminders of more abstract values or emotions. 'Therapists use their creative arts to help clients tap into their inner selves and symbolically represent their feelings, their relationship to the deceased and/or what the individual stood for' (Cook and Dworkin, 1992: 85).

Being creative satisfies an innate urge we have to understand the meaning of an experience. Art therapy provides both a process to clarify and deepen the questions we ask and an awareness of how we create our own life conditions, and points the way to alternative choices. Clay is used especially for its sensory, tactile qualities and its capacity to bring out the unspoken. It can assist in working with individuals who stay away from their feelings by analysing and speculating on the 'whys' of behaviour, and is especially helpful in the exploration of painful or 'negative' feelings. Music can be utilized to highlight positive expectations, to create a mood or support the expression of sadness, loss, and reminiscence, to explore the universality of loss and the paradoxes of life, or just to have fun.

We rely heavily on the use of *metaphors and rituals*. Metaphors can provide a powerful and useful framework for lowering resistance to the pain of grief, fostering mutuality, and facilitating both the universalization and normalization of acute grief. Metaphors offer a graphic non-judgmental framework to help the bereaved cope with the crisis of death (Schwartz-Borden, 1992). Rituals, by contrast, are ceremonious acts endowed with symbolic meaning that facilitate tapping into a deeper level of consciousness and intensity. They are designed to assist clients both to accept the reality of loss and related feelings and to process the tasks of grief.

Rituals involve more than funerals and memorial services. They are connected to transformation and change (Imber-Black, 1991). Rituals are actions specifically designed to change the way we see the world, to allow us to act out inner feelings, legitimize emotional and physical ventilation through symbols, and channel grief into clearly defined, purposeful activities. Rituals also have the capacity to express powerful contradictions simultaneously, making them especially relevant to the mourning process with its inherent ambivalence.

Homework tasks are frequently assigned at the end of therapy sessions. Tasks may involve reading articles, journal writing, talking to someone or writing a letter about unfinished business, writing letters to the dead person, grave visiting, the development of rituals for saying goodbye or to bring manageability to holidays, and self-care activities.

Reweaving a Complex Web: A Grief Model for Survivors

A Contextual Framework

The framework for any therapy rests on the assumptions, beliefs, and theories that inform and give it shape. A major loss is an event that initially diminishes self, reducing a person's dignity, will, and resources. After such a loss, we do not return to 'normal' – we are essentially changed; 'normal' has shifted. But major losses can also be wellsprings of growth and renewal. They are often benchmarks in one's life course. The bereaved are actors, influencing the change process over which they exercise significant control. Bereavement is a fundamentally active process wherein the bereaved must be aware of and responsible for their own thinking and actions (Nerkin, 1993). Our choices can move us forward towards a constructive outcome, or we can become stuck.

The orientation guiding our work is psychodynamic, and is strongly informed by family systems and by developmental, existential, and cognitive behavioural perspectives. It is based on the following principles:

1 Bereavement is a normal and natural, though often traumatic and emotional, experience resulting in profound, permanent changes, sometimes even destructive ones.

2 Grief and mourning follow no timetables or stages, and some losses will never be fully resolved.

3 Grief is a holistic, multidimensional process.

4 Grief and trauma are defined by the meaning the griever attaches to them.

5 Grief is a dynamic process involving choices and the potential for change and growth.

6 Grief is an individual and family developmental process that occurs within a broader social context.

7 We must recognize and honour the natural capacities and resiliency of individuals and families.

8 Human responses to loss, including suicide, vary on a continuum from 'normal' to complicated and post-trauma based.

9 Survivors of suicide may be victimized, but they are not victims.

Our beliefs achieve an extraordinary fit with Attig's (1982) model of grief and personal integrity based on the metaphor of a spider's web. The model rests on the fundamental belief that we are who we are by virtue of our connections with others. Personal integrity is represented by the delicately woven spider's web, composed of enumerable threads radiating from the centre and transverse threads binding them together, and attached to its surroundings at countless points. Individual strands represent the physical, emotional, intellectual, practical, and social ties between individuals, and transverse threads of the web represent the additional complexity of how we are involved with the world. Several aspects of the impact of loss upon personal integrity are reflected through this metaphor. If each wedge of the web represents a valued relationship with another, the death of that person can be imagined as a blow where that wedge is anchored, penetrating to the centre of the web. 'Loose ends would be left hanging where once there was connection. All of the security in the world as well as the structure within the self which had been provided by the relationship is lost ... Such a disorienting blow tears at the very fabric, i.e., the integrity of the grieving person' (Attig, 1982: 65).

Reverberations throughout the web vary with the severity of the blow, the quality and meaning of the relationship, and the nature and extent of the interconnecting relationships. The grieving process can therefore be seen as one of the reintegration of self following a loss – a virtual reweaving of the personal character of the bereaved. Successful grieving may bring a new resiliency and an enhanced capacity to live more fully. But no matter how well spun, the new web will never be the same as the old – something precious has been lost and the new web reflects a new life in which the relationship with the deceased, as well as many other relationships, are forever changed.

Using this model requires basic respect for individual vulnerability (including our own), and the recognition that the anguish of the bereaved is a symptom of the underlying injury to his or her personal integrity in the world. The experiences of grieving under complicated circumstances such as suicide and/or trauma can also be accommodated by the model. The separation, isolation, and broken connections resulting from traumatic death, and the feelings of physical and psychological disintegration where the self has fragmented, speak profoundly to the need for rearranging our human webs (Lifton, 1979).

Tasks of Grief

We are guided in our work by Worden's (1982) four tasks of mourning. Because the psychosocial context is of fundamental importance to the understanding and treatment of grief, we have also incorporated two additional tasks designed to promote grief adaptation within families (Walsh and McGoldrick, 1991):

Task 1: To accept the reality of the loss.
Task 2: To experience the pain of grief.
Task 3: To adjust to an environment in which the deceased is missing.
Task 4: To withdraw emotional energy from the deceased and reinvest it in another relationship.
Task 5: To share acknowledgment of the reality of the death and share the experience of loss.
Task 6: To reorganize the family system and reinvest in other relationships and life pursuits.

Components of After Suicide

While the group process is guided by a defined structure, it is also governed by flexibility and client need. It is structured by five main components, each of which includes a number of sessions designed to address particular issues: (1) understanding grief; (2) understanding grief after suicide; (3) remembering and saying goodbye; (4) human responses to grief and trauma; and (5) reorganizing family and community relationships.

1. Understanding Grief

Normalizing the grief process stimulates participants to share fully in the group. The avoidance of euphemisms and use of clear language about what to expect from, and how to understand, the grief process supports members to accept further the reality of their losses.

Leaders present the principles and model of grief and bereavement as outlined above. The spider's-web metaphor and other metaphors are introduced. Common physical, emotional, cognitive, behavioural, and spiritual reactions to grief, as well as secondary losses that accompany death, are explored while examining how participants have been changed by the death. Past, present, and alternative future coping mechanisms are evaluated. Relaxation exercises, guided imagery, and clay work are utilized to assist participants in the management of overwhelming grief symptoms that may be interfering with necessary daily functioning.

2. Understanding Grief after Suicide

Complications and Trauma in Suicide Bereavement

Suicide is a major risk factor contributing to complicated mourning, and suicide bereavement shares many of the features of complicated grief (Rando, 1993). High-risk factors can be divided into two categories. The first category is associated with sudden, unexpected deaths, which often occur in a constellation of other risk factors including trauma, violence, and mutilation, the loss of a child, the perception of death as preventable, and personal encounters with death. The circumstances of sudden, violent death produce an additional dimension of stress that severely taxes coping mechanisms and forces survivors to give priority to overwhelming feelings and perceptions.

The second category includes factors associated with preceding and subsequent relationship variables and liabilities, including perceived lack of social support. High-risk factors are interrelated and, generally, the existence of more factors increases the risk of complications (Rando, 1993). Many of these factors converge for many survivors of suicide.

Suicide bereavement also frequently meets the criteria for post-traumatic stress reactions or disorder (Figley, ed., 1986; Leenaars and Wenckstern, 1991; Rynearson, 1987), and there are often psychological experiences common to both suicide and trauma (Leenaars and Wenckstern, 1991; Rando, 1993). Rynearson's (1986) watershed article on the psychological effects of unnatural dying links suicide bereavement and trauma, suggesting that unnatural dying is accompanied by factors that can result in post-traumatic stress reactions. In addition, the existential dilemmas that are a defining feature of the trauma experience take on a particular hue determined by the mode and configuration of a suicide death. Essentially, suicide presents an unanswerable existential contradiction (Rynearson, 1981).

The interplay of trauma and grief reaction is complicated and as yet has not been clearly defined. Although grief and trauma are profoundly different human experiences, a single event such as suicide can produce both. What is most important in terms of assisting the survivors is the understanding that coexisting trauma impairs grief work (Pynoos and Eth, 1985; Rando, 1993). While trauma and grief may overlap, each must be attended to uniquely, beginning with an early treatment focus on psychic trauma that will allow grief work to progress, unencumbered by contamination with traumatic issues.

Over the course of several group sessions, similarities and differences between suicide loss and previous losses are explored with a threefold purpose: (1) to explore suicide grief as a form of complicated grief process; (2) to explore suicide grief within the framework of traumatic experience, which is accompanied by identifiable processes; and (3) to emphasize the resiliency and power of survivors.

Participants share their thoughts and feelings about the suicide, especially those that distinguish it from other deaths, according to factors that fall into three general categories. The categories are those factors surrounding the event itself, those that signal internal pain and confusion (including existential issues) but are external to the relationship, and, finally, interpersonal, contextual features involving relationships, including issues of choice and preventability, guilt and responsibility, and powerlessness and lack of control. Trauma features such as intrusiveness, hyper-arousal, and numbing are also explored. Symptoms of complicated grief and trauma – from 'normal' to posttraumatic stress reactions – are accepted as normal coping responses. We emphasize that while survivors may have been victimized, they do not remain victims; while they did not have a choice about their victimization, they have many choices about recovering from it. Coping techniques are discussed and honoured, and methods for coping with trauma features are recommended.

Understanding Suicide

Suicide survivors have a great need to understand why the person they loved would choose to leave them. The question of 'Why?' is often amended to 'Why did he do this to me?' Information regarding the prevalence of suicide and suicidal behaviour, the multidimensional and complex nature of suicide, depression and mental illness, and intergenerational aspects of suicide is presented to group members to aid in their struggle for understanding.

Through the creation of a collage that explores the life and world of their deceased loved ones, group members also examine suicide from the perspective of the deceased in an attempt to understand better the many factors in the deceased's life that led to suicide. In addition, this activity creates an opportunity for reality testing with respect to responsibility, culpability, and guilt.

Survivors are encouraged to develop a gentler and more healing theory about the suicide that allows them to see that the suicide was not their fault, without sullying the reputation of the deceased. This exploration also aids in assessing the degree to which survivors identify with the deceased, potential suicidal thoughts or behaviours, and fear of further suicide by self or other loved ones. Finally, it allows for the examination of the existential issues raised by suicide.

3. Remembering and Saying Goodbye: Telling Stories

It is a normal part of bereavement to talk about the deceased and share the story of the death. Indeed, storytelling can be a central healing force in accepting the reality of the death (Horacek, 1995). We construct stories in the wake of events that require interpretation and cognitive-emotional-behavioural connection in order to decrease their potency and gain a sense of control, peace, or resolution with them, in order to heal and recover (Harvey et al., 1992). As stories are told and heard, over and over again, individuals may gain a new perspective that helps to compensate for their sense of loss. One of the goals of therapy is to construct and complete the story – not a memorized script – of the who, what, when, where, and how aspects of the death (Johnson, 1987). Telling the story can also facilitate the development of a realistic picture of the deceased that includes both positive and negative components. It may be the beginning of a personalized review of the history of loss and the relationship with the deceased, a method of addressing its unfinished business, and another step in the process of saying goodbye.

Participants tell their stories as they are ready over time. They bring pictures of, or items that have special meaning in relation to, the deceased, including music, letters, and poetry. Storytelling includes reminiscing about the positive and not-so-positive characteristics of the deceased and the former relationship, and about what happened leading up to, during, and after the suicide. Through the process, leaders are listening for how the story is constructed, what is included or excluded (e.g., saying goodbye, seeing the body), where the tears come or do not come, where the story is most potent. An affective-cognitive balance is sought.

4. Human Responses to Grief and Trauma

This component explores common and problematic grief responses, including anger, guilt, fear, rejection, abandonment, pain, and sadness. The relationship between feelings and the importance of identifying, labelling, and expressing them appropriately is explored. Sessions are designed to promote the capacity of survivors to experience, express, and integrate the painful affects associated with suicide bereavement by connecting thoughts and emotions; participants also learn to utilize the most adaptive means possible of managing the painful affects that accompany their losses.

While feelings associated with grief are explored throughout all sessions, some require more significant, deeper treatment, particularly anger and guilt. The order in which feelings are explored in detail depends on which seem most potent (intense) to the group. Leaders are cautious about focusing on the exploration of anger early on, especially if some participants have experienced post-trauma symptoms (Everstine and Everstine, 1993).

Denial as Defence

The bereaved must achieve a balance between the demands of reality and the safety of mechanisms that mask bereavement. 'The optimal balance occurs where the bereaved are able to feel their pain, loss, anger, and fear sufficiently to begin to integrate their experience, and yet have available to them a repertoire of protective (defensive) mechanisms to prevent them from being overwhelmed' (Schucter and Zisook, 1987: 178). Therapists must honour all mechanisms as primarily adaptive (though perhaps only temporarily), assist in exploring the efficacy of long-term effects, and support the need to continually adapt, choosing new mechanisms that better serve the demands of reality. Clearly, timing and the accessibility of alternatives are important elements.

Denial, the response that seems to be intrinsic to all defence mechanisms, is explored within several metaphorical frameworks. The roles, uses, and values of common defence mechanisms are discussed and explored both generally and personally. Participants then create clay 'masks' that reflect the various faces each participant presents to the outside world of family and community. This activity illustrates how we use masks to protect ourselves from feeling, and at what cost, as well as illustrating the influences of culture in determining appropriate, often limiting, grieving behaviours.

The exploration of defence mechanisms forms the foundation for sessions dealing with specific and difficult feelings. As denial diminishes, intense and hard-to-handle feelings, especially anger and guilt, frequently surface.

Anger

Anger is a common, complex, and multifaceted companion to the bereaved and to victims of trauma. The root of the word 'bereaved' is 'to rob.' It is natural to feel angry after being robbed of a person who has been integral to one's life. The fact that the deceased has also been the thief may increase the anger – and confusion. Anger is a healthy response to a violation of our personhood and an inspiration to change, a legitimate cue to action.

In situations of complicated grief, angry distortions accompanied by some level of inhibition or suppression of grief are common (Rando, 1993; Raphael, 1983). Anger frequently protects us from the pain and shattered beliefs that underlie it. Frequently there are limited opportunities for the constructive expression of anger, and many suicide survivors have not learned to identify or to express anger. One of the most significant blocks to the expression of anger is the difficulty of experiencing both anger and love simultaneously. Our focus is to assist survivors to understand, own, and express anger without blame, opening the door both to love and care for the deceased and, ultimately, the intense pain of loss.

The 'anger' sessions are introduced with a satirical piece of music that illustrates in a humorous way our unhealthy, confusing, and often gender-based cultural attitudes towards expressing feelings – especially anger. Sessions begin with comfortable cognitive explorations and progress to more expressive dimensions and those related more directly to the suicide.

How group members learned about anger, both culturally and within families, is explored within an interactional, systems-based framework. Alternative ways of expressing clear positions of anger through use of words and tone of voice in role-play are discussed and practised. Art work assists in the identification of the physical components of anger and of constructive methods to work it out through exercise and other techniques. Clay work is the chosen medium for expression of angry feelings related to the deceased and the suicide death.

Guilt

Guilt is an almost universal experience for survivors, and a very intense and troublesome experience for many (Barrett and Scott, 1990), especially since suicide is often seen as preventable. When death occurs by suicide, the issues of how responsible any person is for the lives and choices of others and how much real control we exercise over the lives of others are highlighted.

Guilt is a very interpersonal experience and is related, in part, to the importance of human connectedness and our essential care for each other. Most dimensions of guilt after a death, including feelings of culpability, responsibility, regret, control, and survivor guilt are related to the relationship with the deceased (Rando, 1986). We experience guilt because of our imperfections, unrealistic expectations of our power and control, and the ambivalence natural to some degree in all relationships.

While guilt is intertwined with shame, blame, and anger, the sessions focusing on guilt assist participants to identify the insidious nature, and the meaning and purposes, of guilt in their lives. Explorations of guilt also facilitate further reality testing about the survivors' role in the deaths.

Because survivors often have been traumatized, the relationship between guilt and the need to maintain a sense of control in an otherwise chaotic world is examined in an effort to assist survivors to create a balance between responsibility and vulnerability. An exploration of existential issues can be helpful in establishing that balance. If guilt is unrealistic, the mourner must gradually discover an acceptable balance between feeling the pain of loss and needing to feel that life is meaningful and that events are controllable. If guilt is linked to real, not fantasy, behaviours, the mourner's task becomes one of learning to accept and live with that fact.

Our most powerful tool for dealing with guilt is a guided imagery exercise developed specifically for suicide survivors. The imagery exercise has the following objectives: (1) to help survivors identify the nature of their guilt and its origins – self (internal blame) or other (external blame); (2) to reality test for culpability; (3) to recognize other functions of guilt in the grieving process; (4) to recognize the costs of guilt and the 'price' survivors have paid, and what price they feel is still necessary; (5) to help participants reassign responsibility for the suicide to the deceased.

5. Reorganizing Relationships – Family and Community

Family

Suicide bereavement is a very interpersonal event that must be seen within the psychosocial context in which it occurs. Suicide occurs within a network of complicated family relationships. However, although there are serious impediments to family mourning, family relationships can also be strengthened by crises such as suicide bereavement, and there is potential for transformation and actualization as part of the grief experience for families (McNiel et al., 1988; Valente et al., 1988; McGoldrick and Walsh, 1991).

Many of the significant injuries a traumatized person suffers are systemic, and result in alteration of, or damage to, the victim's family and social systems. Therapy must involve the key external systems with which individuals interact, including family and social systems. We live, die, grieve, and survive within a family context in which intergenerational bonds to both past and future need to be recognized and honoured. Since grief at heart is a family process, injuries to its members are best healed within the family. Not only do individual identities change, but the collective identity of the family also changes. Families must mourn not only for a lost member, but also for the family as it was.

We incorporate into our group framework two major family tasks intended to promote immediate and long-term adaptation for family members and to strengthen the family as a healthy functioning unit (Walsh and McGoldrick, 1991). The first is the shared acknowledgment of the reality of the death and the shared experience of loss. Open, dynamic communication is a key factor promoting family understanding and support. Often 'it is not the death itself, but avoidance of the experience through mystification and myth, that becomes problematic' (Walsh and McGoldrick, 1991: 52). However, we must also understand that when a death occurs within the family, there are powerful competing demands for family members to adapt to each other's attempts to re-establish emotional control and to maintain the stability of daily life while personal as well as family identities are reconstructed. Sharing one's grief and feeling understood minimizes isolation and facilitates recovery; still, 'open emotional exploration and integration of a death and its many implications for every aspect of life is, paradoxically, a necessary developmental luxury' (Shapiro, 1994: 15) that can only occur when there is sufficient access to resources to re-establish and maintain stable family functioning.

The second task involves reorganization of the family system and reinvestment in other relationships and pursuits. Death in a family necessitates major role changes and realignments, both internally and externally, within the community. The objectives for this component involve supporting group members to understand and carry out these tasks. An important first step is understanding individual responses to grief through the lenses of family history, family patterns of communication and interaction, and the impact of current and past losses on family members.

The intergenerational legacy of loss is of particular interest to suicide survivors since there is evidence to suggest that they are at greater risk for suicide than 'normal' grievers (Silverman et al., 1994–5). When death occurs in the context of family conflict, or is stigmatized and surrounded by secrecy, the power of the legacy of death is intensified. If families are unable to mourn and to share acknowledgment of the loss, recovery from loss is impaired and the legacy of death continues.

Genograms can be an effective tool in multigenerational exploration. Art techniques are also utilized to facilitate the process of understanding grief within the family – what is changeable and how it can be changed, both symbolically and in reality. Other important activities associated with how families mourn the loss of a loved one and move forward include the development of new family rituals and making necessary changes in old ones.

Holidays and anniversaries, special events, other deaths, and threatening events may stimulate memories of the one who died and may cause a temporary, short-lived experience of intense grief symptoms, a sort of grief tailspin for family members. Coping with these occasions may involve discussion of old family rituals, precipitating an open sharing of family stories about the deceased loved one and his relationships, and facilitating the mourning process.

Building Bridges
Death shatters a dependable social world and social relationships must be transformed in being rewoven into the web as the bereaved adjust to a social environment in which the loved one is missing. An exploration of how social relationships have been changed by the suicide and the role the survivor may have played in the changed relationships is the first step.

Diverse sources and forms of social support are not only beneficial but essential to the bereavement process. Suicide death often precipitates a longer, more difficult bereavement process that significantly influences, and is influenced by, reactions and relationships with others (Van Dongen, 1993). It is frequently characterized by a lack of social support, rejection, and stigma (Thompson and Range, 1992–3), greater feelings of blame and responsibility (McNiel et al., 1988), and a lack of cultural norms governing social reactions and internal stigma (Dunn and Morrish-Vidners, 1987–8; Gray, 1988). Social support appears to be a multidimensional construct, characterized by a dynamic process between survivors and support system, mediated by taboo, stigma, and conditions of normlessness for survivors and supporters alike.

Though social support is a crucial mitigating factor in the process of mourning, often those who are closest are not aware of the survivor's need for support, or cannot provide it. Indeed, survivors may not recognize or accept support when it is proffered, further jeopardizing social interaction and support. It is not uncommon for misunderstandings and miscommunication to result in damaged relationships, and even the best friendship can be severely tested by a suicide death. A lack of clear norms and expectations regarding appropriate and supportive behaviour frequently puts the onus for clear communication and proactive response on those whose abilities to act are the most severely compromised – the survivors.

Within group sessions, goals for exploring social relationships include (1) identification and exploration of inner resources/external supports and how they have helped participants to cope; (2) exploration of barriers to gaining and giving support and how to overcome them; and (3) solidification of new relationships and supports. Guided imagery or clay work allow for symbolic 'bridge building' to portray damaged, repaired, or new relationships.

Conclusions: Renewal and Transformation

Renewal can be seen as the integration of our old and new selves, a blending of what remains consistent in our identities throughout bereavement and who we have become in the changed, new world. It begins the moment we accept, even in a small way, that our loved one will never be part of our lives in the same way as before. Renewal involves saying goodbye to the old way of life and fashioning a new relationship with the one who has died, recognizing that remembering and sadness may accompany us for many years.

Renewal is also a process of evaluating progress in meeting our goals and determining new ones, and of celebrating achievements while continuing to build on the sense of hope and future so important to healing. As the end of the group approaches, ideas about renewal are incorporated into a discussion of the new spider's web and how each survivor has changed in the past months. Survivors consider what growth has resulted, or might result, from the bereavement experience, and what it would be like to 'complete' the major work of grieving. Envisioning their most optimistic views of the future and how they can make their visions a reality completes the process.

In the final sessions, significant time is spent in preparing survivors for the ending of the group, validating the ability of each one to manage the tasks that yet lie ahead. The transformation intrinsic to the development of a new identity or spider's web has been accomplished each time those who have entered our group as 'victims' emerge as survivors and warriors.

Working with suicide survivors is without a doubt the most intense, stimulating, and satisfying experience in our professional and personal lives. While the work constantly challenges us and highlights our own vulnerabilities, witnessing the growth and transformation of survivors as they reweave themselves and their families is a powerful and dynamic experience that also changes us. The potential of the human psyche to heal and restore itself through its essential connectedness with other human beings, including ourselves, continues to be both a humbling and an awe-inspiring experience.

REFERENCES

Andress, V.R., and D.M. Corey. 1978. 'Survivor-Victims: Who Discovers or Witnesses Suicide?'
    Psychological Reports 42: 759–64.
Appel, Y.H., and A. Wrobleski. 1987. 'Self-Help and Support Groups: Mutual Aid for Survivors.'

In E.J. Dunne, J.M. McIntosh, and K. Dunne-Maxim, eds, *Suicide and Its Aftermath*, 215–33. New York: W.W. Norton.

Attig, Thomas. 1982. 'Grief and Personal Integrity.' In R.A. Pacholski and Charles Corr, eds, *Priorities in Death Education and Counselling*, 61–70. Arlington, VA: Forum for Death Education and Counselling.

Barrett, T.W., and T.B. Scott. 1990. 'Suicide Bereavement and Recovery Patterns Compared with Non-Suicide Bereavement Patterns.' *Suicide and Life-Threatening Behavior* 20(1): 1–15.

Borman, M.A., and L.D. Lieberman. 1979. *Self-Help Groups for Coping with Crisis*. San Francisco: Jossey-Bass.

Brent, D.A., J. Perper, G. Moritz, C. Allman, A. Friend, J. Schweers, C. Roth, L. Balach, and K. Harrington. 1992. 'Psychiatric Effects of Exposure to Suicide among Friends and Acquaintances of Adolescent Suicide Victims.' *Journal of the American Academy of Child and Adolescent Psychiatry* 31: 629–40.

Cain, A.C., ed. 1972. *Survivors of Suicide*. Springfield, IL: Charles C. Thomas.

Cleiren, M., R. Diekstra, A. Kerkof, and J. van der Wal. 1994. 'Mode of Death and Kinship in Bereavement: Focusing on "Who" Rather Than "How."' *Crisis* 15(1): 22–35.

Cook, A., and D. Dworkin. 1992. *Helping the Bereaved*. New York: Basic Books.

Dunn, R.G., and D. Morrish-Vidners. 1987–8. 'The Psychological and Social Experience of Suicide Survivors.' *Omega* 18(3): 175–215.

Dunne, E.J. 1987. 'Special Needs of Survivors in Therapy.' In E.J. Dunne, J.M. McIntosh, and K. Dunne-Maxim, eds, *Suicide and Its Aftermath*, 193–207. New York: W.W. Norton.

Dunne, E.J., J.L. McIntosh, and K. Dunne-Maxim, eds. 1987. *Suicide and Its Aftermath*. New York: W.W. Norton.

Eth, S., and R.L. Pynoos. 1985. *Post-Traumatic Stress Disorder in Children*. Washington: American Psychiatric Press.

Everstine, D.S., and L. Everstine. 1993. *The Trauma Response*. New York: W.W. Norton.

Figley, C.R. 1986b. 'Traumatic Stress: The Role of the Family and Social Support System.' In Figley, ed., *Trauma and Its Wake. Vol. II*, 39–53.

Figley, C.R., ed. 1986a. *Trauma and Its Wake. Vol. II: Traumatic Stress Theory, Research and Intervention*. New York: Brunner/Mazel.

Gray, R.E. 1988. 'Meaning of Death: Implications for Bereavement Theory. *Death Studies* 12: 309–17.

Harvey, J.H., T.L. Orbach, A.L. Weber, N. Merach, and R. Alt. 1992. 'House of Pain and Hope: Accounts of Loss.' *Death Studies* 16: 99–124.

Henley, S.H. 1984. 'Bereavement Following Suicide: A Review of the Literature.' *Current Psychological Research and Reviews* (Summer): 53–61.

Hopmeyer, E., and A. Werk. 1994. 'A Comparative Study of Family Bereavement Groups.' *Death Studies* 18: 243–56.

Horacek, B.J. 1995. 'A Heuristic Model of Grieving after High Grief Deaths.' *Death Studies* 19(1): 21–32.

Horowitz, M.J. 1986. *Stress Response Syndromes*. 2nd ed. Northvale, NJ: Jason Aronson.

Imber-Black, E. 1991. 'Rituals and the Healing Process.' In F. Walsh and M. McGoldrick, eds, *Living Beyond Loss*, 206–23. New York: W.W. Norton.

Johnson, S.E. 1987. *After a Child Dies: Counselling Bereaved Families*. New York: Springer Publishing.

Klass, Dennis. 1988. *Parental Grief: Solace and Resolution*. New York: Springer Publishing.

Leenaars, A., and S. Wenckstern. 1991b. 'Post-Traumatic Stress Disorder: A Conceptual Model for Postvention.' In Leenaars and Wenckstern, eds, *Suicide Prevention in Schools*, 173–9.

Leenaars, A., and S. Wenckstern, eds. 1991a. *Suicide Prevention in Schools*. New York: Hemisphere Publishing Corp.

Lifton, R.J. 1979. *The Broken Connection*. New York: Simon & Schuster.

McGoldrick, M., and F. Walsh. 1991. 'A Time to Mourn: Death and the Family Life Cycle.' In F. Walsh and M. McGoldrick, eds, *Living Beyond Loss*, 1–29. New York: W.W. Norton.

McIntosh, J.L. 1993. 'Studies of Suicide Survivors.' *Suicide and Life-Threatening Behavior* 23(2): 146–61.

McNeil, D.E., C. Hatcher, and R. Reubin. 1988. 'Family Survivors of Suicide and Accidental Death: Consequences for Widows.' *Suicide and Life-Threatening Behavior* 18(2): 137–48.

Matsakis, A. 1994. *Post-Traumatic Stress Disorder: A Complete Treatment Guide*. Oakland, CA: New Harbinger Publications.

Nerkin, I.R. 1993. 'Grief and the Reflective Self: Toward a Clearer Model of Loss Resolution and Growth.' *Death Studies* 17: 1–26.

Nichols, K., and Jenkinson. 1991. *Leading a Support Group*. New York: Chapman and Hall.

Parkes, C.M. 1980. 'Bereavement Counselling: Does It Work?' *British Medical Journal* 281: 3–6.

Pynoos, R.S., and S. Eth. 1985. 'Children Traumatized by Witnessing Acts of Personal Homicide, Rape, or Suicide Behavior.' In S. Eth and R.S. Pynoos, eds, *Post-Traumatic Stress Disorder in Children*. Washington: American Psychiatric Press.

Rando, Therese. 1993. *Treatment of Complicating Mourning*. Champaign, IL: Research Press.

– ed. 1986. *Parental Loss of a Child*. Champaign, IL: Research Press.

Raphael, B. 1977. 'Preventive Intervention with the Recently Bereaved.' *Archives of General Psychiatry* 34: 1450–4.

– 1983. *The Anatomy of Bereavement*. New York: Basic Books.

Reed, M.D. 1993. 'Sudden Death and Bereavement Outcomes: The Impact of Resources on Grief Symptomatology and Detachment.' *Suicide and Life-Threatening Behavior* 23(3): 204–18.

Reed, M.D., and J.Y. Greenwald. 1991. 'Survivor-Victim Status, Attachment and Sudden Death Bereavement.' *Suicide and Life-Threatening Behavior* 21(4): 385–401.

Rudestam, K.E. 1992. 'Research Contributions to Understanding the Suicide Survivor.' *Crisis* 13(1): 41–5.

Rynearson, K.E. 1981. 'Suicide Internalized: An Existential Sequestrum.' *American Journal of Psychiatry* 138(1): 84–6.

– 1986. 'Psychological Effects of Unnatural Dying on Bereavement.' *Psychiatric Annals* 16(5): 172–5.

– 1987. 'Psychological Adjustment to Unnatural Dying.' In S. Zisook, ed., *Biopsychosocial Aspects of Bereavement*, 75–94. Washington: American Psychiatric Press.

Schwartz-Borden, G. 1992. 'Metaphor – Visual Aid Grief Work.' *Omega* 25(3): 239–48.

Scurfield, R.W. 1986. 'Post-Trauma Stress Assessment and Treatment: Overview and Formulations.' In C.F. Figley, ed., *Trauma and Its Wake: The Study and Treatment of Post-Traumatic Stress Disorder*, 219–51. New York: Brunner/Mazel.

Shapiro, E.R. 1994. 'Grief as a Family Process.' New York: Guilford Press.

Schucter, S.R., and S. Zisook. 1987. 'The Therapeutic Tasks of Grief.' In S. Zisook, ed., *Biopsychosocial Aspects of Bereavement*. Washington: American Psychiatric Press.

Silverman, E., L. Range, and J. Overholser. 1994–5. 'Bereavement from Suicide as Compared to Other Forms of Bereavement.' *Omega* 30(1): 41–52.

Solomon, S.D. 1986. 'Mobilizing Social Support Networks in Times of Disaster.' In C.R. Figley, ed., *Trauma and Its Wake. Vol. II*, 232–58. New York: Brunner/Mazel.

Thompson, K.E., and L.M. Range. 1992–3. 'Bereavement Following Suicide and Other Deaths: Why Support Attempts Fail.' *Omega* 26(1): 61–70.

Valente, S.M., J. Saunders, and R. Street. 1988. 'Adolescent Bereavement Following Suicide: An Examination of the Relevant Literature.' *Journal of Counselling and Development* 67: 174–7.

van der Kolk, B.A. 1987. 'The Role of the Group in the Origin and Resolution of the Trauma Response.' In B.A. van der Kolk, ed., *Psychological Trauma*. Washington: American Psychiatric Press.

van der Wal, Jan. 1989–90. 'The Aftermath of Suicide: A Review of Empirical Evidence.' *Omega* 20(2): 149–71.

Van Dongen, C.J. 1993. 'Social Context of Postsuicide Bereavement.' *Death Studies* 17: 125–41.

Walsh, F., and M. McGoldrick. 1991. 'Loss and the Family: A Systemic Perspective.' In Walsh and McGoldrick, eds, *Living Beyond*, 1–29.

Walsh, F., and M. McGoldrick. 1991. *Living Beyond Loss*. New York: W.W. Norton.

Winch, G., and K. Letofsky. 1981. 'The Nature of Suicidal Death as a Factor in Understanding the Reactions of Surviving Members.' In J.P. Soubrier and J. Vendrinne, eds, *Depression and Suicide: Aspects médicaux, psychologiques et socio-culturels*, 523–32. Proceedings of the 11th Congress of the International Association for Suicide Prevention, Paris, 5–8 July. New York: Pergamon Press.

Worden, J.W. 1982. *Grief Counselling and Grief Therapy*. London: Tavistock.

Yalom, I.D. 1975. *The Theory and Practice of Group Psychotherapy*. 2nd ed. New York: Basic Books.

Zisook, S. 1987. 'Unresolved Grief.' In S. Zisook, ed., *Biopsychosocial Aspects of Bereavement*, 21–34. Washington: American Psychiatric Press.

25

Women as Survivors of Suicide: An Experience of Integration*

LOIS SAPSFORD

We are endeavouring to knock out of us all the pre-conceived ideas, emptying ourselves of everything except that nature is here in all its greatness, and we are here to gather it and understand it if only we will be clean enough, and humble enough to go to it willing to be taught and to receive it not as we think it should be, but as it is, and then to put down vigorously and truthfully that which we culled.

F.H. Varley, 1914 (McMichael Gallery)

F.H. Varley spoke these words in 1914 as he described the Group of Seven, and the task they had taken on as like-minded artists in the early 1900s in Ontario, Canada. This task was to paint nature in a clean and pure way, putting aside their British-taught techniques. The challenge was met and the interpretations of these artists are captured forever in a permanent display at the McMichael Gallery in Kleinburg, Ontario. I suggest that it is the same process of knocking out all the preconceived ideas that researchers should seek as they enter into subject-directed qualitative research. It is essential to this process to be humble enough to go to the subject willing to be taught and to receive it not as we think it should be, but as it is.

It is with this humbleness that my research into women's experience of grief after suicide was initiated. Working as a suicide-bereavement counsellor, I found myself challenged by the traumatic stories of the women who attempted

---

*This chapter is dedicated to my co-researchers: Anna, Betty, Connie, and Debbie. Their courage in sharing their stories, their tears, and their wisdom with me creates the essence of this research.

to unravel their confusion in the safety of my office. The greatest challenge was the incongruence between the clients' experience and needs and the grief theory that served as my clinical guide and framework (Glick et al., 1974; Henslin, 1972; McIntosh and Kelly, 1988; Rando, 1984; Shepherd and Barraglough, 1974; Sheskin and Wallace, 1976; Shneidman, 1985; Silverman, 1972; Stroebe, 1983; Whitis, 1968; Wrobleski and McIntosh, 1987; and Zisook and Lyons, 1990).

Clients provided feedback about the written literature I had given them, indicating that it was somewhat helpful ... *but* ... it did not fit their experience. In fact, it often angered them, eliciting accusations that 'They obviously don't understand me.'

Theories of grief posit a three- to six-stage process, beginning with the 'acceptance of the death' and ending with a final stage of 'resolution,' described as a withdrawal of energy from the dead to reinvest it in the living (Worden, 1982), acceptance (Kubler-Ross, 1969), reorganization (Bowlby, 1980) and resolution of grief (Rando, 1988). Without exception, the suicide-bereavement literature approaches the phenomenon of grief based on these 'resolution as goal' models (Barrett, 1989; Hewett, 1980).

The paucity of research and literature regarding the process and outcome of grief beyond the first year was recognized at the 1989 American Association of Suicidology annual meeting. Panel members Dunne, Pfeffer, Farberow, and Rudestam concluded that 'the impact of loss upon all family members; the process and outcome of bereavement beyond the first year; and the impact on the family system required extensive future study' (AAS 1989: 9).

With support and encouragement from my clients, I returned to graduate school to ask the questions they posited it to me: What is the long-term experience of women's grief after the suicide death of a family member? How can such information help me prepare for and understand what lies ahead for me? How can the information gained assist therapists in helping others with their questions centred around the long-term process of grieving?

Method

This study examines the long-term process of grieving in women who have experienced the suicide death of a family member. I chose a qualitative-research design based on the grounded-theory methodology developed by Glaser and Strauss (1967) and Glaser (1978).

Meanings and processes are therefore the subject of inquiry, rather than the prevalence or comparison of particular problems, issues, or responses (Demi, 1978, 1984; and Demi and Miles, 1988).

And so, like the Group of Seven, I was now attempting to knock out of myself all my preconceived ideas (about women and grief after suicide) and to be humble enough to be taught how grief after suicide actually is. Within the boundaries of grounded-theory methodology, my task was to learn from women who had experienced a suicide and to develop a theoretical understanding of their grieving based solely on their accounts. This meant leaving the grief theories on the side as I listened to and questioned their stories.

The focus of my study was on women's experience of grief after the suicide of a male family member. The sample was based on four women from both a clinical and non-clinical sample. The time elapsed since the suicide ranged from three to seventeen years. The purpose of the study was to develop a theoretical understanding of the process of the long-term grief experience in women surviving a family member's suicide.

Feminist research argues for the importance of understanding women's psychological development based on women's life experience rather than as that development has been perceived by external observers (Miller, 1986). This methodology is in keeping with feminist research theory on the perception of meaning. The discovery of knowledge discovered in the course of feminist research is understood as the process of bringing forth certain phenomena rather than the search for the discovery of a single truth.

Data was collected using an unstructured, intensive, in-depth, and qualitative interview that seeks to obtain the information in the respondent's own words (Chenitz and Swanson, 1986). '[T]hose who begin their enquiries with facts will never arrive at essences. The "fact gathering" psychology ... produces a fragmented perception of reality precisely because the aim is to gather isolated data from isolated parts of the organism ... [S]uch facts, documented and "verified" will never be more than facts among other facts, facts closed in on themselves, not permitting a grasp of the totality of the human gestalt' (Suransky 1982: 37).

The constant comparative method of analysis as developed by Glaser and Strauss (1967) was used to analyse the data collected. Following this method, data collection and analysis occur simultaneously, resulting in the generation of theory based on the data in which that theory is grounded. Theoretical sampling continued until the core categories were saturated. That is, 'no new data and no additions are added to the category and one overriding core category can explain the relationship between all of the others' (Chenitz and Swanson, 1986: 8). This method guides the sample size in each study.

Qualitative research must be measured in terms of responsibility and credibility. Responsibility indicates that the researcher must be trustworthy enough to represent the participant's experience. Each piece of emerging theory was returned to the participants for confirmation of the research findings. This was done in a group format, thus confirming the accuracy of my interpretations. One woman in this study cried as she read the first draft of the developing model, exclaiming how good it was to read an accurate account of her experience and to have hers confirmed by reading other voices describing the same process she had lived.

Credibility in qualitative research answers the question, 'If I apply this theory to a similar situation, will it work, that is allow me to interpret, understand, and predict phenomena?' (Chenitz and Swanson, 1986: 13). The procedures of the method of grounded theory can be repeated with reliable accuracy; the methodology is, therefore, reliable and credible.

The Women

Anna

Anna is a thirty-year-old professional woman, raised in a small Canadian prairie town in a family of five. Anna relates that she was close to both her siblings as children; however, she was particularly close to 'Ned,' her now deceased brother. In describing their relationship she stated: 'We were always very close. We were – we just liked one another's personalities – a real connection between the two of us.'

Anna remembered experiencing a 'sixth sense as to something being wrong' on the day her brother committed suicide, although she had no reason to suspect anything had changed. She found herself avoiding answering her phone at work during that day. She stalled going home after work, certain that the telephone was going to deliver a sad message. 'I found myself becoming just more and more saddened, ... and defensive and wanting to protect myself and my time. Finally the news came (he killed himself) ... and – God what was it like – it was horrible!'

Betty

Betty, age forty-two, described an estranged relationship with her parents. The lack of stability and consistent caring by her parents was the main reason she and her brother developed a strong relationship. 'It was Bob and I against the world.'

Betty moved to Europe with her husband after their marriage. She clearly remembers receiving word of her brother's suicide a year later: 'I guess we'd been in Europe about a year and I got really sick one day. I was just laying in the bed, it was really dark, and I just wanted the curtains closed. It must have been a couple of days I was like that until finally, my husband, came home with the padre and said ... [pause] ... your brother's dead. It had happened three days prior, and my parents had already cremated him, and he was gone.'

Betty tried escaping from her feelings. She became dependent on both prescription and street drugs to help her numb her feelings. For fifteen years after her brother's suicide she describes herself as 'absolutely blocking it [the suicide]. I just wouldn't allow it in.' A year later, Betty 'allowed' herself to face her grief. While searching for information about his death, she recalls being told by professionals that after sixteen years her grief should not be as important or as real: 'And I remember being really – I was so angry at them. I thought – it's got nothing to do with whether it's been 16 years ago. It wasn't 16 years ago – that's just the date. It actually happened last month, you know. And that's what was happening. That's exactly – it did happen last month! ... I had nightmares – crying and crying.'

Connie

Connie, age thirty-six, introduced herself through a description of her family: 'I have one brother left, but we're not even close ... and I'm not my Dad's little baby anymore because he's not there and I'm not – never was my Mom's little baby ... She's my little baby, sort of. So I feel old that way.'

Connie's brother Mike committed suicide a couple of years after he had been diagnosed with diabetes. He had become very depressed and underwent a 'whole personality change.' Connie describes her relationship with Mike as 'my closest family connection.' Connie was informed of her brother Mike's suicide by her father: ' And then I got a phone call from my father one day that Mike had shot himself in the middle of the night and it was – I guess – shock, you know, for the whole two weeks.'

Connie recalled a conversation with her brother David just before his suicide, seven years after Mike's suicide: 'We'd been talking about Mike committing suicide and David was saying that he was going to commit suicide and I remember saying to him one night just before he left – you know, he said to me, nobody has any right to tell anybody else that they have to live and I said yes, I realise that but God, you know, if you do this too – like, I've lost Mike and ... it was just like – Oh God, No, like that couldn't happen twice, but it did.'

Connie remembered her initial reaction after hearing about David's death: 'It made me think of it more ... for awhile there I thought that maybe I had to, too, for some reason.'

Debbie

Debbie, a thirty-nine-year-old widow of three years and mother of two pre-teen daughters, related how she wanted to share her experience of her husband's suicide to help others deal with the pain of grief.

Debbie discussed the changes over time in her marriage from mutual caring to her assuming a caretaking role for her husband and children. Her husband had been hospitalized three times for severe depression. 'I felt more like his mother, I didn't feel like a wife anymore.'

Debbie told of an incident that occurred the night before her husband's suicide: 'Gary asked me to read to him, I just thought he really needs a mother right now, so we sat on the couch and he had his head on my lap and I read to him ... That night Gary was up all night pacing and smoking.' He ended his life the next day right after Debbie had left the house to call the physician because of her growing concern for his physical and mental well-being. Debbie returned to their home to discover his body: 'I called his name and looked in the kitchen and bedroom and then I went downstairs. He was laying down on the floor and I thought his head was smashed in, I thought he smashed his head in with something ... [cries] ... and his eye was gone, you could see the brains ... [cries] ... there was no blood ... I ran outside and screamed for help! ... [cries] ... How can I tell my kids that their Dad is gone?'

It is important that these experiences be included in the research at this time, as they remind the reader of the horror and trauma from which this grief-experience takes its beginnings. Horror is a fact of suicide-grief that cannot be overlooked.

Grief Integration: A Theoretical Model

The theory of grief integration is based on the stories narrated by the four women described above. The basic social-psychological process accounted by this model is the experience of *grief integration*. Rather than seeing grief as leading to a finite 'resolution,' this model assumes grief after suicide to be a life-long process. The language of resolution is foreign to this experience. The model also implies that the stages of grief are experienced in a non-linear fashion; each stage within a cycle can be repeated, bringing the woman to a new level of integration. Instead of viewing grief with a finite goal of 'resolution' and 'emotional withdrawal,' the women within this study describe grief as 'maintaining and re-creating the relationship' with the deceased. According to the research participants, it is the emphasis on connection that allows for an integration of the grief. Grief as an integrative process requires a change in the relationship, not an emotional withdrawal from the relationship.

Summary of Model Characteristics

PHASE I – GRIEF SUPPRESSION
- Characteristics:
  - Caretaking
  - Replacement
  - Running/escaping
- Critical condition – Safety to grieve: Safety is a necessary precondition to movement into Phase II.

PHASE II – GRIEF EMERGENCE

Stage 1: Meaning Making
- Focus: Outward / Suicide-related
- Characteristics:
  - Searching
  - Need for information
  - Spiritual questioning
  - Social stigma

Stage 2: Intense Grief
- Focus: Inward / Suicide-related
- Characteristics:
  - Guilt
  - Anger
  - Sadness
  - Fear
  - Shame
  - Unpredictability
  - Preoccupation with deceased
  - Physical health problems

Stage 3: Implications of Self
- Focus: Inward / Self-related
- Characteristics:
  - Abandonment
  - Identity loss

- Connectedness
- Dreams
- Presence felt
- Family re-constellation
- Social expectations

Stage 4: Action in Relation
- Focus: Outward / Self-in-relation related
- Characteristics:
  - Completing picture of the deceased
  - Re-creating existing relationships
  - Authenticity
  - Self-empathy
  - Permission

PHASE III – GRIEF INTEGRATION
- Characteristics:
  - Grief residing with the survivor
  - Altered quality/frequency/duration of grief
  - Re-creation of relationship with deceased
  - Rituals of connection
  - Dreams as connection
  - Replacing the suicide as most important memory

Phase I – Grief Suppression

The grief-suppression phase involved all the participants suppressing their grief at the time of the news of the suicide. Some of the women discussed how their priority function as family caretaker moved them into 'pushing aside' their grief to facilitate the caring for others' pain. Other women described denying the importance of the death by replacing the deceased with another person and attempting to become a new person in a new relationship. Avoidance of grief was achieved by some women through alcohol, drugs, or multiple moves.

Passage out of this phase came when it was safe to grieve. A critical condition of this safety was defined by the research participants as a sense of control over their life or some sense of confidence in one's own and others' survival. This safety was often found in the family system. If the family support system was absent, the women needed to be part of a supportive social network before moving on into the emergence phase.

Phase II – Grief Emergence

The emergence phase involved four interrelated and mutually inclusive stages.

Stage 1: Meaning Making
The focus of this stage was predominantly on the act of the suicide itself. This was a very active stage, with the survivor focusing on following up leads and clues, reading, and general information-seeking that would help her understand or 'make sense' of the fact that someone very close to her had taken his own life.

Stage 2: Intense Grief
During this stage the survivors remained focused on the act of the suicide, as in Stage 1. This stage is different, in that the survivor examines her own emotional response, allowing her to experience the internal pain of grief. For most women, this stage was characterized by feelings of guilt, anger, sadness, fear, shame, unpredictability, idolization of and preoccupation with the deceased, and physical-health problems. It is within this stage that all the survivors reported being at the highest risk of suicide.

Stage 3: Implications of Self
The internal emotional experience is maintained at this stage of the grief experience; however, the focus now shifted from the suicide to the self and to the implications of the suicide on the survivor.

A feeling of abandonment and loss of identity in the absence of the deceased was described by many women. The survivor began to focus on the relationship with the deceased and became aware of the deep sense of connectedness that she experienced in that relationship. There was often a fear of identity loss, as the woman identified her 'self' within the relationship. Each woman became at a loss as to which qualities of herself she would be able to maintain without this relationship, and which (if any) she must lose with the death of the individual. This became a questioning and frightening stage in the survivors' experience. At this stage many survivors acknowledged having thought about killing themselves as they struggled with their identity, their grief experience, and the often contrasting message presented by their social world.

For example, Betty described an overwhelming feeling of loss-of-self as she struggled with the loss of this key relationship: 'I think what happened was – I really had become invisible. I really didn't know who I was because [my brother] was – he was who I could check out who I was with. He made my identity. It was him I relied on. When he was gone, there was nobody – there was nobody there!'

The attitudes of family, friends, clinicians, and society at large were similarly described by all the survivors. All survivors experienced being pushed to 'let go of him,' 'get on with your life,' 'put it behind you,' 'finish your grieving and get on with it.' The women responded to these pressures by cutting themselves off from these relationships. ' It pisses me off. Damn right. What do you mean, let him go – shit. I can't let him go – he's my brother!'

Connie described her struggle through this period of examining her identity and relationships as one not only of being cut off from social supports owing to their 'false expectations' for her grief, but also, as she turned to the clinical literature for support, of being met with the same 'lack of really understanding' her experience ... 'Something is wrong with you. You go through all these steps in this order and – like that grief book makes me sick. The one that tells you what – how you're going to be feeling like this for a month and then you're going to be mad for a month and then you're going to be blah, blah for a month, and then it's going to be over.'

During this period of grief many survivors described a feeling of wanting others to hear how important it was for them to remember and maintain the relationship or connection with the deceased.

Survivors are able to move fully into the next stage of this process (again the overlap inherent within these stages must be stressed) at a time when they are able to accept that they do not need to give up qualities of their selves that were developed in relationship. Their task becomes one of accepting these relational qualities as part of their identity and striving to maintain a connection with the deceased in a new way.

Stage 4: Action in Relation
During the fourth stage of the Emergence phase, survivors typically turned outward and became very active as part of the grief process. The women experienced a self-in-relation focus during this stage.

Survivors at this stage became active in 'completing the picture of the deceased.' It was important for the survivor to be able to expand her knowledge as to who the deceased was outside of their relationship. Completing the picture of the deceased allowed the survivor to begin to establish a qualitatively different relationship with the deceased, to see him in a 'different light.'

The women at this stage began re-creating their existing relationships. Each of the survivors experienced an authenticity and new honesty about themselves and the relationships they chose to maintain or create at this time.

Another common experience of survivors was that of giving themselves permission for the sadness of grief to be a continuing part of their grief, a permission towards self-empathy. Anna described her sadness and pain in these very eloquent words: 'I can't say, like it's a constant state, it's more what I go through at points in time. The missing [him] is probably stronger with the passage of time, rather than reducing. But the missing him doesn't have to be the despairing kind of longing for him to be back like it was at the outset. The missing him now – what accompanies that is the understanding, more understanding of the illness, more understanding of why he made the choice to kill himself and – what he had to offer when he was here.'

During this stage, the women continued to experience social pressure to 'let go.' Their acceptance of their periods of sadness and the continued discussion of the deceased's influence in their lives were viewed by others as pathological. All women found ways to counteract this message. Some found the validation they sought within their new, stronger sense of identity. All recognized their need to listen first to their own experience. Betty describes her desire to be connected with other suicide survivors at this point as a way of adding more strength to her experience. Connie and Debbie both became involved in survivor support groups at this point in their grief.

Phase III – Grief Integration

Integration is seen as a continually evolving state within the surviving woman's life. The key characteristic of this phase is the recognition that grief resides with the survivor on an ongoing basis. Grief was not seen by the survivors as a finite experience, but rather as a developmental process that grief becomes a part of their lived experience. Connie described her thoughts about grief in the following manner: 'I guess mine [grief] is sort of like with me and travelling with me. I guess maybe more in my mind. And just – it's always there and it's coming in and out, in and out, and it will always be there. Sort of like – how would you describe it – *like a circle around you.* A circle that everything is in that circle and it's in your mind, and sometimes it's not, and sometimes it's, like, farther outside of you – sometimes it's closer ... like things sort of cling to you. Like little, maybe atoms, whipping around you.'

Connie's description of her grief 'travelling with' her can be interpreted as an indication that an integration process has taken place. She experiences a continued connection with her deceased brothers: 'It's like it [grief] is a part of me. Everything is connected to me, everything that's ever happened is I guess.' Similarly, Anna discussed her grief as 'residing with' her: 'What's different is I don't feel the sense of horror. It doesn't feel so raw. You know, because I've lived with that for three years, almost three years, so it lives with me, resides with me easier.' A common need throughout this phase for these women was that their experience be respected by others.

All the women in the study reported some continuing concerns about developing new trusting relationships with men. This issue is prominent for women who have experienced a close male family member commit suicide. The issue of trust becomes one of trusting other men in relationships and also a continuing one of self-trust.

Discussion

According to Worden (1982), grieving ultimately requires an 'emotional withdrawal from the deceased person so that this emotional energy can be reinvested in another relationship' (15). This notion of withdrawal, however, does not fit the experiences of the survivors interviewed in this research. Grief was described by them as a life-long process. Many identified the term 'resolution' as inadequate to account for their experience. In Anna's words: 'To resolve [to me] means that something is terminated ... and I think about him every single day, and every day in some way. And so that letting go. I'm not going to let go of the image.' Rather than seeing grief as involving an emotional withdrawal, the women in this study talked about 'maintaining and re-creating the relationship' with the deceased. This difference in terminology is not just a minor nuance in language. Rather, it refers to a different experience in the griever, with unique social and clinical implications.

Without exception, the suicide-bereavement literature approaches the phenomenon of bereavement based on a model of resolution. The most recent comprehensive work in the area of suicide bereavement is Barrett's (1989) *Life after Suicide: The Survivor's Grief Experience*. He defines the grief process as involving a dual process of separation and reconstruction:

Separation: ... Initially, then the function of grief is to help the survivor detach emotionally from the deceased. If detachment does not occur, the survivor will cling both emotionally and psychologically to the deceased.

Recovery: ... the specific purpose of the reconstruction process is to redirect the survivor's emotional investment away from the decedent and toward new relationships. (p. 19)

Barrett's model of the process of grief differs from the model presented here. The widest discrepancy is in Barrett's hypothesis indicating that 'only after emotional detachment from the decedent is accomplished can the task of recovery from grief be earnestly pursued' (106). Thus, the hypotheses of recovery versus integration and of emotional detachment versus redefining the relationship are the key areas of difference within Barrett's (1989) work and this study.

In a review of empirical evidence on suicide bereavement, van der Wal (1990) presents a framework of tasks through which she attempts to examine the literature. The framework includes the language of 'detachment of the deceased,' as well as that of integration.' Van der Wal defines her 'concept of integration as referring to the end of the grief process' (158). In reviewing the empirical evidence to date, in terms of integration, she concludes: 'The studies discussed here do not give clear indications regarding the degree of integration ... The lack of long-term research automatically results in a lack of information with regard to integration of the loss' (158). The present study adds support to van der Wal's comment of her understanding of integration: 'It has been said that death only ends a life; it does not end a relationship' (158). In a recent study, Stroebe et al. (1992), looked at cultural norms of grief and recognized that 'contemporary orientations emphasise the importance of breaking bonds with the deceased and the return of survivors to autonomous lifestyles. Placing this orientation in cultural and historical context reveals that it is largely a product of a modernist worldview. Within the romanticist ethos of the preceding century, such breaking of bonds would destroy one's identity and the meaning of life' (1205). The authors' description of grief ritual in many past and present cultural norms again find support in this study's findings on grief as a life-long integrative process that is all about relationships.

Thinking about grief in terms of integration rather than resolution has also found support in the literature on the psychology of women. The growing body of such research has been born out of the realization that our psychological theories are based largely on men's experience. Thus, until recently women have been measured by men's standards and experiences. Women were understood largely in terms of what they were missing when measured against a male paradigm.

One of the main premises of the emerging women's developmental theory is that, 'women's core self-structure, or their primary motivational thrust, concerns growth within relationship, or what we call the 'self-in-relation' (Kaplan 1984: 3). In this theory, connection with others is a key component of growth. The growth of the differentiated self is seen within the growth of one's relational capacities and relational networks' (ibid. 1984).

The women's experience of grief as a continuous process of change and recreation of the relationship and, subsequently, of their sense of self fits with and adds confirmation to this emerging women's developmental theory. If women's experience in our society is one of connection and growth within relationships, then it follows that, in the case of a loss of a relationship through a suicidal death, there is a sense of loss of self and a strong need to redefine the relationship with the deceased, rather than separating all energy from that relationship.

Clinical Applications

It is useful for counsellors to encourage their grieving clients to reconnect with the deceased as the goal of grieving. Another application is to establish the context of 'grief finding a place to be' with the client as an evolving part of their lives, rather than prescribing the 'letting go' or 'resolution' of a finite sense of grief.

The model itself may be experimented with in the clinical setting. It may be presented to the survivor during the first session and used as a counselling tool to elicit feedback and discussion regarding the survivor's own experience of grief. The model provides a working draft from which the survivor is encouraged to validate her own experience and to continue in the refinement of the model. In this way, it provides a framework within which the therapist and client can enter into discussion and decide on the direction for the therapeutic relationship. If such experimentation occurs with the use of the model, the uniqueness of each woman's grief experience must be stressed and respected. The model is not to be implemented as the normative truth, but rather is to be seen as a continually evolving, working theoretical model. Each survivor's experience and discussion adds to the continual refinement of this theory.

Summary

The model presented in this paper provides a starting point to the understanding of women's experience of grief after suicide. The primary implication for counselling practice is the shift in focus from resolution to integration. The process of connection and reconnection leading towards integration calls forth a different expectation of the griever and demands a different interaction from a social and clinical perspective. The basic social process of grief integration allows the therapist to approach the bereaved woman with an altered expected outcome of grief. The language and expectations of grief as they exist today are challenged by this shift in focus from 'resolution' to 'integration.'

Victoria Alexander (1987) recounts her experience of living through her mother's suicide, and describes her changing sense of self as follows: 'I am not the same person I was before my mother's death, not only because of her loss, but because suicide has become part of the vocabulary of my experience. It has a permanent place at the core of my life, and I am both more vulnerable and stronger for it' (117).

The conceptual model of grief integration presented here speaks to the process that is experienced in reaching that place within the woman's self where grief 'has a permanent place at the core of [her] life.'

It seems only fitting, as our thinking is challenged here in terms of language and process regarding women's experience of grief, that the women who have shared so much of themselves leave us with this challenge in their own words:

I guess my grief is sort of like with me and travelling with me. I guess maybe more in my mind. It's always there and it's coming in and out, in and out, and it will always be there. Sort of like a circle around you.

It's like grief is a part of me. Everything is connected to me.

As for resolved – not applicable!! It's more evenly balanced, stored and filed where it fits in my heart, mind, and life!

You have given me back my husband so he can be a realistic part of who I am!

Connie died by suicide three years after the completion of this study. No one can know what brought her to suicide; as with most suicides, she left behind no definitive explanations. Those of us who had been privileged to know and learn in our relationships with Connie will each struggle with finding a way to remember and integrate Connie into our lives. As a researcher and therapist, I now find myself in the role of suicide survivor. As I remember Connie and reflect on those things I learned about myself and about her experience in this world, I more fully understand the process of finding a place for that grief to be a part of who I am. I am beginning to understand Connie's words: 'It's like grief is a part of me. Everything is connected to me, everything that's ever happened is I guess.'

My hope is that her death will serve to remind all of us of the urgent need to continue to further our understanding of her experience ... and to remember the people who continue to be affected by suicides ... those who are left to grieve.

REFERENCES

Alexander, V. 1987. 'Living Through My Mother's Suicide.' In E. Dunne, J. McIntosh, and K.
   Dunne-Maxim, eds, *Suicide and Its Aftermath*. New York: W.W. Norton.
American Association of Suicidology. 1989. 'Bereavement.' *Newslink* 4(2): 9.
Barrett, T. 1989. *Life after Suicide: The Survivor's Grief Experience*. Fargo: Aftermath Research.
Bowlby, J. 1980. *Attachment and Loss. Vol. III: Loss Sadness and Depression*. New York: Basic
   Books.
Chenitz, W.C., and J.M. Swanson, 1986. *From Practice to Grounded Theory*. Menlo Park, CA:
   Addison-Wesley.
Demi, A.M. 1978. 'Suicide and Non-Suicide Survivors Compared.' *Community Nursing Research*
   11: 91–9.

– 1984. 'Social Adjustment of Widows after a Sudden Death: Suicide and Non-Suicide Survivors Compared.' *Death Education* 8: 91–111.

Demi, A.S., and M.S. Miles. 1988. 'Suicide Bereaved Parents: Emotional Distress and Physical Health Problems.' *Death Studies* 12(4): 297–307.

Glaser, B.G. 1978. *Theoretical Sensitivity.* Mill Valley, CA: Sociology Press.

Glaser, B.G., and A.L. Strauss. 1967. *The Discovery of Grounded Theory.* Chicago: Aldene de Gruyter.

Glick, I., R. Weiss, and C. Parkes. 1974. *The First Year of Bereavement.* New York: Wiley.

Henslin, J. 1972. 'Strategies of Adjustment: An Ethnomethodological Approach to the Study of Guilt and Suicide.' In A.C. Cain, ed., *Survivors of Suicide.* Springfield, Il: Charles C. Thomas.

Hewett, J.H. 1980. *After Suicide.* Philadelphia: Westminster Press.

Kaplan, A.G. 1984. 'The Self-in-Relation: Implications for Depression in Women.' In *Work in Progress* 14. Wellesley, MA: Wellesley College Stone Center for Developmental Services and Studies.

Kubler-Ross, E. 1969. *On Death and Dying.* New York: Macmillan.

McIntosh, J.L., and L.D. Kelly 1988. 'Survivors' Reactions: Suicide vs. Other Causes (Summary).' *Proceedings of the 21st Annual Meeting of the American Association of Suicidology,* 89–90.

Miller, J.B. 1986. *Toward a New Psychology of Women.* Boston: Beacon Press.

Parkes, C.M. 1975. 'Unexpected and Untimely Bereavement: A Statistical Study of Young Boston Widows and Widowers.' In B. Schoenberg, ed., *Bereavement: Psychosocial Aspects.* New York: Columbia University Press.

Rando, T.A. 1984. *Grief, Dying and Death: Clinical Interventions for Caregivers.* Champaign, IL: Research Press.

– 1988. *Grieving: How to Go on Living When Someone You Love Dies.* Lexington, NY: Lexington Books.

Shepherd, D., and B.M. Barraclough 1974. 'The Aftermath of Suicide.' *British Medical Journal* 2: 600–3.

Sheskin, A., and S.E. Wallace. 1976. 'Differing Bereavements: Suicide, Natural, and Accidental Death.' *Omega* 73: 229–42.

Shneidman, E.S. 1985. Some Thoughts on Grief and Mourning. *Suicide and Life-Threatening Behavior* 15(1): 51–5.

Silverman, P.R. 1972. 'Intervention with the Widow of a Suicide.' In A.C. Cain, ed., *Survivors of Suicide,* 186–214. Springfield IL: Charles C. Thomas.

Solomon, M.I. 1981. 'Bereavement Following Suicide.' *Psychiatric Nursing* 22: 18–19.

Stroebe, M., M. Gergen, K. Gergen, and W. Stroebe. 1992. 'Broken Hearts or Broken Bonds: Love and Death in Historical Perspective.' *American Psychologist* 47: 1205–12.

Stroebe, M.S., and W. Stroebe. 1983. 'Who Suffers More? Sex Differences in Health Risks of the Widowed.' *Psychological Bulletin* 93: 279–301.

Suransky, V.P. 1982. *The Erosion of Childhood.* Chicago: University of Chicago Press.

van der Wal, J. 1990. 'The Aftermath of Suicide: A Review of Empirical Evidence.' *Omega* 20(2): 149–71.

Whitis, P.R. 1968. 'The Legacy of a Child's Suicide.' *Family Process* 7: 159–69.

Worden, W.J. 1982. *Grief Counselling and Grief Therapy: A Handbook for the Mental Health Practitioner.* New York: Springer.

Wrobleski, A., and J.L. McIntosh. 1987. 'Problems of Suicide Survivors: A Survey Report.' *Israel Journal of Psychiatry and Related Sciences* 24: 137–42.

Zisook, S., and L. Lyons. 1990. 'Bereavement and Unresolved Grief in Psychiatric Outpatients.' *Omega* 20(4): 307–22.

PART IX: THE RIGHT TO DIE

The right-to-die debate is a critically important issue. 'Rational' suicide, euthanasia, assisted suicide, planned death, and medical withdrawal are all terms that describe forms of death in the right-to-die debate. This debate is one of the most controversial and elusive issues facing suicidology – and the general population – today in Canada and in many other parts of the world.

The right-to-die debate raises new issues. There is growing support for the right-to-die process, even more so in Canada than in the United States. Yet, it is equally clear that Canadians' understanding of what they are considering may not be sufficient. Often people do not know how to define euthanasia or assisted suicide. This observation is even more encompassing, involving people's lack of information about suicide itself.

We need various points of view to understand the issue of the right to die. Coroners and medical examiners, as the prime investigators of death, are in a unique position to observe the circumstances surrounding death and to give some added perspective. Suicidologists, equally, have a place; so does every Canadian. There are arguments in favour and against. The important thing, as recognized by the 1995 report of the Special Senate Committee on Euthanasia and Assisted Suicide, is that the right-to-die issue must be reflected on and discussed. There are numerous questions, such as 'Are we willing to provide the services that terminally ill people need?'

This last section addresses the issue of the right to die. Part nine consists of three chapters: a coroner's view on the right to die, highlighting both a definition of terms and the medical-legal issues; a discussion of the pros and cons of euthanasia and assisted suicide; and an overview of issues and concepts in the area.

26

A Coroner's View Regarding the 'Right to Die' Debate

JAMES G. YOUNG

Currently, there is intense worldwide debate involving the issue of the 'right to die.' Coroners and medical examiners, as the prime investigators of death, are in a unique position to observe the circumstances surrounding death and to give some added perspective to the 'right to die' or euthanasia debate.

Today's Western world is ready for the debate concerning the 'right to die,' and thus it will take place whether opponents to the concept agree or disagree. It is essential that the public and legislators, along with legal and health-care professionals, have as much background as possible concerning the issues involved in this debate in order that the terms of the discussion may be carefully defined and that multidisciplinary public discussions ensue.

What Is the Coroner's Role in the Debate

Coroner's Mandate

Coroners and medical examiners in Canada investigate all sudden and unexpected deaths. This includes deaths where the means may be classified as accident, suicide, homicide, or undetermined. Answering the question of the means of death is often a complex task. This task may be particularly difficult in suspected cases of assisted suicide, where witnesses may be reluctant to speak to the coroner.

Although the organization of provincial coroners' and medical examiners' systems may be quite different, their basic goals overlap. In Ontario, all coroners are qualified medical practitioners legally licensed to practise medicine in

Ontario. They are called to the scene of all sudden and unexpected deaths to begin the task of answering the following questions:

1 who the deceased was;
2 where the deceased died;
3 when the deceased died;
4 how the deceased died (pathological cause of death); and
5 the means of death.

To assist in this task, coroners are vested with investigative powers – such as entry, inspection, and seizure – to be used to fulfill their task. As well, coroners may request and receive assistance from the police to interview witnesses and gather information. The purpose of a coroner's investigation is to obtain the answers to the five questions noted above and to understand the circumstances surrounding the death in order to ensure that the death of no one is overlooked, concealed, or ignored. It is not the purpose of a coroners' or medical examiners' system to find fault or legal responsibility. The system is designed to find the true circumstances surrounding a death and to make positive preventative recommendations. If there are issues concerning potential fault or legal responsibility, they are dealt with in other legal forums. If, for example, a coroner felt that a physician or nurse may have improperly assisted in a patient's death and there was a concern that a potential criminal act existed, the facts of the case would need to be reviewed by the police and the Crown attorney. The case would be referred to the appropriate professional college if the concern was one of professional competence. In the medical coroners' system, the coroner has a role to assist the police and the Crown attorney to obtain information on and understand the medical circumstances of the case. The coroner does not, however, make decisions on whether to prosecute.

Recommendations

In Ontario, the coroner also has a legislated duty (Coroners Act, R.S.O. 1990, c. 37) to examine the circumstances surrounding a death and, if possible, to make recommendations to ministries, agencies, or persons in an effort to prevent similar deaths from occurring in the future. The need to do this in accidental deaths and the potential benefits arising from recommendations are obvious. Less obvious, but equally important, is the ability to make recommendations in cases of homicide or suicide. For example, in the case of suicide deaths occurring in custody, recommendations may be proposed regarding establishing processes and procedures that will lead to improved inmate monitoring and cell design.

Investigations of a high incidence of suicides in a community may result in a redeployment or expansion of medical services in a community. Examinations of homicides may result in recommendations concerning such issues as bail, parole, and police investigative techniques.

The Criminal Code of Canada Regarding Euthanasia

The present Criminal Code of Canada (Criminal Code, R.S.C. 1985, c. 46, as amended) clearly states that assisted suicide or euthanasia are illegal in Canada. Section 14 of The Criminal Code states: 'No person is entitled to consent to have death inflicted on him and such consent does not affect the criminal responsibility of any person by whom death may be inflicted on the person by whom consent is given.' The Supreme Court decision on the Sue Rodriguez case, which will be discussed later, confirms the purpose of this provision.

Investigating Possible Euthanasia Deaths in Private Residences

The investigation of deaths where euthanasia may have occurred in private residences and in public institutions is difficult. Although currently both are clearly illegal, there are important differences with regard to their investigation. Assisted suicide of terminally ill patients in their own homes undoubtedly occurs, but because of the illegal nature of the activity its scope can only be estimated by anecdotal evidence. In most instances of terminal illness, such as cancer or AIDS, the patient has ready access to strong analgesics. As well, there is existing literature and a group of people who are more than aware of the various drug combinations and techniques that may be employed in assisting suicide. In most instances, the death of someone who is terminally ill is not sudden and unexpected, and therefore, in the various provinces, a coroner or medical examiner would not be called to the deceased's home to investigate.

An exception to this is when the death occurs at night or on a weekend and a physician cannot be found to come and certify the death. Since a medical certificate of death must be issued before the body can be moved, it is often necessary to involve the coroner simply to produce the necessary paperwork to allow funeral arrangements to proceed. Undoubtedly, therefore, coroners are from time to time called to the death of terminally ill patients at home where assisted suicide may have been practised. The usual circumstances presented at the scene are those of a history of a long-standing fatal illness and the appropriate medications for the medical condition. The coroner is able to obtain the medication dosage that the deceased was using; however, witnesses certainly do not speak of assisting the death in any way. Coroners in Ontario have been advised to approach such situations with a high index of suspicion and to realize that unless the parties involved wish to publicly challenge the system, therefore admitting to assisting in the death, coroners will likely not receive full and complete information during the course of the investigation.

Even if the coroner investigating such a death at home becomes suspicious, there are problems and limits to the investigation. The first of these, as previously mentioned, is that there will, in all likelihood, be a lack of cooperation and candor by witnesses. Second, a lack of financial resources limit the number of coroner investigations and autopsies of at-home deaths of this kind. However, in death-scene situations where advocates are present or the coroner is suspicious of the circumstances, resources are made available to investigate further.

One such investigative tool is an autopsy. An autopsy attempts to determine whether the death was consistent with the medical condition and also includes toxicology testing. Toxicology, however, has serious limitations. In most instances, the patient would already be taking an analgesic. Therefore, finding such a drug in a specimen is subject to interpretation. Certainly if drugs are found that were not prescribed to the patient, this will be useful in establishing that assisted suicide may have taken place.

All coroners' investigations into potential euthanasia or assisted suicide call for a high degree of sensitivity. The deceased person has generally suffered a chronic illness and survivors have a strong emotional bond to the deceased and are clearly grieving.

In summary, in deaths occurring at home, it is clear that assisted suicide probably does, on occasion, take place, but there are problems and limits to a successful investigation of such events. It is important to note that coroners and medical examiners have the ability to investigate any death that is suspicious. Therefore, persons engaged in the practice of assisted suicide run the risk that they may be discovered, particularly if a relative or someone at the scene decides to disclose the circumstances following the death.

Establishing a Euthanasia Policy in Institutions

Although there is the possibility that an advocate of assisted suicide might impose his or her view on a number of terminally ill, and perhaps not so terminally ill persons, such deaths only occur on an isolated basis in homes. The risk of a person either misinforming patients or imposing his or her view is greatest in an institutional setting. It is a major concern of every coroner's or medical examiner's office that a medical professional working within an institutional setting may unilaterally and arbitrarily perform euthanasia based on his or her own values with or without consulting the patient. Clearly, institutions cannot be run subject to individual whims. For example, in one nursing home the average life expectancy might be years and yet in another, because of individual policy, it might be limited to months. If this were to be the case, it would certainly be necessary to advertise such practices before someone agreed to become a resident in such an institution.

The Evolution of the Right-to-Die Argument

The 'right to die' has long been debated, but the magnitude and urgency of this discussion has increased dramatically in recent times. This is most likely due to a combination of several factors, including medical advances and changes in societal values.

Societal Rights versus Individual Rights

Traditionally, Canadian society was based on a model of societal rights that, at times, overrode individual rights. The sanctity of life was felt to be a societal goal, and therefore suicide, and at one time even attempted suicide, as unlawful. At this time, certainly, the concept of assisted suicide was out of the question. At the same time, medical practice was much less sophisticated and the pattern of practice was for medical practitioners simply to instruct patients as to what they should do. It was not seen as important that patients understand their illness or the reasons for their treatment, but rather they should follow the prescribed treatment regime. Recently, there has been a tendency to consider and recognize individual rights versus societal rights, particularly since the proclamation of the Canadian Charter of Rights and Freedoms. As well, there have been great advances made in medical technology. Decisions such as whether to resuscitate or whether to continue an ailing person on a ventilator have become commonplace. Patients are better informed and now challenge the diagnosis and the treatment and want to understand exactly why certain actions are being taken. These factors and others have combined to make the debate about the 'right to die' unavoidable.

Final Exit

The debate concerning the 'right to die' is happening worldwide. The Hemlock

Society in the United States has been successful in bringing this issue to the public's attention in North America. It is important in any debate that there are strong opponents on both sides of the issue. The Hemlock Society as well as the Dying With Dignity organization in Canada have been strong advocates for their position. The Hemlock Society's book entitled *Final Exit*, however, is a different case and deserves special comment (Secaucus, NJ: Carol Publishing, 1991). A disclaimer at the beginning of the book indicates that the *avowed* purpose of the book is to provide a 'how to method' for those who are terminally ill and wish to end their own life, either with or without assistance. The problem is that the book is also a 'how to' book for those who are not terminally ill. It is the experience of coroners' and medical examiners' offices across North America that this book frequently shows up at suicide scenes open, and often with certain pages underlined. These suicides, more often than not, are not of terminally ill patients, but rather of persons who may be suffering from emotional or psychiatric difficulty. In one instance in the United States, the open book was found, but the case proved to be a homicide committed by the deceased's son. The Office of the Chief Coroner for Ontario recognizes the book author's right of opinion with regard to the right to die. However, it does not believe that the publication of this book detailing how to commit suicide has been a responsible act. Should assisted suicide be legalized? That is up to the Parliament of Canada to decide. If it is, however, a careful set of guidelines will no doubt be created, and there will be no useful purpose served by the existence of a book such as *Final Exit*.

The Kevorkian Experience

Dr Jack Kevorkian, of Michigan, has taken the debate to new heights. This man has unilaterally decided to act as judge and jury and to decide which persons should or should not be allowed the right to die. It is reported that he not only has set up his suicide machine to allow patients to self-trigger fatal injections, but has also actively assisted in the death of patients by administration of drugs either by injection or by an anaesthetic machine. Jack Kevorkian would no doubt be subject to prosecution under the Criminal Code of Canada if he were practising his craft in Canada. It would appear that he has deliberately set out to advance his cause publicly knowing that the state of Michigan has no such law. The state legislature attempted to add a provision to the Michigan criminal code, but this was subsequently struck down because it appeared that it had been written directly to effect Kevorkian. Justice Sopinka of the Supreme Court of Canada noted in the majority decision in the Sue Rodriguez case that many in the medical field are opposed to the liberalization of assisted suicide. He goes on to say that 'this leaves open the potential for growth of a Macabre specialty in this area reminiscent of Dr. Kevorkian and his suicide machine.'

The United States Experience

In several parts of the United States, the issue of euthanasia or assisted suicide has been publicly debated by putting forward referendums to change the law. In Washington State and California such referendums to allow euthanasia have been narrowly defeated. Recently in Oregon, the proposal did receive narrow approval by the voters. There has since been a court challenge as to the constitutionality of this proposed amendment to the criminal code, and in the interim the courts have ruled that euthanasia should not proceed until these arguments have been heard.

The Dutch Experience

The Dutch experience has been the most publicized of the European models. In the Netherlands, assisted suicide and the voluntary act of euthanasia are still officially illegal, but prosecutions are not laid as long as there is compliance with medically established guidelines. These guidelines establish which persons are eligible for assisted suicide, where and how the process will be carried out, and also clear safeguards (such as examinations by multiple psychiatrists) to ensure that the patient is able to make up his or her own mind and has not altered his or her view. Critics of the Dutch system worry that the relaxation of the absolute prohibition begins to take us down 'the slippery slope.' They allege that despite the guidelines there is evidence that there are increasing numbers of involuntary acts of euthanasia being carried out that are not permitted by the Dutch guidelines. They argue that once the prohibition against euthanasia is lifted, the proponents of the 'right to die' will not abide by whatever new guideline is established.

The Italian Experience

The Italian experience is different. In Italy, there remains a statute that says that 'whoever brings about another's suicide or reinforces his determination to commit suicide or in any way facilitates the commission of suicide shall be punished.' With the attempts being made to harmonize the European economies and laws, it may prove most interesting in future to see how such issues as euthanasia are dealt with by different countries.

The Ontario Case Experience

Directives Issued by the Chief Coroner
Ontario coroners have been advised to watch for potential cases of euthanasia
or assisted suicide and to order appropriate testing, including autopsy and toxicology. This directive was issued following several cases where potential euthanasia became a major issue.

The directives start from the point of recognizing that palliative care is a
legally accepted and desirable part of medical practice in appropriate circumstances. Palliative care may be defined as a form of treatment that is offered to
patients who have a definitely diagnosed terminal illness for which there is no
further useful active therapy or where the patient refuses further active therapy.
Palliative care should not be instituted without the informed consent of the
patient or substitute decision maker, usually the next of kin. The general intention of palliative care is to give the patient as good a life as possible with the
least pain or discomfort. It will include many forms of treatment, including drug
therapy. When deciding on a particular drug therapy the physician must be sure
that the therapy is truly palliative and not euthanasia. There is nothing to prevent a qualified medical practitioner from commencing or continuing to administer palliative care that reduces or may reduce a patient's life expectancy
provided the palliative care meets the following criteria:

1 It is administered in response to symptoms or signs of the patient's suffering
   and is commensurate with that suffering.
2 It is intended solely to relieve the patient's suffering.
3 Is not the deliberate infliction of death.

It is also important for physicians to record sufficient documentation on the
patient's chart to show that these criteria have been followed. Generally, a small
dose of drug should be given initially, followed by gradual increases depending
on the response to the previous dose. Concerns have been raised in some
instances where there is no documentation on the chart and where large doses of
drugs were used initially. When investigating deaths, coroners are advised to
concentrate on the need for the drug and the justification in evidence that the
drug has been titrated in its administration rather than concentrate on the actual
dosage of the drug.

After the issuance of these guidelines on palliative care the Office of the
Chief Coroner lectured extensively on this subject. It was clear from this experience that a large number of health-care professionals were having trouble
finding the line separating palliative care from euthanasia. In the Supreme

Court decision on Sue Rodriguez, Justice Sopinka makes clear the fact that palliative care is legal and that the key point in determining when the Criminal Code is breached is the interpretation of when an intent to end life has occurred. He acknowledges that in many instances this may be a subjective judgment; nevertheless, this is the current legal line.

Case Studies: 1/ Christopher Robin Home

The Office of the Chief Coroner of Ontario has dealt with a number of cases in institutions where euthanasia was an issue. The investigation into deaths at the Christopher Robin Home centred around the deaths of fifteen young children in an institution that specialized in the care of severely physically and emotionally challenged children. These children had complex medical problems and shortened life expectancies. Investigation revealed that many of these children had been switched from active medical care, which attempted to cure various medical conditions, to palliative care, without proper medical testing, documentation, and consultation with their families. In addition, many of these children were given morphine as part of their palliative care. These issues were explored at a lengthy inquest, including the propriety of prescribing morphine as well as the particular dosages. Autopsies were not done at the time of death, and given the medical histories of these children, it was difficult to establish exact causes of death. It became obvious, however, that when palliative care was offered it should have been done following proper testing, documentation, and consultation. The investigation clearly illustrated that there is a line that defines proper and legal palliative care, but that when this line is crossed, one is engaging in euthanasia.

Case Studies: 2/ Intravenous Infusion Pump

During the course of the Christopher Robin Home investigation and inquest, three other institutionally based cases came to light in Ontario. In the first of these, a family member increased the dosage from an intravenous infusion pump that was providing morphine to a terminally ill cancer patient. Nursing staff noticed the increased rate of infusion and turned the flow down. The patient died the next day, probably of the illness. The family member was originally charged with attempted murder, but ultimately pleaded guilty to mischief likely to endanger life.

Case Studies: 3/ Potassium Chloride Case 1

The third case was a well-publicized one in Toronto where a male nurse admitted to injecting potassium chloride into a terminally ill patient. The patient had been on a ventilator and was being extubated with the expectation that such a medical act might well result in the patient's death. Physicians had ordered Valium and morphine to make the patient more comfortable. A repeat dose of these drugs had also been given, some moments after the extubation. The nurse did not feel that the patient was comfortable and became alarmed by the length of time the dying process seemed to be taking. He admitted to administering the potassium chloride. Potassium chloride used in this medical circumstance and given in this dose has only one purpose, namely, to cause death. The nurse, who was originally charged with first-degree murder, ultimately pleaded guilty to administration of a noxious substance. He voluntarily agreed to no longer practise nursing.

Case Studies: 4/ Potassium Chloride Case 2

The fourth case involved a physician in a northern Ontario town. The patient was brought to hospital for a bronchoscopy in order to determine the extent of the cancer she had in the throat area. The procedure did not go well and the tube could not be removed nor the ventilator stopped at the end of the procedure. The family was summoned and it was explained that she could not be removed from the ventilator. By the next day, however, the patient had improved and insisted that the ventilator be removed, in spite of any potential risk to her at that time; she was given an analgesic and Valium and the tube was taken out. When this process was finished, she was given further analgesia; according to witnesses she appeared to be surviving the process. The physician asked the nurse for potassium chloride but was refused. He found the potassium chloride on his own and proceeded to administer the drug, which resulted in her death. He was charged with second-degree murder, and ultimately pleaded guilty to administration of a noxious substance.

Case Studies: Summary

In each of these instances, the Office of the Chief Coroner vigorously investigated the death and assisted the police and Crown attorney in understanding the medical evidence. If these cases had been handled without charges a strong message would have been sent to health-care professionals that such practices were desirable and tolerable.

At the same time, the police and Crown attorneys recognize the strong emotional arguments that could be made in these cases; the potential difficulties in securing a conviction on such a serious charge; and the fact that high-profile trials might make martyrs of persons engaging in such practices. Therefore, in each of these instances, a reduced charge was agreed upon and the person pleaded guilty. It is hoped this process still sends the clear message to health-care professionals and families that until the law has changed the limits of legal activity are what constitutes palliative care. Based on these cases, it has become clear that the courts are not the best place to settle issues of assisted suicide or euthanasia. If the law is to be redefined, it should be done with care and appropriate safeguards established.

As a result of the involvement of the Office of the Chief Coroner with these four cases and of subsequent seminars with senior Crown attorneys, it is apparent that there are concerns that euthanasia is currently only treated under the *Criminal Code* as first- or second-degree murder; but, as these different cases have shown, procuring a conviction in such cases is extremely difficult.

Canadian Cases

Nancy B.
Many years ago there was tremendous debate in medical-legal circles in Canada as to whether it was legal and proper to write 'Do Not Resuscitate' orders on medical charts. It came to be recognized that 'Do Not Resuscitate' was merely a medical act and that it was possible to write guidelines as to when such orders should and should not be applied. This is, in fact, part of the greater question regarding the right of refusal of medical treatment. Over time, the concept of refusal of treatment has become medically and legally acceptable. The Nancy B. case in Quebec (*Nancy B. v. Hôtel Dieu de Quebec* (1992), 69 C.C.C. (3d) 450) was further confirmation of this concept. Nancy B. had Guillain Barré Syndrome, which left her ventilator-dependent. She petitioned the court to have the respirator turned off, thereby refusing treatment even though she realized that this would end her life. The court established a decision-making process as a safeguard and did allow the ventilator to be turned off if that remained her wish. It was, and she subsequently died. This case reinforced a practice that was in fact widespread at the time – that the patient had a right to refuse treatment. In future, this right will be further expanded by the widespread use of living wills and substitute decision makers.

Sue Rodriguez
The Sue Rodriguez case (*Rodriguez v. British Columbia (Attorney General)*, [1994] 85 C.C.C. (3d) 15) was the test case for euthanasia. Ms. Rodriguez had Amyotrophic Lateral Sclerosis (ALS). This condition causes rapid deterioration and one loses the ability to swallow, speak, walk, or move the body without assistance. Eventually, one also loses the capacity to breathe without a respirator or to eat without a gastrostomy tube and becomes confined to bed. Ms. Rodriguez asked that a qualified physician be allowed to set up the technological means by which she might, when she was no longer able to enjoy life, by her

own hand, and at a time of her choosing, end her life. In other words, she was asking that an IV be started and that such an IV contain medication that could end her life, at the time that she so chose to activate it. It was argued that under Charter of Rights and Freedoms Ms. Rodriguez did not have to suffer cruel and unusual punishment, that she was entitled to a certain quality of treatment, and that therefore her request should be granted.

The British Columbia Court of Appeal denied Ms. Rodriguez's motion, but the chief justice in a minority ruling agreed to such a process provided certain conditions were met. These conditions were as follows:

1. Ms. Rodriguez must be mentally competent and this must be certified in writing by her physician and a psychiatrist not more than 24 hours before arrangements are to be put in place allowing her to end her life.
2. Physicians must certify:
   a) terminal illness near death and no hope of recovery;
   b) without medication she would be suffering unbearable physical pain or psychological distress;
   c) she is fully informed, she can change her mind;
   d) she is informed she will likely die both with and without palliative care.
3. The Regional Coroner must be given at least three days notice of the psychiatric examination and may be present.
4. One of the physicians giving certification must re-examine Ms. Rodriguez each day to ensure that she has not changed her mind.
5. No one may assist death more than 31 days after certification is granted.
6. The act causing death must be her own unassisted act and not that of anyone else.

These conditions, while not forming the majority opinion in either the British Columbia Court of Appeal or the subsequent Supreme Court of Canada decision, are well worth noting and may form a sensible basis for discussion and guidance should parliament decide at some future date to change the law.

When the case reached the Supreme Court of Canada, there was again a minority opinion supporting the act, but with conditions. The minority opinion said that since suicide is legal, why should assisting suicide be illegal. The following conditions should apply:

a) the applicant must be fully disabled;
b) strict conditions should be set out as to how the assisted suicide is carried out (conditions similar to those imposed by the minority decision in the British Columbia Court of Appeal);
c) Parliament should be given time to write a new law.

In the majority opinion, Justice Sopinka argued that the sanctity of life is a prime pillar of society, and should it be removed or changed there must be careful safeguards to protect the vulnerable. His judgment says:

Assisted suicide, outlawed under the common law, has been prohibited by Parliament since the adoption of Canada's first Criminal Code. The long-standing blanket prohibition is s. 241(b), which fulfills the government's objective of protecting the vulnerable, is grounded in the state interest in protecting life and reflects the policy of the state that human life should not be depreciated by allowing life to be taken. This state policy is part of our fundamental conception of the sanctity of life. A blanket prohibition on assisted suicide similar to that in s. 241(b) also seems to be the norm among Western democracies, and such a prohibition has never been adjudged to be unconstitutional or contrary to fundamental human rights. These societies, including Canada, recognize and generally apply the principle of the sanctity of life subject to narrow exceptions where notions of personal autonomy and dignity must prevail. Distinctions between passive and active forms of intervention in the dying process continue to be drawn and assisted suicide in situations such as the appellant's is prohibited with few exceptions. No consensus can be found in favour of the decriminalization of assisted suicide. To the extent that there is a consensus, it is that human life must be respected. This consensus finds legal expression in our legal system which prohibits capital punishment. The prohibition against assisted suicide serves a similar purpose. Parliament's repeal of the offense of attempted suicide from the Criminal Code was not a recognition that suicide was to be accepted within Canadian society. Rather, this action merely reflected the recognition that the criminal law was an ineffectual and inappropriate tool for dealing with suicide attempts. Given the concerns about abuse and the great difficulty in creating appropriate safeguards, the blanket prohibition on assisted suicide is not arbitrary or unfair. The prohibition relates to the state's interest in protecting the vulnerable and is reflective of fundamental values at play in our society. Section 241(b) therefore does not infringe s. 7 of the Charter.

(Supreme Court of Canada Judgment, *Rodriguez v. The Attorney General of Canada and the Attorney General of British Columbia*; judgment rendered 30 September 1993)

Justice Sopinka further commented that he had several disagreements with the minority opinion. He felt that the minority opinion would recognize a constitutional right to legally assisted suicide beyond that of any country in the Western world and beyond any serious proposal anywhere. As well, it would allow a greater degree of latitude than was even asked for in this case. He further felt that the minority opinion failed to provide safeguards up to the level of either the Dutch or Californian experiences, and in both of these instances there were questions of whether or not the safeguards were adequate. He felt the conditions imposed by the minority opinions seemed vague and in some instances unenforceable.

Both the majority and minority opinions in the Sue Rodriguez case make fascinating reading. As well as discussing important legal concepts, they document many philosophic arguments for and against euthanasia and should be read by all involved in the debate.

Senate hearings concerning euthanasia took place after the Supreme Court decision. The Senate was split on this emotional issue and chose not to suggest changing the law, but did recommend defining euthanasia as a separate category within the Criminal Code. This issue will undoubtedly be raised in the House of Commons in the near future.

The Need for Definitions

Confusion may arise over the euthanasia debate because people interchange terms that do not have the same meaning for each or define the same terms differently. It is essential that everyone uses the same definitions and terminology in order to ensure they are talking about the same thing. For example, one fairly widely accepted definition of assisted suicide says that 'it is an act by a health-care provider which makes the means of suicide available to a client who is physically capable of performing the act.' Some persons, however, consider assisted suicide to be 'the act by any person that makes the means of suicide available to someone else who is physically capable of performing the act.' This is an important distinction, since if safeguards are to be put in place it is presumed it will be health-care providers who are involved in the process, not just 'any person.'

Similarly, voluntary active euthanasia has been defined as 'an act in which the health-care provider makes the means of death available as well as taking the necessary steps' to complete it. Assisted death has been defined as 'an act by a health-care provider that is designed to facilitate the death of a client.' It may be either an assisted suicide or a voluntary act of euthanasia. It is, however, not uncommon for people to use the term 'assisted death' and 'assisted suicide' interchangeably. As one notes from the definition, these terms are not interchangeable and have very different implications.

It is also possible that public misunderstanding of what is being debated could lead to very different levels of support for euthanasia. While the majority of the country might agree with assisted suicide in situations such as terminal ALS or terminal cancer, this number would shift and diminish if the situation was redefined. For example, if one talked of the right to assisted suicide of those diagnosed with AIDS, the answer for many would vary depending on the definition of when AIDS was considered terminal. Is it considered terminal only at the end of the disease process or from the moment it is diagnosed?

It is of some interest that there is quite widespread public support for assisted suicide in cases of ALS and yet the need for assisted suicide is very limited in this disease. An ALS sufferer has the legal right to commit suicide and has the physical ability to do so until the late stages of the disease. In the terminal stages of the disease, the sufferer is usually respirator-dependent and at that point, as in the Nancy B. case, could refuse the respirator as a legal right. Therefore, it is only in the period during which the patient cannot physically commit suicide and has not become respirator-dependent that he or she may require assisted suicide.

The Future

The Supreme Court of Canada recognized in the Rodriguez decision that there needed to be vigorous public debate on the issue of euthanasia and that the issue should ultimately be decided by the Parliament of Canada. In response to the growing public debate on the issue, the Senate of Canada established a special subcommittee on euthanasia and assisted suicide. The background of the senators on the committee is multidisciplinary and includes medically trained persons, lawyers, and senators from a variety of other professions. This group has canvassed interested parties from across Canada and around the world and has certainly heard a divergent set of opinions as to what should be done. The Office of the Chief Coroner of Ontario fully supports this type of process. It is necessary that there be extensive public debate on the issue of euthanasia and, as mentioned, that all parties should be debating from the same set of definitions. The Office of the Chief Coroner of Ontario, on invitation, made a submission to this Senate committee. The position of the Office of the Chief Coroner is that if the law changes very stringent safeguards must be put in place. In this office's view, such safeguards should include an active role by the office of the chief coroner or office of the medical examiner in all provinces. This is a logical role, since these offices are already involved in medical-legal investigations and they also understand the pertinent issues. As well, in a situation such as organ donation these offices function as an arbitrator between the medical and legal systems in trying to promote organ donation and yet ensure that legal criteria have been met. It would appear sensible that these offices would have a role in monitoring (after the court order has been given permitting an assisted suicide) to ensure that all of the prescribed conditions continue to be met.

In the event that Parliament decides not to change the law, the Office of the Chief Coroner believes that an amendment should be made to the Criminal

Code that sets out the offence of assisted suicide with an appropriate punishment. It is this office's experience that this area is not sufficiently covered under the present Criminal Code. It is therefore difficult to prosecute because the penalties currently available appear to be rather draconian when first- or second-degree murder or manslaughter charges are involved. Whether or not the law for assisted suicide changes, it would be useful to define what is not acceptable and to establish a reasonable penalty for those who breach the law.

The issue concerning the 'right to die' is evolving and will continue to do so in the future. It will remain a difficult ethical and legal issue without a unanimous answer.

27

The Right to Die and the Right to Live: Perspectives on Euthanasia and Assisted Suicide*

BRIAN L. MISHARA

During the past few years there has been vigorous debate in Canada on the legalization of active euthanasia. On the one hand, some contend that the right to a self-chosen death by euthanasia is morally just and constitutes an expression of individual freedom guaranteed by the Canadian constitution. Others, who are opposed to legalization of active euthanasia, may be divided into two camps (not mutually exclusive): those who believe that human life is sacred and that it is not morally justifiable to foreshorten life under any circumstances and those who believe that it is impossible to condone active euthanasia without allowing unconscionable abuses. Before examining arguments for and against, this chapter presents definitions of euthanasia and discusses the distinction between euthanasia and other acts that may result in a premature death, such as suicide and homicide. The major arguments in support of and against the legalization of euthanasia are briefly summarized, then considered in terms of human-rights issues involving euthanasia and suicide. The chapter concludes with a comparison of arguments based upon moral and philosophical beliefs and arguments based upon practical concerns.

Defining Euthanasia and Suicide

In Canada, all deaths are classified according to a limited number of generally accepted categories: causes of death may be 'natural,' 'accidental,' 'homicide,'

*This chapter presents some preliminary thoughts on euthanasia based upon a year of study supported by the Bora Laskin National Fellowship for Research on Human Rights, 1994–5, from the Social Sciences and Humanities Research Council of Canada.

or 'suicide.' In some rare cases, the 'cause' of death is 'undetermined,' meaning that the physician or coroner was unable to determine which of the above categories applies. According to this system of classification, when one person kills another, this is a case of homicide; when a person kills himself or herself, this is classified as suicide. At first blush, this seems clear and simple. However, these definitions do not take into consideration the circumstances surrounding the death; all that matters is who conducted the activities that resulted in death. Even if it is a physician who initiates the activities that result in death, the only category that seems to apply is 'homicide.' In Canada acts of homicide may be more or less serious (as expressed in the severity of punishments for these acts), depending upon whether or not the killer intended to end the life of the victim. Thus, manslaughter, in which the victim dies during a violent act but the killer had no premeditated intention of killing the person, is punishable by less severe penalties. However, current Canadian law does not excuse any homicide as justifiable. In contrast, in the Netherlands some homicides may be justifiable by 'force majeure' (major extenuating circumstances), and in some circumstances, if certain guidelines are followed, they are considered as justifiable euthanasia. In Canada, the word 'euthanasia' does not exist in the Criminal Code and suicide is only mentioned in section 241 of the Criminal Code, which states that it is a punishable crime to aid or abet a person in suicide.

The word euthanasia literally translates from its Greek roots as a 'good death.' (Oxford English Dictionary, 1961). The Oxford Dictionary states that the original meaning, 'a gentle and easy death,' has evolved to the recent use of 'the actions of inducing a gentle and easy death.' However, today 'euthanasia' has been used in Canada to refer to all situations where the life of a person who is terminally ill is ended prematurely at the specific request of the patient him- or herself (Canadian Association for Suicide Prevention, 1994). The intention in euthanasia is to relieve uncontrollable pain or suffering, and euthanasia is considered a last resort in certain situations. When euthanasia is involuntary (without the consent of the dying person) it may be called 'mercy killing.' In the case of involuntary euthanasia, someone initiates activities that bring about the death of a terminally ill person who is incapable of giving consent for these acts, usually because the person is unconscious (for example, in an irreversible coma).

In Europe, the difference between euthanasia, homicide, and suicide appears to be relatively clear. However, in Canada and the United States there is much confusion concerning the use of the terms 'assisted suicide' and 'physician assisted suicide.' These terms are often used to describe situations that involve ending the life of a terminally ill person by the direct intervention of a physician. Since suicide literally refers to an individual killing him- or herself, it is difficult to see how a physician who is involved in ending a person's life – for example, by giving a lethal injection – could be 'assisting' in a suicide. Is there a difference between giving a lethal injection and shooting someone with a gun, if the intent is the same, to end the person's life? One may question the distinction between 'assistance' in ending life and homicide.

In North America, terms such as 'assisted suicide' have appeared in the media when some physicians were asked to justify their involvement in the premature deaths of patients who were suffering. The Canadian criminal code specifically states that one may not use as a legitimate defence in a homicide case the 'justification' that the victim requested to be killed or wanted the murderer to commit the act. The physicians' use of terms such as 'assisted suicide' rather than 'euthanasia' or 'justifiable homicide' offered the advantage of possibly avoiding punishment for homicide. While killing (homicide) is considered a heinous crime, suicide is completely legal. Assisting in suicide has a light punishment and convictions are rarely obtained.

In the Netherlands, for example, physician-assisted suicide is defined in a very specific manner: it occurs when a doctor provides the means for a person to commit suicide, for example by prescribing a lethal dose of medication, or gives information concerning how to kill oneself. While this definition seems quite clear and excludes activities where the doctor causes the patient to die by his or her activities, some feel that such a definition is too limiting because some individuals who are severely handicapped may be incapable of committing suicide and thus are in need of 'help' from a physician or other person in order to kill themselves. In response to this objection, the author of this paper contends that the term 'handicap' implies that an individual is incapable of doing certain things. A person in a wheelchair is incapable of walking, but may still get from one place to another. When a person in a wheelchair travels to a destination this is not considered 'walking with the assistance of a wheelchair.' The person is incapable of walking. In the same manner, a person who is incapable of committing suicide because of a severe handicap may resort to being killed by another person in order to attain the desired objective of ending his or her life. In such instances, the person was incapable of committing suicide and opted to ask another person to kill him or her. We suggest that suicide should be used only to describe acts in that a person kills him- or herself; situations in which another person initiates acts that result in death are instances of homicide or of a 'justifiable' homicide, called euthanasia.

Arguments in Favour of Active Euthanasia

Arguments in favour of active euthanasia are generally based upon beliefs concerning individual liberty – what constitutes a 'good' or 'appropriate' death, as well as beliefs concerning certain life situations that are considered unaccept-able. These arguments are generally based upon moral or religious values as well as certain beliefs concerning the value and quality of human life. Many of the arguments in favour of euthanasia are also based upon certain suppositions concerning the nature of rational decision making and the 'usual' extent of suf-fering in the terminal phases of illness. Below are some of the principal argu-ments in favour of euthanasia.

The Good Death

According to this point of view certain ways of dying are better than others. Usually a good death is described as the ideal situation of drifting into death in a pleasing environment as if one is falling asleep. Cicero (1981) described the good death as the ideal way of respecting natural law and public order by departing from earth with dignity and tranquillity. Euthanasia may be seen as a way to ensure that a person dies in a dignified and 'appropriate' manner rather than in a manner that is inconsistent with this idealized concept of how one should depart from life.

Individual Liberty

As Hume (1789) described in his eighteenth-century *Essay on Suicide*, choos-ing the manner of one's death may be considered the right of all individuals in a free society. For Hume and others who use this argument, choosing the time and manner of one's death is a morally sanctioned right of autonomous individuals in any free society and an expression of individual liberty.

Right to Maintain Human Dignity

This argument is similar to the argument for the good death, except that the objective is to *avoid* a poor-quality life before one's death and an undignified dying process rather than to seek out any particular idealized concept of the good death. What constitutes a dignified way to live (and die) varies from one individual to another. Nevertheless, commonly mentioned indignities include being a burden to others, living in a deteriorated state where one is incapable of normal daily activities, the inability to remain at home, and being dependant upon medical apparatus. It is impossible to contest an individual's personal evaluation of what constitutes a dignified life and an acceptable quality of life. Mishara (1994) suggests that the quality of a person's life, even among those who suffer from terminal illnesses or severe handicaps, *may be related to the circumstances in which they live rather than the nature of their illness or handicap.* He proposes that the following generally accepted aspects of the quality of life may be used to assess the circumstances of a terminally ill person and that an analysis of these dimensions may suggest means of improving the quality of life in order to develop alternatives to euthanasia:

– *Control* refers to the impression that people are able to exercise control over important aspects of their personal life on a daily basis. This feeling develops from the ability to make choices in everyday life, including the most minor decisions concerning what to do and how to spend one's time.
– *Security* may be either physical or emotional. Physical security involves all aspects of life that may be physically threatening for an individual. Emotional security is related to having a relatively stable emotional life wherein people perceive that there are others in their lives who love them and that there is no one in their immediate environment who is emotionally threatening.
– *Comfort* also has two components: physical and psychological. Physical comfort refers to having a minimum of aches, pains, and physical problems; psychological comfort involves feeling at ease in one's milieu or environment and in relationships with others.
– *Identity* is the feeling that one is able to maintain her or his unique characteristics in daily life. Identity is expressed in many ways, including the way we decorate our physical environment, whether or not people with whom we have contact treat us as an individual with our own unique history, and so on.
– *Intimacy* refers to the possibility of being able to do what one wants in privacy without being disturbed by the presence or surveillance of others. In institutions such as hospitals, intimacy may be difficult to maintain because of surveillance policies and the lack of private space.

Rather than simply evaluating the extent of deterioration or incapacities in individuals, an evaluation of the presence of the above components of quality of life may determine if improvements in these dimensions of life may temper a desire for euthanasia.

Reduction of Suffering

It is common to justify euthanasia by the belief that it is cruel to have to endure intense and prolonged suffering: when unrelenting suffering is present, euthanasia may be seen as a last-resort means to end a life that is intolerable. Battin (1994) suggests that euthanasia in order to reduce suffering has two components: (1) to avoid pain and suffering in the future, and (2) to end pain and suffering that is currently experienced. The liberal Catholic Thomas More, in his book *Utopia* (1605), describes euthanasia to end suffering as follows: 'Those that are ill from incurable diseases take comfort by sitting and talking with them, and with all means available. But if the disease is not only incurable but also full of continuous pain and anguish, then the priests and magistrates exhort the patient saying that he has become ... irksome to others and grievous to himself; that he ought to ... dispatch himself out of that painful life as out of a prison or torture rack or else allow his life to be ended by others' (186–7).

Justice

Gruman (1973) used the term 'thrift euthanasia' to describe decisions to end the lives of certain patients in situations where there is competition for limited resources in medical care. In a situation where there is a severe scarcity of resources in a society, not all people who are ill can continue to live. In such a situation, one can suggest that 'less valuable' individuals should give up their places to individuals who contribute more to society. An extreme example of this situation is the eugenics programs based upon Darwinian concepts, such as those described by the German biologist Ernst Haeckle (1904). Haeckle was concerned with the great private and public expenditure for welfare and medical costs and suggested that 'hundreds of thousands of incurable lunatics, lepers, people with cancer, etc.' be killed by means of morphine or some other 'painless and rapid poison' (118–20, in Gruman, 1973). This approach inspired the National Socialists led by Hitler in their 'eugenics' program.

Even if one disagrees strongly with any form of eugenics program or massive extermination for economic reasons, one may still consider the fact that social pressures often exist in situations where resources are limited. The concept of 'distributive justice' involves looking at the collective good or general welfare as something to be shared among the total membership of society. When resources are limited, one may question, for example, if it is worth expending tremendous resources to maintain the life of one incurably ill individual in a vegetative unconscious state rather than using those resources to help cure those who have a good prognosis for recovery.

Avoiding Botched Suicides

Molloy (1993) suggests that even if euthanasia remains illegal, some people who desire euthanasia will attempt suicide or request euthanasia from loved ones. In some instances, unsuccessful suicide attempts and botched euthanasia by others may result in a life situation that is worse than before. It can be argued that legalization of euthanasia will avoid suffering from botched attempts and the prosecution of loved ones who are acting sincerely at the request of a family member.

Control of Existing Practices

When the author of this chapter was discussing euthanasia in the Netherlands, a repeated argument expressed by proponents of their practices was that physicians practise euthanasia throughout the world regardless of the laws. As long as euthanasia remains illegal, physicians will camouflage those activities and there will be no monitoring or control of the practice of euthanasia. An advantage to legalizing active euthanasia would be to enact strict controls on the extent of the practice of euthanasia as well as to specify clearly the circumstances under which these practices are permitted. According to this argument, legalization will simply allow for fewer possible abuses and more appropriate practices of euthanasia than exist under the current 'hidden' practices.

Arguments against Active Euthanasia

Sanctity of Human Life

According to this view, human life is considered sacred and inviolable; no person may take the life of another. This belief may be based upon religious values, such as the biblical interpretation by Saint Augustine (1950) that the prescript against killing is absolute and includes taking one's own life. Or it may be based upon a belief that the sanctity of human life is one of the pillars of social order that must be maintained in order to avoid social breakdown. For example, Saint Thomas Aquinus condemned suicide as an act that goes against one's obligations to oneself, the community, and God. Some, further, contend that history shows that when there are abuses of the principle of the sanctity of human life, there have been many other abuses in society.

Wrong Diagnosis and New Treatments

According to this point of view, where there is life there is hope. It is always possible that the terminal diagnosis was due to an error – some people thought to be dying from an incurable disease may learn that the physician made a mistaken diagnosis and continue to live. Also, given the rapid pace of advances in medical science, it is possible that an individual may continue to live sufficiently long for medical science to find a cure for a previously 'incurable' disease. Thus, euthanasia may be a mistake if there is a possibility, however slight, that the ailing person is not really going to die or continue suffering.

The Wedge or 'Slippery Slope'

According to this argument, if one accepts the killing upon demand of certain individuals in certain intolerable situations, there will be abuses, even despite the best controls and regulations. Furthermore, once the door is open to justify murder under some intolerable circumstances, there is the possibility of developing broader criteria and making euthanasia a more widespread practice. For example, in the Netherlands there was a recent case where a physician provided the means to commit suicide to a woman who had no terminal illness but who had a long history of depression (Hendin, 1994). Although this practice differed from previous cases involving terminally ill patients, the physician was not condemned for his act.

Protection of the Weak, Incompetent, and Disadvantaged

Similar to the wedge or slippery-slope argument is the concern that certain people who may be unable to make informed choices concerning euthanasia may be pushed into opting for a premature death. Some people who have severe handicaps or mental illnesses or endure great suffering may be potential candidates for euthanasia 'in their best interest' despite a possible lack of true informed consent. Furthermore, some 'less useful' individuals in the society may be pressured into euthanasia.

Suicide Is Always an Option

Since suicide is not illegal in Canada, one may reason that euthanasia is not necessary because it is quite rare that a person may not find some effective means for committing suicide. Because of various dangers in legalizing euthanasia, one might instead encourage those who desire euthanasia to commit suicide rather than involving others in their deaths. One may further argue that those who 'do not have the courage' to end their own lives may be too ambivalent and should not be put in a situation where they are killed by others.

The Value of Suffering

Some believe that suffering is a heroic act that may even be of value as a human experience. Jesus' suffering on the cross may be seen as an example of an appropriate way to die; suffering may even be seen as the price to pay for our sins in order to guarantee a better life in the hereafter. It is impossible to debate a religious belief concerning the value or utility of suffering. Nevertheless, one can question on a practical level if suffering has positive effects or is an intrinsic and necessary part of the experience of certain illnesses. For example, earlier in this century male physicians felt that pain experienced by women during childbirth was a 'natural' phenomenon that should not be changed. Today these beliefs are considered unjustified, and it is considered unacceptable to not offer pain relief during childbirth. The concept of the importance and value of suffering may therefore change over time within a society and varies according to the social context.

The Message of Euthanasia (to Youth)

One may argue that if euthanasia is accepted as a justifiable recourse in cases of extreme suffering, then other people who are not terminally ill but are feeling psychologically distraught (particularly youth) may conclude that it is better to die than to endure a difficult life. Therefore, one may feel that the acceptance of active euthanasia may serve to condone death as an alternative to suffering and thus increase the suicide rates among younger persons who are experiencing transitory painful and difficult situations.

Practical Considerations Concerning Voluntary and Rational Consent

One may ask if it is possible for someone who is suffering terribly and is in the terminal phases of a debilitating disease to behave rationally and competently in a request for euthanasia. Spinoza (1677) felt that the desire to survive is an essential part of human nature, so essential that humans may not rationally prefer to not survive and to kill themselves. One may further ask if rational decision making is possible for persons whose emotions are terribly upset by pain and suffering. Perhaps pain and suffering lead to impulsive irrational choices where people seek immediate solutions rather than weigh other future options. Furthermore, one may question the criterion of rationality in human decision making in general. Many of the important decisions people make are based upon emotional rather than rational considerations. The choice of a career, marriage partner, where to live, or whether or not to have children may be more emotional than rational. Why then should one be more rational when terminally ill? Also, there are no generally established criteria for what constitutes an acceptable rational argument in favour of euthanasia: what constitutes a logical and comprehensible argument in favour of euthanasia for one person may constitute the reasoning for continuing to fight against death for another person in a similar situation.

Choosing Death for the Wrong Reasons

Many individuals who experience severe suffering consider ending their lives by euthanasia. However, people involved in palliative-care programs that focus upon diminishing the suffering of terminally ill patients contend that better pain control and improvement in the psychosocial situation of the terminally ill can alleviate a large proportion of the suffering. One may question whether or not some individuals who are ready to seek euthanasia may be aware of other means to reduce their suffering by appropriate interventions (such as better palliative care). Ignorance of the availability of other intervention methods may lead some people to choose death. This desire to choose death rather than life-sustaining interventions may also have an unconscious psychological basis. For example, psychoanalysts consider that there is a death instinct that involves both a desire to die and a desire to kill. Menninger (1938) emphasized the importance of understanding our own death instinct in order to better learn about how our unconscious desires influence choices we make in our lives. Such unconscious motivations, which may be resolved by psychotherapy, may push some individuals to seek death by euthanasia when the true unconscious sources of their discontent and desire to die remain obscure.

Undiagnosed Clinical Depression

Athough sadness and grief may be considered normal feelings among persons facing the end of their lives, some terminally ill persons may suffer from the more severe and potentially treatable psychiatric syndrome of clinical depression. Massie (1990) contends that over 25 per cent of patients with advanced cancer suffer symptoms of clinical depression. Wells et al. (1989) report research results which indicate that physicians fail to diagnose clinical depression in over half of their patients who suffer from it. According to this view, accurate diagnosis and treatment with antidepressant medication and/or psychotherapy is a preferable option to euthanasia. However, one may question the efficacy of these treatments with the terminally ill as well as the ability to diagnose depression in someone facing death by using criteria developed in healthy populations. Is it not normal to be depressed when facing our demise and is it justifiable to try to induce a 'happier' state of mind when terminally ill?

Erosion of Confidence in Physicians

Physicians are generally considered people who help others and save lives. Our confidence in physicians may be eroded if physicians are also associated with killing. Perhaps a person who ends someone's life, even in a case of extreme suffering and terminal illness, should not be the same person who is charged with saving lives and reducing suffering. It has even been suggested that 'specialists' in euthanasia be the only people authorized to commit these acts so that physicians will maintain their reputations as helpers in the fight against death and the diminution of pain and suffering.

Critical Analysis of Arguments for and against Active Euthanasia

The majority of arguments in favour of active euthanasia are based upon an understanding of what is correct and appropriate according to the ethics and values that people hold (Mishara and Riedel, 1994). These values include beliefs about what constitutes a good or appropriate process of death, the importance and nature of a dignified life for persons who are terminally ill or incapacitated, and the necessity to reduce suffering, as well as concepts about what is most appropriate in a just society. Such moral values and religious beliefs are often impossible to contest on the basis of facts. For some, these values and beliefs are of long standing and are recalcitrant to change. For others, these beliefs are the result of experiences with publicity about euthanasia, such as the widely publicized case of Sue Rodriguez, and may change depending upon mass-media presentations and personal experiences. Only two of the arguments cited above may be subject to empirical research investigation: the contention that legalization of euthanasia would result in less suffering from botched suicides and the belief that permitting euthanasia would result in an increase in suicide among younger people as a method of dealing with suffering and life difficulties. Little is known about cases of botched suicides. Nevertheless, this matter has not come to the attention of researchers or proponents of euthanasia as a significant problem. Also, reports from the Netherlands indicate that suicide rates in general and youth suicide rates in particular did not increase over the years since the acceptance of the practice of euthanasia and its legalization.

On the other hand, most arguments against euthanasia are not based upon moral or religious values. Nevertheless, the religious or moral belief in the sanctity of life as an inviolable principle recurs often. Another argument based on personal values is that suffering is a positive or acceptable human state, particularly near the end of life. However, each of the other arguments may be subject to empirical validation. Based on empirical evidence, it is quite rare that people would die by euthanasia needlessly just before a new cure is found for an illness: one would have to be a tremendous optimist to hope that such an event would occur. Similarly, wrong diagnoses of terminal illness occur quite infrequently. It is difficult to base a national policy upon such infrequent events.

One of the most common arguments against euthanasia is that of the wedge or slippery slope, which suggests that if euthanasia were to be accepted in certain circumstances, there would be a tendency subsequently to accept or even encourage death by euthanasia in other situations that we are not currently ready to approve. In order to verify this argument, most people look to the Netherlands, where the practice of euthanasia is accepted by jurisprudence and has recently been condoned by legislation. Physicians who practise euthanasia are supposed to follow a number of strict guidelines that include the necessity for a second confirming opinion by another physician, assurances that the decision was freely made by an informed, competent individual, and the obligation to have tried or offered all other possible means of diminishing the individual's suffering before recourse to euthanasia as a last resort. Some claim that there is already much abuse of euthanasia practices in the Netherlands, despite the strong popular support for legislation legalizing these practices. Research studies by van der Maas and colleagues (1992), in which physicians were asked to report anonymously on their experiences with euthanasia and similar practices, suggests that there are numerous cases of active euthanasia that do not follow the legislated guidelines, particularly with individuals suffering during the last phase of terminal illness. The culture and legal system in Canada are quite different from those in the Netherlands. The flexibility within the legal system that permitted the practice of euthanasia by judicial sanction for 'force majeure' does not exist in Canada. In Canada, there is more government control of individuals' activities compared to the more open society in the Netherlands, which greatly emphasizes individual freedom of choice. One cannot easily generalize to Canadian society from the experience in the Netherlands because of differences in the legal systems, the health-delivery systems, and cultural expectations. Some situations in the Netherlands, such as the assisted suicide of a depressive woman who was not terminally ill, which did not create a national uproar in that country, might result in a completely different reaction in Canada. For some, the Netherlands is an example of the risks noted by the slippery-slope argument, while for others the detailed regulations and vast popular support for those practices in the Netherlands suggest that euthanasia may become an acceptable practice with little reason for concern.

It is also difficult to tell if the eventual approval of euthanasia would result in a compromise of the rights of those who are more feeble, incompetent, or disadvantaged. Those in favour of euthanasia insist that it is possible to make laws that have sufficient guarantees of the rights of those who are disadvantaged. Also, if one insists that the choice of euthanasia be 'rational,' some ethical problems arise. We have no generally accepted ethical, moral, or practical guidelines that stipulate when the choice of euthanasia is rational and when it is less reasoned. If we limit our criterion to the capacity for rational thought, there exist judicial means to determine if a person is legally competent to make decisions. However, if we include the criterion that people should not suffer undue influence on their decision making by pressure from others, depression, or considerations that may distort their capacity for rational thought, the situation becomes more complicated. All human decision making is influenced by its context, including the quality of life the person is experiencing at the time a decision is made. Social isolation, pain, suffering, and the feeling of being a burden for caregivers may influence decision making and distort the perspective of the decision maker on what is right or wrong. We know very little about why certain persons desire to end their lives by euthanasia, while other individuals in similar situations choose to continue to live. Studies in the psychology of death suggest that the quality of the psychosocial environment is an important influence on the well-being and happiness of terminally ill individuals. The experience of intense pain may distort one's capacity for rational or logical decision making. Perhaps, then, it is not enough simply to evaluate one's rational capabilities. It is also essential to evaluate the psychosocial and environmental pressures that influence the decision-making process. At present we know very little about the motivations of persons who desire euthanasia and the factors that influence the desire for euthanasia in persons who are terminally ill. This is an important area for future research.

Sometimes what seems perfectly rational for an individual at one time changes later on as the person's illness develops. The author of this chapter has been conducting interviews with people who suffer from the latter stages of symptomatic AIDS. At a time when these people were suffering less and anticipating the evolution of their illness in the future, many of the persons interviewed insisted upon their right to end their lives by suicide or euthanasia, should they reach a level of illness or incapacity where they were incapable of continuing to lead a 'normal' existence. However, one of the unexpected results of this interview study was that some people who had highly articulate, well-justified, and vehemently espoused beliefs and desires concerning suicide and euthanasia *frequently changed their minds* when they actually found themselves to be in a deteriorated state of suffering from the terminal phases of their illness. Some who had planned the details of an assisted suicide or euthanasia decided at the last moment that they would 'hold on' a bit longer and die a natural death. Others, who had asserted that life is sacred, and that they would want to live out their lives to the very end despite their illness, changed their minds when they were greatly incapacitated. These findings suggest that rational decision making at one point in time may not reflect a person's desires when circumstances change later on.

It is curious that many people who choose euthanasia are capable of killing themselves by suicide but prefer to have their lives ended by a physician. In the United States, most of the patients whose lives Dr Jack Kevorkian 'helped' to end (he uses the term 'assisted suicide,' but the descriptions of his practices indicate that he committed acts which resulted in death, thus falling under the category of active euthanasia) were capable of killing themselves, but preferred to have their lives ended by this physician. We know very little about people's motivations for wanting to be killed by a physician rather than committing suicide. Perhaps it is the fear of not being able to complete a suicide attempt and having increased suffering as a consequence. On the other hand, the desire to involve a physician in the process of dying may be due to ambivalence about death: putting the act of ending life in the hands of another person may be a means of trying to resolve or avoid personal ambivalence. For some, death at the hands of a physician may seem less 'scary' (more akin to going to sleep) than death by suicide. The phenomenon of preferring death induced by a physician to self-induced death by suicide is in need of further investigation.

Freedom of Choice: The *Other* Human-Rights Issue in Euthanasia

The freedom to choose in life-and-death issues is a fundamental concept for those who are in favour of active euthanasia. It has been argued that the choice of euthanasia as a means of ending life is a fundamental right that should be protected by legislation approving euthanasia. This theme recurred frequently in testimony before the Special Senate Committee on Euthanasia and Assisted Suicide (Senate of Canada, 1995). Each year thousands of Canadians exercise their freedom of choice in life-and-death issues by taking their own lives by suicide. Some suggest that a large number who kill themselves suffer from mental disorders and may have distorted reasoning (National Task Force, 1994). Nevertheless, suicidologists concur that most suicides are avoidable tragedies – most people can find other ways to resolve their problems that led to suicide. Still, any Canadians who wish to die by suicide may do so as an exercise of their right to choose.

There are at least one hundred suicide attempts for each completed suicide that results in death (National Task Force, 1994). The relatively small death rate among suicide attempters does not indicate that Canadians are incapable of or inept at killing themselves. The relatively small proportion of deaths is due to the fact that the vast majority of persons who attempt suicide change their minds during the attempt, or after the attempt – they stop before they have inflicted so much harm that they will die or they seek help after starting the attempt. Many more people who are highly suicidal change their minds before initiating an attempt despite their strong desire to end their lives. Suicidal people, including those who suffer from terminal illnesses, usually change their minds before, during, or after an attempt because most suicidal individuals experience great ambivalence about dying, even in the most painful and difficult situations.

Changing one's mind about suicide can be considered a fundamental expression of an individual's right to free choice. However, this right may be compromised in situations where the individual is not alone in the process of ending her or his life, when others are involved and present, as in active euthanasia. When another person is present, such as a physician who believes that euthanasia is the correct thing to do at this time, it is not so easy to change one's mind. When other people are around who believe that death is the right choice (and believe it so much that they are willing to aid in this process), there is a tremendous social pressure to complete the act and die. The scene is set, the apparatus is in place, and the person who requested euthanasia and convinced one or two doctors, and perhaps several members of the family as well, that it was the right thing to do, is *expected to die*. It is not so easy to say to the doctor and anyone else present, 'Could you please come back in a few days, I have a few things I'd like to do before I die.' It may not be easy to admit publicly that perhaps death is scary after all and maybe a mistake was made in choosing a premature death by euthanasia. If the physician does come back in a few days, can the person then ask for another few days, and another few days thereafter? When others are involved, the individual plays the role of an actor in a play in which the script has been written: he or she is to die. A decision to change one's mind, after the long process of convincing everyone that this is the right thing to do, is not on the agenda. In this situation, the rights of individuals to change their minds may be compromised by the social pressures to complete the act. For this reason, choosing death by suicide rather than euthanasia better allows for the expression of personal ambivalence and better permits changing one's mind without undue pressure. This analysis suggests that suicide is more respectful of human rights than euthanasia; in euthanasia, the right to change one's mind has a greater risk of being compromised.

Some argue that there are people who are incapable of committing suicide and thus must have recourse to euthanasia if they want to end their lives in order to end unbearable suffering. However, these cases are quite rare: suicide is an available option for the vast majority of Canadians. In the Netherlands, physicians insist upon the necessity of their presence in most cases of euthanasia and point out that in instances of assisted suicide there is a risk of a botched result. These physicians feel that they are necessary to ensure that death will occur and that a prescribed poison not be used on someone other than the person who had requested it for euthanasia. (There have been no documented cases of poison prescribed for euthanasia being used for a homicide, although there appear to be instances of a death by euthanasia occurring as part of a pact between two people, where one person died but the other had no intention of respecting the pact and planned to live after the other had died.)

If suicide offers the advantage of decreasing the risk of compromising one's freedom to change one's mind, then one may ask whether there is a social obligation to make suicide more accessible for the minority who 'truly' decide to die despite their ambivalence. Legalization of assisted suicide would allow physicians to prescribe lethal poisons under certain circumstances. However, what should be the criteria for access to this form of premature death, should such practices be approved? In the Netherlands, reports show that between 50 and 75 per cent of formal requests for euthanasia and assisted suicide are refused, usually for the following reason: other interventions that may diminish the person's pain and suffering have not been tried before recourse to euthanasia or assisted suicide as a last resort. These include medical interventions (e.g., pain relief), psychological help (e.g., to decrease depressive reactions to incapacities), and psychosocial interventions (e.g., reducing the feeling of being a burden to one's family or creating opportunities for contact with others for someone who feels lonely). Debates on euthanasia often emphasize the need to help someone who is suffering seek relief in death, rather than first insisting upon society's obligations to ensure that everything possible has been done to diminish the suffering that leads to a request for euthanasia.

Conclusion

Arguments for or against active euthanasia that are based upon moral or religious beliefs are impossible to contest on the basis of empirical facts or logical arguments, particularly if these beliefs are based upon important core values. However, values change within cultures, and practices that were considered barbaric at one time in history may sometimes become acceptable. Similarly, practices that were once commonplace may be considered barbaric later on. Furthermore, social values may be influenced by public debate and media reports on the issue of euthanasia.

Some common arguments for and against euthanasia may be subject to verification by research studies. We are in great need of more research on the factors that influence the desire to die by euthanasia and the process of choosing this form of death. This article suggests that there is a great risk of compromising the right to change one's mind when euthanasia is practised. This risk is much lower when individuals chose to die by suicide. Furthermore, it is well documented that the vast majority of those who are seriously suicidal or attempt suicide change their minds and continue to live. However, the presence of other persons when active euthanasia is practised, such as doctors or family members, creates social pressures to complete the act. This makes it more difficult to postpone the planned death or change one's mind completely. Since ambivalence and changing one's mind is so common in suicides, even when the suicidal person suffers from a debilitating and painful terminal illness, we may reasonably suspect that a significant number of people who desire a premature death by euthanasia would experience the same ambivalence and want to change their minds at the last moment in order to live a bit longer.

Many of the discussions on euthanasia and assisted suicide emphasize the issue of access to death rather than society's obligations to provide the means for diminishing pain and suffering among those who may develop a desire to die prematurely. A balanced debate on the topic should include considerations of the availability and efficacy of interventions that may alleviate or diminish the pain and suffering that lead to a request for euthanasia. Furthermore, one should analyse the risks of compromising the rights of individuals to change their minds when a social situation is created by involving others in the process of dying by euthanasia.

REFERENCES

Augustine, Saint. 1950. *Augustine: The City of God.* Ed. T. Merton, trans. M. Dods. New York: Modern Library.
Battin, M.P. 1994. *The Least Worst Death: Essays on Bioethics on the End of Life.* New York: Oxford University Press.
Canadian Association for Suicide Prevention. 1994. *Suicide: A Media Resource Book.* Calgary, AB: CASP.
Cicero. 1981. *Caton l'Ancien (De la vieillesse).* On Ageing. Trans. P. Wuilleumier. Paris: Société d'édition 'Les Belles Lettres.'
Gruman, G.J. 1973. 'An Historical Introduction to Ideas about Voluntary Euthanasia: With a Bibliographic Survey and Guide for Interdisciplinary Studies.' *Omega, Journal of Death and Dying* 4(2): 87–138.
Haeckel, E. 1904. *The Wonders of Life: A Popular Study of Biological Philosophy.* Trans. J. McCabe. New York: Harper.
Hendin, H. 1994. 'Seduced by Death: Doctors, Patients and the Dutch Case.' *Issues in Law and Medicine* 10: 123–68.

Hume, D. 1789. *An Essay on Suicide*. Yellow Springs, OH: Kahoe, 1929.

Massie, M.J. 1990. 'Depression.' In J.C. Holland and J.H. Rowland, eds, *Handbook of Psycho-oncology: Psychological Care of the Patient with Cancer*, 283–90. New York: Oxford University Press.

Menninger, K. 1938. *Man against Himself*. New York: Harcourt, Brace.

Mishara, B.L. 1994. *La qualité de vie des personnes âgées*. Working document prepared for Franco-Québécois Seminar on Mental and Geriatric Health, Nantes (France), June.

Mishara, B., and R.G. Riedel. 1994. *Le vieillissement* [Ageing]. 3rd ed., rev. Paris: Presses Universitaires de France.

Molloy, W. 1993. *Vital Choices: Life, Death and the Health Care Crisis*. Toronto: Penguin Books.

More, T. 1605. *Utopia*. New Haven: Yale University Press, 1964.

National Task Force on Suicide in Canada. 1994. *Suicide in Canada: Update of the Report of the Task Force on Suicide in Canada*. Ottawa: Health Canada.

Oxford English Dictionnary. 1961. Vol. 3. Oxford: Clarendon Press.

Senate of Canada. 1995. *Of Life and Death: Report of the Special Senate Committee on Euthanasia and Assisted Suicide*. Ottawa: Minister of Supply and Services.

Spinoza, B. 1677. *The Ethics*. Trans. R.H.M. Elwes. New York: Dover Publications, 1951.

van der Maas, P.J., J.J.M. van Delden, and L. Pijnenborg. 1992. *Euthanasia and Other Medical Decisions Concerning the End of Life: An Investigation Performed upon Request of the Commission of Inquiry into the Medical Practice concerning Euthanasia*. Amsterdam: Elsevier.

Wells, K.B., R.D. Hays, A. Burnam, W. Rogers, S. Greenfield, and J.E. Ware. 1989. 'Detection of Depressive Disorder for Patients Receiving Prepaid or Fee-for-Service Care: Results from the Medical Outcomes Study.' *Journal of the American Medical Association* 262: 3298–302.

28

Suicide, Euthanasia, and Assisted Suicide

ANTOON A. LEENAARS

The right-to-die concept is one of the most controversial and elusive issues facing suicide and suicide prevention in Canada today. Most recently, there has been a focus on euthanasia and assisted suicide (Report of the Special Senate Committee on Euthanasia and Assisted Suicide, 1995). Polls (ibid.) and research (Domino and Leenaars, 1989, 1995; Leenaars and Domino, 1993) have indicated a growing support for the right-to-die concept, even more in Canada than the United States. Yet, a persistent question that has been raised is whether people in Canada have a sufficient understanding of what they are considering. This observation is even broader because people lack in their understanding of suicide itself.

People are perplexed, bewildered, confused, and even overwhelmed when they are confronted with suicide, including the suicide of a terminally ill person. People do not understand suicide very well. The purpose of this essay is to define suicide and to raise some questions about the right-to-die debate. Next, the essay will attempt to provide a few perspectives on the topic. These thoughts are, in fact, not meant to be exhaustive or encompassing. The thoughts are presented only to raise some issues and to offer a few directions in thinking about suicide, euthanasia, and assisted suicide.

Any discussion on the topic of the right to die, I believe, should begin with a definition of suicide. Indeed, Edwin Shneidman (1985) has argued that providing a definition should be the beginning of any discussion on the topic of suicide in general. Thus, my attempt here is to offer a definition with explication of suicide. Next, I will attempt to raise a number of questions, including:

– Do we let the suicidal person die? Or do we provide suicide intervention?

- Is suicide intervention moral?
- Is suicide a civil right?
- How does a definition of suicide apply to euthanasia and assisted suicide?
- Is the suicide of the terminally ill, elderly, and so on, the same as suicide in general?
- How do different cultures approach euthanasia and assisted suicide?
- Would it be more appropriate to call the lethal act in euthanasia or assisted suicide voluntary death or self-determined death than suicide?
- Is there a slippery slope if, for example, self-determined death is introduced for dying, terminally ill people?

It is critical that these and many other questions are addressed in the debate. There is a need to understand better the issues at hand. Again, I offer here only a few thoughts from the perspective of a suicidologist, although some may question whether a suicidologist has a place in the debate.

A Psychological Theory of Suicide

Suicide is defined differently by different people. There is no such thing as *the* definition. However, from a *psychological* perspective, let me offer a working definition of suicide, by Shneidman (1985): 'Currently in the Western world, suicide is a conscious act of self-induced annihilation, best understood as a multidimensional malaise in a needful individual who defines an issue for which suicide is perceived as the best solution' (203). To understand suicide in the terminally ill or any suicide, we need to understand clearly this definition. According to Shneidman, the best way to explicate the definition is to offer some theoretical commonalities of the event.

Suicide is a multidimensional malaise. It is a psychological event with intrapsychic and interpersonal aspects. I believe (Leenaars, 1988, 1989a, 1989b, 1996) that suicide can be best understood as follows:

A. Intrapsychic

1. Unbearable Psychological Pain
The common stimulus in suicide is unendurable psychological pain (Shneidman, 1985). The enemy of life is pain. The suicidal person is in a heightened state of perturbation. It is the pain of feeling pain. Although, as Menninger noted in 1938, other motives (elements, wishes) are evident, the person primarily wants to flee from pain – a trauma, a catastrophe. The fear is that the trauma, the crisis, is bottomless – an eternal suffering. The person may feel

boxed in, rejected, deprived, forlorn, distressed, and especially hopeless and helpless. It is the emotion of impotence, the feeling of being hopeless-helpless, that is so painful for many suicidal people. The situation is unbearable and the person desperately wants a way out of it. The suicide, as Murray (1967) noted, is functional because it abolishes painful tension for the individual; it provides relief from intolerable suffering.

2. Cognitive Constriction

The common cognitive state in suicide is mental constriction (Shneidman, 1985). Constriction, that is, rigidity in thinking, narrowing of focus, tunnel vision, concreteness, is the major component of the cognitive state in suicide. The suicidal person exhibits at the moment before death only permutations and combinations of a trauma (e.g., poor health, rejection by spouse). The person is figuratively intoxicated or drugged by the constriction – and his or her emotions, logic, and perception are all affected. The suicidal mind is in a special state of relatively fixed purpose and of relative constriction. In the face of the trauma – pain – a possible solution becomes *the* solution. This constriction is one of the most dangerous aspects of the suicidal mind.

3. Indirect Expressions

Complications, ambivalence, redirected aggression, unconscious implications, and related indirect expressions (or phenomena) are often evident in suicide. There are complications, concomitant contradictory feelings, attitudes, and/or thrusts, often towards a person and even towards life. The suicidal person is often ambivalent about survival and unbearable pain. The person experiences humility, submission and devotion, subordination, flagellation, and sometimes even masochism. Yet there is much more. What the person is consciously aware of is only a fragment of the suicidal mind. There are more reasons to the act than the suicidal person is conscious of when making their final decisions. Suicide is complex, more complicated than the person's conscious mind had been aware of. The driving force to suicide may well be unconscious processes.

4. Inability to Adjust

People with all types of problems, pain, losses, and so on are at risk for suicide. Although the majority of suicides may not fit best into any specific nosological classification, depressive disorders, the 'down phase' of manic-depressive disorders, obsessive-compulsive disorders, schizophrenic disorders, panic disorders, hysterical disorders, and psychopathic disorders, among others, have been related to some suicides (Leenaars, 1988; Sullivan, 1962, 1964). Suicidal people see themselves as unable to adjust. Their state of mind is incompatible with an accurate discernment of what is going on. Considering themselves too weak to overcome difficulties, these people reject everything except death – they do not survive life's difficulties.

5. Ego

The ego, the part of the mind that reacts to reality and has a sense of individuality, is a critical aspect in the suicidal scenario (Murray, 1967). Ego strength is a protective factor against suicide. Suicidal people, however, frequently exhibit a relative weakness in their capacity to develop constructive tendencies and to overcome personal difficulties. The person's ego has likely been weakened by a steady toll of traumatic events (e.g., loss, rejection, abuse, failure). This implies that a history of traumatic disruptions – *pain* – has placed the person at risk for suicide. A weakened ego correlates positively with suicide risk.

B. *Interpersonal*

6. Interpersonal Relations

The suicidal person has problems in establishing or maintaining relationships (object relations). There is frequently a disturbed, unbearable interpersonal situation. A positive development in those same disturbed relations may have been seen as the only possible way to go on living, but such development was seen as not forthcoming. The person's psychological needs are frustrated. Suicide often appears to be related to unsatisfied or frustrated attachment (affiliation) needs, although other needs may also be evident, such as achievement, autonomy, and dominance. Suicide is committed because of thwarted or unfulfilled needs, needs that are often frustrated interpersonally.

7. Rejection-Aggression

The rejection-aggression hypothesis was first documented by Stekel in a famous 1910 meeting of the Psychoanalytic Society in Freud's home in Vienna (Friedman 1967). Adler, Jung, Freud, Sullivan, and Zilboorg have all expounded variations of this hypothesis. Loss is central to suicide; it is often a rejection that is experienced as an abandonment. It is an unbearable narcissistic injury. This injury is a traumatic event that leads to pain and, in some, to self-directed aggression. In the first controlled study of suicide notes, Shneidman and Farberow (1957) reported, in fact, that hate directed towards others and self-blame are both evident in such notes. The person is deeply ambivalent. Although he or she may be ambivalent, a characteristic in some suicides is the turning back upon oneself of murderous impulses (wishes, needs) that had previously been directed against a traumatic event, most frequently someone who had rejected the individual. Suicide may be veiled aggression – it may be murder in the 180th degree.

8. Identification-Egression

Freud (1974a, 1974b) hypothesized that intense identification with a lost or rejecting person or, as Zilboorg (1936) showed, with any lost ideal (e.g., health, youth, employment, freedom) is crucial in understanding the suicidal person. Identification is defined as an attachment (bond), based upon an important emotional tie with another person (Freud, 1974c) or any ideal. If this emotional need is not met, the suicidal person experiences a deep pain (discomfort) and wants to egress, that is, to leave, to exit, to be gone, to get away, to be elsewhere. Suicide becomes the only solution and the person plunges into the abyss.

These commonalities begin to define suicide. I believe, thus, that suicide is a multidimensional malaise. The suicidal individual is experiencing unbearable pain, is figuratively intoxicated with overpowering emotions, is constricted in logic, and so forth. Suicide is not simply a response to a stressful trauma (e.g., rejection by a lover, unemployment, ill heath). Suicide, in fact, reflects lifelong adjustment patterns (Shneidman, 1985). It has a history. Hopefully the perspective here will provide some thoughts on suicide, although they are not meant to be exhaustive. Yet, regardless of one's definition, a clear understanding of 'Why people kill themselves' is an a priori necessity before beginning to discuss the right-to-die issue.

Suicide is suicide. Yet, there is a question: 'Is the suicide of the terminally ill person the same as other suicides?' Regrettably, to date there is no answer on the question from science. Some say 'yes'; others say 'no.' I will address this question again in the text, turning first to suicide prevention.

Suicide Intervention

The suicidal person *feels* weak, that he or she is defeated and cannot go on, that he or she has experienced unbearable pain, and so on. It would be accurate to conclude that the suicidal person has not only suffered a trauma, but that he or she is not capable, given his/her state of mind, to cope. The situation demands adaptation, but the person sees him- herself defeated and unable to meet the challenge. Do we let that person die? Should we intervene?

Some people such as Szasz (1971, 1986) have argued that we should let suicidal people die. Specifically, Szasz (ibid.) noted that labelling patients as psychiatrically disturbed or suicidal is sometimes done simply to justify forcible intervention into their lives. To force intervention on those who do not request it is demeaning and paternalistic, he believes. Ernest Hemingway, according to Szasz (1971; see Lester, 1987), committed suicide partly to avoid intervention – that is, having to return to a psychiatric clinic for treatment. Szasz believes that intervention is immoral if the person wants to die. Yet, I believe that Szasz is simply wrong! Suicide intervention is not only moral; it is a necessity in a caring, humanistic society.

Let me address these issues from the vantage point of history. In 1972, Edwin Shneidman met Thomas Szasz in a debate on the issue 'Is suicide intervention moral?' This debate on the ethics of suicide prevention was held in San Francisco at the University of California.

Shneidman, the father of suicide prevention in North America, argued in favour of suicide prevention. Thomas Szasz is well known for his unorthodox beliefs that mental illness is a myth and that suicide is a civil right.

Shneidman argued that intervention is needed. He insisted that the therapist-patient relationship should include a sense of responsibility for a life at risk; and that suicide ideation, attempts, and so on are an expression of pain, unbearable mental pain, and thus treatable. Shneidman made the now obvious point that, when a patient talks about suicide, it suggests that he or she is ambivalent. He or she may feel hopeless, yet he/she is ambivalent, even about life and death. A suicidal person who is ambivalent can often be dissuaded. A change, an altered plan, a reduction in the level of perturbation, and so forth is often sufficient to reduce the pain. It should be the psychotherapist's duty to help a person recognize this fact, and guide him or her to the side of life. Szasz, by contrast, argued that suicide should not be seen primarily from the point of view of pain, ambivalence, and so on; rather, it should be seen as a civil right, in accordance with the principles of civil law. He went on to note that the therapist-patient relationship ought to be a contract between equals. Unless it is explicit in the contract that the therapist will intervene on behalf of the patient, the therapist is not obligated to act and indeed should not do so. For Shneidman, it is the healer's duty to intervene, while Szasz considers any treatment that is not specifically contracted for unethical. For Shneidman, when a person is suicidal, he or she is simply not in his or her best state of mind. It is the healer's duty to discuss alternatives. For Szasz this duty to intervene is a violation of a civil right. While Shneidman's view has the potential for meddling, the 'error' is on the side of life. It is on the side of preventing an unnecessary death. The consequences of Szasz's non-interference, when fatal, are irreversible (Shneidman and Szasz, 1972; West, 1993).

My position is akin to Shneidman's: The suicidal mind is often treatable (Leenaars et al., 1994). Suicide intervention is justified.

Euthanasia and Assisted Suicide

To this point, I have been addressing suicide in general. Next, I would like to direct my focus to suicide in the terminally ill, especially in the elderly. There are many questions to consider when attempting to understand the issues involved. The right to die of the terminally ill is not only a controversial and elusive issue; it is a multifaceted one. It cannot be reduced to *one* question such as, Is suicide of the terminally ill rational? The issues are multifarious. Let me again begin, once more, with a brief look back in history.

In August of 1991, Derek Humphry's book, *Final Exit*, reached the best-seller list for advice-books in the *New York Times*. To date, this book has sold more copies than any other book on suicide. The book highlights an issue in the right-to-die debate that all of us working in suicide prevention must face. Specifically, in *Final Exit*, the practicalities for suicide are spelled out. Yet, do people need a guide to practical methods? Do people need a diagram of a gun with an arrow to the trigger stating, 'Pull here'? Humphry says 'yes.' I am not that sure. In fact, the Hemlock Society, which has dissociated itself from Humphry, also raised questions about the publication of 'concrete' methods (*Globe and Mail*, 1994c). Of course, such published information is not unique to *Final Exit*. For example, in a prominent journal in the field, *Suicide and Life-Threatening Behavior*, Kim Smith (Smith et al., 1984) provided a scale to measure risk that consists of a detailed manual on how to kill yourself. He not only provides the method, but also indicates, for example, what to do to not be rescued and how to succeed, although that is not the intent of the author.

What is the importance to us involved in the right-to-die debate of *Final Exit*? What is the importance of other efforts such as those of Jack Kevorkian, who assists terminally ill people to end their lives? Derek Humphry, the Hemlock Society, and other right-to-die groups – there are eight in the United States and four in Canada – do not advocate suicide per se, but many of these groups do believe that suicide and assisted suicide, carried out in the face of terminal illness that causes unbearable suffering should be ethically and legally acceptable. Old age, in and of itself, is *not*, for Humphry, an adequate cause for suicide. But, whether we like it or not, terminal illness in some people is sufficient cause. It is, in fact, the most 'rational' of such people who choose suicide as a final exit according to Humphry. However, views about the right to die are not uniform. Kevorkian (1988), for example, dissociates himself from the Hemlock Society (and other right-to-die groups). He believes that we should, without further debate, provide assisted suicide to those who request such procedures. The positions of Humphry and Kevorkian are quite different and there are conflicts between them (Humphry, 1992). Humphry and most of the right-to-die group advocates argue for democratic reform. Kevorkian has a disregard of the law. The right-to-die movement is not uniform, and that fact is relevant when people try to understand what they are considering in the debate.

Different cultural/international perspectives may provide a larger window to examine the 'right to die' issues. A look at different European countries may help us examine better the considerations raised to this point in the paper. Specifically, the views in the Netherlands and Germany will be briefly presented.

In the Netherlands, lawful euthanasia for the terminally ill is 'tolerated.' A court decision on the practice in that country was in legal limbo for years. However, on 9 February 1993 (*Globe and Mail*, 1993) the court of the Netherlands adopted the most liberal euthanasia guidelines in Europe. Although the legislation stops short of legalization, it guarantees protection from prosecution for the physician who performs euthanasia, provided a rigorous set of guidelines are met (Battin, 1993; Diekstra, 1992, 1993; Kerkhof, 1993). The 'carefulness requirements' approved by the Dutch parliament are as follows:

Voluntary nature – The request for euthanasia must reflect 'entirely the patient's own free will' and not be due to pressure from others. Patients must be spoken to alone to ensure that the decision is voluntary.

Consideration of alternatives – The patient must be well informed about his or her situation and must have been able to consider the alternatives.

Certain decision – The patient should have a 'lasting longing for death. Requests made on impulse and based on a temporary depression cannot be considered.'

Unacceptable suffering – 'The patient must experience his or her suffering as perpetual, unbearable, and hopeless. Although these criteria will always contain an element of subjectivity ... the physician must reasonably be able to conclude that the suffering is being experienced as unbearable.'

Consultation – The physician must consult at least one colleague on the patient's request.

Reporting – A well-documented written report must be drawn up stating the history of the patient's illness and the meeting of 'carefulness requirements.'

Euthanasia is, however, comparatively rare in the Netherlands. Furthermore, recent studies by the Dutch government have found that Dutch doctors are responsible and reticent in advising euthanasia. Although not fully legalized, today in the Netherlands the right to euthanasia is seen as a personal choice, and a physician following the guidelines will not be prosecuted.

In Germany, there is an opposition to euthanasia, probably because of the painful history of Nazism. Although Kevorkian (1988) sees the raising of these memories as propaganda, I disagree. Euthanasia in Germany is viewed as wrong, and is against the law. The Germans see the Dutch falling down a slippery slope. However, assisted suicide is practised (Battin, 1993; Diekstra, 1993), and is seen as quite different than euthanasia. In fact, a private support group, the Deutsche Gesellshaft für Humanes Sterben (DGHS; German Society for Humane Dying) has been established to support choosing suicide as an alternative to the suffering of terminal illness. They publish a booklet, *Menschenwürdiges und Selstverantwortliches Sterben* ('Dignified and Responsible Death'), that gives specific advice about suicide, including methods. There are restrictions to its distribution; for example, only members of the DGHS may obtain a copy. Membership in the DGHS is denied if a person has received treatment for depression or any other 'psychiatric illness' during the last two years. The DGHS gives advice, support for treatment refused, and so on. Still, even though assisted suicide is not illegal, the DGHS remains controversial; indeed, its president, Hans Henning Atrott, has been arrested for selling drugs related to a planned death (Schmidtke, 1993; Wedler, 1993).

Humphry states that such options as practised in the Netherlands and Germany should be available in North America. Kevorkian states that such matters are irrelevant to praxis: 'All of these [issues] have been well debated in the past, and there is nothing new to learn' (1988: 2). Although I strongly disagree with Kevorkian, one needs to be careful in transposing practices, even ethical ones, from one country to another, one culture to another. For example, in 1993, I went to my home, the Netherlands, to attend the funeral of my beloved aunt, Tante Toni. She had died in her eighties from a heart attack. Death in general – like suicide specifically – is understood differently in the Netherlands than in other countries. Dutch doctors practise medicine in their own cultural tradition. To continue my discussion, while at my uncle's home (Oome Martien), his *huis arts* (family doctor) arrived; the *arts* was there at the home when my aunt died. He then, as well as later, provided care to my uncle. One should not underestimate the differences between cultures regarding patient care, including that around death and dying. Culture is critical in addressing death and suicide in the terminally ill. I believe, as a European, that there are good reasons why there are different practices of euthanasia in the Netherlands and assisted suicide in Germany. These countries, despite close proximity, are quite different. Each country, including Canada, thus, needs to carefully reflect on its own as well as studying international views.

The real importance of the right-to-die movement – and these are Humphry's words – is that 'society needs now to come to terms with elderly suicide' (1992: 129). In particular, society needs to come to terms with terminally ill 'suicide' of the elderly.

Alternatives and Applications

Suicide by the terminally ill, requires understanding: Is it 'rational?' What are possible alternatives? Withholding or withdrawing treatment? Euthanasia? Assisted suicide? What do these alternatives mean? We have, in fact, been talking as if we all agree about these terms. Using the writing of West (1993), let me provide a few observations about each of the essential concepts in the field.

Refusal – The patient in this type of planned death refuses life-extending medical treatment. The patient dies because he or she declines to undergo medical or surgical procedures. The courts in Canada have supported the right of fully informed, competent patients to refuse medical intervention. Most democratic countries see this as a civil right. However, there have been numerous challenges to a person's right of refusal, often coming from doctors or family. Often at issue is a person's competency. The best-known examples have been observed in the Jehovah's Witnesses, who reject even basic medical treatment such as blood transfusions. Yet, there are many other examples, such as the terminally ill AIDS patient who refuses hospitalization.

Withdrawal – Another way to die, practised in North America, results from the withdrawal of life-sustaining treatment for patients who may be considered already dead because they have lost all higher brain functions. The landmark case here was an American one, that of twenty-one-year-old Karen Ann Quinlan. In many countries, however, debate continues about whether withdrawal is different than administering a drug. In Britain, for example, there was the recent case of Tony Bland, a football fan who had been tragically crushed in a football disaster. His doctor went to court for two years before the courts allowed Tony's feeding tubes to be removed. The courts allowed withdrawal in this case; yet, in Britain, the court has not allowed the withdrawal of treatment of all patients (*Manchester Guardian Weekly*, 1995). Bland was seen as an exception, unlike Karen Ann Quinlan in America and the closest Canadian equivalent, Nancy B. Nancy B., having Guillain Barré Syndrome, petitioned the court to have her respirator removed. The court established a decision-making process to allow withdrawal in Canada, much like the case of Karen Ann Quinlan had done in the United States. Still, there are questions: Who decides when treatment is withdrawn? Is this action different than administering a drug? Processes such as living wills and durable powers of attorney have attempted to address these issues. Yet, in many countries there is controversy about withdrawal.

Euthanasia – Euthanasia literally means an easy or good death. It refers to a merciful death caused by an intervention, rather than through withdrawal or withholding of treatment. It refers to the practice, after aggressive treatment has failed, of allowing the patient to die with the physician hastening the death. This is illegal in Canada (and the United States). The Netherlands, as discussed, presents a case example where euthanasia is tolerated by the court.

Assisted suicide – Assisted suicide is not performed by the physician; rather the means are provided by which patients can end their own lives. Physicians in North America would do this privately, since it is illegal in America and Canada. The case of Sue Rodriguez is best known in Canada. Ms. Rodriguez, who had Amyotrophic Lateral Sclerosis, asked the courts to allow a doctor to provide the means for her suicide. The court denied Ms. Rodriguez her request. Germany, as discussed, presents an example of a country that is exploring this direction of allowing for assisted suicide.

One concept – rational suicide – however, needs a different presentation. Obviously, my theoretical explication of suicide would suggest that suicidal people are not rational. Yet, is the issue of 'rational or not' relevant to the issues being discussed? Diekstra (1993) has suggested that the issue of 'rational' suicide should be eliminated from our discussion on the right to die. 'Rational' is a mental construction. The important question to be asked is, 'When is any behaviour just "rational" or not?' The debate of rational versus not rational is, I believe, misleading. The figural question should be, 'What are the real critical issues with the topic at hand?'

Elderly suicide, especially of the terminally ill, is a critical issue. Some (e.g., Kevorkian, 1988; Szasz, 1971, 1986) espouse the position that old age by itself may be a legitimate – and they state 'rational' – reason for suicide, regardless of whether one is terminally ill or not. Others (Osgood, 1992; Richman, 1993), and I agree, believe that being elderly is not a reason for suicide and can never be the sole reason for suicide. Suicide, as I have outlined, is complex. Suicide is, to use a metaphor, an intrapsychic drama on an interpersonal stage. It is not a simple choice. Furthermore, recovery from the suicidal state is possible. Suicide prevention is possible (Leenaars et al., 1994).

Joseph Richman (1992) is probably best known for his arguments against the right-to-die movement. In the book *Suicide and the Older Adult* (Leenaars et al., 1992), Richman stated that suicide in the elderly, including suicide of the terminally ill person, is never based simply on being old or even ill. Sigmund Freud is a dramatic example of this fact, since his work in mental health is so influential. Freud killed himself. Was it, as he stated, because of his terminal illness? Or was it because he was severely depressed at the time? He had been overwhelmed by the Second World War and had notable problems in his adjustment to moving to England. Freud left Vienna in 1938, when Hitler took over Austria. Those years were onerous for him not only because of the war, but because, since 1923, he had suffered from cancer of the mouth and jaw. The cancer had progressed to a degenerative stage; indeed, the smell was so bad that even his faithful dog refused to be in the same room with him. The pain was unbearable for him. In an aside in *Moses and Monotheism* (1939), Freud says, 'Do not call me a pessimist.' He died by his own wish, with the assistance of his physician, on 26 September 1939 at the age of eighty-three. Was Freud's suicide due only to his terminal illness? Or to old age? Does Freud's suicide differ in its essence from other suicides? Humphry would say yes; Richman would say no. Does Freud's suicide fit into our theoretical perspective of suicide or not? There are other questions about the example at hand, such as, 'Was Freud's death best described as a suicide?' Would it be more appropriate to call it 'self-determined death,' 'free death,' or 'voluntary death'?

Richman (1992, 1993), in his arguments on suicide in the terminally ill, stated that (1) terminal illness is a crisis and crisis intervention is needed; (2) in crises our thinking is mistaken, narrow, and rigid; (3) one feels distressed, fearful, and lonely; (4) impending death leads to pain and grief in relationships, including the family; and (5) therapy, especially family therapy, and other mental-health work *can* help. Richman's arguments need to be carefully considered. He would, in fact, suggest that the suicide of terminally ill people is the same as the multidimensional theory outlined earlier.

Other well-known suicidologists have made equally relevant comments. For example, Shneidman wrote, in the *New England Journal of Medicine* (1992): 'In human beings pain is ubiquitous, but suffering is optional, within the constraints of a person's personality ... Physicians and other health professionals need the courage and wisdom to work on a person's suffering at a phenomenological level and to explore such questions as "How do you hurt" and "How may I help you." They should then do whatever is necessary, using a wide variety of legitimate tactics ... to reduce that person's self-destructive impulses' (890).

We must first be good interventionists, and that is *not* meddling, according to Shneidman. I agree. Could even Freud's death have been prevented?

The Slippery-Slope Issue

There are other key issues. A most relevant one is, 'Is there a slippery slope' if one introduces self-determined death for the terminally ill? Humphry says 'no.' Kevorkian (1988), of course, believes that all such consideration is irrelevant. We should simply assist people now, without further discussion. The 'slippery slope' issue is seen as an 'absurdity' (ibid.). Is promoting assisted suicide or euthanasia creating the 'wedge'? It is an established fact, I believe, that imitation occurs, including of suicide. Young people are especially susceptible to the imitation phenomenon (Phillips, 1986). Humphry's suggestions, for example, can be – in fact, have been – imitated. Kevorkian's ideas can, as another example, open opportunities not intended. Coroners in Canada and elsewhere have reported deaths in youth who explicitly used the instructions of Humphry's book for their demise. As a further example of such impact, my colleague Susanne Wenckstern (Leenaars and Wenckstern, 1990) was called to intervene in a crisis at a school. The teacher of a grade 12 class had assigned student presentations. A group of the students decided shortly after the release of Humphry's book to tackle suicide prevention. They went to a local bookstore to find a book on suicide and bought Humphry's book. They produced a videotape explicitly showing how to kill oneself. That is, of course, not what Humphry intended; yet it occurred. Should we see this as simply an example of the possibility that anything can be misused, as Kevorkian (1988) has suggested? The students who did the video project received an A, and that is all that would have happened if it had not been for a parent of a student in the class. That student was quite disturbed about this video, which is not surprising because subsequent showings of the video at major national conferences of the Canadian Association of Suicide Prevention and American Association for Death Education and Counselling resulted in numerous adults feeling the pain portrayed in the video. A plan of intervention was developed and a proper prevention program (Leenaars and Wenckstern, 1990) was introduced to the class. I believe that we have to be careful of the imitation effect, especially in young people.

Even in the Netherlands, the issue of the slippery slope is debated. On 23 June 1994 (*Globe and Mail*, 1994a), the Dutch Supreme Court refused to punish a doctor who provided the means for death to a severely depressed patient. The court stated: 'This comes within the existing regulations.' The Netherlands' guidelines for euthanasia are seen to include the mentally or emotionally ill. Some welcomed the ruling, while others see it as a classic example of the slippery slope. Killing, some in the Netherlands fear, is seen as a means to solve problems. Yet, in July 1994 (*Globe and Mail*, 1994b), the court charged a gynaecologist, Dr H. Prins, for killing a three-day-old girl born in March 1993 with multiple physical and mental handicaps. This case is now in the courts. Obviously, it may be assumed that the people of the Netherlands are unsure of where to level off the slope. We in Canada should be equally cautious.

Concluding Remarks

When are suicide, assisted suicide, and euthanasia acceptable and when not? What practice would be acceptable? These are difficult questions that we face in Canada.

To cite a concrete example of these questions, a few years ago, I witnessed the after-effects of a suicide of an elderly male, aged eighty-four. His wife had died three months earlier; he had cancer; his car was in the shop; he had no family; and he chose to jump twenty-two stories to his death. That was tragic. What was even more tragic for me was watching the people in his building, a senior citizens' apartment block with apartments, but no services. I remember seeing an older woman on the fifth floor look for over an hour at the body, as did others. What services had the dead man needed that he did not receive? Could we have helped him with his crisis? And what about the other people? Is it humane to allow these senior people to be forced to witness such a death, or would euthanasia (e.g., by a family doctor) or assisted suicide in privacy be more humane for all concerned?

An important aspect of the right-to-die issue is that it raises questions that we in suicidology must reflect on and discuss (Report of the Special Senate Committee on Euthanasia and Assisted Suicide, 1995). I would like to raise one last question, because it is so fundamental for how we Canadians will define ourselves. Are we willing to provide the services that terminally ill people need, such as social support? Are we, as another example, willing to provide the financial assistance that palliative care (e.g., a hospice) needs? We know, in fact, that often pain can be alleviated in suicidal people by providing the services that such people need. There are many key questions around euthanasia and assisted suicide. I have only offered a few personal reflections and, hopefully, raised some important questions. My main conclusion is simply stated: the right-to-die issue must continue to be discussed among suicidologists and all people, with caution about quick answers and quick acquiescence.

REFERENCES

Battin, M. 1993. 'Suicidology and the Right to Die.' In A. Leenaars, ed., *Suicidology: Essays in Honor of Edwin Shneidman*. Northvale, NJ: Aronson.
Diekstra, R. 1992. 'Suicide and Euthanasia.' *Giornale Italiano Di Suicidologia* 2: 71–8.
– 1993. Personal communication.
Domino, G., and A. Leenaars. 1989. 'Attitudes toward Suicide: A Comparison of Canadian and United States College Students.' *Suicide and Life-Threatening Behavior* 19: 160–72.
– 1995. 'Attitudes toward Suicide among English Speaking Urban Canadians.' *Death Studies* 19: 489–500.
Friedman, P. 1967. *On Suicide*. New York: International Universities Press (originally published 1910).
Freud, S. 1974a. 'Mourning and Melancholia.' In J. Strachey, ed. and trans., *The Standard Edition of the Complete Psychological Works of Sigmund Freud*, vol. 14. London: Hogarth Press (originally published 1917).
– 1974b. 'A Case of Homosexuality in a Woman.' In J. Strachey, ed. and trans., *The Standard Edition of the Complete Psychological Works of Sigmund Freud*, vol. 14. London: Hogarth Press (originally published 1920).

- 1974c. 'Group Psychology and the Analysis of the Ego.' In J. Strachey, ed. and trans., *The Standard Edition of the Complete Psychological Works of Sigmund Freud*, vol. 18. London: Hogarth Press (originally published 1921).

Globe and Mail. 1993. 'Dutch soften law on euthanasia.' 9 February: A8.

- 1994a. 'Dutch expand bounds for aiding suicide.' 23 June: A1.
- 1994b. 'MD faces charge in baby's death.' 19 July: A8.
- 1994c. 'Suicide law falls short, activist says.' 7 December: A17.

Humphry, D. 1991. *Final Exit*. Eugene, OR: Hemlock Society.

- 1992. 'Rational Suicide among the Elderly.' In A. Leenaars, R. Maris, J. McIntosh, and J. Richman, eds, *Suicide and the Older Adult*. New York: Guilford Press.

Kerkhof, A. 1993. Personal communication.

Kevorkian, J. 1988. 'The Last Fearsome Taboo: Medical Aspects of Planned Death.' *Medicine and Law* 7: 1–14.

Leenaars, A. 1988. *Suicide Notes*. New York: Human Sciences Press.

- 1989a. 'Suicide across the Adult Life-Span: An Archival Study.' *Crisis* 10: 132–51.
- 1989b. 'Are Young Adults' Suicides Psychologically Different from Those of Other Adults?' The Shneidman Lecture. *Suicide and Life-Threatening Behavior* 19: 249–63.
- 1996. 'Suicide: A Multidimensional Malaise.' The Presidential Address. *Suicide and Life-Threatening Behavior* 26: 221–36.

Leenaars, A., G. Domino. 1993. 'A Comparison of Community Attitudes toward Suicide in Windsor and Los Angeles.' *Canadian Journal of Behavioural Science* 25: 253–66.

Leenaars, A., R. Maris, R. McIntosh, and J. Richman. 1992. *Suicide and the Older Adult*. New York: Guilford Press.

Leenaars, A., R. Neimeyer, and J. Maltsberger. 1994. *Treatment of Suicidal People*. New York: Taylor & Francis.

Leenaars, A., and S. Wenckstern. 1990. *Suicide Prevention in Schools*. Washington: Hemisphere Publishing Corp.

Lester, D. 1987. *Suicide as a Learned Behavior*. Springfield, IL: Charles Thomas.

Manchester Guardian Weekly. 1995. 'Creeping crabwise towards death.' February: 1.

Menninger, K. 1938. *Man against Himself*. New York: Harcourt, Brace.

Murray, H. 1967. 'Death to the World: The Passions of Herman Melville.' In E. Shneidman, ed., *Essays in Self-Destruction*. New York: Science House.

Osgood, N. 1992. *Suicide in Later Life*. New York: Lexington.

Phillips, D. 1986. 'Effect of the Media.' Paper presented at the conference of the American Association of Suicidology, Atlanta, April.

Report of the Special Senate Committee on Euthanasia and Assisted Suicide. 1995. *Of Life and Death*. Ottawa: The Committee.

Richman, J. 1992. 'A Rational Approach to Rational Suicide.' In A. Leenaars, R. Maris, J. McIntosh, and J. Richman, eds, *Suicide and the Older Adult*. New York: Guilford Press.

- 1993. *Preventing Elderly Suicide*. New York: Springer.

Schmidtke, A. 1993. Personal communication.

Shneidman, E. 1985. *Definition of Suicide*. New York: Wiley.

- 1992. 'A Comment on "Rational Suicide and the Right to Die."' *New England Journal of Medicine* 326: 889–90.

Shneidman, E., and N. Farberow, eds. 1957. *Clues to Suicide*. New York: McGraw-Hill.

Shneidman, E., and T. Szasz. 1972. 'The Ethics of Suicide Prevention.' *Audio-Digest Psychiatry* 1(2), 24 July, cassette. Debate sponsored by the University of California, San Francisco, 29 April 1972.

Smith, K., R. Conroy, and B. Ehler. 1984. 'Lethality of Suicide Attempt Rating Scale.' *Suicide and Life-Threatening Behavior* 14: 215–42.

Sullivan, H. 1962. 'Schizophrenia as a Human Process.' In H. Perry, N. Gorvell, and M. Gibbens, eds, *The Collected Works of Harry Stack Sullivan*, vol. 2. New York: W.W. Norton.

– 1964. 'The Fusion of Psychiatry and Social Science.' In H. Perry, N. Gorvell, and M. Gibbens, eds, *The Collected Works of Harry Stack Sullivan*, vol. 2. New York: W.W. Norton.

Szasz, T. 1971. 'The Ethics of Suicide.' *Intellectual Digest* 2: 53–5.

– 1986. 'The Case against Suicide Prevention.' *American Psychologist* 41: 806–12.

Wedler, H. 1993. Personal communication.

West, L. 1993. 'Reflections on the Right to Die.' In A. Leenaars, ed., *Suicidology: Essays in Honor of Edwin Shneidman*. Northvale, NJ: Aronson.

Zilboorg, G. 1936. 'Suicide among Civilized and Primitive Races.' *American Journal of Psychiatry* 92: 1347–69.

Contributors

Jeannette A. Ambrose   Saskatoon, Saskatchewan
Meeka Arnakaq   Pangnirtung, Nunavut
Nada Barraclough   Toronto, Ontario
Roger C. Bland   Edmonton, Alberta
Menno Boldt   Lethbridge, Alberta
Margaret Boone   Thunder Bay, Ontario
Lucy J. Boothroyd   Montreal, Quebec
Richard Boyer   Montreal, Quebec
Edward A. Connors   Rama, Ontario
Anton F. de Man   Lennoxville, Quebec
Ronald J. Dyck   Edmonton, Alberta
Anne Edmunds   Windsor, Ontario
Naki Ekho   Iqaluit, Nunavut
Christopher Fletcher   Montreal, Quebec
Errol Fletcher   Iqaluit, Nunavut
Patricia Harnisch   Toronto, Ontario
Gerry G. Harrington   Calgary, Alberta
Mae Katt   Thunder Bay, Ontario
Karen G. Kiddey   Calgary, Alberta
Peggy Kinch   Thunder Bay, Ontario
Laurence J. Kirmayer   Montreal, Quebec
Michael J. Kral   Windsor, Ontario
Marcia B. Krawll   Vancouver, British Columbia
Okee Kunuk   Iqaluit, Nunavut
Antoon A. Leenaars   Windsor, Ontario & Leiden, The Netherlands

Gilles Légaré   Montreal, Quebec
David Lester   Pomona, New Jersey
Karen Letofsky   Toronto, Ontario
Sheila Levy   Iqaluit, Nunavut
Peter D. McLean   Vancouver, British Columbia
David Masecar   Sault Ste Marie, Ontario
Bruce Minore   Thunder Bay, Ontario
Brian L. Mishara   Montreal, Quebec
Stephen C. Newman   Edmonton, Alberta
Elisapee Ootoova   Pond Inlet, Nunavut
Helene Orn   Edmonton, Alberta
Bernd Osborg   Annapolis Royal, Nova Scotia
Susan Patenaude   Edmonton, Alberta
Malaya Paptsie   Iqaluit, Nunavut
Michel Préville   Montreal, Quebec
Richard F. Ramsay   Calgary, Alberta
Linda Rosenfeld   Vancouver, British Columbia
Danielle St-Laurent   Montreal, Quebec
Isaac Sakinofsky   Toronto, Ontario
Lois Sapsford   Calgary, Alberta
C. Murray Sinclair   Winnipeg, Manitoba
Lucien Taparti   Rankin Inlet, Nunavut
Steven Taylor   Vancouver, British Columbia
Roger J. Tierney   Calgary, Alberta
Michel Tousignant   Montreal, Quebec
Frank Trovato   Edmonton, Alberta
Neville Twine   Toronto, Ontario
Susanne Wenckstern   Windsor, Ontario
Jennifer White   Vancouver, British Columbia
Gordon Winch   Toronto, Ontario
Joan Wright   Edmonton, Alberta
James G. Young   Toronto, Ontario

Index